ARIANA ANTIQUA

A DESCRIPTIVE ACCOUNT OF THE

ANTIQUITIES AND COINS OF AFGHANISTAN

ARIANA ANTIQUA

A DESCRIPTIVE ACCOUNT
OF THE

ANTIQUITIES AND COINS
OF
AFGHANISTAN

WITH

A MEMOIR ON THE BUILDINGS
CALLED TOPES, BY C. MASSON, ESQ

H. H. WILSON

GYAN

Published by

Gyan Publishing House
5, Ansari Road
Daryaganj, New Delhi-110002
Phone: 011-47034999, 9811692060
E-mail: books@gyanbooks.com

Distribution Network
gyanbooks.com
India, USA, Canada, UK, Australia, France

ISBN : 978-81-212-3137-4 (PB)
First Published, London, 1841

2nd Impression 2020

Printed at: Gyan Press, Delhi.

Ariana Antiqua
Author: H. H. Wilson

TO THE MEMORY

OF

JAMES PRINSEP,

LATE SECRETARY OF THE ASIATIC SOCIETY OF BENGAL,

AND

EDITOR OF THE SOCIETY'S JOURNAL,

IN WHICH PUBLICATION

HE

WITH EXTRAORDINARY TALENT, INDUSTRY, AND ZEAL, PURSUED WITH UNPRECEDENTED SUCCESS

THE INVESTIGATION OF

INDIAN NUMISMATICS AND PALÆOGRAPHY,

AND EFFECTED DISCOVERIES OF THE HIGHEST INTEREST AND VALUE IN

THE HISTORY OF ANCIENT INDIA,

This Work,

FOUNDED UPON HIS LABOURS,

IS INSCRIBED

BY

HIS FORMER COLLEAGUE AND FRIEND,

H. H. WILSON.

London, Sept. 1841.

THE LIST OF SUBSCRIBERS.

	COPIES.
HER MOST GRACIOUS MAJESTY THE QUEEN	2
HER MOST GRACIOUS MAJESTY THE QUEEN DOWAGER	5
HIS ROYAL HIGHNESS PRINCE ALBERT	1
His Grace the Archbishop of Canterbury	1
The Duke of Northumberland	1
The Marquis of Lansdowne	1
The Earl Amherst, Knowle, Seven Oaks	1
The Right Hon. the Earl of Munster	1
The Right Hon. Lord Clare, Belgrave Square	1
The Right Hon. the Lord Mayor of London	1
The Athenæum Library, Waterloo Place	1
Corpus Christi College Library, Oxford	1
India Board	1
The London Institution, Finsbury Circus	1
Oriel College Library, Oxford	1
Sion College, London Wall	1
Trinity College Library, Oxford	1
The United Service Institution, Scotland Yard	1
J. Y. Ackerman, Esq., F.S.A., L. & E., Peckham	1
Dr. Annesley, Oriental Club	1
James Barclay, Esq., Farm Terrace, Clapham	1
Thomas Baring, Esq., Bishopsgate Street	1
William Barker, Esq., Mark Lane	1
Lieut.-Colonel Barnewell, Oriental Club	1
R. Boyne, Esq., 18, Peter's Hill, Doctors' Commons	1
The Rev. Dr. Bull, Christ Church, Oxford	1

	COPIES.
Messrs. Burrows and Sons, Hounsditch	1
R. W. Buttermer, Esq., 11, Copthall Court	1
R. B. Byas, Esq., Whetstone	1
Sir John Campbell, Bart.	1
Sir James Carnac, Bart., Oriental Club	2
Isaac Carr, Esq., Moorgate Street	1
James Carruthers, Esq., Glencraigah, Ireland	1
R. Clarke, Esq., 17, Kensington Square	1
Major Close, Oriental Club	1
Wm. Addison Coombe, Esq., 4, Lawrence Pountney Hill	1
James Dodsley Cuff, Esq., F.S.A., Bank of England	1
George Durant Cummings, Esq., 11, Copthall Court	1
Joseph Curt, Esq., Princes Street, Leicester Square	1
Thomas Curtis, Esq., Southgate, Middlesex	1
The Rev. W. Dansey, Donhead, Wilts	1
John Day, Esq., Tottenham	1
Thomas Dobson, Esq., Forty Hill, Enfield	1
Alexis James Doxat, Esq., Bishopsgate Street	1
Richard Durant, Esq., 11, Copthall Court	1
Richard Durant, Junr., Esq., 11, Copthall Court	1
Captain Eastwick, 22, Sloane Street, of the Bombay Army	1
The Hon. Mount Stewart Elphinstone	5
Sir Charles Forbes, Bart., 9, Fitzroy Square	1
George Forbes, Esq., 9, Fitzroy Square	1
James Stewart Forbes, Esq., 9, Fitzroy Square	1
John Hopton Forbes, Esq., 9, Fitzroy Square	1
The Hon. Colonel Fox, M.P., Ordnance Office	1
J. P. Gassiot, Esq., Clapham Common	1
Messrs. A. A. Gower, Nephews, and Co., Coleman Street	1
H. S. Greene, Esq., Oriental Club	1
Mrs. Greenwood, Cumberland Terrace, Regent's Park	1
S. Gregson, Esq., Upper Harley Street	1
Hudson Gurney, Esq., V. P. S. A., F. R. S., &c.	1
W. D. Haggard, Esq., Lea, near Blackheath, F.S.A., F.R.A.S.	1
W. R. Hamilton, Esq., R.G.S., F.R.S., M.R.S.L., V.P.S.A., &c., Boulton Row, May Fair	1

	COPIES.
Edward Hawkins, Esq., British Museum, F.R.S., F.S.A., F.L.S.	1
Walter Hawkins, Esq., Foulkes Buildings, Tower Street	1
David Henry, Esq., Bush Hill, Enfield	1
Francis Hobler, Esq., 26, Bucklersbury	1
John Jeffkins, Esq., 2, Crosby Square	1
George Jeffkins, Esq., 2, Crosby Square	1
Stephen Jones, Esq., 1, Grange Road, Bermondsey	1
John Kirkman, Esq., 70, King William Street	1
Sir G. H. Larpent, Bart., 8, Austin Friars	1
Mrs. William Martin Leake, 50, Queen Anne Street	1
Dr. Lee, College, Doctors' Commons, L.L.D., F.R.S., F.S.A., F.R.A.S.	1
John Lester, Esq., Aldermanbury	1
C. W. Luscombe, Esq., Clifton, near Bristol	1
Francis Maubert, Esq., Norwood	1
A. A. Mieville, Esq., 11, Angel Court	1
L. L. P. Mortimer, Esq., Great Bush Lane	1
— Moore, Esq., 9, Moorgate Street	1
James Muir, Esq., Edinburgh	1
General Sir Charles Napier, Bart., Commander-in-Chief, Bombay	1
William Newnham, Esq., 4, Park Crescent, Portland Place	1
The Rev. Dr. G. F. Nott, the Close, Winchester	1
J. Horsley Palmer and Company, King's Arms Yard	1
Lewis Hayes Pettit, Esq., 9, New Square, Lincoln's Inn, M.A., F.R.S.	1
Colonel Sir Henry Pottinger, Bart.	2
Rev. Archdeacon Potts, Vicarage, Kensington	1
Thomas Pryer, Esq., 29, Austin Friars	1
William Richards, Esq., Tottenham	1
George Rodwell, Esq., Burnham Deepdale, Burnham Market, Norfolk	1
A. Rogers, Esq., 1, Riches Court, Lime Street	1
Sigismond Rucker, Esq., 12, Tower Street	1
George Rutherford, Esq., Lombard Street	1
Thomas Saunders, Esq., 1, Queen Street, F.S.A.	1
Dr. Simes, Cheltenham	1

	COPIES.
Charles Roach Smith, Esq., F.S.A., Secretary to the Munismatic Society of London	1
John Smith, Esq., Cotton's Wharf	1
Messrs. Smith and Elder, Cornhill	1
Edmund Treherne, Esq., 14, St. George's Terrace	1
— Tringham, Esq., Cunningham Place	1
Timothy Tyrell, Esq., Guildhall, London	1
Godfrey Vigne, Esq., Walthamstow	1
Mrs. Waddle, Beach House, Walmer	1
John B. Walbancke, Esq., Riches Villa, Finchley New Road, St. John's Wood	2
John Wild, Esq., 7, Martin's Lane	1
Mrs. Wild, 2, Gloucester Place, Portman Square	2
Mrs. Wood, Tower Street	1

PREFACE.

The circumstances under which important accessions to Indian Numismatics have been made within the last few years are fully detailed in the following pages; those which have led to the publication of the present work require to be explained.

It is stated in the following account of the progress of the discovery of coins and antiquities in Afghanistan, that one of the most active and successful labourers in the field was Mr. Masson. At an early period of his researches, Mr. Masson proposed to the Government of Bombay, through the Resident in Cutch, Colonel Pottinger, to transfer his actual and all future collections to the East India Company, on condition of their defraying the cost of his operations. The proposal was favourably received, and from the year 1834 until 1837 Mr. Masson was sedulously employed in the pursuit, in which he had engaged with equal intelligence and zeal, on behalf and at the expense of the East India Company. In the course of time the collections he had formed were transmitted to England, and deposited in the Company's Museum.

Although the discoveries of Mr. Masson had been brought to the knowledge of the public by his own descriptions of them, and by the remarks and illustrations of Mr. James Prinsep in the Journal of the Asiatic Society of Bengal, of which he was the able and indefatigable editor, yet as this work was not extensively accessible in England, and as the notices of Mr. Masson's collections were published at different intervals, and were consequently in a detached and inconvenient form,—as the subject also had received much additional light from the observations of scholars and numismatists in Europe, and many of the verifications and conjectures hazarded in the early stages of the inquiry had been corrected by further experience and investigation,—it appeared to me to be likely that a connected description of the principal antiquities, and of the whole of the coins received from Mr. Masson, would be acceptable both to the cultivators of numismatic science, and to those interested in the ancient history of India. I accordingly offered my services to the Honourable the Court of Directors to prepare such an account, if they should think the publication desirable. The suggestion was most cordially and liberally approved of, and as profit was not the aim of either of the parties, the Court resolved, that after appropriating such a portion of the edition as they should think fit to require, the remainder should be presented to the mother of Mr. Masson as an additional mark of the sense they entertained of the merits of her son.

Having accordingly undertaken to publish a description of the antiquities and coins sent home by Mr. Masson, I conceived it to be necessary, in order to enable any who might feel disposed to direct attention towards them the better to appreciate their character and value, to prefix to the account some specification of the steps by which they had been discovered, some proofs of the interest which they had excited amongst the antiquaries and numismatists of Europe, and some particulars of the important elucidations which they had received from many of the most distinguished scholars of the Continent. These form the principal topics of the first chapter of the following work, together with some speculations as to the origin and objects of the Topes, the remarkable edifices in which most of the antiquities and some of the coins have been found.

That the scene of Mr. Masson's labours was the vicinity of Peshawer and Kabul, and that he had opened many Topes in this situation, appeared from occasional passages in his communications to the Bengal Journal, but no detailed description of these buildings had been published by him; and materials were consequently wanting to form any precise notion of their structure or position. I therefore requested him to favour me with a more particular report of his operations; and the circumstantial description which was in consequence received from him, and which occupies the second chapter, together with the sketches of the Topes, which are here engraved, cannot fail to enhance the use and interest of the work.

In the third chapter, which treats of the comparative geography of the countries between Persia and India, to which, upon the authority of classical writers, I have attached the collective designation of Ariana, I have endeavoured to supply materials for a more accurate comparison than has yet been instituted in this country between their present and past topographical distribution. We have had no systematic attempt to verify the ancient geography of this part of Asia since the writings of Major Rennell. Without detracting in any degree from his just claims to distinction as a classical geographer, it is undeniable, as he himself admits, that the means at his command were in this instance wholly incapable of leading to safe and certain conclusions. European enterprise had not then penetrated into districts which offered no prospects of commercial profit, and which were of dangerous access, partly through physical and political difficulties, but still more through the lawless habits and fierce intolerance of their inhabitants: the land was unvisited, unknown. The state of things is now altered; instead of the solitary journey of Forster, performed under great disadvantages in one circumscribed route, the country has been crossed in various directions by able and intelligent Officers; and, since it became the scene of military events, has in many places been surveyed and measured by them. Their proceedings have in many cases been published either in separate works or in the Journal of the Asiatic Society of Bengal; and where unpublished, they have been sent to England and incorporated in the latest Map compiled by the able Geographer to the East India Company, Mr. Walker. Although, therefore, something remains to be effected before the information can be considered as complete, yet, as so much that is authentic and novel has been added to our store, I have thought it would be of service to geographical investigation to bring together the scattered details, and arrange them in a form in which they might be readily consulted by the scholars and geographers of this country. The same purpose influenced the attempt I have also made to follow the marches of Alexander into Bactria, the Paropamisus, and India, until his departure from the latter country.[1]

[1] In the map which accompanies this chapter I have purposely omitted many names found in classical maps, as little dependence can be placed on the positions assigned to them: with a few exceptions, I have inserted only those which seemed to admit of probable identification. Such modern names as are given without any ancient equivalent are those which may assist future comparison. In the course of printing the work additional information was received which requires one or two alterations to be made in this chapter. Thus, the probable route of

The last chapter is devoted to the especial purport of the publication, a detailed description of the different coins collected by Mr. Masson, with an attempt to derive from them some facts relating to the history of the different dynasties who for so many centuries ruled over the countries in which the coins have been discovered. In order to furnish the fullest means of judging of the correctness of my deductions, I have added to the coins sent home by Mr. Masson, descriptions, and, in some cases, delineations, of others belonging to the same family, but not included in his collection. Some of these have been taken from the coins themselves, for the inspection of which I have been indebted to the Royal Asiatic Society or to personal friends whose residence in India had put them in possession of specimens not in the Company's cabinet, particularly Dr. Swiney, Colonel Miles, Mr. Thomas, Mr. Vigne, and Sir A. Burnes. A few, neither in their possession nor in the Masson collection, but which were of more than ordinary interest, I have taken the liberty of repeating from the notices and plates of them elsewhere published, and especially the memoirs and engravings of Mr. Prinsep in the Journal of the Asiatic Society of Bengal, and of M. Raoul Rochette in different numbers of the Journal des Savans. To both these sources I am also indebted for much valuable information, and as they are in most instances entitled to priority of description and deduction, I have thought it my duty to specify under each coin the pages or plates in either of the works named in which some account of it has already appeared. I have also occasionally referred to other contemporary authorities, as the Journal Asiatique and the eighth supplemental volume of M. Mionnet, and have cited them in the same manner. I have not thought it necessary to make the like particular

Craterus was not by the Bolan, but by the Gundava Pass; and the Khoshal Pass in the Himalaya is not open through the whole year. These corrections do not affect the general results.

reference to the works of Professor Lassen and Dr. C. Grotefend[1] on the subject of these coins, as they, like myself, follow the original guides whom I have particularized. I have, however, derived from both much valuable aid, as from time to time I have duly acknowledged.

The coins which are the chief objects of the following descriptions are for the most part Bactrian, whether Greek or Indo-Scythic. The Sassanian, Hindu, and Mohammedan coins which are also noticed are for the most part restricted to those that have been found in Afghanistan, and are far from embracing every variety of each class. The pure Sassanian coins have received much additional illustration from two distinguished numismatists who have recently engaged in this branch of numismatic inquiry, M. Adrien de Longperrier[2] and Mr. R. Steuart.[3] The work of the former only is published, and, although of exceeding merit, leaves much, as its modest title of 'Essai' intimates, for further investigation. There are also several classes of these coins which, although evidently related to the Sassanian, have been apparently struck by Scythic or Indian princes, respecting which nothing positive is yet determined, and which require additional examples and more careful study for their accurate appropriation. The Hindu coins have been treated of by Mr. Prinsep alone. Some of the classes, as those termed

[1] Zur Geschichte der Griechischen und Indoskythischen Könige in Baktrien, Kabul, und Indien durch entzifferung der Altkabulischen legenden auf ihrer Münzen; von Christian Lassen: Bonn, 1838. Die Münzen der Griechischen, Parthischen und Indo-Skythischen Könige von Baktrien und den ländern am Indus; von Dr. C. L. Grotefend: Hannover, 1840.

[2] Essai sur les Médailles des Rois Perses de la Dynastie Sassanienne; par Adrien de Longperrier: Paris, 1840.

[3] The work of Mr. Steuart is not yet published, but I am indebted to his kindness for copies of the plates by which it is illustrated.

Kanoj, Rajput, Saurashtran, and Indo-Mohammedan, were examined by him in great detail, and with very extraordinary success; but they are by no means exhausted, and much respecting them remains for further research. As they are found in Afghanistan only to a limited extent, they scarcely come within the scope of the present work; but they have been described as partly included in Mr. Masson's collections, and partly procured in England from other sources, so that some advance will have been effected, it is to be hoped, in our knowledge of them. Additions to their numbers have been made, however, since these pages were written, which will no doubt reward continued examination with new and important results. One collection of Saurashtran coins brought home by Dr. Burnes may especially be named. The coins of the Mohammedan kings of Delhi, and their predecessors of Ghizni and Ghor, belong to an æra subsequent to that at which our series closes: a few of the earliest obtained at Kabul by Mr. Masson, I have, with the kind assistance of Mr. Shakespear, described: he has also decyphered others in the collection, but mostly of a later æra: the subject, however, has not yet been fully and systematically prosecuted, and, with the materials which are now accessible, deserves to be separately and deliberately considered. This is still more the case with a very extensive description of coins of which scarcely any specimens crossed the Indus: these are Buddhist and Hindu coins, found at Behut and in other places: some of them were described by Mr. Prinsep, but he had latterly become possessed of many more, which his lamented illness prevented him from fully examining and describing. He had delineated and engraved a considerable number, and the Plates are published in the Bengal Journal for December, 1838, with brief descriptions, which, although able and correct, do not enter into that detail which the subject required, and which no one was so competent as Mr. Prinsep to have bestowed upon it. Many of the coins are in his cabinet, which is now in England; many others are in the hands of different collectors, several of whom are still in India, and from their persevering industry we may expect to be put in possession of whatever further elucidation this class of coins can receive.

CONTENTS.

CHAPTER I.

CHAPTER II.

CHAPTER III.

CHAPTER IV.

LIST OF PLATES.

Mem. Where 'Supplemental Plate' is cited, Plate XXI. is intended.

COINS AND ANTIQUITIES OF AFGHANISTAN.

CHAPTER I.

ACCOUNT OF THE PROGRESS OF BACTRO-INDIAN NUMISMATIC AND ANTIQUARIAN DISCOVERY, AND OBSERVATIONS ON THE EDIFICES, CALLED TOPES.

THE history of literature and science abounds with instances of investigation pursued with exemplary patience, unwearied zeal, and eminent ability, for many successive years, yet failing to attain even a prospect of arriving ultimately at the end proposed. At the same time, it would have been matter of great regret had no such seemingly hopeless efforts been instituted, or had the uncertainty or remoteness of success deterred the attempt, or prematurely cut short its prosecution.

It can rarely happen that talent and perseverance toil in vain. Even though the immediate purpose of a pursuit, in which the highest faculties of man's nature are engaged, be not accomplished, yet it is certain that some collateral advantage will be realised of a worth perhaps more real than the object originally started; and although it be true that many and long continued and ably directed exertions have been unprofitable, yet it has not unfrequently occurred that at the moment when interest most languished and hope grew faint, fortune proved propitious, and unexpected success rewarded the resolution that gave not way to despair. The experiments of the alchemists failed to discover the philosophers' stone or the elixir of immortality, but they bequeathed to science many sources of national wealth, many means of alleviating disease and of prolonging life. Scholars and antiquaries have not yet unrolled the entire volume of the Egyptian records, but the labour which so long sought in vain for a key to the characters in which they are concealed, has not been wholly disappointed of its reward, and they may reasonably now look forward to a more brilliant recompense. We seem to be at last upon the eve of becoming familiar with whatever the inscriptions of Babylon and Persepolis may have preserved from periods anterior to authentic history; and the doctrines or facts perpetuated on rocks or columns, or in inscriptions on stones, which so long baffled the industry and erudition of Indian orientalists, have been at last made accessible to the world by the more fortunate application of learning, talent, ingenuity, and perseverance. Instances of this description cannot fail to demonstrate the advantage of not desisting from a course of inquiry, merely because the attainment of its objects is not apparently nigh at hand.

Few inquiries of an archæological purport have been attended with so abundant a harvest of discovery as those of which India has been recently the field. The results do not ascend to so remote a period as is necessary for the illustration of antiquities purely national, or for the determination of the origin and era of the religious or political institutions of the Hindus; but they fill up in the most satisfactory manner an extensive blank in the history of an important part of India at an interesting period, and dissipate the clouds that have hung over the interval between the invasion of Alexander and that of Mohammed Ghori, in regard to the provinces which were the seat of their respective aggressions. They give us for fifteen centuries a variety of important circumstances relating to the political and religious condition of the kingdom of Bactria, and the conterminous regions of Persia and Hindustan, of which we have hitherto had but few and imperfect intimations, or which were heretofore altogether unknown.

A very short period has elapsed since the means of an acquaintance with the history of Bactria and Bactrian India were extremely circumscribed. It was known that after the death of Alexander, Bactria became an independent principality under Greek sovereigns, and the names of a few of them were picked out with extraordinary labour and learning from the fragmentary notices of classical authors, and one or two rare coins. It had been ascertained from the same writers, and from Chinese authorities, that the Greek rule was overthrown by Scythian chiefs, whose sway extended to the mouths of the Indus; and from the Mohammedan historians we had learned that the Arab invaders of Sindh and Afghanistan were encountered by Hindu princes, who had therefore supplanted in those countries both Greek and Barbarian kings. These few leading facts were unaccompanied by details, and scantily occupied the interval that separated the Mohammedan from the Macedonian invasion. Within the last seven years this deficiency has been remedied, this barrenness of events has been changed to abundance. Successful research has not only corroborated all that was before imperfectly known, but has filled up the meagre outline with circumstances and persons of historical truth and importance. The hitherto unnamed or unknown members of successive or synchronous dynasties now pass before our eyes as well-defined individuals and in connected order; and revolutions of a religious as well as of a political origin may be discerned, if not with all the minuteness we could wish, yet with a distinctness that demands unquestioning reliance. The means by which these additions to our knowledge of the past have been effected, are the numerous monuments and coins which have been found within the period above specified in Turkestan, Afghanistan, and the Punjab, and of the discovery of which it is now proposed to offer a summary review.

In the early part of the last century a coin of one of the Bactrian kings, Eukratides, and another attributed to the founder of the monarchy, Theodotus, but which we now know to belong to Menander, suggested to Theophilus Bayer the plan of his Historia Regni Græcorum Bactriani, published at St. Petersburgh in 1738. Something later in the course of the same century, a gold coin, published by the celebrated numismatist Pellerin, confirmed the existence of another Bactrian monarch mentioned by Greek writers, Euthydemus, and here for some time the numismatic illustration of Bactrian history was suspended. In 1799 another addition was made to the list, by a coin bearing the name of Heliocles, who was placed by M. Mionnet amongst the kings of Bactria: the addition was conjectural, being founded chiefly upon the style of the fabrication of the coin, and it was for some time contested; it has since been proved correct. These different coins were described in the numismatic publications of Mionnet in 1811, and Visconti in 1814, and specimens of them were sparingly multiplied in Europe through

Russia and Persia. In 1822, a new king was added to the list by Koehler, Antimachus Theos, and in the following year the same numismatist published a description of a coin of Demetrius procured at Bokhara by the Russian ambassador, Count Meyendorff; at the same time he published several smaller coins of Euthydemus, and some tetradrachms of the same king, but of rude and barbaric execution. A duplicate of the tetradrachm of Heliocles, and one of that of Eukratides, found their way into the collection of R. P. Knight, Esq., and were transferred to the British Museum: they were published in 1830 in a descriptive catalogue of the collection. The tetradrachm of Demetrius passed into the cabinet of Baron Chaudoir, and was described by the Abbé Sestini along with some of the coins of Euthydemus in the same cabinet. The description was published at Florence in 1831.

In the course of the same period a new impulse and accelerated progression were communicated to Bactrian numismatics through the publication in 1824, in the first volume of the Transactions of the Royal Asiatic Society, of a memoir by the late Colonel Tod upon Greek, Parthian, and Indian medals, illustrated by engravings. During the last twelve years of his residence in India, Colonel Tod had directed particular attention to the collection of ancient coins, and had employed persons to search for them at Mathura and other Indian cities of celebrity. In the interval above mentioned he thus accumulated about 20,000 coins of all denominations. He describes the greater number as possessing no interest, but the collection comprised a few of entire novelty, and great numismatic and historical value. Of this description were coins of Apollodotus and Menander, now for the first time discovered. The existence of these kings of Bactria was known from classical testimony, and the author of the Periplus of the Erythræan Sea, who it is supposed visited India some time in the second century, mentions that their coins were current in his time at Barygaza or Baroach. Of the coins described by Colonel Tod, one was found at Mathura and another at Bateswar, a place also on the banks of the Jumna; from which it may be inferred that the circulation of the coins of these princes was not confined to the west of India. None of them had, however, before found their way to modern Europe; and Colonel Tod's discovery of them therefore constitutes an era in the history of Bactro-Indian numismatics.

Besides the coins of Apollodotus and Menander, Colonel Tod also introduced to the numismatists of Europe other coins of scarcely inferior interest, although at the time of their publication imperfectly appreciated, the types being unknown, and the legends undecypherable. They are now familiar to us as Bactrian, Scythian, and Indian coins, bearing the names and titles of the princes in whose reigns they were issued.

The coins described and figured by Colonel Tod became, after no long interval, the subject of an interesting and learned dissertation by Augustus Wilhelm von Schlegel, which was published in the Journal Asiatique, November, 1828. Of the medals of Apollodotus and Menander, Schlegel observes, "ces deux médailles sont pour ainsi dire, hors de prix tant pour la conservation parfaite que pour leur extreme rareté et leur importance historique." Their historical value is undiminished, but nothing is calculated to exhibit the rapid progress of numismatic discovery in respect to Bactrian coins more strikingly, than the alteration which their attribute of rarity has undergone within the last twelve years. Instead of only two medals, the cabinets of Paris and London possess now nearer two thousand of the coins of Menander and Apollodotus, of silver and copper, of a great variety of types, and mostly in excellent preservation.[1]

In addition to his comments upon the coins of these two Bactrian kings, Schlegel partly determined the true reading of the inscriptions on some coins, which, although very numerous and bearing a Greek legend, do not specify the name of any king.[2] He also attempted to appropriate another coin, which he regarded as the most curious of the whole series, to a Gothic king. His reading of the inscription was inaccurate; but his assignment of the coin to a Barbaric prince was ingenious, and has been justified by subsequent discoveries; the coin in question, as well as several following it in Colonel Tod's plate, being the first published, first heard of, coins of kings since determined to be Indo-Scythic, and having the Hellenised names of Kadphises, Kanerkes, &c. They are found in great numbers in many parts of India, but commonly with the letters of the legend more or less effaced.[3]

In the fourth series of his engraved medals, Colonel Tod represented, also

[1] See the description and plates in this work. Plates III. IV.

[2] See Plate IX.

[3] Plates X. to XIV.

for the first time, Hindu coins which have been since abundantly found in India, and are now known as the coins of the Gupta kings of Kanoj.[1] A number of these, but of inferior fabric and alloy, were found in Bengal, near to Calcutta, in the year 1783, on the bank of the river, and were brought to light by the washing away of the soil. They were purchased by Warren Hastings, and sent to the Court of Directors of the East India Company, by whom they were distributed to the British Museum, the Royal Society, the Universities of Oxford and Cambridge, and the Museum of Dr. Hunter. Some of them are engraved in the second volume of Marsden's Numismata Orientalia, which was published in 1825. Marsden's work, which is of the highest merit, relates less to the coins of India than those of Syria and Persia during the Mohammedan rule, commencing with the Khalifs. The coins of India which he describes are those chiefly of the Patan and Mogul kings of Hindustan. The last plates delineate the Gupta coins above mentioned, and some other Hindu coins, but their origin and appropriation had not then been investigated. Of the Gupta coins he observes, "Some learned antiquaries think they discover in them the evidences of a Greek origin," referring to a Paper communicated by Mr. R. P. Knight to the Society of Antiquaries, April 18th, 1822. On this point he expressly refrains from conjecture, almost prophetically "cherishing the hope that future discoveries may throw a light upon the subject, which is in itself of the highest interest."[2]

The success which attended the operations of Colonel Tod may naturally suggest some surprise that similar researches should not have been embarked in earlier, and that his discoveries should have been reserved for so modern a date. There is nothing of numismatic interest in the volumes of the Asiatic Researches of Bengal, until some time subsequent to Colonel Tod's publication. It must not be inferred, however, that the subject was one of easy prosecution, or that it had been entirely neglected. There were not many private individuals in India who had the means or opportunities of forming collections of coins, and it was long after the institution of the Asiatic Society that any attempt was made to form a museum in connexion with it of any

[1] See Plate XVIII.

[2] Numismata Orientalia, vol. ii. p. 726.

description. There is still no other public collection of the same kind in Bengal, and it is believed that a museum of any order is still wholly wanting at the other Presidencies. Private collections are necessarily liable to dispersion, and they are peculiarly precarious in a society like that of British India, the members of which have no permanent interest in a country in which they are only temporary and transient sojourners. Such numismatic collections as had from time to time been made had therefore speedily again disappeared, and no trace of them was left behind. Such was the fate of large and apparently interesting collections made by Mr. Edwards, Mr. Seymour, and Colonel Willoughby,[1] and no doubt of others; and extensive facilities for careful and deliberate examination and comparison were consequently unavailable. There were two collections of a less perishable character, however, made latterly in India; one of copper coins by Dr. Robert Tytler, of the medical service, which he presented to the East India Company, and another by Colonel Mackenzie, which was purchased for the Company on his death. Both these collections are at the India House: they are of a very miscellaneous description, and of partial numismatic value. Dr. Tytler's collection, made chiefly at Benares and Allahabad prior to 1820, contains a number of the Indo-Scythic coins, but from their having been in circulation the edges were so much worn that the inscription was universally obliterated, and they could only, therefore, excite curiosity, not supply information. Colonel Mackenzie's coins were more instructive, but although they embraced a wider range, they did not comprehend any Greek or Indo-Scythic coins of Bactria.

Upon the purchase of Colonel Mackenzie's coins, duplicates were presented to the Asiatic Society of Bengal, as were duplicates of drawings made by his direction from other private cabinets. From these, aided by a few coins in his own possession, and in that of some of his friends, the writer of this notice, then Secretary to the Asiatic Society of Bengal, prepared an account of the Select Hindu Coins in the Society's Cabinet, which was communicated to the Society in 1831, and was published in the seventeenth volume of the Asiatic Researches in the course of 1832. The author was

[1] See drawings of coins from their cabinets, engraved; Asiatic Researches, vol. xvii.

assisted in his undertaking,—in which, without such assistance, he would probably not have engaged,—by his friend and associate the late Mr. James Prinsep, who superintended the engraving of the coins, and delineated and engraved many of them himself. The zealous interest which Mr. Prinsep thus learned to take in the subject of Indian numismatics did not cease with the occasion, and the continuance of his labours in this department of inquiry may be considered as the most important consequence of the publication of the paper in question. It exercised, it is believed, a similar influence in other parts of India, and coincided with circumstances which were at the same time in independent and uncommunicated progress in instigating that spirit of numismatic research which, under the animated and intelligent guidance and assistance of Mr. Prinsep, has been productive in India of such interesting and valuable results.

One of the concurrent events just referred to, was the discovery of some ancient coins by General Ventura, an officer in the service of Maharaja Runjit Sinh, upon opening an ancient monument at a place called Manikyala, in the Punjab. An account of his discovery, which was effected in April and May, 1830, was forwarded by him to Calcutta, and made known there about the end of the same year. In consequence of a communication addressed to him he subsequently forwarded impressions in wax of three of his coins, from which plaster casts were taken by Mr. Prinsep; drawings of them were also made and engraved by him, and they were described in the Paper communicated to the Society (Asiatic Researches, vol. xvii. p. 563. pl. I. f. 1; pl. II. f. 35, 43). They exhibited indications of Greek inscriptions, and, although these were not sufficiently entire or distinct to be satisfactorily decypherable, yet, as their presence was undeniable, they encouraged the expectation that from other and more perfect specimens they might yet be read and interpreted. The expectation was realised by the event, and they are well known now as Indo-Scythic coins. Some of the casts of General Ventura's coins were sent to Paris, and the Journal Asiatique for March, 1832, contains two short notices of them by M. Reinaud and M. Saint-Martin. The latter attempted to make out the legend, and was not wholly unsuccessful, but he justly remarked that more and better specimens were necessary before confidence could be placed in any interpretation.

He ascribed the coins to Greek or Asiatic princes who inherited the authority of Alexander's successors in the countries watered by the Indus.

In the beginning of March, 1832, Lieutenant (now Sir Alexander) Burnes, then on his route to Bokhara, visited Manikyala, and had an opportunity of inspecting the operations of General Ventura. He also collected there some antiques and coins. One of the latter, sent to Calcutta, arrived in time to be engraved and described before the account of the Society's coins was in type.[1] Lieutenant Burnes, during his onward journey, continued to avail himself of such opportunities as offered of collecting coins, and obtained several of great interest and value. The circumstance was alluded to by Mr. Prinsep in the Journal of the Asiatic Society of Bengal, January, 1833,[2] and he noticed at the same time the success of Dr. Swiney at Karnal, in collecting Bactrian or Indo-Scythian coins.[3] A more particular description of the coins of Lieutenant Burnes was published by Mr. Prinsep in the Journal of the Society for June, 1833,[4] as well as of some others with which he had been supplied. On one of the former the name of Kanerkes was for the first time distinctly legible. To his descriptions he added some remarks on the historical bearings of the coins, and some speculations as to the appropriation of such as were least known; accompanying the paper with drawings and engravings of eighteen coins. The coins were afterwards published in London, with the account of Lieutenant Burnes' journey; and the remarks of Mr. Prinsep were reprinted with some further observations by myself. Inquiry in India was now fairly and spiritedly set on foot, and Mr. Prinsep concludes his communication by announcing a supplement containing a selection from Dr. Swiney's and General Ventura's discoveries. "My task," he adds, "increases upon me daily; but I shall be amply rewarded if my humble notice of the discoveries of others shall, by connecting them with ancient history, eventually turn these most interesting relics to the true end of numismatic study." He little anticipated at this time the extent to

[1] As. Res. vol. xvii. p. 575, pl. II. f. 25.

[2] On the Greek coins in the cabinet of the Asiatic Society: Journal of the Asiatic Society of Bengal, vol. ii. p. 27.

[3] Ibid. p. 37.

[4] Note on Lieutenant Burnes' collection of ancient coins: J. As. Soc. B. vol. ii. p. 310.

which materials were about to pour in upon him, or the important conclusions which he was consequently enabled to establish or suggest. He little anticipated also, we regret to think, the amount of exertion which such researches, added to his other numerous occupations, imposed upon him; and which, whilst they obtained for him merited celebrity, contributed, it is to be feared, to shorten his useful and valuable life.

Conformably to Mr. Prinsep's announcement, the August number of the Journal[1] contained a description and engravings by him of eighteen coins, Bactrian and Hindu, chiefly from the collection of Dr. Swiney; amongst which were now made known, for the first time, some of the drachmæ no doubt spoken of by Arrian, those of Menander and Apollodotus. The former are of a type since become numerous; the latter is still rare,—attaching to the name and title of the king the epithet Philopator, and having on the reverse the Minerva Promachos, which is borne by the silver coins of Menander. In illustration of these coins, Mr. Prinsep translated Professor Schlegel's Observations on the History of Bactria, illustrated by the coins discovered by Colonel Tod. Some other coins, since known to belong to Indo-Scythic and Hindu princes, were also now for the first time delineated and described.

An accession of unexpected extent and value was soon, however, about to be made, and in April, 1834, the first account of Mr. Masson's discoveries in Afghanistan was communicated through the Journal to the public.[2] Mr. Masson had resided some time in Afghanistan, and had been engaged either by himself or in co-operation with a medical officer in the service of Runjit Sinh, Dr. Honigberger, in examining the ancient monuments, the topes and tumuli of that country. In the course of these investigations some coins were obtained, but the chief site of Mr. Masson's discoveries was at a place named Beghram. "In July of the present year (1833)," he states, "I left the city of Kabul to explore the districts north of it, at the base of the Hindoo Kush, with the primary object of identifying the site of Alexandria ad Caucasum: although upon this question I defer a decision until I can

[1] Bactrian and Indo-Scythic coins continued: J. As. Soc. B. vol. ii. p. 405.

[2] Memoir on the ancient coins found at Beghram in the Kohistan of Kabul; by Charles Masson: J. As. Soc. B. April, 1834, vol. iii. p. 153.

consult the ancient authorities, there being many spots which would agree with it in a local point of view, I was recompensed by the discovery of numerous interesting objects, and among them of an ancient city, of immense extent, on the plain now called Beghram, near the confluence of the rivers of Ghorbund and Punjshir, and at the head of the high road leading from Khaja Khedri of Kohistan to Nijrao, Taghao, Lughman, and Jelalabad. I soon learned that large numbers of coins were continually found on the plain, and my first excursion put me in possession of about eighty, procured with difficulty, as their owners were suspicious of my motives in collecting them. The coins were of such a type and description as naturally increased my ardor in their search; and, succeeding in allaying the mistrust of the finders, I obtained successive parcels, until up to this time (November, 1833) I have accumulated one thousand eight hundred and sixty-five copper coins, and fourteen gold and silver ones." It may be here observed, that Mr. Masson continued his researches at this place during the four succeeding years, and collected in this interval above thirty thousand coins.

In another communication to the Journal in January, 1836,[1] Mr. Masson gives further details of the topography of Beghram, the plain of which, he states, bears N. 15 E. from the modern city of Kabul, distant by computation eighteen ordinary kos; and as the line of road has few sinuosities or deflections, he estimates the direct distance to be about twenty-five miles. It is a square plain, of nearly six miles in each direction, situated at the north-east point of the level country of the Kohistan, in an angle formed by a ridge of the Hindu Kush and the inferior range of the Siah Koh. The whole extent is covered with fragments of pottery, lumps of iron, and other indications of a numerous population; and in the soil are found coins, seals, rings, and other signs of habitation: some few fragments of sculpture, and some tumuli, are observable; but no vestiges of buildings are discovered, except, at the depth of three or four feet, where are found, lines of cement which seem to be the remains of foundations, and large unburnt bricks forming

[1] Second memoir on the ancient coins found in the Kohistan of Kabul; by Charles Masson: J. As. Soc. B. vol. v. p. 1.

mounds of considerable extent, which have been supposed to indicate the walls of the city. Further research may, perhaps, bring more such remains to light; but, in the mean time, the superficial excavations of the Afghan shepherds, who conduct their flocks to pasture on this plain during the summer months, have for many years past redeemed from the ground vast quantities of copper coins. Mr. Masson estimates the number annually at thirty thousand, which, until they became objects of European search, were melted in the mint of Kabul, or by the coppersmiths of that city and Charikar, who repair to the tents of the shepherds and purchase them by weight. The far greater proportion, judging from Mr. Masson's own collection, must have been too much injured by time and corrosion to have had any other than metallic value; but from the same accumulations we may infer that great numbers of coins, of high numismatic interest, must have perished in the indiscriminate destruction to which the whole have for so long a time been condemned.

It is unnecessary to specify in any detail the coins which were thus first made public by Mr. Masson's investigations and memoirs; they are fully described in the following pages. It may be here mentioned, however, that in addition to new coins of Greek princes already known, he found those of several whose names are not mentioned in history, as Antialkidas, Lysias, Agathocles, Archebias, Pantaleon, and Hermæus. He also found the coins of the king whose titles only are specified as the Great King of kings, the Preserver, and of others whose names, although assuming a Greek form, indisputably denote barbaric or Indo-Scythic princes,—Undapherres, Azes, Azilises, Kadphises, and Kanerkes. Mr. Masson described the most remarkable of these, and furnished linear delineations of them, which were engraved in the Journal, and which, although not pretending to merit as works of art, were satisfactory confirmations of the correctness of his descriptions and decypherings. The first great step in the series of Bactrian numismatic discovery was thus accomplished, and the great object of later investigations has been to complete and extend the structure of which such broad foundations were laid.

A principal labourer in the accumulation of Bactro-Indian medals up to a late date has been Mr. Masson himself, and the Journal of the Asiatic

Society continued to be the medium by which the results were made public.[1] His researches were not limited to Beghram, but extended to the surrounding districts; and from Jelalabad, Peshawer, and Kabul,[2] and from the mountains of the Hazaras, he has drawn important accessions to his collections of Greek, Indo-Scythic, Hindu, Sassanian, and Mohammedan coins, as will be hereafter particularised. We shall, therefore, for the present, return to the collateral progress of Mr. Prinsep.

In consequence of a remark made in a previous number of the Journal (vol. ii. p. 308), intimating the hope that a more precise account of General Ventura's discoveries might be published in its pages, which remark was communicated to that officer, he immediately, with the most disinterested liberality, requested Captain Wade, the political resident at Ludiana, to accept the whole collection. Captain Wade declined the offer in favour of Mr. Prinsep, to whom it was in consequence forwarded through Captain Wade by General Ventura, with the simple request that Mr. Prinsep would favour him with a French translation of any description he might publish. He wrote to Captain Wade, "Veuillez, je vous prie, mon bon ami, vous servir de cette occasion pour faire agréer mon sentiment d'estime à M. Prinsep et de le prier en même temps de m'envoyer une description écrite en Français de ce qu'il pourra déchiffrer des inscriptions et empreintes de ma trouvaille." Mr. Prinsep remarks, "In acknowledging this unexpected and most disinterested offer I could not but disclaim all permanent interest in the relics, and request M. Ventura to consider them still at his disposal, although I should be proud, whilst they were deposited in my care, to do my utmost in making them more fully known to the world." This contest of liberality, equally honourable to all parties, ended in Mr. Prinsep's consenting to retain one or two specimens of such of the coins as were in any number. Two memoirs[3] were devoted by Mr. Prinsep to the subject of General Ventura's

[1] Second memoir on the ancient coins found at Beghram; by C. Masson: J. As. Soc. B. Jan. 1836, vol. v. p. 1.

[2] Third memoir, &c.: ibid. Sept. 1836, vol. v. p. 537.

[3] On the coins and relics discovered by M. le Chevalier Ventura in the Tope of Manikyala: J. As. Soc. B. Jan. 1834, vol. iii. p. 314. Continuation of observations on the coins, &c.: ibid. Sept. 1834, vol. iii. p. 436.

collection. The coins were Sassanian and Indo-Scythic. The Sassanian coins added to their usual characteristic types and legends the peculiarity of a Nagari inscription, of which the term Srí only was legible. A similar coin, however, obtained by Keramat Ali, at Kabul, added to this the Indian name Vasudeva, whilst at a considerably subsequent period some of the same coins enabled Mr. Prinsep to decypher the entire legend round their margin, referring them to Persian princes, though of unknown and uncertain appellations.[1] The Indo-Scythic coins were of the Kanerkes type; and by a comparison of those found at Manikyala with others sent from the Punjab and Afghanistan by Messrs. Masson, Wade, Burnes, and Gerard, and by Munshi Keramat Ali, the intelligent companion of Lieutenant Conolly in his journey overland from Persia to India, the legends on these coins, written in a barbarised form of Greek, were completely decyphered by Mr. Prinsep; that of the obverse being Rao Nana Rao Kanerki Korano, whilst on the reverse occurred Greek or Hellenised native names of the sun and moon, as Helios, Mithro, Mao, &c., and frequently the term Nanaia, in which Mr. Prinsep conjectured a reference to the goddess of the Persians, Anaitis or Anahid. The speculations on those coins are full of erudite and ingenious matter, and his conclusions have been adopted by the more practised and professional scholars of Europe. In a third memoir on the relics of Manikyala,[2] Mr. Prinsep displays acquirements of a different order, in a chemical analysis of a brown liquid found in one of the cylinders, and of some vitreous fragments; the latter proving to be of glass, the former consisting partly of vegetable or mineral matter in solution, with a small quantity of ammonia and phosphate of lime, indicating also animal remains. He also points out the remarkable concurrence of similar objects having been found in barrows or tumuli recently opened in Essex (Archæologia, vol. xxv.), and discusses the character and intention of the structures or topes in which they are found in India.

Besides the memoirs on the coins and relics of the Manikyala Tope opened

[1] J. As. Soc. B. May, 1838, vol. vii. p. 418.

[2] Note on the brown liquid contained in the cylinders from Manikyala; by J. Prinsep: J. As. Soc. B. Nov. 1834, vol. iii. p. 567.

by General Ventura, the same volume of the Journal[1] contains a translation by Mr. Prinsep of a memoir by Captain Court,[2] also an officer in the Sikh army, on other topes at the same place, opened by himself, and a note of some most curious discoveries made by him, especially of the presence of several Roman silver coins, which Mr. Prinsep describes and delineates. A correction of his description,[3] made by Lieutenant Cunningham, was immediately and thankfully published by him; but both have been since criticised, and their conclusions have been perfected by still higher authority, that of M. Raoul Rochette.[4] The general deduction, however, has been confirmed, and the coins in question are admitted to belong to the consular æra of Rome, at a date shortly anterior to the Christian æra.

The success which had attended the operations of General Ventura in exploring the contents of the Manikyala Tope had induced that officer to extend his inquiries, and to enlarge his collection of ancient coins. Being favourably situated for the accomplishment of such a purpose, his researches were rewarded with rapid success, and he very soon formed a valuable assemblage of those specimens of ancient medals which are to be found in the Punjab or between the Indus and Peshawer. The whole accumulation was intrusted to a brother officer, General Allard, who was returning by way of Calcutta to Europe. In Calcutta it was submitted to Mr. Prinsep's inspection, and specimens were also, with General Ventura's usual liberality, placed at his disposal. He prepared at the time a classified list of the collection,[5] and in the following year a more particular notice, with engravings of the individual coins. The collection consisted of several hundred pieces, and added to the Greek and Indo-Scythic series several new and interesting medals. The whole, as we shall have occasion to observe, were also fully described when they reached France. It may also here be mentioned that at a subsequent date, or in 1838, General Ventura himself visited

[1] Further information on the Topes of Manikyala: J. As. Soc. B. vol. iii. p. 556.

[2] Note on the coins discovered by M. Court, p. 562.

[3] Correction of a mistake, &c.; by Lieutenant A. Cunningham: J. As. Soc. B. vol. iii. p. 635.

[4] Journal des Savants, Feb. 1836, p. 71.

[5] Proceedings of the Asiatic Society; Journal, vol. iii. p. 591.

Europe, and brought home the accumulations of the intervening period, from which, while he was in London, he presented to the Royal Asiatic Society a selection containing some important novelties, which are specified in the following pages.

In addition to the coins from the Punjab and Afghanistan thus noticed, others were sent from the same direction by zealous contributors, whom we have already named. The collection of Sheikh Keramat Ali, political agent at Kabul on the part of the British Government, was submitted to the Asiatic Society on the 20th of May, 1834;[1] and another was laid before a meeting in August, brought over by Mohun Lal, a Hindu attached to the expedition of Lieutenant Burnes, and collected by Dr. Gerard and himself.[2] These, amounting to several hundred pieces, comprised specimens of all those discovered by Mr. Masson in the same localities, many of them in excellent preservation. Amongst the coins of Mohun Lal is specified a tetradrachm of Euthydemus, as remarkable for its rich relief and exquisite workmanship.

The interest excited by the coins and relics of the Punjab and the districts beyond the Indus stimulated persons less favourably circumstanced than the officers of Runjit Sinh to look around them for such remains of past times as India Proper might afford; and the search was not in vain. A curious discovery was made in 1833, by Captain Cautley, of the site of an ancient town near Behut in the Doab, which was seventeen feet below the surface of the soil.[3] It was laid bare in clearing out the bed of a canal; and amongst other relics a number of coins were found.[4] These were engraved and described by Mr. Prinsep; some were rude specimens of Indo-Scythic coins, but others formed a new series distinguished by peculiar types and ancient Sanscrit characters.[5] Their publication soon produced others of a similar description: two, procured at Chitore, were sent by Major Stacy;[6] others

[1] Journal, vol. iii. p. 247. [2] Ibid. vol. iii. p. 364.

[3] Discovery of an ancient town near Behut in the Doab; by Captain P. T. Cautley: J. As. Soc. B. vol. iii. p. 43. [4] Further account: ibid. p. 221.

[5] Note on the coins found at Behut; by J. Prinsep: ibid. p. 227.

[6] Note on two coins of the same species as those found at Behut; by Major Stacy: Journal, vol. iii. p. 431; with Observations, &c., by Mr. Prinsep, p. 443.

were obtained by Lieutenant Conolly at Kanoj, and several were comprised in the cabinet of Dr. Swiney. These were described and delineated by Mr. Prinsep, who also pointed out the identity of the letters borne by them to the ancient form of the Nagari alphabet found on the pillar or Lát at Allahabad, and then not decyphered. The alphabet has been since made out, and the legends on the coins have been read by Mr. Prinsep, when sufficiently entire or distinct.[1] They are the names and titles of princes not otherwise known. From the symbols, however, and especially from the Chaitya or Buddhist shrine, the coins of the Behut group are with reason regarded as belonging to a period when Buddhism prevailed in Upper Hindustan.[2]

At the same time another family of Indian coins was brought to notice — the coins of Kanoj. Some specimens of these had appeared, as above mentioned, in Colonel Tod's paper, in Marsden's Numismata, and in the 17th volume of the Researches, but little was known of their appropriation. The fortunate decyphering of the second inscription of the Allahabad column had, however, now given a new value to these coins; for, as pointed out by Dr. Mill,[3] they presented legends in similar letters, and were thus determined to belong to a dynasty of princes bearing the same family designation of Gupta. Some of these Gupta coins found at Kanoj by Lieutenant Conolly are described and figured by Mr. Prinsep in the Journal for May, 1834; and others are mentioned as having been obtained at Jonpur by Mr. Tregear, in a notice, communicated by him to Mr. Prinsep, of an ancient palace at that city.[4] By the end of 1834, or in less than two years from the first attempt made in Calcutta to describe and delineate the ancient coins of India, we had thus become possessed of vast numbers of the Greek coins of Bactria, many bearing the names of kings never heard of before, of equal numbers of the coins of the Indo-Scythic kings who succeeded the Greeks, and of the two families of the coins of Behut and Kanoj,

[1] Application of the Lát alphabet to the Buddhist group of ancient coins: J. As. Soc. B. June, 1837, vol. vi. p. 463.

[2] Coins and relics from Bactria: ibid. Dec. 1838, vol. vii. p. 1047.

[3] Restoration of the Inscription No. 2 on the Allahabad column; by the Rev. W. H. Mill, D.D. J. As. Soc. B. vol. iii. p. 257.

[4] J. As. Soc. B. vol. iii. p. 617.

—acquisitions which might have lingered on unnoticed and unprofitable for an indefinite period, had not the Editor of the Society's Journal been ever at hand to aid and encourage and make known the successful exertions of all who preceded or accompanied him in numismatic research.

The next contribution to the subject by Mr. Prinsep constitutes an important epoch in its history. The coins of Menander and Apollodotus, it had been all along observed, whilst they presented Greek inscriptions on one face, offered on the reverse a legend in unknown characters. The same circumstance was noticeable on the coins of the other Greek and of the Indo-Scythic kings, and the value of this unknown alphabet was a problem for solution. It was resolved by Mr. Prinsep. Having bestowed a deliberate investigation on the Bactrian and Indo-Scythic coins, and himself drawn and engraved no fewer than six plates of them, he published another memoir more fully descriptive of all which had been sent to him, or of which he had any knowledge, up to the middle of the year 1835.[1] The results of his investigation are thus enumerated by himself: "The careful examination of the whole has brought to light the names of several princes unknown to history, and some few not included in the very curious and novel list of Mr. Masson, published in the second volume of this Journal. It has also enabled me to appropriate to their right owners many of the coins of Lieutenant Burnes and other collectors, engraved in former plates. Further, it has furnished me with a clue to the Bactrian form (if we may so call it) of the Pehlevi character which is found on the reverse of many of these coins; and, lastly, it has laid open a perfect link and connexion between what we have hitherto called the Indo-Scythic coins with corrupted Greek inscriptions and the Hindu coins attributed with reasonable certainty to the Kanoj dynasties immediately anterior to the Mohammedan irruptions of the eleventh century. In a few more years we shall doubtless have the whole series, from the time of Alexander downwards, fully developed; at present, in these detached notices, we can do no more than hazard fresh conjectures, and wipe out former errors as we advance."

[1] Further notes and drawings of Bactrian and Indo-Scythic coins; by J. Prinsep: J. As. Soc. B. vol. iv. p. 327.

Of these results the most important was the ascertainment of the unknown alphabet. The circumstances under which it was decyphered are thus described by Mr. Prinsep: " Mr. Masson first pointed out in a note addressed to myself through the late Dr. Gerard, the Pehlevi signs which he had found to stand for the words Menandrou, Apollodotou, Ermaiou, Basileos, and Soteros. When a supply of coins came into my hands sufficiently legible to pursue the inquiry, I soon verified the accuracy of his observation, found the same signs with slight variation constantly to recur, and extended the series of words, thus authenticated, to the names of twelve kings and to six titles or epithets. It immediately struck me that if the genuine Greek names were faithfully expressed in the unknown character, a clue would through them be formed to unravel the value of a portion of the alphabet, which might in its turn be applied to the translated epithets and titles, and thus lead to a knowledge of the language employed. Incompetent as I felt myself to this investigation, it was too seductive not to lead me to an humble attempt at its solution."

Although thus diffident of his own competency, the object was pursued with great patience and ingenuity, and was rewarded with deserved success. Equivalents for the Greek letters were consistently made out, and an alphabet constructed by which the language also was ascertained. The paper from which the above passages are extracted contains an elaborate analysis of the inscriptions on the bilingual coins, and is illustrated by two plates, in one of which (Pl. XIX.) the letters on the coins, and on the cylinders found with the coins, are compared with those of the Zend and Pehlevi alphabets, with the Pehlevi letters on coins and inscriptions, and with the Hebrew. In the other (Pl. XX.) the Greek legends on the coins, as well as detached names, titles, and epithets, are compared with their equivalents in the Bactrian letters. Although not identical with any known letters, yet it was rendered certain that these letters belong to a family of which more modern representatives are found on the rocks of Persia, in inscriptions considered contemporaneous with the first Sassanian princes. Being induced, although doubtingly, from this resemblance of the letters, to refer the language to a Zend or Pehlevi affinity, Mr. Prinsep, in his first explanation of the title corresponding to Basileus, adopted that of Maleka, as read by M. De Sacy on the Sassanian coins; and so far his system was defective, as the consequence was a wrong valuation of several of the letters of the alphabet. He was not slow to perceive this himself, and, at a subsequent period, instituted a careful revision of his verifications, on which occasion he made the necessary corrections and additions, and determined the language to be, as he had always thought it likely to be, an Indian dialect of Sanscrit origin, to which the designation of Prakrit or Pali might be applied.[1]

This was the last great labour which his failing health permitted him to attempt, and it worthily terminated the long series of valuable memoirs through which he had so successfully prosecuted the subject of the numismatic history of India.

The other great object of Mr. Prinsep's conclusions was the connexion that existed between the Indo-Scythic and the Hindu coins of the Behut, Kanoj, Saurashtra, and Lahore families.[2] He traced the connexion through two memoirs, illustrated with engravings, and in the course of them determined several curious and novel facts.[3] The coins of the Behut group, of which he had now before him many additional specimens, are supposed to have originated with the rude pieces of metal (silver) which may be considered as amongst the earliest attempts of the Hindus to fabricate a national currency, and which have been found in all parts of India in considerable numbers.[4] At a later date they were more regularly formed, and when assuming Buddhist symbols, they were probably struck in the monasteries of the period. Those which offer imitations of the Indo-Scythic coins of course followed the establishment of the princes of that nation. From the manner in which the coins of Kadphises, Kanerkes, and Kenoranes are found intermixed, Mr. Prinsep naturally infers their belonging to a connected period, towards the close of which they assumed new types, which

[1] Additions to Bactrian numismatics, and revision of the Bactrian alphabet; by J. Prinsep: J. As. Soc. B. July, 1838, vol. vii. p. 636.

[2] On the connexion of various ancient Hindu coins with the Grecian or Indo-Scythic series: ibid. Nov. 1835, vol. iv. p. 621.

[3] Continuation of Notice of ancient Hindu coins: ibid. Dec. 1835, p. 668.

[4] As. Res. vol. xvii. pp 596, pl. V. figs. 101-108. See also, account of coins found in tumuli in the Peninsula of India: Archæologia, vol. xxii. p. 1.

were repeated in a better style of execution and with some modification upon the coins of Kanoj. The coins of Kadphises and Kanerkes are also connected with the latter, through the common use of a remarkable four-pronged symbol which invariably occurs upon them, whilst in a sitting female figure, on the reverse, they become the prototypes of coins which bear the names of the Rajas of Kanoj at the period of the Mohammedan conquest. Of the Kanoj coins of the middle period, bearing inscriptions in ancient Nagari, Mr. Prinsep gives drawings and descriptions of several, by which the names of eleven princes of the Gupta dynasty, in addition to two others from different authors, are ascertained. The subject of the connexion between the coins of Kanerkes, or, as Mr. Prinsep designates them, the Mithraic coins, and those of Kanoj, is further prosecuted in another memoir subsequently published.[1] In these papers many new and interesting varieties of both kinds are delineated, and important accessions are made to the Gupta dynasty. The coins are also traced to the rude imitations of them, which are not uncommon, but which, as sometimes found in the topes, must be of some considerable antiquity. In the first of the memoirs[2] Mr. Prinsep has paid a deserved tribute, one which he was ever willing to offer, to the exertions of his fellow-labourers in India, and in particular to Colonel Stacy, who had been long zealously and successfully engaged in the collection and study of Indian numismatics, before the existence of the Bactrian coins had been suspected. The field of Colonel Stacy's investigation, prior to his communication with Mr. Prinsep, was restricted to India Proper. It has recently been changed to the countries beyond the Indus; and the same success that attended them in Hindustan cannot fail to accompany them at Candahar, as Colonel Stacy has already given public demonstrations of unimpaired activity and undiminished zeal.

The second memoir, in the 4th volume of the Journal, on the connexion of the several series of coins, also describes those of Kanoj of the eleventh and twelfth centuries,—coins bearing the type of the Varáha or Boar, and coins of Ceylon found in India, the latter of which, offering decypherable legends,

[1] New varieties of the Mithraic or Indo-Scythic series of coins, and their imitations; by J. Prinsep: J. As. Soc. B. Oct. 1836, vol. v. p. 639.

[2] Journal, vol. iv. p. 621.

bear evidence to the truth of the chronicled existence of the sovereigns of that island. Equally curious results were afforded by a still more ample series of those termed Rajput coins, furnished by the collection of Colonel Stacy, and which, whilst they adopt on one face the mounted horseman of some of the Bactrian or Scythian coins, have on the other the Indian bull, and an inscription in Nagari letters of a middle age. These for a while represent the names of Hindu Rajas, but they come in time to denote the names of the Mohammedan princes of the family of Ghor, and of the first kings of Delhi, and, at last, are transformed to Arabic letters expressing the same denominations. These coins are exceedingly numerous, both in silver and copper. One or two had been previously noticed; one as a unique by Mr. Prinsep himself. It was now only, however, that their abundance and true character were made known. They are illustrated by ample historical details, derived from a diligent study of the records of the first establishment of the Mohammedan dominion in India.

Another and equally curious series of coins is the subject of description in the same memoir, the coins found in Surashtra, of which a few detached specimens only had been before published. The character of a head in profile on one side connected them, in Mr. Prinsep's opinion, with coins of Grecian origin. The reverse was marked with characters of which it was observed, "the marginal writing may with certainty be pronounced to be an ancient form of Sanscrit, but I cannot attempt to read it." The attempt was, however, subsequently made, and affords another instance of brilliant success.[1] In the eighth number of the Journal of the Royal Asiatic Society of Great Britain, is published a memoir on Saurashtra coins, with two plates of a considerable number of them, by J. R. Steuart, Esq. Copies of the plates were sent to Mr. Prinsep, and other specimens of the coins having also come into his possession, he had now ample means of examining the legends in a greater number and variety of conditions. This soon enabled him to detect the Nagari letter in a very simply modified form, and to read the inscriptions, which proved to be Sanscrit, expressing the name of the sovereign and his

[1] The legends of the Saurashtra group of coins decyphered; by J. Prinsep: J. As. Soc. B. May, 1837, vol. vi. p. 377.

predecessor. Eleven descents were thus made out of a dynasty bearing the name of Sah, as Rudra Sah and others. The discovery did not stop here. Returning to the subject on occasion of an ancient inscription from Girnar,[1] Mr. Prinsep found reason to correct his reading of one of the terms, which, upon revisal, proved to be the title *Kshatrapa*, so that these coins were proved to belong, not to kings, but to *Satraps* of the provinces at the mouth of the Indus; and the Persian title, so familiar to Grecian history, was thus traced to an intelligible Sanscrit compound, signifying Protector, or chief of the warrior or Kshatra caste. The same paper contains also the first intimation of a discovery which, if confirmed by further research, will be of exceeding importance,—the presence of dates upon the Saurashtra coins expressed in characters previously unknown. These are represented and compared with the numerals of other Asiatic people, and although the forms are unusual, yet their elements may be traced in recognised systems, and there is little reason to question the correctness of the office assigned to the symbols.

Whilst numismatic investigation was thus so vigorously and successfully prosecuted in India, so much of it as regarded the coins of the Greek and Indo-Scythic kings of Bactria and India became equally the object of interest and research in Europe. It is therefore necessary, in order to complete our view of the progress of the inquiry, to advert, however imperfectly, to the contributions made to our knowledge of the subject by the scholars of the West, who entered upon the inquiry with all the advantages derivable from familiarity with numismatic research, from ready access to cabinets and books, from friendly communication with talent and learning similarly directed, and from erudition,—the business, not the amusement of their lives,—advantages which the situation of individuals in India but imperfectly affords, or from which it wholly debars them.

The earliest as well as one of the most eminent European archæologists who resumed the subject of the numismatic illustration of Bactrian history was M. Raoul Rochette. Two medals from St. Petersburgh, a tetradrachm

[1] Examination of the inscriptions from Girnar, in Guzerat; by J. Prinsep: J. As. Soc. B. April, 1838, vol. vii. p. 334.

and drachm of Agathocles, having been purchased for the Royal cabinet, furnished the occasion of two articles published by him in the Journal des Savants, June and July, 1834. In these memoirs he enumerates the Bactrian coins which had been previously noticed, elaborately describes the coins which were the especial objects of his observations, and argues, we must be bold enough to think, with more erudition and plausibility than soundness, that Agathocles, and not, as usually affirmed, Theodotus, was the officer under whom Bactria first became independent, and who assumed the title and station of king. The coins and the arguments founded upon them will be hereafter noticed. Besides the coins strictly Bactrian, M. R. Rochette describes, in the second article, a gold coin brought by General Peyron from India, bearing a name in Greek letters, which he at first read Mokaupsices, but afterwards Mokadphises; the coin being one of the Indo-Scythic family, belonging to the prince whom Mr. Masson and Mr. Prinsep had designated Kadphises. M. R. Rochette repeats also, after Pellerin, the description and delineation of a coin having the head of a king on one side and a figure with a cornucopia on the other. Pellerin, who published it in 1767, observed that it was "une pièce singulière dont la tête lui était aussi inconnue que les legendes lui en paraissaient inintelligible," and he challenged the numismatists of his day to attempt its explanation. It was reserved for Mr. Prinsep to execute the task proposed; for the coin is one of the Indo-Scythic family, having on one side the legend Rao Nana Rao Oorki, and on the other Ardokro. It seems strange, now that we are familiar with the characters, that a corruption of the Greek alphabet, seemingly so palpable, should not have been at once detected. A misappropriation made by the same distinguished numismatist, Pellerin, was more excusable, although it furnishes a warning against confidence in erudition. One of the Rajput coins having come into his possession, he fancied the bull to represent Apis, and the Sanscrit letters to be Egyptian, and therefore ascribed a coin of a Raja of Lahore, of the ninth or tenth century, to Tiridates, the Persian Satrap of Egypt in the reign of Cambyses.

In the course of 1833 Lieutenant Burnes returned to Europe: the account of his travels was published early in 1834. Dr. Honigberger also returned in the same year from India, having travelled leisurely from the

Punjab through Afghanistan, and by way of Balkh and Bokhara to Orenburg, and thence to the capital of Russia, collecting on his route antiquities and coins, the greater part of which, obtained in the vicinity of Kabul, were transmitted by way of Calcutta to Paris. Notices of Dr. Honigberger's travels and collections were published in the Russian and German papers at the end of 1834, and in the following year he repaired to Paris, where his collections had arrived. He also visited London, where he disposed of a few coins; and by this means, and by the plates in Lieutenant Burnes' work, who presented the original coins to the British Museum, the numismatic stores of Bactria and India began to be appreciated. Further knowledge of them was disseminated by an account of Dr. Honigberger's coins, by M. R. Rochette, published in the Journal des Savants in September and October, 1835. The collection consisted, with one or two additions, of the same coins as those which had been found by Masson; but the Journal of the Bengal Asiatic Society was little known; and the commentary of the learned academician, giving them additional value, at once made them objects of attention and interest throughout Europe. The first part of a particular account of Dr. Honigberger's operations and of the antiquities he had discovered, with a biographical introduction, was submitted to the Asiatic Society of Paris in September, 1835, by the late M. Jacquet.[1] It was not published, however, until September, 1836; by which time the Bengal Journal for 1834, the third volume, had reached France, and contributed, as acknowledged by M. Jacquet and by M. Rochette, to elucidate the researches and discoveries made in Afghanistan. M. Jacquet's notice was prolonged through several numbers of the Journal Asiatique, and was finally interrupted, before it was completed, by his premature death.

The arrival of General Allard in Paris, and the presentation of the collection made by himself and General Ventura to the Royal cabinet, again supplied M. Rochette with ample materials for the application of his intelligence and learning to their illustration; and the Journal des Savants

[1] Notice sur les découvertes archéologiques faites par M. Honigberger dans l'Afghanistan; par M. E. Jacquet: Journ. Asiatique, Sept. 1836, p. 234. Suites, Nov. 1837, Fev. 1838, Mai, 1839.

of 1836 contains four consecutive and highly valuable memoirs upon the subject from his pen. Much important verification of the Greek and Bactro-Indian coins is afforded by these memoirs, and will be taken advantage of in the following description. A less elaborate but ingenious and talented account of General Allard's coins, of every class, was at the same time drawn up by M. Jacquet, and published in the Journal Asiatique of February, 1836.

The commendable industry of M. Mionnet included in the eighth volume of the Supplement to his great work on Classical Numismatics, published in 1837, a descriptive list of one hundred and forty-three Bactrian and Indo-Scythic coins. It is compiled chiefly from the memoirs of Jacquet and R. Rochette. It is, however, to be regretted that he should have thought it necessary to engrave the Bactrian inscriptions without making himself acquainted with Mr. Prinsep's unexceptionable order of arrangement. In the chance-medley form in which they appear in Mionnet's table they are worse than useless, and only calculated, if consulted at all, to puzzle and mislead.

We have not the same facility for tracing the progress of the interest excited by the Bactro-Indian coins in other parts of Europe, but the learned men of Germany are always too vigilantly awake to objects of intellectual activity for us to doubt that their attention was at an early date directed to the antiquarian harvests of Afghanistan. M. Rochette, in September, 1835, speaks of a letter from the elder Grotefend on the subject of Dr. Honigberger's collection; and in a subsequent memoir adverts to notices published by Grotefend the younger in 1835, and by Arneth, at Vienna, in the Vienna Jahrbucher of 1837 and 1838. These latter articles are reviews of Mr. Prinsep's papers in the Calcutta Journal, and of M. Rochette's in the Journal des Savants. The celebrated C. O. Muller has also on three different occasions, in 1835, 1838, and 1839, made the Indo-Greek coins the subject of learned disquisitions in the Gottingen Anzeigen. In 1838 a work of exceeding interest and utility was published by Professor Lassen on the history of the Greek and Indo-Scythic kings of Bactria, Kabul, and India, through the decyphering of the old Kabul legends on their coins. In this work, which is less of a numismatic than a historical composition, Professor Lassen investigates the characters upon the coins, and whilst he concurs with Mr. Prinsep in most of them, suggests alterations in others, agreeing in some cases with the changes adopted finally by Mr. Prinsep himself. The work contains also a topographical description of the countries which were the chief sites of Greek and Indo-Scythic rule, and a classification of the different dynasties, with a chronological arrangement of the several individuals. Where the premises are so far from being complete or precise, the deductions are unavoidably liable to question. That Professor Lassen's classification and chronology are susceptible of improvement is admitted by himself; but, although they can scarcely be regarded as conclusive, it is nevertheless difficult to substitute others that will not be equally open to exception. Since the publication of his work Germany has supplied another serviceable contribution to this department of research, in the "Coins of Greek, Parthian, and Indo-Scythian Kings of Bactria and the countries on the Indus," by Dr. C. L. Grotefend, published last year at Hanover.

The cultivation of numismatic studies in this country has been of late years but little prosecuted, and is, when pursued, of a somewhat circumscribed and exclusive tendency. The medals of the East have never been thought worthy of attention, and even for the coinage of the Mohammedan kings of Delhi we must seek for information in continental rather than in English publications. Marsden is the only exception; and his work, although of great merit and extent, is far from enabling us to dispense with the works of Fræhn and other eminent continental numismatists. It is not surprising, therefore, that upon a subject so novel nothing should have been yet published in London beyond the few observations addressed by myself to the Numismatic Society, printed in the Numismatic Journal, January, 1838, and the remarks made upon the paper in the Annual Report of the Society's Proceedings for 1837-1838, by the President, Dr. Lee.

The indifference thus manifested in England is not, however, shared by our neighbours, and this recapitulation of their labours cannot better terminate than with the latest which, as far as I know, has appeared, and which is again from the indefatigable pen of M. R. Rochette. A further collection of antiquities and coins, that made by M. Court, was brought to Paris in 1838: a general list of it was printed in the Revue Numismatique, No. II. for 1839, but a more detailed description of the novelties which it contained, as well as of some others which had come to his knowledge, was immediately undertaken by M. Rochette. Two memoirs have accordingly been published in the Journal des Savants; one in December, 1838, and the other in the February following. The series, however, is yet incomplete,—much, I confess, to my regret; as although I may sometimes take the liberty of demurring to M. Rochette's conclusions, I do not the less prize the extent and depth of classical and antiquarian erudition and numismatic experience by which his papers on the coins of Bactria are so eminently distinguished. This acknowledgment is due for the great advantage I have reaped from his publications, and I have the more satisfaction in making it, that he has in his last memoirs paid a just tribute to the merits of Mr. Prinsep. He thus speaks of his labours: "A l'avantage d'avoir fait connoître le premier par des dessins aussi satisfaisants que possible des monuments si remarquables à tant de titres, avantage qu'il dévait à sa position, ce savant a joint le merite qui lui appartient en propre d'ouvrir la voie au déchiffrement et à l'interprétation des inscriptions en caractères Indo-Bactriens qui ont été pour la science une source non encore épuisée de révélations aussi nouvelles qu' inattendues."

Although the object of the present publication is in an especial degree a description of the coins found in Afghanistan by Mr. Masson, yet, as a scarcely inferior interest attaches to the remarkable monuments in which some of the coins, along with other remains of antiquity, have been met with, and as the two objects have been investigated at the same time and by the same individual, the account of the progress of numismatic discovery in this field, would be imperfect without some notice of that with which it was associated, and from which it in some degree originated. For the monuments themselves, however, at least for those situated in Afghanistan, where they occur apparently in the greatest number, the following memoir of Mr. Masson will furnish more authentic and circumstantial details than have yet been before the public. It is only necessary, therefore, to prefix to them a brief notice of the steps by which they have been brought to our knowledge, and the measures adopted for the determination of their construction and contents.

The edifices which have of late years attracted so much attention in the north-west of India and in Afghanistan, have been known by the general appellation of Topes, a word signifying a mound or tumulus, derived from the Sanscrit appellation Sthúpa, having the same import. The first building of the class which came under observation was one at Sarnath, about four miles from Benares. In 1794 a native, digging for stones from extensive ruins at this spot, discovered, twenty-seven feet below the surface, a stone urn, of the size and shape of the Barberini vase, enclosing one also of stone; within which were some human bones, pearls, gold leaves, and jewels of no value.[1] A statue of Buddha was also found, bearing an inscription which stated that a monastery and a lofty shrine had been built, or rather repaired, here in Samvat, 1083 (A.D. 1026). The inscription terminated with a stanza in honour of Buddha, which is familiar to all Buddhists as a short invocation or prayer in common use, and which was found, when the building was opened in 1835, upon a stone slab in the interior of the edifice.[2] Other specimens of Buddhist sculpture, from the same locality, were presented to the Asiatic Society of Bengal; and left no doubt, therefore, that the structure was a Buddhist monument or tope.[3] Although frequently mentioned, there is nowhere any detailed description of this monument; but some account of it by Mrs. Stewart Mackenzie occurs in Mr. Erskine's valuable paper on the remains of the Buddhists in India;[4] and several circumstances relating to its history and design, as well as to the form and size of the urn, are given by Colonel Wilford.[5] In his latter paper he describes the monument as being about fifty feet high, of a cylindrical shape, with its top shaped like a dome, corresponding in these respects with the ordinary construction of a tope.

A few years after this, the visits of Colonel Mackenzie and Mr. Harrington to Ceylon added to the knowledge of the peculiar form of certain shrines or temples erected by the Buddhists. At Devendar or Dondera the former noticed a low temple, of a circular shape, of about one hundred and sixty feet in circumference, erected on a platform. The structure, it was said, was solid, and had one of the teeth of the sacred elephant enshrined in it.

[1] As. Res. vol. v. p. 131.

[2] J. As. Soc. B. March, 1835, vol. iv. p. 132, and ibid. pp. 211, 712.

[3] J. As. Soc. B. Sept. 1836, vol. v. p. 588.

[4] Transactions of the Literary Society of Bombay, vol. iii. p. 519.

[5] As. Res. vol. ix. p. 203, and vol. x. p. 130.

Mr. Harrington describes a dahgopa at Kalanee as a solid mass of earth and brick-work sixty feet high, and shaped somewhat like a dome, with a cupola above. This monumental temple was said to contain twenty images of Buddha buried underneath it. These accounts were published in 1799.[1] We have, however, much later and fuller information regarding the Ceylon monuments, and they afford most valuable illustrations of the whole class, being situated in a country where they have ever been and are still well-known objects of veneration. We have various notices of them, but the latest and most fully detailed are contained in the Transactions of the Royal Asiatic Society, and in the intelligent work of an officer who resided some years in the island, lately published: both accounts are illustrated with plates.[2] At Anuradhapura, the ancient capital of the island, the Anuragrammam of Ptolemy, are seven dahgopas, some of immense size. One of these, not the largest, but the most elegant, is entitled Topha-Rama, the former member of which is, no doubt, the Pali representative of the Sanscrit Sthúpa, the original of 'tope.' The Tope of Mehetelé, twelve miles north-east of Anuradhapura, although in ruins, is nearly two hundred feet high, and is said to be more than a thousand feet above the level of the sea. Two hundred steps led to the platform on which it stood. It appears also, from Dr. Davy,[3] that the operations which were instituted of late in Hindustan were anticipated in Ceylon, and with similar results. A ruined dahgopa, whose dimensions are not stated, was opened near Colombo by Mr. Layard: in the midst a small square compartment was discovered, lined with brick, paved with coral, and containing in the centre a small cylindrical vase of grey granite covered exactly with a rounded top of the same stone, several small clay images of the hooded snake, a common earthen lamp, and a small obelisk or four-sided truncated pyramid. The vase contained a *small fragment of bone*, bits of thin plate gold, some small gold rings, two or three small pearls, beads of rock-crystal

[1] As. Res. vol. viii. pp. 439, 450.

[2] Some remarks upon the ancient city of Anuradhapura and the hill temple of Mehentala in the island of Ceylon; by Captain J. J. Chapman; read July, 1832: Trans. Roy. As. Soc. vol. iii. p. 468. Eleven Years in Ceylon, &c.; by Major Forbes: London, 1840.

[3] Account of the Interior of Ceylon; by J. Davy, M. D.: London, 1821, p. 221, note, with a delineation.

and cornelian, small fragments of ruby, blue sapphire and zircon, and pieces of glass in the shape of icicles, which were crystalline and opaque. Dr. Davy points out the analogy these relics offered to the articles found at Sarnath; and we shall see that the 'trouvailles' which have been afforded by the topes in Upper India will show that these are precisely the articles found in them, with the addition of coins, of which it is not said whether the Ceylon monuments were productive.

The use of the term tope in connexion with monuments of this shape was first adopted when the next building of the class was discovered in Upper India. In 1808 the embassy to Kabul, conducted by Mr. Elphinstone, when upon their way back to India, arrived at a part of the country between the Indus and the Jhelum,[1] in which, according to the notions of Colonel Wilford, the capital of Taxiles, the ally of Alexander, was situated. A party left the camp to explore the neighbourhood for relics of antiquity, in confirmation of this opinion; and they met with this edifice, the Tope of Manikyala, a solid circular building of masonry, surmounted by a dome, and resting upon a low artificial mound. It was estimated to be about seventy feet high, and was one hundred paces in circumference; it was built of brick cased with stone, but the casing was in some parts apparently unfinished. Some broad steps led up to the base, which was encircled by a moulding about eight feet high. Above this rose a perpendicular wall for about six feet, and thence the building ascended in a spherical form. Those who saw it felt inclined to look upon it as of Grecian architecture; but, although its elevation may have been influenced by a recollection of Grecian buildings, yet it has been since fully proved the work of Indian artists. The building was called by the natives a tope; Manikyala is the name of the village near which it stands. The village lies about forty kos E.S.E. from Attok, on the Indus, and thirty-four N.W. from the town of Jhelum, on the river of that name, the ancient Hydaspes. Its geographical position leaves little doubt of its being the site of the capital of Taxiles, or, more correctly speaking, of the city Taxila—the Tax-sila of the Hindus; and the identity is confirmed by the ancient remains scattered about the country. The party that visited Manikyala saw no other vestiges of an ancient city than the tope: but in this

[1] Elphinstone's Account of Kabul, p. 78.

they were deceived by the hurried nature of their excursion; they had not time to search, and rather hastily inferred that nothing was to be found. Twelve years afterwards, Moorcroft, crossing the spot, was informed by the people that old wells, fragments of pottery, and ancient coins, were frequently discovered.[1] Lieutenant Burnes obtained, whilst there, old coins and antiques;[2] and M. Court, whose opportunities have been still more propitious to discovery, describes the neighbourhood as strewed with ruins, the remains of massive walls, of old wells, and of tombs and temples; he found also and opened no fewer than fifteen topes. With respect to the edifice originally noticed, many years elapsed before its character was ascertained by actual examination; but Mr. Erskine accurately determined it when observing, "although its origin is unknown, yet in its hemispherical form and whole appearance it carries with it sufficient proof that it was a magnificent dahgope or Buddha shrine, constructed at a remote period by persons of the Buddhist faith."

Before the Tope of Manikyala was opened, however, monuments of a somewhat similar description were discovered in other parts of India. One of these was found at Amaravati, a town on the south bank of the Krishna river, in the Guntoor Sircar. Upon the edge of the town rose a remarkable mound named Dipaldinna, or the 'hill of lights;' it was one hundred and twenty-eight feet in diameter and sixteen high; the centre was occupied by a tank, and the base had been enclosed by a double row of stones richly sculptured, but many had been removed or destroyed. There were gateways on four sides, and over one of them was an inscription in old Nagari letters, whilst on a slab of stone near the spot occurred an inscription in ancient but different letters.[3] Near at hand were the remains of an ancient city named Dharani-Kota, considered to have been at one time the capital of Telingana; and at a short distance to the south were a number of circular tumuli, which are yet unexplored. The place was first noticed by the late Colonel Mackenzie and his assistants. I have not found any description of it amongst his papers; but, from a few brief memoranda, it appears to have been

[1] Travels, vol. ii. p. 311.

[2] Travels, vol. i. p. 67.

[3] Decyphered by Prinsep; J. As. Soc. B. March, 1837. The slab itself and several specimens of the sculptures are in the Museum at the India House.

visited by him repeatedly, and in 1816 to have been measured and surveyed. Several of the sculptured slabs were brought away by him, and some of them are now in the Museum of the Asiatic Society of Bengal and in that of the East India Company. The Company's Library also contains a volume of copiously delineated details. From a duplicate of this volume, presented to the Asiatic Society of Bengal, Mr. Prinsep, with his usual alacrity, had the inscriptions engraved in the sixth volume of the Society's Journal. One is in an ancient form of Nagari, and begins with three characters, which are precisely the same as those on a slab at Haburenne, in Ceylon, and as those on the early Kanoj coins. Mr. Prinsep has not, however, offered any interpretation, waiting apparently for a *fac-simile* of the Ceylon inscription. The inscription on the slab he has made out; it is in Sanscrit, and consists of moral precepts of a Buddhist purport. The characters are very remarkable; for they form, as Mr. Prinsep observes, the link between the early Devanagari characters of Northern India, and the more florid and, at first sight, dissimilar alphabets of the South. The coins are rude and worn. Some are stamped on one face only, with the Indian bull, the hooded snake, and a crescent,—types of Siva: others are struck on both sides: one face bears a kind of star enclosed in a circle; the other has a brief inscription in Nagari, of the same date as the inscription on the gateway, but of which Mahá (great) is the only word that can be decyphered. The entire word may have been Mahádeva or Mahánandi. These coins are, therefore, the coins of a Saiva prince. The sculptures, however, are eminently Buddhist, and there can be no doubt that Dipaldinna presents the remains of a Buddhist tope.

Another remarkable monument of the same class was first noticed by Captain Fell, on the west bank of the Betwa river, near Bhilsa. He published a description of it in the Calcutta Journal of the 11th of July, 1819, whence it is reprinted by Mr. Prinsep in the third volume of the Journal of the Asiatic Society of Bengal, p. 490, with additional illustrations and a *fac-simile* of an inscription. This account is sufficient to determine that the building is a tope; but the point has been fully ascertained since by further and more satisfactory investigations. In the sixth volume of the Journal, p. 451, *fac-similes* of several inscriptions at Sanchi or Bhilsa, by Captain

Smith, and drawings of the monument and its sculptures, by Captain Murray, are published, with remarks by Mr. Prinsep; and in the seventh volume, p. 562, a number of short inscriptions taken by Captain T. S. Burt, are published, with translations and remarks by the same indefatigable palæographer. They led to important results, enabling Mr. Prinsep to extend his discoveries, and to complete the decyphering of the ancient alphabet on the staff of Firoz Shah, the Buddhist coins of Behut, and, finally, the inscriptions on the rocks in Orissa and Guzerat. One of the inscriptions at Sanchi or Bhilsa is said to have been made in the reign of Chandragupta.

Whilst, however, the precise nature of the edifices at Benares, Amaravati, and Bhilsa, remained a subject of some uncertainty, their interior structure having been unexamined, the monument at Manikyala was opened, and the contents gave a new impulse, fresh certainties, and additional encouragement to inquiry. The time and circumstance of this occurrence have been already alluded to. The particulars, first published from General Ventura's private correspondence in the Calcutta Journal, were transferred to the Asiatic Researches. A further account, and a description of the articles found in excavating the Manikyala Tope, were published by Mr. Prinsep in the Journal of the Society for July, 1834, and again in November of the same year. General Ventura being encamped with the Sikh force under his command at Manikyala in the beginning of 1830, employed the people at his disposal in the examination of the structure which Mr. Elphinstone's companions had discovered, and which, as far as its exterior denoted, seemed to be a solid mass of masonry. The excavation was commenced on the 27th of April, 1830, at the base of the cupola, but the work was so much interrupted by the falling in of the superjacent materials, that it was found necessary to abandon the purpose, and to recommence at the summit of the building. The following is a summary of the result.

On the 28th of April the cap of the cupola was laid open, and at the depth of three feet six coins were discovered.

On the 1st of May, at the depth of twelve feet, a square mass of masonry of quarried stones in the centre of the building was found; on piercing into which, to the depth of ten feet, a single coin was discovered.

On the 6th of May, at the depth of twenty feet, one silver and six copper coins were discovered.

On the 8th the workmen found, at the bottom of the square mass of masonry, an iron box containing one of gold, in which was a gold coin, a gold ring, a bit of pale ruby, three small silver coins, one large Sassanian coin, two smaller Indo-Sassanian coins, and one rude Hindu silver coin.

On the 12th of May the perforation had reached thirty-six feet, when another copper coin presented itself.

The work proceeded, without any further discoveries being made, to the 25th of May, when a depth of forty-five feet was attained. On lifting up a large quarried stone, another similar to it was found underneath, having a hollow in its centre, in which was deposited a copper vase, and in it were a piece of cloth, a crystal drop, and a cylinder of pure gold. On the 27th of May, at the depth of fifty-four feet, another copper coin was found. On the 29th, at sixty-four feet deep, a copper ring, a cowrie shell, an iron ring, and three broken Sassanian coins, were met with. On the 31st of May the principal discovery rewarded the General's labours. An immense stone slab seemed to cover the whole surface; when this was raised, a small chamber was perceived, a foot in breadth and depth, filled up with stone and lime, in the midst of which, when carefully removed, was found a box of copper filled with a brown compound liquid; in the fluid was a brass cylindrical box, turned on a lathe, having an inscription punched or dotted on the lid: within this box were five Indo-Scythic copper coins, and a gold cylindrical box containing fragments of glass, a small gold coin, and a disc of silver, with characters similar to those on the lid. Outside of the copper box were forty-four coins, of the same description as those within the brass vessel; coins since familiar to us as those of Kadphises and Kanerkes.

The excavations were continued to the 8th of June, twenty feet below the foundation, but only a few more copper coins were found, and it was evidently unnecessary to proceed farther. The articles were sent to Mr. Prinsep, and are described and engraved by him in the numbers of the Journal above referred to.

Animated by the success which had attended M. Ventura's excavation, some of his companions in the service of Runjit Sinh engaged actively in similar researches; for it now appeared that the Tope of Manikyala was not a solitary instance of this kind of edifice in the Punjab. Even at Manikyala itself, others were discovered, smaller, but of similar form. M. Court enumerates no fewer than fifteen which he had opened, and in which he had found coins and antiquities of a similar description. In one of these, situated about a cannon-shot N.N.E. from the village of Manikyala, much dilapidated, but forming a mound about sixty or seventy feet high, M. Court made some singularly interesting and important discoveries. At a depth of thirteen feet, he came to a massive stone slab which was covered with inscriptions on the lower surface, forming the roof of a hollow parallelogram, constructed of stones cemented with mortar. In the centre stood a copper urn enveloped in linen, containing a silver cylinder; in the latter were seven silver coins and a gold cylinder; within the latter were four gold coins of the Indo-Scythic king, Kanerkes. The silver coins were all Roman coins of an early date. This was at once seen by Mr. Prinsep, and his verifications were in part confirmed and extended by Lieutenant Cunningham.[1] But what they left doubtful or erroneous was subsequently amended by M. Raoul Rochette, who identifies the whole seven as Roman coins struck between the years of Rome 680 and 720. One he leaves, from its being too much worn, undetermined; four he recognises as the coins of the Roman families Minucia, Plætoria, Cordia, and Accoleia; one is a coin of Julius Cæsar whilst Proconsul of Gaul, and one of Marc Antony as Triumvir.[2] These coins are therefore of great chronological value, and determine the construction of the monument, in which they were found, to have taken place at a period not very long subsequent to the æra of Christianity.

The existence of topes on the west of the Indus and in Afghanistan had been observed by Messrs. Moorcroft and Trebeck in 1820, on their way from the Punjab to Kabul; but they have lost the credit of priority by the delay which has taken place in the publication of their Travels. The first published intimation of their occurrence in Afghanistan is a short notice of those at Peshawer and Khyber, by Lieutenant Burnes, in the Asiatic Society's Journal, vol. ii. p. 308, at a subsequent period reprinted in his Travels:

[1] J. As. Soc. B. vol. iii. p. 564 and 635.

[2] Journ. des Sav. Fév. 1836.

but this was soon followed by a more ample account of the labours of the two persons who have been most distinguished for their researches amongst the topes,—Dr. Martin Honigberger and Mr. Masson. The first account was drawn up by Dr. Gerard at Jelalabad in December, 1833, and was published in the Society's Journal, July, 1834, along with a letter to Dr. Gerard from Mr. Masson, giving a detail of some of his operations. Dr. Honigberger, as has been mentioned, was a medical officer in the Sikh service, who on his way to Europe spent some time in Afghanistan, where he employed himself in excavating a number of topes in the vicinity of Jelalabad and Kabul. We have also alluded to the detailed and interesting notices of his operations and their results by the late M. Jacquet in the Journal Asiatique. Mr. Masson is an English gentleman who in 1833 had been resident some time in Kabul, and is still in that part of India. The longer duration of his residence has afforded him more numerous opportunities, than his associates possessed, of exploring the topes of Afghanistan, and he has availed himself of them with remarkable perseverance and intelligence. Various notices of his proceedings, drawn up by himself or his friends, appeared in the volumes of the Asiatic Society's Journal; but they were occasional and general, and not designed to supply those minuter details which were requisite for a precise appreciation of the scene and subjects of his labours. That such particulars had been compiled by him was known not only from his own information, but from the delineations of the site of the topes of Kabul, with which M. Jacquet's account of Dr. Honigberger's operations was illustrated, and with which the latter had been presented by Mr. Masson. The want of such illustrations of Mr. Masson's own researches was sensibly felt by M. Jacquet, and he remarks, "Ce grand domaine de l'antiquité ne sera donc entièrement restitué à la science que lorsque M. Masson aura communiqué au public la notice des recherches archéologiques qu'il y a exécutées."[1] Concurring in these opinions, I applied to Mr. Masson for more precise indications than had been yet published, and received from him, in consequence, the memoir and illustrations which follow,

[1] Journ. Asiat. Mai, 1839. Although entitled 'a continuation of the notices of Dr. Honigberger's discoveries,' this memoir is chiefly devoted to an account of Mr. Masson's operations.

with permission to make use of them. I have thought it advisable to print them unaltered, as they supply all the requisite details, and Mr. Masson's own views, which are entitled to the greatest consideration. It is only necessary here to state briefly those which I entertain respecting the construction, date, and objects of these buildings.

A tope is, or has been, a circular building of stone, or brick faced with stone or stucco, erected on a platform which has been built upon either a natural or artificial elevation. It is distinguished, according to Mr. Masson, from a tumulus by having a distinct cylindrical body interposed between a circular basement and a hemispherical cupola. This is, no doubt, the case at Sarnath, and in most of the topes of Afghanistan. In the great Tope of Manikyala, however, the perpendicular part between the basement and dome scarcely constituted a perceptible division. At Bhilsa, Amaravati, and still more in Ceylon, time, vegetation, and decay have effaced these distinctions, and the tope occurs as a mound rising conically from an irregularly circular base. Steps usually lead up to the basement of the building or the platform on which it stands. It seems not unlikely that the cupola was crowned by a spire. Such embellishments usually terminate temples in Buddhist countries, to which these topes are considered analogous, as well as the dahgopas, which present other analogies. They are also found on what may be considered miniature representations of the topes, which have been discovered within them; and the Ceylon topes have evidently been thus terminated.[1] Traces of spires are visible on the summits of the great mounds of Abhayagiri and Jaita-wana.[2] The dimensions of the topes vary considerably. Many of those in Afghanistan are small, and the largest are not of great size: the circumference of few of them at the base exceeds one hundred and fifty feet; and their elevation apparently does not often reach sixty. Sarnath, as above mentioned, is about fifty feet high, and may be as many paces in circumference. The Manikyala Tope, opened by General Ventura, is stated by M. Court to be eighty feet high, and three hundred and ten to three hundred

[1] See accompanying plates. Antiquities, Plate III. fig. 1. See also Plate III. of M. Jacquet's notice in the Journ. Asiat. of May, 1839. The smaller tope, found by Dr. Honigberger within that of Ek-dhara, has a similar spire.

[2] Eleven Years in Ceylon, vol. i. p. 220. Trans. Roy. As. Soc. vol. iii. Plate XIX.

and twenty in circumference; the others at the same place were smaller. The base of the Amaravati Tope is about five hundred feet in circumference, but the elevation is inconsiderable. The Tope of Bhilsa is large, the circumference of the base being five hundred and fifty-four feet, and the height one hundred and twelve feet; but the elevation has been much greater, as the cupola has fallen in. The topes of Ceylon, however, are the first in dimensions. The Abhayagiri, it is said, was four hundred and five feet high, and it is still two hundred and twenty feet in elevation. The Jaita-wana, which it is asserted was originally of the height of three hundred and fifteen, rises to that of two hundred and sixty-nine feet, and is of considerable expansion. A calculation of its solid contents, as cited by Major Forbes, conveys a striking impression of its dimensions. It has been computed that a brick wall twelve feet high and two broad, and ninety-seven miles long, might be constructed with the still remaining materials.[1]

The topes are uniformly asserted to be solid, and the assertion has been verified in all the numerous instances examined. The interior is filled up with stones, rough or hewn, or with bricks cemented more or less compactly by lime or earth. The operations of M. Ventura indicated the presence of a number of small square chambers, formed by the stones being placed on their edges and covered over by a flat slab, along a line drawn through the centre from the summit to the base. This arrangement has suggested to the celebrated geographer Ritter[2] the theory, that a tope should contain a series of chambers or stages, such as are found in the pagodas of the Chinese, and which are typical of the stages by which a Buddha attains perfection. This notion is not, however, consistent with the condition of the topes of Afghanistan: their general principle is the enclosure of a tope within a tope; the larger building being constructed over a smaller,—solid as well as the larger,—but having a well-defined line of separation; within the smaller edifice is the space or small chamber in which the relics are deposited. The situation of the inner tope is either at the lower part of the building or where the cylindrical part and basement story meet. Mr. Masson's sections represent the form, situation, and proportions of several

[1] Eleven Years in Ceylon, vol. i. p. 228.

[2] Die Stupas (Tope); von Carl Ritter. Berlin.

of these chambers: they are usually as high as the basement, and the diameter is sometimes specified as seven or eight feet. The topes of Ceylon in like manner are said to have been erected around a small cell or hollow stone containing relics. In some instances spaces have also been found in the centre or at the summit of the topes: in the centre they are commonly indicated by a large and heavy slab of stone lying over them. In a few cases tunnels leading from the interior cell to the circumference have been met with, as if it had been designed to leave access to the relic. The advantage of this is not very apparent, as the cell itself being solid, the casket, or whatever was enshrined within it, could not have been extracted without the demolition of the cell,—an operation not practicable by such an approach. There are traditions current, however, both in Afghanistan and Ceylon, of passages having been made into the interior of the topes. At Anuradhapura, King Dutagamonoo is said to have opened by divine aid an underground entrance into the interior cell of Rumanwali, by which he entered and worshipped the relics it contained.[1] The proprietor of the land on which the Tope of Chakri-bala, near Kabul, stands, informed Dr. Honigberger that some years before, whilst constructing a subterranean water-course, his workmen came upon a tunnel, which, seeming to proceed towards the tope, he directed them to enter it, and ascertain whether it did so terminate: after penetrating some distance they were driven back, they asserted, by bats; but they soon afterwards left the country without even demanding the wages that were due to them, and it was thence inferred that they had found a treasure, with which they had absconded. The story is rather suspicious; but the existence of underground passages to the bases of the topes is not impossible, especially if, as indicated by the discovery at Sarnath, the essential relic is not within the tope itself, but at some depth under the foundations. That such was sometimes the practice is confirmed by the inscription found at Islamabad (Chittagong), of which a translation is published in the second volume of the Asiatic Researches;[2] in which it is recorded that the Raja dug a cave (or cell) four feet and a half in depth, and as many in diameter, and paved it (rather, perhaps, filled it) with brick, for the purpose of depositing in it

[1] Eleven Years in Ceylon, vol. i. p. 224. [2] As. Res. vol. ii. p. 383.

images of Buddha, with a vessel of brass, in which were deposited two of the bones of the Thacur, with sundry holy texts inscribed on a silver plate; and over this cave was erected a place of worship, probably a tope, for the veneration of the Magas. Colonel Wilford also affirms, upon the authority of oral information received from Buddhists, "the sacred relics are not deposited in the pyramid, but are always placed in a small vault deep underground at some distance from it."[1] This does not seem to have been the case in Afghanistan, or in the Punjab. At Manikyala, General Ventura's excavations descended some way below the foundations, and found nothing. They do not seem to have been prosecuted so far in the Afghan topes; but the presence of the inner cell renders it unlikely that any other place of deposit exists. At the same time it may be desirable to verify the fact, should opportunity occur.

Many of the topes have yielded no return to the labour expended upon them; others have been rich in relics. It is a curious circumstance, noticed by Mr. Masson, that where those substances which appear to be the remains of a funeral pile, as ashes and animal exuviæ, most abound, the relics of antiquity are least abundant. The most conspicuous objects are, in general, vessels of stone or metal: they are of various shapes and sizes; some of them have been fabricated on a lathe. They commonly contain a silver box or casket; and within that, or sometimes by itself, a casket of gold. This is sometimes curiously wrought. One found by Mr. Masson at Deh Bímaran is chased with a double series of four figures representing Gautama in the act of preaching; a mendicant is on his right, a lay-follower on his left, and behind the latter a female disciple: they stand under arched niches resting on pillars, and between the arches is a bird: a row of rubies is set round the upper and lower edge of the vessel, and the bottom is also chased with the leaves of the lotus: the vase had no cover. Within these vessels, or sometimes in the cell in which they are placed, are found small pearls, gold buttons, gold ornaments and rings, beads, pieces of white and coloured glass and crystal, pieces of clay or stone with impressions of figures, bits of bone, and teeth of animals, of the ass and goat species,[2] pieces of cloth, and folds of

[1] As. Res. vol. x. p. 129.

[2] They have been verified by Mr. Clift.

the Tuz or Bhurj leaf, or rather the bark of a kind of birch on which the Hindus formerly wrote; and these pieces bear sometimes characters which may be termed Bactrian, but they are in too fragile and decayed a state to admit of being unfolded or read. Similar characters are also found superficially scratched upon the stone, or dotted upon the metal vessels. In one instance they were found traced upon the stone with ink. Within some of the vessels was also found a liquid, which upon exposure rapidly evaporated, leaving a brown sediment, which, as already noticed, was analysed by Mr. Prinsep, and offered some traces of animal and vegetable matters. Dr. Honigberger succeeded in carrying with him to Paris the unevaporated fluid in a silver vessel, which, upon its discovery, he closed almost hermetically with a coating of gum-mastic. The vessel was opened in Paris, and was found to contain a yellowish-brown fluid emitting a powerful resinous odour; a number of small articles were immersed in it. No analysis was then made, nor does it appear that its nature has been since ascertained, Dr. Honigberger resolving, according to M. Jacquet, "que l'avantage d'analyser la substance liquide contenue dans la boîte d'argent dévait être réservée à la personne ou a l'établissement scientifique qui ferait l'acquisition de sa collection."[1] The fluid, however, is probably nothing more than water holding in suspension the insoluble substances which form the sediment left behind upon its evaporation, and which constitute all that is the object of chemical analysis.[2]

The last article found in the topes that need be specified is that of coins; and they are the most important of all, as affording grounds for conjecturing the chronology of the monuments in which they are discovered. It is essential, therefore, to notice what particular coins have been found. They are,—1. Copper coins of the Hermæus or Eu-Hermæus type, having a profile on one face, and a standing Hercules on the other, very rudely executed.[3] 2. The same coins, with the name of Kadphises in barbarous

[1] Journ. Asiat. Fév. 1838, p. 187.

[2] A selection has been made from the articles discovered and sent home by Mr. Masson, and they have been delineated and engraved. See the plates; and a descriptive list at the end of this chapter.

[3] Pl. of coins V. figs. 8, 9.

Greek letters.[1] 3. Copper coins of Azes, having a rude figure of Victory on the reverse.[2] 4. Copper coins of Undapherres.[3] 5. Large copper coins of Kadphises.[4] 6. Copper coins of Kanerkes.[5] 7. Gold coins of Kadphises, of superior workmanship, and in excellent preservation.[6] 8. Gold coins of Kanerkes, of which the same may be said.[7] 9. Debased and barbarous Hindu coins.[8] These are the only coins of local origin; and it is very remarkable that no coin of a Greek prince of Bactria has ever been met with in any tope. Foreign coins, however, are not rare. We have already adverted to the Sassanian coins found in the Tope of Manikyala by General Ventura, and in those of Afghanistan by Mr. Masson, as well as the Roman coins found in the Tope at Manikyala opened by M. Court. In the Tope of Hidda, opened by Mr. Masson, he discovered a vast number of Sassanian coins of the reigns chiefly of Sapor the Third and Bahram Gor, and in the same edifice he met with five gold coins of the lower empire,—the solidi of Theodosius, Marcian, and Leo, A.D. 407-474. From these contents of the topes, then, we can form some reasonable conjectures as to the approximate dates of their construction. They must have been built some time later than the issue of the coins which are found in them. They were no doubt erected some time prior to the seventh century of our æra. There are several reasons for fixing upon this as the most modern limit that can be ascribed to their erection. The great number of Sassanian coins still procurable at Kabul, mostly of a late date, as may be inferred from their style, indicates the predominance of a Perso-Indian dynasty on the borders of Afghanistan subsequent to the beginning of the Hijra; whilst the same abundance of the Rajput or Lahore coins, found in the west of Hindustan and the Punjab, confirms the testimony of the Mohammedan historians, that Hindu princes were reigning even at Kabul when the Mohammedans first spread their arms in that direction. Neither Guebre nor Brahman was likely to have patronised Buddhist architecture. But, moreover, at the end of the seventh century the Mohammedans commenced their incursions into Afghan-

[1] Pl. of coins XI. figs. 10, 11, 12, 13. [2] Pl. VIII. fig. 1. [3] Pl. V. figs. 12, 13, 14. [4] Pl. X. fig. 15, &c. [5] Pl. XII. fig. 12, &c. [6] Pl. X. figs. 7, 8, &c. [7] Pl. XII. figs. 1, 2, &c. [8] Pl. XVIII. fig. 26, &c.

istan, and thenceforth continued to advance and consolidate their power, until by the end of the tenth century Mahmud of Ghizni had extended his authority and the religion of Islam beyond the Indus, and threatened the whole of Hindustan. It is not possible that in this time of trouble and alarm public monuments of any description should have been constructed. We may therefore confidently assume the eighth century as a limit whence to retrograde. We cannot, however, go back very far. The coins of the lower empire are of the fifth century, to which, therefore, the tope in which they were found is subsequent. The Sassanian coins of Mr. Masson's finding are principally of the fourth century, and those of the Manikyala Tope, opened by General Ventura, are still more modern. The Roman coins found in M. Court's tope are of older date; the most modern is contemporary with the æra of Christianity, but some time must be allowed them before they could have travelled to India, and even in this case the first or second century after Christ is the earliest date that can be assigned to the structure. It seems likely that the interval between the beginning of the Christian æra and the sixth century was the period in which the chief topes of this part of India were built, and the most perfect of them in the present day may be dated about the fourth and fifth centuries. Their date will, perhaps, explain why Greek-Bactrian coins are never found in them, as they had long ceased to be current, although they had, perhaps, not become so scarce as to be thought worthy to be enshrined as rarities.

The chief objection to the modern date of the topes of Afghanistan arises from the possibly higher antiquity of the similar edifices in other parts of India. The building of Sarnath is comparatively modern, at least, if contemporary with the date of the inscription, as already noticed, of A.D. 1026. The monument at Amaravati is, however, more ancient, as the characters of the inscription over the gateway and even on the separate stone slab demonstrate; and that of Bhilsa is older still, many of the inscriptions there being written in the most ancient known form of the Nagari letter: still there is no reason to infer a remoter date for these structures than the early years of the Christian æra. The monument or Tope of Rumanwalli at Anuradhapura, in Ceylon, is, however, said to have been erected by

King Dutagamonoo,[1] who reigned B.C. 161-137, and the smaller one of Topharamaya, in the same vicinity, is referred to B.C. 307. The construction of these edifices seems, therefore, to have accompanied the extension of Buddhism in India. For, there is no difference of opinion on this point: all are agreed that the topes are monuments peculiar to the faith of Buddha: there is some difference, not very material, as to their especial appropriation. Lieutenant Burnes, Mr. Masson, and M. Court, adopting the notions that prevail amongst the people of the country, are inclined to regard them as regal sepultures; but I am disposed with Mr. Erskine and Mr. Hodgson, and, I believe, with those learned antiquaries who have treated of the subject in Europe, to regard them as dahgopas on a large scale, that is, as shrines enclosing and protecting some sacred relic, attributed, probably with very little truth or verisimilitude, to Sakya Sinha or Gautama, or to some inferior representative of him, some Bodhisatwa, some high-priest or Lama of local sanctity. Mr. Prinsep has manifested a disposition to effect a kind of compromise between these opinions, and suggests, after examining some of the circumstances calculated to throw light upon the question, that the two objects of a memorial to the dead, and a shrine to the divinity, may have been combined in the meritorious erection of these curious monuments. The chief reasons for a contrary opinion, and for believing them to be the shrines of supposed relics of a Buddha,—Gautama or his predecessors,—are drawn from the opinions of nations still professing Buddhism, whose sentiments in regard to the origin and purport of their own religious monuments are more entitled to respect, than the careless and loose credence of the Hindus and Mohammedans of the Punjab and Afghanistan.

The Cingalese, for example, are still Buddhists, and they uniformly assert that the mighty mounds, which, although overgrown with vegetation and rendered shapeless by decay, yet preserve, too palpably to be mistaken, the positive outline and general character of the topes of Upper India, are nothing but dagobas or dahgopas erected to receive sacred relics imported into the island. Thus it is recorded, that Devenipiatissa built the dahgopa

[1] Turnour's Mahawanso, Introd. p. LXI. Forbes's Eleven Years in Ceylon, vol. i. p. 222.

of Topharamaya over the the right jaw-bone of Gautama, which was brought from India along with his begging-dish filled with relics, and a branch of the Bo or Indian fig-tree under which he had reclined; and the mound at Mehentelé was erected over a sacred hair that grew gracefully, though rather misplacedly, over Gautama's left eyebrow.[1]

A case equally illustrative of this appropriation occurs in the great monument of the Burmese, the Shwe-da-gon pagoda near Rangoon. This is a mass of solid masonry, standing on an elevated platform; it is more than three hundred feet in height, and its circumference at the base is one thousand three hundred and fifty-five feet.[2] It is not, however, the magnificence of this immense pile that renders it, for so it is, peculiarly an object of national respect and veneration: underneath its stupendous weight are deposited the relics of the four last Buddhas, viz., the staff of Kauk-ka-than, the water-pot of Gau-na-gon, the bathing-garment of Ka-tha-pa, and eight hairs from the head of Gautama. There is no doubt, therefore, of the light in which these monuments are esteemed by the Buddhists of Ava and Ceylon.

That the practice is universal and essential is also confirmed by the written authorities of the Buddhists; and the Lalita-vistára, a life of Gautama, relates that upon his death eight cities disputed for his remains. The contest was appeased by the distribution of a portion to each; and over them each city erected a magnificent shrine. The legend, whatever be the date of the work, not only therefore confirms the usage, but refers it to a period of considerable antiquity, the date of the death of Gautama being B.C. 543.

We have also evidence, from a quarter whence it might be little looked for, of the prevalence of the custom in the very countries where the topes which have given rise to these remarks still stand, and at the period at which it may be conjectured that some of the earliest were built. Clemens of Alexandria, writing in the beginning of the third century, after stating in one place that some of the Indians obey the precepts of Buddha, whom for

[1] Trans. of the Roy. As. Soc. vol. iii. p. 489.

[2] Inscription on the great bell at Rangoon; with remarks by the Rev. G. H. Hough: As. Res. vol. xvi. p. 270.

his eminent virtues they revere as a god;[1] mentions in another, that "there are amongst the Indians some who are called Semni, who cultivate truth, foretell events, and reverence certain pyramids in which they imagine the bones of some divinity are deposited: they observe perpetual continence; and there are also women called Semnæ,[2] who lead a life of chastity." The same authority also informs us that "the Samanæi are the philosophers of the Bactrians."[3] Samanæi and Semni are, no doubt, both corruptions of Sramana, the proper title of a Buddhist religious cœnobite,—the Gelum or Lama of Tibet, the Rahan of Ava, Talapoin of Siam and Ceylon, in the former of which countries may still also be found the Semnæ or Sramaní, women who lead a religious life. The pyramids are undoubtedly our topes, and there is good reason to believe that their object is accurately defined. From this testimony, therefore, we must conclude that in the first or second century of the Christian æra there were buildings of this description in the countries on the north-west of India.

Finally, we may derive the same inference from the analogous though smaller monuments or dahgopas which characterise so decidedly a Buddhist cavern temple. In their general form they resemble topes, and they cannot possibly inurn the remnants of secular individuals, or they would not hold the place they so conspicuously occupy in excavations undoubtedly appropriated to offices of religion.

At the same time it is not to be inferred that the practice of enshrining relics being thus from the earliest date an essential part of the Buddhist religion, no other mode of paying homage to them was permitted. The exhibition of such sacred fragments was too effective and palpable an expedient for establishing popular belief upon popular credulity, to be overlooked by the ministers of the Buddhist religion. Under what circumstances relics were concealed or were displayed we have no explanation, but that both customs were observed at the same time there is satisfactory evidence. Fa-Hian, the Chinese traveller, who visited the countries upon the Indus at the end of the fourth century, speaks of magnificent monuments, which he describes as Thai or towers, and to which, he says, the natives give the

[1] Stromat. I. 15. [2] Ibid. III. 7. [3] Ibid. I. 15.

name Su-tu-pa, undoubtedly Sthupa or Tope. One of these, he asserts, was four hundred feet high,—an elevation rendered not improbable by that of the monuments of Ceylon, although no longer approached by any of the monuments of which the ruins remain in Afghanistan. Fa-Hian does not say much about these topes, however, and is more particular as to the public exhibition of sacred relics, in which, as a good Buddhist, he took a warmer interest. He tells a story also of a vain attempt made by the King of the Yu-chi to carry off Gautama's begging-dish from Foe-leü-sha. A carriage drawn by elephants was provided for its conveyance, but the dish had no desire to travel, and, although it was placed upon the carriage, it would go no further, and the carriage was immoveable. It does not appear that the Getic monarch anticipated Mr. Masson or General Ventura by breaking into a tope; and the vessel must, therefore, have been kept in some more readily accessible shrine. In truth, however, this practice is still known in Buddhist countries; and in Ceylon the dalada or tooth of Gautama, represented by a piece of discoloured ivory two feet long and proportionably thick, being evidently part of an elephant's tusk, is kept in a chamber adjoining to the palace at Kandy, and is produced occasionally with great parade and solemnity for the superstitious veneration of the multitude.[1] Some relics, therefore, were kept for this purpose in open chapels, whilst others were hidden from sight amidst a mass of brick and mortar.[2]

Whilst also it seems most probable that the principal topes in the Punjab

[1] Eleven Years in Ceylon, vol. i. p. 290.

[2] Wilford has some very curious matter upon the subject of the relics of Buddha, and affirms that the Buddhists declare that many of the pyramids (topes) do not really contain the relics, though they are supposed and asserted to contain them: "the real place where they are deposited should remain unknown, in order to prevent profanation, exactly like the various tombs of Osiris." He also states that the original search for the relics of Buddha is annually commemorated by a solemn festival, in which his disciples pretend to look for them, until a priest announces that they are found. "This is practised to this day by several Tartarian tribes of the religion of Buddha."—As. Res. vol. x. p. 128. Unfortunately, Wilford's facts are so blended with his fancies that it is difficult to discriminate them, and, as he rarely specifies his authorities, it is not always easy to verify his citations. It is but justice to him, however, to state, that in many cases where they have been traced, they have been verified, and there is little doubt that he had some authority for the celebration of the festival he speaks of.

and Afghanistan fulfilled these holy purposes of veiling sacred relics from eyes profane, and protecting them from felonious aggression, it is, no doubt, true that they were commonly surrounded by sepulchral structures something similar to them in shape and solidity, though not in size or destination. Mr. Masson informs us that tumuli are commonly observed in the vicinity of the topes, and that although now in most instances mere mounds, yet, where perfect, they offer a regularity of structure which assimilates them to the ordinary dahgopa: they differ from the topes in general in dimension, and in the want of the cylindrical body which intervenes between the basement and the cupola: they are also distinguished by their contents: the fragments of bones and ashes in them are in considerable quantities, whilst they are very sparingly met with in topes. In one instance Mr. Masson found the bones of the entire body, wanting a skull; in another he found a skull only, with some relics beneath it. In general, however, the tumuli are destitute of relics; and it is remarkable that skulls alone are discovered, sometimes in considerable quantities, in the loose soil at the foot of or about the mounds. A tumulus sometimes occurs in an isolated situation; and many tumuli are found where no tope is present, but no tope occurs without the presence of tumuli in its vicinity. These circumstances are sufficiently intelligible, and confirm the notion of sanctity attached to the most conspicuous edifice. The practice of inhumation in the vicinity of holy edifices is not peculiar to the Buddhist religion. Nor is it limited to the Buddhists of Upper Hindustan, for there are many tumuli in the neighbourhood of the mound at Amaravati. The similar character of the tomb and tope is also to be remarked; for in Ceylon "the monumental tombs of Buddha's relics only differ in size and in the durability of their materials from the humble heap which covers the ashes of an obscure priest, or a village chief."[1] The tombs of the kings at Kandy are visibly a collection of minor dahgopas.[2]

In the neighbourhood of the topes and their contiguous assemblages of tumuli, Mr. Masson describes in the following memoir the common accompaniment of caves practised in the mountainous elevations on which the monuments stand, and justly designates them as the abodes of Buddhist

[1] Eleven Years in Ceylon, vol. i. p. 221. [2] Ibid. vol. i. p. 300.

priests. The records of Ceylon confirm the association, and wherever a tope was erected there was also constructed a Vihar (a temple for worship), and cells or caves for the priests. Preparatory to the arrival in Ceylon of the Tooth of Gautama, King Devenipiatissa (B.C. 306), who built the vihar and dahgopa in which the relic was deposited, constructed sixty-eight cells in the Chetíya mountain for the accommodation of an equal number of Arhats or priests.[1]

From these considerations, then, we cannot be at a loss to understand the origin and object of the different monuments which have been recently brought to our knowledge in this part of India. The topes are the shrines of the supposed relics of the last Buddha, Sakya or Gautama; and the tumuli are the tombs in which the ashes of his votaries have been buried, under the protection of his holy shrine. That such shrines and sepultures were coeval with Buddhism in India is highly probable; but the specimens that have been found on the east and west of the upper course of the Indus cannot boast of very remote antiquity, as they are probably all subsequent to the Christian æra. Their prevalence, in all likelihood, originated with the establishment of the Indo-Scythic rule, as the Getæ or Yu-chi, according to Chinese authors, adopted, upon their conquests in India, the religion of Fo.[2]

We have thus brought the account of the discoveries of coins and antiquities down to the period of the late political events, which have unexpectedly domesticated us in countries to which access had long been perilous or prohibited. The time immediately consequent upon hostile aggression, and before our influence has been established, is not very propitious to antiquarian research; but it is to be hoped that the season is not very remote when intelligent and enterprising Englishmen may follow unrestrictedly the footsteps of Mr. Masson, and, prosecuting the researches he has so zealously and ably commenced, complete the restoration to ancient history of the political and religious revolutions of Bactria and Western India.

[1] Mahawanso, vol. i. p. 103.

[2] Histoire des Huns, vol. i. part 2. p. 378.

DESCRIPTIVE LIST OF LITHOGRAPHED ANTIQUITIES.

PLATES I. TO IV.

PLATE I.

Fig. 1. Interior and top of a vase of steatite, found in a tumulus at Darunta. The cover is ornamented and has a hollow at the summit with a lid. The interior is divided into compartments, in which were some minute gold and silver cups, beads of pearls, crystal, agate, and coral; small ornaments of gold and stone, a piece of birch-bark, with characters, and six small coins of the 'nameless' king. See Plates of Coins, Plate IX.

Figs. 2, 3. Lateral view and face of a seal of black earthenware. The inscription is carelessly and blunderingly written in barbarous Pali, and in Nagari letters of the seventh century. (See Prinsep's alphabets, J. As. Soc. B. March, 1838.) It is evidently, however, the sacred formula of the Buddhists, and in modern characters runs thus:

यो धम्महेतुप्रभवो हेतु: सब तथागत स्राह
तस्स च यो निरोध एव वादी महासमणो

"The Tathágata (Buddha) has declared the causes which are the origin of moral merit: what is its obstruction also the great ascetic has explained." See J. As. Soc. B. vol. iv. p. 132.

Fig. 4. A cornelian seal, with an (apparently) female Hindu head. Underneath, in Nagari of the seventh century, is Kusuma-dásasya, '(seal) of the slave of the flower.' The term is used as a proper name, no doubt; but it is that of a man. Mr. Prinsep read it Kesava-dasa, the 'slave of Kesava' (Krishna). J. As. Soc. B. vol. vi. p. 987.

Fig. 5. Gold seal, with cornelian, and a head cut on it; apparently of Greek workmanship. This and the two preceding were procured in the Punjab by General Ventura.

Fig. 6. A bull couchant; cornelian; from a tope at Deh Bímarán. Similar small figures of animals, in metal, stone, or hard clay, are found in several topes, and at Beghram.

Fig. 7. Cornelian, with two figures; in dress and attitude Hindu, and probably intended for Krishna playing on the flute and Rádhá on the tabor.

Fig. 8. Small cornelian, with boar. From one of the topes.

PLATE II.

Fig. 1. Vase of steatite, with inscription on the cover and round the body of the vase, as copied below. The characters are a cursive form of those inscribed on the coins, but their value is not satisfactorily determined. This vase contained the gold cup lithographed in Plate IV. figs. 1, 2, 3. From a tope at Deh Bímarán.

Fig. 2. Vase of copper, gilt; the bottom destroyed. From the large tope at Hidda. It was found within a larger vase, to the side of which it adhered, and was broken on being detached; the lower part being corroded by immersion in a fluid with which the larger vase was half-filled. The fluid, probably water, that had oozed through the masonry, holding in solution some carbonate of copper, evaporated on exposure. Within it were five gold coins of Theodosius, Leo, and Marcian; one hundred and eighty-seven Sassanian coins, which, when not corroded, were cognisable as coins of Sapor III. and Behram Gor (see Plate of Coins XVI. figs. 7, 8, 9, &c.); a couple of rude and debased Hindu gold coins (see Plate XVIII. figs. 26, 28); several gold and silver rings, engraved stones, beads, &c. The smaller copper vessel contained the following:

Fig. 3. A silver casket with lid and spire of fillagree, originally soldered on the lid, but now detached. Within this vessel was the following:

Fig. 4. A small gold casket or portable perfume-box, having four small rings, by which it was, no doubt, suspended; the lid is set with emeralds, and surmounted by a sapphire. Within is a small quantity of aromatic powder, musk and sandal, in which are some small pearls.

Fig. 5. A gold ring with a ruby. From the Hidda Tope.

PLATE III.

Fig. 1. A steatite model of a tope, found in a tope at Sultanpur. It is in four compartments, which may be separated,—the base, the cylindrical body, the dome, and the 'Tee' or spire. There are hollows in the two former, but they were empty.

Fig. 2. A vase of steatite, containing a silver box; in the latter were two thin circular gold ornaments, a gold bead, impression of a seal on clay (see Plate IV. fig. 6), and ten large copper coins of Kadphises. From a tope at Kotpur.

Figs. 3, 4. Gold buttons, of which ninety-six were found in the Tope of Guldára, near Kabul, with eight gold coins of Kadphises and Kanerkes.

Figs. 5, 6. Gold rings, with heads cut on cornelians, of Hindu workmanship. From the Tope of Hidda.

Fig. 7. Cornelian, with head. From Hidda.

Fig. 8. Cornelian, with head. From the Punjab. The inscription gives a name, Ajita Varmma. There were kings of Kashmir, of the family title 'Varmma,' in the ninth century; and one of them was called Nirjita Varmma, bearing the same meaning as Ajita, or 'unconquered.' He reigned, however, but a short time, and the seal is probably none of his. It is, however, no doubt, of his period.

Fig. 9. Iron head of bird; used, perhaps, as a weight, or as the ornamental top of some implement. From Beghram, where similar objects varying in size and outline are found in some number.

Fig. 10. An iron astragalus; used, probably, at some game.

Fig. 11. A piece of birch-bark, with characters, such as has been found in several topes, but in fragments too small and brittle to offer any continuous and legible inscription.

PLATE IV.

Fig. 1. A circular gold casket without lid; found within the stone vase delineated Plate II. fig. 1. The upper and lower rims are studded with rubies separated by ornamental devices. The circumference is divided into eight compartments, enshrining four figures, represented in duplicate. They are separated by pilasters terminating in arches, circular below and pointed above, between which are figures of birds (cranes ?).

Fig. 2. The four figures of the vase represented on the same superficies. The third figure from the left is the principal, and is that of the Buddha Sakya Sinha or

Gautama, in the attitude of pronouncing a benediction. Next to him, on his left, is a lay follower, in the garb of a Rajput Hindu, in the usual attitude of reverential salutation. On his right is a religious follower or ascetic, with his hair twisted, and the water-ewer in one hand; the other is raised as in salutation. Behind him stands a female disciple, perhaps a religious female, such as the nuns still found in Tibet, in act of prayer.

Fig. 3. The ornamented bottom of the cup, representing the pericarp and petals of the lotus. The inner surface of the cup had been lined with a coating of indurated clay, fragments of which were detached, and showed the same design upon the surface in contact with the metal, being in all probability the mould on which the metal had been chased. The workmanship of this casket is very remarkable, and exhibits the character of that style which prevailed in the early part of the middle ages.

Fig. 4. Fibulæ or pins of iron and copper, sometimes with gilt heads. Many of them are found in the plain of Beghram.

Figs. 5, 13, 15. Birds and heads of birds, in iron. Many of them are found at Beghram.

Fig. 6. Impression on indurated clay; from a tope at Kotpur.

Figs. 7, 8. Iron seal; from Beghram.

Fig. 9. Device of a brass seal; from Beghram.

Figs. 10, 11. Cornelian intaglios; from Hidda.

Fig. 12. Cornelian seal; from Beghram: modern. Having the invocation of the Sikh faith,—Sat-Guru, Sat-Nám, 'the holy teacher, the true name,' and the appellation of the owner, perhaps, Jalas Ray.

Fig. 14. A gold ornament; from a tope at Kotpur (Plate III. fig. 2).

Fig. 16. Iron handle of a key (?). Many such found at Beghram.

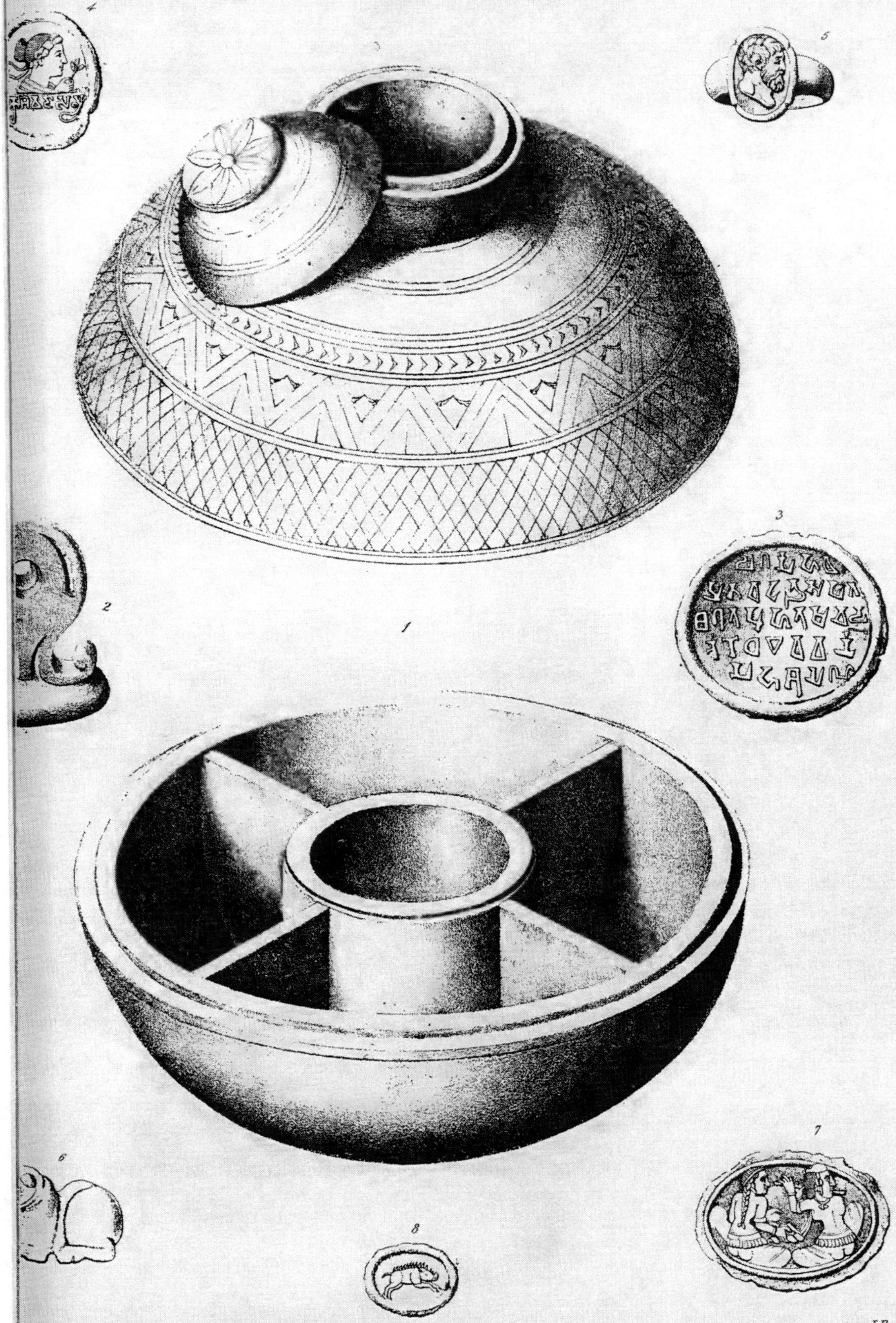

J. Basire, del. et lithog.

J. Bowers del et lith.

J Basire del et sc

J. Basire, del. et lithog.

CHAPTER II.

MEMOIR ON THE TOPES AND SEPULCHRAL MONUMENTS OF AFGHANISTAN.

BY C. MASSON, ESQ.

THE term Tope, which is applicable to the more prominent and interesting of the structures under consideration, is that in ordinary use by the people of the regions in which they most abound. A tope is a massive structure comprising two essential parts, the basement and perpendicular body resting thereon. The latter, after a certain elevation, always terminates after the manner of a cupola, sometimes so depressed as to exhibit merely a slight convexity of surface, but more frequently approaching the shape of a cone. At a particular height, belts of ornamental mouldings enclose the circumference of the superior body, frequently containing a succession of arches supported on pilasters. In some cases the pilasters only occur, and in still fewer even they are omitted, and the belts of mouldings constitute the decorative characteristics. Yet it must be observed that these belts, while they distinguish the earlier and more important topes, are not observable on those of more recent date, nor is it certain that they were ever carried around them. Belts may not, therefore, be considered beyond ornamental appendages, although their presence is general on the more ancient structures, and renders them easily recognisable.

These monuments are substantially constructed of layers of large stones, cemented with well-prepared and beaten earth. In some the stones employed internally appear to have been rudely fashioned; in others they seem to have been selected from the skirts of the surrounding hills. While the interiors of topes are immense masses of stones and earth, regularly however disposed, the exterior surfaces have been objects of particular care. On the upper portions of the greater number of them, from the lower lines of mouldings, concentric lines of fashioned stones, with due intervals between them, have been continued to the summit. The same arrangement is adopted in the ground of the belts within the lines of mouldings, and sometimes for a foot or two beneath them. As the space between these concentric circles is filled up with dark slate, in the most curiously neat manner, topes, at least many of them, present a very singular and striking appearance, from the chequered arrangement of their upper surfaces. The mouldings, pilasters, arches, and other embellishments stand in relief, and are all formed with slate-stones in the same peculiar and neat style. The abundance of primitive slate, of a fine dark colour, in the hills of Afghanistan, has furnished the artists with a plentiful supply of excellent and easily worked materials, of which they have admirably profited to promote the elegance and beauty of these structures. Originally a surface or covering of white cement overspread the superior portions of the topes, including the circumferent mouldings and decorative belts, also, probably, the lower portions, although from the injuries of time this is not so apparent. Another peculiarity must be noted, with reference to the construction of these topes; which is, that in process of their construction, at intervals of one foot, one foot and a half, or two feet, thin layers of pounded slate, yellow sand, red ochreous earth or white cement, have been superposed, so as to form distinct lines of separation between the several strata of stones and earth. In raising these enormous structures it is evident that it became necessary at certain stages of the progress to allow the masses, as they were placed upon each other, to subside and to acquire consistency, as is now observed in the elevation of an ordinary mud wall. Whether these layers mark the several periods of repose granted for the due compression and adhesion of the materials during the course of erection, or whether they have a mystical allusion, cannot be now determined. Topes, of course, vary exceedingly in their dimensions, but these would appear to have been regulated, as every thing else relating to them, on a fixed principle; and although the imperfect condition of most of them may not allow us to define it with certainty, yet it can scarcely be questioned that their proportions were duly regarded. Some of the monuments have a circumference of one hundred and forty-four feet, many that of one hundred and eight feet. Others even exceed or fall short of these dimensions. Topes must be considered as fronting the east, both because many of their basements are provided with flights of steps at that point, and because others of them have niches facing the east, over their ornamental belts. That these niches once held statues is almost certain, from the holes or apertures seen in them, as is observed in the smaller niches among the caves and temples of Bamian, which we know were occupied by statues or idols, from their mutilated remains still to be seen in some of them. Some of the basements of the larger topes had flights of steps at all the cardinal points, others only at the eastern or western points, and others again simply at the eastern points; while some, from their interior elevation, were unprovided with such appendages. There can be no doubt but that every tope was erected on a basement; although, from the casualties of time and the accumulation of fallen materials around, the traces thereof may not be in some few cases recognisable. Many topes have contiguous to them large oblong areas enclosed within huge mounds of earth, which seem on a *prima facie* view to have been intended for reservoirs of water; but in some situations it is difficult to conjecture how they could have been filled. These areas may have some other meaning not yet understood, as it is observable that the earth, of which their enclosing mounds is composed, has been sifted with the greatest care, so that no stone or other extraneous substance is to be detected in it. These areas lie frequently to the south; but as they occur in some instances to the east, also to the west of topes, it is doubtful whether any deduction can be justly authorized from their position. They may, however, afford a fair criterion for discrimination between the topes of various dynasties and epochs. None of the Darunta topes have such accompaniments, while those of Chahár Bágh and Hidda are never found without them. The topes of Kabul are likewise characterized by them. The topes of Hidda display incongruities, to be explained, as that spot may be the more recent as well as more general of the three important ancient places of sepulture in the valley of Jelalabad, distinguished by the actual existence of topes, and may be supposed to have been principally formed in a decline of political power and of religion, when ancient forms would be laxly followed or deviated from, owing to the corruption and degeneracy of the age. In a few of the topes examined, passages or tunnels have been found, extending from the centre towards the circumference. That they had an import or were conducive to some purpose, must be credited, however we may not venture to determine it.

The locality and position of these structures demand attention. The favourite sites selected for them are at the skirts of hills, on elevations separated from each other by ravines. The topes of Kabul, Chahár Bágh, and Hidda, are remarkable for the distinct nature of their situation with reference to each other. This feature also applies to those monuments of the Darunta group which are placed on the summits of eminences, but not so strictly to the greater number seated on the plain. In the neighbouring hills or in the scarps of the adjacent ravines, are invariably found, connected with all topes, a number of samuches or caves. Many of these are important as to extent and arrangement, and all of them were originally lined with cement. The superior caves, which are crowned with a cupola, were probably temples, and many of them have, at their upper extremities, niches which may have been occupied by statues. In many series of these excavations, outward niches are associated with them, which it may with certainty be pronounced were intended to contain statues or idols. The majority of these caves may be, however, conjectured to have been abodes of priests and recluses, who formed the establishment connected with the endowment and consecration of these venerated monuments. A complete series of caves embraced—dwellings for the ministers and attendants; apartments distinguished by a niche at the extremity; an apartment with domed ceiling, and an outward niche for the lodgment of a statue.

Topes are always accompanied by inferior structures, which may be called tumuli: they are known to the people of the country by the name of ráshak. There is a manifest connexion between them, as no tope, however remotely situated, is without its dependent tumulus. In many instances numerous tumuli are near the tope. A tumulus is often isolated, but is never without its cave, proving that it is, under circumstances, an independent structure. Tumuli abound over all the Afghan countries.

Water is constantly found near topes and their appendages, and it would appear to have been a leading principle in the selection of their sites, that springs of water should be at hand. It was, of course, indispensable to the conveniences of the communities secluded in the caves, and to their performance of their rites and ablutions; and it was also necessary that it should be pure and flowing from the rock. In some cases, as at Hidda, water has been conducted in kárrézes or subterranean aqueducts, from remote points, and through a most difficult soil, and at vast labour and expense. They are subjects of wonder to the slothful Mohammedan, who is willing to excuse his inferiority, in the belief that they owe their existence to devs or demons. Some topes may be found which have not, at this time, water very close to them; but the exhausted springs which once supplied the establishments connected with them are obvious.

Having premised these brief and general remarks, upon the form, architecture, construction, and position of these monuments, I shall proceed in like manner to offer a few observations upon the relics or tokens they enclose, and upon the mode of their deposit. The relics generally found in the topes of Afghanistan are mostly discovered in small recesses or apartments in the centres of the buildings, enclosed in caskets or vases of copper, brass, and steatite; the latter mineral, called alg, abounding in the inferior hills of the valleys of Afghanistan. There are exceptions to this mode of deposit, which will be noted when I treat of the particular contents of each tope. These vases, sometimes of a globular, sometimes of a cylindrical form, usually contain smaller cylindrical cases of gold or silver, often of both, distinct, or enclosed the one within the other. In one of these will be generally found a fragment or two of bone, and these appear to have been the essential relics over which the monuments were raised. These fragments are sometimes loose and detached, and sometimes mixed with a small mass of unguents or other doubtful matter, amongst which a bead or gem may be inserted, and the whole carefully wrapped up in an envelope of fine linen or karbás. This name, Sanscrit as well as Greek and Latin, is yet in use to denote the coarse cotton fabrics of the country. In the larger vases is usually discovered a portion of fine pulverized earth or of ashes, amongst which have been placed burnt pearls, beads, rings, seals, and other trinkets, with gems, coloured stones, pieces of crystal, fragments of mother-of-pearl shell, &c. In some examples the deposits have been accompanied by twists of tuz-leaves, inscribed internally with characters.[1] These may have contained the precise information we seek. The only other probable conjecture as to these twists, is that they contain mantras or charms. Be this as it may, it is peculiarly unfortunate that they have become so decayed as to have crumbled away, or to do so when handled. In one or two instances only have we obtained twists in better preservation, their leaf being of coarser texture, and consequently more durable than the finer specimens generally employed. The characters on these leaves are invariably those found on the native legends of our Bactrian and Indo-Scythic coins, and it is clear that the topes were raised during the period when such characters composed the alphabet of the country. In one or two instances I have met with inscriptions: one scratched with a stylet or sharp-pointed implement around a steatite vase extracted from a tope at Darunta; another written in ink around an earthen vessel found in a tope at Hidda; and a third, dotted on a brass vessel, within a tope at Kohwát, in the district of Wardak. The characters of these inscriptions were alike Bactro-Pali. Some topes have small caskets of bark of tree, which, being curiously painted, might be more highly prized than the ordinary ones of metal or steatite; but unfortunately, from their pulverized state, we are enabled merely to carry off their fragments. Topes, in which a large quantity of bones and ashes are discovered, seldom prove productive of other relics: their presence I have learned to consider ominous of ill fortune. The relics are generally lodged in the centres of topes, that is, of the superior perpendicular bodies, on the line where they rest on their basements, sometimes at the centre and bottom of the latter, on a level with the soil. They are mostly enclosed within small chambers formed by squares of slate-stones, and frequently are enclosed within internal topes, or structures of the same form as the outer mass, only wanting the platform. These are sometimes of considerable size, while at others their capacity is trifling. Very many topes, and even tumuli, have these enclosed structures; they are covered with cement, and their separation from the mass of the monuments is often marked by a line of unburnt bricks, sometimes by stones of a

[1] It seems likely that what Mr. Masson denominates 'tuz-leaves' is the inner bark of the bhurj or birch tree, which was very commonly used for writing upon by the Hindus in early times.—H. H. W.

description different to that employed in the mass. If such were composed of hewn stones, boulders might be chosen to define the boundary of the enclosed tope. From trustworthy evidence, I am inclined to believe that deposits of inferior consideration were originally placed at the very summits of many topes. These, from the decay of the buildings, have become self-exposed, and have been carried away. It is probable that in many of them, from the centre of the apex of the dome to the base of the structure, may be continued at intervals deposits of tokens; and that they are placed in other situations, has been proved in course of our examinations. Still we may rest assured that the primary deposit is to be found at the centre of the base of the tope or of its basement. In some topes there is a peculiarity of construction observable in the existence of a shaft or chamber at the summits. The purport of these incisions into the masses is not very evident; but in those occurring in my researches, the spaces described by them were filled up by carefully sifted earth, and their sides were lined by cement; their depth was from six to eight feet. Two of the Darunta topes, provided with them, disclosed that huge stones were deposited beneath them. My plan of operations upon these structures is, if the line of contact or union of the tope with the basement be discernible, there to make way to the centre, and, if the expected results are not found, to descend perpendicularly to the foundation.

TOPES AND SEPULCHRAL MONUMENTS OF JELALABAD.

These occur principally at three localities, viz., Darunta, Chahár Bágh, and Hidda. The Darunta group is, it may be believed, the more ancient, next to it is that of Chahár Bágh, and the more recent is that of Hidda. There can be little doubt that there was anciently a town or city of importance in the valley of Jelalabad, and it might be sufficient to refer to it the mysterious edifices overlooking the valley. As there is the possibility that many of these structures have more than a mere sepulchral character, and that their localities were considered sacred ones; upon inquiry we shall find that they are now so considered by the Hindus of the country, and are visited by pilgrims from various parts of India. At Sultanpur, Chahár

Bágh, and Jelalabad, are religious establishments; and the Jogis of the two latter places are eminent, and receive considerable remittances from their disciples east of the Indus. Sultanpur is distinguished by its beautiful and copious springs, said by the Hindus to have issued at the command of Baba Nanak, to whom the place is sacred; at Chahár Bágh is the shrine called Gaddí Bramdás; and at Jelalabad that called Gaddí Surya. There is also a fourth site in the valley of Jelalabad, esteemed sacred by the Hindus, that of Bishbúlák. This Turki term may not have been its more ancient appellation; and there is the shrine called Darbarra Sinh. At Bishbúlák, where there are no topes, but abundant vestiges of ancient places of sepulture in mounds, caves, &c., the Hindus celebrate the festival of Dímála; at Jelalabad that of Sivarat; at Chahár Bágh that of the Díwálí; and at Sultanpur that of Vaisákh. The topes are in nowise venerated by them. From every circumstance of antiquity, splendour of appearance, and general interest, the topes of Darunta have the first claims to notice; and in the division of our narrative relating to the Jelalabad topes into sections, an arrangement sanctioned by their distinct localities and characters, we shall devote our first section to them.

SECTION I.

TOPES AND SEPULCHRAL MONUMENTS OF DARUNTA.

DARUNTA.

The name Darunta peculiarly applies to a break in the terminating point of a hill-range called Siah Koh (the black hill), through which the river of Kabul and Laghman escapes into the valley of Jelalabad. By custom the name has been extended to that portion of the contiguous plain contained in the angle formed by the Siah Koh on the one side, and the course of the river on the other. The Siah Koh, commencing at Jigdillak, disappears at Darunta, passing under sand-stone elevations, which extend northwards to the hill-range extending from Kargha of Laghman to Khonar. Amongst these elevations are situated the topes of Gudára and Bár Robát, which we have included in this section, although they cannot be considered as on the plain of Darunta, although the first overlooks it. Their style of architecture and general aspect perfectly connect them with the topes of the Darunta group. The remainder of the topes at Darunta are found on the level plain, immediately at the base of the Siah Koh, excepting Nandára Tope and Surkh Tope, which are perched on the hill's lower eminences. The Tope of Sultanpur I have also comprised in this section, notwithstanding its distance from Darunta, as it could not be classed with the group of Chahár Bágh; and presuming it belonged to one of the groups, I have joined it to that which its indications more strongly authorized. The cultivated lands of Darunta are tenanted by a mixture of Galzais and Tajiks, the former now the lords absolute. They are of the Omar Khel tribe, whose principal, Yar Mohammed Khan, has a castle here. Considering the topes as his property, from being on his soil or within his jurisdiction, he being the Naib of the Galzais, he was willing to oppose my operations on them. Indeed, at their commencement, a party of armed men from his castle drove away my working parties, but explanations led to so good an understanding, that his castle thenceforth became my head-quarters. The scenery of Darunta is naturally picturesque; and its interest is, of course, much enhanced by the presence of its topes. The coup-d'œil must needs have been gorgeous when these monuments existed in their original splendour. To exhibit the relative situation of these venerable records of past ages, and to show, better than description may pourtray, the disposition of the neighbouring country, a topographical sketch is annexed.[1] I divide the topes of this section into three classes, as warranted by their comparative dimensions, style of architecture, solidity of construction, &c. The first, or superior class, contains seven; the second class, including those of fair pretensions and appearance, includes six; and the third class, comprising the smaller and inferior ones, comprehends five: in all, eighteen topes. Independently of this artificial division into classes of these monuments, what might be called a natural division may be as readily made from the quality of the relics and the typical characteristics of the coins entombed in many of them.

[1] This and other sketches by Mr. Masson have been incorporated in one general plan. See the accompanying topographical sketch by Mr. Walker, Plates of Topes, I.—H. H. W.

TOPES OF KOTPUR.

Tracing the skirts of the Siah Koh, is a road leading from Bála Bágh to Darunta, and thence across the river of Kabul and Jelalabad to Laghman. From Bála Bágh to the ferry at Darunta may be a distance of seven miles. At about five miles on this road, coming from Bála Bágh, we meet the topes of Kotpur, situated a little on our right hand. The first is in the midst of cultivation, about one hundred yards from the road; a deep ravine, through which flows a stream derived from the Surkh Rúd (red river), separates it from its two companions. These stand on a dák, or barren level, overspread with fragments of potter's ware; and here coins, rings, and other relics are sometimes found. The spot was, therefore, an ancient place of sepulchre. One of these topes is made to form an angular tower to the small deserted castle of Kotpur, the property of Shakúr Khán, Jabár Khel, who resides at Watípur, a castle on the opposite side of the Surkh Rúd.

TOPE NO. 1 OF KOTPUR.[1]

This is a tope of the first class, with a circumference of one hundred and sixty feet; it has an encircling belt of double rows of mouldings, comprising a succession of arches supported on pilasters. From the lower line of mouldings to the summit it was covered with cement, much of which remains. Traces of the basement are preserved, but it has considerably subsided beneath the soil. The building itself has also inclined to the east. M. Honigberger opened this structure from the west, and at the centre came upon a small cupola of burnt bricks; it was removed, but nothing elicited. On digging towards the foundation, two or three fragments of alg or steatite were found, with a silver box containing an unctuous red fluid, which exuded at the line where its cover fitted on; by shaking the box, it was manifest that some other object was enclosed within it. M. Honigberger did not open the box, with a view to the conservation of the fluid. From experience we may conjecture the enclosure to have been a smaller box of

[1] See Engravings of Topes, Pl. II.

pure gold, containing the essential relics,—fragments of bone, with beads, gems, &c. The probability is that no coins would be discovered.

This tope on the eastern side being so dilapidated as to allow access to its summit, I profited thereby to make an excavation into the body of the building from that point. At a depth of six feet the workmen came upon an immense block of stone, which the united efforts of some fifty individuals, collected from the neighbouring villages, could not dislodge. We then dug under it, and found nothing more useful than the beak of a bird, supposed to have been a Maina. This was not an accidental deposit; a similar one having occurred in a tope at Chahár-Bágh, and again in a tumulus at Darunta. The huge stone is alike frequently discovered in topes, having been detected at the summit of the famous Nandára Tope, also in a tumulus at Darunta, and in topes at Hidda.

TOPE NO. 2 OF KOTPUR.[1]

This tope is of the second class, with a circumference of one hundred and eight feet. We have to note in its embellishments the absence of arches in the belt encompassing it, which consists merely of a series of pilasters enclosed between double lines of mouldings. The structure originally stood on a platform, and was surrounded by square walls, of which the foundations are distinctly to be seen. As this tope has suffered much from the assaults of time, the accumulation of fallen stones on every side of it is proportionably great. It was opened, under my direction, from the east, and at the centre was discovered a large cupola, or, in fact, an internal tope, with a diameter of twelve feet, and covered with cement. This continued to the foundation of the structure, where we found a small chamber formed by takhts or squares of slate. In it was a cylindrical box of steatite, with flat ornamented cover: within it was a smaller one of silver, containing the following relics: a small portion of ashes, an impression of a seal on clay,[2]—(unfortunately not entire, but presenting the standing figure of an armed

[1] See Pl. II.

[2] This is apparently fig. 6 of Pl. IV. of Antiquities: the characters of which Mr. Masson speaks are not distinguishable.—H. H. W.

prince with a lance in his hand, the proportions of singular beauty; to the right of the figure was part of an inscription in pure Greek characters, which, from the two or three final letters visible, must have been ΒΑΣΙΛΕΩΣ,) —a small circular piece of silver, (doubtful whether a coin, from its smooth reverse, but on the obverse bearing the bust of a king, whose head was bound with the Greek diadem,) two thin circular golden ornaments, one globular golden bead. Without the superior box of steatite were ten copper coins of some prince of the family whose currency is distinguished by the figure of Hercules on the reverse.[1] The discovery of these coins was satisfactory, as affording data both for the appropriation of, and epoch to which, the monument may be ascribed. Their number also was to be remarked, as I suspect some stress may be laid upon it, as will be hereafter noted. The prince whose cenotaph has been here examined may have ruled ten years: he may also be supposed to have been one of the latest of his race. This tope was constructed of very large round and oval-shaped stones, inserted in regular layers, but loosely cemented together. The excavation was attended with some danger, but happily no accident happened, although twice or thrice large masses fell in.

TOPE NO. 3 OF KOTPUR.[2]

This tope is of the third class, and is found at the north-west angle of the deserted castle of Kotpur. It has a circumference of one hundred and eight feet; its construction was originally very inferior, and it would seem to have been covered coarsely with cement; its decorations, if it ever had any, have disappeared. M. Honigberger opened this tope from within the castle. At the centre was discovered a small cupola, covered with cement, within which was detected merely a small portion of fragments of bones and ashes. The first excavation not having been carried to the soil, I spent a few days more upon this structure, and cleared its foundation, without making any discovery. This tope, therefore, remains unidentified, but we may infer from its contiguity of position, that it refers to the same family of princes as the

[1] Engravings of Coins, Pl. V. fig. 8, &c.

[2] Drawings of Topes, Pl. II.

two preceding; and, looking to the humble pretensions of its appearance and architecture, that it belongs to one of the latest, who may have been honoured after death with a cenotaph.

TOPES OF PASSANI.

Continuing along the line of road at the skirts of the Siah Koh, which, from the parallel of the topes of Kotpur accommodating itself to the direction of the range, slightly inclines to the north, we arrive at the topes and tumuli of Passani. The principal tope is seated immediately on the road to the right. A little west of it is the Mohammedan Ziárat of Hazrat Iliás, above which, leading up to the near hills, is a wide ravine, whose banks on either side are honeycombed with caves. On the high lands stretching from the banks are situated some important tumuli, and amongst those to the right is a dilapidated tope. Above the caves the ravine contracts, and its confined breadth is crossed by a perpendicular wall of yellow rock. Its front has been obviously worn smooth by the passage of currents of water, and it is fair to infer that a rivulet flowed over it when the caves were excavated, but it has long ceased. From the summit of this mass of yellow rock a dark khol or glen ascends up the superior hill. In the lower eminences of the hills at this point are also many caves, and their crests are crowned with a variety of stone walls and parapets. They are indications of ancient places of sepulture, proved by the bones, ashes, and frequently earthen jars containing similar contents, abundantly found within their limits. The old inhabitants of these countries particularly affected lofty and retired spots for their cemeteries, and the eminences selected they girt with parapet walls, filling up the intervals between them and the rock with carefully sifted and cleansed earth from the plain below. The present inhabitants imagine such sites to have been places of defence, and apply to them the general appellation of Káfir Killa, or the Infidel's Fort. The ashes, &c. to be found at all of them are, however, decisive as to their character. Immediately north of the large Tope of Passani is a Mohammedan burial-ground, and the stones employed to construct its graves have been all supplied by the topes and tumuli.

The caves here are during the winter occupied by an humble pastoral tribe of Afghans, called Passani, whose sole wealth consists in their flocks of goats. Their name has been transferred to the ravine, and, for want of a better, we apply it to the topes and tumuli. Around the latter, fragments of pottery abound, and copper coins are occasionally picked up.

TOPE NO. 1 OF PASSANI.[1]

This tope is of the second class, standing immediately right of the road; it has a circumference of one hundred and eight feet: to the south and west it is surrounded by tumuli; to the north a Mohammedan burial-ground separates it from other tumuli: it is still an imposing mass, although so dilapidated that no idea can be formed of its general appearance and decorations. The reports of aged men agree that it was in their remembrance much more entire, and that it had a coating of cement. It had been opened high up some years since on the western side by a villager, who formed an aperture to receive his stock of winter provender. Its unpromising aspect probably deterred M. Honigberger from operating upon it; but as there could be no doubt of its character, I pierced it from the north on a level with the soil. On reaching its centre we found a succession of takhts or squares of slate; these were promising indications, but their removal led to no further discovery. I continued the ineffectual search, until I was satisfied that we had gained the soil on which the tope rested: unwilling to abandon the structure without obtaining some token from it, I perforated it anew from a point higher up on the same side, being guided by a line of cement we detected: the centre of the tope was again reached, but nothing met with. That nothing might be left undone, I continued the aperture made by the villager to the centre of the structure, and then, descending, connected it with the apertures made by my workmen. All my labours proved fruitless, and I was compelled to retire foiled from the hopeless monument. It was wonderfully hard to penetrate, and a month was wasted in its useless examination.

[1] Drawings of Topes, Pl. II.

TOPE NO. 2 OF PASSANI.[1]

This is a small tope of the third class, on the northern bank of the ravine of Passani; it is very much dilapidated, and contiguous to it are many tumuli. M. Honigberger operated upon it, but discovered nothing. As his excavation was not carried to the soil, I judged it warrantable to be continued, under the hope that, if successful, I might be better able to appropriate the larger structure. After a few days' toil the soil was satisfactorily reached, but I gained nought beyond the knowledge that the structure rested upon a foundation of huge boulders.

TOPES OF BÍMARÁN.

Following the high road from Passani, we soon reach the village of Bímarán, containing some twenty houses occupied by Tajik and Afghan families. In the very centre of the village stands a magnificent tope, and its present walls are built on the foundations of the ancient ones enclosing the monument. In the immediate neighbourhood of this tope and village we find four other similar edifices.

TOPE NO. 1 OF BÍMARÁN.[2]

This tope is of the second class, but a superior one of the description; it has a circumference of one hundred and forty-four feet: it is the first one approached from Passani, and stands in the cultivated lands a little right of the road; it is much dilapidated, and a vast accumulation of fallen materials surround it on every side. From the portion remaining entire we are enabled to ascertain the nature of the belt which encompassed it, consisting of a series of plain pilasters, enclosed within double lines of mouldings. I penetrated into this structure from the north, and was gratified to discover in the centre a large cupola coated with cement. After clearing round its summit, I proceeded to open it, and soon beheld flattering omens in square

[1] Drawings of Topes, Pl. II. [2] Ibid.

slates; on their removal, to my joy, the workmen fell upon an apartment formed by slates, but which, on being opened, yielded nothing more than a little loose mould, in which, after the most minute inspection, and subsequent dissolution in water, no fragment of bone or any other débris could be found: the interior surfaces of the slates describing the apartment were coloured with sindúr or red lead. This secluded recess was not untenanted by the living of the creation, however destined to contain only a memento of the dead: a spider had his web there, and sallied forth from his long-concealed retreat when our profane hands had violated the privacy of his asylum and caused the admission of light. Aware that the cylindrical body, crowned by the cupola, descended through the body of the tope, I continued the excavation until we had clearly passed the foundation of the structure, in fact until the internal tope had been fairly hollowed out from the enclosing mass; but no token recompensed the labour. Satisfactory as it would have been to have obtained some evidence of this monument from itself, there can be no danger in classing it with its neighbours.

TOPE NO. 2 OF BÍMARÁN.[1]

This tope is of the second class, and has a circumference of one hundred and twenty-six feet; it is three hundred and sixty yards distant from the preceding monument, and about half that distance from the superior one in the village of Bímarán. To the preceding tope it has much affinity, is of the same kind of construction, and evidently refers to the same epoch. The dilapidation of both structures is also of similar extent. Its embellishments comprise a succession of arches supported on pilasters, enclosed within double lines of mouldings. M. Honigberger opened this monument from the north, and abandoned it, having been induced hastily to repair to Kabul. I continued his pursuit, and in the centre of the tope discovered a small apartment formed as usual by squares of slate, from which were procured some valuable and satisfactory relics. They consisted of a good-sized globular vase, of alg or steatite, with a carved cover or lid, both of which

[1] Drawings of Topes, Pl. III.

were encircled with lines of inscriptions scratched with a stylet or other sharp-pointed instrument.[1] The characters were Bactro-Pali. On removing the cover, the vase was found to contain a small quantity of fine mould, in which were mingled a number of small burnt pearls, beads of sapphire, crystal, &c. In the centre was standing a casket of pure gold;[2] it had no cover: its exterior was embellished with eight figures,[3] in separate compartments, formed by a series of flat columns supporting finely turned arches, the spaces between which were filled by eagles hovering with extended wings. The circumference of the casket at top and bottom was adorned by two lines of láls or rubies of Badakshán, twelve in each, and inserted at intervals; the casket was coated internally with hardened clay. Within the casket and steatite vase, collectively, were contained a small metallic plate,—apparently belonging to a seal, and engraved with a seated figure,—thirty small circular ornaments of gold, sundry beads of burnt coral, numerous burnt pearls, and eighteen beads of nílam (sapphire), agate, crystal, &c. Without the steatite vase were also deposited four copper coins, in excellent preservation, having been inserted new. They were the most useful portion of the discovery, as enabling us with some certainty to assign the monument and its era; they were of the horseman type, and bearing Greek legends on the obverse, corrupt indeed, but allowing the titles ΒΑΣΙΛΕΩΣ ΒΑΣΙΛΕΩΝ to be distinguished on them. The characters of the legends on the reverse are Bactro-Pali: they are fortunately distinct, and point out the commemorated monarch as one of the Azes dynasty.[4] In this tope, it may be observed, there was no interior cupola, and the deposit was found on the line where the cylindrical mass of the structure rested on its basement.

[1] Antiquities, Pl. II. fig. 1.

[2] Ibid. Pl. IV. figs. 1, 2, 3.

[3] There are two sets of four figures repeated, and are evidently intended for Gautama in the act of teaching, having on his right a religious, on his left a lay, follower; the fourth figure is a female disciple. See description of the casket, p. 53.—H. H. W.

[4] Coins, Pl. VIII. fig. 1. See also descriptions of the coins of Azes.—H. H. W.

TÓPE NO. 3 OF BÍMARÁN.[1]

This is a tope of the first class; it has a circumference of one hundred and forty-four feet, and stands a singular and prominent object in the centre of the village of Bímarán; it is encircled with a handsome belt of a succession of arches resting on pilasters within double lines of mouldings. There can be no doubt of its having been erected on a platform, but the houses built around it conceal it from observation. It was surrounded by walls, the foundations of which mark the limits of the present village. This structure has suffered most on the western side, and, notwithstanding its comparatively entire condition, has furnished materials for the construction of the houses and walls of the modern village, and for the graves of the deceased inhabitants. This system of spoliation has probably been carried on for centuries. It was penetrated by M. Honigberger from the west, and in its centre was found a small cupola, which contained a smaller recess, formed as usual by slate-stones: in this was deposited a globular vase of steatite, enclosing a variety of the customary trinkets and ornaments, with a large proportion of burnt pearls. Without the vase was a considerable quantity of fine mould, amongst which was found a handsome pagoda-like ornament of pure gold, other burnt pearls, and twenty-seven copper coins of the great prince, whose coins have on the obverse his bust, and on the reverse a horseman with the Greek legend, varying on different coins as to the corrupt style of the characters, ΒΑΣΙΛΕVΣ ΒΑΣΙΛΕΩΝ ΣΩΤΗΡ ΜΕΓΑC.[2] The coins, I should consider, justify us to assign the monument, or, if we may not be permitted to do so much, they may authorize us to draw the inference that it is a work of the age in which the coins were current. They bear the type, well known, of the genuine Azes family, so far as the horseman is concerned, but they display a bust not usually met with on their prototypes: they have, moreover, a peculiarity in the absence of a native legend. The coins of this prince are found in very great numbers, and over a vast extent of country. From Beghram, in 1833, I procured one hundred and seventy-one; in 1834, two hundred and sixty-seven; and, in 1835, two

[1] Topes, Pl. III.

[2] Coins, Pl. IX. fig. 8, &c.

hundred and fifty-seven. In speculating on the antiquity of the monument, we must bear in mind that it is posterior to the age of the first kings of the Azes dynasty, whose coins, both from their execution and the purity of their Greek legends, must be referred to a period coeval, or nearly so, with the second class of Greek-Bactrian sovereigns, as Apollodotus, Menander, Antimachus, &c. It must further be noted, that the prince and his family, whose coins are found in these topes, will have been a branch only of the great Azes family; for, while the coins of the former are found abundantly in the regions west of Peshawer, similar records of the genuine Azes dynasty are seldom or ever found beyond Jelalabad, and there scantily, while to the north and east of Peshawer, also at that place, they are amongst the most numerous of the descriptions of coins met with. Our king, who seems to have held a very extended rule, may possibly have been a conqueror. His coins are found not only in the countries of Kabul and the Punjab, but in the north-western provinces of India, and generally, it would appear, over the Indian continent. It is a remarkable fact, and illustrative of the value attaching to collections of coins from a known spot, that no moneys of the genuine Azes kings have been discovered at Beghram.

While I would fain believe that coins of the same type, found in any tope, are adequate testimonies to the character and age of the structure, I am in like manner disposed to think that their number may not be an accidental or indifferent circumstance; they may refer to duration of life or reign. The latter hypothesis is suggested by the numbers found in this tope and the preceding one. These remarks cannot, of course, apply to topes which yield a numerous medley of coins of all types and ages, but only to such in which the coins deposited are of one type, and of a certain, definite, and, if we may so term it, applicable number. In the former case, they may be considered the indiscriminate deposit of whatever was at hand, old or curious: still even such collections have their value, as they enable us to decide upon the comparative antiquity of the coins aggregated, as these may fix limits to the epoch of the structure enclosing them. The Darunta topes concur in having contained coins of the same types and of applicable numbers. Those under consideration present in their varieties the bust of a king, from twenty to fifty years of age. What might be inferred from his portraits, granting them fidelity, that he swayed the sceptre of monarchy for a period approaching to thirty years, has been confirmed by the number of coins found in his cenotaph, if such it be. If it have another character, we might conjecture it was erected in the twenty-seventh year of his reign. In both cases the number of coins in the structure were advisedly placed. In the instance of the preceding tope, four coins only were deposited, and the application of this number to the length of rule is strengthened by the few coins of the type discovered at Beghram, or brought to light through other accidents. Beghram in 1833 yielded none, in 1834 but one or two; and Jelalabad has not been more productive, obviously intimating that the period of their currency was brief.

The coins found in the monument giving occasion to these remarks have another peculiarity in the omission of the name of the sovereign. This peculiarity being observable on no other ancient coins is so remarkable, that we should rejoice if it were possible to recognise in the epithet, as it has been considered, of ΜΕΓΑϹ, the nomen. The legend, also at variance with most others, stands in the nominative in place of the genitive case, and might, perhaps, be as justly read The King of Kings, the Saviour Megas, as the King of Kings, the Saviour, the Great.

TOPE NO. 4 OF BÍMARÁN.[1]

This is a tope of the third class, situated amid numerous tumuli, one hundred and twenty yards distant, west of the magnificent tope last described: it is much dilapidated, and its original circumference was one hundred and eight feet. No idea can be formed of its original embellishments. I opened this structure from the north, under the supposition that a connexion would be found between it and the preceding monument, being influenced by its contiguity of position: this the event verified. In the centre, and at the base of the foundation, was discovered a small apartment described by slate-stones, filled with an oblong mass of mould, evidently consolidated and prepared, and made to fit in the recess as in a

[1] Drawings of Topes, Pl. III.

mould. At one of the lower angles of this mass, and inserted therein, was found a silver box, in shape resembling the common steatite vases, which contained a small portion of ashes. This box, from its slightness, had become so brittle, as to shiver into fragments when touched. Without the box, in the same mass of earth, were found seventeen beads of cornelian, agate, crystal, &c., sundry others of burnt coral, &c., the figure of a recumbent bull graven on a green stone,[1] and six copper coins of the same type as those found in the preceding tope, two of the smaller, and four of the ordinary sized moneys of the coinage. Applying the hypothesis as to the meaning which, under conditions, coins deposited in these buildings may have, I am inclined to suppose that the monument now examined had been raised to commemorate a son or child of the great prince to whom tope No. 3 refers. I further, from the number of the coins, conjecture that he may have died at the age of six years. The coins yielded were of the early currency of the prince they indicate; in this respect, therefore, not discountenancing my surmises. The tumuli, all small ones, immediately adjacent, are twelve in number, and run in two straight lines. I could not help looking upon the spot as a family place of interment. About two hundred yards further west of this small tope commence the inferior eminences dependent on the Siah Koh, in the nearest of which, caves of considerable magnitude are excavated in the escarpments: they have all been lined with cement; one of them has a recess at the extremity, and some of them have many apartments. They of course are connected with the monuments below them on the plain.

TOPE NO. 5 OF BÍMARÁN.[2]

This is a tope of the first class, separated from the preceding monuments of Bímarán by the ravine noted in our accounts of the topes of Kotpur. It has a circumference of one hundred and fifty-three feet, and now stands amid cultivated lands. It is very substantially constructed, and is remarkable

[1] Antiquities, Pl. I. fig. 6. The stone, however, is a cornelian.—H. H. W.

[2] Topes, Pl. III.

for the depression of its summit, which merely exhibits a slight convexity of surface. The absence of the usual arches and pilasters may also be noted, the decorative belt consisting merely of two lines of mouldings; the intermediate space, now that the cement once covering it has fallen off, discovering two lines of oblong whitish stones, inserted at intervals in a dark body of arranged slate-stones, producing thereby a chequered appearance. It stood evidently on a platform or basement. A tumulus, somewhat to the south, may be presumed to refer to it. It is known in the neighbourhood by the name of Jání Tope, standing on land formerly belonging to Jání, a deceased husbandman. M. Honigberger opened this structure from the north, and in its centre, near the base, discovered no less than three distinct apartments, formed as usual by squares of slate: each of them furnished a steatite vase, with flat carved covers. One of these, which may be considered the principal deposit, besides a quantity of earth and ashes, in which were mingled burnt pearls, ornaments of gold, beads, &c., contained, as I have been told, a box of bark of tree. Accompanying this deposit were thirty or thirty-one copper coins; twenty-five or twenty-six of that type distinguished by the figure of Hercules with his club on the reverse,[1] four of the horseman type, identical in that respect with those I extracted from Tope No. 2 of Bímarán,[2] and one of the King Unadpherres, Undapherres, or Gandapherres, as it may be.[3] M. Honigberger, upon the supposition that the coins of the Hercules type referred to the same prince, appropriated the monument to Hermæus, whose name is apparent on the earlier and better specimens of the series. On a visit to Darunta, I learned that other discoveries had been made in this tope; first, by some boys of Naib Yár Mohammed's castle, who, amusing themselves in the excavation made by M. Honigberger, by overturning a stone, discovered a fourth apartment, in which were deposited thirty or thirty-one copper coins; secondly, by an A'khund or village-priest, who, encouraged by the success of the boys, made a more formal search with instruments, and was rewarded by finding a fifth apartment, in which was a steatite vase and thirty-one copper coins; thirdly, by one Mulla Abd-ul-rahím, who discovered a sixth apartment, containing a

[1] Coins, Pl. V. fig. 9, &c. [2] Ibid. Pl. IX. fig. 8, &c. [3] Ibid. Pl. V. figs. 12, 13.

steatite vase and thirty or thirty-one copper coins. Of the first parcel of coins I was enabled to recover six, the whole, thirty-one, of the second, and fifteen of the third parcel; the steatite vases had been disposed of, and I was unable to recover them. The parcels of six and fifteen coins were of the Hercules type. The entire parcel of thirty-one coins yielded twenty-six of the Hercules type, four of the horseman type, and one of King Unadpherres, or exactly the number and in the same proportions as had been discovered with the primary deposit by M. Honigberger. I subsequently directed a search to be made at the summit of this monument, which is readily accessible from the east, with the view of ascertaining whether there were grounds for the belief I entertained, that a series of deposits might have been made in it from the top downwards. I was confirmed in my belief, and discovered an apartment containing a steatite vase, in which were a few ashes, one small hollow bead of gold, and one of burnt coral, with sixteen copper coins of the Hercules type: the latter, indeed, were placed without the vase. I thus became possessed of sixty-eight coins exhumed from this tope, those of the dominant type all certainly of the same age, but no one of them permitting the recognition of the name of the prince. They are all of indifferent execution, and plainly refer to one of the later princes of the family. The coins of the horseman type were in excellent preservation, as are all those (few indeed) that we have met with. The coins of King Unadpherres were much worn. I may mention, while treating on Jání Tope, that on an eminence at Hidda stand five or six very small topes, one of which in style of building so nearly resembles it, and is so different from its companions, that on first beholding it I could not forbear to suspect it had some affinity with its superior type at Darunta: the workmen also were struck with the accordance in style, and previous to the examination had given to it the name of the bacha or son of Jání Tope. The results of the excavation of this minor structure furnished sixteen copper coins,—thirteen of the Hercules type, two of the horseman type, and one of King Unadpherres; or just one half of the proportions of coins, both with reference to number and to the types, as were found in the superior monument at Darunta. This circumstance was assuredly not unintentional or accidental, however we may be unable to explain it. It is possible that this small tope at Hidda, as it is the more ancient, has been made the nucleus of the vast accumulation of topes and tumuli which we now behold there.

The coins of the series, to which belong those found in this tope, have only two recognisable names on the leading and earlier specimens, viz., Hermæus and Kadphises. There may be a doubt whether even Hermæus was the name of the king whose coins bear it, or whether the legend was not copied from his predecessor, a prince whose coinage is numerous and satisfactory. The same remark also applies in some measure to the name Kadphises, which is that of a prince whose beautiful coins are abundantly found. One singular fact is, however, given by the corrupt coins of the Hercules type, bearing the name of Kadphises, that they also bear the title Choranes, or military lord, seeming to point to the time when, according to Chinese authors, the Yu-chi, or Massagetæ of Cophene, deposed their kings, and substituted military chiefs or Choranes.[1] This important epoch would appear to have been some time between B. C. 26 and the end of the second century of our era. It was further signalized by the introduction, or rather by the adoption as the religion of the state, of Buddhism, by the Massagetic Choranes; and if these topes be considered as essentially Buddhist monuments, calling to mind the chaityas or consecrated structures raised over the relics of the saints of that religion, and memorably over those of their great incarnation Sakya, we at once become informed of the causes to which we are indebted for so many of these singular edifices. The topes of Darunta I should consider the more ancient of those which have hitherto been discovered, as they indubitably are of the several groups at Jelalabad. Their antiquity also might be offered as a corroboration of the hypothesis, that they are connected with the military chiefs of the Massagetæ, as it must be carried very close to the commencement of our era. Neither would it overthrow the opinion, that many of them are the cenotaphs of kings, to admit that the Buddhist mode of preserving the relics of their saints has originated them. There is no reason to be alleged why kings may not have

[1] Mr. Masson has not given any authority for this historical fact, and I have been unable to verify it. It does not seem to have been known to Mr. Prinsep or to Professor Lassen.—H. H. W.

been similarly honoured, and indeed we know that Menander, one of the second class of Bactrian kings, was so distinguished.

TOPES OF DEH RAHMÁN.

Proceeding a little northerly from the last group of topes at Bímarán, we cross the ravine before alluded to, and a very short distance from it we arrive at a tope situated amid cultivated land; and still a little beyond it, at the small walled-in village of Deh Rahmán, in the centre of which, as at Bímarán, stands an imposing tope.

TOPE NO. 1 OF DEH RAHMÁN.[1]

This tope, the first reached, is of the second class, and is much dilapidated; its circumference was originally one hundred and eight feet. We penetrated it from the north, and, after excavating about eight feet, discovered a small apartment, from which was produced a diminutive steatite vase, containing a number of minute copper coins, much corroded, and so cemented together as to form one mass: one or two of them enabled us to verify them, as of the Hercules type. This deposit could scarcely be considered as the primary one, and the excavations were therefore continued to the centre of the building, where, finding nothing, I changed the direction of our labours with a view of reaching the base of the structure. We had descended some feet, and were gratified by the appearance of slate-stones, an auspicious omen as contrasted with the more substantial masonry of the pile, when, to my disappointment, the tope became filled with water: in fact, we had converted it into a well. I made some ineffectual attempts to drain off the water, but was ultimately compelled to abandon the monument, with, it may be, the primary deposit remaining in it. I had gained, however, one of the secondary deposits sufficient to allow of the appropriation of the edifice.

[1] Drawings of Topes, Pl. III.

TOPE NO. 2 OF DEH RAHMÁN.[1]

This is a tope of the first class, and remarkable for its extraordinary dimensions, having a circumference of one hundred and eighty feet. It is seated in the midst of the small village of Deh Rahmán, from which it soars a conspicuous object. The upper part has suffered much from the assaults of time, and it is easy to ascend to the summit: the decorative belt has also been nearly effaced, although enough of it remains to show its nature; it consisted of double lines of massive mouldings enclosing a succession of flat pilasters. The intermediate intervals, now that the cement has fallen away, exhibits that chequered appearance so common to all topes. This tope had flights of steps to the east and west, perhaps also to the north and south; but on the two latter points their indications are not very apparent. It is to be noted, that these flights of steps ascend up what appears to be the body of the tope to the inferior line of mouldings: in other structures they are found attached to the basements on which they rest. With this tope, indeed, traces of a basement are not perfectly discernible: there may certainly have been one, and it would be singular that so enormous a pile should have been raised on a yielding alluvial soil, without being provided with a secure foundation. The tope has considerably subsided into the soil, as have all the topes of Darunta erected on the same alluvial plain. This monument was originally enclosed within walls of masonry, the foundations of which are still seen: they had a breadth of four feet, and a length on each face of about one hundred and fifty feet. M. Honigberger penetrated this mass from the west, but discovered no relics. I heard, however, from the workmen employed, that in the centre were found three or four large stones, placed in a perpendicular position. I resumed operations, and prosecuted them towards the foundation, until it was passed, or until the masonry had ceased. I was still not satisfied that the earth found was that of the true soil, from its appearing to have been cleansed of all foreign substances, save an occasional fragment of charcoal, in itself a suspicious token. I continued therefore our labours, but they proved fruitless.

[1] Drawings of Topes, Pl. III.

SURKH TOPE, OR THE RED TOPE.[1]

This is a tope of the third class, called Surkh Tope by the natives, from the materials employed in its construction, which are stones broken from the rock on which it stands. It is distant about seven hundred yards west of Tope No. 1 of Deh Rahmán, and is perched on the first eminence of the lower hills of the Siah Koh range. It is much dilapidated, and is remarkable for the peculiarity observable in the encircling belt, a portion of which only remains; each circular arch therein being alternated by one of three sides. Adjacent to the tope are tumuli of the same red appearance, and around the structure are a variety of parapets of masonry, describing apartments, &c. M. Honigberger opened this tope from the north: in its centre was discovered a chamber of larger dimensions than usual, and slate-stones were not employed, while the sides had been lined with cement. On one of the sides was painted a human figure, as I learned from the workmen employed by M. Honigberger, who was not present at the discovery: this was destroyed by the workmen in their endeavours to detach it. From the accounts of the workmen, no very competent judges, it was an erect figure. The eminence on which this tope stands has a perpendicular escarpment towards the plain, and in it are excavated some of the usual caves. There was nothing to tempt a renewal of the examination of this structure; but on wandering about its precincts accident disclosed a coin, which, although much defaced, enabled us to identify it as of the series of the horseman type, from the symbol that was visible upon it.[2]

NANDÁRA TOPES.

On the same line of eminences, on which the preceding or Surkh Tope is erected, stands a very superior tope, called by the natives Nandára Tope or Khásta Tope; the latter term in Pushto signifying wonderful. Beneath it, but on the ascending plain, is a small dilapidated tope.

[1] Drawings of Topes, Pl. III.

[2] From the symbol it was a coin of Azes. Coins, Pl. VIII. fig. 1.

TOPE NO. 1 OF NANDÁRA.[1]

This beautiful tope, of the first class, is seated on an eminence of the Siah Koh, distant about four hundred yards from Surkh Tope to the north, and about five hundred yards to the west of the large tope of Deh Rahmán. It has a circumference of one hundred and forty-four feet. It rests on a magnificent basement, of variable depth, being accommodated to the unequal surface of the rock. A flight of steps is carried up the basement on the eastern side, which we may safely pronounce the superior one. This tope is embellished with a splendid encircling belt, consisting of double lines of mouldings, and a succession of finely turned arches and pilasters. The exterior surface of the pile from the lower line of mouldings upwards is covered with dark and fashioned slate-stones, arranged in the most curiously neat manner, while successive lines of oblong white stones concentrically surround it, being inserted at intervals. The effect produced by this diamond or chequered arrangement is nowhere so advantageously displayed as in this tope. This species of architectural peculiarity we cannot decide to have been general in the ordinary buildings of the epoch to which the tope refers, as none of them remain. We observe it, however, in all sepulchral monuments, and it may have been peculiar to them. This tope, from the lower line of mouldings upwards, was also covered with cement, as was the basement. Its body from the lower line of mouldings to the basement (like those parts of all others) has now so rugged an appearance that we neither discover any traces of its having been covered with cement, or even of its surface having been finished with slate-stones after the manner of the upper part of the tope, yet we cannot positively affirm that it was not so finished. If it were, why the lower portion of the tope's surface should suffer more from the injuries of time than the upper (a fact observable in every tope) is to be determined. The basement is alike embellished with imposing lines of mouldings, enclosing a series of pilasters, with striking capitals and pedestals. On the eastern front, above the higher line of mouldings and the encircling belt, is an aperture. It is probable that

[1] Drawings of Topes, Pl. IV.

there was originally a small niche here, containing a statue or idol, which has been wilfully destroyed at some former period. Similar apertures are found in like situations in many topes. To all of them a common story is attached, which I relate only to omit nothing which is connected with the most tastefully executed of the Darunta Topes.

A certain cunning man of Delhi once inquired of an Afghan whence he was. The reply was, " From Darunta." The cunning man asked if he was acquainted with Nandára Tope, and was answered in the affirmative. The cunning man proffered to the Afghan, that if he would extract from the tope, and bring to him, the stone on the eastern face, first illuminated by the rising sun, he should receive a reward of five thousand rupees. The Afghan returned from Delhi to Darunta, and, having the tope continually in his sight, was as constantly reminded of the cunning man's promise. About to start again for Delhi, without deeming the offer of much validity, he repaired to the tope before sunrise, watched the rising of the luminary, identified the stone, and extracted it. He carried it to Delhi, and presented it to the cunning man, who instantly paid him the promised sum, and, taking a hammer, broke the stone in his presence. The astounded Afghan beheld a quantity of gems and jewels beyond price. The cunning man remarked, " O blockhead! but for your simplicity you had surpassed in wealth the richest monarch on earth."

M. Honigberger opened this tope, or rather its basement, from the north, and penetrated to the centre without discovering any deposit. He then excavated at each angle of the basement, but elicited nothing. I directed operations upon the tope from the east, at the line of its union with the basement, and at the centre found a small cupola, and within it a small apartment described by slate-stones, whose internal sides were covered with sindúr, or red lead. In the mysterious recess was a box of bark of tree, enveloped with tuz-leaves, formed into a twist at the top, and bound with a thread. These originally fragile materials had become so decayed as to crumble on being touched. On their removal it was found that the bottom of the box of bark had entirely disappeared,—the consequence of contact. That contact is a cause of and accelerates decay, we have witnessed in other instances, where even metallic substances have been obviously influenced by it. A few ashes, and a piece of clay, on which was the impression of two figures holding palm branches in their hands, were the only contents of the box. The figures on the clay were very similar, if not identical, with those found on the smaller coins of the Kanerkes family, and probably were, like them, personifications of NANAIA and HΛIOC, or of the sun and moon. In the apartment without the bark casket was a small quantity of loose earth, amongst which were fragments of tuz-leaves, also completely pulverized, but which clearly had been originally formed into a twist, and bound with thread. These contained Bactro-Pali characters, but the state in which the faithless record was found rendered it impossible to do any thing with them, even to copy them. The bark casket had been curiously painted, and, had it been well preserved, might have been more highly prized than a more costly relic. The designs would seem principally to have been circles within circles of various colours, enclosing as their centre a white spot or nucleus; the spaces between them being filled by undulating lines also of divers colours, while the circumference near the top and bottom was encompassed by belts comprising a series of zigzag lines.

The absence of the usual accompaniments of beads, gems, coins, &c., will be here noted. It has led me to suppose that the cenotaph is rather due to a hierarch, or saint, than to a king. The distinct nature of its position on the summit of the rock may also be noted in favour of this conclusion; and it will be remembered that at its neighbouring edifice, Surkh Tope, alike seated on an eminence, and which may also refer to a saint of minor consideration, no coins were found, at least within the structure. Influenced by eminence of position and the absence of coins, I feel every disposition to conjecture that some of these monuments have been dedicated to saints. Applying this conjecture, if I may so term it, practically, I have been enabled, on inspection, indeed at first sight, to pronounce whether I should discover coins or not in many topes previous to their examination; and, as regards the earlier groups, where system and order are preserved, I have been generally correct in my judgment. If the monument in question be that of a hierarch, or holy man, we learn why the spot has been selected for the interment or cremation of others, and the reason of the formation of the group. Even in these corrupt days, and when the land is possessed by races of a different faith, it is customary for the rulers to direct their remains to be deposited in spots already consecrated by the interment of some holy man. Thus the actual chiefs of Peshawer select for the burial-place of their deceased members the supposed grave of the patriarch Lamech in Laghman; and their brethren at Kabul take equal care to repose their departed relatives near the tomb and shrine of the ambiguous saint, Ashak Arífán, presuming that, as at the day of resurrection the holy saint will needs soar upwards to heaven, there is hope that themselves and their friends may accompany him. Being willing to procure a coin, if possible, from this monument, and further to test its character, I continued M. Honigberger's excavation to the rock; but nothing further was discovered. I then directed a descent to be made from the summit into the centre of the tope, and there a shaft was brought to light, filled with carefully sifted mould, the sides being lined with cement. At its bottom was a huge mass of rock, on which was found the iron head of a hatchet. We contrived to dislodge the block, but nothing more was elicited. I have already observed that the peculiarity of a shaft at the summit is to be observed in other topes, but it is not general to all of them. The hatchet may have been that with which the fuel for the funereal pyre was hewn, and it may have been deposited as an emblem thereof.

TOPE NO. 2 OF NANDÁRA.

This tope, of the third class, is much dilapidated, and had originally a circumference of sixty feet. M. Honigberger had unsuccessfully employed some days' labour on its remains, and I continued his excavation to the rock, in hope of, by chance, meeting with some token illustrative in a remote degree of the superior tope, with which it may be supposed to have some connexion, even if erected to perpetuate the memory of some disciple. I discovered no more useful evidence than a stone of the exact size and shape of a common fowl's egg. Other topes and tumuli have yielded stones, generally spherical ones; and as they are always found in the very centre of the structures, their insertion was intentional, and I suppose had a purport, which, however, I pretend not to expound. South of this tope and its superior companion, on other and distinct eminences, are two or three tumuli, and in the escarpments are caves.

It is worthy of observation, that at the foot of the eminence on which this minor tope stands, by a slight removal of the soil, human skulls are found, deposited in apartments formed by arranged stones. No other bones are lodged with them. Similar objects are to be found at Sultanpur Bála, two or three miles south of Darunta, and there it occasionally happens that the grave-diggers in their labours fall upon a skull, the modern Mohammedan place of burial being on the site of an ancient Golgotha. The Surkh Rúd, also south of the town, has sometimes, in washing away the banks, exposed deposits of skulls. A tumulus of Passani has also yielded to my researches a human skull, and beneath it a steatite box with the usual relics. I may also point out, that in numerous topes and tumuli, in which I have met with large quantities of human bones, I have never detected skulls amongst them. These facts merit explanation. Without presuming to afford it, I think it is mentioned in Tooke's View of the Russian Empire, that at the numerous tumuli occurring, I do not exactly remember whether in the Crimea or in Siberia, which have been opened, while multitudes of bones have been discovered, there also no skulls were ever found.

A sketch of this tope is given in the plate of its predecessor, where it is seen beneath; it was hardly worth while to make a distinct one for it.[1]

TOPE GUDÁRA.[2]

This is a tope of the first class, seated on an eminence of sandstone overhanging, to the north, the river of Kabul, which, issuing from the defile of Darunta, forms, in that direction, the boundary of the plain. The eminence towards the river has an abrupt perpendicular descent, and in the steep front have been excavated several important samuches. Beneath this tope, the Surkh Rúd, or red river, effects its junction with the principal stream above noted. The monument itself, although much dilapidated, appears to have been originally constructed with much care, as to its external appearance,

[1] Drawings of Topes, Pl. IV.

[2] Ibid.

but with less as to its solidity; the mass being composed of large oval stones, but indifferently cemented together. Its original form seems to have comprised a succession of basements piled the one upon the other, decreasing in their dimensions upwards, thereby permitting little or no exhibition of the cylindrical body generally so prominent. I opened this structure from the east, and at a point high up, as from its ruinous condition the outlines of the pile were not very perceptible, and from the numerous terraces I was unable to determine the one on which the principal part of the structure rested. I depended on finding some token denoting the centre, when to descend, however laborious, would be practicable; whereas if perforated at a low point, to ascend, from the loose composition of the pile, would have been dangerous. As it was, considerable peril threatened the workmen, but the centre was reached without any more serious accidents than slight contusions; and there we fell upon a cylinder of fine earth, three feet in depth, and the same in diameter. Nothing was found but the earth. One foot and a half below it we found another cylinder of fine earth, of similar dimensions, which alike yielded nothing more. Still one foot and a half lower, a globe, also of fine earth, of a foot in diameter, presented itself; and this being cleared away, there was another, distinct, but touching it. About three feet below this lower globe a small apartment was discovered, formed of slate-stones, in which was deposited a silver casket, which enclosed a smaller one of pure gold. Within the golden casket was some reddish brown substance, probably unguents, two or three beads, a fragment of sadap or mother-of-pearl shell, with the essential relic, a fragment of bone. The squares of slate-stones on the sides and bottom of the apartment were covered with leaf-gold, and the upper slate was alternated with squares of leaf-gold and lapis-lazuli colour. I excavated for some distance below this deposit, although confident it was the primary one, yet nothing further was discovered. In this tope I first met with the novel circumstance of a tunnel running from the centre towards the side. I have since found it in two other instances. The object of these is not apparent, yet they must have some meaning. I believe such passages are found in the pyramids of Egypt, and, what may be more to our purpose, in the Buddhist monuments of Ceylon. The deposit found in this tope does not permit us to identify its origin by any positive evidence; but looking at the nature of the relics enshrined and the absence of coins, I feel an inclination to ascribe it, as that at Nandára, to some hierarch or saint; and this supposition is not discountenanced by the singularity of its position and the presence of the important caves connected with it. Gudára is a Pushto term for 'on the opposite side,' whence, Tope Gudára, or the tope on the opposite side of the river.

TOPE OF BÁR ROBÁT.[1]

This is a tope of the second class, situated on the same line of sandstone elevations as Tope Gudára, but about three miles further eastward. From the last tope the bank of the river is skirted to reach it, and the various escarpments of the eminences are provided with numerous caves, particularly at a central spot, which, seeming to refer to neither of the topes, may probably relate to a celebrated Tappa, or mound, on the plain on the other side of the river, and called Tappa Khwaja Lahoree. From the caves and temples at Gudára, an ancient aqueduct was conducted parallel to the course of the river beyond Bár Robát. In many places, it has been cut through the rock, and the water channel has been lined with cement. The tope of Bár Robát stands on an eminence about eight hundred yards from the river, having contiguous the castle and cultivated lands of Aga Jahán, son of Sirkarda Yusef, of some notoriety in his day for rebellions and murders. This structure was opened by M. Honigberger, who found in its centre, at the base, a small recess, from which he extracted a vase of steatite, containing ashes, &c., with, I believe, a mass of crystal. No coins were discovered. This monument I am also willing to ascribe to some saint, and it will have been observed that the topes of Darunta, pre-eminently situated, have all yielded a certain class of relics, and none of them have yielded coins. There may be more than one sufficient motive given for the deposit of monetary tokens, as to record the age of the building, or that of the founder, or of his rule, even to pay the grim ferryman's fee, but they might well be dispensed with when a holy personage became the object of distinction. South of this tope is a large tumulus on a distinct eminence, no doubt connected with it. On the western acclivity of the eminence of Tope Bár Robát are found

[1] Drawings of Topes, Pl. IV.

numbers of pisolitic pebbles, called sárcham, or 'small shot,' by the natives, and used by them in lieu thereof.

TOPE OF SULTANPUR.[1]

This tope is of the second class, and has a circumference of one hundred and eight feet. It stands amongst cultivated lands belonging to Mohammed Jahán Khán, Galzai, and south of the rivulet formed by the springs of Sultanpur. It is more than a mile distant from Sultanpur, and above two miles from the greatest of the Darunta groups, that of Kotpur. Yet I am inclined to class it with them, from its general appearance, and because, like them, it is unprovided with a contiguous mound-enclosed area, which we shall find characterizes the groups we shall presently have to notice. The tumuli and caves belonging to this structure are seen by directing the eye upon the elevations to the south, and they are nearly a mile distant. They are moreover seated on the same side of the valley, as farther east are the Chahár Bágh monuments; and I might have considered them and their tope as connected therewith, but from the absence, as before noted, of the characteristic area. The distance of this tope from the nearest of those of Chahár Bágh is about the same as between it and the Kotpur group. In this respect, therefore, it is the link between the topes of Chahár Bágh and Darunta. A husbandman had, at some former period, made an opening into this tope from the east, for the purpose of sheltering himself from rain as he watched his lands. I continued this excavation to the centre of the edifice, and there discovered a large internal cupola, at whose apex was deposited a pyramidical ornament of steatite. It was in four detached fragments, and the base was in form a box, which contained a few ashes.[2] In doubt whether this was the primary relic enshrined, I pursued the cylindrical body of the interior tope until it terminated, and even carried down the process for some feet beneath it, till nothing further compensated my search. The interior tope in this structure was arranged peculiarly, as will be seen in the section:[3] instead of regularly descending, it threw off lines of

[1] Drawings of Topes, Pl. IV.

[2] Antiquities, Pl. III. fig. 1.

[3] Drawings of Topes, Pl. IV.

mouldings on a line level with the basement; in fact it rested on the basement or mixed into it.

CONCLUDING OBSERVATIONS ON THE TOPES OF DARUNTA.

It is natural to inquire what information has been gained by the examination of the preceding topes as to their origin and purpose. Without venturing at once to pronounce what these monuments are, we may be allowed to sum up the facts elicited, which may be brought to bear upon that question. Some of the structures have yielded coins,—others none. Those in the former condition I have judged may claim to be considered secular monuments; those in the latter, the more sacred monuments of hierarchs and saints. I have further supposed that the presence of the hierarchal shrine may have induced the assemblage of secular monuments around it. I have conjectured the topes enclosing coins to be due to monarchs, and would believe the number of coins deposited in them to have, in certain cases, a significant import, which it has been surmised may be length of rule. This remark I have pointed out will only apply to such groups of topes as this of Darunta, which is not a miscellaneous but a select collection, where we can distinctly view all the dependent tumuli and caves, and trace the principles of the system which influenced their formation. The latter also are in no greater number than we might look for in the burial-places of sovereigns and their families, and we feel assured that we behold consecrated ground, in which only the privileged by high birth and rank were allowed to deposit their ashes. If it be admitted that the monuments are royal, there can be no difficulty in ascribing them to the two families of princes whose coins have been found in them. That they are of the nature of cenotaphs, seems proved from the fact that no one of them contained bones or ashes in quantity, as would have been the case had entire corpses or their remains been entombed within them. The essential deposit has been found to be a small fragment of bone or a minute portion of ashes. It has been remarked that no tope is without its accompanying tumulus, and in this dependent and inferior structure it has been presumed that we behold the monument raised over the spot of cremation. The caves which never fail to attend these structures are of course the former abodes of the priests and others appointed to watch over them and their preservation. If these views be correct, we have at Darunta five topes referrible to saintly personages, eleven topes to monarchs, and two to the relatives of monarchs. One of the last has been nearly proved to be so, and the other from its diminutive size may be conjectured to stand in the same relation. If it be wished to appropriate to each family of princes the number of topes assignable to them, as every tope did not yield evidences or relics explanatory of its origin, we must avail ourselves of other circumstances. These will be principally found in their relative situation and contiguity, with the liberty to determine the character of unidentified topes by that of identified ones. With these allowances we might make over four topes, viz., Nos. 1, 2 and 3 of Bímarán with No. 1 of Passani to the princes whose coins are of the horseman type; and seven topes, including that of Sultanpur, (whose character is, however, dubious,) to the princes whose coins are distinguished by the Hercules type.

TUMULI OF DARUNTA.

Tumuli, as before noted, invariably accompany topes, yet very many occur as detached and independent structures. They are readily distinguished from the superior monuments, by the absence of the characteristic cylindrical body, and the hemispherical form of their cupolas. Indeed, while topes may be correctly defined cylindrical bodies resting upon basements and terminating upwards conically, tumuli may be described as basements surmounted by cupolas: nor is it impossible that as the tall taper body is the principal part of the tope, so the basement may be that of the tumulus. The belt, so prominent a feature with many topes, is never found on the tumulus, whose form would prevent its exhibition. The only decorations observable are, in one or two instances, cornices which have been carried around the sides of the square basement near the ground. The tumulus has a striking resemblance to the dahgope of Hindustan. True it is that the great proportion of these monuments, at the present time, are merely circular mounds; but the superior, also the more ancient ones, preserve in part their original outline; and if not just to conclude that the whole of them have been similarly constructed, it is allowable to consider that particular form as their primitive type.[1] The character of tumuli will be best understood by the quality of the relics they enclose. Several of them which have been examined have yielded large quantities of bones and ashes, seeming to have been erected over spots of cremation; some have enclosed large funereal jars, containing also bones and ashes, which being pulverized have been of course collected; some have produced simple ashes and bones with mingled fragments of charcoal; and others have been deficient of even these slender indications. In one or two instances an internal gumbuz or cupola has been discovered, while one only of the many tumuli of Darunta, which were opened, afforded relics analogous to those we expect to find in topes, and these were inserted immediately beneath a human skull.

I have observed that no tope is without its tumulus, although numerous tumuli have not corresponding topes: the reason appears to be this. Tumuli, in many instances, are the sole monuments that have been dedicated: topes could only be erected under favourable and concurring circumstances of power and command of treasure, strongly countenancing the opinion that they are royal or saintly monuments in general, were other and more decided proofs wanting. I say in general, because wealth, the essential requisite, might be possessed by private as well as regal individuals; and the same incentives to honour and perpetuate the memories of the dead would influence in former times, as in the present. Still these exceptions will not affect the general conclusions upon the nature of these structures.

It might be questioned whether some of the tumuli have not been raised over the remains of sovereigns, whose memories have not been perpetuated by topes; a point of moment when we would wish to ascertain the numbers of reigning princes. The magnitude and importance of some of them might authorize the affirmative inference, but examination has afforded no confirmation of such a hypothesis.

A peculiarity of internal structure is observed in the superior tumuli of Darunta, which in no instance has been noted in topes. The whole mass of the structures is divided into four quarters, by passages intersecting each other at right angles:[2] the passages extend the entire depth of the buildings,

[1] Drawings of Topes, Pl. IV. [2] Ibid. Pl. V.

and have a breadth of five or six feet or more; their interior surfaces are lined with arranged slates, as neatly and carefully as the exterior of the piles: the spaces formed by these passages are filled with the same materials as the rest of the buildings; the essential relics, of whatever nature, being placed in the centres, where the avenues meet. Inferior tumuli do not always exhibit this peculiarity of construction, which may nevertheless be deemed genuine, and possibly prescribed, being found in the more ancient monuments. Many are also distinguished by slightness of construction, in comparison with topes, as they are chiefly composed of materials loosely arranged, or without that view to solidity and duration so apparent in the erection of the superior structures. On their exteriors the same care has been bestowed, and while their surfaces were covered with arranged slates, they were again passed over with cement. Others again of these tumuli, and at Darunta they are of inferior size, are as substantially built as topes, and these would seem to have a mixed nature: from one of these I obtained a set of relics. In judging as to the character of a tumulus, its solidity may be perhaps a safe guide.

As topes and their dependent tumuli are accompanied by caves, so are detached and isolated tumuli; and this remark applies to all of the vast numbers of such monuments dispersed throughout the Afghan territories. The cave in every case had a similar design: it was the abode of the priest or recluse attached to the funereal endowment, whose employment was to tend the sepulchre and to offer up prayers for the deceased. Similar duties have been, and are, more or less practised in all countries and all ages. The Mohammedans of the present day appoint priests to read the Koran, for certain periods, over recent graves; and the tombs of their kings, and shrines of their saints, are frequently provided with establishments: moreover every village has its takia, or village shrine, with its complement of dissolute and mendicant fakirs. The caves, while attesting that the duties and obligations of their occupants were permanent, indicate asceticism,—a principal feature in the religion of the day: some of them are remarkable enough to merit particular notice.

The tumuli of Darunta principally occur grouped, contiguous to the topes of Passani, Bímarán, &c. They are found usually behind topes, and never to the front or east of them, corroborating that those structures fronted in that direction, as indicated by analogy and confirmed by the occasional presence of niches.

GROUP OF TUMULI ABOUT THE TOPES OF PASSANI.

This group comprises fourteen tumuli, contiguous to the two topes of Passani: some of them are of imposing dimensions. Having failed to procure any tokens from the topes, I examined several of these secondary structures, in hope of eliciting through their medium some evidence respecting the superior ones. It was also an object to determine the true nature of the tumulus.

No. 1. A small tumulus; yielded in the centre a large stone and human bones.

No. 2. A small tumulus; contained in the centre a human skull, and beneath it a large steatite vase, divided internally into five compartments,[1] in which were sundry minute cylindrical boxes of gold and silver, with the usual addenda of ashes, coloured stones, beads, &c. There was moreover a twist of coarse tuz-leaf inscribed with Bactro-Pali characters, and six copper coins, one of which presented a novel type, but apparently of the Azes family. This was the only tumulus at Darunta which furnished this description of relics, and was one of those built compactly: there was no interior cupola.

No. 3. A small tumulus; furnished a large broken earthen jar, containing ashes, but no other deposit.

No. 4. A small tumulus; it produced nothing.

No. 5. A large tumulus; to which a distinct account is due, and will follow.

No. 6. A large tumulus; to be noted again.

No. 7. A large tumulus; to be further described.

No. 8. A small tumulus; it yielded nothing.

No. 9. A small tumulus; some years ago, on being dug into, to prepare

[1] Antiquities, Pl. I. figs. 1, 2.

a grave for a Mohammedan fakir, an earthen jar was discovered with a few copper coins.

Nos. 10 to 14 are small tumuli; unexamined, as nothing profitable could be expected from them.

TUMULUS NO. 5 OF PASSANI.[1]

This is a large tumulus standing with its débris on a circumference of two hundred and twenty feet. It was opened at the summit, near which we found a few corroded copper coins; amongst them was one of the horseman type or of the Azes family. Some distance below them was found a small spherical stone or marble, an intentional deposit, being placed exactly in the centre. Finally, towards the base, surrounded by very large stones or boulders, was a cupola of six feet in diameter and about eight feet in depth; the conical portion of which was coated with cement, and decorated with coarsely coloured flowers. Nothing was found in the materials filling it but the beak of a bird, supposed to have been a Maina,—a deposit, whatever signification may attach to it, which has been found elsewhere, as in Tope No. 1 of Kotpur. On this tumulus a greater expense was necessary than on any of the topes we had examined.

TUMULUS NO. 6 OF PASSANI.[2]

This is the largest tumulus of the group and has not been opened, the results of its neighbour, the preceding one, not being such as to induce me to incur the heavy expense which would have been required to have penetrated into it. A sketch of it is given, in which the advantage has been taken of showing a great part of the plain of Darunta with its topes and villages.

TUMULUS NO. 7 OF PASSANI.[3]

This is a large tumulus near the minor Tope No. 2 of Passani. In its centre was found a large stone covered with layers of plain tuz-leaves, or perhaps the smooth internal bark of some tree. Beneath it was a large apartment, in which were deposited the entire bones of a corpse, regularly

[1] Drawings of Topes, Pl. V. [2] Ibid. [3] Ibid.

extended, save the skull. I was at a loss to decide whether these bones had been burned, from their state of preservation and from their integrity; the roof of the apartment was indeed smoked. This tumulus, with its predecessors Nos. 5 and 6, enables us accurately to determine the original outline of its construction.

GROUP OF TUMULI AT BÍMARÁN.

This group comprises twelve small tumuli. As the two topes near which they are situated have been satisfactorily identified, I did not examine these inferior tumuli, having no idea that they cover any thing more useful than funereal jars, some of which during the last few years have become self-exposed, and have been removed by the inhabitants. Of their connexion with the adjacent topes there can be little doubt, and it might be supposed they are assignable to the members of the family of the great prince commemorated by Tope No. 3.

GROUP OF TUMULI NEAR SURKH TOPE.[1]

This group comprises five tumuli, two of considerable size, one of which I examined, but no token was yielded. I was willing to have proceeded with the inspection of the other, although I could scarcely calculate on its proving more productive, being anxious to verify, if possible, the age of the tope to which it and the others may be supposed to have more or less relation, when close to that building I picked up a copper coin, which, with the precise type unrecognisable, disclosed the symbol which is found on coins of the Azes family.[2] I accepted this fortuitous testimony as an indication of its epoch.

GROUP OF TUMULI AT NANDARA TOPE.[3]

This group has three tumuli, all small ones. I did not examine them, from the conviction of their being like the topes to which they relate, of a holy nature, and that no profitable tokens would be gained from them.

[1] Drawings of Topes, Pl. V. [2] Coins, Pl. VIII. fig. 1. [3] Drawings of Topes, Pl. V.

ISOLATED OR UNGROUPED TUMULI.

These are all unexamined. One near Deh Rahmán manifestly refers to the huge tope which stands in the centre of the village. A tumulus near the junction of the Surkh Rúd with the Kabul river seems to refer to Tope Gudára on the opposite side of the stream. Near Jání Tope are two tumuli which may be reasonably assigned to that structure, whose examination has proved satisfactory. On the immediate bank of the Surkh Rúd is seated a large tumulus, which I suspect to have been the burial-place of a village, rather than belonging to topes or of the character of ordinary tumuli.[1] It bids fair to be washed away by the river, which has already assailed its southern face. On its summit is a Mohammedan burial-place, distinguished by its venerable gaz or tamarisk trees, and one of those graves of extraordinary dimensions, common in this part of the country, which are generally revered as shrines by the Mohammedans, and mostly connected with their legends of Hazrat Ali; although in some cases they are carried much farther back, as in Laghman, where one of them is supposed to be the grave of Métar Lam, or Lamech the father of Noah, and another near Bála Bágh has the reputation of covering the remains of Lút Paighambar, the Lot of Scripture. Abounding in the valleys of Jelalabad and Laghman, they are less numerous at Kabul, where they are called Chehel Gazzi (forty cubits). They are also found in the Hazáraját sparingly, but wherever they occur have been converted into shrines. They appear Mohammedan, if their position from north to south be a valid proof. The tumuli of Sultanpur Tope, five in number, are on the eminences above a mile from it, with their caves.

CAVES OF DARUNTA.[2]

I have already noted that some of the caves attached to tumuli and topes deserve notice. In proportion to the circumstances under which they were excavated, they exhibit many various aspects and combinations, besides

[1] Drawings of Topes, Pl. V. [2] Ibid. Pl. IX.

differing in the natural qualities of extent and number. The solitary and obscure tumulus may have its humble and single cave, but the magnificent tope has a series of caves, some of them of large dimensions and of many apartments; and these are sometimes distinguished by particular features in their construction, which, while they intimate some reason for deviation from the simple forms, also explain it. Amongst them are frequently one or more crowned with cupolas, which may reasonably be concluded to have been temples; and in line with the caves we often see mere niches, which we may suppose once contained statues or idols. The complete range of excavations, it is manifest, included, besides apartments for priests and their attendants, temples and niches for the statue of the person commemorated or the idol of his deity. These collections are miniature representations of the vast assemblages at Bamian; and while their affinity is too apparent to be doubted, they attest the character of those important vestiges of ancient superstitions. There are no topes at Bamian, because the monarchs there distinguished were probably of a peculiar faith, which did not permit the burning of their bodies; therefore there was no need of the tumulus to cover the spot of cremation, or of the tope to receive some consecrated relic of their materiality. Caves are always lined with cement, but are otherwise devoid of ornament. Some of them have a recess at their upper extremities,—a feature also to be remarked in many caves at Bamian. The domed caves or temples only have, in some cases, been surrounded with belts of mouldings or distinguished by ornaments at their apices. The most interesting of the Darunta collections of caves is that attached to Tope Gudára, and excavated in the scarped front of the eminence confining the river on which that structure stands. It exhibits all the peculiarities observable in such evidences, and may be worthy of representation. Sketch No. 1 shows the idol niche, and the view, from the opposite side of the river, of a suite of apartments, connected their whole length by two internal galleries: they are called by the natives the bazar. Sketch No. 2 shows the entrance to a large cave with a dome, therefore the temple of the ancient establishment, called on account of its size by the natives, the fil khána, or elephant stable.[1]

[1] Drawings of Topes, Pl. VI.

TUMULUS OR TAPPA ASHRAK.[1]

Eastward of the Surkh Rúd, and on the plain stretching to Jelalabad, are dispersed many tumuli. Amongst the more remarkable of these is one called Tappa Ashrak, a little north of Chahár Bágh, being separated therefrom by a broad and deep ravine, through which flows the rivulet of Sultanpur. It is surmounted by a square building called Burj Jemadár, believed to have been raised by a Galzai Jemadár in recent times, as the tappa is ascribed to one Ashrak, a modern Galzai Khán, but erroneously, as manifested by the fragmentary portions of the fine slate covering which once enveloped it. This structure has not been examined, and I should not have noticed it but for its large dimensions, and as serving to introduce another huge mound with which the Darunta section will close. Both, I am aware, are foreign thereto, but they conduct to the site which may have been the chief city of this country at the period when the topes were erected.

TAPPA KHWAJA LAHOREE.[2]

This mound is one of the most extraordinary objects on the plain of Jelalabad, from its huge dimensions. Its base has a circumference of one thousand eight hundred feet; it stands near the Kabul river, and on the skirt of the site called Beghram, where tradition assigns an ancient city called Lahore. From the remains of masonry scattered about its sides, we may readily conjecture it to have been an ancient place of sepulture. The character of these remains is at once decided by the chequered arrangement of the exteriors,—a fashion prevalent in all sepulchral monuments, and, for aught we know, peculiar to them. The presence of the caves in these vestiges and on the sides of the mound also indicates the purpose which it has served. Coins, trinkets, and other relics are found here, generally at any time, but particularly after rains. Jars are also frequently disinterred, and point out that it was not a particular cemetery, but the common one of a community. Adjacent to it are many tumuli, particularly near a hamlet named Chakanór.

[1] Drawings of Topes, Pl. VI. [2] Ibid.

SECTION II.

TOPES AND SEPULCHRAL MONUMENTS OF CHAHÁR BÁGH.

The topes and sepulchral monuments of Chahár Bágh are situated about a mile south of the town of that name, on a line of low eminences, which form, in that direction, the boundary of the cultivated valley of Jelalabad. From the ambiguous tope of Sultanpur, the nearest tope of Chahár Bágh is distant about a mile and quarter; and from the nearest of the Darunta group, viz., the topes of Kotpur, it is distant about two miles and a half.

The Chahár Bágh Topes are dispersed over a space, extending from east to west, of a mile and half. Beyond them, to the west, are isolated tumuli, connecting them as it were with a large tumulus, or perhaps dilapidated tope, named Tappa Ahinposh, south of the town of Jelalabad, and on the same continuous line of eminences. From this last structure, proceeding south for about three miles, we reach the multifarious assemblage of topes and tumuli at Hidda, to be hereafter noticed.

The topes of Chahár Bágh are inferior monuments in comparison with those of Darunta; no one of them had originally a greater circumference than one hundred and twenty feet: it is probable that one hundred and eight feet was the precise circumference of all of them. In the case of some of the Darunta topes we have found occasion to note this standard of dimension, and we may well conceive that these monuments were constructed on some principle of proportion and gradation. At present no embellishments are observable on any of the group under remark, neither are any traces visible of the coatings of cement, which we may yet conclude once covered them: they are rude, naked structures, composed of fragments of the calcareous conglomerate on which they stand. These topes are distinguished by an accompaniment, generally to the south, of a large square or oblong space, enclosed by lofty and ample mounds: such appendages are not found with the Darunta topes. What these enclosed spaces were intended for, may be difficult to determine; but the encompassing mounds are composed of earth carefully sifted, and cleansed from foreign substances. It obviously occurs to reflection, that as such accompaniments were necessary to these monuments, and not so to those of Darunta, there must have been a sufficient reason for the distinction: this may possibly be sought in the difference of the religions followed by the reigning families under whom the two groups were respectively raised.

That a difference prevailed, we might argue from the types of the coins elicited from the two groups. Those of Darunta exhibit on their reverses the figure of Hercules; the last vestige, perhaps, of the mythological system introduced by the Macedonian conquerors, or of the ancient and possibly very analogous one of the native Indians, in which Balarám was equivalent to Hercules; and who, as Arrian says, was worshipped in the hill countries, as Bacchus was similarly honoured on the plains. The coins enclosed in the monuments of Chahár Bágh announce very different objects of worship, in the sun, moon, and elements; of which their reverses bear the personifications. This form of religion, it will be remembered, was that in vogue amongst the ancient Persians and Scythians.

The topes at Chahár Bágh, considering those only as such whose outlines permit the clear recognition of the basement and cylindrical body, are six in number; and there are twelve superior tumuli, which, from being accompanied by enclosed spaces, may be conjectured to have an approximate character.

In the position of these topes, distinctness is a characteristic feature, each being separated from the other by a ravine. The same peculiarity is not so palpably exhibited by the topes of Darunta.

All the sepulchral monuments of Chahár Bágh have their caves, and the scarped sides of the several ravines afforded convenient sites for their excavation. Some of these are spacious, but devoid of ornament, and the entrances of many of them are formed after the manner of Egyptian caves.

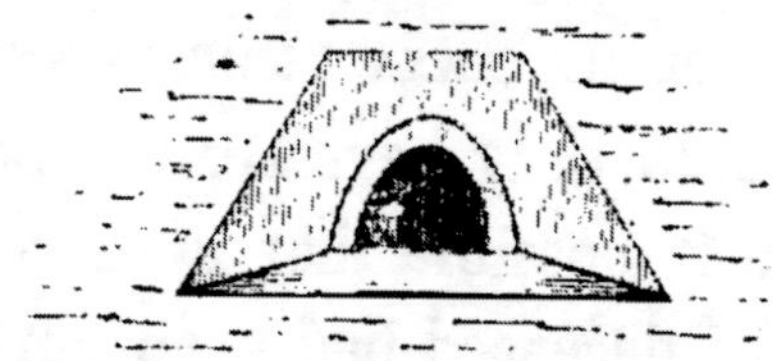

The examination of the topes of Chahár Bágh did not prove very productive in results, but these enabled us to assign the structures to the epoch of Mokadphises, and the successors of Kanerkes. As coins of the same type have been discovered in superior monuments at Kabul, we are not permitted to consider these inferior ones as dedicated to the honour of those princes. If it were imperative more definitely to designate them than as structures of a certain epoch, we have the alternative of conjecturing them as due to the memories of prince viceroys of the families.

This group, like that of Darunta, agrees in having afforded simple and unmixed deposits of coins, from which greater dependence can be placed on their testimony, and we derive a corroboration of the hypothesis that their deposits are significant.

TOPE NO. 1 OF CHAHÁR BÁGH.[1]

This tope, much dilapidated, is the first approached from the west, and is found on the ascending plain, just at the skirt of the low line of eminences. It has a remarkable depth of basement, and to the south is a large oblong square area described by huge mounds. I opened this structure from the north, and in its centre was discovered a large mass of black, greasy earth, emitting a most fetid smell. Ashes and fragments of charcoal were mixed up with this corrupt deposit, but no bones were discovered. After clearing it away, and it occupied a very considerable space of the body of the tope, we descended towards the foundation, where was discovered a small cupola. On being examined it afforded a small apartment formed of slate-stones, where, to my disappointment, no relics had been placed. This tope exhibited a new feature in the mass of funereal earth and ashes placed within it, and if we could suppose that they belonged to the person commemorated, there would be no reason to enshrine a choice portion or relic of the body when its entire remains were entombed. The mass, it need not be observed, could only have been deposited after the structure had been well advanced. Is it possible that at a certain stage of the erection some of the slaves of the deceased had been immolated?

TOPES NOS. 2 AND 3 OF CHAHÁR BÁGH.[2]

These topes are seated on the eminences south of the preceding tope. They have south of them the characteristic enclosed areas. They had been

[1] Drawings of Topes, Pl. VI.

[2] Ibid.

opened from their summits at some former and unknown period. I resumed their examination, and excavated to their foundations, but gained nothing more satisfactory than the knowledge that No. 3 was superposed upon a layer of enormous boulders.

TOPE NO. 4 OF CHAHÁR BÁGH.[1]

In the examination of this tope we fell upon a globe of pure cleansed earth at the centre, a species of deposit that had before been found in Tope Gudára of Darunta. The excavation was extended to the base, where we discovered a gumbuz or cupola. This contained no relics, but without and adjacent to it was a steatite vase, enclosing a very small cylindrical case of gold, without cover; and near to this vase were lying twenty-eight Indo-Scythic copper coins, whose obverses present the intelligible Greek legend ΡΑΟ ΝΑΝΑ ΡΑΟ ΚΑΝΗΡΚΙ ΚΟΡΑΝΟ, and whose reverses exhibit the personified types of the elements in ΜΑΟ, ΜΙΙΡΟ ΑΘΡΟ, ΟΚΡΟ and ΟΑΔΟ.[2] In this tope I again met with an example of the tunnel found before in Tope Gudára; a tope which also, as noted above, resembled the present one of Chahár Bágh in the deposit of a globe of earth. I was very willing to have verified the nature of the tunnel, and, as it appeared to extend beyond the circumference of the tope, I ordered the soil, or rather rock, to be laid open; but, after some days' labour, it was clear that with the implements and appliances at our command the task was impracticable. If this tunnel proceeded to any distance, it would have run under the mysterious enclosed area belonging to this monument, and a solution of the enigma of one might have led to that of the other.

TOPE NO. 5 OF CHAHÁR BÁGH.[3]

This is a dilapidated tope, with its successor No. 6, the most westerly of the Chahár Bágh group. It engaged the attention of Dr. Gerard, being

[1] Drawings of Topes, Pl. VII.

[2] Coins, Pl. XI. fig. 15, &c.

[3] Drawings of Topes, Pl. VII.

seated near the high road, as he passed through Jelalabad in 1833, and he set about its examination. In the centre he discovered a large square apartment, or rather, I suspect, a cupola, which was removed, but no relics were procured to recompense his researches. I carried on the excavation to the base of the structure, at which was found a small steatite vase, which covered some ashes and fragments of bones, with an animal tooth, perhaps that of a camel, and one copper coin of Mokadphises. This tope has its enclosed area to the east instead of to the south, as in the other topes to the west; and there is just a suspicion that it and its companion may have a priority of epoch, referring more particularly to that of the prince whose coin it enclosed.

TOPE NO. 6 OF CHAHÁR BÁGH.[1]

This tope is situated about five hundred yards from its predecessor, and, like it, underwent the examination of Dr. Gerard. I continued the excavation to the base, and found there a small steatite vase, enclosing a small cylindrical case with cover of gold. Beyond a sprinkling of ashes, there was no further deposit. This tope and the former one were originally of the same dimensions; they now show a circumference of ninety feet, but it is probable their genuine one was one hundred and eight feet. It has also, as No. 5, its enclosed space to the east. Contiguous to these two topes are eleven large tumuli and a few inferior ones.

TUMULI OF CHAHÁR BÁGH.[2]

I have before noted that as many of these secondary monuments have the accompaniments of enclosed areas, there is the probability that they may have in such cases a character analogous to topes: examination, however, produced nothing to verify this conjecture; for the few I opened were barren of results. Still a tumulus with an enclosed area attached, may be a structure of higher import than a tumulus without one. A sketch is subjoined, to show the nature and appearance of these monuments.

[1] Drawings of Topes, Pl. VII. [2] Ibid.

SECTION III.

TOPES AND SEPULCHRAL MONUMENTS OF HIDDA.

This miscellaneous collection of topes, tumuli, and caves, is situated on the same line of conglomerate elevations as those of Chahár Bágh, from the nearest of which they are above three miles distant. From the present town of Jelalabad they are south, and distant about five miles.

As those of Chahár Bágh, they present no traces of embellishment, or of the coatings of cement, by which they were probably once covered. They are rude piles, formed of the fragments of the conglomerate rocks on which they stand in most instances. In some of the topes, the original outlines are imperfectly preserved; but in many and the greater portion they are obliterated, and the tumuli have generally become mere mounds. This is not owing to their possessing antiquity above the superior structures, as at Darunta, for they are much more modern in nearly all cases, but by reason of their less substantial construction.

They are scattered about a small village called Hidda, but there is no tradition to assist us in the appropriation of the antiquities, beyond the unsatisfactory one which assigns them to Raja Udí. This prince, or some other under the name, has attained a great traditionary fame in the countries between Jelalabad and the Hydaspes.

It is however, I think, proved by the examination of the structures at Hidda, that they relate to whatever city was flourishing on the plain of Jelalabad at the period of the Mohammedan inroads, although it may also be considered as proved that the site had been honoured by notice during the epoch of one of the families commemorated at Darunta.

TOPES NOS. 1 TO 7 OF HIDDA.

These are small topes seated on the summit of an eminence called Gundi Kabul, or the hillock of Kabul. They are the first we approach coming from Chahár Bágh: the eminence on the higher parts near the topes has had many parapets carried along it, traces of which remain. The summit of this eminence barely affords space for the structures on it, and to the south has an equally abrupt descent as on the northern side, and is perforated with caves. I examined all these topes, and shall detail the results.

Tope No. 1 contained a small steatite vase, within which was a small silver cylindrical case, with a twist of tuz-leaf. The leaf was inscribed with Bactro-Pali characters, but I fear it is too much to expect that it could be unrolled and deciphered.

Tope No. 2 contained the fragments of a casket of bark of tree, but unfortunately it did not appear to have been deposited in a distinct recess, as usual in most other topes. Accompanying it were twenty-seven large coins of the Indo-Scythic prince Mokadphises.

Tope No. 3. This monument has a striking resemblance to the great Tope No. 5 of Bímarán, or Jání Tope, which induced the workmen to name it the Bacha, or 'child' of Jání Tope: the result of the examination proved that it had an affinity. In the interior we found, also placed in the bulk of the structure, without being deposited in a distinct chamber, the fragments of a large steatite vase; also the fragments of a small silver casket, containing three crystal beads, a piece of green stone, two white substances, an entire small shell, and a fragment of another. There was, moreover, a very small cylindrical case of gold, with a small globular ornament of gold, a pale ruby, a bead, and two seeds. Accompanying these deposits, were sixteen copper coins, one square coin of Hermæus, one of Unadpherres, two of the Azes dynasty, identical in type with those found in Tope No. 2 of Bímarán, and again in Jání Tope, and the remaining twelve coins of the exact type and kind as those found also so numerously in Jání Tope.

Tope No. 4. This structure yielded the fragments of a bone or ivory casket, alike deposited without the precaution having been taken to form an apartment for its better preservation. Accompanying it was a small cylindrical golden case, containing an apparently incinerated mass of unguents. There were also a ruby set in gold, a small globular bead of gold, a bead of crystal, small lumps of sindúr, or 'red lead,' or some such pigment, and one seed. In addition to these were five copper coins; one of Mokadphises, and four, of the successors of Kanerkes.

Topes Nos. 5, 6, and 7. From these structures no relics were procured; from one a copper coin was obtained near the summit.

Of this group of topes two sketches are given, one showing the appearance of them and Gundi Kabul from the north, the other exhibiting the same objects from the south.

TOPE NO. 8 OF HIDDA.[1]

This is a dilapidated tope surmounting an eminence immediately behind, or south of, Gundi Kabul. In course of our excavation to its centre, but very wide of it, we fell upon an apartment in which was deposited a massy copper gilt lamp with stand: the upper receptacle for the oil still contained a portion of the fluid matter, and the wick was in as fresh a state apparently, as if it had become extinguished during the night; on exposure to the air, however, the oil speedily evaporated, and the wick crumbled. With the oil were brass pins, such as might have been intended to adjust the wick. On arrival at the centre we found a huge boulder, covered with tuz-leaves, which I carefully examined, but found no characters upon them. Upon this mass were lodged a few fragments of bones. Supposing it probable that other relics might be deposited at the foundation, I resolved to penetrate to it. The removal of the stone became necessary, and was effected, but not without perilling the workmen: at the foundation nothing further was elicited. The examination of this structure showed that deposits are sometimes irregularly made; and if I had opened it from any other point than that fortunately selected, I should have missed the lamp.

TOPE NO. 9 OF HIDDA.[2]

This structure had as much the appearance of a mere tumulus as of a tope,[3] still there were certain indications of its original outlines, which made me suspect it to be one of the superior monuments. It was formed of successive layers of round and oval stones, faced on the exterior only with the conglomerate of the locality. In descending to its foundation, one

[1] Drawings of Topes, Pl. VII. [2] Ibid. Pl. VIII. [3] Ibid.

copper Indo-Scythic coin was found, but no other discovery rewarded my labours. The foundation consisted of a layer of enormous boulders.

TOPE NO. 10 OF HIDDA.[1]

This tope is the most important and prominent of the Hidda monuments. From its most imposing appearance and superiority of size, it is called Tope Kelán, or the Great Tope; yet in these respects it may not compete with the splendid edifices of Darunta, neither can it, like them, boast of any architectural embellishments. We may suppose it to have been originally covered with cement, but no traces of it remain; and a naked exterior is presented of a succession of layers of stones, superposed the one upon the other, with the intervening lines of cement, pounded slate, &c., distinctly shown. It stood on a basement, whose outlines are very intelligible. We penetrated this structure on a line nearly on a level with that of contact between the superior cylindrical body and the basement, and found at the centre a large deposit of fetid earth and ashes. We then descended towards the foundation, and there was found a large copper jar or vessel. Without it were thirteen copper coins, four pins of brass or copper gilt, three silver rings, and sundry minute ornaments, beads, &c. On opening the copper vessel it was discovered to be half-filled with a liquid as fluid as water, but discoloured by the verdigris of the metallic jar. In this liquid was deposited first a cylindrical copper gilt case, whose bottom, the effect of contact, had become corroded, and fell away as the case was extracted.[2] This enclosed a series of deposits: first, a silver casket with cover, containing four thin silver coins which we have been accustomed to call Sassanian, a small blue stone, and a mass formed probably of unguents: then, beneath it was a cylindrical mass of crystal, with a smaller incision therein, as would have fitted it to have been inserted on a cane or walking-stick: next, beneath this mass of crystal was a larger silver casket, the cover terminating upwards in a pyramidal form;[3] enclosed within it was the principal and more costly portion of the deposit in a golden casket, the cover of which was surmounted by a handsome jewel, I believe a sapphire, and which was

[1] Drawings of Topes, Pl. VIII. [2] Antiquities, Pl. II. fig. 2. [3] Ibid. fig. 3.

encircled by seven small emeralds.[1] This golden casket contained a colourless limpid fluid of the most delightful musk fragrance, but it soon evaporated: it contained three small beads and a mass of unguents. Within the silver casket, and filling the space unoccupied by the golden enclosed one, were fifty-two golden or gilt beads, with a proportion of unguents. The larger copper vessel contained amongst its discoloured fluid an ample store of numismatic and antiquarian curiosities, as follows:

5 gold solidi of the eastern emperors Theodosius, Marcian, and Leo.
2 gold (alloyed) Kanoj coins.[2]
202 silver coins of what we have been accustomed to call, I think unjustly, Sassanian coins.[3]
1 gold ring set with engraved gem.
1 gold ring set with sapphire.
1 gold ring, without gem.
7 gold rings, plain, with 2 fragments.
1 gold cylindrical case, small.
2 engraved gems, very interesting and beautiful ones.
3 rubies, plain gems.
7 gems, various.
13 beads, various.
13 gold ornaments.
1 fragment sadap, or mother-of-pearl.
1 fragment coral bead.
1 silver ring set with gem.
62 silver rings, plain.
1 silver cylindrical case, without cover.
Sundry fragments of rings, silver ornaments, beads, &c.
11 copper coins.[4]

Here was a sufficient harvest of antiques and curiosities to repay my exertions; still when I wished to apply their results to the determination of the character and epoch of the monument so fertile in its varied treasures, I had no decisive indication. A tope is of course either coeval with

[1] Antiquities, Pl. II. fig. 4. [2] Coins, Pl. XVIII. figs. 25, 26.
[3] They are undoubtedly Sassanian coins. See Pl. XVI.—H. H. W.
[4] These articles are now in the Museum of the East India Company.—H. H. W.

or posterior to the coins enclosed in it. Here they were so numerous and of so many divers species, that we could not pronounce it coeval with any of them; but the coins of three successive Greek emperors, Theodosius II., Marcianus, and Leo, who flourished from A.D. 408 to A.D. 474, enable us to affirm that the structure was erected subsequent to the latter date: how long subsequent, I dare not conjecture. Amongst the coins which have been called Sassanian, were none of the most recent description, and none of those we often meet with, having marks punched on their margins, which were unquestionably impressed on them by the first Mohammedan invaders. We might hence infer that this tope was raised at some period prior to the Mohammedan inroads, and might obtain the interval between A.D. 474 and A.D. 690, as embracing the epoch of its construction. It were needless to enter fully upon the nature of the various coins deposited, as they have been transmitted for more mature consideration. It is clear that the greater portion, if not all of them, were curiosities at the time of deposit; but as the age of them, if ascertained, will bear on that of the tope, so the period of the tope determined, will be of service in fixing the antiquity of the coins.

TOPE NO. 11 OF HIDDA.[1]

This structure is seated on a mound north of the village. Its examination proved that in the centre was an interior cupola, which contained, amongst the mass, some human bones, and two or three animal teeth, which we conjectured to be those of a camel.[2]

TOPE NO. 12 OF HIDDA.[3]

This structure, on being penetrated, yielded a few copper coins near the summit: they were Indo-Scythic, but of the more recent classes. Nothing further was elicited. All the topes of Hidda have enclosed areas

[1] Drawings of Topes, Pl. VIII.

[2] They have been examined by Mr. Clift, along with others elsewhere found by Mr. Masson, and are the teeth of the ass, the goat, and of a species of deer.—H. H. W.

[3] Drawings of Topes, Pl. VIII.

attached to them, but indiscriminately situated with regard to them. The present monument actually stood in one of them, unless indeed the sides formed an enclosure or wall. About fifty feet north of this tope was formerly a small tumulus of sifted earth, which, becoming accidentally exposed, disclosed a circular bhút khána, or house of idols. It may have had a diameter of nine feet, and a depth of about three or four while it was covered with a cupola. The idols would appear to have been twelve in number, seated figures, with their heads of hair covered with leaf gold, and of the same description as those frequently dug up near the village. This discovery occurred a short time before my visit to Hidda; and I was enabled, from the fragments of the idols I saw, and from an inspection of the place where they were found, perfectly to comprehend its arrangement. The idols were separated from each other by tablets of hewn and ornamented stone.

TOPE NO. 13 OF HIDDA.[1]

This tope is situated on the brink of a water-course, more than a mile from the village of Hidda. In our progress towards the centre we fell upon a small earthen jar, enclosing a stone wrapped in tuz-leaves. This simple deposit was perhaps the most useful that any of the many topes examined had yielded, for it was encompassed with a Bactro-Pali inscription, written with a pen, but very carelessly. Fearful that this testimony might become obliterated, or suffer in its journey from Kabul, I copied it at the time as well as I could, under the hope that, if necessary, a transcript would be serviceable. At the centre of the building we found a large quantity of fetid matter mixed with ashes and bones. Here was another instance of good fortune in having selected a certain point for the course of our excavation. Had I chosen any other, we had missed the inscribed jar.

TUMULUS OR TAPPA KELAN OF HIDDA.[2]

I opened several of the Hidda tumuli, but with unsatisfactory result. On some of them an Indo-Scythic copper coin or two, always of the lower series, would be discovered near the summits; and I heard from the

[1] Drawings of Topes, Pl. VIII. [2] Ibid.

natives accounts of the exposure of earthen jars which had been removed in their time, and even by some of the narrators. Nothing, it was asserted, was found in them but bones and ashes. One of the more conspicuous of this class of monuments, and which had possibly been cased with hewn stones, if I might so infer from the number of them strewed about, I examined with higher hopes, but to meet disappointment. A sketch of this tumulus is given.

CAVES OF HIDDA.[1]

The topes and tumuli of Hidda have an abundance of accompanying caves: they are none of them very remarkable: the more curious are found in the escarpment of an eminence called Tappa Zurgaran, or the goldsmith's mound. Of a portion of these a sketch is given, with the caves numbered, to assist explanation. No. 1 of these caves is a square apartment, surmounted with a cupola: it was covered with cement, and starred with patches of yellow paint. I presume it to have been a temple. No. 2 is a niche, clearly for the reception of a statue or idol. Nos. 3, 4, and 5 are ordinary caves, twenty-four feet in length, ten feet in breadth, and six feet in height, with circular ceilings. To the left of these caves, in the same mound, are seven or eight other caves, amongst which are three crowned with cupolas; and they have been highly painted. With water I was able to freshen the colours; but to form an idea of what subjects were represented, was impossible. The last of these caves has many branches, and strange tales are told of its interminable extent.

FUNEREAL JARS OF HIDDA.

Large numbers of funereal jars may be found in a mound behind the village of Hidda, near Tappa Kelán, whose acclivity would seem to have been devoted to their reception. They vary much in size, from a depth of three feet to six inches: they have all been covered with white paint, and generally are marked with some ornamental lines around the head and shoulders. Some of them are further adorned with flowers of varying colours; and a common device on many of them is a succession of circles,

[1] Drawings of Topes, Pl. VIII.

the inner one, or nucleus, ever white. They contain merely ashes and bones in greater or less quantity, and their mouths are invariably covered with stones. Around the necks, in almost all, it is easy to distinguish a green verdigris-coloured patch, proving that coins have been deposited with them, and at that particular part; yet I have never been able to procure one. They have been deposited sometimes in regular succession, distinct indeed from each other, but resting on a common line of cement, seeming to show that such deposits are those of a family. It is very difficult to obtain one entire, as, although preserving their integrity of form in the soil, they have become so fragile by absorption of humidity, and age, as to fall into pieces on the attempt being made to disengage them. The greater portion are of common baked potters' ware, but few occur of a stronger species. A sketch of the better jars, exhumed under my inspection, will best show the nature of their ornamental appendages.[1] On one an inscription was scratched, which I copied.

IDOLS, ETC., OF HIDDA.

On the mound on which the village is built, under the walls to the south, idols in great numbers are to be found. They are small, of one and the same kind, about six or eight inches in height, and consist of a strong cast head fixed on a body of earth, whence the heads only can be brought away. They are seated and clothed in folds of drapery, and the hair is woven into rows of curls. The bodies are sometimes painted with red lead, and rarely covered with leaf gold: they appear to have been interred in apartments, of which fragments are also found.[2] I know not whether coins were deposited with the idols, but in the course of my search for them two or three Indo-Scythic coins were detected.

[1] Drawings of Topes, Pl. IX.

[2] Ibid.

SECTION IV.

TOPES OF KABUL.

The plain which lies to the east of Kabul is bounded on the south by a ridge of mountain extending for about ten miles. Its western extremity, called Shákh Baranta, is of fair altitude, and about five miles south from the city. On the northern base of this ridge, along its skirts, are dispersed some eleven or twelve topes, two or three of them only of considerable magnitude: they occur as it were in three groups; the first and nearest from Kabul overlooking that portion of the plain called Shevaki. Amongst these is the principal monument of the kind,[1] with five or six inferior structures, seated in the recesses of the hills adjacent to it. Below or east of this group, south of the village of Kamari, are two other topes, one of them a large one; and still farther to the east are three topes, called from their number Seh Topan. The whole of these edifices were examined by M. Honigberger, and only two of them, the principal tope of Shevaki, and the superior one of Kamari, yielded results to him. The first gave a steatite vase with a Bactro-Pali inscription written in ink, and the latter a gold medal of Mokadphises. Amongst the topes of the Shĕvaki group, and immediately contiguous to an inferior one, is a column of masonry called Surkh Minar, or the red pillar, from the colour of the materials employed in its construction, which were taken from the rock on which it stands. It is clearly of the same age as the topes, and, from its position and amalgamation with them, may be calculated to participate in the character attaching to them. It, moreover, displays the chequered arrangement of its surface, as respects the insertion of pale-coloured stones at intervals and in concentric lines, as I have shown is general upon the upper and conical portions of topes and upon their basements. On the crest of the range also above the principal tope of Shevaki is another column called Minar Chakri,[2] superior in altitude and in preservation. Of this I annex a sketch, the better to convey an idea of it. The original form of Surkh Minar was probably identical, but its upper parts have fallen beneath the injuries of time. The principal of the topes of these

[1] Drawings of Topes, Pl. IX.

[2] Ibid.

three groups are respectively seated at the bottom of roads leading across the ridge of mountain; they are all, as the monuments of Chahár Bágh and Hidda, accompanied by enclosed areas, and have the usual appendages of caves, &c.[1]

In a valley called Guldára, or the vale of flowers, on the opposite side of this ridge, is a tope which was also examined by M. Honigberger. As he had penetrated only the basement, I directed it to be re-opened at the line where the superstructure reposes on it. My search was successful, and at the centre were discovered in an apartment mingled with ashes, gold medals of Kadphises, and of the earlier princes of the Kanerki family, which it was interesting to meet with in company with each other, and numerous ornaments of gold, apparently buttons, resembling such articles even to being provided with shanks.[2]

South of the eastern extremity of the ridge, at the termination of a valley opening upon a plain in which is situated the village of Khúrd Kabul, or little Kabul, are also four or five topes, one of them only tolerably preserved, but of small dimensions. I was unable personally to superintend the examination of these structures; and the parties I deputed, it is very probable from the retired situation of the locality, and from their apprehensions of being disturbed, carried on their operations with more haste than was necessary to their successful issue. However this may have been, no results were obtained but two copper Indo-Scythic coins, of a type more recent than may be supposed the age of Mokadphises. It might have been satisfactory had a greater number of the Kabul topes proved productive of the usual tokens; yet from those yielded it may be inferred that they are of the age of the coins enclosed in them, which were unmixed with those of prior dynasties. The inscription found by M. Honigberger on the Shevaki vase, if it escaped obliteration, may unfold their origin and epoch. The man employed by M. Honigberger, some year and a half after that gentleman had left Kabul, brought to me for sale two or three gold Indo-Scythic coins, of the same species as those found in these topes, with a gold coin of Trajan. I suspected he had obtained them in a manner he was not likely to avow,

[1] Sketches of the Kabul Topes were given by Mr. Masson to Dr. Honigberger, and have been etched in the J. Asiatique, Sept[re]. 1836.

[2] Antiquities, Pl. III. figs. 3, 4.

but if I could have been certain that the Roman coin had been found in one of these topes, it would have at once fixed a limit to their age, and have brought it to the second century of our era, the period at which, weighing other circumstances, our conjectures would place it. The lamented Jacquet supposed Mokadphises to be the Sanscrit Mahatrisha: if such a prince be known, it will be useful to compare his age with the inferred one of the topes.

The topes on the northern base of the Shákh Baranta ridge overlook the portion of the plain, in which we find a modern village retaining the name of Beghram, or the chief city. There are abundant vestiges in mounds, &c., to testify the existence anciently of some considerable place here, had we needed the corroborating evidence of tradition. To it we may with some confidence assign the residence of the monarchs whose topes we behold in the contiguous hills, and, until disproved by stronger testimony, we may feel justified to consider it as having been the capital of Mokadphises. The Hindus of Kabul and the vicinity celebrate on the banks of the river of Loghar, which winds through the meadows of Beghram, their annual festival of Vaisákh.

SECTION V.

TOPES OF KOH DÁMAN AND THE KOHISTÁN.

To the north of Kabul, and in the districts of Koh Dáman and the Kohistán, are three detached topes. The first occurs at Korrindar, about twelve miles from the city: it was examined by M. Honigberger, who discovered nothing within it to reward his toil: it had, however, been penetrated at some unknown and former period.[1] The next occurs at Dara,[2] about twenty-five miles from Kabul, and is perhaps the most complete and beautiful monument of the kind in these countries, as it is one of the largest. I examined it in 1833, and found in the centre a small apartment, formed by slate-stones, and containing the same materials as the mass of the building; amongst them I detected a fragment of bone, but no more

[1] Drawings of Topes, Pl. IX.

[2] Ibid.

useful result: the inner surfaces of the slate-stones had been covered with red lead. This was the first tope I opened, and subsequent experience led me to believe I had not proceeded far enough in the examination of the structure; at all events, it would have been satisfactory to have continued it. The duties imposed upon me by the Supreme Government of India prevented me from the opportunity of again visiting the spot, and I was careless of sending people, who, while they might have been permitted to have completed the excavation, would scarcely have been suffered to carry off the results, had any been yielded. The third structure is found at the extremity of a small ridge of hill called Koh Bacha, traversing the northern line of the site of Beghram, and the tope may be about thirty miles distant from Kabul: it became indispensable to open it, at any chance, from its position on so interesting a site. I made the best arrangements in my power with my friends in the neighbourhood, and sent a party from Kabul to operate upon it. An internal cupola was discovered at the centre, but beyond bones and ashes in some quantity, nothing decisive was obtained from it.

There is still another tope, it is said, about twelve miles east of the last, at the gorge of the valley of Alisai, the southern extremity of Nijrao, and opening on Tagao; and in the latter valley, if there be not a tope, we may glean from the vague accounts of the natives that there are considerable vestiges of ancient sepulchral sites, which yield also casually great numbers of coins.

TOPES OF KOHWAT IN THE DISTRICT OF WARDAK.

These topes are situated on the course of the river, which, having its source in the Hazáraját, flows through Loghar into the plain east of Kabul, where it unites with the stream passing through the city. They are distant about thirty miles to the west of Kabul. There are five or six topes, strictly so called, with numerous tumuli. Unable, from the insecurity of my situation, and the nature of my occupations at Kabul, to superintend the examination of these monuments, and yet anxious to ascertain their character, I used my influence with the authorities, and with the principals of the district in which they are located, to insure the success and safety of the people I proposed to depute on the task. Satisfied that nothing on my part had been omitted, I sent them from Kabul. While the operations were being carried on, I rode over to the place, to obtain an idea of the locality and of the structures, as well to confirm the good dispositions of the natives, and to increase the confidence of my own people. I was received with great cordiality, and found it difficult to excuse my abrupt visit. The same necessity for caution, however, which had caused me to leave the city without informing any one, precipitated my return to it, and I reached it without having been missed. I found that three or four of these structures had been opened at some unknown period; and before the present Afghan inhabitants had dispossessed the former occupants, Hazáras, about one hundred years since. It was also apparent that they had been excavated precisely on the plan I had followed in the examination of these buildings; and my workmen, who were old ones summoned from Jelalabad, agreed that Feringhis had been here before. In the principal tope an internal cupola was enclosed, or rather had been; and one of those unexplained tunnels or passages led from it towards the circumference. I directed certain operations to be pursued, even with the opened topes, and pointed out a number of tumuli which I wished to be examined, as they were very substantially constructed: the results proved successful, in great measure, and comprised seven vases of metal and steatite, with other and various deposits. One of the brass vases was surrounded with a Bactro-Pali inscription, of which I did not take a copy, as to have done so I must have cleansed it. I was averse to take this liberty, being aware that the characters being firmly dotted in could by no chance be obliterated. The coins found in these monuments were of the Indo-Scythic class; and it may be remarked, that in the several groups of topes explored at Kabul and Jelalabad, coins of all the primary and generic Indo-Scythic types have been found, whose imitations are so numerously discovered in Hindustan.

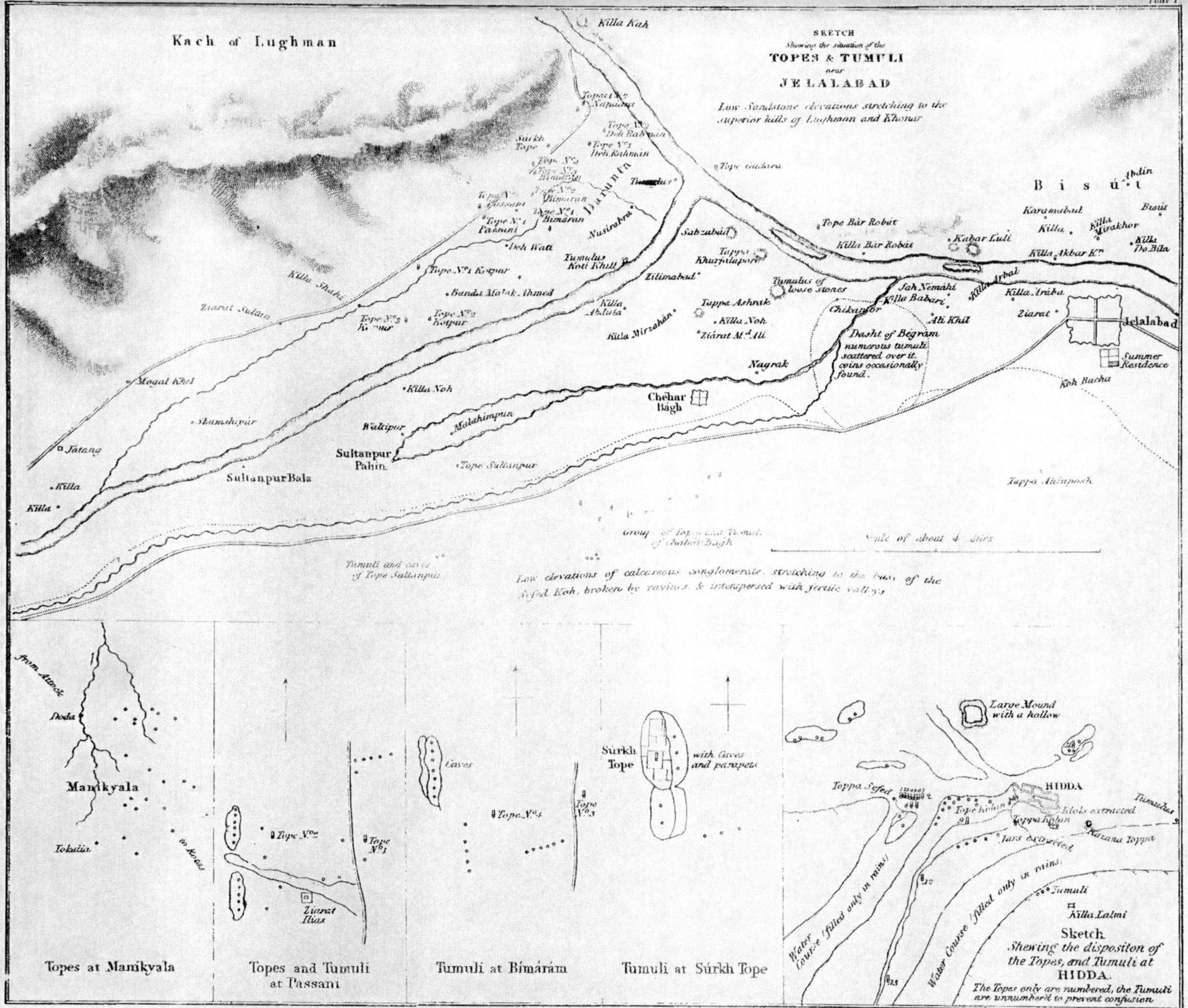
SKETCH
Shewing the situation of the
TOPES & TUMULI
near
JELALABAD
Kach of Lughman
Low Sandstone elevations stretching to the superior hills of Lughman and Khonar
Bisút
Jelalabad
Summer Residence
Dasht of Begram numerous tumuli scattered over it. coins occasionally found.
Chehar Bagh
Sultanpur Pahin
Sultanpur Bala
Darunta
Low elevations of calcareous conglomerate stretching to the base of the Sefid Koh, broken by ravines & interspersed with fertile valleys
Topes at Manikyala
Manikyala
Topes and Tumuli at Passani
Tumuli at Bimáram
Tumuli at Súrkh Tope
Súrkh Tope
with Caves and parapets
Large Mound with a hollow
HIDDA
Sketch
Shewing the dispositon of the Topes, and Tumuli at HIDDA.
The Topes only are numbered, the Tumuli are unnumberd to prevent confusion
J. & C. Walker Sculp.

Plate II.

J. Basire lith.

Plate III.

Section shewing the interior disposition of Tope No. 1 at Bimaran.
Tope No. 2 at Bímarán.
Tope No. 3 at Bímaran.
Tope No. 4 at Bímaran.
Tope No. 5 at Bimarán
Jani Tope.
Tope No. 1 at Déh Rahmán
Tope No. 2 at Déh Rahman
Surkh or Red Tope
J. Basire lith

Plate IV.

Topes 1 & 2 Nandára
Tope Gudára
Section shewing the disposition of the interior of Tope No. 1 at Nandára
Section shewing the disposition of the interior of Tope Gudára
Tope Bar Robat with its Tumulus.
Tope at Sultanpur
Section shewing the primitive form of the Tumulus.
Section shewing the interior disposition of Tope Sultanpur.
J. Basire, lith.

Plate V

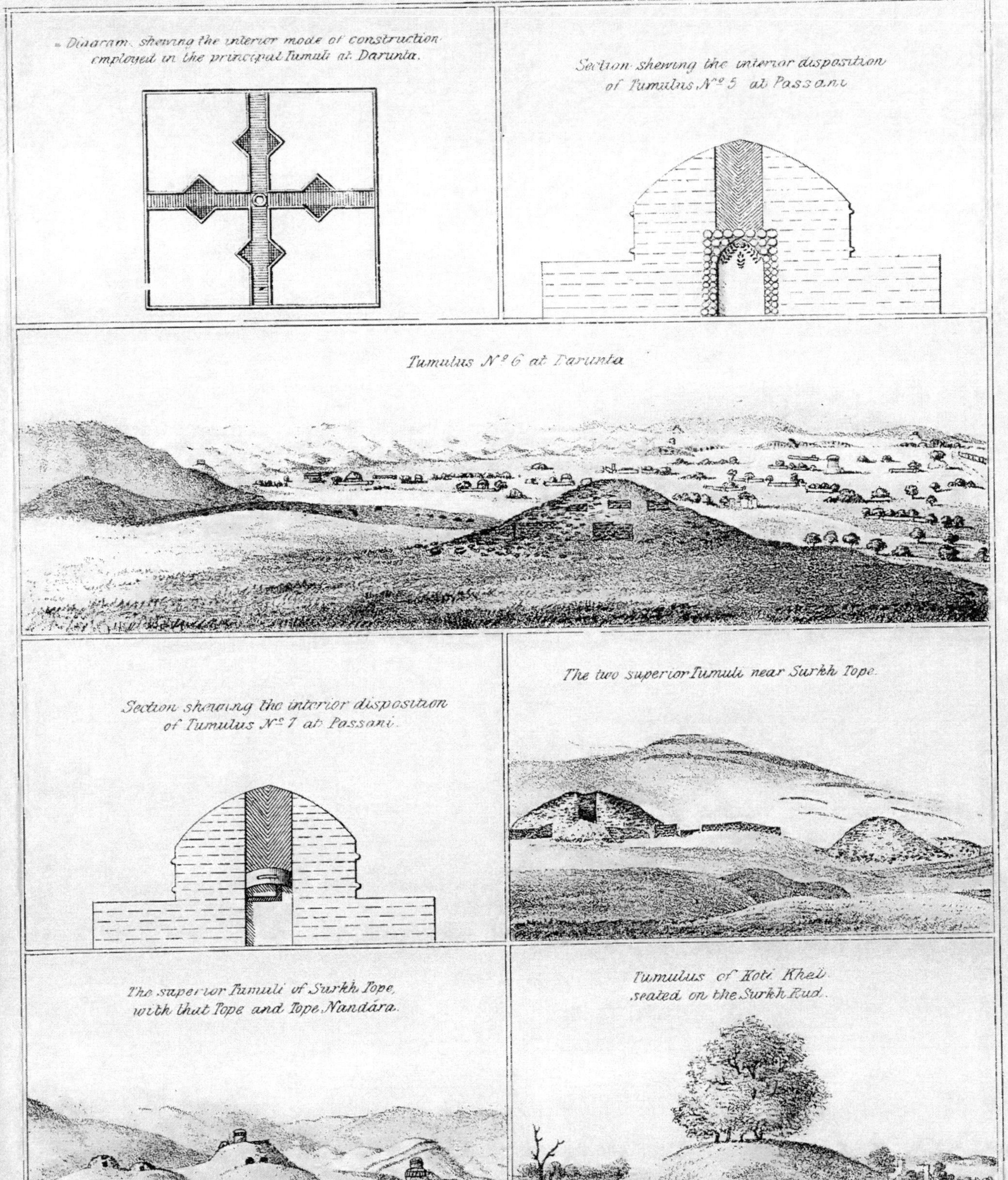

Diagram shewing the interior mode of construction employed in the principal Tumuli at Darunta.

Section shewing the interior disposition of Tumulus N.º 5 at Passani

Tumulus N.º 6 at Darunta

Section shewing the interior disposition of Tumulus N.º 7 at Passani.

The two superior Tumuli near Surkh Tope.

The superior Tumuli of Surkh Tope, with that Tope and Tope Nandára.

Tumulus of Koti Khel seated on the Surkh Rud.

J Basire lith

Plate VI.

Tope No. 4 at Chahár Bágh.

Section shewing the interior disposition of Tope No. 4 at Chahár Bágh

Tope No. 5, at Chahár Bágh.

Tope No. 6 at Chahár Bágh.

Tumulus of Chahár Bágh.

Tumuli of Chahár Bágh.

Groupe of seven Topes and Gundi Kabul from the north.

Groupe of Topes and Gundi Kabul from the south.

J. Basire, lith.

Plate VII.

Caves of Darunta No. 1 shewing the Idol niche and the grand suite of excavated apartments.

Caves of Darunta with Tope Gudára No. 2.

Tumulus or Tappa Ashruk, with Búrj Jemadár.

Tumulus or mound of Khwaja Lahoree.

Tope No. 1 at Chahár Bágh

Section showing the interior description of Tope No. 1 at Chahár Bágh

Tope No. 2 ab Chahár Bágh.

Tope No. 3 at Chahár Bágh

J. Basire, lith.

Plate VIII.

Tope N.º 8 at Hidda.

Tope N.º 9 at Hidda

Tope N.º 10 at Hidda

Tope N.º 11 at Hidda

Tope N.º 12 at Hidda

Tope N.º 13 at Hidda

Tumulus or Tappá kulán at Hidda

Caves at Hidda

J. Basire lith.

Tope of Shevaki opened by M. Honigberger

Column or Minár Chakri

Tope at Korrndar.

Tope of Tope Darrah from the front or east.

Cave Temples at Daranta, known by the Native by the name of Feel-kham or the Elephants Stables _ the apertures 1 & 2 are evidently receptacles for Statues, and the Cave N.° 3 is called the Feel-kham, from the capacity of its interior dimensions

Funereal Jars exhumed at Hidda

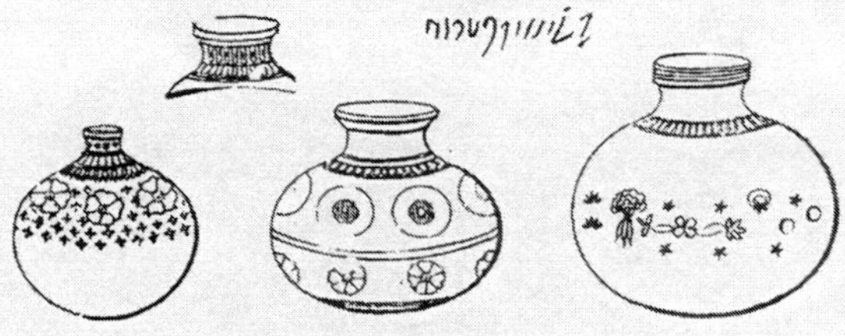

Fragments dug up at Hidda

Profile of bark casket found in Tope N.° 1 at Nandara.

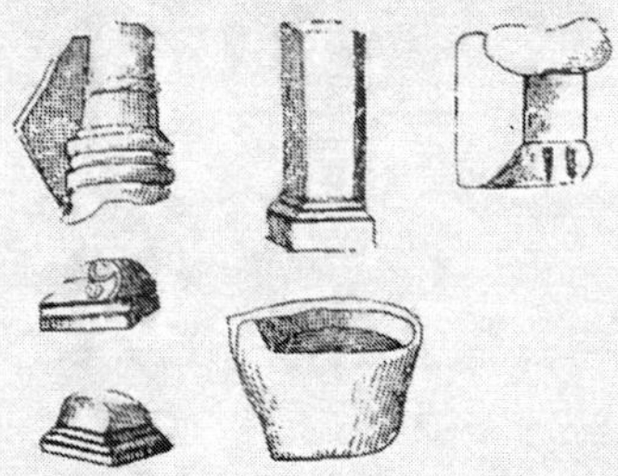

J. Basire, lith.

CHAPTER III.

ANCIENT NOTICES OF ARIANA: THE COUNTRY BETWEEN PERSIA AND INDIA, WITH REMARKS UPON ALEXANDER'S MARCH FROM THE FORMER TOWARDS THE LATTER.

THE extent of the kingdom founded by the successors of the Greek governors of the province of Bactria considerably exceeded the limits assigned to the province by classical geographers. Its precise boundaries cannot be satisfactorily determined, but the numismatic illustrations which the history of the Bactrian kings has received render it likely that at different periods, and under different dynasties, the Bactrian monarchy comprised not only Transoxiana, but the countries to the south and south-west, to the confines of Persia on the one hand, and of India on the other. It is not likely, indeed, that the whole of this tract was at any one time under one sovereign; and the coins to be hereafter described show that there must have been several distinct dynasties of more or less contemporary existence. The country was therefore, no doubt, partitioned amongst different branches from the original stem; but in its undivided form it was in all likelihood co-extensive with the modern kingdom of Kabul, and with the Ariana of the ancients, in the widest application of the term.[1] It is therefore advisable, before describing the coins of the several dynasties which held domination in this quarter of the globe, to attempt to determine what that designation imported, and what was the ancient condition of the countries over which the sway of the Bactrian Greeks was for a short season extended.

The denomination of Ariana has perhaps been rarely used with the

[1] So Strabo says; the Greeks of Bactria made themselves masters of Ariana and India, Ἕλληνες τῆς Ἀριανῆς ἐπεκράτουν, καὶ τῶν Ἰνδῶν. Book XI. 11. 1.

precision it deserved either by ancient writers or their modern expounders. It is often confounded inaccurately by both with Aria; and although the difference has been occasionally recognised, it has not in general been very decidedly marked. Whether it was known at an early date to the Greeks, is doubtful. Ariana is not mentioned by Herodotus, although he speaks of the Arii: he seems however to have had some imperfect intimation that this appellation, or something similar to it, was susceptible of a more comprehensive application than to the people of a single district, as he mentions that the Persians formerly called themselves Artæi, and that the Medes were originally denominated Arii.[1] At a later date the distinction was better understood; and although Ptolemy takes no notice of Ariana, it is fully described by Strabo, and is mentioned as including the Arii with other people by Pliny. It may therefore be inferred that it was known to their chief authorities, the contemporary narrators of Alexander's expedition, and that they derived it from the natives of the country, amongst whom it was always familiar, being, in fact, the same as IRAN, the proper appellation of ancient Persia.

Although some difficulties perplex the text of Strabo in regard to the boundaries of Ariana, yet they are not of a very important nature, nor do they materially affect the general extent and position of the country so called. On the east and south there is no disagreement. The eastern boundary of Ariana is the Indus; the southern is the Indian Ocean,[2] from the mouth of the Indus to the Persian Gulf. The western limit is said in one place to be an imaginary line drawn from the Caspian gates to Carmania. In another, Eratosthenes is cited as describing the western boundary to be a line separating Parthiene from Media, and Carmania from Parætakene and Persia[3]—that is, taking in the whole of Yezd and Kerman, but excluding Fars. The northern boundary is said to be the Paropamisan mountains, or the same mountains of which the continuation forms the northern limit of India.[4] It is elsewhere observed, upon the authority of Apollodorus of Artemis, that the name is applied

[1] Book VII. 61. 62. [2] Book XV. 2. 1. [3] Book XV. 2. 8.
[4] Book XV. 2. 1 and 8.

to some parts of Persia and Media, and to the northern Bactrians and Sogdians,[1] and it is specified of Bactriana that it is a principal part of Ariana.[2] The nations by whom Ariana is inhabited, as enumerated by Strabo, in addition to the Persian and Bactrian, who are occasionally included, are the Paropamisadæ, the Arii, Drangæ, Arachoti, and Gedrosi. Pliny specifies the Arii, Dorisci, Drangæ, Evergetæ, Zarangæ, Gedrusi, Methorici, Augutturi, Urbi, the inhabitants of Daritis, the Pasires, and Ichthyophagi.[3] The additional tribes may be regarded as those others, besides the Gedrosi, who, according to Strabo, were the inhabitants of the coast.[4] Elsewhere Pliny speaks of India comprehending four satrapies beyond the Indus; Gedrosia, Arachosia, Aria, and the Paropamisus; although, according to some, these belong to Ariana.[5] He does not differ essentially from Strabo, therefore, south of the Hindu Kush. One reason, apparently, for Strabo's comprising some of the eastern Persians, and the Bactrians and Sogdians, with the people of Ariana below the mountains, was the affinity of their languages; "for they are, as it were, for the most part, of one speech;"[5] an assertion which there is every reason to believe perfectly correct, to the guarded extent to which it is made. The languages of the people were, no doubt, for the most part, very much akin, as they were in fact natives of one and the same country.

It cannot now be reasonably doubted that Aria and Ariana, and a variety of ancient denominatives, of which Aria is a component element, are, as pointed out by M. Burnouf, connected with the Hindu term Arya, 'excellent, honourable.' According to Manu, Arya-vartta, 'the country of excellent men,' extends between the Himalaya and the Vindhya mountains, or rather between

[1] Book xv. 2. 8.

[2] Καθ' ὅλου δέ φησιν ἐκεῖνος ('Απολλόδωρος) τῆς συμπάσης 'Αριανῆς πρόσχημα εἶναι τὴν Βακτριανήν.—Book xi. 11. 1.

[3] Book vi. 25.

[4] Εἶτ' ἐφεξῆς πρὸς νότον Γεδρωσηνοὶ σὺν τοῖς ἄλλοις τοῖς τὴν παραλίαν ἔχουσιν.—Book xv. 2. 9.

[5] "Plerique ab occidente non Indo amne determinant (Indiam), sed adjiciunt quatuor satrapias, Gedrosios, Arachosios, Arios, Paropamisadas, ultimo fine Cophete fluvio:" (Book vi. 23.) he adds, "quæ omnia Ariorum esse, aliis placet;" but, as the Scholiast observes, "laxiore nunc vocabulo utitur pro Arianorum."

[6] 'Επεκτείνεται δὲ τοὔνομα τῆς 'Αριανῆς μέχρι μέρους τινὸς καὶ Περσῶν, καὶ Μήδων, καὶ ἔτι τῶν πρὸς ἄρκτον Βακτρίων, καὶ Σογδιανῶν· εἰσὶ γάρ πως καὶ ὁμόγλωττοι παρὰ μικρόν.—Book xv. 2. 8.

the same parallels of latitude, to the Western Sea; that is, to an indeterminate boundary westwards. The ancient Persian term for the same region west of the Indus is, according to its Zend form, as represented by Du Perron,[1] Eriene-veejo, in which we have the Sanscrit Arya-vartta, or varsha. M. Burnouf gives it the appellation Airyana, or Airya-dagya;[2] in the latter of which we have the Sanscrit Arya-désa. He also explains the names to signify "l'Arie dans sa plus grande étendue, c'est à dire le pays habité par la race des Arya ou des hommes nobles." The same with the negative prefixed, Anairyya, denotes "les provinces non Ariennes," an expression, the use of which has been verified by MM. de Sacy and St. Martin, who found the word Aniran on the coins of the Sassanian kings of Persia, and in the literature of Armenia, to signify countries not included in Ariana or Iran,—that is, in ancient Persia. Now, whatever doubts may be suggested by much that is given in the religious text-books of the Parsees of India, as Zend, it is highly probable that their ancestors carried with them the genuine names of places, persons, and things; and that all such terms, still preserved in their extant sacred writings, are genuine relics of their ancient nomenclature. We may, therefore, admit that Airya, or Airyana, are old Persian words, and the names of that region to which the Hindus extended the designation of Arya, which the coins of the Sassanian princes denominate Iran, and which the Greeks of Alexander's time understood by Ariana.

With regard to the affinity of the language from Bactria to the Persian Gulf, it would of course follow, that the country being that of the ancient Persians, the Persian language would be spoken in it, varied as to dialect, but radically the same. If the language of Persia was Zend, this would have been in use throughout Ariana; and its strong affinity to Sanscrit would justify the extension of Strabo's remark even to the Indians of the Paropamisus and the west bank of the Indus. With all the other divisions of Ariana there is no difficulty, even if the Persian of ancient did not materially differ from that of modern times; for Persian is still the language

[1] Vendidad Sade; Fargard, vol. i. Zendavesta, vol. i. part 2. p. 262.

[2] Commentaire sur le Yaçna, lxii.

of the inhabitants of the towns of Afghanistan and Turkestan—of Kabul and Bokhara.[1] It enters largely also into the composition of the Pushtu and Baluch dialects. Where it has been supplanted by Turki dialects it may be suspected that the alteration is of comparatively recent date. It is, therefore, not at all unlikely that the people of Ariana, extending that term to Bactria and Carmania, did, for the most part, employ a similar form of speech, and that the affinity is a valid argument for regarding them as one people—the inhabitants of ancient Iran or Persia.

There seems to be no sufficient reason for refusing to admit as the earliest authentic accounts of the political condition of the countries included within the limits of Ariana, with such reservation only as a regard for possibility imposes, the traditions which were adopted by the Mohammedan writers of the ninth and tenth centuries, and have been repeated by their later historians. According to them,[2] and in consistency with classical notices, the greater portion of Ariana was Iran or Persia. Balkh, which is usually identified with the capital of Bactria, was founded, according to some traditions, by Kaiumars, the first Peshdadian king.[3] Other accounts ascribe its foundation to Tahmuras,[4] the third of the dynasty; others, to Lohrasp,[5] of the Kaianian race. Balkh continued to be a chief city of the early Persian monarchs for some time, but fell with Transoxiana under the power of the Turks, typified by their

[1] Klaproth on the Language of the People of Bokhara: Journal Asiatique, vol. ii. p. 154. Burnes says, the aborigines of Turkestan are Tajiks, whose language is Persian, which is that of the country: Travels, vol. ii. p. 268. Mr. Elphinstone also observes, that the vernacular language of the Tajiks of Kabul and Turkestan is Persian: Account of Kabul.

[2] Firdusi in the Shah Nama, the Tarikh Tabari, Rozat-us-safa: Malcolm's History of Persia, vol. i. Vans Kennedy on the Chronology of Persian History: Transactions of the Bombay Literary Society, vol. ii. p. 109. Heeren's Researches, translation, vol. i. p. 232.

[3] History of the Early Kings of Persia, translated from the Rozat-us-safa of Mirkhond, by David Shea, published by the Oriental Translation Fund, p. 58.

[4] Shea's Mirkhond, p. 81.

[5] "Some historians maintain that Lohrasp was the founder of Balkh, but it is probable that such an event must have happened at a much later period:" Shea's Mirkhond, p. 59. The Persian author explains the name to have originated in an exclamation of Kaiumars, Bal-akh, 'O brother!' on receiving unexpectedly a fraternal visit. D'Herbelot, repeating the story, says, 'balkhíden' or 'balgíden' signifies "en langue Persienne accueiller et embrasser un ami." There are no such words in Persian, and the learned Orientalist was probably thinking of

longæval King Afrasiab, as they encroached upon Persia. It was recovered to the latter by Kai-Khosru, and was made his capital.[1] Lohrasp was entitled Balkhi, because the greatest part of his reign was passed in that region.[2] The reign of his son and successor Gushtasp was signalized by the reformation, or possibly the institution, of the Magian religion, by Zerdusht or Zoroaster, whom classical and oriental writers concur in designating as a native of Bactria or Balkh.[3] Gushtasp was one of Zerdusht's most zealous proselytes; he erected fire-temples in all parts of his dominions, and put to death so many of those who opposed the new doctrines, that his subjects were intimidated into the universal adoption of the worship of fire. These traditions, as well as similarity of name, identify Gushtasp, or, as he is also termed, Vishtasp, with the Darius Hystaspes of the Greeks.

The same accounts which testify the extension of Iran to the Oxus particularize Kabulistan as occupied by Hindus. The prince is named Mihrab; whose daughter Rudábá became the bride of Zaul the son of Saum, and prince of Sejestan or Seistan. Her son was the celebrated hero Rustam, who, from the country of his mother, was denominated Kabuli.[4] Zaul was appointed by Manuchehr governor of Seistan, Kabul, and the countries northward of the Indus. Local traditions indicate many vestiges of the presence of Rustam in the districts both immediately north and south of the Hindu Kush, or amongst the mountains.[5] The son of Gushtasp, Isfendiar, it is said, invaded Hindustan, and compelled the Hindus to acknowledge his father's supremacy and conform to his religious faith.

بغل *bughul*, 'an arm-pit,' whence بغل نمودن *bughul nimuden*, 'to show the arm-pit,' signifies 'to embrace.' Another etymology says, Tahmuras called it Talkh, 'bitter;' his predecessor, Hoshung, having been killed there; but that in time the word was changed to Balkh: Mirkhond, p. 81. Persian historians, however, are very imaginative etymologists.

[1] Mirkhond, p. 258.

[2] Ibid. p. 272.

[3] Zerdushti seu Zoroastris vita: Hyde, Religio veterum Persarum, p. 312. Zerdusht Nama; cited by Du Perron: Vie de Zoroastre, Zendavesta, vol. i. part 2. Also a memoir by the same in the Mémoires de l'Académie des Inscriptions, vol. xxxvii. The latter is translated and inserted by Mr. Shea in his translation of Mirkhond, p. 274.

[4] Shea's Mirkhond, p. 171.

[5] As the takht or throne of Rustam, near Aibek; Moorcroft's Travels, vol. ii. p. 403. And the cave of Rustam in Suwat; M. Court's Map: J. As. Soc. B. April, 1839.

The traditions of the Hindus concur with those of the Persians in considering the tribes immediately west of the Indus, and even those towards the Oxus, as their countrymen. Those of the Paropamisus are termed by them Gandháras, of which the modern Kandahar possibly preserves a vestige; but those of Bactria or Balkh are apparently intended by Bahlíkas, a term of frequent occurrence in the legendary histories of the Hindus. Bahlíka, from whom the Bahlíkas sprang, is called the son of Pratípa, of the family of Kuru.[1] In the Mahábhárat he is one of the allies of Dhritaráshtra. The same work classes the Bahlíkas with the Gandháras and other tribes beyond the Indus, specifies the country as difficult of access, and mentions its being famed for its breed of horses,—a reputation which it still enjoys.[2] In some of the Puranas there seems to be an allusion to the Greek princes of Bactria, but the passages are obscure, and, in all probability, corrupt.[3] These notices are of no great value, except that they confirm the antiquity of Balkh as the seat of an independent kingdom at some remote date, and tend to prove that it was connected in the relations of both peace and war with Hindustan.

Although there can be little doubt that the country which was known to the Persians as Balkh, and as Bahlíka to the Hindus, was in geographical position the same to which the name of Bactria was assigned by the Greeks, yet it is questionable how far this name is derived from an Asiatic original. The only approach to such an appellation known to the people of the country is the word Bakhter, which, according to Burnes, is applied by them to the tract between Balkh and Kabul.[4] The term Bakhter, also with the long vowel Bákhter, is Persian, and is used by the poets to denote most usually the east.[5] It also signifies, according to D'Herbelot, the eastern

[1] Translation of the Vishnu Purana, p. 457. [2] Ibid. p. 191, note.

[3] Ibid. p. 478, and note.

[4] The country from Kabul to Balkh is yet styled Bakhter Zumin, or Bakhter country: Travels to Bokhara, vol. ii. p. 268.

[5] In the Furhung Rashidi it is affirmed that Bakhter is used by old authors for either east or west, but most commonly for the former. In the Glossary of the Desatir, vol. ii. p. 7, Mulla Firoz restricts the sense to 'west,' and says, that the authors of the Furhungs or Poetical Lexicons, who give it the meaning of east, are in error. باختر بمعني مغرب است و انكه ارباب فرهنگها از لغات الاضداد شمرده بمعني مشرق نيز اورده اند سهو است

parts of Persia. If the language of Bactria, as part of Ariana or Iran, was Persian, as is not unlikely, there would be no incongruity in admitting the origin of Bactria from the Persian word Bákhter, if it had not been maintained that the Persian language has undergone such a change as could have brought it in its extant condition out of Zend. That such a metamorphosis has occurred is, however, matter of doubt, and we may be content to take Bákhter as the origin of Bactria until a more plausible derivation is proposed. A more weighty objection, however, arises from the absence of any competent standard authority for the employment of Bákhter to denote the country to which they apply the denomination of Balkh. In the time of Ibn Haukil[1] the province of Balkh included Ghizni and Kabul, but he has no such word as Bákhter for any part of it. Moses of Chorene applies the designation Apakhtaria to the countries to the north of Aria; and M. Burnouf refers this to a Zend word, Apakhtara, which he explains 'north.' Bactria, as derivable from Apakhtara, means therefore 'la ville septentrionale.'[2] It may be doubted, however, if the Apakhtaria of the Armenian annalist be any thing more than his mode of expressing the Greek Bactria.

The first occasion on which the Bactrians make a figure in Grecian history is not irreconcileable with the oriental traditions, which represent them as little, if at all, different from the Persians. They were invaded, it is said, by Ninus, king of Assyria, with an army which bespoke the arduousness of the enterprise against their independence. According to Ctesias, as quoted by Diodorus Siculus,[3] his forces amounted to two millions. Oxyartes made head against this host with indomitable courage, but was compelled to retreat into his capital, and was there besieged. The city was strong and vigorously defended; and Ninus despaired of its capture, when Semiramis, who had joined her husband Menon, an officer in the Assyrian army, proposed a plan of attack by which the city was taken. Her share in the exploit introduced her to Ninus, and she became his queen and successor. Bactria continued to be a dependency of the Assyro-Persic empire, and there, it is said, Semiramis fitted out her expedition against India, which,

[1] Geography, p. 223. [2] Commentaire sur le Yaçna, cxii. [3] Book II. c. 1.

notwithstanding the enormous extent of her preparations, terminated in her discomfiture. No detail of these transactions is preserved in the traditions collected by Firdusi, but it seems not improbable that the conquests of Ninus the Assyrian may have some connexion with the legend of the defeat of Jamsheed, and the subjugation of Persia by Zohauk the Arabian or Abyssinian. Zohauk was destroyed by Feridun, who, according to some traditions, was the grandson of Jamsheed, and, to others, was eight generations removed;[1] and the uncertainty which attaches both to the individual and the period intimates obscurely the duration of the Assyrian supremacy, and its final overthrow by a native chief.

The recovery of the independence of Iran, and the re-establishment of the capital at Balkh by Kai-Khosru, as related by oriental chroniclers, are probably the same events which Ctesias has recorded of Bactria. It appears from him that the Bactrians became independent upon the decline of the Assyrian empire, and continued so until the reign of Cyrus.[2] He is said to have made war against them without success, until they found that he had married Amytis, the daughter of Astyages, when they submitted to his power, and became part of the kingdom of Persia. Upon the death of Cyrus, in consequence of his being wounded in battle with the Scythians, he left to his youngest son, Tanyoxartes, the sovereignty over the Bactrians, Khoramnians, Parthians, and Karmanians. This prince was murdered treacherously by Cambyses, according to Ctesias; but one of the Magi, Sphendadates, who resembled him so strongly that the people perceived no difference, became king of Bactria. He was, however, eventually discovered and put to death, and Bactria was once more a province of Persia, under Darius Hystaspes. So it continued in the reign of Artaxerxes Mnemon, at which time Ctesias made a journey from Ephesus to Bactria. It is much to be regretted that the title only of this journey has been handed down to us.[3] The wars of Cyrus with the Scythians are evidently those of the Persian with the Turanian kings; and although

[1] Shea's Mirkhond, p. 134.

[2] Excerpta ex Ctesiæ Persicis.

[3] Amongst the fragments of Ctesias, collected by Photius, occurs, Ἄφεσις ἀπὸ Ἐφέσου μέχρι Βακτρῶν.—Frag. lxiii.

Kai-Khosru is represented as having defeated Afrasiab, yet he is said to have ultimately disappeared, and no one ever after found a trace of him. His followers, including many of the most distinguished nobles of his court, are also said to have perished in a dreadful tempest; traditions which seem to have some connexion with the Greek accounts of the defeat and slaughter of the Persian army. Of his successor, Lohrasp, also, it is related that after he had retired from power to a life of religious seclusion, he was put to death at Balkh by the Scythian prince, Arjasp;—incidents possibly connected with the story of Tanyoxartes and his Magian likeness, although in both the oriental and Greek accounts much distorted by the inevitable inaccuracy of merely traditional record.

The inclusion of Bactria amongst the provinces of Persia is confirmed by the statements of Herodotus, to whom we may now have recourse,[1] not only for such particulars as were known of the Bactrians in his day, but also for all that can be ascertained of their neighbours, the people comprehended within the limits of Ariana, taken in its widest extent, or those upon its immediate confines. Of the tribes so situated, the geographical position cannot be always satisfactorily determined, but in some instances it may be verified from incidental notices in the same writer, on which conjecture may be based, or from the recurrence of the same names in other authors, accompanied by indications more or less positive of the site of the people whom they designate. In attempting, however, to identify nations and countries mentioned by classical geographers and historians, it is sometimes important to remember, that although those authorities are separated from us by a long interval, yet they are not contemporaries of each other. Many centuries intervene, for instance, between Herodotus and Strabo, and in that period many alterations must have occurred, particularly in a region of the East, where, both from physical and political causes, change has been great and frequent.

In the enumeration of the satrapies into which the Persian kingdom was divided in the reign of Darius Hystaspes,[2] we find that the sixteenth associates the Sogdians and Arians with the Khorasmians and Parthians. The

[1] Thalia, 92, &c. Polymnia, 86, &c.

[2] Thalia, 94.

Sogdians, as is specified by subsequent writers, occupied the country between the Oxus and Jaxartes, the fertile vale of Soghd of the Mohammedans, so that the name has suffered no change for two thousand three hundred years. The Arians were of course the people of Aria, a province more particularly described in after times, and still recognisable in Herat. In the Khorasmii we have another example of the longevity of a name, as their position, intimated by their combination with the Sogdians and Parthians, shows that they were the people of Khwarizm. Their locality is confirmed by some circumstances mentioned in another passage,[1] where they are associated with the Hyrcanians, Parthians, Sarangæans, and Thomanians. They are there described as the inhabitants of a plain encircled by mountains, and dependent for the productiveness of their lands upon canals cut from the river Akes, either the Ochus or the Oxus. The same is the case still with the countries upon the Oxus, or between it and the Caspian; and the neglect of the system of irrigation, which has followed the defective administration of the government, has converted many fertile lands into barren wastes, as happened when the Persian king, as Herodotus relates, dammed up the issues of the river.[2]

The position of the Sarangæi and Thomani[3] is thus likewise determined to be somewhere in the neighbourhood of the Oxus or the Caspian. They are elsewhere again named in concert, and also with tribes called Sagartii, Utii, and Myki or Meki, and those inhabiting the isles of the Erythræan sea, indicating therefore a different locality; and, if the author has not erred in his nomenclature, the appellations must be applicable to different people. Both Rennell and Heeren consider the Sarangæi to be the people of Seistan; the latter regards the Utii and Meki as neighbours of the Thomani, who, he imagines, dwelt on the banks of the Oxus, a site no doubt appropriate to

[1] Thalia, 117.

[2] Heeren observes, it has been frequently maintained that the Akes is the Ochus; but the opinion of Gatterer, who takes it for the Oxus, appears more probable: vol. ii. p. 276. M. Ste. Croix conceives that the lake which the waters of the river are said by Herodotus to have formed was the Aral: Historiens d'Alexandre, p. 714. The story of the stoppage and loss of the waters of the Akes, found in Herodotus, appears to have had an extraordinary duration, being to the same purpose as the local traditions, which are still repeated in order to account for the altered course of the river.

[3] Thalia, 93. But the word which in the former passage is Θωμάνιοι is here Θαμάναιοι.

one tribe so called, but very inapplicable to another: he adds a loose guess that the Utii may be the same as the Uzes, the ancestors of the Turks. Rennell has a different locality for them, identifying them with the Uxians or Bakhtiyaris in Persia; but this is not better founded than Heeren's conjecture; they should rather be the people of Mekran, from their being classed with the islanders of the Indian Ocean; and, as far as any conjectural etymology is admissible, it is quite as likely that we have a trace of the Meki in Mekran, as that of the Utii in Uzes or Uxians. We may be very well content, however, after so long an interval to be able to identify so many of the tribes that are mentioned, and need not wonder to have lost sight of some that may have been extinct for centuries.

The same remark applies to many other tribes of which the names and little else are given by Herodotus. Thus, along with the Utii and Meki marched the Parikanii, and these again are associated in the tenth satrapy with the Orthokorybantes.[1] Heeren places them on the lower Jaxartes; upon what grounds does not appear. According to Rennell, we should look for them in Persia, towards Susiana, as they are connected with Ecbatana and parts of Media. The Parikanii are also classed in the seventeenth satrapy with the Asiatic Æthiopians.[2] In the former case Rennell regards them as the people of Parætakene, or Eastern Media; in the latter as inhabitants of Mekran.

In the eleventh satrapy of Herodotus we find a series of tribes, who, as Heeren affirms, wandered along the shores of the Caspian sea, between it and the Aral lake; these were the Caspii, Pausikæ, Pantimathi, and Daritæ. There is no evidence of this locality. That the Caspians bordered on the sea so named, may be admitted; but Heeren allows that they were found at a later period in a different vicinity, or on the west and north of the Caspian; and Rennell places them in Ghilan. Herodotus has also other Caspii associated with the Sakas, forming the fifteenth satrapy, and these were, no doubt, the eastern Caspians who in the army of Xerxes were clad in skins and armed with sabres and with bows. The Pausikæ are conjectured to be the same with the Pasikæ and Aspasiakæ of Ptolemy and Strabo.[3]

[1] Polymnia, 68. Thalia, 92. [2] Thalia, 94. Geogr. of Herodotus, p. 270, 304.

[3] Rennell, Geography of Herodotus, p. 276.

In the interior of Great Bokharia and on the east were, according to Heeren[1], the Gandarii, Aparytæ, Dadikæ, and Sattagydæ; they are classed together as forming the seventh satrapy. The Gandarii and Dadikæ are named again in the catalogue of the troops in connexion with the Sogdians and Khorasmians,[2] and they are said to be armed like the Bactrians.[3] Instead of the east, Rennell[4] would place them on the west of Bactria in the province afterwards called Margiana; but we can scarcely doubt that the Gandarii of the classical geographers were the Gandháras of the Hindus, and these were people south of the Hindu Kush, from about the modern Kandahar to the Indus, and extending into the Punjab and to Kashmir.[5] It seems likely, indeed, that both the authorities referred to have erred in placing most of these tribes to the north of Khorasan; and perhaps, as intended by Herodotus, they may be better located amongst or in the vicinity of the Paropamisan mountains, being the predecessors, if not the ancestors, of the modern Hazáras.[6]

In addition to these tribes, whose general position is sufficiently well ascertained, the Hyrcanians, Parthians, Khorasmians, Bactrians, and Sogdians, to those connected with them apparently by contiguity, as the Thomanians and Sarangæans, and to the Eastern Caspii, we have abundant means of filling up the vacant space between the Paropamisan mountains and the sea of Aral with the Sakæ and Massagetæ of Herodotus. The former, in conjunction with the Caspians, constituted the fifteenth satrapy.[7] In the army they were brigaded with the Bactrians under the same commander, Hystaspes the son

[1] Vol. ii. p. 277. [2] Herodotus, Book III. 91. [3] Ibid. Book VII. 66.

[4] Geogr. of Herodotus, p. 295.

[5] As. Res. vol. xv. p. 103: on the Gandháras or Gandarii and other people of the Punjab. So also M. Troyer, in the Appendix to his excellent edition and translation of the Raja-Tarangini, observes of the seventh satrapy, that it "s'étendait peut-être du Kandahar jusqu'à Pechaver. Les Gandarioi peuvent avoir occupé la partie orientale de cette satrapie, et s'être étendus de l'Indus, jusqu'au Kachmir:" tom. ii. p. 319. See also Vishnu Purana, trans. p. 443 and p. 191 and note.

[6] A term which has been said to indicate the numerous tribes or clans who inhabit the mountains: from the Persian word هزار *Hazár*, 'a thousand.'

[7] Herodotus, Book III. 93.

of Darius and Atossa the daughter of Cyrus, and were well accoutred with pointed helmets surmounted by a crest,[1] with slender bows, bills, and battle-axes; and they wore breeches. These were a particular tribe, however, of Scythians called Amyrgii; for, as Herodotus observes, all those whom the Greeks called Scythians the Persians denominated Sakas; so the same may be said of the Hindus, whose Sakas are undoubtedly the Sakas of the Persians, and the Scythians of the Greeks.[2] The Scythians of Herodotus were principally situated more to the west, between the Danube and the Don; but his classing the Sakas with the Caspians in one case, and with the Bactrians in another, intimates what is positively affirmed by other writers, that the Sakas were situated on the east of the Caspian also. The locality of the Massagetæ is still more positively pointed out. "Some assert," says Herodotus, "that they are a warlike nation established on the eastern side of the Araxes, and near the Issedones; others, that they inhabit an immense plain on the east of the Caspian sea." The Araxes in this place is shown by both Rennell and Heeren to be necessarily the Jaxartes; and the plain, according to the latter, is that steppe land which at this day includes Sungaria and Mongolia, touches on the frontier of Eygur, and extends to the Altaic chain.[3]

The remaining people in this quarter were the Indians who formed the twentieth satrapy, which was as wealthy and as populous as the other satrapies together. It is clear, however, that even at the time of Alexander's invasion little or nothing was known of the interior of India, and we may suppose that he was in possession of all the information which the Persians could give him. These Indians consequently could not have dwelt far from the Indus, and the major part of them were, no doubt, on the west of that river. The most easterly tribe of the satrapies not Indian were the Sarangæans. If these were, as is likely, the people of Seistan, there remains a considerable tract between that district and the Indus to be filled up. In truth, there is every reason to believe that a great part of the modern kingdom of Afghanistan and its dependencies, from Kabul to the sea, was occupied

[1] Herodotus, Book VII. 64.

[2] Vishnu Purana, trans. p. 188, note.

[3] Heeren, vol. ii. p. 278.

by an Indian population for many centuries after as well as before the invasion of Alexander. He found Indians in the Paropamisus. Pliny, as above mentioned, notices the common opinion that four satrapies west of the Indus, extending even to Aria, belonged to India. Reference has also been made to the tradition preserved by Firdusi that the king of Kabul in the time of Rustam was an Indian. At the end of the seventh century the Mohammedans found idolaters at Kabul, and even to the north of the mountains, under a prince with a genuine Indian appellation, Retna-pála;[1] and Ibn Haukil, who is supposed to have written in the middle of the tenth century, observes that at Kabul, although the castle was occupied by Mohammedans, the town was still possessed by idolaters, that is, by Hindus.[2] It is very probable that in Kandahar we have some trace of the Sindhu or Indo-Gandháras of the Sanscrit writers: in Sewestan and Kuch Gundawa, and even in Baluchistan and along the coast, we still have Hindus; and the historical traditions of both Baluchis and Brahuïs show that they are of comparatively recent origin.[3] On the borders of Mekran is a celebrated Hindu place of pilgrimage, Hinglaj, a temple dedicated to the goddess Kali, which is considered of high antiquity.[4]

How far Indians extended to the north and north-west, cannot be satisfactorily determined: according to Heeren[5] the whole of the mountainous region above Kashmir, Badakhshan, Beloor-land, the western

[1] The name is variously written by Mohammedan writers, Rateil, Ratpeil, Ratbal, Rantal, Zantil, &c.,—variations easily accounted for by the nature of the Persian letters. Price says the name bespeaks him either a Tartar or a Hindu; and there is no doubt that he was the latter, the name being, in fact, Rutun-pál or Retna-pála. It appears, as Price remarks, that the family of this prince had possessions in Bokharia: Mohammedan History, vol. i. c. 1. p. 454. See also Gildemeister's Scriptorum Arabum de rebus Indicis, &c., p. 5, and Abulfazl, Ayin Akbari, ii. 184.

[2] He also observes that Khorasan is bounded by Sejestan and Hindustan, because all that lies beyond Ghaur may be considered in Hindustan; p. 212. Ghaur is mostly inhabited by infidels; p. 226.

[3] Pottinger's Baluchistan, p. 274. He refers them in some places to colonies from Sindh, as late as the first Mohammedan invasion of that province; but in Kuch Gundawa and Sewestan, and other districts, there is no tradition of a recent immigration.

[4] Journey to Beylah. Memoir on the province of Lus; by Lieut. Carless: J. As. Soc. B. March, 1839, p. 193.

[5] Vol. i. p. 279.

boundary mountains of Little Bokharia or Little Tibet, and even the desert of Cobi, were all considered to belong to India. His only authorities for this extension are Herodotus and Ctesias, and their information could not have been very authentic: it was probably, however, not wholly erroneous, as traces of Sanscrit may be found along this track. According to Remusat,[1] upon the authority of Chinese writers, Khoten is properly Ku-sthana, a Sanscrit appellation; and he affirms that the Sanscrit language prevailed in the province. At a later period this does not seem to have been the case; for Fa-Hian, travelling in this direction, observes, that the people speak different dialects: their religion and literature, however, were Indian; Buddhism being established throughout the whole extent.[2] The present occupants of Little Tibet are, however, as is proved by their language, of an entirely different race, and the occupation of the other countries by Turk tribes of Uzbeks and Kirghiz is matter of modern history. The Indians, therefore, if they ever held the regions on the north of the Indian Caucasus, must have been dispossessed of them by the tribes that successively rolled over them in consequence of the convulsed state of Eastern Tartary and China for two or three centuries before until five or six centuries after the Christian æra.[3]

Without extending the limits of India, however, too far to the north, there is no reason to doubt that the valleys of the Indian Caucasus were properly included within them, and that their inhabitants, as far as to the Pamer mountains and Badakhshan, were Indians, who may have been at first tributary to Persia, and afterwards subjects of some branches of the Greek race of Bactrian kings. This forms a very extensive tract of country, which is yet but imperfectly known to us, never having been traversed by Europeans. The latest authority for the portion immediately north and west of the Indus is that of native information collected under the direction of M. Court, and compiled by him from the reports of the surveyors he employed.[4] We are indebted to

[1] Histoire de la Ville de Khoten.

[2] Foe-koue-ki, ou Relation des Royaumes Bouddhiques, p. 16.

[3] Histoire des Huns.

[4] Collection of Facts which may be useful for the comprehension of Alexander the Great's exploits on the western bank of the Indus; by M. A. Court, Ancien Elève de L'Ecole Militaire de St. Cyr: J. As. Soc. B. April, 1839.

the same intelligent officer for a map and description of the country between Peshawer and the Indus, and between that river and the Hydaspes, as well as for some information relating to the districts between the Indus and Kashmir.[1] Some illustration of this latter portion is also furnished by the travels of Forster and Moorcroft, whilst to the latter we owe the only satisfactory details we have of the country of the Durds, extending along the northern ranges of the Hindu Kush from Kaferistan to Little Tibet. From the language of Kaferistan we may also infer that the people of that region are of Hindu descent. These countries are more thickly peopled than might be suspected from their generally rugged outline; and on the southern slopes not only are the existing towns numerous, but there are the ruins of many others which must have once been of considerable extent and population.

In this situation then we have the northern Indians of Herodotus conterminous with Paktyika and the city of Kaspatyrus, extending to the confines of Bactria on the one hand, and to the gold plains on the other, that is, between Badakhshan and Little Tibet. In the gold desert are placed the gold-making ants as large as dogs, some of whom, Ctesias asserts, were to be seen in the menagerie of the kings of Persia, and who were so dangerous to the Indian gatherers of the precious metal. The story has an Indian foundation, although it has been embellished by Grecian fancy, and in its native form occurs in the Mahábhárata.[2] "At the solemnity of the inauguration of Yudhishthira as universal emperor, his feudatories, princes, or people, bring him the natural or artificial products of their several countries, as com-

[1] Memoir of a Map of Taxila and Peucelaotis: J. As. Soc. B. Aug. 1836.

[2] Mahábhárata, Sabhá Parva, printed edition, vol. i. p. 373.

मेरुमन्दरयोर्मध्ये शैलोदामभितो नदीं। ये ते कीचकवेणूनां छायां रम्यामुपासते । खसा एकासना ह्यर्हाः प्रदरा दीर्घवेणवः । पारदाश्च कुलिन्दाश्च तङ्गणाः परतङ्गणाः । तद्वै पिपीलिकं नाम उद्धृतं यत् पिप्पीलिकैः । जातरूपं द्रोणमेयमहार्षुः पुञ्जशोः नृपाः ॥ "Those tribes who dwell between Meru and Mandara, and upon the Sailodá river, under the shadow of the Bambu forests, Khasas, Ekásanas (in some MSS. Ekáyanas), Arhas, Pradaras, Dirgha-venus, Páradas, Kulindas, Tanganas, Paratanganas: the kings (of those tribes) verily presented in lumps of a drona weight that gold which is dug up by Pippílikas (ants), and is therefore called Pippílika (ant-gold):" Mahábhárata, Sabhá Parva, vol. i. p. 375.

plimentary offerings. Various mountain tribes bring him large lumps of the native gold denominated 'Pippílika,' because it is excavated by Pippílikas," that is, by large ants, such being the meaning of the term; the Hindus apparently imagining that the ants cleared away the sand or soil, and left the ore exposed, and this simple notion was wrought into the extravagant marvels of Ctesias and Herodotus.

With regard to Paktyika and Kaspatyrus, they must be sought for on the south of the mountains, and apparently comprehend Kashmir, with the countries adjacent to it on the south and on the west. Rennell supposed Paktyika to be identifiable with Pakheli or Pakheri, a district on the upper part of the Indus above Attok.[1] The sircar of Pakheli, in the time of Akbar, embraced the country between Kashmir and the Indus;[2] and the position is compatible with the account of Herodotus. It is not impossible that in earlier times the district extended across the river, and thus included the town which seems to have given name to the modern sircar, Peukelaotis or Pushkala-vatí.

There is a general disposition to dislodge Kaspatyrus, and fix it on some other river than the Indus; I think, unnecessarily. Wilford transferred it to the Jhelum, in which he had the countenance of a modern town called Kashab-pur.[3] Heeren and Mannert look for it in the modern Kabul, or its vicinity; and Wahl places it with confidence at the fort of Kuttver. The only reason, apparently, for seeking for Kaspatyrus in this direction, is the averment of Herodotus that the river ran towards the east; but this, as I have elsewhere conjectured, appears to have been suggested by the prevailing belief that the Indus ran into the Eastern Ocean. None of the feeders of the Kabul river have an easterly course, and this part of the description would apply, therefore, to that river alone. None of its feeders are navigable; they are rapid mountain-streams, studded with

[1] Memoir of a Map of Hindustan, p. 146.

[2] Ayin Akbari, vol. ii. p. 155. Gatterer is cited by M. Troyer as identifying Paktyika with Badakhshan, and Mannert and Lassen as placing it west of the Indus. The latter affirms that the Paktyiens undoubtedly dwell upon one of the rivers which join the Indus on the west, perhaps on that of Kabul: Translation of Raja-Tarangini, vol. ii. p. 305.

[3] Troyer's Raja-Tarangini, vol. ii. p. 305.

rocks, on which no vessels could float. The Kabul river itself forms numerous rapids and whirlpools; and, although it is descended from Jelalabad on rafts, the descent is not without danger, from the rocks and the violence of the current:[1] in fact, it is practicable for boats of any burthen only to within five kos of Peshawer, or about forty miles from the Indus.[2] It offers no advantage, therefore, over the upper part of the Indus, which was descended to Attok by Alexander in boats, and which is, in fact, navigable forty miles above that fortress to the vicinity of its débouche from the mountains, a spot likely to have been selected by Scylax; for, as it was his object to survey the river, he would of course have commenced his voyage as near to what was considered the source of the Indus as possible.

It may also be urged that we have no traces of any such place as Kaspatyrus west of the Indus. Alexander and his generals met with no such city, nor is there any other notice of it in this direction. On the east of the river we have some vestige of it in oriental appellations, and Kaspatyrus is connected apparently with Kashmir. The preferable reading of the name is Kaspa-pyrus.[3] It was so styled by Hecatæus, and the alteration is probably an error. Now Kasyapa-pur, the city of Kasyapa, is, according to Sanscrit writers, the original designation of Kashmir; not of the province of the present day, but of the kingdom in its palmy state, when it comprehended great part of the Punjab, and extended no doubt as far as, if not beyond, the Indus.[4] The site of the particular city that gave its name to the country is not ascertainable; but the general position of Kashmir and Pakheli, on the Indus, is in sufficient agreement with that which is assigned to Kaspatyrus and Paktyika by Herodotus, to satisfy us that Scylax, if he ever navigated the Indus at all, commenced as well as prosecuted his voyage on that river.

To return, however, to the countries between India and Persia, the most precise accounts we have of their distribution are given by Strabo, and from

[1] Elphinstone's Kabul, 8vo edition, vol. i. p. 150. [2] Moorcroft's Travels, vol. ii. p. 338.

[3] On the authority of Stephanus of Byzantium, Κασπάπυρος πόλις Γανδαρική.

[4] In the reign of Akbar, the Soobah of Kashmir included Kabul and Kandahar: Ayin Akbari, vol. ii. p. 134.

him, therefore, we shall next endeavour to form a view of their situation, comparing his descriptions with those found in other writers.

On the left, then, sailing across the Caspian, Strabo, like Herodotus, places nomadic Scythians, extending, he says, to the Eastern Sea and to India.[1] The ancient historians of Greece, according to him, called all the Scythians east of the Caspian, Sakas and Massagetæ; and such continued to be their appellations when known to the Macedonians under Alexander, and, at a period something later, to the Hindus and Chinese. The character of the countries which they occupied seems to have been in all ages essentially the same,—extensive steppes and plains of sand, interspersed at intervals only with water and verdure, and compelling the inhabitants to lead a migratory life, in quest of pasture for the cattle on which they themselves chiefly subsist. Such were the Sakas and Massagetæ of the Caspian plain, and such are the Turkman tribes of the present day.[2]

In like manner, as the Caspian Turkmans are distinguished into clans and tribes under different denominations, as Yimuts, Goklans, and Tekkahs on the west,[3] and Arsaris, Sakars, Salores, and Saraks on the east of the Desert,[4] so, as we have already seen, the Sakas or Scythians were divided into a number of tribes or petty nations, bearing different specific appellations; although it often happens that the generic term is applied to a particular nation or clan.[5] Thus it is said that the Sakas and Sogdians occupied the left bank of the Jaxartes, and that they and the Massagetæ were situated more to the east than another nomadic tribe, the Daæ. In ancient as in modern times, no doubt, there were many fluctuations of strength and authority amongst these kindred nomadic tribes, and one or other appropriated a larger share of territory, and took the lead in predatory excursions, giving its own name to the host assembled under its paramount guidance. Hence the Sakas were best known to the Persians

[1] Book XI. 6. 2.

[2] Travels overland from England to India; by Lieut. Conolly: and Travels to Bokhara; by Lieut. Burnes. See also Fraser's Travels in Khorasan.

[3] Conolly, vol. 1. p. 35.

[4] Burnes, vol. ii. p. 253.

[5] Pliny has a long list of the names of these nomadic races: Celeberrimi eorum, Sacæ, Massagetæ, Dahæ, Essedones, Ariacæ, Rhymmici, Pasicæ, &c. Book VI. 19.

and Greeks when Herodotus wrote, and in those days when they invaded and subdued countries far removed from their usual abodes. For, as Strabo relates, they subjugated the best part of Armenia, which derived from them its name of Sakasene. They thence penetrated into Cappadocia, but were surprised and defeated there with great slaughter; in commemoration of which the Persians built on the spot two temples, one to the goddess Anaitis, and the other to Omanus and Anandata, and established an anniversary festival known by the name Sakaia. Another story attributes the institution of the Sakaia to Cyrus: neither, possibly, may be true, but the traditions evince the migratory march of the Sakas, and the terror which was attached to their name.

At a later period the Sakas invaded and conquered Bactria; and here we have an instance of a subdivision of appellations, or rather of clans aggregated under a common name; for Strabo, who states that the Sakas subdued Bactria, also observes that the nomads who took Bactria from the Greeks were the Asii, Pasiani, Tokhari, and Sakarauli. These, according to the same writer, were the tribes best known.[1] Their sites, before or after their incursion, have not been very satisfactorily determined, but we are not without traces of them in countries comprised in or conterminous to Bactria. The Sakarauli are possibly the same with the Sagaraukæ of Ptolemy, situated near the mountains at the head of the Oxus. Relics of the Pasiani may possibly exist in the Pashais, who occupy the seven valleys of Nijrao, and are considered by the Afghans as a kind of Tajiks[2]—meaning a people older than themselves. Their language is chiefly a mixture of Persian and Sanscrit.[3] The Tokhari are very probably the Tusharas, or Tukharas, of Hindu geography,[4] from whom the country of Tokharestan, the Sthána, or place of the Tukharas, derived its appellation; and this is consistent enough with other indications of the position of the Sakas of whom Strabo speaks. They were conterminous with the Sogdi, and opposite

[1] Quoique dit Strabon ces quatre peuples sont peu connus: Trad. de Strabon, tom. iv. p. 255, note 3. The reading of some of the names varies, as Takhari, Takhori, and Thogari, and Sarakauli, Sakarangi, Sakauraki, and Sardukhæ.

[2] Description of the Siah-posh Kafirs; by Sir A. Burnes: J. As. Soc. B. vol. vii. p. 329.

[3] Vocabularies of Seven Languages spoken in the countries west of the Indus; by Lieut. Leech.

[4] Vishnu Purana, p. 195, note 157.

to the Massagetæ: but it is clear from other considerations that the Massagetæ spread from the right branch of the Jaxartes to the Aral sea and to the Desert; therefore the Sakas were on the east of the Sogdians, extending to the country at the sources of the Jaxartes and Oxus, Karatagin, Hissar, Kutlan, and Darwaz, the greater part of which is comprehended in Tokharestan. In another place it is said they are separated from the Sogdians by the Jaxartes; which is rather at variance with what is said above, and cannot be strictly correct, though it might be in part true on the upper part of the course of the river. These limits agree with the position assigned to the Sacha regio of Ptolemy, to the east of Sogdiana, and are not incompatible with the assertion of Eratosthenes, that they were fronting India, if by India we may understand the people along the foot of the Pamer mountains.

The Massagetæ are placed by Strabo upon the Araxes or Jaxartes, following in this respect Herodotus; and, as before observed, he says they were opposite to the Sogdians and Sakas; but amongst the Massagetan tribes were the Khorasmii, consequently they extended to the Aral, commonly called by oriental geographers the Darya or Sea of Khwarizm. This situation agrees with what Arrian relates of Spitamenes, that he was assisted by the Massagetæ in his repeated attacks on the places and detachments left by Alexander in his rear when he advanced to the Jaxartes: his operations must have consequently proceeded from the west and north, the direction of the Sea of Khwarizm, or from Khiva and Bokhara. Another tribe was that of the Attasii, called also Augasii and Auzasii, and another that of the Aspasiakæ, called also Aspasiatæ, Aspassiakæ, Aspasiatræ, or Pasiatæ.[1] In all but the last we have the word Aspa, which occurs so constantly in the names of these Scythic tribes, and not without national fitness; for it is the Persian and Sanscrit word Asp or Aswa, a horse. These people were warriors on horseback, and the horse was held sacred by them as a victim especially offerable to the sun, whom they are said to have worshipped.[2]

The Scythian tribes who occupied the Caspian plain to the west of the

[1] Eratosthenes associates also with the Massagetæ the Arakhoti, but it is doubtful if the reading be correct: Trad. de Strabon, tom. iv. p. 263, note. Arachosia is also called a city of the Massagetæ, but this refers to a later period when Scythian tribes had crossed the mountains. Lassen, Zur Geschichte der Griechischen Könige in Baktrien, p. 252.

[2] Herodotus, Book I. 216. Strabo, XI. 8. 6.

Massagetæ, extending to the Oxus or even to the Jaxartes, in which case they must have blended with the Massagetæ, bore the general appellation of Daæ. They were also called Parni or Aparni, or that name was applied to a particular tribe amongst them, said in one place to be seated on the Oxus, and to have aided Arsakes in his invasion of Parthia, and in another to dwell nearest to Hyrcania and the coast of the Caspian. Other tribes, as the Xanthi and Pissuri, extended towards Aria, having formerly been situated beyond the Palus Mæotis. The Daæ generally seem to have swept round the northern extremity of the Caspian, and prolonged their migrations to the south. They were separated from Hyrcania, Parthia, and Aria by an extensive desert, which, however, they occasionally crossed, and levied contributions on the countries beyond it; being, like their present representatives, the Turkmans, continually at war with their neighbours. It is conjectured, and not without probability, that these people have left traces of their name in the province of Dahestan adjoining to Asterabad, a rather more southerly position than might be assigned to the Daæ or Dahæ, but within the limits of their migratory range.[1] That the Daæ were a powerful tribe, and that they were in juxtaposition and alliance with the Massagetæ, we have confirmation from Chinese writers; for, according to them, the Yu-chi, Yu-tí, or Getæ (Massagetæ), being driven to the west by the advance of the Hi-ung-nu, formed a union with the Ta-hi-a (Daæ), and the combined tribes forced the Sakas before them to the south, in consequence of which their tribes again pressed into Bactria, and finally overturned the kingdom which the Greeks had founded there.[2] In the name Daæ, Dahæ, however, or Ta-hi-a, it is commonly inferred that we have the term Tajik, that is, Persian; but we have already shown that there is good reason to place Persians even in Transoxiana long before the barbarous tribes of the Caspian plain were heard of. After their irruption the same state of things took place probably that exists in the present day, and a political combination of distinct and even of different tribes, constituted, as it still constitutes, the kingdom of Persia. In this

[1] Kinneir, Geographical Mem. p. 168. D'Anville and Tzschucke, cited in the French translation of Strabo, tom. iv. p. 243, note.

[2] Remusat, Nouvelles Mélanges Asiatiques, tom. i. p. 205.

loose combination the designation of one member of the aggregate may have been applied to all, and the Daæ may have given a name to the Persians on the Oxus, although they became a constituent portion of the Persian state long after it had held a prominent rank amongst the monarchies of Asia.

On the south of the Caspian plain we have the Hyrcania of Strabo: he carries it, however, farther to the north than is consistent even with his own statements. He describes it as watered by both the Ochus and the Oxus on their way to the Caspian sea. This would extend Hyrcania to the Balkan, and would make it the country of the Daæ and other Scythian tribes. He also says of it that it is separated from the Desert by the Sarnius or Sarnæus, by which may be understood either the Gurgan river or the Atrek. The Turkomans are met with on the former, but the Desert can scarcely be said to commence until the latter has been forded. There are, however, remains of ancient towns even beyond it,[1] and in former times the southern limit of the sands may have been situated more to the north. The name of Hyrcania is still preserved in Gurkan or Hirkan or Jorjan, a town to the east of Asterabad, but the cities named by the Greek geographer cannot be satisfactorily identified. His capital is Tape; the site however is that of Zadrakarta, which was the name of the capital in Alexander's time, and was situated not far from the Caspian gates.

Nesaia, the next district, is by some included in Hyrcania; but, according to others, it was a separate province. It should, however, be more properly comprehended in Parthia, being identified with the modern Nissa, a small town or village on the north of the Alburz mountains, between Asterabad and Meshed.[2]

Modern geography is in no instance more at variance with ancient than in respect of the rivers of this part of Asia. Besides affirming that the Oxus flowed through Hyrcania to the Caspian or Hyrcanian sea, Strabo adds,

[1] Conolly, vol. i. p. 50.

[2] Kinneir, p. 174. It has been a question, what is the proper reading of this name, Νησαια or Νισαια? the latter occurring in a subsequent passage of Strabo, Book XI., as well as in Herodotus, Book III. 106, and Book VII. 40: Trad. de Strabon, tom. iv. p. 248. The question is unnecessary, as it is clear that two different places are intended; one Nissa on the north of the mountains; the other on the south, not improbably Nishapur.

upon the authority of Aristobulus, that it was one of the largest rivers of Asia, that it was navigable, and that by it much valuable merchandise was conveyed to the Hyrcanian sea, and thence distributed to Asia Minor, or conveyed to the Black Sea for transport to the country on its borders.[1] So Pliny affirms that it was ascertained at the time when Pompey was carrying on hostilities in the East against Mithridates, that a journey of seven days from the frontiers of India brought the traveller to the Icarus, which flowed into the Oxus: the voyage continued along that river into the Caspian, and across it to the Cyrus, from whence a land journey of no more than five days carried Indian merchandise to Phasis in Pontus.[2] It would appear also that Patrocles, the admiral of Seleucus and Antiochus, had navigated the Caspian, and that the results of his observations were in perfect accord with these statements. There could scarcely have been any mistake.[3]

The country between the Caspian and the Oxus has, however, in late times, been crossed in various directions; and not only has the Oxus been unseen, but its course has been ascertained to take a north-westerly instead of a south-westerly direction, and it flows not into the Caspian but into the sea of Aral. One of our latest and ablest travellers not only concurs in this statement, which is unquestionably correct, but expresses his doubt if it ever could have been otherwise.[4] Physical obstacles, according to Sir A. Burnes, oppose the entrance of the Oxus into the Caspian south of the bay of Balkan, and north of that point its natural receptacle is the Aral; and that this has been the case for nine centuries at least, we have the evidence of Ibn Haukil, who traces the river from its source in Badakhshan to its débouche into the sea of Khwarizm.[5] His testimony is of great importance in invalidating the evidence of modern local tradition, which pretends that the course of the river was diverted by an earthquake, or by the labour of man, as late as the sixteenth century.[6] If the course of the river underwent a

[1] Book XI. 7. 3.

[2] Pliny, Book VI. 20.

[3] Strabo, Book II. Pliny, Book VI. 21.

[4] Journey to Bokhara, vol. ii. p. 188.

[5] Oriental Geography, p. 239.

[6] Between 1642 and 1643, according to Abulghazi Khan; Mémoire sur l'ancien cours de l'Oxus; par M. A. Jaubert: Journ. Asiatique, Dec^{re}. 1833, p. 493. Jenkinson, who visited the Caspian in 1559, also observes that the Oxus formerly fell into the Gulf of Balkan. He is the author of the story that the Turkmans dammed up the mouth of the river in the hope of

change, it must have happened before the date at which Ibn Haukil wrote. A Turkish geographer, Kateb Chelebi, opposing to the statements of Ibn Haukil and Abulfeda the assertion of Hamdallah, a geographer of the fourteenth century, that a branch of the Oxus entered the Caspian, concludes that it is possible that both may be true, and that although the principal branch falls into the Aral, there was a branch which pursued a westerly course to the Caspian. This opinion is adopted by M. Jaubert.[1]

In confirmation of the westerly course of the Oxus, it has been observed that extensive excavations have been met with, which must have been part of the bed of a considerable river, in the direction which the Oxus may be supposed to have followed. Sir A. Burnes considers them to be no more than the remains of the canals of irrigation, which from the days of Herodotus to the present time have been the only means of fertilizing the barren plains of Khwarizm. Their extent, however, exceeds the probable limits of a canal. At ten days' march from the Balkan, Mouravieff, on his way to Khiva, came to what he considered the bed of the Oxus, where it was six hundred and fifty feet wide, having steep sides overgrown with brushwood, and being one hundred feet below the level of the plain: it accompanied the march for six or eight miles. Lieutenant Conolly crossed a similar bed in a different direction about one hundred and sixty miles from Asterabad. It was a thousand paces broad, with high banks, and had every appearance of having been the bed of a large river. He concludes, "there seems to be no great reason to doubt that a branch of the Oxus once flowed westwards into the Caspian."[2]

Evidence still more positive, however, of the débouche into the Caspian of a considerable river, which is now dry, is afforded by observations on the

preventing the diminution of its waters in the upper part of its course; a story repeated by Woodrooffe and Thompson. See Hanway's Travels.

[1] Mémoire, p. 498. Zimmerman, in his account of Khiva, also leans to the same notion, and, in answer to the objection to such a divergence, from the distance of the Caspian, conjectures that the shores of the sea have receded. The early notices of the outlet of the Oxus into the two inland seas having been navigable are rendered more probable by supposing them to have been less distant from each other in former times than at present. Memoir on Khiva, by Lieutenant Zimmerman, translated by Captain Morier, p. 19. Had, however, the shores of the Caspian receded, they would not have left traces of water-courses or river-beds actually entering into the sea.

[2] Travels, vol. i. p. 50.

sea-coast, particularly in the bay of Balkan. The earliest of these is the survey of the bay made by Captain Woodrooffe, in 1743, by order of Nadir Shah, who lays down the embouchure of a river which he was told was the Oxus.[1] The accuracy of his survey has been confirmed by more elaborate surveys since made by Russian officers, the results of which are embodied in the Periplus of the Caspian compiled by Professor Eichwald;[2] and these leave no doubt that a river, which could have been no other than the Oxus, formerly entered the Caspian at the south-eastern part of the bay of Balkan, by two branches; in one of these there are still pools of water, the other is dry: how far they may be traceable inland, is yet to be ascertained, but enough has been determined to justify the belief of the ancient world that the Oxus was a channel of communication between Asia Minor and India.[3]

A similar difficulty applies to the Ochus, a river which, according to some ancient geographers, rising in Parthiene, flowed through Nesaia and Hyrcania to the Caspian sea; or, according to others, formed the western boundary of Bactriana, and fell into the Oxus.[4] The former course is assigned to it by Kinneir, who, identifying the Ochus with the Te-zen or Te-jend, states that it appears to have its source near Surukhs, and after receiving the accession of many streams, one of which is the river of Meshed, falls into the Caspian in north latitude 38° 41′. In concurrence with this statement, Sir A. Burnes observes, "At the third mile from Surukhs we crossed the dry and pebbly bed of the Tejend, which rises in the neighbouring hills, and is lost in the sands. This is not the Herat river, nor is it the Ochus; for no such great river, as appears in our maps, has existence." Mr. Elphinstone, again, considers the Tejend *to be* the river of Herat, and that to

[1] Hanway's Travels, vol. i. p. 130.

[2] This work, entitled a Periplus and Monography of the Caspian Sea, with a Map, by Professor Eichwald, is quoted as one of the authorities of Zimmerman on Khiva. Being dated in 1834, it is the latest authority except Zimmerman's own map.

[3] In a memoir on Western Central Asia, by Count Cancrin, furnished to Lieut. Zimmerman by A. von Humboldt, and inserted in his Memoir, the Count gives a preference to the gulf of Kara-Bughaz, which is more to the north than that of Balkan, "if," he remarks, "the maps may be depended on;" p. 64.

[4] Strabo, Book II. 7. 3. Pliny, Book VI. 18. Ptolemy, Book VI. 11.

be the Ochus, either now lost in the sands or going to the Oxus.[1] The identity is far from satisfactorily shown, and, at any rate, it affects only the upper part of the supposed course of the Ochus. Mohun Lall, whose authority is quoted by Mr. Elphinstone, in asserting that the Tejend falls into the Oxus, agrees with those ancient writers who affirm the same of the Ochus. There is, however, some evidence of the accuracy of the account which carried the Ochus into the Caspian, in the spacious river-bed which, as has been already noticed, was traversed by Lieutenant Conolly, and which, as it was a considerable way to the south of the bay of Balkan, was not likely to have been a branch of the Oxus.[2] There is also the Atrek river, which rises near Kuchan to the north-west of Meshed, and falls into the Caspian about twenty-seven miles from Gurgan.[3] The passage of the Ochus through Nesaia would bring it on a line near to the sources of the Atrek. Either of these may be taken in evidence that there was a river, known to the ancients as the Ochus, flowing into the Caspian to the south of the Oxus.

The prolongation of the Alburz mountains, called by the ancients Taurus, constituted in their opinion part of a continuous chain from the Taurus of Pamphylia and Cilicia to the Paropamisan and Imaus mountains: the range forms the southern boundary of Mazenderan or Hyrcania: it proceeds thence in a south-easterly direction to Herat, whence it turns something to the north of east to meet the mountains of Ghaur or the Paropamisus. The mountains decline in elevation from the parallel of Mazenderan and beyond Meshed, where they again attain a respectable height: the intermediate space opposes little difficulty to the passage of caravans or incur-

[1] Elphinstone's Kabul, 8vo edition, vol. i. p. 155. [2] Conolly, vol. i. p. 49.

[3] Burnes, vol. ii. p. 101. Conolly, vol. i. p. 41. On this subject Count Cancrin remarks, "the possibility of there ever having been a river called Ochus, besides the Oxus, is by the maps rendered very doubtful, as the gulf of Balkan and the supposed double embouchure of the Amu (the Oxus) approach to within a very short distance of the limitrophe rivers of Persia, the Atrek and the Gurgi, with the boundary wall of Kizil Alan. But the southernmost of these two mouths, which is out of the limits of the gulf, has not been examined, and it is just possible that the Ochus and the Oxus may terminate in these two mouths." He points out some difficulties and objections, but concludes that the various questions connected with the subject can be cleared up only by further researches. Memoir on Khiva, p. 65.

sions of plunderers. From Armenia to the boundaries of Parthia the range was called Parakhoathras,[1] and was the seat of various barbarous tribes, whose exact position it is not easy to verify. They begin, according to Eratosthenes as cited by Strabo, with Albani and and Kadusii, the latter of whom are placed by M. Ste. Croix in Ghilan;[2] then follow the Anariakæ, Mardi, and Hyrcani, along the coasts of the Caspian for about five hundred and fifty miles, bringing them to the mouths of the Oxus or the bay of Balkan, the seat, as already noticed, of the nomadic Da-hæ. The distance is as near the truth as possible; but the position of the people is incompatible with the general distribution of the country, and with subsequent accounts of it given by Strabo. The mountains of Media and Armenia, which encircle the southern portion of the Caspian, are chiefly, he says, inhabited by Gelæ, Dokuseni, Amardi, Vitii, and Anariakæ;[3] these then are evidently tribes in Ghilan and Mazenderan on the south, not the east, of the Caspian: and the same is indicated in another passage, where it is stated that the length of the mountains of Taurus in Hyrcania is occupied by Gelæ, Kadusii, Amardi, and Hyrcani.[4] It seems likely that the Amardi of Strabo, and Mardi of Eratosthenes and Arrian, were the same people, as being equally contiguous to the Hyrcani; but this has been questioned, and much erudition has been unsuccessfully employed in determining the country of the people bearing either denomination.[5] Between the Hyrcani and Arii dwell the Tapyri, or they are placed between the Derbices, who are on the east of the Hyrcani and the latter. The position of the Tapyri, however, evidently varied at various times; and even Strabo places them subsequently in Media. The truth

[1] Strabo, Book XI. 8. 1. Also read Parokhoaras, Parokhoatras, Parkhoathras, and Parakoatras; all very like some such term as Pára-khetra, an allowable Sanscrit compound for 'a country beyond' a river or sea.

[2] Mémoires de l'Académie, tom. i. p. 126.

[3] Book XI. 7. 1.

[4] Book XI. 8. 1.

[5] "Personne n'ignore combien depuis plus d'un demisiècle on a fait des efforts pour concilier les divers témoignages des anciens relativement à des peuples mentionnés par eux dans cette double dénomination (Mardi, Amardi), et qu'ils placent tantôt dans la Medie, tantôt dans la Parthyæa, tantôt dans l'Arménie, tantôt dans la Perse, tantôt plus près du Pont Euxin:" Trad. de Strabon, tom. iv. p. 239, note, and the authorities there referred to.

seems to be that the information respecting these tribes occupying mountain-tracts of limited extent, was at no time very precise, and amounted to scarcely any thing else than the knowledge that the Hyrcanian mountains and their skirts were occupied in various parts by tribes of whom little more than the names had been ascertained.

The country next to Hyrcania, between the mountains and the Desert, was Parthia, the original country of the Parthians,[1] or, perhaps, only the cultivated part of it; for the Parthians themselves, as we have seen, were associated under the Persian government with the tribes of the Caspian desert. As a province, according to Strabo, it was of little extent, and usually joined into a satrapy with Hyrcania. It was mountainous, woody, and so poor, that the kings of Persia in passing through it journeyed as quickly as possible, as the country could not furnish provisions for their suite. The name of Parthia or Parthiene, after the revolt of Arsakes, was very differently applied, and comprised the greater part of Media and other provinces of Persia. The original district must have been situated amongst the mountains to the north and west of Meshed, as the district of Nesaia was distinct from it, or was included in Hyrcania.

The province on the north of the mountains adjoining to Parthia, according to Strabo, was Margiana. In early periods it seems to have been unknown as a distinct province, and was, no doubt, in part at least, comprised within the limits of Parthia. In the days of the later geographers it had undergone the very reverse relation, and had, to all appearance, extended its boundaries so as to include great part of the original Parthia. It is evident, from Strabo's notice of the latter, that there was left little of it except the name; and in Ptolemy no part of Parthia appears above the mountains.[2] The western boundary of Margiana was Hyrcania; the eastern, Bactriana; the northern, the Desert; and it was divided on the south, from Parthia and Aria, by the Sariphi mountains. It included Nesaia amongst its cities, and it was watered by the Margus, whence the province derived its name. It was a country divided between mountain and valley in some parts, and

[1] Strabo, xi. 9.

[2] Pliny also places Margiana immediately next to the Hyrcanian tribes. It was separated from them, however, by a Desert of one hundred and twenty Roman miles. Book vi. 18.

fertile plains in others; and in site and character corresponds to the tract which stretches from Bujnurd on the west to Merv and the Murghab, the Margus, on the east, and from the skirts of the Desert on the north to the mountains on the south:[1] a tract remarkable for its beauty and fertility in many places, and for cities celebrated in Mohammedan history; in some of which the site of others of earlier renown may perhaps be traced. One of these was founded, or, according to Pliny,[2] restored by Antiochus Soter, having been originally built by Alexander: its name was accordingly changed from Alexandria to Antiochia. Strabo also notices its foundation by Antiochus; and, according to him, it was situated on a plain enclosed by a wall, through a circuit of one hundred and seventy miles. The city was eight miles in circumference. There can be little doubt that in Antiochia, or, as it was afterwards called, Seleucia, we have Meru, Merv or Merv Shah Jehan, one of the four imperial cities of Khorasan, and long the seat of many of the sultans of Persia, particularly those of the Seljukian dynasty.[3] It is now a dependency of Bokhara, and in a state of great decay.[4] The Margus, the Murghab or Meru Rúd, rises in the mountains of the Hazaras, and loses itself in the sands about fifty miles north-west of the city.[5]

Another region of greater note, Aria, it is said, was conterminous with Bactriana and the mountains surrounding that province,—that part of the mountains of Ghaur which proceeds towards the south-west and meets the Alburz chain above Herat. Alexandria in Ariis is said to be situated six thousand stadia from the Caspian, or above six hundred and eighty miles, which is as nearly as possible the distance of Herat from Asterabad.[6] The boundaries of Aria are not very clearly defined by Strabo, although they may be made out from different passages. It was contiguous on the north and north-west to Margiana and Hyrcania, extending apparently to Meshed and the adjacent hilly country, and therefore lying to the north of some part of

[1] Travels of Burnes, Conolly, &c.

[2] Book VI. 18.

[3] Oriental writers ascribed it to Tahmasp or to Alexander Zul Karnin. Ibn Haukil, p. 215.

[4] Kinneir, p. 179.

[5] Burnes, vol. ii. p. 35.

[6] A Geographical Memoir in the Library at the India House, compiled from the latest information, gives two routes from Herat to Asterabad: one by Sharood is but five hundred and thirty-three miles, but the other by Meshed is six hundred and eighty-eight miles.

the mountains of Taurus or Parakhoathras.[1] On the south-east it had Drangiana, running up towards the Paropamisan mountains, and separating by a narrow interval Aria from Arachosia. There does not appear, however, to be so much difficulty in adjusting these positions, as some of Strabo's translators and commentators seem to have imagined.[2] According to Strabo, Aria was two thousand stadia (two hundred and twenty-nine miles) in length, and three hundred stadia, or little more than thirty-four miles in breadth in the level country. If these measurements be correct, we must contract the limits of Aria much more than has been usually done; and Aria will be restricted to the tract from about Meshed to the neighbourhood of Herat,[3] —a position well enough reconcileable with much that Strabo relates of Aria; its similarity to Margiana in character and productions, its mountains and well watered valleys, in which the vine flourished, its position as much to the north as to the south of the chain of Taurus or Alburz, and its being bounded by Hyrcania, Margiana, and Bactriana on the north, and Drangiana on the south. As Margiana was watered by the Margus, so Aria was traversed by the Arius, the Hari Rúd, or river of Herat, another stream, of which the notices are discordant. According to Strabo, the Arius was lost in the sands; and Arrian agrees with him. Ptolemy makes it terminate in a lake; and hence Rennell carried it south into the lake of Seistan. Kinneir also gives it a southerly course, although he mentions this as doubtful.[4] The notion possibly originated from confounding the river of Herat with that of Furrah, which last pursues a southerly course, and falls into the Zarah lake. The course of the Herat river is now determined. It rises at Oba in the Paropamisan mountains, and having run westerly past Herat, it turns to the north-west, and at no great distance is lost in the sands.[5] If the Tejend is to be considered as the Ochus, the river of Herat is not the Tejend; and

[1] Strabo, Book XI. 10.

[2] Trad. de Strabon, tom. iv. p. 276, note 1.

[3] The distance from Meshed to Herat is about two hundred and thirty-two miles according to Conolly, vol. i. p. 414; by a different route it is two hundred and seventy-nine miles: Geographical Memoir.

[4] Memoir of a Map of Persia, p. 172.

[5] Account of Kabul, vol. i. p. 155, and note.

as there appears to be, from the accounts of Fraser[1] and Burnes, a different river, that which rises near Surukhs, to which the name of Tejend is more correctly applicable, it is in that river, as above remarked, that the upper part of the course of the Ochus must be looked for. However this may be, it is evident that the Arius or river of Herat never could have run into the lake of Zarah, as has been sometimes thought probable: neither can the Ilmend or Helmund have any thing in common with the Arius;[2] they are expressly distinguished by Arrian, and are in very different directions.[3]

The boundaries of Aria, as described by Ptolemy, agree very tolerably with those specified by Strabo. Aria, he says, has Margiana and Bactriana on the north, Parthia and the great Desert of Carmania,—that is, the great Desert of Yezd and Kerman,—on the west, Drangiana on the south, and the Paropamisan mountains on the east; limits which correspond sufficiently with those above noticed. The long list of cities which he recapitulates it is not possible to verify, but a number of small towns occur on the road from Meshed to Herat, and thence towards Kandahar or Kabul. There can be no reasonable doubt that in Herat, or, as it is called by oriental writers, Heri, we have the Aria of the Greeks; but there is a difficulty in determining what particular city it represents. The capital of Aria, according to Strabo and Arrian, was Artakoana, also read Artakakna. Strabo specifies as other cities, Alexandria and Akhaia. Isidore of Charax has three cities, Kandake, Artakauan, and Alexandria. It is only in Ptolemy that we have an Aria civitas, as well as Alexandria and Artakaudna. Which of these is Herat? According to a memorial verse current amongst the inhabitants, Herat unites the claims of the ancient capital and the city built, or rather repaired, by Alexander.[4] "It is said that Hari was founded by Lohrasp, extended by Gushtasp, improved by Bahman, and completed by Alexander."[5] The distance from the Caspian gates to Alexandria is in favour of the identification of that city with Herat; and its

[1] Travels in Khorasan, Appendix, p. 57.

[2] Heeren, vol. i. p. 255.

[3] Book IV. 6.

[4] لهراسپ نهاده است هري را بنياد گشتاسپ براو بناي ديگر بنهاد بهمن پس
ازان عمارتي ديگر كرد اسكندر رومي اش همه داد بداد

[5] Letters from Mohun Lall: J. As. Soc. B. Jan. 1834, p. 9.

traditional attribution to Alexander may not be wholly unfounded: Artakoana could not, however, have been very distant from it. According to Barbié de Bocage it was situated at a place he calls Fusheng,[1] the Busheng or Pusheng of Ibn Haukil, one stage from Herat, on the borders of the Heri river. M. Court proposes to place it at Obeh or Oba, ten farsangs from Herat. The same officer mentions, that on his route from Isfahan to Yezd he came to a town called Ardekoun, which is valuable testimony for the genuineness of the appellation Artakoana, showing it to be a Persian word, although it is quite impossible that any city of Aria could be situated in this direction. According to Pliny the river flowed by Artakoana, which will apply either to Herat or Pusheng. M. Jacquet seems to attach weight to Ptolemy's position for Alexandria on the Arian lake;[2] but this proves no distinction, for his Artakaudna is even still more immediately on the borders of the same lake. D'Anville proposed Parra or Phurrah for the site of Alexandria; but this is beyond the probable limits of Aria, and was in all likelihood always known by something like its actual denomination, as we shall presently observe. In Heeren's estimation, Alexandria was the same with Artakoana; for, as he remarks, Arrian does not inform us of the foundation by Alexander of any new city in this country, nor does his rapid march through it countenance such a supposition. Several ancient cities received new names from the Macedonian conquerors.[3] This confirms the tradition; and notwithstanding, therefore, the specification to the contrary, it seems not unlikely that Artakoana, Alexandria, and Aria are aggregated in Herat.

We have in Strabo only incidental notices of the province contiguous on the south-east to Aria,—Drangiana, the country of the Ẓarangæi, or Sarangæi, or Drangæ. Heeren affirms that although the Zarangæi and Drangæ have been frequently confounded, they were perfectly distinct.[4] They were first identified by D'Anville, whose opinion is maintained by his learned countrymen

[1] Analyse de la Carte des Marches et de l'Empire d'Alexandre le grand: Historiens d'Alexandre, App. p. 193.

[2] Notes by M. Jacquet on M. Court's conjectures sur les Marches d'Alexandre: J. Asiatique, Oct[re]. 1837.

[3] Vol. i. p. 256.

[4] Vol. i. p. 275.

Burnouf[1] and Jacquet;[2] and apparently with justice, for a variety of considerations indicate the position of the Sarangæi of Herodotus,[3] the Zarangæ of Arrian and Pliny, to be in the province of Drangiana; although it is true that a tribe of mountaineers called Drangæ are also noticed by Arrian somewhat more to the east, and the same people are distinguished by Pliny from the Zarangæ.[4] Their independent existence may be therefore admitted without separating the Zarangæ from the province of Drangiana.

Drangiana, from the occasional notices of it by Strabo, was conterminous on the north-west with the mountains in which Aria was situated, but it extended below the mountains to the south, where its western boundary was Carmania or Kirman; on the east lay Arachosia, and Gedrosia was its limit on the south. The road from Aria to India, by the southern route, passed through Drangiana. The same boundaries are assigned to it by Ptolemy.

According to M. Burnouf, the name of the province is derived from the Zend word Zarayo, 'a lake,' a word still retained in the lake Zarah in Seistan, which corresponds in general position and extent with Drangiana; the term Zarangæ denoting the inhabitants of the country of the lake. This, according to Heeren, is the same with the Aria palus, separating Aria from the province of the Zarangæ; but this is incompatible with the contiguity of Drangiana to the Arian mountains, the latter being considerably to the south of Herat. The capital was Prophthasia, distant, according to Eratosthenes, one thousand five hundred or one thousand six hundred stadia from Alexandria Ariorum. Isidore of Charax says the name of the ancient capital was Phra;[5] but, according to Plutarch, Alexander founded the city, or at least converted an insignificant village into a town of note. In Phra

[1] Commentaire sur le Yaçna, Notes, p. xcvii.

[2] Jacquet asserts, "L'identité absolue des Zaranges et des Dranges est admise par presque tous les critiques modernes:" J. Asiatique, Oct[re]. 1837.

[3] See what is said of the Sarangæi of Herodotus, p. 129.

[4] He enumerates them, Drangæ, Euergetæ, Zarangæ. The Scholiast observes on the latter: quæ de Zarangæis Arrianus prodidit, hæc de Drangis Strabo, Curtius, aliique. They, as well as the Euergetæ, were, no doubt, equally people of Drangiana, and essentially the same.

[5] Phrada: Trad. de Strabon, tom. v. p. 103, note.

we have very possibly the Furrah of modern times, one hundred and thirty miles south of Herat;[1] but the capital of Seistan is Dushak, which is supposed to be Zaranj or Zarang, the residence of Jacob Ben Leith, and in this name the Zarangæ of antiquity is unquestionably preserved. In the neighbourhood of Dushak, however, are the remains of several ancient cities:[2] Captain Christie, who travelled through the country, saw an astonishing number. At Pulki he describes the ruins as immense; and about half-way between Dushak and Furrah he found the relics of a very large city named Peshawarun.[3] Now the first of these accords as closely as possible, as to distance, with Prophthasia; for Dushak is about two hundred and ten miles from Herat, Pulki is something more; but Peshawarun is about twenty-seven miles north of Dushak: it is consequently one hundred and eighty-three miles from Herat, and this is identical with the longer of the ancient measurements of the distance of Prophthasia from Aria, which, as one thousand six hundred stadia, is equal to nearly one hundred and eighty-three miles.[4] Ibn Haukil mentions that in his time there were the remains of a considerable city more to the west, by the people of which Zaranj was built: he calls it Ram-shehristan, a curious compound of Indian and Persian appellatives. In the army of Xerxes the Sarangæi were distinguished by the beauty of their coloured vestments, either having manufactures of their own, or obtaining them by the course of commerce between India and Persia. One main road from India to Herat, and through it to Persia, still passes by Dushak and Furrah; but the country has been for some time in great

[1] The routes, in the Memoir already cited, make it little more than one hundred; but the distances from Kandahar to Herat have subsequently been measured by the perambulator.

[2] Kinneir, p. 191.

[3] There is a shade of affinity between the meaning of this word and Prophthasia, the Persian Peah-áwaran, 'bringing before,' and the Greek προφθάνω, 'prævenio, præoccupo.' The Greeks sometimes translated.

[4] Heeren, or rather his authority, Mannert, has erred strangely in making Dushak or Zaranj only thirty-six miles from Herat. Kinneir makes the difference above three degrees. In the map attached to Burnes' Travels the latitude of Dushak is 32°, and that of Herat 34° 15′. The Memoir above cited makes the whole distance from Herat to Dushak but one hundred and sixty-eight miles. The distance in the text is computed from the actual measurements last referred to.

disorder. Recent political events will have secured it from all external violence, and its continued decay will be the effect only of its internal mal-administration.

• Pliny, in one place, calls Prophthasia the capital of the Zariaspæ, but in another he agrees with other authorities, in placing it in the country of the Drangæ.[1] Geographers have agreed also that the former name is more correctly that which is found in Arrian, Ariaspæ or Agriaspæ. Ptolemy again calls Ariaspa the second city of Drangiana, meaning, no doubt, the site of the Agriaspæ, called also by Arrian the Euergetæ, and placed by him on the Etymander, between the Zarangæ and the Drangæ. Strabo places them between the Drangæ, meaning clearly Drangiana, and the Arachoti, thus concurring with Ptolemy in extending the province to the district of the Ariaspæ. It is only a question, therefore, of the precise extent of the boundaries of Drangiana eastward, and does not occasion any perplexity as to the actual position of these people on the Helmund or Etymander river, supposed by Arrian to be lost in the sands, but, in truth, flowing into the Zarah lake. The Euergetæ are said to have been so named from the seasonable supply of corn furnished by them to the army of Cyrus when in distress, whence they were called the 'benefactors' of the king. The Greek word must have been a translation of some native term; and M. Burnouf, although he does not find any equivalent for it as the name of a people, discovers that such epithets as 'bienfaisant' are used as topographical designations;[2] such being the sense of 'Hukairya,' the name of a mountain of some celebrity in Zend books.[3] The other name of this people, Ariaspæ, is unexceptionably Indian, being resolvable without any etymological extravagance into 'Aryáswa, 'the rearers or riders of excellent horses.'

[1] Prophthasia oppidum Zariasparum, Book. VI. 25. Inde ad Prophthasiam Drangarum: Book. VI. 21. [2] Comm. sur le Yaçna, p. xcix.

[3] According to Herodotus, however, those who have deserved well of the king are called, in the Persian language, Orosangai, which is not Zend; and either, therefore, M. Burnouf is wrong in his etymology, or Zend was not the language of Drangiana. In justice to M. Burnouf it must be added, that he himself has pointed out this difficulty: Comm. sur le Yaçna, Notes et Eclaircissements, p. c., note.

In like manner the boundaries of Arachosia are to be extracted from Strabo only by his occasional notices of them in relation to other provinces. It is said to be at the foot of the southern face of the mountains extending to India, and not far from Drangiana, with which it formed one satrapy. The distance from Prophthasia to the chief city of the Arachoti is said to be four thousand one hundred and twenty stadia, about four hundred and seventy miles, which, in a direct line, would bring us to the Indus. The measurement is along the great road to Bactria, and is derived from the itineraries of Alexander's marches: it, no doubt, diverged to the south and east, so as to have added to the actual distance.

If we turn to Ptolemy for our guide, he describes the province of Arachosia as bounded on the north by the Paropanisan mountains, by India on the east, by Drangiana on the west, and by Gedrosia on the south, being separated from it by the Bœtian mountains, the range which, branching off from the Brahoik range, runs westward and then north-westward to Kirman: the central portion has the name of the Washati mountains in Pottinger's map.[1] Ptolemy also mentions a river, different, he says, from the Indus, called the Arachotus, rising in part from a lake. The chief difficulty here is to determine what river is meant; for the country which corresponds with Arachosia presents several. The principal of these is the Helmund,—the Etymander, Hermandus, or Erymanthus of the ancients,—which descends from the mountains west of Kabul and runs to the south-west close upon the Desert, when it changes its course to the north-west, and passes through part of Seistan into the Zarah lake. M. Burnouf considers this to be the Arachotus, giving its name to the province, and finds its original appellation in the Zend word Haraquaiti, representing the Sanscrit Saraswatí, a name common to a river, and implying connexion with a lake. Except, however, in the lower part of its course, the Helmund flows amidst the mountains of the Paropamisus, and can scarcely be regarded as within the northern limits of Arachosia, the river of which, both in name and direction, appears to be the modern Urghundab or Arkand-ab, especially if we include under that name the Turnuk, which rises more to the east near

[1] Account of Baluchistan.

Ghizni, passes through a small lake (the Dooree lake of Elphinstone's map), and then loses its identity in the Urghundab; circumstances which in some manner authorize Ptolemy's description of the Arachotus. The Urghundab passes by Kandahar; and whether it or the Helmund be the Arachotus, it equally follows that Heeren is wrong in restricting Arachosia to Sarawan or Kelat.[1] The Arachotus is also celebrated as the site of a city said to have been founded by Semiramis;[2] the remains of which, M. Court says, are to be seen on the Arghasan river, four farsangs from Kandahar, on the road to Shikarpur. This appears somewhat incompatible with the Arachotus being the Urghundab; but, in fact, the Arghasan unites with the Turnuk,[3] and both with the Urghundab; and as they are rivers of about the same volume, it is possible that the name under which they are now combined may have been formerly indiscriminately applied to either or to all of them, especially as no very precise knowledge seems to have been possessed of the exact sources or course of the Arachotus.

Amongst the towns enumerated by Ptolemy are an Alexandria, which is usually considered to be Kandahar. That the city lay upon the route of the Macedonian is, no doubt, true; but the name bears a closer affinity to Gandhara than to Alexandria. The name of the capital, Arachotus, as well as that of the province, is preserved in Arokhaj, according to Rennell, or Roh Kaj, according to Wilford.[4] Jacquet says the Arabic term Al-rokhaj is derived from the Greek. The authority for this oriental name does not appear: there is no such word in Ibn Haukil; but we have on the road

[1] Vol. i. p. 274, and note. At the same time there can be no doubt that these districts were included in Arachosia; for Alexander, whilst on his progress down the Indus, below the confluence of the Akesines, dispatched Craterus to the confines of the Arachosians and Drangians on a military expedition, from which Craterus had returned and rejoined the king before he advanced to Patalene; he could not have been long absent: Arrian, Book VI. 15.

[2] Pliny, Book VI. 25. He says, some called the river the Kophen. According to Stephanus it was the name of the city. Some MSS. read Cutin. Notes on Pliny, Book VI. note 70.

[3] The source of the Turnuk on the opposite side of the high ground about Ghizni from that on which the southern branch of the Kabul river or the Kophen rises, may have led to some confusion in the name of the Arachotus, as if it was the same with the Kophen.

[4] Rennell, p. 169. D'Anville, Géographie Anc. tom. ii. p. 291. As. Res. vol. viii. p. 336. Trad. de Strabon, tom. iv. p. 267.

from Seistan to Ghizni,[1] at a distance of thirteen marches, the city Roha or Rohaj, or, perhaps, Rokhaj, which may offer some trace of the ancient appellation. There is also said to be in Afghanistan a district called Roh, whence the Rohilla Afghans derive their origin and name. There can be little doubt that in one of the modern denominations, Beest or Bost, on the Helmund, at the confluence of the Urghundab, we have the Beste, Abeste, or Parabeste, by which the Erymanthus flowed, according to Pliny.[2]

On the south of Arachosia and Drangiana was situated Gedrosia, an extensive district, bounded on the west by Carmania, on the south by the Indian ocean, and on the east by the Indus. Strabo differs from Ptolemy in some slight degree, by interposing along the southern coast some maritime tribes, as the Arabiæ or Arbii between the Indus and Arabis or Arbis, or Purali river, in the province of Lus, and the Oritæ between them and the head of the Persian gulf. It is not likely that many vestiges of antiquity should remain in so rude a country, especially as it seems to have been taken possession of in comparatively modern times by colonists from Persia, which the Baluchis appear to be from their language. Puhra, however, a town visited by Captain Pottinger, appears to be the Paura, the capital of Gedrosia, if the latter be not merely the Sanscrit word Pura, *a* or *the* city, reached by Alexander on his march along the coast.[3] M. Gosselin, as quoted by the translators of Strabo, finds the name of Orites in Hor or Haür, which, he says, is the capital of the country.[4] There is no such name in Pottinger. Beyond the Orites the sea-coast was inhabited by the Ichthyophagi.[5] Gedrosia, however, was the country to the north of these tribes, and extended far up, or, as Baluchistan still does, to the desert skirting the southern portions of Seistan and the kingdom of Kabul.

Returning to the north, we come to the range of mountains which is continuous from the Parakhoatras, or from the extremity of the prolongation of the Alburz mountains to the north of Herat, and which passes on one hand to Ghaur and Bamian and the Kohistan of Kabul, and on the other to

[1] Oriental Geography: Route from Bost to Ghizni, p. 210. [2] Book VI. 25.

[3] Heeren, vol. i. p. 270. [4] Trad. de Strabon, tom. v. p. 95.

[5] Pliny calls the Oritæ, Ichthyophagi, and observes, they speak a language of their own, not an Indian dialect: Book VI. 25.

the mountains of Ghizni and the Suliman range, branching off to the south. The whole of the northern chain was called Caucasus by the Greeks; but they adopted distinctions borrowed, according to them, from the Barbarians, by whom the mountains were differently named in different places; as Paropamisus, Emodus, Imaus, and the like.[1] The first extended from the confines of the Arii to where the line turned to the north; the second was the central portion of the range running to the east from the Kohi Baba to the Indus; and the third, the eastern and south-eastern portion of the chain, the Himalaya. The limits of each division were not, however, very precisely defined, but it is clear that the Paropamisus is commonly used to denote all the mountains west of the Indus and north of the Kabul river as far as to the vicinity of Herat, and that it was applied also to the western extremity of the Suliman range or the Kohi Baba and its ramifications, where the line of demarcation between the northern and southern chains ceases to be distinguishable. The whole chain comprises then the Hindu Kush and the mountains on the west to which the name of Paropamisan has been lately applied, and which, independently of the Kabul range, extends over a space of three hundred and fifty miles from east to west, and two hundred from north to south, and is occupied in its eastern parts by Hazáras, and western by Aimaks. The country is said to be difficult, and the people barbarous; but it has never been visited by any European travellers, and an extensive tract, very important, perhaps, for the elucidation of Bactrian history, has yet to be explored. It may be observed, that great numbers of some of the most interesting coins, particularly the silver coins of Menander, have been obtained from the Hazáras.

Ptolemy calls the people Paropanisadæ, and this may be a correcter mode of representing the original term, as Professor Lassen has supposed.[2] The Hindus place a range of mountains called Nishadha north of the Hemakuta and Himalaya ranges;[3] and although these chains, as they represent them, form part of their mythological geography, yet the names, as well as that of the Himalaya, may have been borrowed from mountains actually existing. According to this classical geographer, the Paropanisadæ were

[1] Strabo, XI. 8. 1. [2] Zur Geschichte, &c., p. 128. [3] Vishnu Purana, p. 167.

bounded on the west by Aria, on the north by Bactria, on the east by India, on a line perpendicular to the sources of the Oxus, and on the south by Arachosia, at a line drawn across the Parueti mountain, or *the* mountain; for Parueti is, no doubt, the Indian word Parvata, ‘a mountain.’ Ptolemy also speaks of a river, the Gardamanis, or Dargamanis, flowing from Bactria, the Khoe falling into it; which may be either the Dehas or the Gori River; and if the Gori be intended, the Khoe will be the river of Bamian or Surkhab. The tribes he names are the Bolitæ, Aristophyli, Ambastæ, perhaps for Ambashthas, Paroetæ, and Parsii. The chief cities are Naulibis and Karura or Kabura, called also Ortospana, on the high road to Bactria. To this latter we shall have occasion to revert, and it is sufficient at present to have named it. It may be remarked, that the names of towns and tribes specified by Ptolemy differ materially from those given by Arrian in his account of Alexander's movements through the country.

It is agreed by the classical geographers, that after crossing the Paropamisan mountains we come to Bactria; but it does not appear how far the mountain tract extends before the limits of Bactria are reached. After crossing the pass of Akrobat on the road by Bamian, the Hindu Kush is considered to be cleared, and the kingdom of Turkistan commences. Although, however, the mountains diminish in height, they do not terminate until farther onwards in the vicinity of Khulm, and we may therefore presume that to be the original limit. At the same time there is no doubt that the political limits included a considerable portion of the territory within the mountains; and it is so stated by Strabo, who observes that the northern portion of the Paropamisan mountains belongs to Bactria. On the west the boundary was Margiana, Aria, and the Caspian desert; and the Oxus separated it from Sogdia and the Scythians on the north. The eastern limits were less precisely known, but they extended to the tracts occupied by Scythian tribes, or were in some parts conterminous with the country of the Indians. They no doubt included Kunduz, and perhaps Badakhshan.

The chief cities of Bactria mentioned by Strabo are Bactra, called also Zariaspa, Darapsa or Adrepsa, and Eukratidia, so named from the name of its founder Eukratides. Bactra is distinguished from Zariaspa or

Zarispa by Ptolemy; but Pliny, and apparently Arrian, affirms their identity: and Pliny states that Bactra was the later appellation.[1] Heeren affirms that the followers of Alexander speak of Bactra and Zariaspa as two different places,[2] and that they are distinguished by Cellarius.[3] Bayer proposes Hazarasp; but this is apparently too far to the north-west for Zariaspa, and would have been either in Sogdiana or the country of the nomadic Scythians. Burnes suggests[4] that Zariaspa may be traced in Shehr Subz; but that would be to transfer it to Sogdiana, as Shehr Subz is on the north of the Oxus. The same objection applies to Farab, which has also been proposed for it,[5] as that lies near the Ailak country towards Ferghana, north-east of Samarkand.[6] Zariaspa was undoubtedly south of the river, as Alexander returned to winter there after his campaign beyond the Oxus.[7] Bactra is usually identified with Balkh.[8] According to Quintus Curtius, it was close under the mountains: it is about six miles from the last hills.[9] Zariaspa was watered by a river of the same name, flowing into the Oxus: the Dehas or river of Balkh, coming from the Hazara mountains, is now expended in irrigation, and finally lost in the sands. Of the site of Adrepsa and Eukratidia, no satisfactory indication can be offered: it has been conjectured that the first is represented by Bamian.[10] Bayer identifies it with Anderab.[11] As the same with the Drapsaca of Arrian, it was one of the first cities taken by Alexander after crossing the mountains, and its position depends upon the point where the passage was effected: it was not unlikely to have been somewhere not far from Anderab, as will be hereafter noticed. Ptolemy has various other names of cities, as Khatra-karta or Kharra-karta, Ebusmi, Alikodra, Khoana, Menapia: he also includes Marakanda in Bactria, whilst he transfers Drepsa to Sogdiana, both irreconcileable with the military movements of Alexander. The Macedonian conqueror is said to have founded several cities in Bactriana, and destroyed others, as Kariata, Marakanda, and Cyra. It is doubtful if traces of those

[1] Bactri, quorum oppidum Zariaspe (quod postea Bactrum) a flumine appellatum est: Book VI. 18.

[2] Vol. i. p. 258.

[3] Vol. ii. p. 711.

[4] Vol. ii. p. 7.

[5] Memoir on Khiva, p. 19.

[6] Oriental Geography, p. 209.

[7] Arrian, Book IV. 1. 7. 15.

[8] Burnes, vol. i. p. 241; vol. ii. p. 163.

[9] Ibid. vol. ii. p. 162.

[10] D'Anville, Anc. Géog. tom. ii. p. 200.

[11] Page 20.

which he built will ever be discovered; but, at any rate, no chance of discovery offers until the localities of the country can be safely and deliberately explored,—a condition never yet realized. It is only of importance to remark that in some of the names we have intimations of a prevailing form of speech connected with Turkish, in such words as karra, karta, and kand, signifying, in that dialect, severally 'black,' 'snow,' and 'a town or city.' The latter, or khand, is also an Indian word for 'a district or province;' and Mara-kanda, or Samar-kand, may be interpreted without any etymological extravagance by Samara-khanda, 'the war, or warlike province.' At any rate this is preferable to the Mohammedan explanation of the term, 'the city of Samar,' which is undoubtedly a modern fancy. Amongst the tribes specified by Ptolemy are also several names of very Indian aspect; as the Khomari or Kumáras; as Raj-Kumars, a tribe of Rajputs still in India; Thokari, Thakurs, another warlike tribe; Varni, for Varna, simply 'a tribe or caste.' Strabo names two satrapies taken from the Bactrians by the Parthians in the reign of Eukratides, Aspionia and Turiva. The latter is variously read Tokariva, Taguria, or Tapuria. Polybius also mentions a Taguria or Ta-gauria, in which perhaps some indication of Ghaur may be conjectured, or the satrapy may have been farther to the west, and may have left traces in the name of Ghorian, which is one of the dependencies of Herat. Ptolemy names also different rivers, as the Dargamanis, Atarmes, Dargis, and Artemis. The first, called also the Orchomanes, is said to flow from the Paropanisus, and after uniting with the Ochus, to fall into the Oxus, circumstances which distinguish this river from the one similarly named, that is said to flow from Bactria into the Paropanisan country. The Artemis flows into the Zariaspa, and may be the Dakash. The Dargis follows the course of the Gori or river of Kunduz; but no great reliance can be placed on Ptolemy's geography of these countries.

The language of Quintus Curtius has been employed by Sir A. Burnes to describe the general character of the country from Balkh to Bokhara, in which oases of the most productive soil alternate with wastes of sand. Strabo speaks of the great fertility and wealth of Bactria, by which its Grecian rulers were enabled to become so powerful as to be able to extend their sovereignty to other countries. Nor was its prosperity owing only to its natural productiveness; but it seems to have been the chief seat of commerce between the east and west of Asia; the manufactures of India, and perhaps of China, being conveyed from thence, according to ancient writers, to the Caspian sea, and to the north of Persia.[1]

Heeren dwells repeatedly upon the natural and commercial advantages of this country. It was destined by nature, he says, to be the first place of exchange for the productions of India, which it purchased with those of its own climate. The great highways of communication from east to west ran towards its capital, and the gold mines of India were in its vicinity. In another passage he observes, "The city of Bactra must be regarded as the commercial entrepôt of Eastern Asia: its name belongs to a people who never cease to afford matter for historical details from the time they are first mentioned. Not only does Bactra constantly appear as a city of wealth and importance in every age of the Persian empire, but it is continually interwoven in the traditions of the East with the accounts of Semiramis and other conquerors. It stood on the borders of the gold country 'in the road of the confluence of nations,' according to an expression of the Zend-avesta; and the conjecture that in this part of the world the human race made its first advance in civilisation, seems highly probable from the facts which have been mentioned in the preceding investigation."[2]

Whatever may have been the civilisation attained by its settled inhabitants, the Tajiks of later times, the Persians of primitive, this seems to have been overwhelmed, in ancient as in modern ages, by barbaric immigration; so that, according to Strabo, the manners of the Bactrians differed in little from those of the Scythians in their vicinity.[3] The old men, Onesicritus asserted, were abandoned, whilst yet living, to the dogs, who were thence called 'buriers of the dead;' and the town was filled with human bones, though the suburbs were quite free. Why this should have been the case, does not appear, and the whole story may perhaps be referred to the prevalence of practices yet in use amongst the followers of Zoroaster,—to the exposure of bodies to spontaneous decomposition in the air, with less precaution perhaps

[1] Heeren, vol. ii. p. 297.

[2] Vol. ii. p. 211, and vol. iii. p. 387.

[3] Book XI. 11. 3.

than is now observed, so that dogs might have had access to the funereal ground: and it is worthy of observation, that in the present ritual of the Parsis the dog plays a very prominent part. Amongst other curious particulars relating to the animal, it is enjoined that dogs of different colours should be made to see a dead body on its way to be exposed, either thrice, or six, or nine times, that they may drive away the evil spirit, the Daruj Nesosh, who comes from the north, and settles upon the carcass in the shape of a fly.[1] Now was this the practice at Bactria, which has given rise to the tales of the Greeks? or is it the relic and representation of some such usage as giving not old men, but dead bodies, to dogs to be devoured?

The adjacent province of Sogdiana is classed by Strabo with Bactriana as having many features in common, and being inhabited by a kindred people. Of its limits we learn from him only that it was divided from Bactria by the Oxus, and bounded on the north by the Jaxartes; and that it was surrounded, and in part at least inhabited, by nomadic tribes. Ptolemy concurs with this definition, placing part of Scythia on the west and north, Sakas on the east, and Bactria on the south. The name has been preserved through all ages in that of Soghd, by which the country along the Kohik from Bokhara to Samarkand has been known to the present day.

Ptolemy places the Sogdian mountains at the sources of the Oxus, and the mountains of the Comedi between the sources of the Oxus and Jaxartes. The former are the Pamer, and the latter probably the range of the Ak-tagh or white mountains. The chief cities are Cyreskhata, Oxiana, Maruca, Alexandria Oxiana, Drepsa (called by Pliny, Panda), and Alexandria ultima. The tribes are Pasikæ, near the Oxian mountains; Thakori, on the Jaxartes; and Augali, near the Sogdian mountains; the Oxydrankæ, Drybaktæ, and Kandari, under the mountains; the Mardyeni, Oxyeni, and Khorasmii, near the Oxus; Drepsiani and Anienses to the east; the Kirrodes, near the Oxus, and a country between the Caucasus and Imaus, called Vandabanda, in which perhaps some imperfect indication of Badakhshan may be conjectured. Some of the other names are very like Indian; as the Kandari may be the Gandháras; the Mardyeni, the Madras; the Thakori, as before

[1] Vendidad Sade; Fargard viii. Anquetil du Perron, vol. i. part II. p. 332.

observed, Takurs; and we can scarcely doubt that we have in Kirrodes the Kirátas, or foresters and mountaineers.

It is, however, from the historians of Alexander that we derive the fullest information relating to Sogdiana, as the Macedonian spent the best part of three years in military operations in that country and the adjacent kingdom of Bactria. The first city he came to after crossing the Oxus was Nautaka, which must have been somewhere in the neighbourhood of Karshi, or Naksheb, as the first habitable oasis in the sandy tract north of the river. After wintering here he advanced to Marakanda,—the Parakanda of Strabo, and Samarkand of modern times,—a city sixty-four stadia, or above seven miles, in circumference. Baber, by whom the ramparts were measured, says the circumference was five miles.[1] From hence Alexander marched to the Jaxartes, or Sihun, the distance of which is said to be one thousand five hundred stadia, or one hundred and seventy-one miles. The merhelehs, or stages, specified by Ibn Haukil, from Samarkand to Khojend, are seven, which at the rate subsequently estimated, of fourteen miles to a stage, would be but ninety-eight miles:[2] so Baber affirms that the distance from Khojend to Samarkand is but twenty-five farsangs, or about one hundred miles.[3] This appears to be too little, as the least distance in our most recent maps is one hundred and forty-six miles, whilst in others it is two hundred.[4] The exact estimate of the distance depends however upon the point where the river was first reached by the Greeks, and their measurement was probably near the truth. Along the Jaxartes were seven cities, the chief of which was Cyro-polis, the Cyreskhata of Ptolemy, the foundation of which, as well as of the rest, was ascribed to Cyrus, with a view of checking the incursions of the Barbarians from beyond the river: of these, Gaza and four others were taken in two days. Traces of Gaza, it has been conjectured,[5] may be found in the name of Ghaz, or Ghazna, which is given to the desert country west of Ur-tappeh by Mohammedan geographers.[6] This, in the time of Ibn Haukil, does not seem to have been

[1] Memoirs of Baber, p. 48. [2] Ibn Haukil, p. 273. [3] Memoirs, p. 4.

[4] Map to Memoirs of Baber. Ditto to Description des Kirgez Kazakes de Levchine. Ditto to Burnes' Travels.

[5] Thirlwall's History of Greece, vol. vi. p. 286. [6] Memoirs of Baber, Introduction, p. xii.

a desert, but a populous principality, and he describes the capital, Ghaz, as the summer residence of its kings.[1] If the identification be correct, the operations of Alexander would lie to the west of Khojend; which is doubtful, as the general character of the strongholds which he captured corresponds better with that of the villages and towns not in the desert level, but in the hilly tracts of Urtappeh and Ferghana. Thus Ibn Haukil, describing the district of Setrushta, or Urtappeh, remarks that the villages of the mountainous parts are situated on steep hills, and the cold part of the country has many strong fortresses.[2] Baber also describes some strongholds, which agree very well with the fortified posts and rocks besieged by the Macedonians. The city of Cyrus must have been a place of greater extent than the rest, as it was defended by eighteen thousand Barbarians, and was not reduced without danger and loss. The western course of the Sihun, or Jaxartes, towards the sea of Aral, is across a desert; and for the inhabited part of its course we look to the eastward in the direction of Ferghana, where we have Khojend, Kokan, Marghinan, and other towns of note. Of these, Khojend is said by Baber to be a very ancient city; and Thirlwall supposes it may have been the city founded on the Jaxartes by Alexander.[3] There does not appear to be any local tradition of this nature, but the position is not unfavourable to the conjecture. Marghinan offers an affinity to the Marginia of Curtius,[4] although he has made an evident blunder in asserting that Alexander, marching to it from Bactria, crossed both the Ochus and Oxus; as, if he went southwards to Margiana, he could not have crossed the latter; if he marched northwards, the former was not in his path. The operations of Alexander were, however, chiefly in Sogdiana during the whole of his residence in this quarter. The towns and forts of Cyrus Alexander destroyed with circumstances of remorseless ferocity, which would have been held up to execration had they been narrated of a Jangiz or a Timur, but which are passed over almost unnoticed by historians when they are told of the type of classical civilisation, a Greek. Yet it is evident that the son of Philip, and pupil of Aristotle, was as great a savage in his military character as an untutored Tartar or Turk.

[1] Ibn Haukil, p. 270.
[2] Ibid. p. 264.
[3] History of Greece, vol. vi. p. 284.
[4] Book VII. 11.

Besides the fortified posts along the river, we have notices of several detached hill forts, the accounts of which are so contradictory that it is now perhaps impossible to determine their position. They have always, however, been common in these countries, as has already been noticed, and as may be inferred from the frequent recurrence of the term Tippa, Tuppa, or Tappah, which is the Turkish word for a 'mound' or 'hill.' If we follow Curtius, we have first the hill fort of Arimazes the Sogdian; the situation of which is not particularized. Droysen, as quoted by Thirlwall, proposes for its site the pass of Kolugha or Derbend in the Kara-tagh mountains, between Kish and Hissar, and points to a hill, on the map near it, called Kohi-ten. Thirlwall seems inclined to concur in the position.[1] Strabo, however, observes that the rock of Arimazes is called by some the rock of the Oxus,[2] and we must therefore look for it on that river. There is no want of analogous posts, and perhaps we have the rock of Arimazes in Kurghan-Tippa on the Amu or Oxus. Thirlwall, apparently following Arrian, refers to the capture of the fort of Arimazes the marriage of Alexander with Roxana;[3] but Strabo states that this occurred upon the capture of the stronghold of Sysimithres, which he places in Bactriana. Curtius describes it as situated at the entrance of a defile, and strengthened by a river in its front. The governor, Sysimithres, in which name we have the Indian Sasi-mitra, 'the friend of the moon,' is called by Curtius the satrap of Naura; which is very probably the same as the hill tract of Nura north of Bokhara, in which such a defile is not unlikely to be met with: in this case Strabo is wrong in placing the rock of Sysimithres in Bactriana. There is an indistinct account of a third hill fort in Curtius, the governor of which he calls Cohortanus, and in which he places Roxana: but little dependence can be placed on an account inconsistent with that of other writers, and even with his own in other passages. A more definite character attaches to the rock of Chorienes, as described by Arrian, which he places in the country of the Parætakæ. Sir A. Burnes conceives that the country of the Parætakæ and the rock of Chorienes may be looked for in the country of Karatagin. That it was in the country between

[1] History of Greece, vol. vi. p. 300.

[2] Book xi. 11. 4.

[3] History of Greece, vol. vi. p. 301.

the Oxus and Jaxartes is little doubtful; as Alexander marched thither from Nautaka, and no notice occurs of his crossing the Oxus, which he must have done had he gone back to Bactria.[1] Thirlwall observes, that the description which Curtius gives of the rock of Sysimithres in general belongs to that of Chorienes;[2] which is rather inconsistent with his previous remark, that Parætakene appears from Curtius to have been situate in the vicinity of the Sakæ, whose seats unquestionably lay to the east of Bactria and Sogdiana, and consequently in a very different direction from the mountains of Nura. The fortresses must therefore be regarded as distinct. Droysen identifies Chorienes with Hissar; and Thirlwall observes, the conjecture is probable enough. Alexander had to cross some difficult mountains to reach it, which would have been the Kara-tagh mountains. It is only a question perhaps between Hissar, or rather Cheghanian, (for Hissar means merely *the* castle,) or Derbend. It seems unlikely that this pass should not have been defended. If we are to look for a fortress in such a position, it must have been the hold of Chorienes, rather than that of Sysimithres, the satrap of Naura.

Whether the position of these hill forts be rightly determined or not, there can be no hesitation in recognising the identity of the Polytimetus and the Zar-afshan, or river of Samarkand, called also the Kohik, or more correctly the river of *the* Kohak; being so termed from its passing by a rising ground, a koh-ak, a 'little hill' or 'hillock,' which lies on the east of the city.[3]

According to Strabo, this river traversed Sogdiana and was lost in the sands: Curtius describes it as entering a cavern and continuing its course underground. The river actually terminates in a small lake to the south of Bokhara, the Dangiz, but in the dry weather the supply of water is too scanty to force its way to the lake, and it is dispersed and evaporated in the sands. What the original appellation may have been does not appear, but the denominations given by the Greeks and Persians, 'the much-honoured,' or 'the gold-shedding' stream, convey the same idea, and intimate the

[1] The Hindu geographers enumerate amongst the barbarous tribes of the mountains, Tanganas or Tankanas, and Paratankanas, also Páratakas, in which we may have the Parætakenæ of the Greeks. Vishnu Purana, p. 193.

[2] Vol. vi. p. 312, note.

[3] Memoirs of Baber, p. 49. Ibn Haukil, p. 254. Burnes, vol. i. p. 350.

benefits it confers upon the region which it waters, and which would be a sterile waste without it.

On the borders of Bactria, conterminous with India, is the district of Choarene, the nearest country to India occupied by the Parthians: according to Strabo, it is nineteen thousand stadia from Ariana, and yet he says Craterus marched through it on his way from India to the country of the Arachoti; which would bring it within the limits of Ariana itself. The statements are clearly incompatible, and it is not easy to conjecture a situation for a province of which no other notice occurs. It has been proposed to identify it with Ghor or Ghaur, but upon no better grounds apparently than the supposed affinity of the names.[1]

Sogdiana formed the utmost limit on the north and north-east to which the princes of Bactria extended their sway, and the remaining seats of their power must be sought in the districts bordering on the Indus. That the Greek kingdom of Bactria, however, comprehended districts to the north of the Indus or Badakhshan, and across the Pamer mountains, Chitral, Gilgit, and other mountain districts little known to Europeans, is probable, not only from geographical contiguity, but the traditions of the presence of Greek princes still alive amongst the mountaineers. The chiefs of Badakhshan, Durwaz, Hissar, as mentioned by Sir A. Burnes, and before him by Mr. Elphinstone, and earlier still by Marco Polo, pretend that they are descended from Alexander. The tradition, although it is little likely to be literally correct, may not be wholly without foundation, and singularly preserves the memory of a time when these countries were subject to princes sprung from the countrymen of the Macedonian conqueror.

It is not the object of the present memoir to follow the Greek geographers in their descriptions of India in general. The only portions to which it is necessary to advert are those which describe such parts of India as were connected with the dominion of the Greek and Scythian princes of Bactria. The territories of these princes were chiefly confined in India to the course of the Indus, which they accompanied to the sea, and extended more to the west than to the east of it, although they may for some time have included

[1] Trad. de Strabon, tom. v. p. 107.

districts in the Punjab, and in Cutch. They followed, upon the whole, the course of Alexander's invasion, and may be best apprehended by attempting to trace his steps; a task often undertaken, but never very successfully accomplished, partly from the imperfections of the accounts preserved of them, and partly from our own defective acquaintance with the countries which the invaders traversed. Much has been done towards removing the latter of these impediments, but much yet remains to be ascertained. The recent political events in Afghanistan will be likely to have one good result at least, and cannot fail to be productive of rich accessions to geographical information.

The great roads from Persia to India and Bactria have always, of necessity, followed the direction to which the natural features of the country confine them; and as these have undergone little material alteration since the Greeks marched to Bactria, there should be no great difference in the routes which are open to travellers in the present day. Passes through mountains, and paths across deserts, afforded access, no doubt, in various situations; but the roads available for commerce, or for war, for caravans or armies, are in all probability much the same now that they always were. The general bearings and stages cannot be very dissimilar. With regard to distances, however, ample allowance must be made for the inexactness of both ancient and modern measurements. The intervals have, for the most part, been fixed not by survey, but by the variable scale of the space which a camel or a horse can traverse in a given time; and no two bodies of men, or even individuals, will go over the same ground in precisely the same period. It is, therefore, idle to expect that the distances of ancient itineraries shall correspond exactly with the computations of modern travellers; and it may rather excite our surprise, than disappointment, that even so much congruity as appears to exist between them should be found.[1]

According to Strabo, there was but one road from the Caspian gates to Alexandria in Ariis: it traversed the country of the Parthians,[2] and must

[1] There were surveyors, or royal geographers, *βηματισταὶ*, attached to Alexander's army, and from two of these, Bæton and Diognetus, Pliny has preserved an itinerary. Book VI. 21.

[2] *Μέχρι μὲν Ἀλεξανδρείας τῆς ἐν Ἀρίοις ἀπὸ Κασπίων πυλῶν διὰ τῆς Παρθυαίας μία καὶ ἡ αὐτὴ ὁδός.* Book xv. 2. 8.

have corresponded, therefore, with that taken by Alexander,—by Hyrcania, or Gurkan, above the mountains. There seem, however, to have been two modes of reckoning from the Caspian gates; and this intimates two roads in ancient as well as in modern times, one above, and one below the mountains, although, strictly speaking, one only, the upper road, should be reckoned from the Pass. By one measurement,[1] that of the upper road apparently, the whole distance from the Caspian gates to Alexandria in Ariis is called six thousand four hundred stadia, or seven hundred and thirty-one English miles. According to the other, the distance from the Caspian gates to Hecatompylos is said to be one thousand nine hundred and sixty stadia, or two hundred and twenty-four miles, and thence to Alexandria four thousand five hundred and thirty stadia, or five hundred and eighteen miles; a total of seven hundred and forty-two miles. Again, in the itinerary of Pliny, the distance from the Caspian gates to Hecatompylos is but one hundred and thirty-three Roman, or about one hundred and twenty-two English miles;[2] that from the latter place to the Arian Alexandria is the same as Strabo's;[3] making a total of only six hundred and forty miles, or between ninety and one hundred miles less. As however the distances generally agree, there is possibly an error in this item of Pliny's itinerary. There can be no hesitation in admitting the identification made by all recent travellers of the Caspian gates with the Gaduk pass.[4] Hecatompylos, the residence of the kings of the Parthyæi, has been supposed to be Damghan: the distance of this place, however, is much less than that assigned to the former capital by Strabo, and his measurements would carry us to the neighbourhood of Jah Jirm: the distance from this to Meshed is about two hundred miles, and from Meshed to Herat it is two hundred and seventy-nine miles;[5] making the whole then,

	Miles.
From the Caspian gates to Jah Jirm	224
Jah Jirm to Meshed	200
Meshed to Herat	279
	703

---

[1] Strabo, from Eratosthenes, Book XI. 8. 9.

[2] Book VI. 17. [3] Book VI. 21. [4] Burnes, vol. ii. p. 129.

[5] Geographical Memoir before cited. Fraser's computation of the distance from Meshed to

which is as near an approximation to the ancient measurement as can be expected.

Again, from Tehran to Herat, it is said, the caravan road is two hundred and fifteen farsangs, or eight hundred and sixty miles;[1] from this ninety miles are to be deducted, the interval between the Pass and Tehran, and the remainder is seven hundred and seventy miles, not more than between thirty and forty in excess of the ancient measurement.

The modern measurements last referred to regard the lower road, or that along the south of the Alburz range, and it is likely that the ancient applied to the upper or northern road. Now, according to the latest accounts, the distance from the Gaduk pass to Asterabad is about one hundred and twenty miles; that from Asterabad to Meshed, three hundred and eighty-nine; and that from Meshed to Herat, two hundred and seventy-nine; making a total of seven hundred and eighty-eight miles,[2]—exceeding the longest of the routes of Eratosthenes by no more than forty-six miles,—an approximation sufficiently close.

At Alexandria in Ariis we have notices of three different roads: the first of these goes direct from Aria to Bactria or Zariaspa,[3] and is said to be three thousand eight hundred and seventy stadia, or four hundred and forty-two miles.[4] The road distance from Herat to Balkh has been usually reckoned at above four hundred miles, but it is scarcely perhaps so much: neither in ancient nor modern times, however, has the distance been verified by actual observation.[5] But besides the direct road to Balkh, there were from Aria two roads to India: one of these led direct through

Herat is, by one route, two hundred and twenty-one, and by another, two hundred and thirty-eight miles: Travels in Khorasan, Appendix, p. 118.

[1] Kinneir: Memoir of a Map of Persia, p. 399.

[2] Geographical Memoir.

[3] Strabo, Book XI. 8. 9.

[4] Heeren has, from two thousand eight hundred and seventy to three thousand stadia; perhaps this is an error of the translation: vol. ii. p. 497.

[5] According to a route given to Mr. Fraser, the distance by way of Andkoï is one hundred and twenty-eight farsangs, or five hundred and twelve miles, but it is doubtful if this route can be relied on: Travels in Khorasan, Appendix, p. 120. By Maimana and Andkoh, Burnes' map makes it about four hundred and twenty miles: later observations reduce it to about three hundred miles.

Bactriana, and over the mountains to Ortospana, across the point where the trivium from Bactria was situated, which was amongst the Paropanisadæ.[1] It is remarkable that no distance is specified; the road, in fact, being then, as it still is, untravelled by Europeans, although it is well known that such a road through the Hazára mountains is practicable:[2] the distance is said to be four hundred and eighteen miles. The other road turned to the south, and was that which Alexander followed, as it is still the principal line of communication between India and the frontiers of Persia, in the direction of Herat. The reasons for the preference are sufficiently obvious, as the southern route turns a rugged and difficult country, and its greater practicability more than compensates for the enhanced distance consequent upon its more circuitous direction.

From Herat to Kabul, by the usual road through Girishk, the distance is six hundred and eighty miles.[3] The distance from Aria to Ortospanum, in which we shall find reason to place the modern Kabul, is, according to Eratosthenes, seven thousand seven hundred and twenty, or seven thousand six hundred and twenty stadia, respectively eight hundred and eighty, or eight hundred and seventy miles. It is not difficult, however, to reconcile the two statements; for Alexander's march, from which the ancient measurements are taken, followed a much more circuitous route than that of which the modern measurement has been made, having led him nigh to the confines of Gedrosia.

In examining the particulars of which the total is composed we find them to be as follows:

From	To	Stadia.	Miles.
Alexandria in Ariis, or Herat,	Prophthasia or Peshawarun	1600	183
Prophthasia	Arachotis or Arkandab	4120	469
Arachotis	Ortospanum or Kabul	2000	228
		7720	880

[1] Εἶθ' ἡ μὲν ἐπ' εὐθείας διὰ τῆς Βακτριανῆς καὶ τῆς ὑπερβάσεως τοῦ ὄρους εἰς 'Ορτόσπανα, διὰ τὴν ἐκ Βάκτρων τρίοδον, ἥτις ἐστὶν ἐν τοῖς Παροπαμισάδαις. Strabo, Book xv. 2. 8.

[2] Elphinstone's Kabul, 4to. edition, p. 633.

[3] By perambulator: From Herat to Kandahar, three hundred and seventy-one miles; from Kandahar to Kabul, three hundred and nine miles; total, six hundred and eighty miles. The

In the first of these we have already observed, that the actual distance agrees precisely with the ancient measurement. The next stage is to Arachotis, and it is difficult to determine where we are to look for the capital of Arachosia. It was four hundred and sixty-nine miles from Prophthasia, and two thousand stadia, or two hundred and twenty-eight miles, from Ortospanum.

The best means we have of making a comparison with Alexander's march is afforded by the itineraries of Ibn Haukil.[1] In one of these he specifies the stages from Sejistan, Seistan, or Dushak, the capital of the province, to Bost; and in another he continues them from Bost to Ghizni. From Sejistan to Bost there are nine manzils or merhilehs; from Bost to Shehr-Rohaj or Rokhaj, four; in all thirteen. From Rokhaj to Ghizni are twenty-six merhilehs. Now, as Sir William Ouseley, the translator of Ibn Haukil, observes, the terms merhileh and manzil, which are indifferently employed by the Mohammedans, signify properly, the halting place after a day's journey, and thence denote the distance travelled in a day, which is a somewhat indefinite scale. A merhileh is said by Al-Edrisi to be equivalent to thirty miles (ثلثون ميل);[2] but the word *mil* is also of vague application, and thirty English miles would be a long day's march. The term merhileh often alternates in Ibn Haukil with stages of three or four farsangs, or from twelve to sixteen miles, and it probably intends something of the same space. If we take the medium or fourteen miles, the distances will be, from Dushak to Bost, one hundred and twenty-six miles; thence to Rokhaj, fifty-six miles; thence to Ghizni, three hundred and sixty-four miles; total, five hundred and forty-six miles; to which, the distance from Peshawarun being added, we have five hundred and sixty-six miles, which is more than we require: whilst, if we stop at Rohaj, the distance is in a still more considerable proportion too small, being only two hundred and ten miles. We must look for Arachotis, therefore, somewhere to the north of Rokhaj, and south of Ghizni.

There is another objection to Ghizni, which, if we assume Ortospanum

Geographical Memoir has for the two items severally, four hundred and four, and two hundred and thirty miles; total, six hundred and thirty-four.

[1] Oriental Geography, pp. 209, 210.

[2] Geography of Al-Edrisi: Preface to Ibn Haukil, p. xvii.

to be Kabul, is still more decisive against its idendity with Arachotis: the latter was two hundred and twenty-eight miles from Ortospanum; Ghizni is only eighty-eight from Kabul. According to former routes, the distance of two hundred and twenty-eight miles would have placed us at Kandahar; but the recent measurements have made that city three hundred and nine miles from Kabul. The claims of Kandahar to antiquity are very doubtful, and it is worthy of remark that it is not mentioned by Ibn Haukil, either in his itineraries or in his description of Seistan, in which Ghizni is included. We must look for Arachotis, therefore, somewhere else, and it seems not unlikely that traces of it will be discovered about the place now termed Arkandab, when opportunity shall allow the investigation to be made.

Arkandab or Urghundab is the name assigned in the map to a small town or village situated on the river of the same name. In a direct line it is about one hundred and forty miles south-west from Ghizni, and consequently two hundred and twenty from Kabul: by the road it would be something more, and consequently corresponds sufficiently well with Arachotis in its distance from Ortospanum.

In calculating the distance from Prophthasia or Peshawarun to Arkandab, if we follow the itineraries of Ibn Haukil, we have, as above mentioned, nine manzils from Dushak to Bost, or at the estimated extent of fourteen miles to a manzil, one hundred and twenty-six miles; or from Peshawarun, one hundred and fifty-three miles. From Bost to Kandahar by the map it is about one hundred and twenty miles, and from Kandahar to Arkandab about eighty; making altogether about three hundred and fifty-three miles. It seems likely, however, that the manzil is rather undervalued; for by the map, the distance from Dushak to Bost is about one hundred and sixty-five miles, which would make the total three hundred and ninety-two miles. It appears from the map, however, that the direct route to Arkandab would be something less than even this computation, which would fall short considerably of the distance assigned to it by Eratosthenes. There is no doubt, however, that Alexander's march did not follow the direct route, but diverged to the south to the confines of Gedrosia, by doing which it was very possible to add a hundred miles to the road to Arachotis. The name of the town and of the river confirm this view of the position of the ancient capital; and it may be remarked that the last syllable *áb*, 'aqua,' is an addition, giving to the modern term the sense of 'the waters or river of Arkand or Arakand.'

The next point is Ortospanum, which, as being situated two hundred and twenty-eight miles from Arachotis, nearly agrees, as has been shown, in that respect, with Kabul, as reckoned from Arkandab. It is quite clear that Mannert's conjecture, as cited by Heeren, of its being fifty miles south of Kandahar, is wholly inadmissible. This would throw us back to some insignificant town on the Arkandab river.

From Ortospanum to the Indus the distance was considered to be one thousand stadia, or one hundred and fourteen miles; the actual distance is two hundred and five miles, which is a greater difference than we should have expected. The matter will not be mended by adopting any other place to the west, as it would be still farther from the river, whilst any town more to the east would not combine the characteristic feature of Ortospanum, would not be the spot where the Bactrian road divided into three, or rather where the three roads, one coming directly from the west, another from the east, and another from the south, met and constituted Ortospanum, the trivium of eastern traffic. Now the statement of Strabo clearly intimates that the roads in question were not three, but four; not the road from Aria by the south, and that from India, meeting and blending into that to Bactria, but three several roads meeting the Bactrian road going thither, or, as he describes it, branching from it, regarded as coming from thence. These three roads are still extant; the road from India, that from Herat by Kandahar, and that from Herat across the Hazára mountains. This conjunction of the three roads clearly designates the site of Ortospanum and Kabul to be essentially the same. Ptolemy gives it the name also of Karura or Kabura, and defines it a city in the Paropanisus; and in the latter denomination an approximation is made to the modern name, whilst it is very possible that we have in Ortospanum (read also Ortospana and Orthospana, and which may be conjecturally corrected to Orthostana,) nothing more than the Sanscrit Urddhasthána, or 'high place,' in allusion to the elevated plain on which Kabul is situated.

It is not consistent with the design of this memoir to trace the march of

Alexander in the early part of his route, or until we find him within the boundaries of Ariana. On his arrival at Susia, on the confines of Aria,—six hundred stadia, or sixty-nine miles from Artakoana, which is about the distance of a place called Zuzan from Herat,[1]—it was Alexander's purpose to have pursued Bessus by the road he had taken, or that leading direct to Bactria. The revolt of Satibarzanes, the satrap of Aria, compelled him, however, to proceed to that province, as it would have been dangerous to have left an enemy in such a position. Alexander accordingly advanced to the capital, Artakoana, the identity of which with Herat or its immediate vicinity is confirmed by the course of this movement, and by that which succeeded it,—the march of the Macedonian army to the south, to the capital of the Zarangæ, to Prophthasia or Peshawarun, the metropolis of Drangiana or Sejistan.[2]

From the capital of the Zarangæ, Alexander advanced to the east, to the district of a people called by the Greeks Euergetæ, and, as above mentioned, Agriaspæ, Arimaspi, or which is no doubt the correcter reading, Aryaspæ or 'Aryáswas, 'the riders of excellent steeds.' These people did not occupy a separate province, but were included in Drangiana, in which their city called Ariaspe is placed by Ptolemy. The Euergetæ were also situated on the Etymander or Helmund river.[3] According to Diodorus they were close upon Gedrosia, and were included with it in one satrapy under Tiridates by Alexander.

From the country of the Euergetæ, Alexander, following no doubt the general direction of the river, and indeed confined to it by the character of the country,[4] proceeded north to Arachosia, subduing on his way the Drangæ

[1] Kinneir, p. 184. Thirlwall, History of Greece, vol. vi. p. 260, proposes Tous; but the remains of this city are seventeen miles on this side of Meshed, and, consequently, two hundred and ninety-six miles from Herat. It may be objected, however, that the distance specified by Arrian refers not to Susia, but to the place whither Alexander had advanced on his way towards Bactria. It does not appear, however, nor is it likely, that he had gone far from Susia, where he halted for some time to concentrate his forces: Arrian, Book III. 25.

[2] Arrian, Book III.

[3] Καὶ 'Ετύμανδρος ὃς δι' Εὐεργετῶν ῥέει. Arrian, Book IV.

[4] The Helmund river at Poollaluk is above four hundred yards wide, very deep, with uncommonly fine water. About half a mile of the country on each side is cultivated by irrigation,

and Dragogi. The former are noticed by Strabo,[1] as well as by Arrian, but the second name appears in the latter author only; and both Curtius and Diodorus carry Alexander at once from the Ariaspians to the Arachosians. The Drangæ are repeatedly identified by other writers[2] with the Zarangæ or the people of Drangiana; and the same inference may be drawn from different passages of Arrian as collated with parallel passages in other writers.[3] There seems no reason to conclude, therefore, that these tribes, even if the notice of them be not regarded as superfluous or erroneous, were not, like the Euergetæ, included within the limits of Drangiana.

The next people reduced to submission by Alexander were the Arachoti, for whom, as we have already seen, we must look to the country about Kandahar and the Arkandab river; and from them he came to the Indians, races dwelling amongst the snows in a rugged and barren country, and who were reduced to submission with much difficulty.[4] The position of these Indians was, no doubt, the rugged country about Ghizni, where the western heights of the Soliman Koh are blended with those of the Hazáras or Paropamisus. Alexander might have found a road across the latter by Deh Zungee to Balkh, but it is afterwards said that he advanced to the Caucasus, and in this direction he would have left the Caucasus, understanding by that term the Hindu Kush, on his right; neither would the transactions that ensued be reconcileable with this route: it is, therefore, little doubtful that after leaving Arkandab he came upon the road from Kandahar to Ghizni, which the character of the country recommends, and must have formerly recom-

and the Desert then rises in perpendicular cliffs; until the last stage, which is short, the preceding stages, for forty-five miles, have no water: Pottinger's Baluchistan, p. 405. It is evident that Alexander must have stopped at this very point, the banks of the Helmund. On the southern bank, where first reached by Captain Christie, he has marked the existence of 'ruins.' See Map.

[1] Book xv. 2. 9. 10.

[2] Curtius and Diodorus. So Strabo also has, "He (Alexander) came to Ariana, thence to the Drangæ, where the conspiracy of Philotas was discovered; from the Drangæ he came to the Euergetæ, so called by Cyrus, and thence to the Arachosi." And in other passages he describes the Drangæ as bordering Arachosia and Gedrosia on the west, as being partly on the north of Gedrosia, and as having Aria on the east and north: Book xv. 2. 8. 9. 10.

[3] In his fourth book Arrian says, Stasanor was appointed satrap of the Drangæ; elsewhere he says, Stasanor was appointed satrap over the Arii and Sarangæ: Book VI. And Curtius says, Stasanor was prefect of the Drangæ.

[4] Arrian, Book III.

mended; being confined on either hand by lofty mountains of considerable elevation and arduous access. That Indians should have been encountered here is no more than might have been expected; for we have seen that even as late as the tenth century the population of Kabul was Indian, and that the same authority observes of the neighbouring hill country of Ghaur, that although there were Mussulmans in the places about it, it was mostly inhabited by infidels.[1] From Ghizni, Alexander marched to the Caucasus, and there built Alexandria ad Caucasum; the exact site of which it is exceedingly difficult to determine, although it is not possible now to stray so widely from the spot, as geographers of the first merit deviated some few years ago in fixing Alexandria ad Caucasum at Ghizni or Kandahar.

According to Arrian, Alexander, after subduing the Indians bordering on Arachosia, and making arrangements which must have occupied some interval, advanced to the Caucasus, and built a city; after which he crossed the mountain. Strabo also says that he spent the winter amongst the Paropamisadæ, in whose country the towns were numerous, and supplies of every kind, except oil, abundant.[2] From hence he crossed the lofty mountains to Bactria: on the fifteenth day he arrived at Adrapsa or Drapsaka, the first city of Bactriana. Curtius[3] says, Alexandria was at the foot or roots of the mountain. Diodorus has the same, with the additional remark, that the city was near to a pass which opens a way to Media: he also mentions that in the neighbourhood was an excavation which the Greeks imagined was the cave of Prometheus. Curtius and Diodorus apparently intend to say that Alexander built the city after a march of sixteen or seventeen days; but possibly this is a mistake for his subsequent march to Bactria. Pliny says that the city was under the Caucasus, 'sub ipso Caucaso;' and the itinerary of Bæton places it fifty Roman miles from Ortospanum.

Gosselin and Rennell[4] suggested some time since that Alexandria ad Caucasum should be looked for at the entrance of the road to Bamian. Sir A. Burnes suggests that Bamian itself may be the site,[5] and his opinion

[1] Ibn Haukil, p. 226.

[2] Πυχνὰν μέντοι κῶμαι δεχόμεναι, πάντων εὔποροι, πλὴν ἐλαίου. Book xv. 2. 10.

[3] "Condendæ in radicibus montis urbi sedes electa est."

[4] Trad. de Strabon. Memoir of a Map of Hindustan.

[5] Travels, vol. i. p. 184.

is repeated by Mr. Vigne.[1] It is also maintained by the celebrated geographer C. Ritter.[2] On the other hand, Mr. Masson proposes Beghram for one of the situations in which Alexandria may be looked for,[3] and Professor Lassen is disposed to concur in that opinion. There are some considerations, no doubt, in favour of Bamian, but they are more than counterbalanced by others adverse to its claims.

The situation of Bamian on the high road to Bactria, and the junction of a road from Herat, the excavations in its vicinity, and its reputed antiquity, are some of the chief arguments in its behalf. The distances, as far as we can compare them, are of a mixed character. If Ortospanum is to be regarded as Kabul, Bamian is more than fifty Roman, forty-seven English miles, distant; it is from eighty to eighty-five miles. Again, Sir A. Burnes proceeded from Bamian to Khulm, the first town beyond the mountains, in seven days, and there seems no good reason why Alexander should have been fifteen in clearing the mountains in that direction. His marches were generally long; he must have been anxious to get out of a barren country; and he was eager to attack Bessus. It is stated, it is true, by Arrian, that when Alexander returned to Alexandria he crossed the Caucasus in ten days, which would be a not improbable time for reaching Bamian from Khulm with an army. It is not clear, however, whence the ten marches are to be reckoned from.[4] It is worthy of remark also, that Arrian here calls the city, Alexandria in Paropamisadis, consistently with the accounts which place the city on the south of the Caucasian chain. The limits of this range are not very exactly defined, but it is evident that the Greek writers do not restrict the term Paropamisus to the Hazára mountains, nor the Caucasus to the Hindu Kush. They seem to understand by Caucasus the loftiest and most rugged part of the mountain range to the north of the Paropamisus, which latter comprehends the lower elevations on either hand of the Kabul valley, being bounded by the

[1] Visit to Ghuzni, Kabul, and Afghanistan, p. 198.

[2] Ueber Alexander, M. Feldzug, referred to in his work on the Topes: Die Stupas, p. 32.

[3] J. As. Soc. vol. v. p. 6.

[4] Thirlwall says he crossed the mountain by a 'shorter' route: Hist. of Greece, vol. vii. p. 5.

Indus.[1] Consequently, Bamian cannot be Alexandria, for it is not on the south, but the north of the loftiest points of the Hindu Kush, the heights of Hajiguk and Kalu. Sir A. Burnes observes, that the everlasting snows of the Hindu Kush had been surmounted before reaching Bamian. "There are, certainly," he adds, "mountains beyond Bamian, but we have no longer the towering tops of the Himalaya."[2] This description is utterly irreconcileable with the position of Alexandria at the foot of the Caucasus, or the dearth of vegetation, fuel, and provisions, which the army experienced in marching not to, but from, Alexandria to Bactria.[3] The same objection may be urged against the place proposed by M. Court, Sighan; as, although there may be the ruins of a fortress attributed by the natives to Alexander, yet it is still farther beyond the summits of the Caucasus than Bamian.[4] The tradition is not of much value, except as a proof that the country preserves the memory of Alexander's invasion of Bactria. It may also be admitted as a corroboration of the assertion of Diodorus, that Alexander built other cities, each distant a day's journey from Alexandria.

It seems likely that we have not sufficient data upon which to form a conclusive opinion as to a preferable site for Alexander's colony. Beghram, although undoubtedly the situation of an extensive city, is out of the probable direction of Alexander's march, and is too near to Kabul, being not above twenty-seven miles distant from it on the north-east. Mr. Masson has suggested other localities, of which Perwan might be preferred, as being eight miles north-west of Beghram, and so much nearer to the Caucasus; but he mentions various indications of extensive sites of ancient cities in the Kohistan and the Koh-daman; the latter of which, from its very appellation, the 'mountain-skirts,' comes recommended by its agreement with the 'sub-Caucasian' position of Alexandria. "Here we discover two very important sites, which unquestionably refer to once capital cities."[5] At the second of these, about sixteen miles from Beghram, is a stupendous

[1] So Strabo: *παρὰ μὲν τὸν Ἰνδὸν οἱ Παροπαμισάδαι*: Book xv. 2. 9. And Ptolemy says the Paropanisus is bounded on the east by India.

[2] Vol. ii. p. 239.

[3] Strabo, Book xv. 2. 10.

[4] J. As. Soc. B. vol. v. p. 390.

[5] J. As. Soc. B. vol. v. p. 5.

artificial mound on the west bank of the river, constructed with elaborate care: the base appears to have been surrounded by a magnificent trench, and it was, no doubt, some important structure—a palace or a citadel. Again, in the district of Ghorbund, west of the low mountains which branch from the Hindu Kush, and form the western boundary of the Koh-daman, many important vestiges of antiquity are said to be discoverable. The distances would nearly correspond, as to Charikar in the plain of Beghram, and to Ghorbund in the valley of that name;[1] the distances from Kabul are between forty and fifty miles. We have yet no authentic information of these remains, but the recent journeys of different officers from Kabul to Kunduz have put us already in possession of many new and valuable topographical particulars. We now learn that roads pass through Koh-daman and Ghorbund to the foot of the loftiest parts of the Caucasian chain, and that it is crossed by various practicable passes, the principal of which is the Pass of Khoshal, which is open throughout the year. This leads into Kunduz, where there are several roads to Balkh.[2] These routes lie directly onward from Kabul, whilst the road by Bamian is extremely circuitous, and requires in the beginning a retrograde movement, which Alexander was not likely to have taken, if avoidable. The road by the Khoshal Pass, or some of the others running perpendicularly across the mountains, are much more likely to have been followed by the Macedonian army.

By taking some spot at the foot of the mountains, in the direction of Ghorbund, we shall also avoid another difficulty which has been objected to Beghram. Alexander, on his return from Bactria, came to his city, and, having remained there a short time, advanced against India: from Alexandria he went to Nikæa, and thence to the Kophen. Now it may be reasonably enough urged, that if Beghram were Alexandria, there would be no place in which we could expect Nikæa, no site in which, with reference to

[1] J. As. Soc. B. vol. v. p. 6.

[2] The plain of Koh-daman, about forty miles in length by sixteen or eighteen in breadth, stretches to the very foot of the Hindu Kush, and gives exit at its northern end to four several routes, by which that chain may be passed: Account of Koh-daman, by Dr. Lord: J. As. Soc. B. vol. vii. p. 521. Baber enumerates seven principal and various other minor passes from Kabul to Kunduz and Balkh: Memoir, p. 139.

Alexander's movements, it would be likely to be found. This difficulty is obviated by proposing Beghram for Nikæa, and to this there is no great objection. The Greek name does not imply a Greek city, and it was probably a translation of some such appellation as Jayapur, 'the city of victory,'[1] which is common in India. M. Jacquet infers[2] that it was some distance from the Kophen; but that does not necessarily follow from Arrian's simple intimation, that he proceeded to that river from Nikæa.

From Nikæa, Alexander went to the Kophen—a river respecting which there is as much uncertainty as Alexandria. Rennell very strangely identified it with the Gomul, which rises some way to the south-east of Ghizni, and, crossing the Soliman range, enters the Indus at least one hundred and fifty miles below Attok. It is utterly impossible that Alexander should have entered India by this route, whether he marched from Bamian or Ghorbund; and the supposition can only be explained by the total want of correct information as to the topography of the country. A similar deficiency explains D'Anville's even more erroneous notion, that the Kophen was the Arkandab. Now there can be no doubt that by the Kophen is to be understood the Kabul river; for Arrian says,[3] that having received the Malamantus, Suastus, and Garœus, it mixes with the Indus in the country of Peukelaotis; and the latter part of Alexander's operations west of the Indus, shortly before he crosses that river, are carried on in the same district along the Indus and the Kophen.[4] At the same time there are some statements which apparently authorize a different inference: the incompatibility, however, is perhaps more apparent than real, and has arisen from the conflicting statements being applicable to different portions of the same river. Thus Arrian himself states that the Astakeni and Assakeni occupy the country

[1] Thirlwall supposes that Nikæa was a new name given to the city otherwise called Ortospana or Cabura, the site of the modern Kabul: History of Greece, vol. vii. p. 5. But the identification is unnecessary, and there is no authority for it.

[2] Ἀφικόμενος δ' ἐς Νίκαιαν πόλιν καὶ τῇ Ἀθηνᾷ θύσας προὔχωρεν ὡς ἐπὶ τὸν Κωφῆνα: Book IV. 23. 7. On which M. Jacquet observes, "Ce passage parait indiquer que Nicée, ville sans doute dépendante des Paropamisades, mais plus avancée a l'est qu'Alexandrié était encore éloignée du cours superieur du Cophes:" J. Asiatique, Oct^{re}. 1837, p. 379, note.

[3] Indica, IV. 11.

[4] Book XV. 1. 26.

beyond the Indus to the west as far as to the Kophen, making therefore the latter the western boundary. So Strabo calls the Kophen the western boundary of India; yet he adds, that with the Khoaspes flowing into it, it runs past the cities of Plegerium and Gorydale, and the districts of Bandabene and Gandaritis; and therefore, it is to be inferred, intimates its junction with the Indus. Pliny also has a Kophes as the boundary between the Paropamisus and Aria, intending, probably, the Kophen, but placing it somewhat far to the west. The Kophen was considered also as the eastern limit of the Paropamisus; but that is, of the satrapy of the Paropamisus formed by Alexander.[1] The Khoes of Ptolemy is also the Kophen of Arrian, as it runs into the Indus.

The formation of a boundary by the river Kophen, however, is not irreconcileable with its course from west to east, and its termination in the Indus, if the formation of the Kabul river is considered. The upper part of that river is composed of two main branches; one on the north, the other on the south. The southern portion is formed also of two branches, one of which comes from the vicinity of Ghizni;[2] and running up therefore from south to north, it is joined on the east of Kabul, near the city, by a stream from the Kohi Baba.[3] The united stream continues to the east to Barikab, where it meets a still more considerable river formed by the junction of the Ghorbund and Punjshir rivers, and which comes from north-west to south-east. The united streams then run to the east as the Kabul river. The branches constituting this river, therefore, run, before they assume in combination an easterly course, nearly at right angles with it from south to north and from north to south; and this direction (the circumstances of which were not perhaps very accurately investigated) may have very probably suggested the notion that the northern and southern streams were one river, which formed a boundary line separating India extra Indum from Arachosia and Bactria on the west. Either of the principal branches may be regarded as identical with the main stream, but the character is more especially appropriate to the

[1] Arrian, Book IV. 23. 6.

[2] From the Hazára mountains, according to M. Court, it is called the river of Sheikhabad.

[3] M. Court says it rises from Meidan on the road to Balkh, between Kabul and Bamian.

united Ghorbund and Punjshir river,[1] and to this may be assigned the denomination of Kophen as well as to its continuation as the river of Kabul: the latter is also, no doubt, the Khoaspes of Strabo and Khoes of Ptolemy; or, if a distinct application be wanted for the former, it may be thought most appropriate to the southern branch or river of Sheikhabad. The Punjshir river is further identifiable with the Kophen if Beghram be Nikæa, as it flows some short distance to the eastward of the plain of Beghram, and consequently Alexander must have passed through the plain before he reached the river.[2]

When Alexander arrived at the Kophen, intending, there can be little doubt, the place where the Punjshir river becomes the Kabul river, he received Taxiles and other Indian princes. He there also divided his forces, sending Hephæstion and Perdiccas to the country of Peukelaotis towards the Indus, that they might prepare materials for the passage of that river by the army. Taxiles accompanied the Macedonian generals to the Indus, and contributed whatever assistance they needed. Astes, king of Peukelaotis, refused submission, and fortified himself in his city, which was besieged and taken after a siege of thirty days. Astes was put to death, and Sangæus was appointed his successor. In these denominations we have no hesitation in recognising familiar Sanscrit appellations. Astes is most probably Hasti, a name borne by several individuals in the dynasties detailed by the Puranas; and Sangæus is, no doubt, the same as Sanjaya, of which appellation there occurs a familiar instance, in the Mahábhárata, in the person of one of the interlocutors of that poem, the charioteer and counsellor of King Dhritaráshtra. Peukelaotis is obviously the Puskhara, Pushkalá, or Pukkala-vati of the Hindus, a city already remarked as known to their topographers, and placed by them in the country of the Gandháras,—

[1] So Thirlwall considers the Kophen to be the river formed by the confluence of the Kabul river with the Punjshir, a larger stream, which meets it from the north-west: History of Greece, vol. vii. p. 5.

[2] In a map sketched by M. Court, published in the J. As. Soc. B. April, 1839, Beghram is placed east and north of the Punjshir river; but this is a mistake, perhaps of the engraver. Mr. Masson says, "The site of Beghram has to the 'north' the river formed by the junction of the Ghorbend and Punjshir streams:" J. As. Soc. B. vol. v. p. 5.

the Gandaritis of Strabo,—a district immediately on the west of the upper course of the Indus. Peukelaotis, or Peukela, as the name also occurs, is described as a large city not far from the Indus.[1]

Strabo says that Alexander crossed the Kophen, which of course he would do, regarding that as the Punjshir branch of the Kabul river. Arrian conducts him from the Kophen without stating that he crossed it against the Aspasii (also read Hippasii), Guræi, and Assakani, to the Khoes river over difficult mountain-paths. The river was also crossed with difficulty. As M. Court no doubt accurately concludes, Alexander took the upper road by Laghman, which, although rugged, he tells us is practicable for cavalry.[2] The Khoes has been supposed to be the river called Khoaspes by Curtius and Strabo; but the Khoaspes of the latter seems preferably assignable to the river of Kabul, at least the upper part of it, as already noticed; and the details given by Curtius are in this part of his narrative of little value. Professor Lassen considers the Khoes to be the Káma or Khonar river, and the opinion has been latterly adopted by M. Court:[3] on a former occasion he identified it with the Punjshir.[4] There seems to be no better reason, however, for supposing the Khoes to be the Khonar river than the concurrence of the initial letter. The river, it is said, is so named from a town on its banks; but we know too little of the origin or purport of the term to express any opinion as to its antiquity; and the resemblance, slight as it is at best, may be accidental. The situation of the river, with relation to Alexander's subsequent movements, strongly indicates the Alishung river, which falls into the river of Kabul at the southern extremity of the Laghman valley, to be the Khoes. The Khoes of Ptolemy evidently comprehends under one name the Kabul river and all its feeders west of the river of Sewat; but in placing the Lam-

[1] Arrian, Indica, I. 8.

[2] Memoir on the Marches of Alexander; by M. Court: J. As. Soc. B. vol. v. p. 391. This road seems to be also the most practicable in the winter, as is evidently the meaning of Baber. He says, "In the winter season they cross the river Sind (the Khonar?), the river of Sewad, and the river of Kabul, above the conflux of this last river with the Sind (the Indus). In most of the expeditions which I made into Hindustan I forded these rivers in the way:" Memoir, p. 140. So it is said that one of Alexander's reasons for keeping the upper road was his expectation that the rivers would be more easily crossed nearer to their sources: Strabo, Book xv. 1. 26.

[3] J. As. Soc. B. vol. viii. p. 306.

[4] Ibid. vol. v. p. 392.

bagæ or Lambakæ about its sources, he possibly indicates the position of the Lampakas of the Hindus, the inhabitants of Lamghan.[1]

After crossing the river, the Macedonians took a town the name of which is not particularized. M. Court, following the usual but questionable reading of the text of Arrian, calls the people of the country Aspii, Thyræi, and Arsaki, and proposes to identify the two former with the Oozbin and Toori tribes, which, according to him, occupy the mountains that separate the valleys of Lamghan and Jelalabad from that of Kabul. With the corrected reading of the text, however, these identifications fall to the ground; and it may also be objected that according to Mr. Elphinstone, although the Oozbin Ghilzeis occupy a short valley between Alishung and Tagao, yet in his map the Tooris are situated on the south of the Kabul river. Both terms have also the appearance of being Pushtoo or Afghan; and the identity of the Afghan clans with the mountain tribes of the days of Alexander is somewhat problematical.

In the Aspasii we have the term so often met with amongst these tribes, of Aspa or Aswa, 'a horse;' and that it occurs in a similar sense is proved by Strabo's translation of it, 'Hippasii.' Professor Lassen conjectures that they may be the Aswasilas of ancient Hindu geography.[2] After destroying the city, Alexander took possession of another, named Andaka by Arrian, and apparently Akadera by Curtius, which he garrisoned. Either of the names may be Indian; and there is still a town, named Adrek, not far from the confluence of the Alishung with the Kabul river, although, being south of the main stream, it is not exactly in the situation of Andaka. Another account represents him as taking Gorydale,[3] on the eastern bank of the Khoes; but Gorydale should be, agreeably to Strabo's description, in the valley of the Kabul river.

Hence Alexander marched to the Euaspla river,[4] and apparently crossed

[1] The country now called Laghman is always termed by Baber Lamghan. He says it is so called from Lam or Lamech, the father of Noah, whose tomb is in the district of Alishung: Memoir, p. 143.

[2] Zur Geschichte, p. 133.

[3] Thirlwall's History of Greece, vol. vii. p. 7.

[4] Thirlwall identifies the Khoes and Euaspla, but they are unquestionably distinct rivers: History of Greece, vol. vii. p. 6.

it, as no notice is taken of its subsequent passage. In two days' march he came to the principal city of the Aspii, but it does not appear whether the city was on the river or beyond it; it was probably not far from the river. If we adhere to the order in which these mountain-streams run from north to south, and consequently across Alexander's route, the Euaspla will be the Khonar or Káma river. Euaspla, Professor Lassen observes, is sometimes read Euaspes: he considers it as a half-Greek translation of an Indian name, Su-aswa, and equivalent to Khoaspes. Having identified the Khoes with the Káma, he is obliged to suppose that the Euaspla is a feeder of that river, or rather one of its upper branches, the Sisa. The supposition is however wholly improbable; for it is very unlikely that Alexander would or indeed could have penetrated into the rugged and almost inaccessible country through which this branch of the Khonar flows, so far from the line of route which he was following towards the Indus. It is evident that he pursued a direction nearly parallel with the valley of Kabul, crossing the lower ridges which separate the several valleys that open from the north into it, and diverging sometimes to the left, where the country became more practicable, in order to bring the mountain tribes under nominal subjection. After crossing the Euaspla, he met with a numerous and brave population, and with more resistance than he had before encountered; and these circumstances are in confirmation of the Euaspla being the Khonar, as beyond this river the main branch of the Hindu Kush recedes considerably to the north of east before it turns again to the east, and forms, with the Indus river on the south, four sides of an irregular square, containing an extensive tract comprehending the valleys of Punjkora, Sewat, Buner, and Chumla, occupied by various divisions of the Yusef-zei tribe of Afghans, in which there are some considerable towns, and in many places of which there are extensive vestiges of ancient population and prosperity.[1]

The Barbarians, on perceiving Alexander's approach, set fire to the city, and retired to the mountains, where they found rugged and almost inaccessible places of retreat, such as abound at the present day along the course of

[1] Elphinstone's Kabul, p. 328. Court on Alexander's exploits on the west of the Indus: J. As. Soc. B. April, 1839.

the Khonar river, especially about the actual capital of the district, also termed Khonar. Alexander passed one of the mountains, and came to the city of Arigæum, which was deserted: this he occupied and strengthened. M. Court suggests that Arigæum may be found in Arichand; but this is on the east of the Lundye river, to which it is doubtful if we have yet arrived. There is a considerable town, however, in this direction, Bajour, and several ruins; and some of these may be the relics of Arigæum. The name of the place is apparently Indian,—Arijaya or Arinjaya, 'the foe-vanquishing city.' From Arigæum, Alexander marched to a neighbouring mountain, where the Indians made a vigorous stand: they were defeated, with the loss, it is said, of forty thousand men and about two hundred and thirty thousand head of cattle.

The next march was against the Assakeni, the Aswa-senis, 'those fighting on horseback,' who were said to have an army of twenty thousand horse and thirty thousand foot, besides eighty elephants. Before entering the country, the Macedonians passed through the territories of the Guræi, and crossed the river of that name with much difficulty, not only from its depth and rapidity, but from the vast numbers of round and slippery stones at the bottom. Now this will agree very well with the district and river of Punj-kora, the five Koras, Goras, or Guræi. This river is the most considerable next to that of Kabul: "without being very deep, its current is very rapid, and its bed is so sown with rocks and slippery stones, that of ten persons that wade it, when its water is low, half are sure to stumble." M. Court concludes, apparently with justice, "I am inclined to think it is the Guræus of the Greeks."[1]

The first place attacked by the invaders after crossing the river was Massaga,—read also Mazaga, Masaca, Masoga, and even Magosa. The probable appellation was Maha-gram, or, in the spoken dialects, Maha-ga-on. A possible corruption of Maha-gram or Ma-gram occurs in Mount Maram, where ancient remains are observable:[2] there was a hill in the neighbourhood

[1] In his first memoir M. Court suggested its being the Khonar, and M. Jacquet concurred in the conjecture: J. Asiatique, 3rd series, tom. iv. p. 387. He mentions also, J. As. Soc. B. vol. v. p. 393, that the Siah-posh Kafirs consider themselves "descendants of the Ghoris, which name resembles greatly that of Guræi." If, however, by this is intended the Ghor of the Mohammedan writers, that district lay too far to the west to have had any thing to do with Kaferistan.

[2] Court on Alexander's exploits.

of the city to which the Indian mercenaries retreated, and where Alexander surrounded and cut them off. Another not unlikely situation for Massaga is that of Ashnagar, written also Hushtnagar, and Ashtnagar: the ruins in the vicinity of this town are very extensive; and in the name it is not improbable that we have a trace of the classical appellation of the people, Assa-keni, the term implying the city, 'nagara,' of the Asti or Assi. According to native information, a city called Masiangar or Maskhina exists close to Kara Baba, on the frontiers of Kaferistan, which M. Court conjectures may be Massaga. To this situation, however, it may be objected that Alexander would not need to have passed the Punjkora river on his way to it, and the declaration of the historian is explicit as to the passing of the river. It is also to be observed, that the Guræus is the last river passed before Alexander comes to the Indus; and it is therefore to be inferred that Alexander crossed the river which is formed by the junction of the Punjkora and Sewat rivers, otherwise he must have passed the latter river as well as the former. The united stream is called either the Punjkora or Sewat river; and this may explain why Arrian in his Indica speaks erroneously of a Suastus as well as a Garæus, whilst in Ptolemy we have no other river than the Suastus described.

That Alexander's operations were continued in the direction of the Indus rather than of Kaferistan, we may infer from other considerations. He marched next upon Ora, hearing that succours had been sent thither by Abisarus: now Abisarus is undoubtedly the Abhisara of the Hindus,—the country west of Kashmir, confounded by the Greeks with the name of its prince. An alliance between Abhisara and Ora renders it certain that they must have been contiguous, and consequently that the latter was not far west of the Indus. The people of Bazira, when they despaired of defending their city, fled to the rock of Aornus. Bazira was conjectured by Rennell to be Bajore, to the north of Khonar, and accordingly he placed Aornus to the north of Bajore, in which he was followed by Barbié du Bocage; but there can be no doubt that Aornus was not far from the Indus, and Bazira therefore could not be in the situation which Rennell proposed; neither is it likely that Alexander would have recrossed the Guræus to occupy Bazira, which he must have done had it been the same with Bajore. It might with more consistency be looked for at a place termed Bazar by M. Court, situated on the southern face of the Koh-Ganga mountain, where are very extensive ruins. Bazar, in its ordinary sense, signifies 'a market,' and it may thence have been applied to a market-town: it appears, however, in this place as a proper name, and is not more unlike Bazira than Bajore.

However this may be, it is certain that we must look for Aornus not far from the Indus. Curtius asserts that the river ran so close to the rock on one side, that many of the Macedonians fell into it and were drowned: and although this is incompatible with the account given by Arrian, and with other statements of Curtius himself, yet he is so far borne out, that Strabo specifies the rock to have been upon the bank of the Indus, not far from its sources; meaning, of course, not far from its passage through the mountains at Derbend.[1] Diodorus also states that the Indus ran past the foot of the rock. It is further stated that Alexander at this period of his campaign took possession, in person, of Peukelaotis, and that, attended by Kophes and Assagetes (Aswajit), the two princes of the province, he reduced many small towns situated upon the Indus. He arrived next at Embolima, a city not far from Aornus; for which M. Court proposes Ambar, a town not far from the west bank of the Indus, or it may be Amb, higher up.[2] Whether either identification be allowable or not, it is clear that Alexander's latter operations, before he crossed the Indus, were carried on in the country lying between the Punjkora and that river.

The tract of country occupied by the Momends and Yusef-zeis has been so wholly unexplored by Europeans, that it is impossible to say whether any vestiges of the towns named by Arrian exist. The information furnished by M. Court, to whom we are indebted for almost all we know of these regions, was chiefly gained from native reports, and we have not the advantage of his personal investigation. According to statements communicated to him,

[1] Thirlwall calls Aornus a hill-fort, on the right bank of the Indus, not far from its junction with the Kophen: but this is incompatible with Strabo's notice of it: *Ἄορνον δέ τινα πέτραν, ἧς τὰς ῥίζας ὁ Ἰνδὸς ὑποῤῥεῖ πλησίον τῶν πηγῶν.* Book xv. 1. 8.

[2] Curtius apparently places it sixteen days' march from the Indus, which is utterly irreconcileable with any place in this part of the country: he also makes Alexander's march to Embolima, after, not before, the capture of Aornus; in which, again, he is probably in error.

there exists a town called Oora, in the district of Buner, and there are various elevated rocks which correspond in character with that of Aornus, and more or less closely with its probable position.[1] In all likelihood, indeed, Aornus was not a proper name. We know that the Macedonians met with more than one fortified mountain to which they gave the appellation: there was one, for instance, in Bactria, which Alexander took on his march from Drapsaka. It is not difficult to explain the occurrence. Aornus is, in all probability, only the Hellenised form of the vernacular corruption of the Sanscrit term 'Awara, or 'Awarana, 'an enclosure,' 'a stockade;' and which, as 'Awur, or, as Europeans write it, 'ore,' forms the concluding syllable of so many towns in this part of India, as Rajore and Bajore, which should be, if correctly written, Rájawur and Bájawur. Aornus, therefore, was nothing more than a stockaded enclosure, situated on a detached hill or mountain of difficult approach.[2] This stockade Alexander placed under the command of the Indian, Sisicottus, or preferably Sisicoptus, in which we have Sasi-gupta, a name that, like Chandra-gupta, means the 'Moon-protected.'

After the capture of 'the' Aornus, Alexander marched in a retrograde direction from the Indus again into the territories of the Assakeni, who had risen in arms. As we have already seen, Massaga was one of the chief cities of the Assakeni. On this occasion he marched against Dyrta,—a place we might conjecture to be identifiable with Dhyr, only that this city is too remote from the Indus; the proximity of which Alexander did not quit, as he captured the elephants of the chief of the Assakeni in the thickets bordering on the river, and presently afterwards embarked upon it, and sailed down to the bridge which his officers had built during the occupation of Pushkalavati.[3]

It is next said that Alexander, on his way to the bridge constructed by his

[1] J. As. Soc. B. April, 1839, p. 309.

[2] This is not inconsistent with the origin of the term suggested by Thirlwall: "Its Indian name," he says, "seems to have been slightly distorted by the Greeks, according to their usual practice, into that of Aornos, which answered to its extraordinary height, as above the flight of a bird:" History of Greece, vol. vii. p. 8.

[3] Strabo, Book xv. 1. 27. Arrian, Book v. 3.

officers, having entered that part of the country which lies between the Indus and the Kophen, the present district of Chumla, came to the city of Nysa or Nyssa,[1] founded by Bacchus; as was proved, according to Acuphis, the head of the deputation sent to Alexander by the Nysæans, by the proximity of Mount Meros, and the presence of the ivy, which grew nowhere else in India. Mount Meros was ascended by Alexander, with his auxiliary horse, and a detachment of infantry; and the Greeks crowned themselves with garlands of ivy, and celebrated sacrifices to Bacchus. Nyssa should be, therefore, upon the west of the Indus, above Attok, or at least not far from the river. M. Court would look for Nysa at Ashtnagar; but this seems to be too far from the Indus: he has in his map a place somewhat lower down, called Nicetta, but whether the name or place is of any antiquity is to be ascertained. Nysa, consistently with Arrian's statement, could not have been far from the Indus; but the whole story has the air of a Greek fiction, founded possibly on some slight resemblances of sounds or usages. It is rather a fanciful etymology to derive Nysa from Paropanisus, or Paropa-nishadha,[2] but the name of Mount Meru may have furnished a hint of Meros. Ivy, as far as is yet ascertained, does not grow in the Kabul valley, but the grape flourishes and abounds in all the valleys of the Hindu Kush.[3] The Kafirs, or people who dwell on the north of the Afghans, make wine; and old and young of both sexes amongst them drink it.[4] They are very fond of drinking-parties, and of music and dancing. As they are not improbably the remains of tribes which in the time of Alexander inhabited the valleys now occupied by the Afghans, these practices might seem to identify them in Grecian estimation with the votaries of Bacchus.

Arrian conjectures, and Curtius asserts, that the Macedonians crossed the Indus on a bridge of boats; and there can be little doubt of the fact:

[1] Curtius places Alexander's visit to Nyssa much earlier in his campaign; but the account given by Arrian is more probable.

[2] Bohlen; Alte Inden, vol. i. p. 143.

[3] According to a local tradition, Chitral was the wine-cellar of Afrasiab, the king of Turan: Moorcroft's Travels, vol. ii. p. 271.

[4] Elphinstone's Kabul, p. 626. Burnes on the Siah-posh Kafirs: J. As. Soc. B. vol. vii. p. 328.

such a bridge has been constructed in modern days for the same passage; and travellers have been impressed with the coincidence between the structures of the Sikh prince and the Macedonian conqueror,[1]—the contrivances of ancient and modern times; the rapidity of the river, in fact, constituting the same cause and producing the same effects. Alexander, it is generally admitted, crossed at the usual place, or opposite to Attok.

Although the route thus traced for the operations of the Macedonian detachment, under its enterprising prince, presents some difficulties, yet there is little reason to question its general correctness, as it harmonizes with the permanent topographical features of the country. Alexander crossed, according to Arrian's narrative, four rivers before he reached the Indus; and these, the Kophen, Khoes, Euaspla, and Guræus, we have still in the Punjshir, Alishung, Khonar, and Punjkora. This recapitulation in the course of the narrative is more likely to be correct than a description compiled from the narrative, in the preparation of which the geographer may err or forget. Thus even Arrian is better authority as an historian than as a geographer, for he describes in the latter character the Kophen as bringing with it to the Indus the Malamantus, Suastus, and Garœus; two of which he does not name at all in his narrative, and of which the third is probably the same with the second. The Malamantus, as not specified on the north of the Kabul river, has been looked for to the south; and M. Court suggests its being the Bahrah river, which flows from the Khaiber mountains.[2] The name is apparently Indian, but there are no means of verifying the river. Ptolemy, as already intimated, is still less exact, mentioning only the Khoe and Suastus as west of the Indus; and Strabo is not much more precise, specifying west of the Indus only the Kophen and the Khoaspes, which falls into it.[3] After the Kophen comes the Indus. Of his cities, Plegerium, Gorydale, Bandobene, and Gandaritis, by which the united stream flows, little can be conjectured: the second is also read Goru and Gorus, in which we may have the Guræi of Arrian. Bandobene occurs, also Bardebene, but neither is verifiable. Of Gandaritis, as synonymous with Gandhar, mention has been made above.

[1] Burnes' Travels, vol. iii. p. 284.

[2] J. As. Soc. B. April, 1839, Map.

[3] Book xv. 1. 26.

The geography of the Punjab has been the subject of repeated and able investigation;[1] and with respect at least to its 'five' rivers, the accounts derivable from classical authorities are found to agree with the topographical description of original Sanscrit writers. There are many other circumstances, however, which yet require elucidation; but it would lead us too far from our principal object, the determination of the provinces subject to the Bactrian kings, to attempt any detailed elucidation of the districts east of the Indus. There can be no doubt that in the Hydaspes of Strabo and Arrian, or Bidaspes of Ptolemy, we have the Bitasthá or Vitasthá, the Behut or Jhelum of the Hindus. The Akesines, possibly for the 'Apa or Aqua of the Sinæ, is the Chin-ab of the present day, or more classically the Chandrabhága, which is traceable in the Sandabala of Ptolemy, and which name, according to Ritter, was known to Alexander, but was changed, as a term of ill omen.[2] The Hydraotes, or Hyarotes, or Rhuadis, is undeniably the Sanscrit Irávatí; the Iraotee of the natives,[3] and Ravi of Mohammedan geographers. The Hyphasis, or Hypanis, or, as Ptolemy again more correctly names it, the Bibasis, is the Vipásá, the Byas or Beyah of the maps. The historians of Alexander have nothing certain to relate of the country beyond the Hyphasis, as that was the boundary of the Macedonian invasion.[4]

Subsequent information, although of a less precise and authentic character, was obtained by the classical geographers; and in the Zaradrus of Ptolemy, and Hesidrus of Pliny, we need not hesitate to acknowledge the Sanscrit Satadrus, 'the hundred-channeled river,' the modern Set-lej. The Jomanes of Pliny is still more distinctly the Yamuná or Jumna; and it cannot be doubted that Arrian intends the same river by the Jobares, which he describes as flowing past Methora and Kleisoboras, the chief towns of the Suraseni, the former of which is, no doubt, Mathurá, the capital of the Surasena tribe.[5] Colonel Tod notices another ancient city on the Jumna, near Bateswar, between Agra and Etawa, called Sura-pur; but, as he

[1] Rennell, Memoir of a Map of Asia; Vincent, Voyage of Nearchus; and later by Professor Lassen; see Pentapotamia Indica: see also M. A. Court in the Memoirs already cited.

[2] It might have been corrupted into Sandrophagos, 'Ανδρο- or even 'Αλεξανδρο-φάγος, 'man- or Alexander-eater.' History of Greece, vol. vii. p. 25.

[3] Burnes, vol. iii. p. 124.

[4] Arrian, Indica, IV.

[5] Vishnu Purana, p. 185, note.

observes, this can scarcely be regarded as the original of Kleiso-boras.[1] The latter may possibly be a blundering attempt to express Krishna-pura, the city of Krishna, a term peculiarly applicable, although I do not know that it has ever been so applied, to Mathurá.

Of the two chief cities mentioned by Alexander's historians, we need be at no loss to identify Taxila with the Taksha-silá of the Hindus, a city between the Indus and Hydaspes, and the extensive ruins of which are still found in the vicinity of Manikyala.[2] The name of the king, Omphis, or Mo-phis, has more the aspect of an Indo-Scythic than an Indian appellation; but it is doubtful if at this early period the northern Barbarians had obtained footing in India. It is not without countenance, however, from original authorities, as the Chronicle of Kashmir records the occupation of that country in the third century B. C. by Turushka or Turk princes.[3] Chiefs of the same race may have found their way to the Punjab.

The appellation of another principal city in the Punjab, Sangala, appears to be traceable in the Sanscrit Sákala, a city of which mention is made in the Mahábhárata as similarly placed, and as remarkable for the loose and Bacchanalian manners of its females.[4] Professor Lassen infers, from a like description being given of the behaviour of the women of a tract of country beyond the Irávatí in the same passage, that the Hindu author intends to place Sákala on the west of the Hydraotes,[5] whilst, according to Arrian, Sangala was situated on the east bank of that river.[6] It does not necessarily follow that the same place is intended by the Sanscrit text; and the females, who are spoken of in the latter of the two passages, are described as living in

[1] Transactions of the Royal Asiatic Society, vol. i. p. 315.

[2] Memoir on a Map of the Provinces of Peucelaotis and Taxila; by M. A. Court: J. As. Soc. B. vol. v. p. 468. Thirlwall observes that the Tope of Manikyala does not seem to have pretensions to such high antiquity. That is true, but he might have known that the tope described in Mr. Elphinstone's Kabul, to which alone he refers, is not the only vestige of an extensive and ancient city in this position. It may be objected to the historian of Greece in this part of his work, that whilst he goes to German compilers for his information, he neglects the English materials at hand from which their information has been derived.

[3] Asiatic Researches, vol. xv. p. 23.

[4] Ibid. vol. xv. p. 108.

[5] See original, quoted in Lassen's treatise de Pentapotamia Indica, p. 65. v. 16.

[6] Arrianus Sangala in orientali Hydraotis ripa collocat. Pentapotamia, p. 20.

woods, not in a city. There is no great objection to the identity of Sákala and Sangala on this account. The Mahábhárata, however, as it alludes to Yavanas, or Greeks, even on the lower course of the Indus, appears to have been compiled subsequently to Alexander's invasion, prior to which the Hindus are not likely to have known any thing of the Greeks; but this being the case, it cannot refer to the actual Sangala of the Greek writers, as Alexander destroyed that city. The name may have been retained, but it was applied probably to another city rebuilt in a somewhat different position, as it might have been considered of ill omen to have re-constructed it on the site where it originally stood. The manners described as prevailing not only at Sákala but throughout the Punjab, the people of which are denominated Bahíkas, 'Aráttás, and Jártikas, show that these tribes had adopted usages not strictly Hindu when the Mahábhárata was written, the consequence, very possibly, of either Greek or Indo-Scythic influence. The description is no doubt exaggerated, and the tone may be derived from the animosity felt towards the Buddhist heresy, which, we have seen, prevailed in the Punjab soon after, if not shortly before, the Christian æra.

According to Sir A. Burnes, the Cathæi, of whom Sangala was the capital, are still recognisable in the Kattias, the name of the pastoral tribe which forms the chief population of the country from the Hydaspes to Delhi:[1] the ordinary derivation has been from Kshattá, or, as pronounced, Khatta, a mixed tribe, of military habits: the term Kattia may have a similar origin.[2] Sangala, Burnes identifies with Lahore,[3] but Arrian places Sangala three marches from the Irávatí, and two on this side the Hyphasis, or rather the united stream of the Beyah and Setlej, the modern Garra. According to Mr. Masson, this position agrees precisely with that of Harípa, which he therefore suggests for the site of Sangala.[4] The topogra-

[1] Travels, vol. iii. p. 130.

[2] Supposed to be the Murdhabhishikta of Menu; but there is a tribe called Kshattá in the same work, the progeny of a Sudra by a woman of the Kshatríya or military caste, and consequently of degraded occupations, which may be the origin of the name. x. 12.

[3] Travels, vol. iii. p. 182.

[4] Extracts from Notes of a Journey from Lahore to Kerachee; by C. Masson: J. As. Soc. B. vol. vi. p. 57.

phical features of the place, the hill or rising ground, and a swamp, with the remains of a brick fort, suit very well with the description of Arrian. It is said to have been the site of a very extensive and ancient town, destroyed, according to local tradition, by divine wrath, in punishment of the iniquity of its sovereign. It is something more than sixty miles southwest of Lahore, and nearly fifty miles from the Garra. If the first distance, however, is to be considered as equivalent to Alexander's three marches, we must interpret the latter not as so many marches from the river, but from the place where the river was crossed, as Harípa is close to the Ravi. That Alexander must have taken a direction obliquely to the south is evident; as, from the Ravi at Lahore to the Garra, just below the accession of the Beyah, where the distance is as considerable as at any other point in a direct line, the whole is something less than sixty miles, which is scarcely enough for five camps or marches. It is therefore undeniable that the Macedonians marched in a southerly direction, although, whether they followed the course of the Irávatí to Harípa, may be reasonably doubted. Better acquaintance with the country will probably bring other vestiges of antiquity to light in a more central position.

The river which arrested the advance of Alexander was passed, according to Strabo, by the Bactrian kings, who, in this direction, crossed the Hypanis, and extended their conquests to the Isamus.[1] It may be doubted if their conquests were more than incursions; for the coins of the Greek kings of Bactria have not been found in any such numbers in the Punjab as to justify the belief that they ever constituted the currency of the country. Some, of course, would find their way there through the intercourse that must have resulted from contiguity and commerce; and they found their way much farther, even to Mathurá; but the instances are rare, and not more than are referable to such contingencies. The Isamus, it has been supposed, is the Jumna, or Jomanes:[2] the correction is rather a violent one, although, geographically, the conjecture is not improbable. The Bactrian princes also subjugated the country along the Indus to Pattalene, and the rest of the seacoast, including the kingdoms of Sigertis and Tessariostus. For a verification

[1] Book XI. 11. 1.

[2] Mannert: Geographie der Griechen und Romer, vol. v. p. 295.

of the former we must again have recourse to the movements of Alexander, comparing the notices given by the classical writers with those to be found in original authorities.

After reaching the confluence of the Akesines with the Hydaspes, Alexander made a retrograde march towards the Indus, upon an incursion against the Sibæ, who, from being clothed in skins and armed with clubs, the latter of which they stamped upon their cattle, the Greeks fancied to be the descendants of Hercules.[1] These are, no doubt, the Sivis of the Hindus, who are often named in the Mahábhárata, and are associated usually with the people of the north-west, or of the Punjab; and who, as the descendants, not of the deity Siva, but of King Sivi, the son of Usínara, are also called Saivas. Several of the other tribes of the Punjab are also called the progeny of this prince; and the existence of a people of this name in the proximity of the Indus is fully confirmed by Sanscrit writers.[2]

The Malli, who were next assailed, were situated in the country about the approach of the Hydraotes to the Akesines, towards the point of their confluence; and their northern, or rather north-eastern frontier, was protected by a tract of desert. It is generally supposed that we have a trace of the name of this people in Multan, or, as it is still called by the people, Mallithán, 'the place of the Malli.'[3] As this city is now about thirty miles below the confluence of the rivers, Ritter supposes that they formerly met a great way to the south of their present point of junction;[4] whilst Rennell, on the contrary, would have placed the capital of the Malli on the Ravi, above the present confluence, at a place now called Tulamḅa. It is clear that the country of the Malli was not limited to the north of the Ravi, but extended some distance also to the south of the river; as Alexander crossed it, and captured and destroyed several towns in that direction before he came to what

[1] Strabo, Book xv. 1. 8. 33.

[2] Vishnu Purana, p. 444. See also Mahábhárata, Vana Parva, 'the rape of Draupadí,' where Jayadratha, king of the Sindhus, also called Sauvíras and Sindhu-Sauvíras, is accompanied by Kotikásya, the prince of the Sivis, and who is thence addressed by Draupadí as Saivya. See also Zeitschrift fur die Kunde der Morgenlandes, 'On the ancient Indian tribes,' by Professor Lassen, vol. iii. p. 183.

[3] Burnes, vol. iii. p. 114.

[4] Thirlwall's History of Greece, vol. vii. p. 36.

appears to have been the capital.[1] This was deserted, and the Malli then retreated to the Ravi, and crossed it, and attempted to make a stand on the northern bank. Upon their defeat they fled to the fortress, in the assault of which the life of Alexander was in such extreme peril that it is difficult to comprehend how he escaped. He was conveyed from thence to the confluence of the rivers. There does not seem to be sufficient reason, therefore, for conjecturing an alteration in the course of the rivers to have taken place, nor have recent travellers noticed the existence of any thing like deserted river-beds in this vicinity. The territory of the Malli lay on both sides of the Ravi; and their capital, or at least their largest city, was on the south.[2] This, it is possible, may not have been exactly in the position of Multan, although there are many considerations in favour of the identification.[3] It is not unlikely that some confusion may have occurred in regard to the names of the rivers, and the denomination of the Hydraotes may have been applied to the united stream below its confluence with the Akesines instead of the latter appellation; although more correctly, according to Arrian, the Akesines preserves its name until it unites with the Indus. Multan is about ten miles distant from the Chinab, after it has received the Ravi; and the former stream was, consequently, more likely to have been taken as a line of defence than the latter. However this may be, the chief evidence for the presence of the particular tribe in the Punjab is the present popular appellation; for although there is a tribe termed Malla in Sanscrit geography, yet they are described as being situated in a different region.[4] There is another tribe in this quarter of India of which the name may bear some relation to it, the Madras, who were a people of the Punjab, and whose monarch, Salya, is one of the heroes of the Mahábhárata.[5]

Confederated with the Malli were the Oxydrakæ, whose name and situation, it has been supposed, are traceable in Ooch, a town on the left bank of the Akesines, after it has collected the waters of the other streams of the Punjab, and is conveying them to the Indus at Mithan-kole, about forty miles

[1] Arrian, Book VI. 8.

[2] Αὐτὸς δὲ ἦγεν ἐπὶ τὴν μεγίστην τῶν Μαλλῶν πόλιν. Arrian, Book VI. 8.

[3] Burnes, vol. iii. p. 114.

[4] Vishnu Purana, p. 188, note 52.

[5] Asiatic Researches, vol. xv. See also Vishnu Purana, p. 177.

lower down. The locality is probable; the agreement of name is very slight; but in the corrected reading of the denomination to Sudrakæ, we have a precise agreement with a nation or tribe named Sudras or Sudrakas, who are placed by Hindu geographers in the west of India.[1]

Alexander was conveyed down the Ravi to a point some short distance above its confluence with the Chinab. He halted some time there, and received the submission of the Malli and Oxydrakæ, which he might well do from tribes inhabiting the neighbouring districts of Multan and Bhawalpur. Falling down the Akesines to the Indus, Alexander was joined at their confluence by Perdiccas, who brought him the submission of the Abastani, and by a reinforcement of boats built in the country of the Xathri. The Ossadii also sent ambassadors, tendering allegiance. Who these different tribes were, it is not possible to ascertain; their names are apparently Indian. The Ossadii may have been the people on the west of the Indus—the Aswádhyas, the 'rich in horses.' The Xathri must have been situated on the Chinab, as the boats came down that river, and they were possibly Kshatriyas, or Kshattas, or Kattias. The Abastani were probably situated in the Doab, between the Jhelum and the Chinab, and were the 'Apa-sthánas, people whose site was upon the waters of the Punjab, or Ava or Apa-sthánas, those on the 'off,' or opposite side of the river.

Sailing down the Indus, Alexander came next to the capital of the Sogdi, who offered him no opposition, but allowed him either to build a city of his own, or erect a citadel, and call their city after his own name: he also constructed additional boats there. The city of the Sogdi is left undetermined by Rennell: Vincent placed it at Bukkur. Colonel Tod and Captain McMurdo imagined that the Sogdi might be recognised in the Sohdas, a Rajput tribe now found much more to the south-east, in the Thul, or Desert bordering on Marwar, but who, according to these authorities, were once sovereigns of an extensive country extending to the Punjab and Kashmir, of which the capital was Alore or Arore, a city the ruins of which are observable a few miles south-east of Bukkur.[2] It is worthy of remark,

1 Vishnu Purana, p. 195, note 153.

2 Account of Rajasthan, vol. ii. p. 310. Journal of the Royal Asiatic Society, vol. i. p. 33.

however, that the Sogdi of Arrian are the Sabrakæ of Curtius, the Sambestæ and Sodræ of Diodorus;[1] and that those writers describe them as living under a republican form of government, a peculiarity attributed by Arrian to the Oxydrakæ. This circumstance, as well as the similarity of the name, renders it possible that the same people are intended, and that the Sogdi were a tribe of the Oxydrakæ, or of the Sudrakas of the Hindus. We should expect to find them, therefore, nearer to the Akesines, and there are other considerations which render this site more probable than Bukkur.

An interesting memoir by one of the writers just named, the late Captain McMurdo,[2] has been published in the Journal of the Royal Asiatic Society, on the lower course of the Indus, with particular reference to the notices of the country found in classical and Mohammedan authors. One principal object of his dissertation is to establish the fact, that even so late as the seventh century, the date of the Arab invasion of Sindh, the main stream of the Indus did not flow in the same direction in which it now runs, but pursued a more direct course to the sea, at the distance, in some parts, of from sixty to eighty miles to the east of its present channel. The bed of the river is still to be seen, and is known as the Purana Deria, or 'old river;' and on its banks stand the ruins of Arore, which was a large and flourishing city when captured by the Mohammedans. If this was the case, Bukkur could not have been visited by Alexander; for the old course of the river turned to the south forty miles above it. It is a confirmation of this view, that whether it be considered, with Vincent, as the city of the Sogdi, or with Rennell as the capital of Musikanus, no notice is taken, by Alexander's historians, of topographical features so remarkable as those of Bukkur, an insulated rock of flint in the river, past which the Indus flows with much noise and violence; a precipitous rocky bank on the east, forty feet high, and a sloping bank on the west.[3] It is scarcely likely, little as Alexander's historians indulge in such details, that they should have altogether omitted them. It is also asserted by the Mohammedan chroniclers of the conquest of Sindh, that Alore was deserted in consequence of the alteration of the course

[1] Vincent's Nearchus, p. 141.

[2] Dissertation on the river Indus; by the late Captain James McMurdo: J. R. As. Soc. vol. i. p. 20.

[3] Burnes' Travels to Bokhara, vol. iii. p. 72.

of the Indus, and that Bukkur was constructed out of its ruins. This was of course a comparatively recent event. If there is any truth in these statements, the capital of the Sogdi was not Bukkur. Nor does it seem to have been Alore; for Alore was a celebrated city, the capital of Sindh at the time of the Mohammedan conquest, whilst the city of the Sogdi, which does not seem to have been of any great note at the time of Alexander's visit, must have been absorbed by his city, and been transmuted into an Alexandria. That traces of such an Alexandria did exist at a later date, is also testified by the oriental authorities. After taking Alore, the Mohammedan army, it is related, proceeded to Multan, and on their way they besieged, and with some difficulty took, Ashkandra or Sekandra,[1] an extremely strong town, which was defended by some of the family of Raja Dahir after the overthrow of the capital: here, then, probably was the city of the Sogdi. The whole of the river's course at present, from Bukkur to Mithan-kote, is skirted by jungle; whether any ruins exist in it, there has been no opportunity of inquiring. The distance in a straight line is about one hundred and forty miles, which would have afforded space for the position of a petty tribe, especially as their habits were then, as they still are in this vicinity, nomadic and pastoral.[2]

The traditional extent and opulence of Alore recommend it as the capital of Musikanus, to which Alexander next proceeded, and which Arrian specifies as the object of the conqueror's admiration. The kingdom of Musikanus was said to have been one of the richest of India, a character it would not now merit, but which might not have been wholly undeserved, when many tracts now arid and waste were irrigated from the Indus.[3] It is not easy to conjecture an Indian original for Musikanus, or, as he is also

[1] J. R. As. Soc. vol. i. p. 31.

[2] Lieutenant Wood, in his Travels to the Source of the Oxus, mentions the frequent appearance of herds of buffaloes on this part of his route, and the pastoral occupations of the people of Sindh: the same circumstance is mentioned by Abulfazl, Ayin Akbari, and was noticed by Strabo:—a curious chain of evidence of the permanence of customs enforced by peculiarities of situation.

[3] In the vicinity of Arore itself the country is still productive. "The soil is of superior quality, and when I visited the spot, it was covered, south of the causeway, with crops remarkable for their healthy and luxuriant appearance." Lieutenant Wood's Journey to the Source of the Oxus, p. 49.

termed, Postikanus and Portikanus. Mahàsena is the nearest Indian name I can propose for the first; and for the second I know of no possible equivalent. The same is to be said of his neighbour Oxykanus; his name is also a problem for solution. Neither can have any possible connexion with the Turkish title Khan.

Whilst residing at the capital of Musikanus, where also he built a citadel, Alexander moved against Oxykanus, and took his two principal cities, as well as the chief himself. It has been proposed to look for the territory of Oxykanus on the west of the Indus; but this seems unadvisable, for not long before the subjugation of the Raja by Alexander in person, Craterus had been despatched across the Indus with the larger portion of the army as far as to the confines of Arachosia; and that he had returned is evident, from its being stated that he was put in command of the new citadel. Had the principality of Oxykanus been on the west of the Indus, opposite to that of Musikanus, it must have been twice traversed by the Grecian army, and the question of its chief's dispositions would have been earlier disposed of. Again, Sambus, whose government was undoubtedly towards the Halla mountains, was afraid of the enmity of Muṣikanus. Had Oxykanus been between him and Musikanus, he would have had more to apprehend from the former than the latter. It seems not unlikely, therefore, that the district of Oxykanus lay to the south-east of Alore. The objection to this position has arisen from the contiguity of the Great Desert; but when the eastern channel of the Indus was well supplied with water the limits of the Desert must have been thrown back also to the east of their present line. Curtius calls the subjects of Oxykanus, Præsthi. Prasthas or Prasthalas might be applied to a people occupying the 'Thuls' or oases of the Desert.

The capital of Musikanus is placed by Dr. Vincent at Sehwan, principally in consequence of Strabo's testimony that the territory of Musikanus joined to Pattalene.[1] But this, although possibly true of the country subject to Musikanus, was certainly not true of the city; for it afterwards appears from Arrian, that the passage by water, either from the city, or more probably from a point even farther to the south, occupied more than three days, implying a distance of at least one hundred miles. Besides which, the

[1] Πρὸς αὐτῇ δ' ἤδη τῇ Παταληνῇ τήν τε τοῦ Μουσικανοῦ λέγουσι. Strabo, Book xv. 1. 33.

adjustment depends upon what is to be considered the northern limit of Pattalene, a point by no means determined; and, finally, if the Indus did not follow its present course, it did not flow by Sehwan. The capital of Musikanus was upon the river, and it was therefore not Sehwan.

That Sehwan, however, is the representative of an ancient city is very probable, and its situation and its name point it out as the Sindomana of Arrian, the capital of Sambus, the prince who was confirmed by Alexander in the command of the mountainous districts adjacent to the kingdom of Musikanus. Sehwan stands close under the Lakhi mountains, and presents many vestiges of antiquity, especially its castle, which Sir A. Burnes observes, is in all probability as old as the age of the Greeks.[1] Sindomana is readily recognisable in a very allowable Sanscrit compound, Sindhu-mán, 'the possessor (the capital, or Raja) of Sindh,' with which 'Sindhu-ván' is synonymous, and the latter may have been softened in common speech to the modern Seh-wan. The palpable objection to the identity of Sehwan and Sindomana was the apparent fact that the latter did not stand upon the Indus. The objection vanishes with the removal of the ancient course of the Indus to the east. Sambus is a genuine Indian appellation; it is the name of one of the sons of Krishna.[2]

From Sindomana, Alexander marched against a city which had revolted; and, having taken it, he seized some of the Brahmans, whom he suspected of having instigated the temporary defection of Sambus.[3] It does not follow that the city was a city of Brahmans, as has been sometimes stated; nor even would that follow from the name Bahmanabad, applied occasionally to towns in India: it is merely an honorific denomination. If we are to understand that the city thus taken by Alexander was near Sindomana, it was not the city of the Brahmans so designated by the Mohammedans. We might rather look for it in the position of Amree (Amari, 'the immortal city'), eighteen miles below Sehwan, which, although now an insignificant village, is said to have been once a large city, and the favourite residence of former kings.[4]

[1] Travels to Bokhara, vol. iii. p. 37.

[2] Vishnu Purana, p. 591.

[3] Diodorus calls it Harmatelia, a city of the Brahmans: Dr. Vincent's Voyage of Nearchus, p. 136.

[4] Burnes, vol. iii. p. 59.

Whilst Alexander was engaged in this expedition, Musikanus revolted. Python was sent against him, took him prisoner, and returned with him to the camp and fleet, where he was crucified. The Macedonians were, therefore, again upon the Indus. After the death of Musikanus, Alexander despatched Craterus with the elephants and worn-out troops to Carmania, by way of Arachosia and Drangiana. They might have marched from Sehwan through the Lakhi Pass, or gone upwards to Larkhana, whence the great road westward branches and crosses the mountains to Kelat, by the Pass of Bolan, which is the route to Kerman.[1]

We now come to Pattalene, the conquest of the Bactrian kings, and difficulties increase as we advance. Whilst in the country of Musikanus, the Raja of Pattalene, called Mœris (Maha-raja or Maha-rai) by Curtius, came on a visit to Alexander, and professed his readiness to become one of his vassals. His submission was graciously received, and he returned to his city. Alexander, after sending off Craterus to Persia, gave the command of those troops he did not take on board, to Hephæstion, and, with the rest, sailed down the river. On the third day he heard that Mœris had thrown off his fealty, destroyed Pattala, and fled into the deserts. He hastened his course, and arrived, it is not said in what further time, at Pattala.

The specification of three days' navigation might seem to furnish a scale by which to measure the interval between the capital of Musikanus and Pattala. It must first, however, be determined whence we are to reckon. Supposing it to be about midway between Sehwan and Arore on the Purana Deria, it would be about thirty miles south of the former. The time of the year was July, when the river was full, and when it would not have been impossible to have sailed down it at the rate of one hundred miles a day; but it appears that the fleet, for the first three days at least, was accompanied by the army, and the progress of the one must have in some degree retarded the advance of the other. In three days then the distance traversed probably had not exceeded fifty miles in a direct line. When the news arrived that the capital of Pattalene was deserted, Alexander left his land force to follow, and accelerated his voyage; and even had he advanced as far as to Tatta, as there were

[1] Burnes, vol. iii. p. 80.

not above one hundred miles to travel, his arrival would not have been long delayed. It is by no means so clear, however, as has been supposed, that Tatta and Pattala are the same.

The situation of Pattala, at the head of a Delta, and that of Tatta, at the head of the actual Delta of the Indus, have induced all former writers on the subject to consider them as the same. Dr. Vincent indeed proposes Brahmanabad, but that is much the same thing, as it is only four miles south-west from Tatta. Sir A. Burnes has concurred with D'Anville, Robertson, Rennell, and Vincent, in this locality.[1]

On the other hand, Captain McMurdo has maintained that the commencement of the Delta of Pattalene began much higher up, and in the ancient or Purana Deria, at a city known as Brahmanabad to the Mohammedans, which was situated a few miles to the westward of the river, upon a branch formerly called the Lohana river, but now generally known as Bahmanawa or the canal of Bahmana.[2] This branch, constituting the western boundary of Pattalene, fell into the present river below Khodabad, and, crossing its course, flowed by Bhambora, and emptied itself into the sea at Dibal.[3] A creek, terminating in a sandy channel, communicating with the sea, is said to be still seen in this direction, which the tradition of the country asserts to have been a mouth of the Indus.

The extent of the Delta is nowhere exactly defined. Arrian says it was not smaller than that of the Nile, a comparison wholly inapplicable if Tatta is to form the apex of the Indian Delta. Again, he asserts that the base is one thousand eight hundred stadia, rather more than two hundred miles. This is exaggerated, no doubt; for the whole interval from the Kharee of Lukput (Lakshmi-pati) to Cape Mouze is not above one hundred and forty miles; but the opening at Lukput is not connected with Tatta: and if we take the base of the Delta from the Mull channel to that of the Piti, the

[1] "The antiquity of Tatta is unquestioned. The Pattala of the Greeks has been sought for in its position, and I believe with good reason, for the Indus here divides into two great branches." Travels to Bokhara, vol. iii. p. 81. See also his remarks on the observations of Captain Pottinger on the present state of the Indus: J. R. As. Soc. vol. i. p. 207.

[2] J. R. As. Soc. vol. i. p. 24.

[3] Ibid. p. 25.

eastern and western branches of the Bagar and Sata, into which the Indus separates below that place, the extreme distance between the mouths will be less than seventy miles, an extreme of disproportion which is unprecedented in any of the accounts of Alexander's movements towards India. Again, it is impossible to reconcile the accounts of Alexander's military and naval operations in Pattalene with the very narrow limits which the Tatta Delta offers; the arms of the triangle not exceeding sixty miles. Even Vincent computed the length of the western limb at one hundred and forty-four miles,[1] and Rennell made that of the eastern branch one hundred and seventy-five; much above Tatta, as he admits. It is evident, therefore, that the weight of both these authorities is decisive against their own conclusions, as by their computation of distances they have shown that Pattala must have been much farther from the sea than Tatta; with the exact position of which they were imperfectly acquainted. Their distances would, in fact, bring us very near to the spot proposed by Captain McMurdo —the site of Brahmanabad.

Although many circumstances are detailed of Alexander's voyage down the western branch, they have not led to any verification. Nearchus sailed out of the same branch, and it is agreed that the mouth could not have been far from Karachi, as his description of the bay of Krokala identifies it beyond question with Karachi.[2] It was only thirty stadia from the bar of the river which he had crossed, or less than four miles: and there are several openings still from the Piti to the Garah, which falls into the bay, one or other of which would answer to this distance: the bed of the former is now dry at no great distance from its mouth. The Piti is a branch of the Bagar, the western arm of the Indus below Tatta; and it is therefore into the former that the course above described by Captain McMurdo, for the western division of the Purana Deria, led. How far the intermediate river-line may be verifiable by observation is to be ascertained; at any rate there is no difficulty in admitting a possible communication between a river so

[1] Voyage of Nearchus, p. 144.

[2] Captain McMurdo: J. R. As. Soc. vol. i. p. 42. Lieutenant Wood, p. 12.

situated as the Purana and the present Indus, some way above Tatta; in which case the actual main channel would form the lower portion of the great western branch, the Sagapa of Ptolemy.

Captain McMurdo is not the only authority for the existence of the bed of the Purana Deria to the eastward of the present course of the Indus. Captain Pottinger, in a paper on the present course of the Indus,[1] mentions in a note that Lieutenant de L'Hoste, who surveyed this part of Sindh, obtained information of the bed of a river which the natives called Puran, which lies a long way east of the Narra, a river which branches off from the Indus a few miles above Bukkur. His description, however, identifies the Narra through part of its course at least with the Puran; for he states that it flows to the south, and, passing about fifty miles east of Hyderabad, falls into the ocean near Lukput-Bundur, the place of the embouchure of the Puran. In a manuscript map, constructed by Lieutenant de L'Hoste, the Narra is made to join the bed of the Purana much higher than is stated by Captain Pottinger, and the two are continued under one name, either that of Purana or Narra, to Lukput-Bundur and the sea. We have also the authority of Sir A. Burnes for the existence of a great eastern branch of the Indus;[2] and although his observations are confined to the lower part of its course, yet the account he gives of a remarkable inundation, the effect of an earthquake in 1826, which reached to Omerkote in the Desert, testified the existence of channels by which the waters of the Indus passed much higher up. He also elsewhere mentions, that formerly a branch of the Indus passed through the valley of Alore or Arore, the waters of which fertilised the desert, and reached the sea by Omerkote and Lukput;[3] a channel through which they still find egress in a great inundation. The Lukput river, he affirms, does not under ordinary circumstances at present communicate with any other branch of the Indus, although it once discharged a portion of the waters of the Fulailee, which passes by Hyderabad, as also of a branch that quits the Indus near Bukkur, and traverses the

[1] J. R. As. Soc. vol. i. p. 200, note.

[2] Memoir on the eastern branch of the river Indus: Trans. R. As. Soc. vol. iii. p. 550. Also Memoir on the Indus, in the third volume of his Journey to Bokhara.

[3] Travels, vol. iii. p. 77.

desert during the swell. This latter is the branch termed Narra by Lieutenant de L'Hoste, and a former connexion is thus admitted by Sir A. Burnes between the Indus above Bukkur and the Lukput mouth, which he calls the Kori: it is more properly the Khári, which means merely a 'salt' creek or estuary of the sea. Of this creek, which, no doubt, once received the eastern arm of the Indus, Sir A. Burnes remarks, that of all the mouths of the Indus it gives the grandest notion of a mighty river. A little below Lukput it opens like a funnel, and at Koteswar is about seven miles wide, and continues to increase till the coasts of Cutch and Sindh are no longer visible from one another.

To place the head of the Delta of Pattalene above Bukkur, however, and maintain that either the Purana or Narra was the eastern branch of the Indus, whilst the actual river was the western, would be open to valid objections on the score of its remoteness from the sea. This is obviated by adopting Captain McMurdo's theory that the Purana was the main stream, and that it did not divide until it had reached the latitude of Bahmanabad. There, according to him, the Indus first separated into two branches, of which the course of the western is described above; whilst the eastern, passing by the head of the Run and Lukput-Bundur, fell into the Khári or creek above mentioned. Whatever may be thought of the course of the western branch, there seems some reason to expect the eastern in this situation. The large salt-water lake described by Arrian as connected with this branch of the river is not improbably to be looked for in the ancient condition of the Run, as Captain McMurdo and Captain Pottinger have conjectured,[1] and as Sir A. Burnes represents it when he maintains that it was once an inland navigable sea. The Greek historian asserts that it was so navigated by Alexander, and that a port and citadel were established on its shore.[2]

It thus seems very probable that the lower part of the present course of the Indus formed the western boundary of Pattalene, and that its eastern limit was the southern course of the Narra or Purana river. The point of the apex of the triangle is not so satisfactorily determinable, although most

[1] J. R. As. Soc. vol. i. p. 41. Ibid. p. 205.

[2] Trans. R. As. Soc. vol. iii. p. 571.

authorities seem now agreed that it must have been to the north of Tatta. Captain McMurdo, as has been stated, proposes Bahmanabad, the precise site of which does not appear to be fully verified. Captain Pottinger suggests that Jarak, or some place even more to the northward, where the ruins of towns are still visible, may be fixed upon with propriety as the site of Tatta; in which case the Pinyari branch of the Indus, terminating ultimately also at Lukput, would be the eastern branch navigated by Alexander. So also Lieutenant Wood observes, "supposing the Pinyari to have been the eastern arm of the Delta in the days of the Greeks, then we should fix the site of Pattala where now stands the modern town of Jerk."[1] Another recent visitor, Dr. Kennedy, would place Pattala even at Sehwan;[2] but this would leave us scant room for the territories of Musikanus, Oxykanus, and Sambus. Without pretending, therefore, to affirm that the northernmost point of the Delta was so far north as the Bahmanabad of McMurdo, it may be assumed conjecturally, until some more positive information can be obtained. It can scarcely be expected, however, that any site shall be proposed to which no objections will apply, as the channels of the lower part of the Indus are perpetually shifting; and it may be doubted if any one of them now follows precisely the same direction that it took when the vessels of Alexander floated down the stream.[3]

The name of Pattala is no doubt Indian: it has been derived from Pátála, mistakingly identified with the infernal regions. Pátála is the realm of the Snake-gods, or Nágas, under the earth, and is a place of enjoyment, not of suffering. A preferable derivation of it would be Potálaya or Potála, 'a harbour;' and it is curious that the name Potala, the 'harbour,' is applied to a city in the Delta of the Indus in the Buddhist writings of Tibet. It is

[1] Journey to the Source of the Oxus, p. 12.

[2] Late Campaign in Afghanistan, p. 104.

[3] Alexander is said to have taken a three days' journey along shore after his voyage down the eastern channel, and it is matter of keen dispute whether he travelled east towards Cutch or west across the lower part of the Delta. It seems likely that his anxiety to explore the country would have rather carried him onwards towards Cutch than brought him back to what he might consider as already traversed. The question is, however, of no importance to the topography of Pattalene.

said to have been the original site of the Sákyas before they migrated to Kapila-vastu, where Sakya-Sinha, 'the lion of the tribe,' the last Buddha, was born.[1] The truth of the legend may be questioned, but it not improbably intimates some connexion with the Sakas or Indo-Scythians, who were masters of Pattalene subsequent to the Greek princes of Bactria.

From Pattalene the extension of dominion to Cutch and Guzerat was most readily to be effected, and we must therefore look to the east for the territories said to have been annexed to the Bactrian kingdom.

In the realm of Sigertis, we have very probably the name of the country mis-stated as that of the prince,—a practice not infrequent with the Greek writers. Colonel Tod, however, following the Ayin Akbari, in which it is stated that in ancient times a prince of the name of Sehris reigned at Alore, whose dominions extended from Kashmir to the sea, considers him to be the Sigertis of the Greeks. Professor Lassen[2] conjectures the original to be Sri-gartta, and to be applied to the sea-coast towards Barygaza or Baroach. This is not unlikely, as gartta, properly 'a hole or cave,' is used in composition, as in the word Tri-gartta, to denominate a country: we might propose Tri-gartta for Si-gertis, but that the name belongs to a principality in the north of India, that which is now termed Chamba. The locality is more likely to be on the coast than in the direction of Alore, which, as we have seen, was inland, and above Pattalene; but it was perhaps more westerly than is here supposed, being identical with the province of Cutch, the Sanscrit Kach-cha. For Tessariostus some MSS. of Strabo read Saraostus,[3] and there can be little hesitation in admitting the superior accuracy of the latter, as it is evidently the Sanscrit Su-rasthra, the Surastrene of Ptolemy and the Periplus, the country adjacent to the kingdom of Sigertis on the east, or the modern Guzerat.

The extension of the sovereignty of the Greek Bactrian kings over people termed by Strabo Phryni and Seres, has much perplexed the most eminent

[1] On the Origin of the Shakya Race; by M. Csoma Körösi: J. As. Soc. B. Aug. 1833.

[2] Geschichte der Könige in Bactrien, p. 231.

[3] Ex codicibus Medic. vol. iii. p. 4. Paris. Moscov. Σαραόστου, ut vetus interpres, sic ut τε vel adhæserit ex priori voce, vel negligenter omissum sit. Utrum statui debeat in obscura hac ambiguitate incertum. Siebenkees, vol. iv. p. 510, note.

scholars, some of whom have carried the Bactrian supremacy to the Chinese on the one hand, and the Phœnicians on the other. By the Seres, however, Professor Lassen observes, may be understood the people of the Serica of Ptolemy, which may be identified with Kashgar and Yarkand, and then there would be nothing improbable in their having felt the Bactrian power; and the position is confirmed by the passage he cites from the Periegesis of Dionysius, in which the Phryni and Seres are associated with the Tokhari, or people of Tokharestan.[1] This leaves little doubt that some of the Bactrian princes attempted to establish their authority over the nations to the north-east of Transoxiana, although the precise extent of their conquests in that direction was not very distinctly defined. Whatever accessions to their territory they may have thus acquired were not long enough in their possession to become familiar to their historians.

In the first century of the Christian æra the Greeks had been dispossessed of the countries along the Indus by the Scythians; and accordingly, by the geographers and travellers of that period, we find the Indo-Scythi located in this direction, and the denomination Scythia applied to the province of Sindh.[2] It would seem, however, that, by the time of the author of the Periplus, some other political revolutions had been effected, as he describes the government of the country as being in the hands of a tribe of Parthians, divided into two parties: each party, as it prevailed, chose a king out of its own body, and drove out the king of the opposite faction. The account may perhaps admit of correction upon the evidence afforded by the coins of this period; and, instead of two factions of Parthians, we may rather suspect that the contest alluded to was a struggle between Parthian and Scythian princes for the possession of Sindh.

The capital of Indo-Scythia was Minnagara, a city the situation of which, as Dr. Vincent remarks,[3] it is not easy to determine. He is inclined to place

[1] Καὶ Τόχαροι, Φρουνοί τε, καὶ ἔθνεα βάρβαρα Σήρων. Book v. 752. Geschichte der Könige, p. 230.

[2] Ptolemy; Dionysius Periegetes; and the Arrian of the Periplus of the Erythræan Sea. Dr. Vincent, both in the Voyage of Nearchus, p. 141, and the Periplus, vol. ii. p. 345, endeavours to prove that Scythia and Scythians are errors for Sindh and Sindhians. Information subsequently obtained, however, justifies the accuracy of the term Scythians.

[3] Periplus, p. 349.

it about sixty miles above Tatta, upon the authority of M. De la Rochette's map, in which a place called Minhavare, by a Mohammedan geographer, Al-Biruini, is so situated; or he would carry it farther north, to the "modern Loheri, at the south extremity of the Isle of Behker." There is nothing in the notice given of it in the Periplus to direct us to its position, further than that goods were carried up to it from Barbarike, a port at one of the 'middle' mouths of the Indus. The name is, no doubt, partly of Indian origin, for Nagara is a common term for 'city;' and Ptolemy has other Minnagaras—one in Guzerat, and one in the Bay of Bengal. The first syllable, however, is obviously some corruption, and it is not improbably intended for some such term as Swami-nagara, the 'city of the Lord,' the city either of Vishnu or Siva. Sami-nugar is a name still applied to Tatta, or to remains of reputed antiquity in its immediate neighbourhood;[1] and the communication of Minnagar by a central channel, such as the Richel or Hajamri, with the sea, renders it not unlikely that it stood in this vicinity. Captain McMurdo proposes for it a different position, and places it on the Lohana river, not far from Bahmana; but in this he identifies it with the Bi-nagara or Agri-nagara of Ptolemy, which appears to be a different city from the Scythian capital.[2] We should certainly look for the latter nearer to the sea.[3]

[1] Wood, Travels, p. 19; also Burnes, who says, "The Jharejas of Cutch, who trace their lineage from Tatta, invariably designate it in these days by the name of Sami-nugur, of which Minugur is evidently an abbreviation:" Travels, vol. iii. p. 79. McMurdo says of Tatta, it was founded by one of the Samma dynasty, near the site of the capital, which was Sámai-nugur: J. R. As. Soc. vol. i. p. 30.

[2] Ibid. p. 31.

[3] In a communication made to the Geographical Society, Major Rawlinson, it is said, expresses his belief that he has found the site of Minnagara on the confines of the Manchor lake, through which the Aral branch of the Indus passes. The details are not yet available.

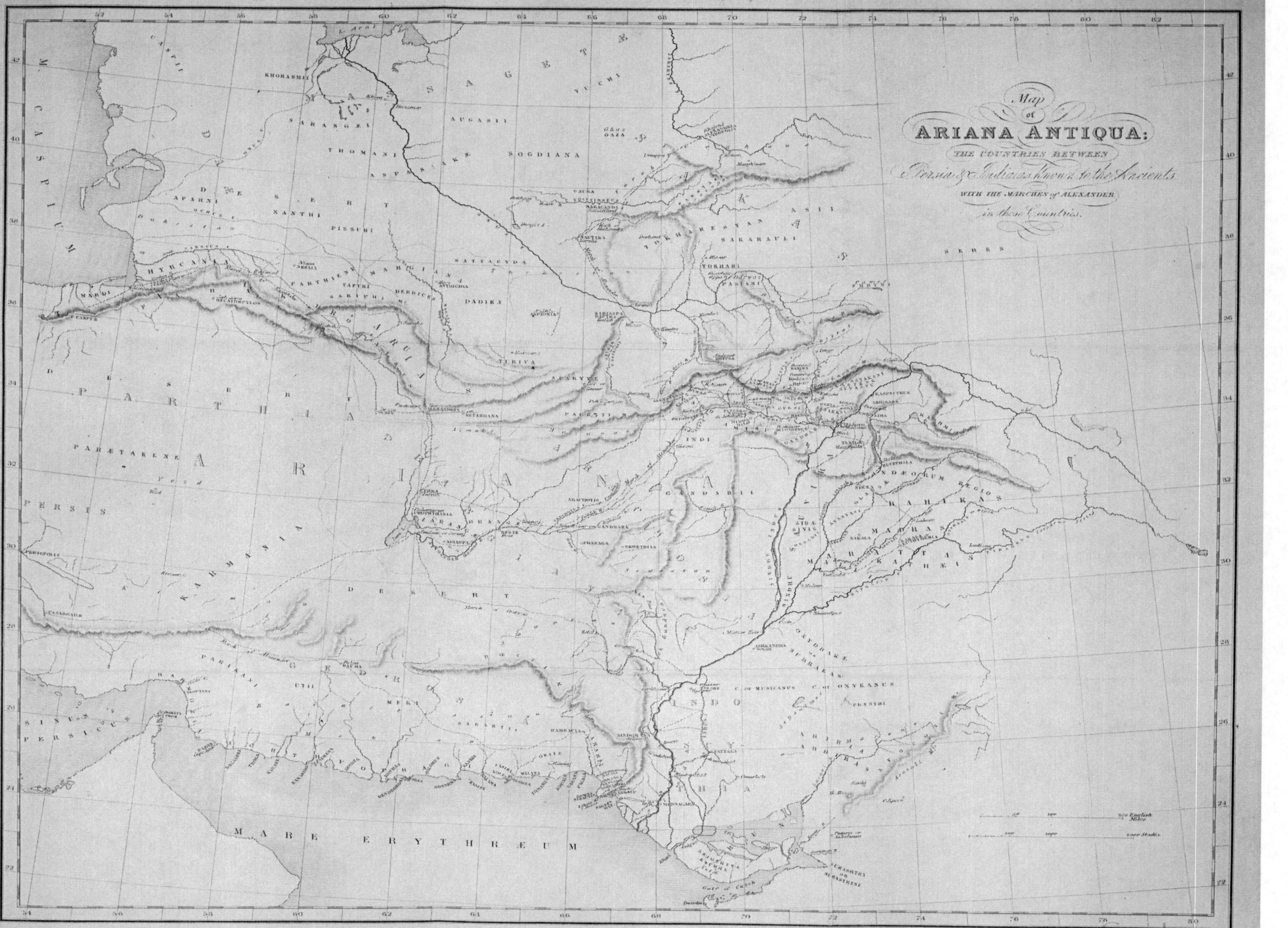
Map of
ARIANA ANTIQUA:
THE COUNTRIES BETWEEN
Persia & India as known to the Ancients
WITH THE MARCHES of ALEXANDER
in those Countries.
M. CASPIUM
SOGDIANA
PARTHIA
ARIANA
PERSIS
KARMANIA
GEDROSIA
INDO SCYTHIA
MARE ERYTHRÆUM
SINUS PERSICUS
SERES

CHAPTER IV.

OF THE SOVEREIGN DYNASTIES OF BACTRIA AND THE CONTERMINOUS COUNTRIES, FROM THE DEATH OF ALEXANDER THE GREAT TO THE MOHAMMEDAN INVASION OF INDIA; WITH DESCRIPTIONS OF THEIR COINS.

SECTION I.—GREEK DYNASTIES.

THEODOTUS I., B.C. 256.

UPON the subjugation of Bactria by Alexander, he appointed Artabazus, a Persian, governor of the province.[1] Being advanced in years, Artabazus held the office but for a short time, and was succeeded by Amyntas, the son of Nicolaüs.[2] Authorities differ with regard to the name of the individual who was governor of Bactria after Alexander's death. According to Arrian, Stasanor, a native of Soli, in Cyprus, was appointed to the government of Bactria and Sogdiana by Antipater.[3] Diodorus calls him Philip,[4] (the governor of Parthia according to Arrian,[5]) and he assigns Aria and Drangiana to Stasanor, in which Dexippus concurs. Justin and Orosius term the governor of the Bactrians, Amyntas.[6] Whoever it might be that was entrusted with the charge, he was, during the contests amongst Alexander's generals, but little interfered with, and enjoyed real if not nominal sovereignty. When Seleucus engaged in his Indian expedition, which ended in his alliance with Chandragupta,[7] he took that opportunity of recalling

[1] Arrian, Exped. Alex. Book III. 29.
[2] Ibid. Book IV. 17.
[3] Arrian, apud Photium, Book IX.
[4] Book XVIII.
[5] Apud Photium, Book XXVII.
[6] Book III. 1.
[7] Justin, Book XV. 4. Strabo, Book XV. 2. 9.

the governor of Bactria to a sense of subordination, and very probably recruited his army with the martial inhabitants of the country. The victory over his competitors, which soon followed his return to Babylon, gave him the undisputed mastery of Asia, and Bactria continued for about fifty years to be, as it had before been, a province of Persia.[1] In confirmation of this dependence, the coins of Seleucus and Antiochus have been found in some numbers at Balkh and Bokhara.

In the reign of the third prince of the Seleucidan dynasty, Antiochus Theus, advantage was taken of his wars with Ptolemy Philadelphus by the governors of the remote provinces to throw off their allegiance, and amongst others the governor of Bactria, Theodotus, or, as he is also named, Diodotus, set the example of revolting, and proclaimed himself king.[2] The death of Antiochus, and the hostilities in which his successor, Seleucus Callinicus, was at first engaged with Ptolemy Euergetes, and then with his own brother, Antiochus Hierax, afforded to Theodotus an opportunity of gathering strength; and he possibly was in some sort confirmed by Seleucus, as an inducement to him to combine in operations against the second Arsacidan king, Tiridates. Whether he assisted Seleucus in that invasion of Parthia by which Tiridates was compelled to become a fugitive, is nowhere stated; but it seems not unlikely, and his death may have been one of the causes which facilitated the recovery of Parthia by Tiridates, as is intimated by Justin.[3] These transactions enable us to form a plausible conjecture as to the termination of his reign, which has been placed B.C. 243.[4] This

[1] Seleucus Nicator's invasion of India took place some time between B.C. 312 and 306, according to the authors of the Ancient Universal History; Clinton, between 312 and 302; and, according to Thirlwall, History of Greece, it was between 311 and 301. The independence of Bactria dates, according to Bayer, B.C. 255; according to Visconti, who is followed by modern scholars, B.C. 256.

[2] In eodem tempore etiam Theodotus mille urbium Bactrianarum præfectus defecit, regemque se appellari jussit; quod exemplum sequuti totius Orientis populi a Macedonibus defecere: Justin, Book XLI. 4. In Bactrianis rebus ut a Diodoto constitutum imperium est: Prol. Trog. Pompeii, Book XLI.

[3] Book XII. 4.

[4] Bayer. According to Vaillant, Historia Arsacidarum, it was 234, but this is, no doubt, too recent.

may be a very few years too soon; for, as Seleucus Callinicus ascended the throne only B.C. 246, it may be doubted if in three years subsequent he was at leisure to prosecute schemes of conquest on his eastern frontier.[1] The difference, however, cannot be considerable; perhaps B.C. 240 may be taken as an approximation.

THEODOTUS II., B.C. 240.

That the accession of the second Theodotus took place in the interval between the first and second expedition of Seleucus into Parthia cannot be doubted, from the change that has been recorded of Bactrian policy in the commencement of his reign.[2] Seleucus having been recalled to Syria by new commotions, afforded Tiridates the means of recovering his dominions. In this he was aided by the second Theodotus, who made common cause with the Parthian, and probably enabled him to defeat and take prisoner the Seleucidan monarch. It has been conjectured that the captivity of Seleucus took place in the middle of his reign, or B.C. 236, and continued to the end of it, or B.C. 226.[3] There is no sufficient authority for these dates, but it seems not unlikely that the capture of Seleucus occurred after the earlier of the two.

That Tiridates availed himself of his triumph over Seleucus to extend and consolidate the Parthian monarchy, was no more than was to have been expected from his vigorous character and long reign; and there is no improbability in the assertion that his alliance with Theodotus II. did not long continue uninterrupted, and that he deprived his former ally of a portion of his possessions. It was chiefly, however, to the west and south, in Hyrcania and Media, that Parthia spread at this season; and Bactria was not seriously endangered. The hostile disposition of Tiridates may, however, have favoured, and his policy may have fomented, discontents in Bactria

[1] He founded the city of Callinicopolis, B.C. 242, at which date he was in Western Asia.

[2] Arsaces exercitum parat metu Seleuci et Theodoti Bactrianorum regis, sed cito morte Theodoti metu liberatus cum filio ejus et ipso Theodoto fœdus ac pactum fecit: Justin, Book XLI. 4.

[3] Froelich, Annales Regum Syriæ, as cited by Clinton, Fasti Hellenici, vol. ii. 'Kings of Syria.'

which cut short the reign of its king, and led to an interval of domestic anarchy, which ended in the accession of a stranger to the throne. Such an inference is warranted by a notice of Euthydemus, which will be presently cited at length from Polybius; and it is to be concluded that he acquired the sovereignty by the suppression of contending rivals for power amongst the descendants of Theodotus.[1]

COINS OF THEODOTUS I.

It is only very recently that a coin of one of the princes named Theodotus has been discovered. Bayer, indeed, gives a plate of a small copper coin, having a barbarously executed head on one side, and on the other the club of Hercules, with letters perpendicularly arranged on each side of it, ΔΙΟ—ΔΙΟΥ. Alluding to this coin, without having it before me, I have rather unwarrantably called it a coin of Menander (p. 3). It corresponds with à small copper coin of Menander in the device of the 'club,' but not in other respects if it is correctly delineated. Its appropriation to Theodotus, however, is very doubtful.

This is not the case with a very different coin, for the following account of which I am indebted to the kindness of M. Raoul Rochette, whose description and delineation of the coin, although anxiously expected, are not yet made public. In a letter with which he has favoured me, he observes, "The gold medal of Diodotus, recently obtained, corresponds entirely in weight, fabrication, and style with the gold coins of Antiochus II. The portrait also bears so close a resemblance to the portraits of Antiochus, that it is

[1] This depends, however, upon the meaning given to the word ἐκγόνους, which Bayer argues denotes in this place 'a son,' (p. 67,) maintaining that Theodotus II. was deposed and put to death by Euthydemus. The form of the word, however, perfectly authorises the equivalent 'progeny or descendants:' so the French translation of Strabo explains the passage, "Euthydème devint maître de la Bactriane par la destruction des chefs de parti qui avaient herité de la puissance des premiers usurpateurs." And M. R. Rochette understands the word in the same sense, although he applies it to the first and second Theodotus, as descendants of Agathocles, who, according to an hypothesis he has started, as we shall hereafter more particularly mention, was the founder of the Bactrian kingdom: J. des Sav. Oct. 1835, p. 594.

likely the artist copied the head of that prince. The obverse is occupied by the head of the king. The reverse has a naked figure of Jupiter erect, with his back to the spectator, and turned to the left; he is in the act of hurling his thunderbolt from his right arm raised, whilst his left arm extended bears the ægis: on one side, in the field of the coin, is a crown, and at the foot of the figure an eagle. The legend on either margin of the reverse is ΒΑΣΙΛΕΩΣ ΔΙ°Δ°Τ°Υ, perfectly distinct. The coin is in excellent preservation. It was procured, along with other coins of less interest, by an Armenian, at the fair of Nishni Novgorod, for a private collector at St. Petersburgh; from him it passed into the possession of M. Rollin of Paris, by whom it has been sold to the Royal Cabinet of Paris.

In a notice of this coin published in the Revue Numismatique, the editor, M. Longperrier, observes, that we have in this country, without knowing it, a coin of the same prince, in a silver tetradrachm, presented by Sir Alexander Burnes to the British Museum. It is figured in the plates of the second volume of his Journey to Bokhara, Pl. III. fig. 8, and is designated by the late Mr. Prinsep and myself as a coin of Antiochus. It corresponds, no doubt, with the description above given of the gold coin of Diodotus in all particulars except the legend, which is distinct as far as it extends, and is clearly ΒΑΣΙΛ - - - ΑΝΤΙΟ - - -, identifying the coin with the coins of that prince. At the same time it seems probable that there is no incompatibility between these currencies, but that they may be reconciled by referring them to different periods in the history of Diodotus. As long as that prince professed obedience to the Seleucidan king, he struck coins in the name and with the device appropriate to Antiochus; when he declared himself independent, he continued the same coin, but substituted his own name for that of his liege lord. The silver coin is, therefore, the Bactrian coinage of Diodotus the satrap; the gold, the Bactrian coinage of Diodotus the king.

EUTHYDEMUS, B.C. 220-190.

It has been affirmed[1] from a passage in Strabo,[2] that Euthydemus was the founder of the Bactrian kingdom; but this is irreconcileable with the positive assertions of other authorities, and the passage probably refers only to his having founded a new dynasty by wresting the sovereignty either from Theodotus II. or some of his descendants,—a transaction which, when hard-pressed by Antiochus the Great, he pleaded in deprecation of that prince's resentment.

Although not in possession of any connected account of the reign of Euthydemus, various interesting circumstances relating to it have been preserved by Polybius; and as he flourished but a few years subsequent to the events he records, he may be regarded as sufficient authority as far as the imperfect remains we have of his writings extend. According to him, Euthydemus was a Magnesian, who, upon being defeated by Antiochus, sent to him to represent that the king acted unjustly towards him in seeking to dispossess him of his dominions, for he was not the author of the revolt of Bactria, but had acquired that kingdom by overcoming the descendants of those who had first rebelled.[3] This serves as a satisfactory comment upon the text of Strabo.

After the partial subjugation of Artabanus, the third Arsacidan prince, Antiochus moved eastward against Bactria.[4] Euthydemus stationed a body

[1] Vaillant, Historia Arsacidarum, Annales, p. 1.

[2] *Νεωτερισθέντων δὲ τῶν ἔξω τοῦ Ταύρου διὰ τὸ πρὸς ἀλλήλους εἶναι τοὺς τῆς Συρίας καὶ τῆς Μηδίας βασιλέας, τοὺς ἔχοντας καὶ ταῦτα, πρῶτον μὲν τὴν Βακτριανὴν ἀπέστησαν οἱ πεπιστευμένοι, καὶ τὴν ἐγγὺς αὐτῆς πᾶσαν (χώραν) οἱ περὶ Εὐθύδημον.* Book XI. 1. 2. On this the French translation remarks, D'après un autre passage les mots, *καὶ τὴν ἐγγὺς*, annonçant des faits posterieurs à la première defection des satrapes de la Bactriane et même de la révolte d'Arsaces, doivent être regardé comme une espèce de parenthése; a phrase borrowed from Bayer, p. 46. See also Ste. Croix, Mém. de l'Académie, tom. l. p. 49.

[3] *Καὶ γὰρ αὐτὸς ἦν ὁ Εὐθύδημος Μάγνης· πρὸς ὃν ἀπελογίζετο φάσκων, ὡς οὐ δικαίως αὐτὸν Ἀντίοχος ἐκ τῆς βασιλείας ἐκβαλεῖν σπούδαζει· γεγονέναι γὰρ οὐκ αὐτὸς ἀποστάτης τοῦ βασιλέως ἀλλ' ἑτέρων ἀποστάντων ἐπανελόμενος τοὺς ἐκείνων ἐκγόνους, οὕτω κρατῆσαι τῆς Βακτριανῶν ἀρχῆς.* Book XI. 34.

[4] Polybius, X. 49.

of horse to guard the banks of the Arius, and encamped with his main army at the city of Tapauria. In this we have, no doubt, some trace of the modern name of the province of Taberistan, whilst the Arius is the river of Herat; showing that the kingdom of Bactria extended in this direction to the Alburz mountains at least, and in all probability it had been, prior to the invasion of Antiochus, carried into Drangiana and Arachosia. Antiochus marched to the river, and, in an action with the Bactrian cavalry, was wounded in the mouth; but he defeated them, and Euthydemus, alarmed, fell back upon Zariaspa, the capital of Bactria.[1] Hence he sent the remonstrance above cited, and a solicitation to be permitted to retain the name and authority of king; urging that his independence was of political importance to Antiochus as well as to himself; as if his principality was enfeebled, it would no longer be able to act as a barrier against the Nomadic Scythians on the frontier, and the provinces of Persia would speedily be overrun by them: thus indicating the perilous position of the Bactrian princes, and the proximity even at this early period of the enemies by whom they were subsequently overpowered. Antiochus admitted the reasonableness of the plea, and, having demanded from Euthydemus all his elephants, crossed the Caucasus on his expedition to India, where he formed an alliance with Sophagasenus, a name undeniably of Indian origin, although not identifiable with any in the usual lists of kings.[2]

The accession of Euthydemus, as calculated by Bayer, and adopted by Visconti, is B. C. 220. M. R. Rochette would carry it a few years farther back, but he proposes no fixed limit, and offers no positive objection.[3] Professor Lassen, on the other hand, reduces it as low as B. C. 209; but this is scarcely reconcileable with the invasion of Antiochus, which must have been prior to this date, and which found apparently Euthydemus fully in possession of the sovereignty of Bactria. There is nothing im-

[1] If this is correctly stated, we should expect to find Zariaspa somewhat more in the direction of Herat than Balkh, as it would have indicated little courage or conduct in the Bactrian to have at once fallen back so far. Zariaspa would be rather in the situation of Meru or Andkoh.

[2] These events must have taken place about B. C. 211 or 210, as the eastern campaigns of Antiochus commenced about B.C. 212.

[3] J. des Sav. Oct. 1835, p. 594.

probable in his having been king for some years at that period. That he reigned also for a like term subsequently is also probable, as the return of Antiochus to Western Asia in B. C. 205, and his engaging in schemes for the extension of his dominions towards Egypt, must have first favoured, or indeed permitted, the attempts of the Bactrian king to extend his authority in the direction of the Paropamisus, either in person or by the instrumentality of his son.

The coins of Euthydemus confirm the notices which antiquity has preserved. The silver coins are found in considerable numbers and variety; some of them are of great beauty, and belong to the purest, and therefore, no doubt, to the earliest style of the Bactrian coinage. Some of the coins are of a less careful execution, whilst a third class is in every respect of barbaric origin, and may have been struck by some of the bordering Scythic chiefs, in imitation of the currency of Bactria. The silver coins have been almost without exception found on the north of the Hindu Kush, in Kunduz, at Balkh, and Bokhara, or within the limits of Bactria proper. Some have been purchased at Kabul, but they were probably brought from the north. A few copper coins have been found on the south side of the mountains, but only at Beghram, and may have been brought there in the course of trade. The title when legible, as it is in all the best executed coins, is simply 'King Euthydemus.' The head is bare, but bound with the ribband or fillet, which with both Persians and Hindus denoted sovereignty; the features of the profile are strongly marked, but the face is beardless. On the copper coins it is bearded, and it is evident that upon them the head of Jupiter is substituted for the head of the king. The prevailing device on the reverse of the silver coins is the figure of Hercules, sitting on a rock; representing him resting upon Mount Atlas from his labours, according to M. R. Rochette. The same authority informs us that the device was not uncommon upon the coins of Greek cities.[1] It also occurs upon the coins of Antiochus Theus, of Syria, and may have been imitated from them.[2] In a few instances Hercules is represented standing, holding a wreath; and one silver coin is specified, in which the head is that of Apollo, and the

[1] J. des Sav. July, 1834, p. 385, note.

[2] Mionnet, v. p. 16, also Supplem. viii. p. 14.

reverse represents a tripod: a similar coin occurs in copper, and in another we have a standing figure of Apollo. The reverse of the copper coins found at Beghram bear a horse galloping, a device perhaps connected with that of Apollo as the sun. Traces of both types, of Apollo and the horse, are found on the coins of the first Seleucidan kings. The monograms vary, but amongst them are the letters Κ Φ Ν and the syllable Kra, denoting probably the places where they were coined.

COINS OF EUTHYDEMUS.

GOLD.

1. Head of king to the right, beardless, with fillet. R. Hercules naked, sitting on a rock on which his left hand rests, his right holds his club, the large end supported on a pile of stones. ΒΑΣΙΛΕΩΣ ΕΥΘΥΔΗΜΟΥ. Monogram 1. Pl. I. fig. 1.

This coin, which is still unique, was first figured and described by Pellerin, Additions aux Médailles des Rois. It has since been noticed by different writers: Mionnet, vol. v.; Visconti, Iconographie Grecque; and R. Rochette, J. des Sav. June, 1834.

SILVER.

2-4. Tetradrachm. Head of king to the right, beardless, with fillet. R. Hercules to the left, seated on a rock, over which the lion's hide is thrown; his left hand is on the seat, his right holds his club, the butt-end of which rests on his right knee. ΒΑΣΙΛΕΩΣ ΕΥΘΥΔΗΜΟΥ. Mon. 2, 3. Pl. I. figs. 2, 3, 4.

These coins are no longer very rare. Those represented are from coins in the British Museum, of which No. 3 belongs to the collection of R. P. Knight, Esq., and has been engraved, Numi Veteres, p. 194. The others were brought from Bokhara by Lieutenant (now Sir Alexander) Burnes, by whom they were presented to the Museum: J. As. Soc. B. June, 1833. Burnes's Travels to Bokhara, vol. ii. Appendix. Similar coins have been described and figured by Koehler, Médailles Grecques des Rois de la Bactriane, St. Petersburgh, 1822, and Supplement, 1823; by Sestini, Collezione di Barone Chaudoir; and by R. Rochette, J. des Sav. July, 1834.[1]

5-8. Tetradrachm. Similar devices with the preceding, but of ruder execution, and more or less worn. Pl. I. figs. 5, 6, 7, 8.

These are also from the donation of Sir A. Burnes to the British Museum. In his supplemental collection there are ten coins of this kind, of different degrees of rudeness, and of standard purity: on some of them the inscription is distinctly legible. Similar coins are figured and described by the authorities last referred to. Besides the degree of merit in the execution, they differ from the more perfect coins of Euthydemus in the features and expression of the countenance, in the attitude of the seated Hercules, and the disposition of the lion's skin. When they present legible legends the characters are either Greek or are unknown, but, in the latter case, are probably intended for Greek. Even where the inscription is wanting, the general appearance of the coins indicates their belonging to Euthydemus. Sestini, who has engraved three specimens, was disposed to think them the coins of a different and unknown prince, "sono di ré incognito dalla Battriana;" but M. R. Rochette regards them as "la monnoie d'Euthydème alterée dans la type comme dans la légende par des mains ignorantes," and conceives them to have been current amongst the Barbarians to the north and east of the Greek kingdom of Bactria, having been chiefly found in that direction: J. des Sav. June, 1834, and September, 1835, p. 515. Sestini concurs in their locality, "per quanto sappiamo vengono questi ritrovati nella Bucaria dove i Battriani si crede che avessero fondata una colonia al mare Caspio." In the Supplement to the corrections and additions to his account of the collection of Baron Chaudoir, M. R. Rochette's view of the origin of these coins is adopted.

[1] Subsequently to the notice in the text, an extensive and interesting supplementary collection of coins, procured by Sir Alexander Burnes, chiefly from Kunduz, Badakhshan, Balkh, and Bokhara, has been sent to the India House; amongst them are many of the coins of Euthydemus, of each description, as will be particularised. There is one well-preserved specimen of the coin here described. A subsequent supply of coins also, from Mr. Masson, includes five of these tetradrachms of Euthydemus, purchased at Kabul.

9, 10. Tetradrachm. Head of king to the right, wearing a sort of cap or crown, as well as the fillet. R. Sitting Hercules; barbaric inscription. ꓶJUUႶИMH ·Pl. I. figs. 9, 10.

These were brought from Bokhara by Sir A. Burnes; and several others procured from the same place, as well as from other places north of the Hindu Kush, occur in his supplemental collection. They are apparently classed by M. R. Rochette with the preceding, J. des Sav. Sept. 1835, p. 515. They are allied to them by the rudeness of their execution, and by the device of the reverse, but the costume of the head is very different from that of Euthydemus, and so is the expression of the face. It is also worthy of remark, that they bear a legend which, as far as has yet been observed, is always the same. It is so in the two specimens of the Plate, and in one represented in Baron Chaudoir's Supplement. He also observes, that the legend "est toujours figurée avec les mêmes caractères." The inscription may possibly be intended for ΕΥΘΥΔΗΜΟΥ, but, if so, the modification of the Greek letters is curious. In the rude delineation of the Hercules they resemble the coins of the kings of Characene.

11. Tetradrachm. Head of Euthydemus as before. R. Hercules as before, but his seat is uncovered by the lion's skin, and his club rests on a pile of rocks or stones, as in the gold coin. ΒΑΣΙΛΕΩΣ ΕΥΘΥΔΗΜΟΥ. Mon. double, 4, 5.

Described and delineated, J. des Sav. July, 1834.

12. Tetradrachm. Head of king as before; Hercules seated on a pile of rocks, the end of the club on a similar pile in front of him. ΒΑΣΙΛΕΩΣ ΕΥΘΥΔΗΜΟΥ. Mon. 6, 7.

One specimen of this coin, procured near Kabul by Mohun Lall for Dr. Gerard, was described and engraved by Prinsep, J. As. Soc. B. June, 1835, Pl. XXV. fig. 1. Another has been since received from Sir A. Burnes. Supplemental Plate, fig. 1.

13. Tetradrachm. Head of king to the right, with part of the bust clothed with the chlamys. R. Hercules standing, front view. The left hand holds the club, and the lion's skin hangs over the arm; the right hand is extended, and holds a wreath. ΒΑΣΙΛΕΩΣ ΕΥΘΥΔΗΜΟΥ. Mon. 8. Pl. I. fig. 11.

This coin, which is unique, was procured at Kabul by Karamat Ali, and sold to Dr. Swiney, from whose collection it is here engraved. It is also described by Prinsep, J. As. Soc. B. Nov. 1836. Pl. XLVI. fig. 3.

14. Drachm. Head of king to the right, with fillet and chlamys, as in the preceding. R. Hercules standing as in the last. Pl. I. fig. 12.

This coin differs from the preceding only in size. The devices are the same, but there is no monogram on the reverse. It was brought from Bokhara by Dr. Honigberger, and is described, J. des Sav. Sept. 1835, Pl. I. fig. 3, and by Mionnet, Supplement, vol. viii. p. 463. Pl. XXI. fig. 3.

15. Drachm. Head of king to the right. R. Hercules seated, and resting his club on a pile of rocks. ΒΑΣΙΛΕΩΣ ΕΥΘΥΔΗΜΟΥ. Supplemental Plate, fig. 2.

From the supplemental collection of Sir A. Burnes.

16. Didrachm. Head of laurelled Apollo to the left. R. Tripod. ΒΑΣΙΛΕΩΣ ΕΥΘΥΔΗΜΟΥ.

Described by M. R. Rochette, J. des Sav. Dec. 1838, p. 741.

COPPER.

17. Round, middle size; convex on the face, slightly concave on the reverse; head to the right, bearded, and without fillet. R. Horse galloping to the right. ΒΑΣΙΛΕΩΣ - - - - - Pl. I. fig. 13.

18. Round, irregular, middle size; head to the right, bearded. R. Horse galloping. ΒΑΣΙΛΕΩΣ ΕΥΘΥΔΗΜΟΥ. Pl. I. fig. 14.

19. Round, small, flat on both sides; head to the right, bearded. R. Horse galloping. ΒΑΣΙΛΕΩΣ -ΥΘΥΔΗΜΟΥ. Pl. I. fig. 15.

Of the larger of these there are about twenty, more or less worn, in the Masson collection. They were all found by Mr. Masson at Beghram, and have not been yet met with elsewhere. The small coin, which is unique and of superior execution, is also in the same collection, and was procured at Jelalabad. The legend identifies them all with the silver money of Euthydemus, but the character and expression of the head are very different from the heads on the silver coins, and it may be doubted if the portrait is not intended to represent that of Hercules, or on the small coin at least, of Jupiter, rather than of the king.

20. Round, small; head; but very indistinct. R. Standing figure of Apollo to the left; head rayed; the right hand holds his arrow, the left his bow resting on the ground. - ΑΣΙΛΕΩΣ ---- ΔΗΜΟΥ. Pl. II. fig. 1.

This coin, which is in the Masson collection, and was found at Beghram, is so much corroded on the obverse as not to admit of any representation. There is little doubt, however, that the device was a head like that on the preceding coins. The reverse is also much worn and indistinct, but the final letters of the name may be made out, leaving no uncertainty as to its appropriation. The form of the coin corresponds also with that of Nos. 16 and 17, being slightly convex on one side, and still less concave on the other. The coin is unique.

21. Small, round; laurelled head of Apollo to the right, with the hair carefully arranged. R. Tripod. ΒΑΣΙΛΕΩΣ ΕΥΘΥΔΗΜΟΥ. Mon. Φ.

Noticed by M. R. Rochette, J. des Sav. July, 1834; described by Mionnet from Koehler, Supplement, vol. viii. p. 465.

22. Section of a large round coin; head of king to the right. R. Part of a standing figure. ---- ΕΥΘΥΔΗΜΟΥ.

The injured condition of this coin deprives it of interest, further than as it affords a probability that copper coins of Euthydemus, differing from any of the above, may yet be found. There is no doubt of the appropriation, as the name is distinctly legible. It was amongst Mr. Masson's last supply of coins from Beghram and Kabul.

DEMETRIUS, B.C. 190.

After the negotiations between Euthydemus and Antiochus had been carried on for some time, the former sent to the camp of the latter his son Demetrius, to bring them to a conclusion. Antiochus, according to Polybius, was much pleased with the youth, and pronounced him, from his appearance and manners, worthy of royalty: he also promised to give to him one of his daughters in marriage.[1] We have, therefore, full evidence of

[1] Ἐπηγγείλατο δώσειν αὐτῷ μίαν τῶν ἑαυτοῦ θυγατέρων.

the relation borne by Demetrius to Euthydemus, and that about the year B. C. 210 he was very young, probably little more than a boy, and not of marriageable years.

The place filled by Demetrius in the history of Bactria is a subject of some difficulty. The notices of him by classical writers are few and scanty, and connect him less with Bactria than with India. Bayer therefore concludes that he never reigned in the former country;[1] in which he has been followed by Visconti[2] and other eminent scholars. Now these conclusions are proved to be wholly erroneous; for all the coins of Demetrius designate him as 'king,' and represent him with the fillet of royalty, and hitherto they have been almost wholly found in Bactria proper. He was, therefore, undoubtedly 'king,' and was as certainly king of Bactria after his father.

But there is positive testimony that he effected conquests and held sovereignty in India, that is, on the south of the Hindú Kush. Strabo, speaking of the extension of the territories of the Bactrian kings towards India, says, some of them were acquired by Menander, some by Demetrius, the son of the king of Bactria, Euthydemus;[3] and Justin terms Demetrius king of the Indians, who besieged Eukratides for five months in vain, and in the end was deprived by that prince of his Indian possessions.[4]

It has been concluded from the first passage, that Menander was contemporary with Demetrius, and that he usurped from him the succession to the Bactrian kingdom; but this by no means follows from Strabo's text,

[1] "Demetrium Euthydemi filium neque successisse Menandro neque omnino Bactriorum fuisse regem, veterum testimonio constat; suspiciones deinde faciunt graves ut non fuisse concludam."

[2] "On peut cependant assurer que Demétrius son fils ne regna pas après lui sur la Bactriane, quoiqu'il paroit vraisemblable qu'il s'empara d'une région de l'Inde d'ou quelque temps après il fit la guerre aux successeurs de son père." And the French translation of Strabo has, "Demétrius ne paroit point avoir jamais porté la couronne." So also Schlegel, "Demétrius ne succéda point à Euthydème dans la Bactriane:" J. Asiatique, Nov. 1828.

[3] Τὰ μὲν γὰρ αὐτὸς, τὰ δὲ Δημήτριος ὁ Εὐθυδήμου υἱὸς τοῦ Βακτρων βασιλεως. Book XI. 1. 1.

[4] "Multa tamen Eucratides bella magna virtute gessit: quibus attritus cum obsidionem Demetrii regis Indorum pateretur, cum trecentis militibus sexaginta millia hostium assiduis eruptionibus vicit. Quinto itaque mense liberatus Indiam in potestatem redegit." Book XLI. 6.

which simply states that the two princes specified were conquerors in India, without regard to their chronological order.[1] It may indeed be inferred, that the conquests of Demetrius were made not whilst he was king, but in his father's lifetime, since Strabo designates him as the 'son of the king;' and this will explain why none of his coins have been found even at Beghram, where those of his father are comparatively not uncommon. That the Indian victories of Demetrius are alluded to upon his coins, by the peculiarity of his helmet, which is formed in imitation of the head and trunk of an elephant, is not improbable; but the use of the elephant in war was not unknown to the Bactrian kings, as Euthydemus is said to have been compelled to relinquish all his elephants to Antiochus. No great weight, therefore, can be attached to this peculiarity. If any extension of territory in India was effected by Demetrius during the life of Euthydemus, it must have been towards the close of that king's reign, as the prince would have been too young to have been sent upon such an expedition at an earlier period. There was also at this time additional inducement to an invasion, not of India proper, but of the countries on the west of the Indus, south of the Paropamisus. Antiochus, on his return to India, had ceded these provinces to his ally, Sophagasenas, and the Greek princes of Bactria must have looked upon this cession with uneasy feelings, as it was a mutilation, not only of their own dominions, but of the general body of the Greek eastern empire; and it was to be expected that they would endeavour to effect their recovery. It is likely therefore that the Paropamisus, Arachosia, and Drangiana would have been the direction to which the arms of Euthydemus and Demetrius were chiefly carried; and the persevering attempts of the latter to recover their southern provinces may have afforded an opportunity to Eukratides to dispossess him of Bactria itself.[2] After a short reign, therefore, in his patri-

[1] So Grotefend, replying to Müller, remarks, "Ich kann in diesen worten nicht finden dass Demetrios und Menandros ihre grossen Eroberungen zugleich und selbst in einem gewissen zusammenhange mit einander in einer stillschweigenden uebereinkunft unternahmen." Die Münzen der Könige von Baktrien, p. 96. Lassen is also of this opinion; Zur Geschichte, p. 234.

[2] Lassen conjectures that he reigned in Bactria for ten years, from about 185 to 175, when he was dispossessed and driven to the south by Eukratides. Zur Geschichte, p. 282.

monial possessions, he was driven to fix himself to the south of the mountains, as Bayer suggests, and where it is said stood the city of Demetrias, of which he was possibly the founder.[1] In this position he remained for the rest of his life, persisting in fruitless attempts to harass Eukratides, especially when the latter also crossed the mountains, and established his authority in the Kokistan of Kabul.

To this view of the case it has been objected that there is evidence of Demetrius having held dominion even on the east of the Indus, as he gave the appellation Euthydemia to the Indian city of Sagala, on the Hydaspes, in honour of his father.[2] There is not the slightest evidence, however, that the change of name was the work of Demetrius; and in the interval that elapsed between his date and that of Ptolemy there was space enough for vague and unfounded traditions of the conquests of Euthydemus himself, to have occasioned the adoption of his name for a city which had been rebuilt. Neither from a consideration of probability, nor from the evidence afforded by the coins of Demetrius, can we attach any credit to his Indian sovereignty.

Another objection is drawn from his probable age at the supposed date of his hostilities with Eukratides. As it appears from the manner in which they are referred to by Justin, that the Indian wars of Eukratides shortly preceded his assassination and the succession of his parricidal son, they occurred, according to Bayer, not long before B.C. 148, at which time Demetrius could not have been less than seventy-eight years of age, when it is supposed he would have been too old to have been engaged in hostilities.[3] If Justin's story is true, that Demetrius besieged Eukratides with sixty thousand men, and was repulsed by him with no more than three hundred, he displayed little military skill or prowess, and the infirmities of age may be thought to have affected his operations. That however would not necessarily

[1] Isidore of Charax enumerates Demetrias amongst the cities of Arachosia: Φάρσανα πόλις καὶ Δημητριὰς πόλις, εἶτα Ἀλεξανδρόπολις, μητρόπολις Ἀραχωσίας, ἔστι δ' Ἑλληνίς. Bayer, p. 64.

[2] Ptolemy has Σάγαλα ἡ καὶ Εὐθυμεδεία, "Sagala, which is also Euthumedia." The latter is corrected with much probability of accuracy to Εὐθυδημεία. Bayer, p. 233. This proof is justly considered by Lassen to be inconclusive: Zur Geschichte der Könige von Bactrien, p. 233. Grotefend attaches more importance to it; p. 95.

[3] Bayer, p. 92.

second coin of the same kind is described by M. R. Rochette, from the collection of M. Court, J. des Sav. Dec. 1838, p. 743.

2. Tetradrachm. Head of king, with fillet and chlamys, to the right. R. Helmeted Minerva, front view; her right hand rests on her spear, her left on her shield. ΒΑΣΙΛΕΩΣ ΔΗΜΗΤΡΙΟΥ. Mon. 9, 10. Pl. II. fig. 3.

Brought by Dr. Honigberger from Bokhara; described, J. des Sav. Sept. 1835. Pl. I. fig. 4.

3. Obolus. Head of king, with elephant casque and fillet, to the right, neck bare. R. Standing Hercules, as in No. 1. ΒΑΣΙΛΕΩΣ ΔΗΜΗΤΡΙΟΥ. Mon. 3. Pl. II. fig. 4.

From the collection of Dr. Swiney.

M. R. Rochette calls this a hemidrachm or triobolus, and yet he specifies the weight twelve grains. The actual weight of this coin is rather more than 10·5 grains. The weight of the obolus is 11·08 grains: Hussey on ancient Weights and Money, p. 23.

4. Obolus. Head of king as in the last, but the bust clothed. R. Standing Hercules as before. ΒΑΣΙΛΕΩΣ ΔΗΜΗΤΡΙΟΥ. Mon. 11. Pl. II. fig. 5.

From the collection of General Ventura; J. As. Soc. B. June, 1835, Pl. XXV. fig. 2; J. des Sav. Feb. 1836, Pl. II. fig. 2; J. Asiatique, Feb. 1836, p. 156. These two small coins, although bearing the same devices, are evidently of different dies; the monograms also are different. A coin corresponding in all respects with the second of them is in Sir A. Burnes's supplementary collection, and another in Mr. Masson's last supply.

COPPER.

5. Head to the right, bearded, and crowned with laurel; the end of a club over the left shoulder. R. Figure (of Apollo ?) partly clothed, standing to the front, head rayed; the right hand raised to the head, the left, hanging down, holds a bow (?). ΒΑΣΙΛΕΩΣ ΔΗΜΗΤΡΙΟΥ. Mon. 12. Supplemental Plate, fig. 3. There is an indistinct appearance of characters in the exergue. The style of the figure, although the attitude is different, resembles that upon the coin of Euthydemus, Pl. II. fig. 1. It has in some respects the appearance of a female.

This is amongst the coins last sent home by Mr. Masson, and was procured from Beghram. Another specimen, but in less perfect preservation, arrived with Sir A. Burnes's supplemental collection.

6. Head of elephant to the right. R. A caduceus. ΒΑΣΙΛΕΩΣ ΔΗΜΗΤΡΙΟΥ.

A description and drawing of this coin are given in the J. As. Soc. B. of January, 1840. It was found at Bamian by Captain Hay, and is remarkable as offering the types found on the coin of a prince of probably later date. See Mayes.

EUKRATIDES, B.C. 181.

We cannot hesitate to place Eukratides as a Bactrian king after Demetrius, although it does not appear that he stood in any degree of consanguinity to Euthydemus. During a portion of his reign, at least, he was also contemporary with Demetrius, whom he supplanted; first probably in Bactria, and afterwards in Paropamisan India.

The story told above of his discomfiting with a small band the numerous forces of Demetrius looks as if he was commencing the career of a military adventurer, whilst the Bactrian king was in possession of considerable power, and may therefore be presumed to have been some time on the throne. This furnishes one clue to the date of the accession of Eukratides: another is derived from his being expressly described as reigning about the same time as Mithridates, the sixth Arsacidan prince; and Mithridates reigned from about B. C. 165 to B. C. 135.[1] It seems likely, if we believe the accounts that are given of the eastern conquests of Mithridates, that he must have flourished towards the close of the reign of Eukratides, and subsequently to its termination, as the extension of his arms to India, even to the

[1] Eodem fere tempore sicuti in Parthis Mithridates, ita in Bactris Eukratides, magni uterque viri, regnum ineunt: Justin, Book XLI. 6. His death is sometimes placed about 141. A coin, preferably attributed to his successor, Phraates II., bears the Parthian date 173, which corresponds to B. C. 140: Mionnet, Supplement, viii. 432. There seems reason, however, to think that he lived some years longer, as the captivity of Demetrius Nicator did not occur until 138, and Mithridates died after that event, some time between it and 130. Clinton, Fasti Hellenici, 'Kings of Syria.'

Hydaspes, is quite incompatible with the character given to Eukratides, with his victories over Demetrius, and with the position which his coins assure us he occupied on the upper course of the river of Kabul.

For the commencement of his reign, then, there is no reason to dissent from the valuation conjectured for it by Bayer, or B. C. 181.[1] The close of it is less satisfactorily appreciable: if the conquests of Mithridates occurred in his reign, it must have extended to some period between B. C. 160 and 135; the former is preferred by Lassen. M. R. Rochette suggests 155, and Bayer 147. If, as is most likely, the Indian victories of the Parthian occurred in the reign of his successor, and after the captivity of Demetrius Nicator, the latter will be the least exceptionable date.

That the reign of Eukratides was a long one is evidenced by the abundance of his coins. They are found plentifully in Bactria proper, and in immense numbers at Beghram, affording evidence both of his Bactrian and his Indian sovereignty. According to Strabo, his authority extended beyond the Indus, where he was lord of a thousand cities.[2] This has not been confirmed by the discovery of his coins in the Punjab, but undoubtedly he was sovereign of the country west of the Indus, and may have held possessions on the east of the river. According to classical authority, his Indian conquests were amongst the last acts of his life, as upon his return from them he was put to death by his son.[3] It is not likely, however, that he would have engaged in such enterprises if Mithridates had been pressing upon him in a different direction; and still less is it possible that he and the Parthian at the very same time subjugated the very same country. The Indian victories of Eukratides must have been effected before Mithridates advanced so far to the east; and if he died on his return from them, he died some years earlier than his Parthian contemporary.

Although we cannot admit that Mithridates invaded India during the reign of Eukratides, yet there is little reason to doubt that under him the provinces contiguous to Parthia on the east and north-east, Aria, parts of Drangiana and Arachosia, Margiana, and part of Bactria proper, were annexed

[1] Lassen says 175: Geschichte, p. 282. R. Rochette, 170: J. des Sav. Oct. 1835.

[2] Εὐκρατίδαν γοῦν πόλεις χιλίας ὑφ' ἑαυτῷ ἔχειν. Strabo, Book III.

[3] Unde quum se reciperet, a filio, quem socium regni fecerat, in itinere interficeretur: Justin, Book XLI. 6.

to the Parthian kingdom. It is also highly probable, from historical evidence, that the Scythians took advantage of the contests, first between Eukratides and Demetrius, and then between Bactria and Parthia, to encroach upon the northern boundaries of the former. A passage is usually cited from Justin to show that the Bactrian kingdom was nearly destroyed in this reign; but the description is incompatible with the character given by the same writer to Eukratides, with his success against Demetrius, and with his conquests in India.[1] It no doubt refers to a later period, if it be not oratorically exaggerated: at the same time there is positive testimony, and it is consistent with probability, that the Parthians dismembered Bactria, and detached from it two of its satrapies, even in the reign of Eukratides. It is not specified under what Parthian king, but it may have been under Mithridates. It is also said they made war upon the Scythians; in which case either they or the Scythians may have been masters of part of Bactria.[2] It is therefore conformable to history, to probability, and to numismatic illustration, to conclude that Eukratides, master at first of Bactria, when weakened by his contests with Demetrius on the south, and the Scythians on the north, and by previous attempts upon India, was exposed, towards the close of his reign, to the superior strength and activity of Mithridates, and was compelled to relinquish a considerable portion of Bactria proper; and that in consequence, restricted to the mountains of the Paropamisus, he sought to indemnify himself by carrying his arms across the Indus: on returning from whence, after a successful incursion, rather than a permanent conquest, he returned to be put to death by the son whom he had associated in the kingdom; a practice he had possibly learned from his Indian neighbours, amongst whom the appointment of the heir-apparent to a joint sovereignty, in the father's declining age, was an ancient and authorized usage.

The coins of Eukratides have been found in some numbers on either side of the Paropamisan mountains. Those brought from the north are chiefly

[1] Bactriani per varia bella jactati non regnum tantum, verum etiam libertatem amiserunt, siquidem Sogdianorum et Arachotorum et Drangianorum Indorumque bellis fatigati, ad posterum ab invalidioribus Parthis velut exsangues oppressi sunt: Book XLI. 6.

[2] Ἀφείλοντο δὲ καὶ τῆς Βακτριανῆς μέρος, βιασάμενοι τοὺς Σκύθας καὶ ἔτι πρότερον τοὺς περὶ Εὐκρατίδαν. Strabo, Book XI. 9. 2. And again, it is specified what satrapies were lost: ὧν τήν τε Ἀσπιώνου καὶ τὴν Τουριούαν ἀφῄρηντο Εὐκρατίδην οἱ Παρθυαῖοι. Book XI. 11. 3.

silver tetradrachms, of which some have found their way to Europe through Persia, and others have been obtained at Kunduz. Silver oboli have been procured by purchase on the south of the mountains at and near Kabul. The most numerous, however, are copper coins, of which hundreds have been found in the earth at Beghram. The prevailing devices on both silver and copper coins are the helmeted head of the king, and on the reverse the Dioscuri charging, with the legend ΒΑΣΙΛΕΩΣ ΜΕΓΑΛΟΥ ΕΥΚΡΑΤΙΔΟΥ. On the small silver and copper coins the bonnets of the Dioscuri are substituted for the horsemen, and the epithet 'Megalos' is omitted. On some of the tetradrachms the head of the king has the royal fillet instead of the helmet, and on the reverse is the figure of Apollo, with the legend in two perpendicular lines, ΒΑΣΙΛΕΩΣ ΕΥΚΡΑΤΙΔΟΥ. Some of the oboli have the same head, but the bonnets of the Dioscuri on the reverse. It has been thought by M. R. Rochette[1] that the use of the fillet or of the helmet indicates two different princes, one of whom was a second Eukratides, the son and successor of the other; which distinction is confirmed by the adoption of the different types of Apollo, or the Dioscuri on the reverse: that the fabrication of the coins approximates in regard to style in a different ratio to the age of Euthydemus, and that the adoption of the title 'Great' on the coins with the helmeted portrait, corroborates the opinion that they belonged to a later and more turbulent period, when the Indian victories of Eukratides II. authorized him to take the title of Megalos. We have, however, on some of the oboli the filleted portrait, with the types of the Dioscuri; nothing conclusive can therefore be drawn from its concurrence with that of Apollo. M. Mionnet sees no difference in the style of the coins; and certainly the beauty of those with the helmeted head, and the title of 'Great King,' is not surpassed by any of the Bactrian coins. We have no evidence of the Indian victories of a second Eukratides, whilst we have of those of a first; and one and the same prince may have added to his name the distinction of Great after his Indian victories, as Bayer has supposed,[2] as well as the use of Indian characters for the legends of his copper coins. Not that these indications always go together, as we have a round copper coin with the helmeted head, and the

[1] J. des Sav. [2] Page 106.

Dioscuri charging, where no Indian legend occurs, but the margin is occupied, as in the tetradrachms, by **ΒΑΣΙΛΕΩΣ ΜΕΓΑΛΟΥ ΕΥΚΡΑΤΙΔΟΥ.** There does not seem to be, therefore, sufficient reason for assigning the coins of Eukratides to two different princes of the name; and the successor, if not the son of Eukratides, appears to have borne the denomination of Heliokles, as will be hereafter noticed.

The tetradrachm of Eukratides that bears the helmeted head is the coin that formed the corner-stone of Bayer's work.[1] It was brought from Astrakhan or Casan, and is in all respects the same as those here delineated. He supposed the monogram to represent **Η Ρ**, which he thought denoted a date,—108 of the Bactrian æra. It may be doubted if the monogram is accurately expressed; but as it seems to be repeated on the coins of different princes, it cannot represent a date, nor have we any other authority for a Bactrian æra.

COINS OF EUKRATIDES.

SILVER.

1. Tetradrachm. Head of king to the right, with helmet ornamented above the temples with the ear and horn of a bull, and surmounted by a crest; bust clothed with the chlamys. R. Castor and Pollux on horseback, charging, with lances in rest; wearing conical caps, each surmounted by a star, and carrying branches of palm over their shoulders. **ΒΑΣΙΛΕΩΣ ΜΕΓΑΛΟΥ ΕΥΚΡΑΤΙΔΟΥ.** Mon. 13. Pl. III. fig. 1.

This is a coin of very great beauty; the drawing is from a specimen in the cabinet of the East India Company, brought from Persia by R. Steuart, Esq.

2. Tetradrachm. Head of king as before. R. Dioscuri charging. Inscription as before. Mon. 14. Pl. III. fig. 2.

3. Tetradrachm. Head of king as before. R. Dioscuri charging. Inscription as before. Mon. 15. Pl. III. fig. 3.

Coins in the British Museum: although agreeing in type, the portraits vary, and the monograms are different. Another coin of this description was procured from Kunduz by Sir A. Burnes, and is in his supplemental

[1] Tab. I. ad p. 100. Fig. 1.

collection. The monogram, No. 16, differs. Another is in the cabinet of the East India Company, presented by Sir H. Willock, and procured by him in Persia; and it may be observed that one of the preceding, that which is in the cabinet of R. P. Knight, was originally obtained also in Persia by Sir H. Willock.

4. Tetradrachm. Similar to the preceding, but the legend blundered. ΡVΣΙΛΕΩΣ ΜΕΓΑΛΟΥ ΕΊΚΡΑΤΑΟΥ.

Collection of General Ventura: J. As. Soc. B. June, 1835, Pl. XXV. fig. 5. J. Asiatique, Feb. 1836.

5. Tetradrachm. Head of king to the right, with fillet only, and with chlamys. R. Standing Apollo, front; the arrow, with the point downwards, in his right hand; his left leaning on his bow. A robe crosses his shoulders, and hangs down the back to the middle of his legs; he has buskins on his feet. ΒΑΣΙΛΕΩΣ ΕΥΚΡΑΤΙΔΟΥ. Mon. 17. Pl. III. fig. 4.

Published originally by Koehler. It is repeated after one brought home by Dr. Honigberger; J. des Sav. Sept. 1835, Pl. I. fig. 5. And by Mionnet from one belonging to Mr. Steuart; Supplement, tom. viii. A fourth has been obtained by Dr. Lord at Kunduz; J. As. Soc. B. July, 1838, Pl. XXVII. fig. 2.

6. Drachm. Head of king with helmet to the right. R. Dioscuri charging. ΒΑΣΙΛΕΩΣ ΕΥΚΡΑ - - ΙΔΟ - - -. Mon. 18.

From the collection of General Ventura; J. des Sav. Feb. 1836, Pl. II. fig. 3. A similar coin, but one more worn, and therefore appearing to offer a different portrait, was previously described in the same work; J. des Sav. Sept. 1835, Pl. I. fig. 8. A copper coin, exactly similar to it, is figured in our Plate III. fig. 8.

7. Drachm. Head helmeted, to the right. R. Dioscuri charging. ΒΑΣΙΛΕΩΣ ΕΥΚΡΑΤΙΔΟΥ. Mon. 19.

Described in the J. des Sav. July, 1834, Plate, fig. 5. Also figured by Koehler and Mionnet. M. R. Rochette considers it to be the type of the coin originally figured by Bayer.

8. Didrachm, square. Helmeted head of the king. ΒΑΣΙΛΕΩΣ ΜΕΓΑΛΟΥ ΕΥΚΡΑΤΙΔΟΥ. R. Dioscuri charging. [Kharoshthi legend] Supplemental Plate, fig. 4.

From the supplemental collection of Sir A. Burnes. The type is in all respects that of the copper coins to be presently described, but this is the only instance yet known of a square silver coin of this prince, and its authenticity is questionable.

9. Obolus. Head of king, with fillet, to the right. R. Bonnets and palm-leaves of the Dioscuri. ΒΑΣΙΛΕΩΣ ΕΥΚΡΑΤΙΔΟΥ. Mon. 20. Pl. III. fig. 5.

10. Obolus. Head of king to the right, with helmet. R. Bonnets and palm-leaves of the Dioscuri. ΒΑΣΙΛΕΩΣ ΕΥΚΡΑΤΙΔΟΥ. Mon. 21. Pl. III. fig. 6.

The originals of both these are in the Company's cabinet; two of the former, and six of the latter: one of the latter was obtained from Mr. Steuart, the others have been all sent home by Mr. Masson, and have been procured by him at Kabul.

COPPER.

11. Round, middle size. Head of king, with helmet, to the right. R. Dioscuri charging. ΒΑΣΙΛΕΩΣ ΜΕΓΑΛΟΥ ΕΥΚΡΑΤΙΔΟΥ. Pl. III. fig. 8.

Several of these are in the Masson collection; others were obtained by General Ventura: they are usually worn, so that the legend is seldom complete: J. As. Soc. B. April, 1834, and June, 1835; J. Asiatique, Feb. 1836; Mionnet, Supplement, viii. p. 471. He notices one with the legend ΒΑΣΙΛΕΩΣ ΣΩΤΗΡΟΣ ΕΥΚΡΑΤΙΔΟΥ, (litt. fugit.): so that the reading is doubtful.

12. Round, small. Laurelled head of Apollo (?) to the right. R. Horse standing to the left. ΒΑΣΙΛΕΩΣ --ΚΡΑΤΙΔΟΥ. Pl. III. fig. 7.

From the Imperial Cabinet of Vienna; described, J. des Sav. May, 1836; figured, J. des Sav. April, 1836; vignette, fig. 21. M. R. Rochette considers the head to be imitated from that on the coin of Euthydemus, No. 19.

13. Square. Head of king, with helmet, to the right. ΒΑΣΙΛΕΩΣ ΜΕΓΑΛΟΥ ΕΥΚΡΑΤΙΔΟΥ. R. Dioscuri charging. [illegible] Mon. 21. Pl. III. figs. 9, 10.

These coins are very numerous: there are several hundreds in the Masson collection, found principally at Beghram. The collections of Ventura, Honigberger, and Court, offer equally abundant specimens procured in the Punjab and towards Kabul and Peshawer. They are in different states of preservation, of different styles of execution, and of different sizes. The faces vary in expression, and still more in age; in some the countenance is very youthful. The monograms vary, but the prevailing character is a modification of the letter M. Nos. 22—25. They have been repeatedly delineated and described, especially by Messrs. Masson and Prinsep; J. As. Soc. B. April, 1834, p. 164, Pl. VIII. figs. 8, 9, and p. 338, Pl. XXV. figs. 8, 9, 10; also same Journal for January, 1836, Pl. IV.; and by R. Rochette, J. des Sav. Sept. 1835, Pl. I. fig. 7; and Mionnet, Supplement, viii. p. 470.

14. Square. Head of king, helmeted, to the right. ΒΑΣΙΛΕΩΣ ΜΕΓΑΛΟΥ ΕΥΚΡΑΤ - - - -. R. Seated figure to the left, indistinct, but apparently a Victory with the palm-branch; front of an elephant's head at her foot on the left, and one of the usual bonnets on the right. Legend in Indian characters, imperfect. [illegible]. Mon. 26. Pl. III. fig. 11.

This coin is in the Masson collection: it has been described by him; J. As. Soc. B. April, 1834, Pl. VIII. fig. 11. The coin is much worn, and the inscription on the reverse is defective: such characters as appear, differ from those on the coins of Eukratides, but the Greek letters give his name sufficiently distinct. A second coin, of the same kind, has been subsequently received from Mr. Masson, in which the figure has more the character of the seated Jupiter as it appears on the worst executed coins of Hermæus. This coin is, however, also very much defaced.

15. Square; small. Head bare, with fillet, to the right. ΒΑΣΙΛΕΩΣ ΜΕΓΑΛΟΥ ΕΥΚΡΑΤΙΔ - -. R. Bonnets and palm-leaves of the Dioscuri. [illegible] - [illegible] - -. Pl. III. fig. 12.

There are several pieces of this type in the Masson collection.

16. Square. Head with helmet, to the left, the back and shoulders bare; the right hand is raised, and grasps a javelin. R. Dioscuri charging. ΒΑΣΙΛΕΩΣ ΜΕΓΑΛΟΥ ΕΥΚΡΑΤΙΔΟΥ. Mon. Φ.

Described by Mionnet from Koehler; Supplement, viii. p. 470. The type of the obverse is common on the coins of Menander. Like the round coins, Nos. 10, 11, it has no Indian inscription.

17. Middle square. Head of king to the left, as in the last. Inscription as before. R. A winged Victory to the right, holding out a fillet.  Mon. 27. Supplemental Plate, fig. 5.

From Mr. Masson's last dispatch.

18. Middle square. Head of king to the right. ΒΑΣΙΛΕΩ - - - ΕΥ-ΚΡΑΤΙΔΟΥ. R. A winged Victory to the left, her right hand holding the wreath and fillet. 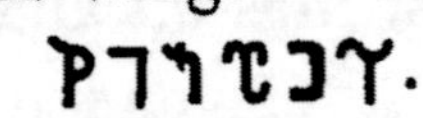 Mon. 28. Supplemental Plate, fig. 6.

From the more distinct of two coins in Mr. Masson's last dispatch.

M. R. Rochette ascribes to this prince a coin on the face of which occurs "une palme posée en travers," on the neck of the king; with the legend ΒΑΣΙΛΕΩΣ - - - - - ΙΔΟΥ. J. des Sav. Oct. 1835, Pl. II. fig. 15. It is undoubtedly, however, a coin of Antialkides.

ON THE ARIANIAN ALPHABET.

It is upon the square copper coins of Eukratides that we first notice the invariable occurrence of a bilingual inscription. It is not found upon even the round copper coins which have been picked up in the same locality, and it does occur upon the only silver coin which is square, as if the foreign letters and foreign shape had been adopted simultaneously. Upon the coins of the kings succeeding to Eukratides, the inscription in the new characters is borne by either round or square coins. It is never single: wherever there is a legend on one face in Arianian letters, there is one on the other in Greek, however barbarized. An Arianian inscription has not yet been found on any of the coins of Euthydemus or Demetrius, nor on the silver coins of Eukratides, with the solitary exception of the somewhat doubtful square coin. It does not occur, as far as has yet been observed, upon the larger and handsomer silver medals, the tetradrachms, even of those princes on whose smaller silver coins it is found, as Heliokles and Antimachus. It evidently, therefore, indicates a subsequent date, and a change of territory; a decline in the power of the Greek kings of Bactria, and the transference of their rule to people on the south of the Hindu Kush, whom it now became their policy to conciliate.

The first attempts to decypher these novel letters originated, as already noticed, with Mr. Masson and Mr. Prinsep, and was prosecuted by the latter with remarkable success. Conceiving, however, that the language was probably Zend, he assumed a valuation for some of the characters which his further experience induced him to alter. His corrections, which were published in the Journal of the Asiatic Society of Bengal, for July, 1838, leave few of the letters subjects of doubt, except from those variations which arise in the inscriptions, either from local modifications, or from the carelessness or ignorance of the engravers of the original dies. This alphabet has also been made the subject of careful investigation by Professor Lassen and Dr. Grotefend, who concur in most of its elements with Mr. Prinsep. The different schemes have been collected with great care and accuracy by Mr. Cullimore, in a Table published, with remarks upon the subject, in the Proceedings of the Numismatic Society of London for 1839. From these sources, and a diligent examination of the coins, I shall now proceed to offer some observations on the characters which are met with on the reverses of the coins to be subsequently described.

In commenting on the probable powers of the letters, it will be convenient to follow the order of the Nagari alphabet, as that which is most appropriate to the language which the characters are used to express.

VOWELS.

A, is uniformly represented, when a syllabary initial, by ; when it is combined with consonants it is, agreeably to the spirit of the Sanscrit alphabet, left without any indication. Nor is it satisfactorily established that any difference is made whether it be long or short: thus the character  may be either the syllable *ka* or *ká*. Mr. Prinsep, however, suggests that the long *á* may be denoted by a dot to the left, as  when initial, and, when conjoined with a consonant, by a line at the foot of the latter, as  *ká*. He also notices that *An* is represented by , as in the first syllable of Antialkides 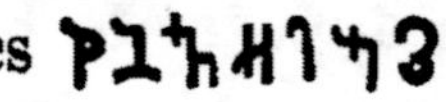 and of Antimachus . The distinction, however, is noticeable on single specimens only, and in all the other coins of these princes the initial is 𐨀.

I, as an initial, does not occur on any coin; but a letter common on inscriptions 𐨀𐨁, Mr. Prinsep thinks may be set down as *i*, whether short or long. Lassen and Grotefend employ 𐨀𐨂 to represent I, but when met with it is rather the equivalent of U, as in the name of Eukratides 𐨯𐨡𐨟𐨁𐨐𐨿𐨪𐨀𐨂𐨀𐨅. Its form, in conjunction with a consonant, is undoubtedly that of a short perpendicular or oblique stroke, attached to it or carried across it, as 𐨟 *ta*, 𐨫 *la*, 𐨟𐨁 *ti*, 𐨫𐨁 *li*.

U, in the representation of the name Eukratides, is represented by 𐨀𐨂; in combination by a loop under the letter, as 𐨐𐨂 *ku*.

E, 𐨀𐨅 or 𐨀𐨅, is constantly employed, according to Prinsep, for the initial E of Greek words, as in the same name Eukratides: in combination it is expressed by a small detached stroke behind or above, as 𐨐𐨅 *ké*.

O, as an initial, does not occur: as following a consonant it is evidently considered as identical with the short *a*, and without any other equivalent. Prinsep, however, suggests its being indicated by a short line to the right of the head of the letter, as 𐨐𐨆 *ko*. As a terminating letter, it was at first conjectured by Prinsep that it was represented by 𐨯, a character which terminates all the names and epithets of the reverses of the coins. He has been followed in this by Lassen and Grotefend; but his final determination of the value of this letter, as will be hereafter mentioned, was that not of *o*, but of *s*.

CONSONANTS.

K. There can be no doubt that this is always represented by 𐨐. The combinations of it with the vowels are already given, but there are also combinations of it with consonants in the Greek names, which we should expect to find repeated in the Indian, as ΚΡΑ and ΚΛΑ in Eukratides and Heliocles. In the former the combination is expressed by 𐨐𐨿𐨪: the form of *kla*, as it occurs in Heliokles, is 𐨐𐨿𐨫. The same in Agathokleia is somewhat differently represented, X; and this appears to be also used for *kra*, as in the coin of Eukratides, No. 17. Prinsep observes, that there are other forms; but these are conjectural, taken from the inscriptions, and do not appear upon any of the coins examined on the present occasion.

Kh is represented by Prinsep by 𐨑, as it occurs on the coins of Antimachus: it is also met with on the coins of Archebius. In some specimens of the former there are modifications of the form, but they are either unimportant or blunders. According to Prinsep, the inscriptions offer other varieties, and in the name of Abagasus 𐨑 appears to be used for *g*.

G, or *gh*, are conjecturally supplied by Prinsep from the inscriptions, as they do not occur on the coins. The forms he proposes, which are given in the accompanying Table, are appropriated to *g*, because they bear some resemblance to the *g* of the Pehlevi.

Ch, and *Chh*, are also conjecturally valued by Prinsep from the inscriptions.

J is represented by him by 𐨗, 𐨗, or 𐨗, and this is one of the great improvements in his latest readings, as he had at first ascribed to it the force of *a* long, and accordingly read the title 𐨨𐨱𐨪𐨗𐨯 corresponding to ΒΑΣΙΛΕΩΣ, Malakáo; his later reading is Maharajasa. The valuation of 𐨗 by *j* was, about the same time, proposed in Europe by Professor Lassen,[1] who has therefore also the merit of having made this important and unquestionable correction.

It is doubtful if the cerebral class of letters of the Nagari alphabet has any representatives in the Bactro-Indian alphabet, nor apparently is any distinction made in the nasals. Prinsep thinks that from the variety of symbols to which the force of *t* and *d* must be applied, the alphabet has the cerebral as well as the dental forms of those letters; and it is possible. At the same time it is not necessary, as some of the derivative alphabets from the Sanscrit omit the cerebral letters, and the alphabet of the Bactro-Indian coins may partake of the same peculiarity.

There is no doubt, however, much confusion in the forms representing *t* and *d*, 𐨟 or 𐨡, so much so that they are evidently used indiscriminately for either. There is also no difference between them and the ordinary form of *r* 𐨪: for the convenience of expressing them typographically, however, we may render them severally, *t* by 𐨟, *d* by 𐨡, and *r* by 𐨪. They

[1] Zur Geschichte, p. 33.

have other forms, either singly or in combination, which will be found in the Table; and the forms of *d* are frequently interchanged with those of *n*.

Dh is represented by various forms, especially by , , and , and *Dhi* by .

For N we have also different forms,   , but they are evidently modifications of what appears to be the correct form, ; accordingly as the two parts are more or less curved, and the bottom stroke is omitted. One of the modifications possibly sometimes represents the compound *nd*.

P has an equivalent respecting which no uncertainty remains, . It has been discovered also as inflected, as *pi*, and perhaps as *pha* or *spa*. Prinsep suspects also that in other forms we have *pá* and *pra*.

Pha is represented by : it seems in some places to take the power of *v*.

B is still undetermined, but the forms given in the Table are proposed for it. In Archebius and Abagasus it is replaced by or .

M is also ascertained to be , sometimes with a dot or a long perpendicular line below it, as , or , with the dot sometimes converted into an indistinct oblique or horizontal stroke, . In the name Menander, which is one of those which first afforded evidence of the value of the characters, represents *me*. According to Prinsep, *mi*, which was at first ascribed to it, is somewhat differently formed, but the distinction is slight, and is not very carefully preserved, and the first form is undeniably of current use for *mi*. The form bears some analogy to the old Sanscrit *m* .

Y has for its equivalent , but the power of it also corresponds with that of *ts* or *z*, as the Greek name Azes is always written . It also expresses the diphthong *ai* before a vowel, as in Hermaiou, which is written . It represents *y* in the Sanscrit word jaya, or . It occurs with the vowels *i* and *u*, as and .

R is most usually expressed by a character which, in general, cannot be distinguished from those by which *t* and *d* are represented, or . Prinsep considers the *d* to be distinguishable from it by the footmark, as in , which however is often omitted. Other forms occur; we shall confine it to . The usual equivalent for *l* is , but occasional modifications of it are met with. For *v* and *vi*, Prinsep proposes the forms in the Table, founding them on the equivalent of ΑΝΙΚΗΤΟΥ, which he reads Apavihata, but the word most usually occurs [Kharoshthi], and may be correctly read Apatihata for Apratihata, 'invincible.' It is therefore doubtful if the power of *v* is so expressed, although in the absence of any preferable conjecture it might be allowed to remain; and there is reason to think that some such letter was used for *b*, as in the name Arkhebius [Kharoshthi]. Professor Lassen proposes [Kharoshthi] for *v*, and reads [Kharoshthi] Jayavatasa; but there is no doubt that [Kharoshthi] has the power of *dh*, as in [Kharoshthi] Dhamikasa, and it is not necessary to suppose that there is but one symbol for two such different sounds.

In Prinsep's first scheme he assigned to [Kharoshthi] the value of *o*. He inferred, upon perfectly sound premises, that as all the words of the unknown legends, whether names or epithets, terminated with this letter, it must denote some masculine inflection; and finding that nouns masculine in Zend formed the nominative case in *o*, he concluded, as he had adopted the conjecture that the language was Zend, that the character [Kharoshthi] was the termination *o*. Professor Lassen, on similar grounds, but substituting Prakrit for Zend, has continued this valuation, in which he is followed by Dr. C. L. Grotefend. Mr. Prinsep, however, in his last corrections proposes, as more analogous to the construction of the Greek inscription, in which not the nominative but the genitive case is employed, and, having relinquished the theory of the Zend for Prakrit, infers, no doubt with more truth, that the letter [Kharoshthi] is the equivalent for the sign of the genitive case of the Prakrit noun or *sa*. That he is correct in his valuation is proved by the use of the same character as a medial, where it must express the sound of *s*, as in the proper names Lysias and Azilises read [Kharoshthi] and [Kharoshthi]. In Philoxenes it occurs with the vowel *i*, or it may be used as *sh*, as [Kharoshthi] Pilishinasa. In the coins of the Indo-Scythic princes the form of this letter is variously modified, but the modifications are, no doubt, chiefly the effect of inaccurate workmanship. Some of them may represent variations of the sibilant, as Prinsep conjectures. Thus [Kharoshthi] may correspond to the Sanscrit palatal *sa* श, and [Kharoshthi] to the cerebral ष or *sh*, but it is a question if this is not rather a variation of [Kharoshthi] *y*.

There can be no hesitation in admitting [Kharoshthi] or [Kharoshthi] to have the value of *h*.

The determination of the value of the letters was derived from a comparison of those words which invariably occurred as the counterparts of the names and titles which were inscribed in Greek characters. The names were an unequivocal test: for the titles it was necessary to take an additional element into consideration, and ascertain the language in which the purport of the Greek words was expressed. The Zend was tried, and failed. The Prakrit form of the Sanscrit, or a dialect of Sanscrit which probably was the spoken language of the people along the foot of the mountains, an Indian people amongst whom the coins were current, furnishes us with equivalents, to most of which there is no reasonable objection, and which, in one or two instances, are conclusive. In some cases, however, there still remains considerable difficulty, and in the names and titles of the barbaric or Indo-Scythic kings the powers of many of the letters have not yet been determined, either because new elements have been introduced, or the old ones have undergone material alterations. It is worthy of observation, that the native characters on the coins appear to have deteriorated in execution as much as the Greek upon the later medals. A brief examination of the equivalents on the several coins will obviate the necessity of recurring to the subject in detail.

It may be necessary here to observe, that the readings about to be particularized are taken, in every case where the coins were in my possession, from a careful examination and collation of the coins themselves. It will be found in general that they agree with the engravings, but there may be sometimes slight differences. I exercised no control over the engraver; he followed his own eye and judgment without any interference, and, in most cases, with great accuracy. No delineation of a single specimen, however, can be held of weight in contradiction to a sufficient variety of good coins; and without any disparagement of the merits of the deserving artist employed on this occasion, or of the talents and accuracy of those who have executed a similar task in other publications, I must propose the verifications which I have derived from the coins themselves, as alone worthy of credit whenever any difference prevails.

There is an immense number of the square copper coins of Eukratides in the Company's cabinet. The major portion are much worn at the edges, but many are perfectly legible. The name usually occurs 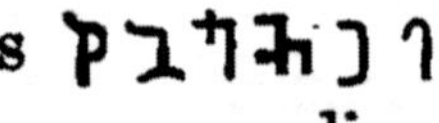 Eukratídasa. There are some variations in the three letters preceding the final, but they are slight and unimportant, and are evidently mere faults of workmanship or impression. The penultimate and antepenultimate are commonly undistinguished, except by the vowel-mark, as , but in good specimens they occur . The title is that of the Greek legend, 'great king,' which is generally expressed with perfect clearness Maharajasa, the Prakrit genitive of the Indian term Maharaja. The *j* has commonly a second transverse stroke, but not always, and this is mostly omitted in the coins of the subsequent princes. It may be possible that the Indian word Maharaj suggested ΒΑΣΙΛΕΥΣ ΜΕΓΑΛΟΣ. In oriental phrase, although literally 'great king,' it imports no more than king. The natives of India would have never used 'Raja' alone as the epithet of majesty; they would have called their Greek sovereign Maharaj as a matter of course, and in their employment of the term may have originated its translation into Greek.

Of Heliokles we have but few coins: one of silver, and one of copper, with bilingual inscriptions, have been collated. The letters on the copper are less cleanly executed than on the silver, and have in some respects been ill represented in the delineation; there is no difficulty, however, about their value. The letters of the silver coin are very distinct. The name occurs Heliyaklayasa. The titles are Maharajasa as before, and for ΔΙΚΑΙΟΥ, , Dhamikasa, for the Sanscrit Dhármikasya, 'pious, just.'

Two silver and several copper coins of Lysias furnish very legible inscriptions. In one of the silver coins the name is apparently written Lisi-asa, but in all the rest it is clearly Lisikasa. In no one instance have I found any thing like , the form which Professor Lassen derives from the engraving of the coin published by M. R. Rochette, and confirmed, as he mistakingly supposes, by Prinsep's engraving, in which the elements of ∇ for *s* occur. They seem to be merely, however, the rudiments of a corruption of , and I doubt if any such letter as ∇ ever occurs. I have not met with it on any of the coins I have examined, although the is sometimes so formed as to approach to an irregular triangle. The form Lisikasa is most consonant to the spirit of Sanscrit construction, the *k* being inserted to obviate the hiatus occasioned by the concurrence of two open vowels not coalescing: its omission, again, in such a situation is equally consistent with Prakrit. The equivalent for the epithet ΑΝΙΚΗΤΟΥ is Apatihatasa, for Apratihatasya, 'undefeated, unconquered.' Prinsep has proposed, as has been mentioned, to read this Avihatasa, making the first letter a *v*, but there is no necessity, as already objected, to adopt this reading. Lassen reads the epithet Apalihata, which is also a Prakrit form of Apratihata, 'non repulsus.' In no case, however, have I met with the transverse bar of the curving upwards, which the third letter of this word invariably does; and we may therefore leave it unaltered as the representative of *t*.

Amyntas offers but two coins, and neither of these is in the Company's cabinet; of one only has an engraving been yet published, of which a cast taken by Mr. Prinsep himself has been subsequently consulted. The letters are for the most part distinct, and give for the name Amitasa. The titles are Basileos Nikatoros, for which we have Maharajasa Jayadharasa. As previously noticed, Professor Lassen reads this epithet Jayavatasa; but there is no good reason for such a reading, Jayadhara meaning 'having victory.'

The name of Antialkides occurs on several silver and many copper coins in good preservation. There is no important variety in the legend. The name is written Atialikitasa, or, as the penultimate may be read with equal correctness, *d*, Atialikidasa. In one instance, that which has been engraved, the initial is slightly varied to , to represent, as Prinsep supposes, *An*. The *ti* in some of the copper coins occurs . For the epithet ΝΙΚΗΦΟΡΟΥ we have the same word as was given for the ΝΙΚΑΤΟΡΟΣ of Amyntas, Jayadharasa. In different specimens the *dh* occurs as and .

For the determination of the value of the next name, that of Arkhebius, two silver coins have been consulted. The greater part of the legend is perfectly distinct, Maharajasa Dhamikasa Jayadharasa. There is a difficulty in the name, which in one coin is very legibly as if it was Akhatiyasa. We can scarcely admit the correctness of the syllable *ti*, for there is no doubt that on both the silver coins the reading of the Greek is ΑΡΧΕΒΙΟΥ, although in one of them the indistinctness of the Β has led both Mr. Masson and my engraver to represent it as an Λ.

Lassen, following Masson's drawing, reads the antepenultimate syllable *li*, in Indian as well as Greek  liyasa, but the transverse stroke turns up, not down. In the engraving of the coin in Pl. II. it is made straight, but that is an inaccuracy. In the second specimen the letter is unfortunately somewhat indistinct, but it looks like a modification of the *ti*. It is possible, however, that a letter somewhat similar to the *t* has been used to express *b*, and they have been confounded by the engraver of the original die.

Seven silver coins of Antimachus have been examined; there are none of copper: on two the legend is entire; on all such parts as are preserved it is distinct, and the whole is 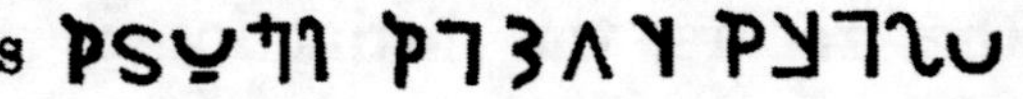 Maharajasa Jayadharasa Atimakhasa. In one instance the initial is varied, as in a coin of Antialkides,  as if it represented *An*. For *ti* also, in some cases, occurs 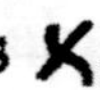, which is evidently a mere deflection from the usual form, which the others present, of 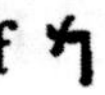; the horizontal and perpendicular lines being run into a continuous curve.

The inscription on the coins of Philoxenes is read from one silver and two copper coins, all with distinct legends. Maharajasa Apatihatasa Pilashinasa, 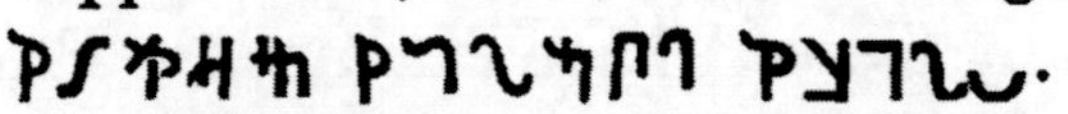. The *l* is formed on these coins more like a *j* in the upper portion; the transverse stroke, although not curved, being placed obliquely upwards.

We next come to the coins of Menander, which we count by hundreds. The legends on the silver coins are in general very distinct. They are occasionally more or less effaced upon the copper. The name is in the most perfect specimens written , possibly intended for Minandasa. There are some modifications of the two middle letters, but those of the antepenultimate are merely varieties of *n*. Those of the penultimate are in general varieties of *n* also, which induced Mr. Prinsep to propose for the reading Minano. Professor Lassen affirms that the most usual form of the penultimate is , which he reads *d*, making the word Minado. Not having the coins before him he has erred in his statement of the fact, as the  is of comparatively rare occurrence, and is, no doubt, an error for 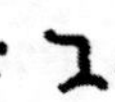. The prevailing form, particularly on the silver coins, is , a letter which does not occur elsewhere, and which must therefore be the equivalent of the letters *ndr*. Professor Lassen, however, rightly objects to this that the combination would be uncongenial to the Prakrit, although not uncommon in Sanscrit, and that the former would substitute for it *nd*, as in Chando for Chandra. The same substitution has probably taken place here, and in the letter [Kharoshthi] we have not *d*, but *nd*, making the equivalent of Menandrou, Minandasa.

The first of Menander's titles, Maharaja, requires no remark, but the equivalent of Soteros is not satisfactorily determined. Although sometimes represented as if three of the four letters of which it consists were the same, [Kharoshthi], yet on all the best specimens of the coins of those princes on which the epithet recurs, the distinction is very perceptible, and is very legibly marked: the word is there written [Kharoshthi]: the first differs from the *t* in being slightly curved at the bottom; in the second we have what usually represents *d*; the third may be either *t* or *r*. What can be made out of these premises? What has been made out of them? Prinsep's first reading of the epithet was Rakako, but this he relinquished for Ladatasa or Nandatasa. Neither is satisfactory, and it is evident that he had not any very good specimens of the coins under his inspection, as the forms which he represents do not occur on any of the many pieces I have examined. Professor Lassen, upon the authority of a coin engraved by Mr. Prinsep,[1] belonging to a king of doubtful name, but having Soter for one of his titles, reads the title [Kharoshthi], which he proposes to read tádáro, the Prakrit form of the Sanscrit trátá, 'preserver.' None of the coins in the cabinet, of this type, have this portion of the legend distinct; but a single coin of barbarous execution cannot be opposed to at least fifty of a purer style. The preferable form of the legend is, therefore, that which is given above; but that is not incompatible with Professor Lassen's reading, since, as already suggested, the two middle letters are likely to be *d* and *r*. The difference between the first letter and *t* is not very considerable, and in the absence of any more probable conjecture the epithet may be Tadarasa.

The coins of Apollodotus are also numerous, and the inscriptions are legible upon many. We have, as in the coins of Menander, [Kharoshthi] [Kharoshthi] for the titles, and for the name [Kharoshthi] Apaladatasa. There are varieties

[1] J. As. Soc. B. vol. iv. Pl. XXIII. fig. 23.

in the forms of the first, third, and fourth letters, but they are not embarrassing. The letters on the coins of Apollodotus are in general inferior in execution to those on the coins of Menander.

There are two copper coins of Diomedes in the collection. On one the only legible part of the Indian inscription is the epithet Soter ᑭ7ᒣᒐ : on the other we have the name sufficiently distinct ᑭʃωΛʃ Dayamedasa.

Hermæus is illustrated by a number of coins both of silver and copper, which leave no doubt of the equivalents. The titles are the same as those of Menander; the name is written ᑭΛυ7ᒐ Hermayasa.

A numerous series of copper coins, and one or two silver, afford specimens of the names and titles of Azes with very tolerable distinctness and precision. The legend is seldom complete on any one coin, but the whole may be made out by a comparison of different specimens, and runs thus, Maharajasa Rajadhirajasa Mahatasa Ayasa, ᑭΛ1 ᑭ7ᒐυ ᑭᒧ7Xᒧ7 ᑭᒧ7ᒐω 'Of the great Aya the great king, the supreme king of kings.' There are some varieties in the legend as well as in the letters; in some the second epithet is Rajaraja, 'king of kings;' and in one set the epithet ᑭhυ? dhamikasa is added. In place of *dhi* in Rajadhiraj the letter may be read *ti*, being either X or ᒉ. This however may be no error, but a provincialism, in which *ati* is pronounced for *adhi*.

Of the coins of Azilises the same may be said as of those of Azes. They offer no difficulties, although the letters are sometimes ill formed and corrupt. The titles are the same; the name occurs ᑭTHXΛ1, in which we have a new form for *s* in the penultimate, or it may be intended for the syllable *si* or *se*.

As we proceed beyond Azilises we meet with new and unexpected difficulties. In some instances the names on the two faces of the coins do not correspond, and in others we have new characters or modifications of the old without adequate means of assigning to them their probable value.

A solitary coin of Queen Agathokleia[1] has on its reverse an inscription which, as far as decypherable, has been regarded as inconsistent with the Greek legend, the **ΒΑΣΙΛΙΣΣΑΣ ΘΕΟΤΡΟΠΟΥ ΑΓΑΘΟΚΛΕΙΑΣ** of which is

[1] Pl. VI. fig. 10.

represented by 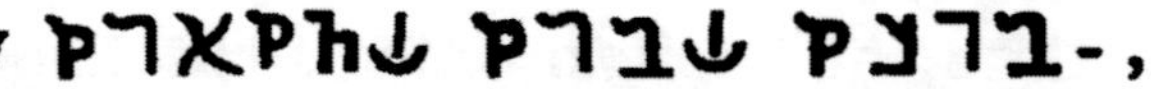, which may be intended for Maharajasa Midatasa (?) Mikasaklatasa. Prinsep reads it Maharajasa - - - tasa Fakasaglitasa (or yasa), making the first letter , in which he certainly is mistaken. Lassen has for the second epithet tádáro; the name he reads Mikonido, in hopelessness of making any thing better of it. Grotefend reduces the name to the syllables *ta sa*, leaving the antepenultimate undecyphered, and making a word out of the three preceding by the conjectural insertion of  *dh*, thus,  dhamikasa-tasa. He is undoubtedly wrong, as there is no room for the additional *dha*. After all, however, there is less incongruity perhaps than there seems to be, and such as is obvious may be owing to the error of the original die-engraver. The name may be easily made to agree well enough with the Greek, except in the first letter, which we must somewhat arbitrarily convert to  *a*; for then if the penultimate were, as it possibly should be,  *ya*, we should read Akas'aklayasa; *k* being substituted for *g*, and the palatal *s'* for *th*.

Abagasus is met with on one coin only, and on that the Indian inscription is imperfect. Prinsep represents the name , which he corrects to  Abhakhasasa.[1]

Several coins of a prince named Mayes have been described, but there is only one instance in which the legend on the coin has come under observation: in that it is complete with the exception of the first letter, and tolerably distinct. The titles are 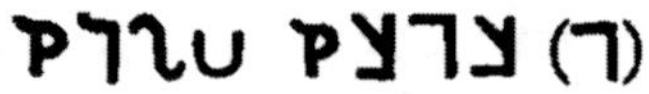 'of the sovereign king of kings the great.' The name is read  Ma-a-sa. Prinsep delineates it as if it was the usual form  with a foot-stroke to the left, as intended for *a* long. The engraving, Pl. VIII. fig. 10, is a faithful representation of the original. In either case there is a new form of the initial *m*: the arrangement of the vowels, which is consistently Prakrit, omits the *y* of the Greek.

Vonones offers, on the reverse of his few coins, a name which is apparently different from its Greek form. Five have been compared, and agree as far as the inscription is legible in each. In one the name is beautifully distinct, and is . There is some difficulty with regard to the first letter, as

[1] J. As. Soc. B. July, 1838, p. 654. Pl. XXVIII. fig. 16.

it presents analogies to two different letters, *k* and *p*. Dr. C. L. Grotefend follows the former, and makes it Kalaharasa. Professor Lassen, depending on ill-executed delineations, and his own theory of the representative of *v*, converts it into Valaharo or Valahado. Prinsep, in his revised reading of the name, adopts a somewhat similar equivalent, and makes it Balaharasa. From a comparison with other names it seems probable that the initial is used indifferently for *p*, or for some of its nearest modifications, as *b*, or *v*, or *f*, or *sp*; and in the present case it may be intended for a *v*, or for an *f*. The penultimate is the usual form of *t* or *r*, but we have seen it used for *n*; and after all, perhaps, the word is not so unlike its Greek form, as it appears to be, admitting of being read Bala- or Valahanasa. The elder Grotefend may have been nearer the truth than any one else when he proposed to read it Vonohno.[1]

The names in which a letter like that of the Indian initial of Vonones occurs are in Greek letters, Hipalirisus and Spalyrius or Spalyris: for the first we have 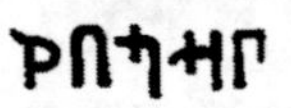 Palirisasa; for the second 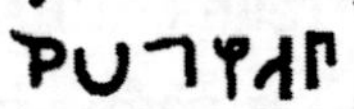 Pala- or Spalapharamasa. The coins are not very scarce: above a dozen of the former, and half that number of the latter, have been collated, all more or less distinct, leaving no doubt of the forms of the letters of the inscription. Prinsep reads the names Spalirishasa and Spalafaramasa. Lassen here adopts *k* as the equivalent of the initial, and makes the names Kalyriso and Kalyrimo, in which he is unquestionably wrong. If any departure from the Greek initials, Hipa and Spa, were allowable, a preferable reading might be conjectured for the second of these names in a common Indian name for a warrior and a prince, Balavarma-sa. If this were the original name, however, it is very unnecessarily transformed in the Greek.

The coin of Spalyris is not the coin of the king, but of the brother of the king: **ΣΠΑΛΥΡΙΟΥ ΔΙΚΑΙΟΥ ΑΔΕΛΦΟΥ ΤΟΥ ΒΑΣΙΛΕΩΣ**. For 'just,' we have as before 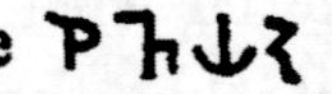 Dhamikasa. We may expect an equivalent also for 'brother,' and there is a word in its place perfectly distinct and consistent in all the specimens, Alabarapatasa . In one case only is the *p* elongated as if the syllable was *pu* ; in one the penultimate is more

[1] Zur Geschichte, vol. iv. p. 65.

decidedly *t* or *r*; but in general the letter is exactly of the form which commences the equivalent of Soter. If it could be considered as *h*, and the following dot as a mark of quiescence, we should have for the last syllables phasa, the same as the last syllable of ΑΔΕΛΦΟΥ; and it seems not improbable that the word is a blundering attempt to represent the Greek epithet of 'brother.' This conjecture may, however, be quite as unprofitable as those of others. Prinsep read Balaharaputasa, 'of the son of Balahara.' Grotefend writes it Kalaharapatasa. Lassen leaves it to a luckier guesser or more acute discerner than himself,—an individual not very easy to be met with.

Coins of other princes of barbaric races and of doubtful appropriation are not wanting. Of these the coins of Undophares are most numerous. They are, in general, in indifferent preservation, and are always of the very worst fabric. The inscription is never perfect, and presents new or probably corrupt forms. The name generally appears as , which Prinsep reads Pharahetisa; it also occurs Pharahetasa. The same name appears on the reverse of some coins on which the name of Gondophares is legibly read in Greek characters Pharahatasa. Lassen and Grotefend both decline any attempt to decypher this denomination.

Immense quantities of copper coins exist in the collection, which bear on one side, in corrupt Greek, the name and titles ΒΑΣΙΛΕΩΣ ΣΩΤΗΡΟΣ ΕΥ ΕΡΜΑΙΟΥ, alternating with other names and titles with the very same type, and which, as far as can be decyphered, are ΚΟΡΣΟ ΚΟΖΟΥΛΟΥ ΚΑΔΦΙΣΟΥ. And again, there are a few coins which have the Greek legend distinctly ΖΑΘΟΥ ΚΟΖΟΛΟΥ ΚΑΔΑΦΕΣ ΚΟΡΑΝΟ. On all these the Arianian inscription appears to be intended to be one and the same, although it is in general so imperfect and indistinct, and abounds so much with new or corrupt letters, that it cannot be entirely decyphered with any confidence. Prinsep himself, in his latest memoir, observes of it that the title Maharaja is not to be found in it, nor is it easy to determine where to commence either the Greek or the Arianian reading. As he decyphers the latter, it is Dhamaratá Kujulakasa Sabashakha (?) Kadaphasa. Lassen has taken considerable pains with these barbarized legends, and thinks that the third and fourth letters [Arianian characters], which he places first, stand for Nara, 'man;' that [Arianian characters] kayala, as he reads it, represents Kozoulo, and that the four last and two first letters, which he reads [Arianian characters], correspond to yhovomo, or ΟΟΗΜΟ, which is found on other coins of Kadphises. It is not strange that Grotefend differs from him.

From examining a great number of these coins, I have no doubt of the forms of the letters, and little of their order: the inscription is [Arianian characters]. Of the value of some of the characters there is more doubt. The third, which Prinsep leaves undetermined, is in all probability *pi*. The same form very nearly commences the equivalent of Philoxenes, *q. v.* The next letter is of the usual form of *n* or *d*, and the first word may be read Dhama-pidasa, 'parent of justice;' or if the fourth letter might be changed to [Arianian characters] the term would be Dhama-piasa, 'the friend of justice.' The word is a common form of a common Sanscrit compound, dharma-priya. Of the next word there is no doubt; it is always very distinctly Kujulakasa, the obvious equivalent of Kozoulo. The next word is doubtful, Sakus′a. I cannot pretend to explain it any further than by a conjecture that it is intended for the equally unintelligible ΖΑΘΟΥ. The first letter of the concluding word is uncertain; it is in general indistinct. It may possibly however be intended for *k*, and then the term is the equivalent of the name Kayadaphasa, for Kadaphes, Kadphis, or Kadphises.

We next come to the better defined though not thoroughly explicable legends on the best preserved coins of this same prince Kadphises. The coins are sufficiently numerous, both gold and copper. It does not often happen that we have the Indian inscription entire, but there are instances, and the whole is established beyond doubt by numerous concurring portions which have escaped obliteration. The inscription is nearly complete on some of the gold coins, and upon the only silver coin which has been found.

The engraving of the large gold coin in Pl. X. is copied from M. R. Rochette's, and is of no use as far as regards the Arianian inscription: the duplicate of it, lately obtained by Mr. Masson, and engraved in the Supplemental Plate, will be consulted with more advantage. The first part of the inscription has the upper portion of the letters excluded from the die, but they are

2 L

easily supplied from other coins, and the remainder is perfect. The inscription is this, 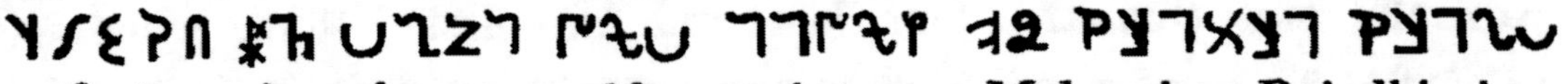 : in the two first words we have our old acquaintances Maharajasa Rajadhirajasa; then follow a group of words which present new elements, to which there is no clue. Prinsep represents them somewhat differently, 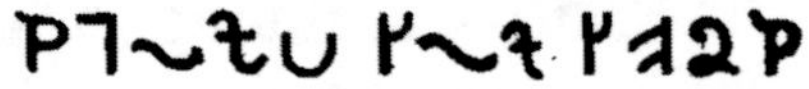 , and reads them Sabatra cha, iha cha, Mahiharasa-dhima; but they can scarcely be so decyphered even upon his values of the letters as they stand, and by which they would give Sabatrapha ihatara Mahihasa dahama: neither is convertible into good English. It is very possible that we have in 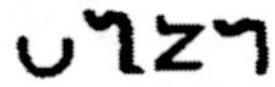 the ΟΟΗΜΟ of the Greek, though what either may mean has not yet been divined. There is no reason to question that we have in  Kapsisasa, or Kapsises: the three last letters should correspond to those generally employed for Soter, but they do not; they are rather dhanasa. The only word in such a position, however, that could be used with propriety, would be devasa, 'god' or 'king;' whether such be their purport must be left uncertain. The objections taken to Professor Lassen's reading of this legend by Dr. C. L. Grotefend are well founded, but it is to be feared that no further elucidation will be derived from the multiplication of specimens. The letters are sufficiently legible,—the difficulty is to determine their power.

Reference has been made in these observations on the legends of the coins to inscriptions in similar characters found in other situations. Of these, three have been published by Mr. Prinsep: one transcribed from characters on the lid of a brass vessel found in the great Tope of Manikyala by General Ventura;[1] one copied from the stone cover of a vase found by M. Court in the second Manikyala Tope;[2] and one from the stone vase found in Tope No. 2 at Bímáran.[3] Amongst his papers also is found a transcript of an inscription on a stone slab at Kapurdegiri. The inscription on the vase in the tope at Bímáran is carefully repeated in our Plate of Antiquities, No. II. Mr. Masson has also forwarded an inscription of some length, written with pen and ink, on an earthen jar from Tope No. 13 at Hidda; and upon the lid of a brass vase sent home by Mr. Masson is a short inscription in similar

[1] J. As. Soc. B. vol. iii. Pl. XXII.

[2] Ibid. Pl. XXXIII.

[3] Ibid. Pl. XXII. See also in this work, Plates of Antiquities, No. II., and p. 70.

characters, dotted. The latter are very indistinct; and the characters, written with a pen upon the jar, are evidently of careless execution: neither, therefore, is calculated to assist in the determination of the alphabet, although some of the letters are evidently the same as those on the coins.

The inscriptions on the brass cylinder and the stone vase of Manikyala are not of much greater legibility. In the former we have what might be read 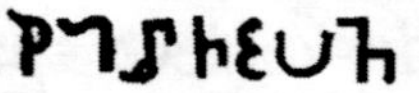 Kamandapa putasa, and in the second we have clearly enough 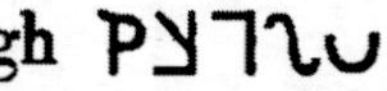 Maharajasa, but I cannot pretend to verify any other intelligible combination. The inscriptions on the stone vase from Hidda are more consistent and distinct than the rest; and in that on the lid and on the body of the vase the same words are evidently repeated; with some additions in the latter. The inscription on the lid may be read, in a great degree conjecturally, Kapharda shatinikhi (sa), pidaramitasa, dhamika putasa, ending with four letters, of which I can make nothing: that on the body, Kapharda shatinikhisa, kradhunapusha-a, pidaramitasa, dhamika putasa; and then follow eight characters I cannot venture to guess at in combination. The meaning of part of the legend may thus be, '(gift?) of the virtuous son, the friend of his father:' some of the other words may be proper names. In some instances Mr. Prinsep's valuation of the letters in these legends differs from mine, but there is room for wider difference still in the perusal of sentences for which we have no probable equivalents in an accompanying inscription in some known alphabet, and in the uncertainty which still in some degree attaches to the language of the legends, whether on the vases or the coins.

If an analogy of grammatical construction prevails in the coins between the inscriptions on the two faces, as is most probable, the termination of the genitive case will be employed for the names and titles of the Arianian as well as of the Grecian legend. If this be, as has been conjectured, 'sa,' it affords a reason for concluding that the names and titles of the king have been made to assume that form of inflection which Prakrit nouns derive from Sanscrit declension; and other considerations deduced from the representation of the names themselves, as Minada or Minanda for Menander, Ati-ali-kido for Antialkides, and the like, confirm the conjecture. The same conclusion is corroborated by the terms which seem to be employed as translations of the Greek epithets, as Dhamiko for Dikæos, Apatihasa for

Aniketou, &c.; and these coincidences furnish plausible grounds for the belief that the language of these coins, during the existence of the Greek princes and their immediate successors, was a vernacular dialect of Sanscrit, to all the varieties of which the appellation Prakrit is applicable. With the Indo-Scythian kings, words borrowed from Turk or other Asiatic dialects may possibly have been intermixed with those of Indian currency; and we have in the inscriptions on the vases possibly a different dialect sparingly intermingled with words of Sanscrit origin.

Another question is, what is the character in which these names and epithets are inscribed? And it is somewhat unaccountable to find that it is not such as is usually regarded as Indian. There is one characteristic difference which is obvious at first sight. That it is written from right to left is unquestionable, from the regular recurrence of certain letters at what must be the close of the words to which they belong, as it is impossible that various names and epithets should begin with the same letter, although, as taking the like inflections of gender and case, they would most probably end alike. Now, in this characteristic it differs from all the alphabets in use amongst the Hindu nations, as they are invariably written from left to right. It belongs, therefore, to a different family; to that of the Semitic alphabets; and we must look for it, if it is to be found any where else, in the more western provinces of Asia.

It is obvious that two or three of the letters, as ד נ ק ר, are like the daleth, koph, nun, and resh, of the Hebrew alphabet; but of these, the two intermediate ones correspond, if the letters on the coins have been rightly read, of which there can be little doubt in these two instances, with *u* and *s*, and consequently they have very different values from the Hebrew letters, however similar their forms. The same may be said of some of the characters of the Phœnician alphabet. There is a resemblance of the shapes, but the sounds cannot be the same, or the language has yet to be ascertained. Although, therefore, of the same family, the alphabet is neither Phœnician nor Hebrew. Falling back more to the east, we find that it offers some analogies of form to the Pehlevi, particularly as the latter appears in inscriptions on sculptured rocks in Persia, and as our character presents itself on the vases in the topes and the later Indo-Scythic coins. We find also what appears to be the medium by which it merged into the Pehlevi of the Sassanians. In a cave at Hajiabad there is a long double inscription,[1] neither part of which is yet decyphered. Although many of the letters are common to both, yet, as Sir Robert Porter observes, they differ widely from each other. One of them approximates very closely to the inscriptions on the vases, and we find in it the characters 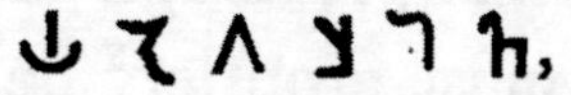, and even some consonants with vowel combinations, as 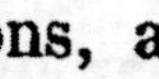, besides other letters which perhaps vary only in the fashion of writing. Again, on the sculptured equestrian figures at Nakshi Rustam there are double inscriptions, in the native character,[2] separated by one in Greek, which has been conjectured by M. De Sacy to express the meaning of its companions. These inscriptions, which are short, are severally analogous to the two at Hajiabad, and they form apparently two additional stages in the transmutation of the characters on the coins of the Greek kings of Bactria to those on the coins of the Sassanian kings of Persia. There is also another point worthy of remark. The inscriptions at Nakshi Rustam, and probably at Hajiabad, appear to express two different languages, allied, but not identical. M. De Sacy himself states this difference to exist; and, whilst he decyphers nearly the whole of the inscription which approaches most closely to Pehlevi, attempts to read but few letters in that which most differs from it. It seems doubtful also if in this case such equivalents for the letters as he does propose can be depended on: if they are correct, our readings of the analogous characters on the coins are wrong, which seems scarcely possible. The interpretation of the legends at Nakshi Rustam requires revision. M. De Sacy admits that he does not feel assured of the language which those most allied to the tope alphabets express, and suggests the possibility that one of the inscriptions may be in the language of Dilem,[3] that is, of the country along the Alburz mountains. This will bring us into Ariana or Iran proper; and possibly a further examination of the inscriptions at Nakshi Rustam in comparison with those of Kabul and Jelalabad, will throw some light on the affinity of dialect which from the earliest times, as we have seen, was said to prevail in Ariana. At

[1] Porter's Travels in Persia, vol. i. p. 512, Pl. 15. [2] Ibid. vol. i. p. 548, Pl. 23.

[3] Plusieurs écrivains orientaux nous parlent d'une langue particulière aux habitans de Dilem. Les inscriptions de la seconde classe ne seroiènt elles point écrites en cette langue? Mémoires sur diverses Antiquités de la Perse, p. 123.

any rate this much is ascertained, that we have on the coins of Menander and his successors one of the earliest specimens of a well defined alphabet of the Semitic family.[1]

Another question, although one of no great importance, is the denomination that may with most propriety be applied to the legends on the coins, seeing that the language belongs to one family, and the letters to another. The language, as far as it can be determined, is Indian. It is not Sanscrit, but Prakrit, a spoken dialect of the former language. We cannot consider the letters to be Indian, for we have in use at or about the same period an alphabet which is read from left to right, and which is unquestionably an ancient form of the current Devanágari alphabet. The letters can scarcely be Bactrian, or we should probably have met with specimens on the coins of those princes of whose rule in Bactria we have historical evidence. To call them Bactro-Indian is objectionable, as it involves a double inconsistency; as they are certainly not Indian, and are probably not Bactrian. They might, without impropriety, be termed Persic; but then we have one term for the letters, and another for the language,—an inconvenience which may be avoided by calling them Arianian, as that will comprehend the entire region from the Hindu Kush to the vicinity of Persepolis, in which the characters have been employed upon coins and sculptures, and in the whole of which, it is to be inferred, both letters and language were once intelligible to the people.

We shall now resume the description of the coins of the Greek princes of Bactria.

HELIOKLES, B.C. 147.

It has been stated above, that in the opinion of Bayer the parricidal successor of Eukratides bore the same denomination, and that the high authority

[1] Gesenius considers the characters on the Bactrian coins to belong to this class of alphabets. " Specimens of the ancient Persian writing distinct from and subsequent to the arrow-headed letters are found on coins of the kings of Persia prior to Alexander, on the coins of some of the Arsacidan kings, and on the coins of kings of Bactria:" Gesenius, Scripturæ Linguæque Phœniciæ Monumenta, pars prima, p. 74. He refers to Mionnet's plates for the characters on the Darics and the Arsacidan coins: vol. v. Pl. XXIX. See also our Pl. XV. figs. 2, 3, 4, for illustrations of the latter.

ARIANIAN ALPHABET.

Vowels A AN I U E AU

Consonants Common | Simple Varieties & Doubtful | Compounded with vowels or consonants.

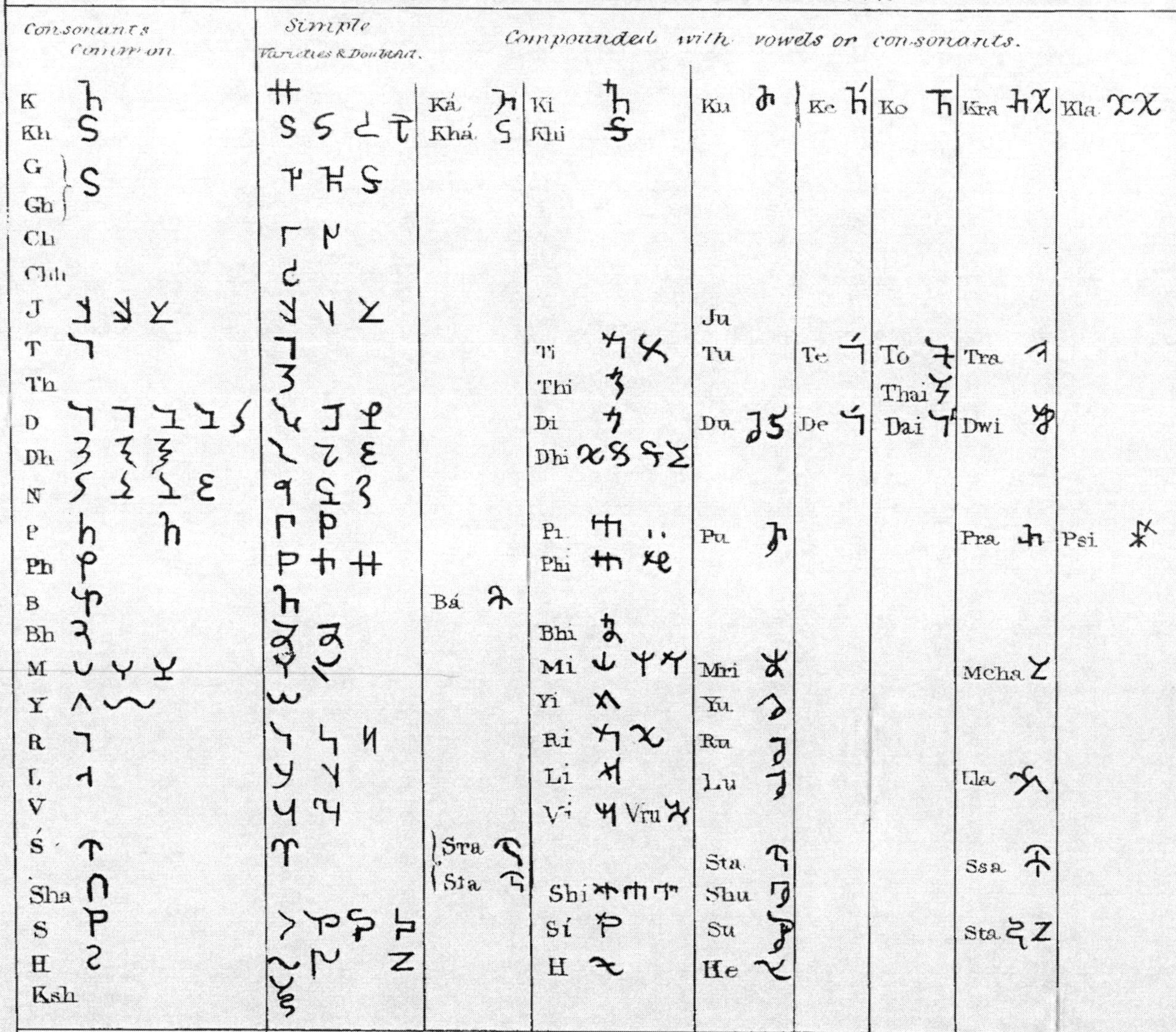

The varieties are taken partly from the Coins, partly from the inscriptions: in the latter case they are chiefly conjectural and are given as valued by Mr. Prinsep
The order is that of the Sanskrit Alphabet.—

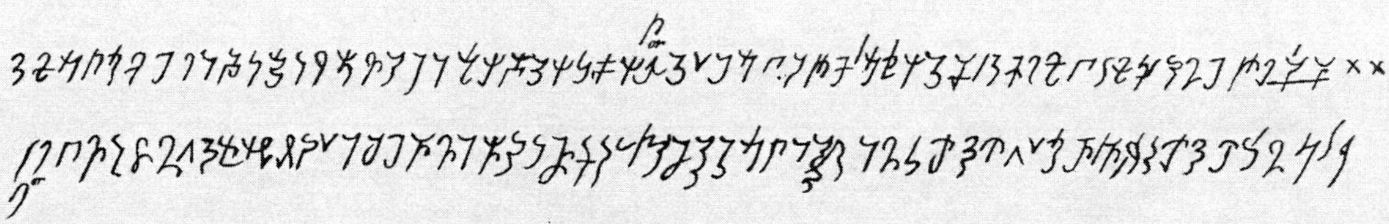

Inscription on earthen Jar found in Tope No. 13 of Hidda.

J. Basire lithog.

of R. Rochette was arrayed on the same side. Dr. C. L. Grotefend entertains the same view, as did Visconti. On the other hand, Mionnet, Lassen, and Müller incline to the belief that Heliokles was the successor of Eukratides.

Ancient authority is silent in regard to the name of the successor of Eukratides. The arguments in favour of a second Eukratides, drawn from coins, have been noticed above. Bayer rested his upon historical evidence. According to him, sundry particulars are recorded of a Eukratides, which are incompatible with the circumstances of the prince who was so named, and which must therefore apply to another of the same appellation.[1] He has not, however, established those distinguishing peculiarities; they are mere assumptions. The cause of the father's murder, he observes, appears to have been his being well affected towards the Parthians, by whom he was assisted, and to whom his son was an enemy, as was proved by his alliance with Demetrius Nicator in his unsuccessful campaign against Mithridates, about the year B. C. 139. There is no such proof. It nowhere appears that any prince named Eukratides was an ally of Demetrius. We learn from classical writers no more than this, that the Greek princes of Eastern Asia, dreading the power and ambition of Mithridates, excited Demetrius to attack the Parthians,[2] and that amongst the allies of the Syrian monarch the Bactrians were included.[3] There is no reason why the Bactrians should not have joined Demetrius in the reign of a Heliokles as well as of a Eukratides. The name of their king is left undetermined.

In the uncertainty which attended the appropriation of a coin of Heliokles when first made known to numismatists, M. Mionnet, judging from the style of its execution, pronounced it to be a Bactrian coin, and proposed to place

[1] Quædam de Eucratide dicuntur quæ in illum superiorem non cadunt; fuit igitur, cui illa conveniunt, et ipse dictus Eucratides: p. 95.

[2] Ejus adventum non invitos orientis populos vidisse et propter Arsacidæ regis crudelitatem et quod veteri Macedonum imperio adsueti novi populi superbiam indigne ferebant: Justin, Book XXXVI. 1. Josephus has a passage to the same effect: Book XIII. 9.

[3] Demetrium adjutum Persarum, Elymæorum, et Bactrianorum auxiliis fuisse: Justin, Book XXXVI. 1. This passage by no means warrants Bayer's assertion, Eucratidem cum ceteris contra Parthos pro Demetrio conspirasse, Justinus in hunc modum fatus diserte demonstrat: p. 95.

Heliokles subsequently to Eukratides, as his son and successor.[1] The justice of the conjecture has been proved by additional discoveries.

History records nothing of the reign of the son of Eukratides except his attribute of parricide, with the further statement that he justified the deed as the destruction not of a parent but of an enemy. What were the grounds of his justification does not appear, but they may have been his inability or his disinclination to engage in hostilities against the Parthians, as Bayer affirms. It seems possible, indeed, upon this supposition, to give consistency and connexion to some of the scattered and conflicting notices of classical writers. Mithridates compelled Eukratides to relinquish to him some of the western satrapies of Bactria, by which his forbearance during the remainder of the life of the Bactrian prince was purchased. Impatience of such subservience to Parthia, and the hope that Demetrius would triumph, may have led the successor of Eukratides to remove him as an obstacle to such a consummation, and to enter into a confederacy with the Seleucidan. The result proving fatal to the latter, Mithridates may have retaliated upon the Bactrians by that invasion of their Indian territory, the evidence for which leaves scarcely any doubt of its occurrence, although 'the glorious old age' which Mithridates is said to have attained, and his death not long afterwards, prevented him from giving the character of permanence to his conquests.

That Heliokles was contemporary with Eukratides, and associated with him in power, as asserted of that prince's son and successor, is placed beyond doubt by a very important medal discovered by the late Dr. Lord at Kunduz. On one side we have the usual helmeted head of Eukratides, with the legend, 'Eukratides, the Great King;' on the reverse is a double profile, with the inscription, 'Of Heliokles and Laodike.' Heliokles is without a fillet; he was not king. Eukratides was king when the medal was struck; but it is not a coin 'of' Eukratides, it is a coin 'of' Heliokles; and his exercise of the regal function of striking money in his own name, whilst he acknowledged the supremacy of Eukratides, proves that although he

[1] In his fifth volume, in a note on the tetradrachm of Heliokles, the only one of his coins then known, M. Mionnet observes, "Dans une courte description de médailles grecques que j'ai publiée en l'an 8 (1799), la fabrique de ce médaillon m'avoit déjà déterminé à le ranger parmi les rois de la Bactriane." See also Supplement, vol. viii. p. 469.

was not yet invested with the title, he was possessed of some of the powers of royalty, not as co-equal, but as—nominally at least—subordinate, as Yuva-Raja, 'prince regent,' or Cæsar. This is, no doubt, the character in which he appears upon the coin in question, and it very remarkably confirms the statement of ancient history that the son of Eukratides was his associate in the kingdom.

The other coins of Heliokles furnish some additional illustrations of his history. They are not numerous, from whence we may infer his reign was neither long nor prosperous. The large silver coins belong to the period of the Bactrian kings, and he, no doubt, held territory north of the mountains. There are, however, also a few bilingual copper coins, showing that he exercised Paropamisan sovereignty.

Upon whatever plea Heliokles pretended to vindicate the murder of his father, and in confirmation of which he possibly assumed the title of 'Dikæus,' there can be no doubt that the transaction must have injured his reputation and weakened his authority, and contributed, with his impolitic demonstrations against Mithridates, to accelerate the subversion of the Greek kingdom of Bactria. The Scythians were still advancing from the north, and the Parthians from the west; and the power of the Greeks was not only curtailed by foreign foes, but was still more fatally impaired by domestic dissension. It may be doubted if the Greeks held any territory north of the Hindu Kush long after the reign of Heliokles, and even on the south of the mountains they soon afterwards were confined to the territories nearest to India. The durability of the Parthian conquests over them in that direction has been already questioned upon a consideration of historical probabilities; and that their occupation, if ever it occurred, was transient, is established by the absence of all Arsacidan coins, except some small copper coins of uncertain attribution individually, which have been picked up at Beghram. It may be confidently asserted, upon numismatic testimony, in opposition to the statements of classical writers,[1]

[1] As Justin, speaking of Mithridates, asserts, Imperium Parthorum a monte Caucaso, multis populis in ditionem redactis, usque flumen Euphratem protulit: Book XLI. 6. And Diodorus, Ὁ Ἀρσάκης ὁ βασιλεὺς τὴν βασιλείαν ἐπὶ πλεῖον ηὔξησε· μέχρι γὰρ τῆς Ἰνδικῆς διατείνας, τῆς ὑπὸ τοῦ Πώρου γενομένης χώρας ἐκυρίευσεν ἀκινδύνως. Fragm. ed. Bip. Book x. 91. Orosius is also cited

that the Arsacidan kings never reduced for a protracted period any provinces of India to their authority.

The aggressions of the Parthians, however, no doubt combined, with other causes, to produce a state of general confusion, in which different members of the reigning dynasty, or mere military adventurers, erected petty independent principalities. It is in this way only that we can explain the existence of the many Greek princes whose names are preserved in the Bactrian coins, and who are posterior to historical identification. They flourished in all probability in the brief interval that separated the death of Eukratides, about B. C. 155, from the total subversion of the Greek Bactrian kingdom by Barbarians. This event is dated, upon good authority, B. C. 127, leaving, therefore, no more than twenty-eight years for the several dynasties. This, however, can be true only of Bactria proper. The Indian branches from the Bactrian stock must have survived this event; and we may not much err in deferring their extinction till some fifty years before our æra, leaving about a century for the total extinction of the relics of Greek domination on the confines of India.

The silence of history throws us almost wholly upon the hints furnished by the coins that have been discovered for the determination of any of the transactions of the interval thus proposed. We have for the period of probably about a century, at least twelve princes of genuine Greek nomenclature, of some of whom it may be inferred that they governed for many years extensive territories. They cannot, then, have reigned in succession; some of them must have been contemporary from the time of Eukratides or even earlier. They were, no doubt, often hostile, setting up and putting down dynasties. Which of them were connected, which distinct, it is no easy matter to conjecture; and all conjectures hazarded upon the imperfect data in our possession must be liable to so many sources of error, that they cannot be offered with courage or confidence. It is necessary, however, for the sake of perspicuity, to adopt some principle of classification, and the following appears to be open to

as authority for a similar extension of the Parthian empire: Omnes præterea gentes quæ inter Hydaspem fluvium et Indum jacent subegit (Mithridates), ad Indiam quoque extendit imperium. As Lassen remarks, the authority is of no great weight.

the fewest objections. It is founded, as will be explained under each separate head, upon a collation of the style, portraits, types, and inscriptions of the coins in our possession; and independently, therefore, of the uncertainty which must attach to all deductions from such narrow premises, it is exposed to the not unlikely contingency of being completely invalidated by additional discoveries. This is a fate which must be risked as long as we shall not have exhausted the stock of materials; and all that may be at present expected is that a careful, and by no means positive, application shall be made of the materials in our possession.

Retrograding, then, to the Bactrian princes of whom we have already spoken, the classification here proposed is the following; it is restricted, for the present, to the kings whose Greek descent appears indisputable:—

Euthydemus.				
Demetrius.	Eukratides.			
Lysias.	Heliokles.			
Amyntas.	Antialkides.	Antimachus.		Agathokles.
Agathokleia.	Arkhebius.	Philoxenes.	Menander.	Pantaleon.
			Apollodotus.	
			Diomedes.	
			Hermæus.	
			Su-Hermæus?	

COINS OF HELIOKLES.

SILVER.

1. Tetradrachm. Head of king, with helmet and fillet, to the right. ΒΑΣΙΛΕΥΣ ΜΕΓΑΣ ΕΥΚΡΑΤΙΔΗΣ. R. Two heads to the right, male and female; the former has no fillet, and is dressed in the chlamys. ΗΛΙο-ΚΛΕοΥΣ ΚΑΙ ΛΑοΔΙΚΗΣ. Mon. 14. Supplemental Plate, fig. 7.

This unique and most important coin was procured by Dr. Lord at Tash-Kurghan. It was first made known to us by the activity of Mr. Prinsep, J. As. Soc. B. July, 1838, Pl. XXVII. fig. 1, whence it was repeated in the Proceedings of the Numismatic Society. It is now engraved from the original, which has been sent home by Dr. Lord. It is in perfect preservation, having been worn as an ornament probably, as it has a loop attached to it.

2. Tetradrachm. Head of king to the right, with fillet and chlamys. R. Jupiter standing, to the front; his left hand holds a spear or sceptre, his right the thunderbolt. ΒΑΣΙΛΕΩΣ ΔΙΚΑΙΟΥ ΗΛΙΟΚΛΕΟΥΣ. Mon. 29. Pl. II. fig. 6.

From a coin in the British Museum, in the collection of R. P. Knight, Esq. A coin of similar type was first published by Mionnet in 1799, who, from its fabrication, inferred its belonging to a king of Bactria, in which he was followed by Visconti, Iconographie Grecque. Other similar coins have been since found, and one was brought from Kabul by Dr. Honigberger: J. des Sav. June, 1834, and September, 1835.

3. Hemidrachm. Head of king, with fillet, to the right. ΒΑΣΙΛΕΩΣ ΔΙΚΑΙΟΥ ΗΛΙΟΚΛΕΟΥΣ. R. Standing figure of Jupiter, his spear in one hand, his thunderbolt in the other. 𐨨𐨱𐨪𐨗𐨯 𐨢𐨨𐨁𐨐𐨯 𐨱𐨅𐨫𐨁𐨩𐨐𐨿𐨫𐨩𐨯 Maharajasa Dhamikasa Heliyaklayasa. Mon. 30. Supplemental Plate, fig. 8.

From Masson's additional supply.

COPPER.

4. Square; middle size. Head of king, with fillet and loose robe, to the right. ΒΑΣΙΛΕΩΣ ΔΙΚΑΙΟΥ ΗΛΙΟΚΛΕΟΥΣ. R. Elephant to the left. Inscription as in 3. Mon. Σ. Pl. II. fig. 7.

From a unique coin presented to the Royal Asiatic Society by General Ventura: it is also figured, J. As. Soc. B. July, 1838, Pl. XXVIII. fig. 7.

5. Square; middle size. Elephant to the right. ΒΑΣΙΛΕΩΣ ΔΙΚΑΙΟΥ ΗΛΙΟΚΛΕΟΥΣ. R. effaced.

A coin presented by General Ventura to Mr. Prinsep, and described by him in the J. As. Soc. B. July, 1838, Pl. XXVIII. fig. 8.

LYSIAS, B.C. 147.

A variety of considerations seem to connect this prince with Demetrius and Euthydemus. We are not told that Eukratides put an end either to the life or reign of Demetrius: he dispossessed him of Bactria, and repulsed his attempts to gain a footing even at the base of the Caucasus. Whilst

Eukratides maintained his own possession of the Paropamisus as well as Bactria, he may have been obliged to leave Demetrius a part at least of his principality. Demetrius must have died, however, shortly afterwards, as conjectured above.

In evidence of the affinity between Lysias and Demetrius, we find upon the silver coins of the former the same elephant-shaped helmet that characterizes the silver coins of Demetrius; and on the reverse we have the same type, the standing Hercules. On the square copper coins the head has much the character of that on the copper coins of Demetrius; and the club borne by the king again alludes, no doubt, to Hercules, who seems to have been the favourite divinity of Euthydemus and his son. The type of the elephant on the reverse of the copper coins is in harmony with that of the crest. The use of the Arianian characters places Lysias on the south of the mountains, out of Bactria proper. The additional title he adopts, of Aniketos, may refer to victories over Heliokles or his successor. The silver coins of Lysias are rare, and the copper, though not scarce, are not numerous; from which a reign neither long nor extensive may be inferred. The monograms of the coins of Lysias comprise the letters Τ, Α, and Σ, but these offer no satisfactory elucidation of his history.

At the same time, however, that the costume of the head and the types of the reverse indicate some connexion with Demetrius, there are other considerations which militate against an immediate succession. The fabric of the coins, the square form of the copper coins, and the presence of Arianian letters, show both place and period different from that of Demetrius; and, whilst they confine Lysias to the south of the mountains, render it likely that he was subsequent to Eukratides, and contemporary with Heliokles. Although, therefore, possibly connected with Demetrius, and perhaps reigning over part of Arachosia, or a tract to the east of it along the Gomul river, he may have succeeded to power only after the death of Eukratides, when the retreat of the Parthians and disaffection to Heliokles offered him a favourable opportunity of regaining a portion of his patrimony. It may be observed, also, that the elephant on the reverse of his copper coins, as well as the monogrammatic Σ, occurs on the copper coins of Heliokles. If the latter intimate similarity of place, Lysias may have won the town in which the coin was struck, from Heliokles.

COINS OF LYSIAS.

SILVER.

1. Hemidrachm. Head of king, with fillet and chlamys, to the right: the head is covered with a helmet in the shape of an elephant's head, like that of Demetrius. ΒΑΣΙΛΕΩΣ ΑΝΙΚΗΤΟΥ ΛΥΣΙΟΥ. R. Hercules standing, to the front; the club and skin, with a palm-branch, in his left hand, his right placing a chaplet on his head. Maharajasa Apatihatasa Lisiasa. Mon. 31. Pl. II. fig. 9.

A coin presented by General Ventura to the Royal Asiatic Society; also described by Prinsep, J. As. Soc. B. July, 1838, Pl. XXVIII. fig. 4. Mr. Masson's last dispatch contains another well-preserved specimen of this coin. The monogram is double, and is the same as that of the following copper coin. The Prakrit inscription is more distinct. The name is distinctly read Lisikasa. See Supplemental Plate, fig. 9.

COPPER.

2. Square; middle size. Head to the right, bare and bearded; bust clothed; head of a club behind the left shoulder, and shaft in front. ΒΑΣΙΛΕΩΣ ΑΝΙΚΗΤΟΥ ΛΥΣΙΟΥ. R. Elephant to the right. Maharajasa Apatihatasa Lisikasa. Mon. 32, double. Pl. II. fig. 10.

These coins are not rare; there are several in the Masson collection: they are described and figured, J. As. Soc. B. April, 1834, Pl. IX. figs. 15, 16, and Pl. XXII. fig. 12; J. des Sav. March, 1836; J. Asiatique, Feb. 1836; and Mionnet, Supplement, tom. viii. The latter describes the obverse as having "tête de Lysias represéntée en Hercule, la massue sur l'épaule gauche,—la peau de lion nouée autour du cou." The objects before and behind the neck are indistinct in every specimen, but they seem to be intended for the two ends of the club. The Hercules on the reverse renders it probable enough that Lysias affected the character and wielded the weapons of that god. The types are probably borrowed from the copper coins of Demetrius. The French numismatist refers to Lysias a coin that belongs to a different prince, as will be subsequently noticed.

AMYNTAS, B.C. 135.

There is but one coin of this prince, of which only two specimens have been found. In placing him as the successor of Lysias, the chief motive is not knowing what better to do with him. The Minerva on the reverse offers some affinity to the coin of Demetrius. The character of the head-dress, however, would bring him down to a more barbaric period, to which also the monogram mostly belongs.

COIN OF AMYNTAS.

COPPER.

Square; middle size. Head of king to the right; the upper part of the head-dress effaced. ΒΑΣΙΛΕΩΣ ΝΙΚΑΤοΡοΥ ΑΜΥΝΤ - - . R. Minerva to the left, her lance resting across her right side; drapery (? or shield) behind her.  Maharajasa Jayadharasa Amitasa. Mon. 33. Pl. II. fig. 14.

The first specimen of this coin was procured by Colonel Stacey, and is here copied from the drawing in the J. As. Soc. B. Nov. 1836, Pl. XLVI. fig. 1. It was erroneously stated by me, on a former occasion, that this coin belonged to Dr. Swiney; Numismatic Journal. Colonel Stacey's coin was lost, but a cast of it is preserved in Mr. Prinsep's cabinet, taken by himself. Another specimen is described by M. R. Rochette, in which the head-dress is "une tiare recourbée en avant et ornée de rayons sur les côtés, avec les rubans qui l'attachent pendants par derrière:" J. des Sav. Feb. 1839, p. 90. He also mentions the receipt, from General Allard, of an impression of a silver medal, so exactly the same, even as to its defects, that it has been evidently fabricated from the copper coin.

AGATHOKLEIA.

A solitary copper coin presents us with the portrait of a queen, Agathokleia, 'the servant of God.' Where and when she reigned it is not possible to conjecture with any sort of confidence, and her being placed here is upon the same principle as the position of her predecessor. It might be supposed she was connected with a prince to be hereafter noticed, Agathokles, but the very different style of the coins, and the use of different letters for the Indian legend, forbid the association. By Professor Lassen she is placed after Apollodotus and Diomedes,[1] and he is followed by Dr. Grotefend. No reason is assigned for her being so located. To classing her with the descendants of Euthydemus, the type of the sitting Hercules on the reverse of her coin is an inducement. The helmet she wears is, however, rather that of Eukratides, but the type is a preferable analogy. The square shape of her coin, the irregularity of the Greek letters, and the use of Arianian characters, show that to whichever dynasty she belonged, she was not of an early date: her reign must have been brief.

COIN OF AGATHOKLEIA.

COPPER.

Square; middle size. Head of queen, with helmet, but no fillet, to the right ΒΑΣΙΛΙΣΣΑΣ ΘΕΟΤΡΟΠΟ - ΑΓΑΘΟΚΛΕΙΑΣ. R. Seated Hercules, with his club on his knee. [Arian legend] - Maharajasa Midatasa Mikasaklayasa. Mon. 34. Pl. VI. fig. 10.

From a unique coin in the possession of Dr. Swiney; obtained by Syed Karamat Ali in Afghanistan. The same coin is described by Prinsep; J. As. Soc. B. November, 1836, Pl. XLVI. fig. 2.

ANTIMACHUS, B.C. 140.

One of the coins of this prince is a tetradrachm of great beauty, which, both by its denomination and execution, belongs to pure Bactrian art. He cannot, therefore, have been long subsequent to Heliokles, after whom no such description of coin has yet been met with. It was brought from Bokhara. There are also smaller silver coins, with a bilingual inscrip-

[1] Zur Geschichte, p. 202.

tion, of which a few have been found at Beghram, but more have been brought from the Hazára country. There is only one copper coin, but that has also a bilingual inscription.

Considerable difficulties attend the determination of this prince's place and period. He may be considered a conqueror, and as the founder of a dynasty, as the reverses of his different coins bear a palm-branch or a Victory with a palm-branch and a regal fillet. The bilingual inscription indicates a date posterior to Eukratides, if, as seems probable, the use of Indian characters originated with that prince. M. Rochette[1] refers him to an earlier date, or B.C. 170, from his bearing the titles of Theos and Nikephoros, which were the titles of Antiochus Epiphanes, B.C. 175-164. The coincidence renders it likely that Antimachus was posterior to Antiochus; but how long subsequent, it leaves undetermined. The figure on the reverse of the tetradrachm is considered to represent Neptune holding a palm-branch—a type of a naval victory, from which M. R. Rochette suggests the possibility of an allusion being intended to assistance given by Antimachus to Antiochus in his Egyptian victories, although he admits that history is silent on the subject. Lassen also supposes that 'a naval victory' is alluded to by this type; but, as he places Antimachus in Drangiana, it is not easy to understand where the scene of such triumph could have been. He makes his date B.C. 165, and assigns to him the foundation of a new principality in Drangiana, a conjecture he supposes strengthened by the attitude of Antimachus as a mounted horseman; whence the device was adopted by the Barbaric kings of Ki-pin, who, according to Chinese authorities, were represented as cavaliers on their coins; and Ki-pin he considers as precisely equivalent to Sejistan. According to Klaproth it is rather Arachosia, comprising Ghizni and the course of the Gomul; in which case Lassen's verification fails, and it may be reasonably doubted if at the date suggested, when Parthia was powerful, any Bactrian princes could have held territory so near to Persia as Sejistan. Considering also that the ground to the eastward was occupied by Demetrius and Eukratides from B.C. 170 to 165, it is difficult to find at that period a territory for Antimachus. It seems, therefore, more probable that we may

[1] J. des Sav. Feb. 1836, p. 82.

place his date somewhere about the latter part of the reign of Heliokles. The Neptune would tempt us to carry him towards the mouth of the Indus, but the localities in which his coins are found indicate a more northern situation, and we may imagine his founding a principality immediately above the Hazára mountains, on the west of the Balkh road, and his making a stand for some time against the advance of the Scythians from the north.

COINS OF ANTIMACHUS.

SILVER.

1. Tetradrachm. Head of king, with fillet and Macedonian hat, to the right; bust clothed with the chlamys. R. Standing figure, to the front, in a mantle which covers the lower part of the body; the right hand leans on a trident, the left holds a palm-branch. ΒΑΣΙΛΕΩΣ ΘΕΟΥ ΑΝΤΙΜΑΧΟΥ. Mon. 35.

This description is taken from Mionnet, Supplement, vol. viii. p. 466, who copies it from Koehler, by whom the coin was first described and figured. The figure on the reverse is considered to be that of Neptune. It was brought from Bokhara, and is yet unique.

2. Hemidrachm. Winged Victory, to the left, holding a palm-branch in her right hand, and a fillet in her left. ΒΑΣΙΛΕΩΣ ΝΙΚΗΦΟΡΟΥ ΑΝΤΙΜΑΧΟΥ. Mon. 36. R. King, with Macedonian cap and fillet, on a galloping horse, to the right. 𐨨𐨱𐨪𐨗𐨯 𐨗𐨩𐨢𐨪𐨯 𐨀𐨟𐨁𐨨𐨑𐨯 Maharajasa Jayadharasa Atimakhasa. Pl. II. fig. 15.

Several of these have been found by all the collectors. Mr. Masson procured a number from the Hazára country; they are of different execution, although they all bear the same monogram. The coin is described, J. As. Soc. B. June, 1835, Pl. XX. fig. 3, and January, 1836, Pl. II. fig. 9; J. des Sav. and J. Asiatique, February, 1836.

3. Obolus. Head of king, with hat, to the right. R. Standing figure of Neptune (?), with sceptre in his right hand, and palm in his left. ΒΑΣΙΛΕΩΣ ΘΥ (*sic*) - ΝΤΙΜΑΧΟΥ. Mon. Κ. Supplemental Plate, fig. 12.

This, which is unique, was contained in Mr. Masson's last dispatch.

COPPER.

4. Square; large. Female figure (Ceres?), to the front, with a cornucopia (?) in her left arm. - - ΕΙΛΕω -. R. Winged Victory, to the left; a rod or sceptre in her left hand, her right extended. Ƥ7ΥX1 - - - Ƥ37ʼn7Υ Maharajasa - - - - Atimakhasa. Mon. Σ. Pl. II. fig. 16.

This coin, belonging to General Ventura, is known only by Mr. Prinsep's figure, here copied: J. As. Soc. B. June, 1834, Pl. XXI. fig. 4. It is described by M. R. Rochette, J. des Sav. March, 1836, p. 131, note; he refers it to Philoxenes. M. Jacquet, J. Asiatique, Feb. 1836, thinks it likely to belong to Lysias. The characters on the reverse give, with exception of but one letter, the Indian equivalent of Antimachus; and the penultimate, which appears in the coin to be 7 *t* or *d*, may have been easily blundered for Ϛ *kh*.

PHILOXENES, B.C. 130.

The several scholars and numismatists who have investigated the subject agree in recognising this prince as the successor of Antimachus. The representation of him, as mounted on a galloping courser, is very much the same as that of Antimachus, except that he wears a helmet instead of the Macedonian hat. His epithet, Aniketos, allies him to Lysias, but the figure of Ceres on his copper coin is a further coincidence with a coin of Antimachus. The humped Indian bull is possibly known to the Eimaks and Hazáras. His coins are very rare; arguing a reign of limited extent and duration: if his kingdom was situated above the mountains, as seems probable, his reign must have ended about B. C. 125.

COINS OF PHILOXENES.

SILVER.

1. Didrachm. Head of king, with helmet and fillet, to the right. ΒΑΣΙΛΕΩΣ ΑΝΙΚΗΤΟΥ ΦΙΛΟΞΕΝΟΥ. R. Mounted horseman, to the right. Ƥ/ϯ1ϯ Ƥ7ʅ7ƚ1 Ƥ37ʅω Maharajasa Apatihatasa Pilashinasa. Mon. 37. Pl. II. fig. 17.

A coin in the possession of General Ventura, described by Prinsep, J. As. Soc. B. June, 1835, Pl. XXI. fig. 1; M. R. Rochette, J. des Sav.

March, 1836, Pl. II. fig. 5; Jacquet, J. Asiatique; and Mionnet, Supplement, vol. viii. p. 481.

2. Hemidrachm. Square. Head of king, with fillet, to the right. ΒΑΣΙΛΕΩΣ ΑΝΙΚΗΤΟΥ - ΙΛΟΞΕΝΟΥ. R. Horseman galloping. [Kharoshthi legend] Maharajasa Apatihatasa Pilashinasa. Mon. 38, and Σ below. Supplemental Plate, fig. 13.

From Masson's last dispatch. A similar coin is described by M. R. Rochette, J. des Sav. February, 1839, p. 89.

COPPER.

3. Square; middle size. Female figure, front view, with cornucopia (?). ΒΑΣΙΛΕΩΣ ΑΝΙΚΗΤΟΥ ΦΙΛΟΞΕΝΟΥ. R. Humped Indian bull, to the right. [Kharoshthi legend] Maharajasa Apatihatasa Pilashinasa. Mon. Σ. Pl. II. fig. 18.

From a coin presented to the Royal Asiatic Society by General Ventura. A similar coin is in the collection of Dr. Swiney; described, J. As. Soc. B. June, 1835, Pl. XXI. fig. 2, and July, 1836, Pl. XXVIII. fig. 12. Another specimen is described by Messrs. Rochette and Jacquet, J. des Sav. March, 1836, and J. Asiatique, Feb. 1836; also by Mionnet, Supplement, viii.; and another is contained in Mr. Masson's last dispatch. The female figure is considered to represent Ceres Carpophoros. The monograms vary. Nos. 39, 40.

ANTIALKIDES, B.C. 135.

The style of the copper coins of this prince so much resembles that of the copper coins of Lysias, that the two princes have been uniformly considered as connected. According to Lassen, Antialkides founded a principality in Arachosia and West Kabul, B. C. 160, in which he was succeeded by Lysias. There are some considerations which are opposed to this classification.

The portrait of Antialkides on his silver coins wears either the plain fillet or the Macedonian hat; that of Lysias, the Demetrian elephant-casque: various types on the coins of the latter are the same as those of Demetrius, whilst Jupiter and the bonnets of the Dioscuri indicate the former's belonging to the hostile family of Heliokles and Eukratides. Antialkides may have succeeded the former, although not by direct inheritance; as the emblems of victory, and the wreath offered by the elephant, denote his achieving sovereignty. It may be imagined that the transfer of the wreath from the elephant's trunk to the Victory held in the hand of the sitting Jupiter is not without significance, and intimates the final overthrow of Lysias or his immediate successors, by Antialkides.

COINS OF ANTIALKIDES.

SILVER.

1. Hemidrachm. Head of king, to the right, with Macedonian hat, fillet, and chlamys. ΒΑΣΙΛΕΩΣ ΝΙΚΗΦΟΡΟΥ ΑΝΤΙΑΛΚΙΔΟΥ. R. Jupiter, seated in a chair with a high back; the left hand, resting on his left knee, holds his sceptre; the right, extended, holds a Victory with palm-branch and fillet; underneath the right hand is the head and fore-part of the body of an elephant with the trunk raised. [Arianian inscription] Maharajasa Jayadharasa Antialikitasa. Mon. ΚΡΑ. Pl. II. fig. 11.

From the Masson collection, procured at Beghram. Another has been presented to the Royal Asiatic Society by General Ventura; a third, in the possession of Dr. Swiney, has been described by Mr. Prinsep, J. As. Soc. B. Sept. 1836; a fourth, given to that gentleman by General Ventura, is also described and figured by him, J. As. Soc. B. July, 1838, Pl. XXVIII. fig. 1; and three others have been recently sent home by Mr. Masson. The epithets "unique et inédite," therefore, applied to a specimen represented by Mionnet, Supplement, vol. viii. p. 520, no longer appertain to it. The inscription on the reverse of Masson's coin is very imperfect.

2. Hemidrachm. Head of king, with fillet and chlamys, to the right. Inscription as in the last. R. Seated Jupiter, as before; the Victory has a double palm-branch, and the fillet is ornamented; the fore-part of the elephant is in profile to the right. Arianian inscription entire and distinct: Maharajasa Jayadharasa Atialikitasa. Mon. 31. Pl. II. fig. 12.

Unique; presented to the Royal Asiatic Society by General Ventura.

3. Hemidrachm. Head of king, with helmet, to the right. R. Seated Jupiter. Mon. ΚΡΑ.

Sent home recently by Mr. Masson. It differs from the preceding only in the helmet being worn by the king: the helmet is of the form of that of Eukratides.

4. Didrachm. Square; base metal. Head of king, to the right. Inscription imperfect. R. Bonnets of the Dioscuri.

Three of these coins are part of Mr. Masson's last supply. They are, no doubt, counterfeits, but two of them do not appear to be modern fabrications; they are probably of the time of Antialkides, and are so far instructive that they testify the existence of a square silver coinage: they are about the weight of the didrachms, something lighter. Of the third, however, which is of a purer silver, it may be pronounced that it is a modern cast from a copper coin. The coiners of Hindustan are beginning to take advantage of the anxiety of collectors to procure 'rare' coins, and are evidently at work to supply them. Some palpable instances of the modelling of specimens of silver upon copper are exposed by M. R. Rochette, J. des Sav. Feb. 1839, in regard to coins of Menander and Amyntas. The recent collections of Sir A. Burnes and Mr. Masson furnish instances of square gold coins of Apollodotus which have evidently been cast in a mould formed with the silver coin; and from Mr. Masson we have a large silver coin of Kadphises unquestionably a cast from an indifferent specimen of his copper. It is necessary now, therefore, that collectors in India should be on their guard against the dexterity of these native dealers.

COPPER.

5. Square; middle size. Head of king, to the right, with fillet; carrying a club across his left shoulder; the face is sometimes bearded. ΒΑΣΙΛΕΩΣ ΝΙΚΗΦΟΡΟΥ ΑΝΤΙΑΛΚΙΔΟΥ. R. The bonnets and palm-leaves of the Dioscuri. 𐨨𐨱𐨪𐨗𐨯 𐨗𐨩𐨢𐨪𐨯 𐨀𐨟𐨁𐨀𐨫𐨁𐨐𐨁𐨟𐨯 Maharajasa Jayadharasa Atialikitasa. Mon. 41. Pl. II. fig. 13.

These coins are in some number in all the collections, and were first described in the J. As. Soc. B. April, 1834, Pl. IX. figs. 13, 14, and June, 1835, Pl. XXVI. figs. 9, 10, 11. They were subsequently described, J. Asiatique, Feb. 1836, and J. des Sav. March, 1836, p. 132, Pl. II. fig. 7. M. R. Rochette is uncertain if the object seen before and behind the neck, as in the coins of Lysias, is a "palme, thyrse, ou massue." M. Jacquet considers it to be a palm-branch; but where most distinct it can scarcely be any thing else than a club.

6. Round; middle size. Head as before. R. As in the preceding.

Unique; in the Masson collection. It differs in no respect except in being round, and in the monogram 42, from the square coins. It has been described, J. As. Soc. B. Jan. 1836, p. 24.

7. Square; middle size. The hide of an animal? - ΑΣΙΛΕΩΣ (*sic*) ΝΙΚΗ-ΦΟΡΟΥ ΑΝΤΙ----. R. A wreath and palm-branch. Inscription incomplete. Supplemental Plate, fig. 11. See also some late observations by Captain A. Cunningham; J. As. Soc. B. April, 1840, p. 393.

From Mr. Masson's last dispatch.

ARCHEBIUS, B.C. 125-120.

The name of this prince has been variously read upon different coins—Archelius, Archerius, and Archebius, the latter of which appears to be preferable; but the various readings of the Greek are seemingly corroborated by the Arianian letters. The silver coins of this prince have the type of Jupiter, and he bears as one of his titles Dikæos, both of which ally him to the family of Eukratides. Another of his titles is Nikephoros, which he shares with Antialkides, who is also connected with the Eukratidan line, as we have seen. It seems unlikely, however, that he followed Heliokles; for on one of his coins we have an attitude borrowed from the coins of Menander, to whom therefore he must be subsequent, or with whom he must during a part of his reign have been contemporary. The copy of the attitude is so exact that it may be intended for the portrait of Menander himself, and may intimate the dependent position of Archebius during part of that prince's sovereignty.

COINS OF ARCHEBIUS.

SILVER.

1. Hemidrachm. Head of king, to the right, with fillet. ΒΑΣΙΛΕΩΣ ΔΙΚΑΙΟΥ ΝΙΚΗΦΟΡΟΥ ΑΡΧΕΛΙΟΥ. R. Jupiter standing, the lower part of

his body dressed; his right hand holds a sceptre, his left, the thunderbolt. PΛHS1 P-JΛ3 PhJZ P3T1ᒐ Maharajasa Dhamikasa Jayadharasa Akhaliyasa. Mon. ΚΡΑ. Pl. II. fig. 8.

From the Masson collection; also J. As. Soc. B. Sept. 1836, Pl. XXXV. fig. 1. The name is read as here represented on the coin; and the Indian legend, although imperfect, and, in some of the letters, unusual, gives the name also with an *l*.

2. Hemidrachm. Head of king, to the left; the bust is in armour, and the right hand is casting a javelin. The type is in all respects the same as one that is frequent on the coins of Menander. ΒΑΣΙΛΕΩΣ ΔΙΚΑΙΟΥ ΝΙΚΗΦΟΡΟΥ ΑΡΧΕΒΙΟΥ. R. Jupiter, as in the preceding. PhJZ P3T1ᒐ PΛ†S1 PTZΛ3 Maharajasa Dhamikasa Jayadharasa Akhabiyasa. Mon. ΚΡΑ and 43. Supplemental Plate, fig. 10.

This is an interesting and curious coin, and clears up the difficulty as to the name. It was procured by Mr. Vigne, who has kindly allowed it to be engraved.

COPPER.

3. Winged Victory, to the right, holding a fillet. ΒΑΣΙΛΕΩΣ ΔΙΚΑΙΟΥ ΝΙΚΗΦΟΡΟΥ ΑΡΧΕΡΙΟΥ. R. Owl. Mon. 44. ΜΙΚ.

Described, from a coin in M. Court's collection, by M. R. Rochette; J. des Sav. Feb. 1839, p. 106. It is engraved as the vignette of Dr. C. L. Grotefend's work.

MENANDER, B.C. 126.

We have now again some help from history.

According to Strabo, Menander was one of those Bactrian kings by whose victories the boundaries of the kingdom were chiefly extended towards the east. He crossed the Hypanis, and passed eastwards as far as to the Isamus river:[1] the latter, as we have already seen, is considered to be the Jumna, the Hypanis being the Setlej. It appears likely, also, from what follows, that the occupation, if not the conquest, of Pattalene, is ascribed to Menander; and this harmonizes well enough with the fact mentioned by the author of the Periplus, that, in his time, the end of the

[1] Εἴγε καὶ τὸν Ὕπανιν διέβη πρὸς ἕω, καὶ μέχρι τοῦ Ἰσάμου προσῆλθε. Book XI. 11. 1.

first century after Christ, the drachms of Menander and Apollodotus were still current at Barygaza or Baroach on the coast of Guzerat.

Menander is spoken of by Arrian as a king of Bactria, and Plutarch gives him the same designation. The title, however, is applied by them without any consideration, and it may be doubted if he ever reigned in Bactria. Bayer, following Valens, makes him either the brother or a kinsman of Euthydemus; and his successor:[1] he calls him also king of India and Bactria; assuming the former from the record of his Indian victories, and a passage in the summary of a chapter of Trogus Pompeius,[2] which, however, does not necessarily indicate the reign of Menander in India. The only authority, therefore, we have for his ruling over any part of India is the writer of the Periplus.

Upon examining the coins, however, of this prince we have every reason to believe that he never was king of Bactria, but that he reigned over an extensive tract from the foot of the Paropamisan mountains to the sea. How far he held sovereignty on the east of the Indus, or even in the delta of that river, is somewhat doubtful, as his coins have not been found in those directions; they are most abundant in the vicinity of Kabul, in the Hazára mountains, and at Beghram; they are obtained in the Punjab, but apparently they are brought thither for sale. Colonel Tod, however, discovered his coins of Apollodotus and Menander on the Jumna, and there is no reason therefore why they may not be dug up in any of the intermediate spots. The chief seat of their issue was, however, the neighbourhood of Kabul, and here was in all probability the royal capital of Menander.

That Menander was never king of Bactria is to be inferred from the total absence of any tetradrachms or any other coins, silver or copper, with a mono-lingual inscription. The largest coin found of this prince is a didrachm, which, although of neat workmanship, is inferior in spirit and execution to the tetradrachms of Heliokles: it bears also an Arianian as well as a Greek legend. His smaller silver coins are very numerous, and the copper are in great variety, as well as number; from which we may ascribe to him a long and prosperous reign. That it was a reign of active

[1] Bayer, p. 74.

[2] Indiæ quoque additæ res gestæ per Apollodorum (Apollodotum) et Menandrum reges.

military exertion is also deducible from the portraits of the king, who not only wears the fillet of peaceful rule, or the helmet and defensive armour, but is exhibited in an attitude of attack, or as lancing a javelin in battle. His coins, therefore, give precision to the indications of history, and leave little doubt that he was a king of Paropamisan India, and a conqueror of the neighbouring provinces. His progress to the north was probably checked by the advancing power of the Scythians, whose contests with the Arsacidan monarchs deterred both from molesting Menander: his arms were therefore turned against his own countrymen, as well as against Indian princes; and such fragmentary portions of Greek dominion as may have subsisted to his day were perhaps once more consolidated under his reign.

It does not appear that there is any satisfactory ground for making Menander a brother of Euthydemus, and the style of his coins is evidence of his being subsequent not only to that monarch, but to Eukratides and Heliokles. Whether he was of kin to either of the two families to which most of the preceding princes have been ascribed, cannot be conjectured with any confidence from the titles or types of his coins. He first adopts the title 'Soter,' which may have been suggested to him by the example of Demetrius, Soter of Syria, to whom however, if the conjectural date here given is near the truth, he was considerably subsequent. His extensive conquests in India cannot well have been anterior to those of Mithridates, which makes him posterior to B. C. 137; and the probability that he was preceded by petty dynasties to which he put an end, cannot allow us to date him much earlier than B. C. 126. The prevailing device on his coins is the Minerva Promachos, which is found on Thessalian, Macedonian, and Seleucidan medals, generally executed in a much more masterly manner. Some of his coins offer a similar indication, and denote his attachment to the same goddess by the representations of her attributes, as her owl, and her ægis. On a small copper coin, which is very abundant, we have the head of an elephant on one side, and the club of Hercules on the other; and these, as well as the Minerva, connect him, if they have any such purport, with Euthydemus, or, rather, with Demetrius. The presence of a winged Victory offering a regal diadem on some of his coins may, however, as conjectured in regard to other princes, intimate his being the founder of a new dynasty.

Of others of his devices the import is not obvious; as the dolphin, boar's head, and the wheel: of the first of these the style is more like Roman than Greek, though distinguished from both by the usual quadrangular shape. A single coin has been found bearing the title ΔΙΚΑΙΟΣ, and having on the reverse a panther; a title and a type which would seem to connect him with Heliokles and Agathokles, but which may merely indicate his being posterior to both those princes.

An anecdote is related of Menander by Plutarch, which is curiously analogous to one of an Indian origin, although relating to a different individual. Menander, it is said, enjoyed such favour with his subjects, that upon his death, which happened in camp, different cities contended for the possession of his ashes, and the dispute was only adjusted by their agreeing that the relics should be divided amongst them, and that they should severally erect monuments to his memory. This story, as has been already noticed, is told of Gautama or Sakya Sinha in all the traditional biographies of him which are current amongst the nations following the faith of Buddha. Upon his death, and the cremation of his corpse, eight cities contended for the ashes; the precious remains were divided amongst them, and each built magnificent shrines or 'topes' for their reception. The existence of such monuments in Bactria and Paropamisus was known in the second century, as has already been mentioned, and the persons with whom the knowledge of the fact originated may have mistaken or mis-stated the object of these posthumous honours.

COINS OF MENANDER.

SILVER.

1. Didrachm. Head of king to the right, with fillet and chlamys. ΒΑΣΙΛΕΩΣ ΣΩΤΗΡ°Σ ΜΕΝΑΝΔΡ°Υ. R. Thessalian Minerva, to the left; back view; the ægis in her left, and thunderbolt in her right hand; the ends of her garment hanging from her shoulders. 𐨨𐨱𐨪𐨗𐨯 𐨟𐨡𐨟𐨯 𐨨𐨁𐨣𐨡𐨯 Maharajasa Tadatasa (?) Minadasa. Mon. 23, and the letter Σ. Pl. III. fig. 13.

This beautiful and hitherto unique coin is in the collection of Mr. Masson, and was purchased by him at Kabul. It is also delineated, J. As. Soc. B.

January, 1836, p. 22, Pl. II. fig. 15. The device on the reverse is borrowed from the Macedonian coins. The attitude, M. R. Rochette remarks, "est consacrée par un long usage sur les monnaies de la Thessalie et sur cette des rois d'Epire et de Macédoine."

2. Hemidrachm. Head of king, with fillet, to the right. Inscription as before. R. Minerva Promachos, and inscription as before. No monogram. Pl. III. fig. 14.

3. Hemidrachm. Head of king, with helmet, to the right. R. Minerva Promachos. Mon. 45. Pl. III. fig. 15.

4. Hemidrachm. Head of king, bare, but with fillet, to the left; back view; the shoulders covered with armour; the right hand is raised, and grasps a short javelin as in act to throw it. Inscription as before. Mon. 45. Pl. III. fig. 16.

5. Hemidrachm. Head as in the last, grasping the javelin: the inscription differently disposed. R. Minerva Promachos; front view, and turned to the right. Mon. 21. Pl. IV. fig. 1.

6. Hemidrachm. Back view of the king's head and shoulders, as in the last, but the head is armed with a helmet. R. Minerva, to the left; the lower part of her dress looks like trowsers. Mon. 46. Pl. IV. fig. 2.

These are delineated from coins of which a considerable number exists in the collection; of these Mr. Masson procured one at Kabul, one at Beghram, and above one hundred from a Hindu, who had purchased them in the Hazára country to the north-west of Kabul. They are all in excellent preservation; and, although agreeing in their devices and legends, are evidently struck from different dies: the minor varieties of execution being very numerous. Of those which bear different representations of the king, those with the arm raised to throw or to stab with the javelin are much the most numerous. The helmeted head in the same attitude, No. 6, is rare; it was unique till a duplicate was presented by General Ventura to the Royal Asiatic Society. The helmeted head to the right, No. 3, is next in number; and the head with the fillet, No. 2, least numerous. The countenance of the last is, in general, juvenile; and that of the helmeted head is also often young. The countenance in the coins which represent the king combating is in general, but not always, that of a man of mature years: in none does the face bear the character of age. The attitude of the combating king occurs on a coin of Alexander in the Hunterian collection, Mus. Hunter, Pl. XXXIV. fig. 15, and on a copper coin of Eukratides, as above, p. 241, No. 16. The figure, attitude, and dress of the Minerva offer many minor diversities; the upper part with pendulous wings or pteryges constitutes the chlamyde Thessalienne, according to Mionnet. The monograms vary considerably; some of those which are found on the coins of other princes, as ΚΡΑ and Σ, as well as Nos. 21 and 23, recur, and others are Nos. 47 to 56. The Arianian inscription always follows the order of the Greek. The order of either inscription places the name in the exergue.

The coin of type No. 2 was the first silver coin of Menander published. It was obtained by Dr. Swiney at Subathu, and described and figured by Prinsep; J. As. Soc. B. August, 1833, Pl. XIV. fig. 6. Since then the coins of Menander have been procured in various parts of Afghanistan and the Punjab: J. As. Soc. B. January, 1836, and July, 1838, Pl. XXVIII. figs. 5, 6; J. des Sav. Sept. 1835, and March, 1836; J. Asiatique, Feb. 1836; Mionnet, Supplement, vol. viii. Pl. XXIII. fig. 1, &c.

COPPER.

7. Square; large. Head bare, to the right; there are traces apparently of the fillet at the back of the neck, but indistinct. ΒΑΣΙΛΕΩΣ ΣΩΤΗΡοΣ ΜΕΝΑΝΔΡοΥ. R. A dolphin. 𐨨𐨱𐨪𐨗𐨯 𐨟𐨡𐨟𐨯 𐨨𐨁𐨣𐨡𐨯 Maharajasa Tadatasa Minandasa. Mon. 57, 58. Pl. IV. fig. 3.

Masson collection, unique, and a remarkable coin. It is also figured; J. As. Soc. B. vol. v. Pl. II. fig. 5, and Pl. XLVI. fig. 8.

8. Square; middle size. Head helmeted, to the right; hair at the back of the neck braided (?). Inscription as before. R. Winged Victory to the left, with palm-branch in her left hand, and a wreath in her extended right. Inscription as before. Mon. 46, and the letter B. Pl. IV. fig. 4.

9. Square; middle size. Head as before. R. Victory, with palm-branch and wreath, to the right. Mon. 59. Pl. IV. figs. 5, 6.

Coins of the type of the two last described, differing only in the position and form of the Victory, are numerous. The monograms, 59, 60, vary, but are commonly indistinct, as the coins are more or less worn. They have been described from the collections of Masson, Honigberger, Ventura, &c., in the J. As. Soc. B. April, 1834; J. des Sav. Sept. and Oct. 1835; J. Asiatique, Feb. 1836; Mionnet, Supplement, vol. viii. The first brought to notice was in the possession of Colonel Tod, and was obtained by him at Mathura; Trans. R. As. Soc. vol. i. p. 313, Pl. XII. fig. 2. See also J. Asiatique, Nov. 1828, for remarks upon it by Professor Schlegel, and Lassen's Pentapotamia Indica, p. 53.

10. Square; middle size. Head bare, to the left; arm raised, grasping a javelin. Inscription as before. R. Minerva Promachos, to the right; her breasts bare, and the ægis on her wrist. Inscription as before. Mon. 60. Pl. IV. fig. 7.

There are three of these coins in the Masson collection; they agree in essentials with the silver coins of the fighting king, but offer some peculiarities, especially in the garb of the Minerva. The Indian letters, which in the specimen engraved are very bold and distinct, present some differences, as will be seen in the Plate; the legend is the same. Maharajasa Tadatasa (?) Minandasa - - . It does not appear that Masson has noticed this coin. A similar one is described by Mionnet, with a different monogram, 61; Supplement, vol. viii. p. 476.

11. Square; middle size. Head, with helmet, to the right; face very effeminate, and hair falling down the back of the neck. Minerva? Inscription as before. R. An owl. Inscription as before. Mon. 62. Pl. IV. fig. 8.

From the Masson collection. It was for some time unique, but a second has been recently received. The first is figured, J. As. Soc. B. April, 1834, Pl. VIII. fig. 4, and Nov. 1836, Pl. XLVI. fig. 6.

12. Square; middle size. Head of a boar, to the right. - ΑΣΙΛΕΩΣ ΣΛΤΗ°Σ (*sic*) ΜΕΝΑΝΔΡ - -. R. A plant. Inscription indistinct. Mon. 63. Pl. IV. fig. 9.

Unique; Masson collection: also J. As. Soc. B. Nov. 1836, Pl. XLVI. fig. 9. Mr. Masson considers the reverse to bear a palm-leaf; but the coin is much worn, and the device is doubtful.

13. Square; middle size. Head, with helmet, to the right. Inscription

as before. R. The shield of Minerva, with Medusa's head. Inscription as before. Mon. 52. Pl. IV. fig. 12.

From a coin of Dr. Swiney's collection; there is one in the Masson collection, but the reverse is less distinct: also J. As. Soc. B. Nov. 1836, Pl. XLVI. fig. 5. Another coin of the same type, from M. Court's collection, is described by M. R. Rochette. That learned numismatist observes, "le travail y rappelle tout à fait celui du même emblème qui forme le type de toute une nombreuse classe de monnaies de bronze autonomes appartenant à des villes de la Paphlagonie et du Pont:" J. des Sav. Dec. 1838, p. 750.

14. Square; small. The head of an elephant, to the right, with proboscis raised, and a bell pendulous from his neck. **ΒΑΣΙΛΕΩΣ ΣΩΤΗΡΟΣ ΜΕΝΑΝΔΡΟΥ.** R. The club of Hercules. Inscription as before. Mon. double, 64, 65. Pl. IV. fig. 10.

Masson collection. These coins are very numerous, and of various execution; many are beautifully struck, others are as rude. They are described by all the authorities referred to. Mionnet has one with the massue couchée; Supplement, vol. viii. p. 476, No. 43.

15. Square; small. Wheel with spokes and studs. **ΒΑΣΙΛΕΩΣ ΣΩΤΗΡΟΣ ΜΕΝΑΝΔΡ - - .** R. A palm-branch. Inscription as before, but imperfect. Mon. 60. Pl. IV. fig. 11.

16. Square. Male figure, to the front, with helmet, short tunic, and buskins; left hand resting on a lance placed obliquely. **ΒΑΣΙΛΕΩΣ ΔΙΚΑΙΟΥ ΜΕΝΑΝΔΡΟΥ.** R. Panther on his hind-legs, to the right. Arianian inscription.

New and unique. Described by M. Rochette, J. des Sav. Dec. 1838, p. 751, who remarks the analogy offered by the title Dikæus to the title of Heliokles, and by the type of the panther to that of Agathokles. The figure he regards as that of Mars; not of the king in that character, as the practice of representing monarchs with the attributes of divinities belongs to a later epoch. "L'usage de représenter les princes sous les traits et avec les attributs d'un dieu est d'une autre époque que cette à laquelle appartiennent les médailles Grecques de la Bactriané."

APOLLODOTUS, B.C. 110.

The same authorities that have been cited for Menander bear witness to the existence of this prince; and that the two were connected in the order of time, as may be inferred from the mention of their coins by the author of the Periplus, and of their names by Trogus Pompeius, is also testified by their coins.

The coins of Apollodotus bear the title Soter, which is one point of coincidence. On one of them, of which it may be observed that a specimen comes from Guzerat, is added the epithet Philopater. It bears also the type of the fighting Minerva, showing another analogy to the medals of Menander, who, it seems to be admitted generally, was probably the predecessor and father of Apollodotus. There is no class of coins from which it might be supposed that any other prince stood in this relation to Apollodotus. That he was of late date is also deducible from his other silver coins, which differ from all other coins of this period in being square: hitherto the quadrangular form has been restricted to copper coins; they differ also from most of those hitherto observed in omitting the portrait of the king, having on one side an elephant, and the humped Indian ox on the other; types that also evidence the Indian dominion of Apollodotus.

The copper coins of this prince, both round and square, are a tangible illustration of his name, and, in like manner, prove his devotion to Apollo. One face presents a figure of that deity, the other his tripod. The only prior instance of the Bactrian use of this type is in a rare coin of Eukratides, who may have adopted it from some of the Syrian coins; and it may only in the present instance argue a later date. The epithet Philopater occurs on the coins of more than one Seleucidan prince, especially of Antiochus IX., on which also an armed Pallas appears. This prince is nearly contemporary with the date conjectured for Apollodotus, or B.C. 114. That Apollodotus was close upon a barbarized period is confirmed by the coin lately described by M. R. Rochette, in which his title appears to be 'king of kings,' and his costume is Scythian. In these round copper coins also we have the Arianian letters first employed as monograms.

COINS OF APOLLODOTUS.

SILVER.

1. Hemidrachm. Head of king, with fillet, to the right; bust clothed in a tight dress. ΒΑΣΙΛΕΩΣ ΣΩΤΗΡΟΣ ΚΑΙ ΦΙΛΟΠΑΤΟΡΟΣ ΑΠΟΛΛΟΔΟΤΟΥ. R. Thessalian Minerva, to the left. [illegible] Maharajasa Tadarasa Apaladatasa. Mon. 66. Pl. IV. fig. 13.

From a coin in the collection of Colonel Miles. A similar coin, belonging to Dr. Swiney, procured by him from Karnal, was the first silver coin of Apollodotus made known: it was described and figured by Prinsep, J. As. Soc. B. August, 1833, p. 406, Pl. XIV. fig. 4. Others in the collection of General Ventura have been described, J. As. Soc. B. June, 1835, Pl. XXVI. fig. 4; J. Asiatique, Feb. 1836; J. des Sav. March, 1836, Pl. II. fig. 13; Mionnet, Supplement, vol. viii. p. 477, Pl. XXIII. fig. 4.

2. Hemidrachm. Square. Elephant walking, to the right. ΒΑΣΙΛΕΩΣ ΣΩΤΗΡΟΣ ΑΠΟΛΛΟΔΟΤΟΥ. Mon. K. R. Humped Indian bull, to the right. Inscription as before. Mon. Δ.

From the Masson collection, in which these coins are in some numbers; they are also in other collections. J. As. Soc. B. June, 1835, Pl. XXVI. fig. 5, and Jan. 1836, Pl. II. fig. 3; J. Asiatique, and J. des Sav.; Mionnet, Supplement, vol. viii.

3. Hemidrachm. Round. Elephant and inscription as before. R. Bull and inscription as before, but no monograms.

This, from the Masson collection, is unique. It differs from the square coins, not only in shape, but in the absence of the monograms and the style of the execution.

COPPER.

4. Round; large. Apollo, to the right, holding his arrow with his right hand, and supporting it with his left; a robe hangs down his back. Mon. 67. ΒΑΣΙΛΕΩΣ ΣΩΤΗΡΟΣ ΑΠΟΛΛΟΔΟΤΟΥ. R. Tripod. [illegible] Maharajasa Tadarasa Apaladatasa. Mon. double, 68.

This, which is the first known coin of Apollodotus, was published by Colonel Tod, Trans. of the R. As. Soc. vol. i. p. 313, Pl. XII. fig. 1. It was procured by him at Mathura. Similar coins have since been found, but apparently in a less perfect condition. A very good specimen, but unfortunately fractured on the edge, is in the collection of Colonel Miles. One belonging to Mr. Millingen is described and figured by M. R. Rochette, J. des Sav. June and July, 1834, Plate, fig. 6. M. Jacquet, describing one of General Ventura's collection, states that the Apollo has " la pharétre attachée sur le dos ;" and Mionnet, speaking of the same piece, has " le carquois derrière le dos." The coin was " très fortement oxydée," and it is possible that the monogram has been mistaken for the quiver.

5. Round ; large, but smaller than the preceding. Apollo, to the right, as before. Inscription imperfect and blundered. **- - - ΤΕΣΑΤΡ ΑΠ - - Μ.** (*sic*). Mon. **Β.** R. Tripod. Inscription, like the Greek, indistinct and imperfect, and possibly erroneous. Mon. double, 69. Pl. IV. fig. 16.

From the Masson collection. It is, no doubt, intended to be the same as the preceding, but is of rude and careless fabrication.

6. Round ; large. Apollo, to the right, holding the arrow in the left hand, the right leaning on his bow. Inscription as in No. 4. Mon. also the same. R. Tripod, as in No. 4. Inscription indistinct.

A coin belonging to Dr. Swiney ; J. As. Soc. B. June, 1835, Pl. XXVI. fig. 6. This coin corresponds in all respects to No. 4, except in the attitude of the right hand.

7. Square ; large. Apollo naked, to the left ; his right hand holds his arrow pointing downwards, his left leans on his bow. **ΒΑΣΙΛΕΩΣ ΣΩΤΗΡΟΣ ΑΠΟΛΛΟΔΟΤΟΥ.** R. Tripod, inclosed in a dotted frame. [illegible] [illegible]. Pl. IV. fig. 17.

8. Square ; middle size. Apollo, &c., as before. R. Tripod, of a different form. Inscription as before. Mon. 70. Pl. IV. fig. 18.

9. Square or oblong ; small. Figure of Apollo and inscription as before. R. Tripod, variously formed. Inscription incomplete. Mon. 71. Pl. IV. fig. 19.

These coins, both large and small, are very numerous, and in very different degrees of execution and preservation. The monograms are in some wanting ; they differ in others, as Nos. 72 to 76, besides the letters **Κ** and **Σ.** Mionnet gives three others, Nos. 77, 78, 79, which are worthy of remark, as connecting the coins of Apollodotus with those of the Indo-Scythian princes; Supplement, vol. viii. p. 478, Pl. V. fig. 1. These monograms, however, have not been observed upon any of the pieces in the Masson collection, nor have they been noticed by any other person; J. As. Soc. B. April, 1834, Pl. VIII. fig. 6; Ibid. Pl. XIII. figs. 5, 6, 7; Ibid. June, 1835, Pl. XXVI. figs. 7, 8; J. des Sav. Oct. 1835; J. Asiatique, Feb. 1836.

10. Square; middle size. Male figure of Apollo standing, to the left, clothed in the anaxyris, with chlamys behind, a quiver at his back; an arrow in his right hand, his left resting on his bow; inclosed in a frame of oblong globules. ΒΑΣΙΛΕΩΣ ΒΑ - - - - ΑΠ°ΛΛ°Δ°Τ°Υ. R. Tripod; in the field a symbol which seems to be a military ensign. Arianian inscription imperfect.

Unique; described by M. R. Rochette, J. des Sav. Dec. 1838, p. 752. The fabric inferior. The Scythic dress of Apollo, and the title of 'king of kings,' render it likely that this coin is of a late period of the reign of Apollodotus. "Tout se réunit pour nous faire considérer cette médaille comme un des derniers monumens numismatiques du regne d'Apollodote."

DIOMEDES, B.C. 100.

In placing this prince after Apollodotus the chief motive is his adoption of the title 'Soter,' although no doubt Dr. Grotefend is quite right in affirming that the use of a common title is no positive evidence of identity of dynasty. There is also a community of device in the Indian ox on the reverse. The figures of the dismounted Dioscuri on the obverse ally Diomedes to Eukratides. It matters not much, however, where this prince is classed; for only two coins have been discovered; and it may be inferred that his reign was of the briefest.

COIN OF DIOMEDES.

COPPER.

Square; middle size. Two warriors standing, each leaning on his spear: the Dioscuri dismounted? ΒΑΣΙΛΕΩΣ ΣΩΤΗΡ°Σ ΔΙ°ΜΗΔ°- . R. Humped

Indian bull, to the right. [Kharoshthi legend] - - - [Kharoshthi legend] Maharajasa Tadarasa Tayamidasa. Mon. 80. Pl. V. fig. 1.

From the Masson collection; described also, J. As. Soc. B. Jan. 1836, Pl. II. fig. 10, and Sept. 1836, Pl. XXXV. fig. 3. It was unique till lately, when a duplicate was sent home by Mr. Masson.

HERMÆUS, B. C. 98.

The title 'Soter' may perhaps intimate a descent from Menander and Apollodotus, and the connexion is rather confirmed by the character of the coins, by the form and style of the didrachm, and the expression of the portraits both on it and the smaller silver coins. On the copper coins the character of the head is different, and on one appears rayed, which is unusual on the Bactrian coins. The prevailing type of the reverse is Jupiter seated in a chair with a high back; a piece of furniture first observable in the coins of Alexander Zebina of Syria, who died B. C. 123. On one silver coin the obverse bears a double portrait, or that of Hermæus and his wife Kalliope, which is also a novelty, and may have been suggested by the heads of Cleopatra and Antiochus VIII. of Syria, B. C. 125, only that in this case the lady being the wife, her name follows that of the king. The reverse of this coin is remarkable as offering a mounted figure, the same in costume and attitude as that seen on the coin of Philoxenes; from which we may at least infer that Hermæus was subsequent to Philoxenes. Some of the square coins have on the reverse the figure of a horse walking. Vast quantities of coins are discovered on which the name and titles of Hermæus, variously modified, occur; but as these are evidently of the last age of Greek rule, even if they are not wholly barbaric, we shall suspend the notice of them until we have dismissed two other princes who are unquestionably of Grecian descent—Agathokles and Pantaleon.

COINS OF HERMÆUS.

SILVER.

1. Didrachm. Head of king, beardless, with fillet and chlamys, to the right. ΒΑΣΙΛΕΩΣ ΣΩΤΗΡΟΣ ΕΡΜΑΙΟΥ. R. Jupiter seated on a chair

with high back and arms; rays round his head; his sceptre is behind him; his right hand is extended. PΛU7Ƭ PT⅃7 Pⅎ7Ꞁᴗ Maharajasa Tadarasa Ermayasa. Mon. 81. Pl. V. fig. 2.

From a coin in the Masson collection, which contains several others, on one of which is a different monogram, 82. This coin is remarkably perfect, and the Indian letters are singularly bold and distinct. The coins were procured at Kabul: J. As. Soc. B. June, 1833, Pl. XXIV. fig. 1; also Mionnet, Supplement, vol. viii. p. 23, fig. 5.

2. Hemidrachm. Head of king, with fillet, to the right. ΒΑΣΙΛΕΩΣ ΣΩΤΗΡοΣ ΕΡΜΑΙοΥ. R. Seated Jupiter; he holds his sceptre, the top of which is in the shape of a cross, in his left hand. PT⅃7 Pⅎ7Ꞁᴗ PΛU7Ƭ Maharajasa Tadarasa Ermayasa. Mon. 83. Pl. V. fig. 3.

Several of these are in the Masson collection; others have been procured by Dr. Honigberger, and described, J. des Sav. October, 1835, Pl. I. fig. 13; also by Mionnet.

3. Hemidrachm. Double profile, to the right. ΒΑΣΙΛΕΩΣ ΣΩΤΗΡοΣ ΕΡΜΑΙοΥ. In the exergue ΚΑΙ ΚΑΛΛΙοΠΗΣ. R. King on horseback, galloping. PΛU7Ƭ PT⅃7 Pⅎ7Ꞁᴗ Characters of the exergue effaced. Mon. 84. Supplemental Plate, fig. 14.

This is a singular as well as hitherto a unique coin. It was one of Mr. Masson's collection.

COPPER.

4. Round; middle size. Head of king, with fillet, to the right. ΒΑΣΙΛΕΩΣ ΣΩΤΗΡοΣ ΕΡΜΑΙοΥ. R. Seated Jupiter, with a crown on his head. Inscription imperfect. Mon. 85. Pl. V. fig. 4.

5. Round; middle size. Head of king, to the right, with fillet. - - ΣΙΛΕΩΣ ΣΩΤΗΡοΣ - - - - Υ. R. Seated Jupiter, with crown. PT⅃7 Pⅎ7Ꞁᴗ PΛᴗ7Ƭ Maharajasa Tadarasa Ermayasa. Mon. 86. Pl. V. fig. 5.

6. Round; small size. Head of king, with fillet, to the right. ΒΛΣΙΛΕΩΣ ΣΩΤΗΓ□Σ ΕΓΜΑΙοΥ. R. Seated Jupiter, with crown. P~77 Pⅎ - - - PΛᴗ7 - Mon. 85. Pl. V. fig. 6.

These coins, found at Beghram and Kabul chiefly, are numerous in all the collections. The character of the face in general agrees, being marked by a very long nose and chin. In No. 5, however, these features are much changed, if the portrait be not that of a different person.

7. Square; middle size. Head of king, with fillet, to the right. ΒΑΣΙΛΕΩΣ ΣΩΤΗΡΟΣ ΕΡΜΑΙΟΥ. R. Horse, walking, to the right. [Kharoshthi legend] Maharajasa Tadarasa Ermayasa. Mon. 87. Pl. V. fig. 7.

From the Masson collection, which contains three coins of this description: one was described, J. As. Soc. B. April, 1834, Pl. XI. fig. 38, and Jan. 1836, Pl. XI. fig. 12; also by Mionnet, Supplement, vol. viii., who, following Masson's drawing, imagines the head to be covered with something like a Phrygian bonnet.

8. Square; middle size. Head of king, with rayed crown, to the right. ΒΑΣΙΛΕΩΣ ΣΩΤΗΡΟΣ ΕΡΜΑΙΟΥ. R. Horse, walking, to the right. [Kharoshthi legend] Mon. 87. Supplemental Plate, fig. 15.

This, which is from Mr. Masson's last supply, is the same as the preceding, with exception not only of the distinct form of the crown, but of the whole character of the head and face, which is something like that of the first Sassanian kings.

9. Round; large. Head of king, to the left. Legend imperfect [ΒΑΣΙΛ]ΕΩΣ [ΕΡ]ΜΑΙΟΥ. R. Victory, dressed and winged, to the right; right hand extended, with crown and fillet.

Described by M. R. Rochette, J. des Sav. Feb. 1839, p. 95. It may be remarked, that according to the description, the Victory corresponds with that on the square coins of Mayes. See Pl. VIII. fig. 10.

AGATHOKLES, B.C. 135.

Two drachms of Agathokles having found their way from St. Petersburgh to Paris, they were made the subject of an elaborate dissertation by M. Raoul Rochette in the Journal des Savants,[1] and his observations were further developed upon the occasion of his describing a tetradrachm of the same prince. He pronounced the coins, upon the evidence of their fabric

[1] June, 1834.

and mythologic types, to be of Bactrian origin, and to belong to a prince who was the founder of the independence of Bactria, preceding Theodotus.

The commencement of the Parthian kingdom is ascribed by Arrian, in the Fragments preserved by Photius, to the vengeance exacted by two brothers, Arsaces and Tiridates, for an insult offered to the latter by Pherekles, the Macedonian governor of Upper Asia under Antiochus II. They slew the governor or eparch, and set up the standard of revolt. Syncellus, reciting the same event from the same authority, the Parthia of Arrian, is somewhat more circumstantial; he calls the brothers the satraps of Bactriana, and he styles the Macedonian the governor of Persia, and names him Agathokles. That such was his name is also urged by M. R. Rochette as probable, from his finding amongst the principal officers of Alexander an Autolykus, son of Agathokles, whose son would, agreeably to the custom of the Greeks, be called after his grandfather Agathokles, and in rank and age would be a very likely individual to have held the station of eparch at the time required, and consequently to have been the Agathokles in question. This Agathokles, the eparch of Persia, he maintains, was no doubt the Macedonian officer who took advantage of the disorders in Western Asia to establish a new kingdom in Bactriana, one of the satrapies subject to his authority. This conclusion has been adopted by M. Mionnet, who places Agathokles first in order of the Bactrian kings. It has not received the concurrence of Messrs. Lassen and Grotefend, and is opposed by such weighty considerations that it cannot be admitted without hesitation.

Admitting the correctness of the change of name from Pherekles to Agathokles, and that an eparch of Persia so called was the son of Autolykus, it by no means follows that he laid the foundation of the kingdom of Bactria. It is positively affirmed by history that the first Bactrian king was named Theodotus; and the very story told by Arrian, and repeated by Syncellus, is fatal to the theory, as the Arsacidan princes murdered, not a king of Bactria, but a governor of Persia. This Agathokles, then, was slain whilst he was yet only eparch: that Agathokles of Bactria lived to be 'king' is evidenced by his coins.

The coins of Agathokles are of two descriptions; those which are of a pure Bactrian type, and those which have an Indian character. The style of the first is that of the best Bactrian coins. Even the copper coins are of the same description; round, well executed, with a Greek legend only. All these, however, are rare. The more numerous coins, which are far from rare, are copper, of a truncated elliptic form, and rude execution. That they belong to the same prince, however, is proved, not only by the identity of name and title, 'King Agathokles,' but by the prevailing type on one face, a panther; a type found on the small silver and round copper coins of the same prince, intimating, along with the head, which is that of Bacchus, the preferential adoration, by Agathokles, of that divinity: but these copper coins have a peculiarity which distinguishes them from all other Bactrian coins, in the legend of the reverse. They have a bilingual legend, but the equivalent of the Greek is no longer an alphabet of Semitic origin, one introduced from the confines of Persia into the Paropamisan regions, but one of a genuine Indian family, being precisely the character which is found in the most ancient Hindu inscriptions, and which is the remote but unequivocal ancestor of the alphabets still used in Hindustan for Sanscrit and various vernacular dialects. Now that this was certainly not in use in Persia we have undeniable proof in the prevalence of the totally dissimilar letters on the other bilingual coins, and we must therefore look for the currency of Agathokles within the limits of India proper. Where his kingdom was situated, it is not easy to conjecture. His silver coins have been brought to Europe apparently through Russia, with the exception of one procured in the Punjab; from whence it might be inferred he ruled on the north of the mountains. His copper coins, however, of both styles have been found at Beghram, and he could not have been very far off. The worship of Bacchus intimates a country in which the vine flourished; and this would bring us especially to the yet unexplored tracts under the Pamer mountains, or into parts of Little Tibet, Hounz, Gilgit, and Chitral,[1] into the wine-cellar of Afrasiab, or at least into Kaferistan.[2] That

[1] See p. 193, note.

[2] An interesting illustration of the extension of the worship of Bacchus in this quarter is possibly furnished by the patera found in Badakhshan by the late Dr. Lord, of which an engraving is published in the J. As. Soc. B. Dec. 1838. The patera itself, on which a bacchanalian procession is embossed, is now in the East India Company's Museum.

the people of these tracts are of Indian descent seems probable from the little that is yet known of their manners and language, but further investigation is necessary to decide the point. Professor Lassen would place him at Nyssa, the city on the Kabul river, in which the companions of Alexander fancied they found vestiges of Bacchus, and which he identifies with the Nagara of Ptolemy, called also Dionysopolis, in reference to the same worship. This is not impossible; but Nagara is so near to the spot which seems to have been the chief site of the Bactro-Indian mintage, that it is probable we should find the same alphabet in use there as on the preceding coins, and that we must go farther off to find a character so totally different as that of the coins of Agathokles in current use. The question of place, therefore, is somewhat doubtful: as to time, it may be conjectured that Agathokles was nearly contemporary with Heliokles, and that he either founded or usurped a principality amongst the mountains during the confusion occasioned by the murder of Eukratides, and the subsequent quarrel with Parthia.

The type of Jupiter holding the three-headed Diana is the subject of much learned speculation by M. R. Rochette in confirmation of his theory.[1] He sees in this the Diana of the Persians, who was distinguished by holding a torch in her hand, and was named Zara or Azara; whence the appellation Zariaspa was, he conjectures, applied to Zariaspa, the capital of Bactria; which in his first essay he identifies with Bactria, but in his second, places, with Arrian, in Sogdiana; making that "le siége principal de la puissance des Grecs, le berceau de la dynastie d'Agathocle et de celle d'Euthydème." In his second memoir,[2] the tetradrachm of Agathokles, which had been procured, it may be observed, in the Punjab by M. Ventura, enabled M. R. Rochette to distinguish on the figure upheld by Jupiter three heads, and 'without ceasing to be Artemis,' the Diana thus becomes, according to him, "une Artémis Hecaté porte-flambeau; une divinité lunaire dont le culte propre à l'Asie n'avait pu être apporté aux Grecs du premier age que par des navigateurs de cette partie du monde, et dont à une autre époque les Grecs conduits par Alexandre dans la Bactriane retrouvérent le type primitif dans sa

[1] J. des Sav. June, 1834, p. 339.

[2] Ibid. Feb. 1836.

patrie même tel qu'ils le produisoient à leur manière sur la monnaie d'Agathocle, comme un premier hommage rendu à leur conquête nouvelle en même temps que comme une réminiscence de leur vielle croyance." Without questioning the accuracy of the identification of the mythological type, it is doubtful if the Greeks would have met with any thing of the kind in Bactria; and most certainly they would have found no such divinity in India, where the moon is a male divinity.

Professor Lassen has suggested the possibility, that in consequence of some confusion of appellations Agathokles may be the prince known in Hindu history as Suyasas, 'the well-renowned,' which again he conjectures may apply to the prince known to the Greeks as Sophagasenos, which was supposed by A. von Schlegel to represent an Indian appellation, Subhágasena.[1] Suyasas was the son of Asoka,[2] and, according to Buddhist authorities, was king of Gandhára, which would bring him west of the Indus. In that case Agathokles would be the contemporary and ally of Antiochus the Great. The identity of nomenclature, however, is too purely conjectural to authorize much reliance on this theory, and it is very doubtful if any of the Greek Bactrian princes could at so early a period have established themselves within the limits of India proper. That Agathokles was of Greek and of Bactrian origin is proved by the silver coins with the type of Jupiter on the reverse: Suyasas must have been a Hindu.

COINS OF AGATHOKLES.

SILVER.

1. Tetradrachm. Head of king, with fillet, to the right. R. Jupiter in the pallium, with wings on his ankles; his left hand leans on a sceptre, his right, extended, holds a figure of the three-headed Artemis (?) with a torch in either hand. ΒΑΣΙΛΕΩΣ ΑΓΑΘΟΚΛΕΟΥΣ. Mon. 88. Pl. VI. fig. 3.

From an engraving by Prinsep of a coin obtained by General Ventura; J. As. Soc. B. June, 1835, Pl. XXV. fig. 3; also described in the J. Asiatique, February, 1836; J. des Sav. February, 1836, Pl. II. fig. 1;

[1] Indische Bibliothek, vol. i. p. 258.

[2] Vishnu Purana, p. 470. Foe Kue Ki, p. 67.

and Mionnet, Supplement, viii. It is added by the latter, that each head is surmounted by a disc or modius.

2. Drachm. Head of king, as before. R. Jupiter, as before. The Diana has apparently but one head, though holding two torches, as before. **ΒΑΣΙΛΕΩΣ ΑΓΑΘΟΚΛΕΟΥΣ.** Mon. 89. Pl. VI. fig. 4.

Described and engraved, J. des Sav. June, 1834, Plate, fig. 2; Mionnet, Supplement, viii. p. 461, Pl. XXI. fig. 1.

3. Drachm. Head of king, or Bacchus (?), with fillet, to the right. R. Panther, to the right, with a bunch of grapes in his fore-paw. **ΒΑΣΙΛΕΩΣ ΑΓΑΘΟΚΛΕΟΥΣ.** Plate VI. fig. 5.

From the engraving of M. R. Rochette, J. des Sav. June, 1834, Plate, fig. 1, and Mionnet, Supplement, viii. p. 461. Both these coins are in the Royal Cabinet at Paris. According to Mionnet, the panther is standing before a young vine.

COPPER.

4. Round; middle size. Head of king (as Bacchus ?), with fillet, and a chaplet of ivy-leaves, and the thyrsus behind his shoulder. R. The panther, to the right, before a standard vine, from which he is plucking the fruit. **ΒΑΣΙΛΕΩΣ ΑΓΑΘΟΚΛΕΟΥΣ.** Mon. 90. Pl. VI. fig. 6.

The coin which is engraved, and corresponds precisely with the silver coin No. 3, except in having a monogram, is in the Masson collection, where it had not apparently been observed by the collector, as it had nowhere been mentioned by him: it was found amongst a great number of Indo-Scythic coins from Beghram. Since its delineation, however, others have been found and sent home by Mr. Masson.

5. Oblong; round at one extremity, or square at both, thick. Panther, to the right. **ΒΑΣΙΛΕΩΣ ΑΓΑΘΟΚΛΕΟΥΣ.** R. A female figure, with turban and fillet on her head, large ear-rings, the breast bare, but a scarf or shawl over the shoulders, and large loose Asiatic trowsers; her right hand holds a lotus (?), part of her shawl is thrown over her left, whilst her petticoat (?) gathered round her waist projects to the right. **ꓘΛ٩ᏧJᒪƐ** Agathakalyaja. Mon. 91. Pl. VI. figs. 7, 8, 9.

Several of these are in the Masson collection. They have been described and delineated, but from less perfect specimens, J. As. Soc. B. April, 1834, Pl. IX. fig. 17, November, 1836, and June, 1837; J. des Sav. September, 1835, Pl. I. fig. 1; and Mionnet, Supplement, viii. Pl. XXI. fig. 2.

PANTALEON, B. C. 120.

A few copper coins attest the existence of this prince, and, as they are in every respect but the name the same as the copper coins of Agathokles, there can be little doubt that he was his successor. The coins are rare, and indicate a short reign: and the principality founded by Agathokles was possibly subverted in the reign of Pantaleon by the arms of Menander, in the progress of his Indian conquests; a circumstance that is in harmony with the dates assigned to those two kings.

COIN OF PANTALEON.

COPPER.

Irregular; square. Panther, to the right. ΒΑΣΙΛΕΩΣ ΠΑΝΤΑΛΕοΝΤοΣ. R. Female figure, with turban, ear-rings, and trowsers, as on the coins of Agathokles, to the left. [Brahmi legend] Patalavatá. Pl. VI. fig. 11.

Several in the collection, but, with one exception (that engraved), the name is imperfect: represented or described, J. As. Soc. B. April, 1834; J. des Sav. February, 1836; Mionnet, Supplement, viii.

SECTION II.—BARBARIC KINGS.

The adjustment of the order of those kings, who by their names and titles are evidently of barbaric origin, is still more perplexing than that of the Greek princes, as we have little assistance from history, and the indications furnished by the coins are not sufficiently precise, either as to the individuals or to the country to which they belonged.

That the Scythians overturned the Greek empire of Bactria is known from

Chinese authorities; but, as intimated above, this applies alone to Bactria proper, for the Greek rule must have continued and spread for some years longer on the south of the Hindu Kush. The reason of this we learn from history. The advance of the Scythians was delayed by the opposition which they encountered from the Parthians. Phrahates, the successor of Mithridates, when about to carry his arms against the Syrian king, was recalled to the defence of his north-eastern territories by the Scythian incursion. The war continued for two years, at the end of which, B. C. 128, Phrahates was slain. The same fate befel his successor Artabanus, who was killed B.C. 125. The next Arsacidan king, Mithridates II., was more successful, and gained some advantages over the Scythians. As they had also at this time apparently an active and warlike adversary in Menander, they were probably confined for some years to the consolidation of their power upon the Oxus, in Bactria and Sogdiana. As Mithridates was latterly involved in contests with Armenia, Syria, and with Rome, the Scythians were exposed to less danger from his power; and, although they may have left Parthia unmolested, they now, about the year B. C. 90, began to advance into the Paropamisus, and towards the close of the reign of Hermæus had fully established themselves in the vicinity of Kabul, and probably about Ghizni and Kandahar; from whence, towards the beginning of the Christian æra, they spread to the mouth of the Indus,—the country near to which, we know from the testimony of Ptolemy and the Periplus, was under the sway of Indo-Scythian princes in the first century of our æra.

We have already seen that the tribes conterminous with Sogdiana on the north and east were the people whom the Greeks and Hindus called Sakas; and it appears, as might have been expected, that tribes of these Sakas were the first who recovered Sogdiana and Bactriana from the Greeks. It were probably more correct to say, at least of some parts of Bactria, that the Scythians wrested them from the Parthians; but the interposition of the latter was from the first contested, and as it was a struggle for the remnant of the Greek power which was carried on for some time between the Sakas and Parthians, in which the former ultimately prevailed, there is no great impropriety in referring to the Sakas or Scythians the downfall of the Greek kingdom of Bactria.

The nomadic tribes, to whom this catastrophe is ascribed by Strabo,[1] are named the Asii, Pasiani, Tokhari, and Sakarauli. According to Trogus Pompeius they were termed Asiani and Sarankæ;[2] but he elsewhere mentions the Tokhari, with the addition that their kings were at one time, at least, from the Asiani.[3] The Tokhari, as already observed, appear to be the people after whom Tokharestan is named. It was in battle with these that the Parthian Artabanus received his death-wound. The Sakarauli, in whom the name of Sakas is properly comprised, appear subsequently in Parthian history as the hosts and confederates of Sanatrokes, giving him an asylum for many years, and afterwards placing him on the throne, B.C. 76. The Sakas appear to have extended themselves more to the west and south; they settled in Parætakene, which was thenceforth called Sakastene or Sakasthán, 'the land of the Sakas,' whence, very probably, the modern denomination of Sejistan or Seistan. The Sakas, however, were not restricted to this province, but penetrated eastwards, and formed at first the Indo-Scythic principality of Sindh. They attempted to advance still further east, or into the interior of India, and their repulse is attributed by Hindu writers to Vikramaditya, king of Avanti or Ujayin, fifty-six years B.C. To the æra which is thence derived, and which is commonly in use in India, the term Saka is applicable; a word having no import connected with chronological reckoning, but which is explained by more than one writer to designate the 'Saka bhupa-kala,' or the 'Saka nripanta kala,'—"the time when the Barbarian kings called Saka were discomfited by Vikramaditya," or "the end of the reign of Vikramaditya, who slew a people of Barbarians named Sakas."[4] He is also commonly termed Sakári, 'the foe of the Sakas.'

The invasion of the Sakas was not merely the overflowing of an enterprising nation; it was the effect of other convulsions in Central Asia, by which fresh hordes of Barbarians were impelled upon those who had for

[1] Μάλιστα δὲ γνώριμοι γεγόνασι τῶν νομάδων οἱ τοὺς Ἕλληνας ἀφελόμενοι τὴν Βακτριανὴν, Ἄσιοι, καὶ Πασιανοὶ, καὶ Τόχαροι, καὶ Σακάραυλοι, καὶ ὁρμηθέντες ἀπὸ τῆς περαίας τοῦ Ἰαξάρτου, τῆς κατὰ Σάκας καὶ Σογδιανοὺς, ἣν κατεῖχον Σάκαι. Book XI. 11. 2.

[2] Quo repugnante Scythiæ gentes Sarankæ et Asiani Bactra occupavere et Sogdianos. Prol. xli.

[3] Reges Thocharorum Asiani. Prol. xlii.

[4] Colebrooke, Introduction to Indian Algebra, p. 43.

ages occupied the right bank of the Jaxartes and the Caspian plain. According to Chinese authorities, a nation called Yu-chi[1] were expelled about B.C. 200 from their territory on the west of Chen-si by the Hiung-nu or Huns. The Yu-chi separated into two bands: the smaller descended southwards into Tibet; the larger passed westwards, and after a hard struggle dispossessed a people called 'Su' of the plains west of the river of Ili. These latter advanced to Ferghana and the Jaxartes; and the Yu-chi not long afterwards retreating from the U-siun, another nomadic race, passed the Su on the north, and occupied the tracts between the Oxus and the Caspian. The Su, also called Szu, Se, Sai, and An-szu, by different writers,[2] according to M. De Guignes, were thus in the vicinity of the Greeks, the Yu-chi in the neighbourhood of the Parthians. The former conquered Ki-pin, the latter Ta-hia; by the latter of which is to be understood great part of Khorasan. These events must have occurred some time anterior to B.C. 126, as that is assigned for the date of the return to China of Chang-kian, the officer who thirteen years before had been sent on a mission to the Yu-chi, had accompanied them in their expedition, and upon whose authority the history of their migrations depends. Ki-pin, as has been mentioned above, is considered to be the country of the Hazáras, including Ghizni and Kandahar: but at the period particularized we should scarcely expect to find any barbaric races so far south of the Oxus, as we had Greek kings apparently both above the mountains and at Kandahar. According to Chinese geographers cited by M. De Guignes, we should rather look for Ki-pin in Sogdiana; and he concludes, that it could be situated nowhere else than in Mawerrunnahar, the tract between the Oxus and the Jaxartes. To the occupation of this region by the Su, about B.C. 140-130, there is no obvious objection. The aggressions of the Yu-chi upon the Tahia, which must have occurred about the years B.C. 129-127, agree well enough with the season of active hostilities between the Scythians and Parthians, in which the kings of the latter, Phrahates and Artabanus, were successively slain.

Although, however, the Chinese accounts are so far corroborated by

[1] This is read also Yue-chi, or preferably, according to Klaproth, Yuei-chi, Yu-ti, and Yutti: Foe Kue Ki, p. 83. Tableaux Historiques de l'Asie, p. 288.

[2] Foe Kue Ki, pp. 39, 83.

Parthian history, they are not easily reconcileable with the information derived from classical writers. We have unquestionable evidence of the presence of Sakas and Massagetæ on the upper course of the Oxus, on the Jaxartes, and on the Caspian plains, long before this irruption of races, apparently the same, from the confines of China. What became of those who were previously settled in these countries? Were they dispossessed and driven onwards, of which we have no proof, or were they amalgamated with the new comers? The Scythians of Sogdiana commenced their encroachments on Bactria as early as the reign of Euthydemus, and no doubt, in the following reigns of Demetrius and Eukratides, wrested great part of Bactria proper from the Greeks; but this must have been about the time that they would have been invaded by the Su, if the Chinese accounts are to be depended upon. These accounts, too, seem to disagree; for M. De Guignes carries the Yu-chi beyond the Su, and engages the former, as is conformable to history, in war with the Parthians;[1] but M. Remusat states that after conquering the Tahia they had established themselves on the north bank of the Mei, or Oxus, and subjugated the An-szu, before the visit of Chang-kian, or at the very time when they were at war with the Scythians. Again, the notices of the Scythian tribes in Strabo, which apply to the Sakas, and which seem to import their settling in Sejistan, are at variance with the Chinese assertion, that the Yu-chi established themselves in the same quarter, or on the borders of Persia. And, lastly, if we are to believe Chang-kian, at the time he visited the Yu-chi they occupied five cities, one of which was Kao-fu, or Kabul, where resided the tribe of that name. We cannot believe that at that time any part of Kabulistan was in the possession of any tribe of Scythian origin. M. De Guignes, indeed, obviates this last difficulty by stating, upon the authority of a Chinese historian, that Kao-fu was not one of the cities of the Yu-chi until afterwards. These are some of the considerations by which the narrative is perplexed, and which cannot but inspire doubts of the accuracy of the Chinese accounts. All that can be safely concluded, perhaps, is that there was a political movement about the period indicated, by which nomadic

[1] Foe Kue Ki, p. 83.

races in Eastern Asia, which were of kin to those already settled on the Jaxartes and Oxus, marched westwards, and united with their countrymen; that some of them fell upon the Bactrian, and others upon the Parthian empire, and wrested extensive possessions from both; that when this was accomplished, some of the leaders of such of them as had moved westwards directed their ambition towards India, reduced to their power the other barbaric tribes, and, about the beginning of the Christian æra, laid the foundations of a principality corresponding in its general extent with the territories of the king of Kabul; and that this extension was facilitated by the essential identity of the different immigrant tribes, who, although distinguished by various denominations, and often at variance with each other, were branches of that great Turkish race which, according to Persian tradition, occupied Turan or Central Asia from the Caspian to China. It seems most consistent with the historical facts which are derivable from the Byzantine writers and Indian traditions, to believe that in the series of irruptions from the north-east which commenced about a century before our æra, the Sakas took the lead, that they were repelled from the frontiers of India, and fell back towards Persia, with which kingdom they are found connected as late as the third and fourth centuries.[1] After them came the Yu-chi, who established themselves along the course of the Indus between the Sakas and India, where they were in power for several centuries, constituting the Indo-Scythi of the classical geographers, and not improbably leaving traces of their designation as Getæ in the Jits, Jats, or Juts, who are found in Western Hindustan, and particularly on the Indus.

From the period of the union of the Su with the Sakas of Sogdiana, which could not have been much later or much earlier than the latter part of the reign of Eukratides, or about B. C. 160, the greater part of the eastern provinces of Bactria were, no doubt, occupied by these tribes, and they may have cultivated or allowed their Tajik subjects to cultivate the arts of peace. It was in this interval, possibly, that in imitation of their predecessors they struck coins of gold and silver, as the Chinese report of the people of

[1] Ipsos Persas ipsumque regem ascitis Saccis, et Russis, et Gellis, petit frater Ormies. Panegyr. Vet. quoted by Gibbon, vol. ii. p. 139. At the siege of Amida, A. D. 359, the Segestans or people of Sacastene acted as the allies of Sapor II.

Ki-pin, on one side of which was a mounted horseman, and on the other the head or the figure of a man.[1] The particulars recorded, by Chinese authors, of two of the kings of the Su, named U-teu-lao and In-mo-fu, are of little general value, and can be true only of tribes much nearer to China than those settled in Ki-pin. All that we can venture to believe of them, therefore, is, that they had occupied the greater part of Bactria proper about the end of the reign of Heliokles, that they were checked awhile by Menander, but that in the reign of Hermæus they had established themselves in Kabulistan, where they were subsequently reduced under the authority of the Yu-chi.

Lassen thinks that the description of these coins applies to the coins of Eukratides, but it may possibly have a wider application. The characteristic of a mounted horseman on one face, however, will not decide the question: for the same is said by the Chinese to be the case with the coins of the Tiao-chi or Tajiks;[2] and, by Mohammedan writers, to have been the type of the coins of the ancient Persian kings. Thus Tabari[3] says that in these coins was represented on one face the king seated on his throne, with the crown on his head, and on the other the same king on horseback, with a lance in his hand. This type was, therefore, not confined to the Sa-i.

From the same authorities we learn that about a century[4] after the Yu-chi had established themselves in Khorasan, one of their kings, named Kiu-tsiu-kio or Khiu-tsyu-khi, extended his authority over the neighbouring tribes, including Ki-pin and Kao-fu; by the latter of which it is conjectured that Kabul is meant, not without probability, although, as the Chinese describe it, it should lie in a very different direction. This prince died at the advanced age of eighty-four, and was succeeded by his son, Yun-kao-ching: the latter conquered Tien-so, or India, or, rather, Sindh, a country watered by a great river called the Sin-teu. M. De Guignes thinks that

[1] De Guignes says the figure; Remusat, the head.

[2] Remusat, Nouv. Mél.

[3] از یك طرف ملك بر تخت نشسته و تاج بسر نهاده و از یك طرف ملك براسپ و نیزه در دست گرفته

[4] De Guignes; which brings the events to B.C. 29. Klaproth has B.C. 80; Remusat has, in the first century of our æra.

they spread towards the Ganges, and they may have passed into the Punjab. They did not remain, however, in this position long, as at the end of the fourth century the king of the Yu-chi was certainly on the west of the Indus.[1] There is no reason, however, to question the accuracy of the general narrative; and the coins we are about to describe corroborate the fact that princes of a barbarous and Scythic descent did conquer the countries east and west of the Indus in the course of the century preceding the Christian æra, or after the reign of Hermæus. It is not impossible that we have traces of the very prince to whom the conquest is ascribed by the Chinese.

SU-HERMÆUS.

KADAPHES. KADPHISES.

The great number of the coins of Hermæus which bear a sitting Jupiter on the reverse, and the situations in which they are found, indicate his having reigned in Kabulistan and the Punjab for a term of longer than average duration; but, besides these coins, a still greater number are found which differ from them materially in their types, and still more in their execution. On the obverse of them, the name Hermæus, variously modified, is decypherable, and the character of the portrait is somewhat similar, though rude; but the Greek letters are of a late and corrupt period, the title is very commonly blundered, and the syllable ΣV follows the epithet 'Soter.' With rare exceptions the device on the reverse is a very rude representation of a standing Hercules.

Reasoning from the great dissimilarity that prevails between this coin and the genuine Greek coin of Hermæus, Mr. Masson thought he distinguished three several princes bearing the same name,[2] whom, from the circumstance of these coins being found in greatest abundance about Jelalabad, he calls kings of Nysa. Dr. Grotefend distinguishes also three kinds; but the first two have the same portraits, the same legends, and the same types, and differ only in the substitution of the square for the round omicron. These

[1] Foe Kue Ki, ch. xii. p. 76.

[2] J. As. Soc. B. April, 1834, p. 167.

are substantially the same; and there are but two kinds decidedly distinguishable from each other, of which one is Grecian, and one barbaric.

If any additional evidence of this were needed, it is supplied by the Arianian inscription. The coins with the sitting Jupiter have, as we have seen, on the reverse the precise equivalent of the Greek inscription Maharajasa Tadarasa Hermayasa; those with the Hercules type have a legend entirely different, or, as above intimated, Dhama-piasa Kujulakasa Sakusa Kayadaphasa, in which we have names and titles in an undoubtedly barbaric dialect; proving therefore, beyond reasonable question, that Hermæus was succeeded by a prince of one or other of those tribes by whom history tells us the West Sindhic provinces were subdued, by either a Saka or a Yu-chi prince, and who, for a considerable portion of a long reign, imitated the portrait and legend on the coins of his predecessor, whilst he borrowed a device from the family of Euthydemus, and inscribed a legend of his own.

It appears, however, that the degenerate artists of this same prince did not confine themselves to this one form of imitation, but ventured on others. Thus whilst they retained both the portrait and the device, they introduced upon the obverse the name apparently of the king, Korso Kozolou Kadphizou; and in another they changed both the portrait and type, and inserted round the former, Zathou Kozolou Kadaphes Korano. In these three varieties, however, the Arianian legend is still the same; and whatever may be its purport, there can be little doubt that Kujulaka Kayadapha are the original words which the Kozolou Kadaphes of the Greek express with as much fidelity as can be expected. These three coins are, therefore, assignable to the same prince, or at least to princes nearly connected in time and place; and it is not impossible that we may here have the monarch of the Yu-chi whose name the Chinese endeavoured to express, at least as it comes to us through the French translation, by Kiu-tsiu-kio.

To this identification, however, may be reasonably objected the occurrence of those other words which in one instance we know to be a proper name, and which is most probably so in the other. Kadphises we shall have presently occasion to speak of, and Kadaphes seems to be an appellation of an analogous description. He is therefore considered as a different prince by all who have described his coins. What connexion either of them could have had with the prince or princes in whose time these coins of Su-Hermæus were current, is very inexplicable. It may, however, furnish some clue to the origin of these coins, that as far as we can conjecture the purport of their legends, the title of king is wanting on the reverse of all, and also on the obverse of the coins which bear the names of Kadaphes and Kadphises. What may be the meaning of Zathou, Korano, or Korso in the Greek, it is impossible to say, or whether either of them be equivalent to king; the latter recurs in the coins of Kanerkes in a position where it cannot well have that signification. Neither of the others bear a resemblance to any known Turkish title, as Beg or Khan. Korano is said by Mr. Masson to imply a military chief. It is said, indeed, that the Sakas when subdued by the Yu-chi had no king;[1] and it is elsewhere mentioned, that in the century before our æra they had abolished royalty, and remained under the command of military chiefs; and hence, possibly, the adoption by them of the portraits and types of Hermæus at various periods, and the insertion of names and epithets unconnected with royalty. These coins might, therefore, be the issues of different military officers of the Sakas during the latter half of the century that preceded the Christian æra, and the establishment of the kingdom of the Yui-chi; in which case the conjecture that these coins bear the name of the Yu-chi prince, Kiu-tsiu-kio, would fall to the ground.

COINS OF SU-HERMÆUS.

COPPER.

1. Round. Head of king, with fillet, to the right; the bust, covered with the chlamys, is presented to the front. - - ΕΙΛΕΛΕ ΣΤΗΓΟΣ (*sic*) ΕV ΕΓΜΑΙΟΥ. R. Standing Hercules, to the front, with fillet; the lion's skin hangs over his left wrist; the right hand rests on his club, the butt-end of which is on the ground. Inscription in corrupt Indian characters. It is not found complete in any one coin, but from a comparison of many the whole appears to be intended for 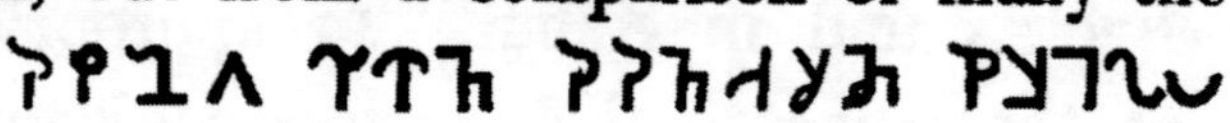

[1] Foe Kue Ki, p. 83.

Maharajasa Kujulakasasa Kashae Yadaphasa. See the coins of Kadphises. Pl. V. figs. 8, 9, 10. No monogram is decypherable.

These coins are found in great numbers, not only in the ground or in the bazars, but in the topes about Jelalabad and Kabul, mixed with others of the Indo-Scythic type. The best are of rude execution, but they offer many varieties of degenerate workmanship, indicating a later and barbarous period.

2. Round; small. Head of king, with fillet and chlamys, to the right. ---- Σ ΣV ΕΓΜΑΥΟΥ. R. Sitting Jupiter, as on the coins of Hermæus, but rudely executed. Inscription imperfect. - [Kharoshthi legend] Ermayasa. Mon. double, 92. Pl. V. fig. 11.

From the Masson collection. The device and legend on the reverse connect this with the coins of Hermæus, but the inscription contains the syllable ΣV. It is, however, of the best order of the coins of this class, and may have been amongst the earliest after the reign of Hermæus, being an imitation of his coins.

The coins of the Hermæus and Su-Hermæus types have been described, J. As. Soc. B. April, 1834, Pl. IX. and X.; June, 1835, Pl. XXIV.; and Jan. and Sept. 1836, Pl. III. and XXXV.; by Messrs. Masson and Prinsep: also by M. R. Rochette and M. Jacquet, J. des Sav. April, 1836, and J. Asiatique, Feb. '1836. They consider the letters on the obverse of the ruder coins to be imperfect attempts at representing Greek characters.

COINS OF THE SAKAS OR SAI (?).

(King's name uncertain.)

The period conjectured to have elapsed from the conquests of the Sakas in Bactria to their settlement in Khorasan is one of some duration, and must be that to which the Chinese descriptions of the kingdom of Ki-pin apply. We may, therefore, expect to find specimens of the coins of these kings in Bactria and in Kabul. In appropriating from the variety before us any of the coins to this source, conjecture is very vague, and no confidence can be attached to the appropriation. There are some coins, however, which it is difficult to know how else to dispose of, and they may be ascribed to this series. They are undoubtedly barbaric; they are comparatively rare; they are not found in any of the topes, and seldom, if ever, east of Beghram. Many of them bear, in common with others possibly connected with them, the devices which it is recorded were used by the Szu,—a mounted rider on one side, and a portrait or a figure of a man on the other.

In supposing the coins, of which the description follows, to belong to this class, and to be one of the earliest, the motives are their barbarous style, the type of the horse on the reverse, and the inscription being solely Greek. As noticed below, M. Rochette attributes these coins to Heliokles; and he may be right: but the costume and character of the portrait are not Grecian; and the inaccuracy of the legend is scarcely indicative of Greek fabric at this period. There is no incorrectness in the Greek inscription even of the bilingual coin of Heliokles. M. Rochette's own explanation of the barbarous coins of Euthydemus may, perhaps, be equally applicable here; and these coins may be the issue of a Barbarian or Saka prince of the time of Heliokles, who imitated the title 'Dikæos' and the general character of the Bactrian coins of that king. The absence of an Arianian legend renders it probable that these coins were struck in Bactria proper, at a season when the greater part of it was no longer under Greek sway.

COINS OF UNCERTAIN NAMES.

SILVER.

1. Round; large. Head of king, to the right. R. Horse walking, to the left. - - ACIΛC - - HΛI IΛC. Edge broken.

COPPER.

2. Round; large. Head of king, to the right, beardless. R. Horse walking, to the left. BACIΛЄΛ C - - - - ΛAIY. Pl. VIII. fig. 15.

3. Small; round. Head, as before. R. Horse, as before. - ΛCIΛEΛC - CIΛEΛN (*sic*) ΔIIAIY. Pl. VIII. fig. 14.

The silver coin is in Mr. Masson's last collection, but several of the small copper and one large were formerly obtained by him, and have been described, J. As. Soc. B. April, 1834, and June, 1835. The Greek letters are distinct, although they give no legible name, and are, no doubt, blundered. M. R. Rochette conjectures that they are intended for coins of Heliokles, reading the legend as corrected, ΒΑΣΙΛΕΩΣ ΔΙΚΑΙοΥ ΗΛΙοΚΛΕοΥΣ. The conjecture is ingenious, and the identification is not improbable, but it requires further investigation: J. des Sav. Dec. 1838, p. 746.

4. Round; large. Head of king, as before, but the upper part has the appearance of being covered with a cap. R. Standing figure, to the front, in a tunic; his left hand grasps a sceptre or spear, his right holds a thunderbolt. - ΑCΙΛΕΥ - ΑCΙΛΕΩΣ - ΗΔΙΙΛΙΥ. Mon. m. Pl. VIII. fig. 16.

From a drawing of a coin in the possession of M. Court; J. As. Soc. B. Sept. 1836, Pl. XXXV. fig. 4. Mr. Prinsep conjectures that the letters in the exergue for the name may be intended for ΔΙΚΑΙοΥ. M. Mionnet refers these coins to Heliokles, Supplement, viii.; and his opinion is confirmed from an inspection of the coin itself by M. R. Rochette, who considers it, as well as the foregoing, " provenir d'une fabrique barbare établie ailleurs que dans le siége même de la dynastie d'Heliocles;" a fact analogous to the concurrence of the barbarous tetradrachms of Euthydemus with those of the most finished execution: J. des Sav. Dec. 1838, p. 478.

5. Round; large. Horseman, to the right, with bow-case or quiver behind him; right arm extended. Legend, imperfect and corrupt, of Greek and Indian letters mixed. Mon. 93. R. Hercules (?) in the garb of an Indian athlete, to the front, crowned by a winged Victory on his right, and a male figure on his left. Inscription incomplete. [illegible] - - - [illegible] Mah - - - - - Yatibadhikhasa (?). Mon. 94. Pl. VIII. fig. 17.

Copied from the engraving of the coin which belonged to M. Court, by Mr. Prinsep, J. As. Soc. B. vol. v. Pl. XXXV. fig. 5, p. 550. From an inspection of the coin itself, M. Rochette thinks he can decypher the Greek words ΜΕΓΑΛοΥ ΜΑΥοΥ on the face of this coin, but this is not confirmed by the Prakrit inscription, if it is correctly delineated.

MAYES, B.C. 100.

The style of the first discovered coin of this prince intimated its being also of Bactrian currency alone, as it bore no inscription in a native character; the title was merely that of king; and the general form and execution of the coin argued a better and earlier period of art; at the same time the name indicated a Barbaric prince. M. Rochette conjectured in the appellation some connexion with the Zend name of the moon, Mao, and, referring the use of such words to a Sol-lunar worship, suggested the possibility of its being the equivalent of Apollodotus.[1] Mr. Torrens, reasoning from the caduceus on the reverse, infers the name to have rather a relation to Mercury; he at the same time admits it to be a coin of the period of Apollodotus, but would attribute it to a Demetrius, the elder brother of Apollodotus.[2] It is remarkable that a coin with precisely the same types has been found at Bamian,[3] which, if correctly delineated, has the name Demetrius upon it; and it may therefore be a coin of that prince, who by the caduceus, if not by the appellation, had added Mercury to his guardian divinities.

Whatever inferences, however, were thought deducible from the purity of the style and the singleness of the inscription have been annihilated by the discovery of other coins of Mayes of as barbarous an execution as any others, and bearing an Arianian legend. We have both in it and in Greek the pompous title, 'the great king of kings.' The types of these coins are various, but they seem to intimate that in time at least this prince is connected on one hand with Menander and Apollodotus, and on the other with Azes. Thus the elephant's head, and bell suspended from it, is found on the small copper coins of Menander; the standing Apollo and tripod, and the walking elephant, are types of Apollodotus; and the very curious coin in which Neptune is introduced is exactly similar to one of Azes. We may, therefore, conjecture that Mayes was nearly contemporary with Hermæus, but reigned at Bamian or Kunduz, and that he was followed by Azes, who, although of foreign origin, was more properly a king of India than of Bactria; the

[1] J. des Sav. May, 1836. [2] J. As. Soc. B. Jan. 1840, p. 70. [3] Ibid. p. 68. Pl. IV.

fortunes of the Sakas having followed the course of their predecessors, and after placing them in the seats of the Greek kings above the mountains, compelled them to recede before more powerful competitors, and establish themselves on the confines of India, to be there again lost in a kindred but conquering tribe.

COINS OF MAYES.

1. Square; large. Male figure, front view; a serrated club or sceptre in his right hand; a trident behind his back, floating drapery from his shoulders and arms. **ΒΑΣΙΛΕΩΣ ΒΑΣΙΛΕΩΝ ΜΕΓΑΛ°Υ ΜΑΥ°Υ.** R. Female figure (Victory), to the right, with fillet (?) [illegible] - Rajadhirajasa Mahatasa Ma-a-sa. Mon. 95. Pl. VIII. fig. 10.

Unique; presented by General Ventura to the Royal Asiatic Society. The same coin is described and figured by Prinsep; J. As. Soc. B. July, 1838.

2. Round; large. Head of elephant with trunk raised, and bell under the throat. R. Caduceus. **ΒΑΣΙΛΕΩΣ ΜΑΥ°Υ.** Mon. 96. Pl. VIII. fig. 11.

3. Square; middle size. Male figure, with trident, treading on one beneath. **- - - ΓΑΛ°Υ ΜΑΥ°Υ.** Mon. 97. R. Figure, to the right, amongst bushes. - [illegible] Mahatasa Ma-a(sa).

A coin in the possession of Dr. Swiney, agreeing in all essential respects, except the name, with one of Azes. See Pl. VII. fig. 5.

4. Square; middle size. Standing Apollo, naked; arrow in his right hand, left resting on his bow. **ΒΑΣΙΛΕΩΣ ΒΑΣΙΛΕΩΝ ΜΕΓΑΛΟΥ ΜΑΥΟΥ.** R. Tripod. Mon. **MI.** Prakrit legend.

Described by M. R. Rochette, J. des Sav. Feb. 1839, who remarks the identity of the types of this coin with those of coins of Apollodotus.

5. Square; middle size. Elephant, to the right, in a frame. **ΒΑΣΙΛΕΩΣ [ΒΑΣΙΛΕΩΝ ΜΕΓΑ]ΛΟΥ ΜΑΥΟΥ.** R. Figure sitting cross-legged on a couch (?), with sword before him.

Described by M. R. Rochette, J. des Sav. Feb. 1839, p. 100. As he observes, a similar coin was figured by Prinsep, J. As. Soc. B. vol. iv.

Pl. XXI., but containing only the first two words of the legend; the coin was left unappropriated. A coin of the same type, but wholly devoid of legible characters, is in the Masson collection. M. Rochette seems to refine too much in supposing the seat on which the figure is placed to represent the omphalos of the Pythian Apollo.

6. Figure seated on a throne; a smaller figure in front. ΒΑΣΙΛΕΩΣ ΒΑΣΙΛΕΩΝ ΜΕΓΑΛΟΥ ΜΑΥΟΥ. R. Macedonian Pallas.

Described, from an impression sent by General Allard, by M. R. Rochette, J. des Sav. Feb. 1839.

PALIRISUS, B.C. 80.

If the date conjectured for the accession of Hermæus be near the truth, a sufficient interval separates it from the probable date of the Indian conquests of the Yu-chi to allow of an intervening government or governments of Barbaric kings; and one of them may possibly be found in the person of this prince, whose name, as well as the style of his coins, indicates no Grecian descent. There is some indistinctness in the first letter of his name, and it has accordingly been read Ipalirisus and Spalirisus. In most cases, however, there is no room for any letter to precede the Π, and the addition of any other character is owing to an inaccurate representation of the lower stroke of the B of Basileos. The Arianian inscription confirms this, by reading Palirisasa [Arianian characters]. Professor Lassen considers the initial of the latter word to be *k*, and makes the name Kaliriso, which he considers the equivalent of Spalirisus, agreeably to the analogy of the substitution of *k* for the Sva or Spa of Zend words. He has discussed the subject at some length,[1] but there does not seem to have been any occasion for the alteration. As noticed below, the name in one instance has been found to be as it occurs on the coins of the next prince, Palapharama.

The type on the reverse of the coin of Palirisus is the sitting Jupiter, so precisely like that on the coins of Hermæus that it must be imitated from

[1] Zur Geschichte, p. 73.

them; and Palirisus may possibly have immediately succeeded him, if not in all, in parts of the territory subject to him. The obverse has the figure of the king, whose costume is neither Grecian nor Hindu, and is as much evidence of his barbaric origin as his name. Another evidence of his barbaric origin is his adoption of the title, 'great king of kings,' a title first used by Mithridates II. of Parthia, who reigned from B.C. 123 to 96. The coins, although not very rare, are not very numerous, and are of limited discovery, being found chiefly about Kabul. The reign of Palirisus was, therefore, probably not long, nor were his dominions extensive.

COIN OF PALIRISUS.

COPPER.

Square; middle size. Figure of king, to the left, dressed in tunic and scarf; behind his back, a bow and quiver (?); his right hand holds a sort of axe: in a frame. ΒΑCΙΛΕѠΣ ΒΑCΙΛΕѠΝ ΜΕΓΑΛΟΥ ΠΑΛΙΡΙCΟΥ. R. Jupiter seated in a high-backed chair, like that on the coins of Hermæus; his right hand extended, sceptre in his left. 𐨨𐨱𐨪𐨗𐨯 𐨨𐨱𐨟𐨐𐨯 𐨤𐨫𐨁𐨪𐨁𐨯𐨯 Maharajasa Mahatakasa Palirisasa. Mon. 98 repeated. Pl. VIII. fig. 12.

Several good specimens in the Masson collection; some also presented by General Ventura to the Royal Asiatic Society; others have been delineated and described, J. As. Soc. B. April, 1834, June 1835, and J. des Sav. Oct. 1835. The legends were in all instances imperfect, and the name was not made out until more distinct specimens were procured by Mr. Masson in 1835, and described, J. As. Soc. B. Sept. 1836, Pl. XXXV. He reads the name Ipalirisus. There is decidedly a stroke before the *p*; it cannot be intended for Σ, for the sigma on both these coins takes up a large space, as C. The legend in Indian characters makes the first letter also either *Sp* or *P* ħ, as in the next coin.

M. R. Rochette is of opinion that this is the same as the coin of the succeeding prince, and that the differences arise only from the blunder of the engraver; but the names are essentially different in the Indian letters, one being Palirisa, the other Palapharama. The whole purport of the legend, also, is different; this is the 'great king of kings,' the other is the 'brother of the king.' The similarity of the style of these coins confirms their connexion. M. Rochette also accuses the artist of having intended to represent in the figure of the man with a bow and quiver, a Victory with wings and a palm-branch. The execution of the coin is no doubt faulty, but still we cannot think that it exhibits such a strange metamorphosis. J. des Sav. Feb. 1839, p. 94.

SPALYRIUS, B.C. 75.

There can be no doubt of the proximate or contemporary currency of this and the preceding coin, as, although the type differs, the style is obviously the same. It is, however, in many respects of a singular description. The Greek legend shows that it is not the coin of the king, but of the just Spalyrius, the brother of the king. The legend in the Arianian characters on the reverse begins with an uncouth word, Alabaraputasa, which is possibly intended to represent the Greek term Adelphos. The name of the prince occurs with a difference, and seems to be Palapharama, or, as Prinsep reads it, Spalapharma. Lassen again proposes to read the first letter as a *k*, and to correct the penultimate to *y*, so as to make the word Kaliriyasa; the letters are, however, too distinct to admit of such conjectural alterations.

The obverse of this coin bears within a square frame, which is common to it and to the last, and is observable also on some of the coins of Mayes, a king on horseback, with lance in rest, agreeably to the description given by Tabari of the old Persian coins. On the reverse is the seated Hercules, imitated, no doubt, from the coins of Euthydemus.

If any doubt could remain as to the connexion of these two princes, it would be removed by the second of the coins described below, in which, whilst we have the same inscriptions on both faces of the coin, and the mounted king on the obverse, we have the seated Jupiter of Hermæus on the reverse. It seems not impossible that this seated figure may be meant, by the assertion of Tabari, that on one side of the coins of the old Persian kings the monarch was represented seated on his throne.

The coins of Spalyrius are less numerous than those of Palirisus, but are generally found along with them. It is not impossible that the 'brother' was the king *de facto*, although he left for a season the title to Palirisus.

COIN OF SPALYRIUS.

COPPER.

Square; middle size. King on horseback, to the right, with lance in rest; in a frame. **CΠAΛYPIOC ΔIKAIOY AΔEΛΦOY TOY BAΣIΛEΩC.** R. Figure seated, to the left; intended, no doubt, for Hercules sitting on a rock with his club in his hand, as on the coins of Euthydemus; but the figure is of effeminate proportions; fillet on the head. 𐨀𐨫𐨦𐨪𐨤𐨂𐨟𐨯 𐨢𐨨𐨁𐨀𐨯 𐨯𐨤𐨫𐨥𐨪𐨨𐨯 Alabaraputasa Dhamiasa Spalapharamasa. Mon. 98. Pl. VIII. fig. 13.

Several very perfect specimens in the Masson collection; described also by Masson and Prinsep, J. As. Soc. B. June, 1835, Pl. XXI. fig. 9, Sept. 1836, Pl. XXXV. fig. 6, and July, 1838, Pl. XXVII. fig. 3. The inscription on the obverse is generally distinct; and, from the various specimens, is read without question. The inscription on the reverse is equally perfect and distinct by the comparison of different specimens. The first word looks as if it was a blundering attempt to represent the Greek term **AΔEΛΦOΣ** by Alabaraputasa. Mr. Prinsep, in his latest remarks upon this coin, July, 1838, judging from the less complete specimens he had seen, in which the first letter was deficient, thinks it may have been the initial of the name on the reverse of the coin of Vonones, and reads it Balahara putasa, 'of the son of Balahara;' but in our coins the first and third letters are what he has given the value of *a* and *b* to. In the engraved specimen the final letter of the name is indistinct, but in two others it is plainly 𐨯 *sa*.

This is the coin which MM. R. Rochette, Jacquet, and Mionnet wrongly ascribe to Lysias, reading the legend, with some variations, thus: **BACIΛEΩΣ BACIΛEΩN** (?) **ΛYCIOY ΔIKAIOY AΔEΛΦOY**, J. des Sav. March, 1836; **BACIΛEAC** (?) **ΛYCIOY ΔIKAIOY** (**ΦIA**?) **AΔEΛΦOY**, J. Asiatique, Feb. 1836; and **BACIΛEΩΣ BACIΛEΩN ΛYCIOY ΔIKAIOY AΔEΛΦOY.** M. R.

Rochette takes great credit for his discovery of a coin which had "restée inconnue à tous les savants et voyageurs Anglais," although the drawing of the very same coin, which he erroneously described, had been engraved by Mr. Prinsep, J. As. Soc. B. June, 1835. Mr. Prinsep, however, was too conscientious a describer of what he saw to have conjectured a name when there was no trace of it upon a coin; and he therefore left it to more practical numismatists to fall into such a mistake.

M. R. Rochette has since corrected his reading after a more perfect specimen from the collection of M. Court; J. des Sav. Feb. 1839, p. 93.

AZILISES, B.C. 60.

The position of this prince appears to be determined by his coin last discovered, in which we have the precise character and types of the coin of Spalyrius, with the name of Azilises distinct on the reverse. Captain Cunningham, by whom the coin is described, notices two others of the same type, which, although less perfect, assist and confirm the reading of the inscription. He conceives Azilises to have been the king alluded to in the legend of the preceding as the brother of Spalyrius; but the similar character of his coin with that of Palirisus would rather indicate his relationship to the latter. Azilises may have been his son or his nephew, and, at any rate, was probably his successor.

On the other hand, the more frequent of the coins of Azilises connect him unequivocally with a different prince, Azes, who stands to him therefore in the character of his successor: the identity of the types and monograms fully establish this connexion, and it is finally proved by a coin which comprises the names of both princes, having Azes in the Greek, and Azilises in the Arianian inscription. That the reign of Azilises by himself was not long, is probable from the comparative infrequency of his coins; and that his association with Azes was still more brief, is intimated by the singleness of the coin bearing both their names. He may have taken Azes as his colleague in the decline of life, and both life and reign may have been cut short by the impatience of his successor.

COINS OF AZILISES.

SILVER.

1. Didrachm. King on horseback, with lance couched, to the right, with cap and fillet. ΒΑΣΙΛΕΩΣ ΒΑΣΙΛΕΩΝ ΜΕΓΑΛοΥ ΑΖΙΛΙΣοΥ. Mon. X. R. Victory in robe, to the left; a palm-branch in her left hand, a peculiar symbol in her right. Inscription imperfect, but first title and name distinct. PTHXΛ1 PY7Ꞁu Maharajasa Ayilisasa. Mon. double, 99. Pl. VIII. fig. 5.

From a coin presented by General Ventura to the Royal Asiatic Society. It agrees in all respects with the didrachm of Azes, except the name; J. As. Soc. B. June, 1835, Pl. XXIII. fig. 27; J. des Sav. April, 1836; J. Asiatique, Feb. 1836; Mionnet, Supplement, viii.

2. Didrachm. Horseman, to the right, as before. R. Victory, to the left, as before, except that she holds a fillet in her right hand. Mon. 100. Pl. VIII. fig. 6.

From a coin belonging to Dr. Swiney. These two coins are alike in the device and legends, and differ only in the substitution of the fillet for the symbol.

COPPER.

3. Square; large. King mounted, to the right. ΒΑΣΙΛΕΩΣ ΒΑΣΙΛΕΩΝ ΜΕΓΑΛοΥ ΑΖΙΛΙϹοΥ. R. Indian bull, to the right. Mon. double, 101.

Delineated by Prinsep, J. As. Soc. B. June, 1835, Pl. XXIII. fig. 28; described also by the other authorities from several in the Ventura collection.

4. Square; middle size. King mounted, to the right. - - - ΜΕΓΑΛοΥ - ΖΙΛΙϹοΥ. R. Elephant, to the right. - - - - PTHXΛ1 Ayilisasa. Mon. double, 99. Pl. VIII. fig. 7.

From an undescribed coin in the Masson collection.

5. Square; middle size. King on horseback, to the right. - - ΣΙΛΕΩΝ ΜΕΓΑΛοΥ. R. Sitting Hercules, with club on his knee. - THXΛ1 PY7Ꞁu Maharajasa Ayilisa - . Mon. double, 99.

This coin has been recently described by Captain Cunningham from a collection made at Bamian by Captain Hay; J. As. Soc. B., New Series, No. XVII., p. 532.

COIN OF AZES AND AZILISES.

Round; large. King on horseback, as before. ΒΑΣΙΛΕΩΣ ΒΑΣΙΛΕΩΝ ΜΕΓΑΛΟΥ ΑΖΟΥ. R. Victory, to the right; her right hand holds a symbol, her left a palm-branch and fillet. Maharajasa Rajarajasa Mahatasa Ayilisasa. Mon. double, 102.

This coin is described and delineated by M. R. Rochette, J. des Sav. Oct. 1835, Pl. II. fig. 16. The name of Azilises on the reverse was pointed out by Professor Lassen and M. Jacquet: Grotefend notices a second.

AZES, B.C. 50.

The coins of this prince, comprehending a greater variety of devices than any other, show him equally to have been of barbaric race and of later date. They are very numerous, and denote a long reign; but there is one remarkable peculiarity to be borne in mind respecting them: according to Mr. Masson,[1] the coins of the genuine Azes dynasty are seldom or ever found beyond Jelalabad, and there scantily; while to the north and east of Peshawer, and also at that place, they are numerous. They have never been found at Beghram, but are not uncommon in the Punjab. It may be a question, therefore, whether Azes should not be regarded rather as a native of India than of Scythia.

Another peculiar characteristic of these coins is the absence of a portrait, unless the figure on horseback, which is common, and in one specimen a sitting figure, be so considered. We have no head of an individual on any coin.

The coins of Azes are mostly of copper, but there are some silver, and several plated, which is another novelty in the Bactro-Indian coinage. The

[1] Masson on the Topes, p. 73.

prevailing form of the silver and plated coins is that of the didrachm, and the most common device on the obverse is the Szu or Saka type of the king on horseback, with his lance in rest. The title is 'the great king of kings,' and the name is more or less distinct, AZΟY, with the square omicron. It also occurs, however, not unfrequently round, but small; and on most of the coins the Greek letters are distinctly inscribed, but in some they offer no legible legend, being evidently most ignorantly and unsuccessfully imitated. The reverse of those coins on which the horseman appears is commonly a Victory with the diadem; whence it is to be inferred that Azes was a conqueror. The title in Arianian letters corresponds with that of the Greek, 'the great king, the king of kings, the great.' The name is Aya-sa or Aya. It is necessary to suppose that the Y in this case was pronounced as if it was J, a change which does take place in some Indian dialects; and the name being read Aja, furnishes the original of the Greek Azes. Aja, it may be remarked, is a genuine Hindu name, but it is difficult to understand why it should have been converted into Aya in this part of India. There is a king celebrated in the annals of the Buddhists, who is called by the Chinese A-yu. The Buddhists, indeed, seem to identify him with Asoka, the grandson of Chandragupta, who lived, therefore, in the third century B. C., and of whom it is fabled that he erected eighty thousand monumental towers in various parts of India. This was certainly not the Azes of the coins, but there may have been some confusion either in the traditions picked up by the Chinese or in the manner in which they have been transferred into European languages. Whether the Aya of the coins be the A-yu of Fa-Hian or not, it may be confidently affirmed that he flourished not very long before, and possibly after, the Christian æra, from the frequency with which some of his coins are found in the topes. The topes are undoubtedly all subsequent to the Christian æra; and it seems probable that the coins buried in them were invariably selected from the prevailing currency which was not of any remotely previous issue.

The great variety of devices on the coins of Azes renders it impossible to select any that may be considered as characteristic: the king on horseback is one: in others we have obvious though very rude and barbarous imitations of the coins of the Greek kings of Bactria; such as the Minerva with spear and shield, as on the coins of Demetrius; and the Hercules raising a fillet to his head, as on coins of the same prince; the fighting Minerva of Menander, and Jupiter holding a Victory, as on the coins of Antimachus. The elephant and Indian bull may be either copied from the coins of Apollodotus, or may be original. The Victories are also taken from Greek coins, although very rudely represented; and in some instances they hold not only a fillet, but a symbol of very uncertain import.

In addition to types for which prototypes may be suggested, we have a number of others which seem to be of Indian origin, such as the lion and the camel; the latter sometimes with a rider on his back. In one case we have the figure of the king sitting cross-legged on a cushion, after the Indian fashion, with his sword apparently lying before him,—an oriental, though not exclusively an Indian usage of royalty; the dress is completely Indian. The reverse of this coin offers what seems to be intended for Mercury, but it is rather inexplicable. It has not, as has been conjectured by several eminent numismatists, any vestige of Siva; it has more the character of Mercury.

One very remarkable coin of this prince is the first of the copper coins described below, the figure on the obverse of which cannot well be intended for any thing but Neptune; from which it might be inferred that Azes reigned at the mouth of the Indus on the sea-coast,—a supposition not improbable, but which would lead us to expect to find his coins in Sindh, where they have not been discovered. As mentioned above, we have also a similar type on a coin of Mayes, whose other coins would seem to limit him to the mountain regions north of Kabul. We can scarcely, therefore, venture to offer any conjecture as to the purport of this type.

The monograms of Azes are as diversified as his types; and as if they were not sufficiently varied, they are multiplied to an extraordinary extent on individual coins, so that we have them frequently double on both faces. They are, however, not Greek; the prevailing forms are those of Nos. 104 and 109, or their modifications. Several of them are intended apparently for Arianian letters. No. 118 is an additional agreement with the coin of Mayes with the type of Neptune. Others will recur on the coins of succeeding princes, intimating, at least, community of local rule.

COINS OF AZES.

SILVER AND PLATED.

1. Didrachm. King, with fillet, mounted, to the right; lance couched. ΒΑΣΙΛΕΩΣ ΒΑΣΙΛΕΩΝ ΜΕΓΑΛΟΥ ΑΖΟΥ. Mon. 103. R. Victory in a long robe, to the left; her right hand holds a peculiar symbol, her left a palm-branch, and a fillet hangs from her wrist. 𐨨𐨱𐨪𐨗𐨯 𐨪𐨗𐨪𐨗𐨯 𐨨𐨱𐨟𐨯 𐨀𐨩𐨯 Maharajasa Rajarajasa Mahatasa Ayasa. Mon. double, 104. Pl. VI. fig. 12.

From a coin presented to the Royal Asiatic Society by General Ventura; also described, J. des Sav. Oct. 1835, Pl. II. fig. 16; but the coin there represented is only copper, silvered. Another silver coin of this type is contained in Mr. Masson's last collection.

2. Didrachm. Plated. King on horseback, with fillet, to the right, holding up his right hand; the lower edge of his garment is ornamented; behind him is an object not determined. ΒΑΣΙΛΕΩΣ ΒΑΣΙΛΕΩΝ ΜΕΓΑΛΟΥ ΑΖΟΥ. R. Minerva, to the right, with spear and drapery on her left. Maharajasa Rajarajasa Mahatasa Ayasa. Mon. double, 105. Pl. VI. fig. 13.

From the Masson collection; delineated by him, J. As. Soc. B. April, 1834; name not legible: identified by Prinsep, J. As. Soc. B. June, 1835, Pl. XXIII. fig. 15; also J. des Sav. April, 1836; and Mionnet, Supplement, from coins of Honigberger and Ventura. These coins vary in their degree of perfection and their monograms. Jacquet, J. Asiatique, Feb. 1836, conjectures the object behind the king to be "un arc placé dans un étui." The right hand raised in most of these coins, and others of the same type, usually holds an object which sometimes looks like a whip, a bird, a short sword, or a Victory. According to Mionnet, his coin is of silver; Prinsep describes his as of copper covered with a layer of billion. Jacquet also terms it "bronze revêtu d'une lame d'argent."

3. Didrachm. Plated. King on horseback, as before, but in a different costume, a sort of surtout. Legend as before. Mon. indistinct. R. Male

figure in a long robe, front view, but looking to the left; part of a trident visible above the right shoulder. Inscription as before. Mon. double, 106. Pl. VI. fig. 14.

4. Didrachm. Plated. King on horseback, as before; whip in his right hand. R. Male figure in a short robe, front view; right hand extended, left raised to the head: an object indistinct, part of his sleeve, on the right. Inscription imperfect. ϷΛ1 ϷУ7Ն Maharajasa Ayasa. Mon. various, 107. Pl. VI. fig. 15.

From coins figured by Prinsep, J. As. Soc. B. June, 1835, Pl. XXIII. figs. 16, 17. Except in size they agree with Nos. 46 and 47 of Masson's, Pl. XI. J. As. Soc. B. April, 1834. The latter is also probably the same coin as Jacquet's No. 27. He calls the male figure "Jupiter Nicephore debout, tenant le sceptre de la main gauche, portant sur la main droite un petit simulacre de la Victoire qui lui présente une couronne." At any rate this description, except in size, applies to the two following.

5. Drachm. Plated. King on horseback; his right hand holds a whip. Legend imperfect and corrupt. Mon. various, 108. R. Male figure in a long robe, with a sceptre in the left hand, and a Victory on his extended right. Legend imperfect, but the name ϷΛ1 traceable. Mon. various, 109. Pl. VI. fig. 16.

From the Masson collection; represented by him as fig. 46 of Pl. XI. referred to above. It is also Mionnet's No. 77.

6. Drachm. Plated. King on horseback, as before. ΒΑΣΙΛΕΩΣ ΒΑΣΙΛΕΩΝ ΜΕΓΑΛΟΥ ΑΖΟΥ. In front ɧ. R. Jupiter (?), to the left; his sceptre behind him; part of his robe or his sleeve hanging on the right; his right hand, extended, holds a winged Victory presenting a wreath. Legend imperfect, but name distinct, ϷΛ1. Mon. various, 110. Pl. VI. fig. 17.

Described and figured from the Ventura collection; J. des Sav. April, 1836, Vignette, fig. 19.

7. Hemidrachm. Silver. King mounted, with lance in rest; the horse's head decorated with a plume. - - - CΙΛЄΩΝ ΜΕΓΑΛ. R. Victory, to the left, with palm-branch and symbol. Inscription imperfect. Mon. various, 111. Pl. VI. fig. 18.

This coin corresponds in most respects, except size, with No. 1. It is described, J. des Sav. March, 1836, Pl. II. fig. 11, and J. Asiatique, Feb. 1836. MM. Rochette and Jacquet ascribe it to Vonones: the name is wanting, it is true, but its exact conformity to the didrachm identifies it with the coins of Azes or Azilises.

8. Hemidrachm. Silver. King on horseback, to the right, in a chequered dress, holding a whip. Legend rude and corrupt. Mon. 112. R. Minerva, front view, her spear behind her; the ægis on her left arm, and her right hand raised. ᑭΛ٩ - - - ᑭꓘ7ꓘ7 ᑭꓘ7ᒪᴗ Maharajasa Rajarajasa - - - Ayasa. Mon. various, 113. Pl. VI. fig. 19.

From the Masson collection; also J. des Sav. March, 1836, Pl. II. fig. 15; Mionnet, Supplement, No. 74; J. Asiatique, No. xxvi.

9. Triobolus. Silver. King on horseback, with couched lance; object in his left hand, apparently resembling a bow (?); horse's head dressed. - - - - ΛΕΩΝ ΜΕΓΑΛΟV. R. Thessalian Minerva, to the left. Inscription imperfect; name beneath, ᑭΛ٩. Mon. double, 114. Pl. VII. fig. 1.

Presented to the Royal Asiatic Society by General Ventura. A similar coin is described by Mionnet, Supplement, Bactrian Coins, No. 75.

10. Triobolus. Silver. King on horseback, to the right; a whip in his hand, and a feather or tuft of hair on the top of his head; dress chequered. Inscription imperfect. Mon. ٦. R. Male figure, Jupiter (?), to the left, sceptre behind; his right hand holds a Victory with a wreath. Inscription imperfect; but name ᑭΛ٩ distinct. Mon. various, 115. Pl. VII. fig. 2.

From a coin of Dr. Swiney's collection.

11. Triobolus. Plated. King on horseback, to the right. Inscription imperfect and corrupt. Mon. double, but indistinct. R. Male figure, with a cap and trowsers, to the left; holding a palm-branch (?) in his right hand. Inscription imperfect; name traceable, ᑭΛ٩. Mon. various, 116. Pl. VII. fig. 3.

From a coin in the collection.

12. Triobolus. Plated. King on horseback, to the right. Inscription imperfect and corrupt. R. Male figure, to the left, with a Victory on his extended right arm. Inscription imperfect; name traceable, though indistinct. Mon. various, 117. Pl. VII. fig. 4.

From a coin in the collection. This and the preceding are figured by

Prinsep, J. As. Soc. B. June, 1835, Pl. XXIII. figs. 20 and 21. It is evident that although varying in execution and size, Nos. 4, 5, 6, 10, 11, 12, correspond generally in type.

COPPER.

13. Square; large. Male figure, to the front, with fillet, and dressed in a long mantle; his left hand holds a trident, the right rests on his right thigh, as it is raised to trample upon a naked figure with horns (?) on his head, prostrate. ΒΑΣΙΛΕΩΣ ΒΑΣΙΛ--- --ΓΑΛΟΥ Α--. R. Female figure, to the front, with fillet, in a long robe, surrounded by branches of a plant, of which she holds the stem with either hand. Inscription imperfect. [Kharoshthi] --- tasa Ayasa. Mon. 118. Pl. VII. fig. 5.

From a coin in very good preservation in the collection of Dr. Swiney. A less perfect specimen has been presented to the Royal Asiatic Society by General Ventura. It was first described by Prinsep, from six specimens in the Ventura collection; J. As. Soc. B. June, 1835, Pl. XXIII. fig. 14. The inscription is entire on both faces of his coin, giving the name Azes distinctly. The same is the case with others described, J. des Sav. April, 1836, Pl. II. fig. 17; J. Asiatique, Feb. 1836; and Mionnet, Supplement, viii. Prinsep terms the male figure a soldier trampling on a prostrate enemy. Jacquet describes him as "posant le pied droit sur l'épaule d'une autre figure représentée à mi-corps et dans l'action de nager." M. R. Rochette considers also the prostrate figure to be swimming, and to represent the river Indus, on which Neptune sets his foot; the standing figure being analogous to that of Neptune on the coin of Antimachus. Mionnet adopts the idea, and terms the figure on the reverse "l'Inde personnifiée." The fillet on each figure denotes royalty, and the male may be the king, under the type of Siva, trampling upon a defeated prince, represented as an Asura.

14. Square; large. Figure, with extended hand, holding a whip or wreath (?), mounted on the double-humped or Bactrian camel. ΒΑΣΙΛΕΩΣ ---ΣΙΛ --ΑΛΟΥ ΑΖΟΥ. Mon. (?). R. Humped Indian bull, to the right. [Kharoshthi] ---. Mon. 119. Pl. VII. fig. 6.

From a coin in the Masson collection; unique.

15. Square; large; apparently cut. Standing Hercules, to the front,

with club and skin in his left hand, raising a wreath and fillet to his head with his right. Inscription imperfect. Mon. 120. R. Horse standing, to the right. ΡΛ٩ Ρ٦Ն - Mon. 121. Pl. VII. fig. 7.

From a coin presented by General Ventura to the Royal Asiatic Society. A similar coin was described by Prinsep as doubtful, J. As. Soc. B. June, 1835, Pl. XXI. fig. 8; but this coin is represented by him as a coin of Azes, J. As. Soc. B. July, 1838, Pl. XXVIII. fig. 9. The standing Hercules is the same as that on the coins of Demetrius.

16. Round; large. Indian bull, to the right. ΒΑΣΙΛΕΩΣ ΒΑΣΙΛΕΩΝ ΜΓΑΛ□V (*sic*) ΑΖ□V. Mon. double, 122. R. Lion, to the right. ΡΣ٦ՆՍ ΡΛ٩ Ρ٦ՆΟ ΡΣ٦Σ٦ Maharajasa Rajarajasa Mahatasa Ayasa. Mon. 123. Pl. VII. fig. 8.

Many of these are in the Masson collection, as well as in others. Three are engraved by Prinsep, J. As. Soc. B. June, 1835, Pl. XXII. figs. 1, 2, 3. The monograms vary. Mionnet has others; the legends are rarely entire, but the name is generally distinct.

17. Round; small. Indian bull, to the right, as before. Mon. 124. R. Lion, to the right. Mon. 125. Pl. VII. fig. 9.

Several in the collection. The inscriptions are always more or less defective and corrupt.

18. Round; large. Elephant walking, to the right. ΒΑΣΙΛΕΩΣ ΒΑΣΙΛΕΩΝ ΜΕΓΑΛ°Υ ΑΖ°Υ. R. Indian bull, to the right. Inscription as in No. 16. Mon. double, 126. Pl. VII. fig. 10.

Several in the collection. Delineated also by Prinsep, J. As. Soc. B. June, 1835, Pl. XXII. figs. 4, 5. Described also by Jacquet, &c. The drawing is from a very perfect specimen belonging to Dr. Swiney.

19. Round; large. Bactrian camel, to the right. Legend imperfect and corrupt. Mon. 127. R. Bull (Indian?), to the right. Legend defective. Mon. ħ. Pl. VII. fig. 11.

From a coin belonging to Dr. Swiney. Several in the Ventura collection have been described by Prinsep, also by Jacquet and Mionnet. They agree in ascribing them to Azes, although the inscriptions are always worn and imperfect, and do not present the name.

20. Round; large. Figure seated cross-legged on a cushion; cap on the

head, with ribbon or fillet tied behind; dressed in a quilted jacket with sleeves, and the Indian dhoti round the lower extremities: the right arm, extended, holds a whip (?); the left hand grasps the lower part of a sheathed sword, placed transversely behind the waist. ΒΑΣΙΛΕΩΣ ΒΑΣΙΛΕΩΝ ΜΕΓΑΛΟΥ ΑΖΟΥ. Mon. 128, 129. R. Standing figure, to the front, looking to the left; naked, but with floating drapery behind the shoulders, hanging down to the ground; the legs have ornaments (or wings?); the right hand holds a fillet, the left a rod (a caduceus?) or trident. Inscription imperfect, but name distinct, 𐨀𐨩𐨯 Ayasa. Mon. in each double, 130, 131. Pl. VII. figs. 13, 14.

21. Round; small. Sitting figure, as before. R. Standing figure, as before; worn.

Several of these, both large and small, are in the Masson collection, as well as in others: J. As. Soc. B. June, 1835, Pl. XXII. figs. 12, 13; J. Asiatique, Feb. 1836, No. XXXVII.; J. des Sav. April, 1836; Mionnet, Supplement, Rois de la Bactriane, 83-90. The coins bear various monograms, and the legends are commonly defective and corrupt: the descriptions of the device do not always agree. The object in the right hand is called a sceptre or a hook; the sword is said to lie on the lap. The floating drapery behind the shoulders of the figure on the reverse is considered by M. R. Rochette to represent arms, and he terms it "figure virile à quatre bras." Jacquet regarded them as the wings of Mercury, and the instrument in the left hand of the figure as a caduceus. Mionnet denominates the figure Siva, "les épaules couvertes d'une longue bandelette qui flotte derrière ses épaules et pend de chaque coté presque jusqu'à terre." In one (85) he finds the caduceus. Grotefend regards the figure as representing Siva.

22. Round; large. A figure, apparently female, sitting on a chair with a high back; the lower part of her body is clothed; her right hand is raised, her left holds a cornucopia (?). ΒΑΣΙΛΕΩΣ ΒΑΣΙΛΕΩΝ Μ - - - - ΑΖ - -. R. Standing figure, to the left; right arm raised, holding an arrow (?); the body is partly clothed, and the left hand holds some of the drapery; an instrument, like a caduceus, projects from behind the left shoulder. 𐨨𐨱𐨪𐨗𐨯 𐨪𐨗𐨪𐨗 - - - 𐨀𐨩𐨯 Maharajasa Rajaraja - - - Ayasa. Mon. double, 132. Pl. VII. fig. 12.

From coins in the Masson collection. One has been engraved by Prinsep, J. As. Soc. B. June, 1835, Pl. XXII. fig. 10; and described by the French numismatists, who consider the figure on the obverse to be Ceres. Mionnet, No. 93, finds " le modius ou le canistrum sur la tête, et un épi dans la main droite." The figure on the reverse he terms " Siva la main droite levée, la gauche appuyée sur une massue posée à terre; dans le champ à droite une espèce de caducée." Prinsep thinks it doubtful whether the figure represents Hercules or Mercury. His drawing delineates the lower object as a club, with the butt-end on the ground; but, in four tolerably perfect specimens consulted, it seems to be nothing else than the skirts of the robe. M. R. Rochette calls the figure, Hercules with the club; Jacquet, Mercury with the caduceus. Prinsep gives a second coin with similar devices, but it either is much worn or rudely fabricated. The name on both faces is usually distinct, and it was on this coin that the name of Azes was first read by Mr. Prinsep; J. As. Soc. B. June, 1835, p. 344.

23. Square; large. Horseman with lance couched, to the right, in a frame. ΒΑΣΙΛΕΩΣ ΒΑΣΙΛΕΩΝ ΜΕΓΑΛ°Υ ΑΖ°Υ. R. Indian bull, to the right. Inscription imperfect, but name distinct, ϷΛϠ. Mon. double (?), 133. Pl. VII. fig. 16.

Ventura collection. Described by Prinsep, June, 1835, Pl. XXII. fig. 9; and previously, Sept. 1834, Pl. XXVI. fig. 2; also by Jacquet, Pl. XXXIV., and Mionnet, 79, 80.

24. Round; middle size. Horseman in chequered garb, to the right, with helmet and fillet; his right hand holds his whip or a wreath (?), and on his left appears the top of his quiver (?). Inscription blundered. Mon. 134. R. Minerva, to the right; her spear and shield are on her left; her right hand holds a Victory. Inscription corrupt, but apparently the name is Azes, ϷΛV (*sic*). Mon. double, 135. Pl. VII. fig. 17.

From a coin in the possession of Dr. Swiney. A similar one has been presented to the Royal Asiatic Society by General Ventura. There may be reasonable doubt as to the appropriation of this coin, as no name is satisfactorily made out, but it corresponds in its general character with the plated didrachm, No. 3.

25. Round; middle size; thick. King on horseback, with his right arm extended. Greek inscription imperfect and corrupt, ωΕΙΛΟΝωΕΟΛΛω

NIOCΛΛC (*sic*). Mon. 136. R. Female figure in long robe with floating lappets; the right arm is extended, the left holds a rude cornucopia. [Kharoshthi] Maharajasa Mahatasa Dhamikasa Rajadhirajasa Ayasa. Mon. double, 137. Pl. VIII. fig. 1.

These coins are very numerous in all the collections, and have been found in most of the topes in considerable quantity. They are evidently of a later and more barbarous period than most of the preceding, and are probably the coins, not of Azes, although his name appears upon them, but of some of his successors. The Greek is invariably an unmeaning assemblage of rude letters; and the Indian legend, although not very faulty, seems to be carelessly and incorrectly cut. Mr. Prinsep, from a tolerably perfect specimen of a coin belonging to General Ventura, reads the Indian legend Maharajasa Mahatasa Dhamikasa Rajadhirajasa Ayasa; J. As. Soc. B. July, 1838, p. 655, Pl. XXVIII. fig. 17. He first described the coin in the Journal, from Mr. Masson's drawing, April, 1834, Pl. XI. fig. 47; and again, June, 1835, Pl. XXIII. fig. 22. It has been described also, J. des Sav. April, 1836. Jacquet, J. Asiatique, Feb. 1836, regards it as of doubtful attribution; but the name in Indian characters is clear enough on many specimens. Mionnet ascribes it to Azes, from the reading which he finds in one instance in the Greek legend of HΣYΩ. Nos. 107, 108.

26. Square; middle size. Lion, to the right. Inscription imperfect and corrupt. Mon. [Kharoshthi]. R. Humped bull, to the left. - [Kharoshthi] Aya - . Mon. [Kharoshthi]. Pl. VIII. fig. 3.

In the Masson collection.

27. Square; middle size; irregular. Horseman, to the right. Legend imperfect. Mon. 138. R. Lion, to the right. Legend imperfect. Mon. 139. Pl. VIII. fig. 2.

From a coin in Dr. Swiney's collection.

28. Round; small. Horseman, to the right. Inscription imperfect. Mon. 140. R. Standing figure holding a Victory, to the left. Inscription imperfect. Mon. various, 141. Pl. VIII. fig. 4.

From the collection of the Royal Asiatic Society. The coin bears no name, but it is essentially the same with the small silver and plated coins, Nos. 10, 11, 12.

GREAT KING OF KINGS, THE PRESERVER.

This prince can be designated by his titles only, as his coins offer the characteristic peculiarity of being without a name. It is also characteristic of the same coins, with a very few and doubtful exceptions, to have a Greek legend only.

At the same time the forms of the Greek characters are indisputable evidence of the late date of the coins, as we have the C and ϵ for the Σ and E on some of them, and C and E on others; M is usually H; Y is always V; and Ω is represented by ω. The inscription is in the nominative case, as CωTHP MЄΓAC BACIΛЄVC BACIΛЄωN, and for the latter we have sometimes BAЄIΛЄVωN. In many instances the characters are altogether barbarous and illegible.

There is no great variety in these coins, although they are infinitely numerous, and are, with very few exceptions, of copper; and these latter are found, to use Mr. Prinsep's expression, 'by bag-fulls' at Beghram, in many of the topes in the Punjab, and even in Central India, as at Benares, and in Malwa. Although the legend is barbarized, the execution of the coins is not bad, and the relief is vigorous and bold. The type on one face is universally the mounted monarch, as on the coins of the preceding princes. On the other we have in a few instances the figure of a man in a long robe, apparently a priest, with a fire-altar; but the device on those coins which are so numerous is the head of the king, occasionally, though rarely, with a helmet; but in general with either a kind of turban, or his hair dressed in a peculiar manner. He holds a short spear.

The absence of a name has induced M. Rochette to conjecture that these coins were struck by a federal association of different independent states, who assumed an ideal monarch as the emblem of the majesty of their union. We can scarcely, however, suppose that they would have adopted such a type, or made use of such a legend as 'the great king of kings.' The portrait is, therefore, in all probability the representation of a genuine king, although who or what he was it is difficult to conjecture.

He must have reigned chiefly, if not altogether, in India, at least in the

Punjab, by the abundance of his coins in the west of Hindustan. The same consideration, as well as the freshness of the coins and the style of the inscription, combine to place him subsequent to the Christian æra, although possibly within the first century. Was he a Scythic prince, as Professor Lassen[1] supposes? The type of the mounted monarch is in favour of the supposition; but, as already remarked, it is doubtful if the Indo-Scythians spread far into India, and the coins of this prince are found extensively in India. It may be observed that the character of the portrait is very different from that which we find on coins of whose Scythian origin no reasonable doubt can be entertained. The head-dress is very peculiar, and there is especially one decoration which is decidedly Indian, the use of large ear-rings,—a practice which is constantly alluded to in Sanscrit heroic poetry as an attribute of princes, and which is so far universal in the present day that every man has in his youth his ears pierced for such an ornament, and many men wear them. The features of the face are also Indian. It is doubtful if the same portrait occurs in all the coins: it is sometimes dissimilar, but the difference is possibly the effect of difference of years; at the same time the great quantities in which the coins are discovered argue a duration of more than one reign, and we may have a dynasty rather than an individual prince.

The position of the first of the series, if there was a succession, or of the individual, if alone, is undoubtedly subsequent to the æra of the Greek kings of Kabul. That it was not very remotely so may be inferred from the use of Greek letters, and from the epithet 'Soter,' which must have been borrowed from the last of the Greek princes. The title 'great king of kings' connects the prince with Azes; and that he was posterior to Azes is indicated by the appearance of a very peculiar symbol,—a trident of three prongs, the short staff of which has a cross-bar, and terminates in a circle. Now on one of the coins of Azes, and in the right hand of the Victory on the reverse of some of the coins of him and of Azilises, we have what may be considered the rudiments of this symbol. What it may designate is uncertain, but it is there rather less perfectly developed, whilst, as it appears

[1] Zur Geschichte, p. 183.

on the coins of the 'nameless' king, it recurs for a considerable period on the coins of princes undoubtedly much more modern. This renders it likely that the coins of the 'great king of kings, the preserver,' occupy an intermediate position between those of Azes and of Kadphises. There is a further concurrence with the coins of the latter in the presence of Arianian letters, especially of ␣ *ta* or ␣ *ti* in the field of the coin. I am therefore disposed to conclude that these are the coins of an Indian prince or princes who in the first century of the Christian æra reigned in the Punjab, and at first held possessions west of the Indus, until compelled to fall back before the concentrated efforts of the Yu-chi or Indo-Scythic prince Kadphises.

COINS OF THE GREAT KING OF KINGS, THE PRESERVER.

SILVER.

1. Drachm. Head of king, with rays, to the right, with chlamys. R. King on horseback, to the right. - - - ΓΑC ΒΑCΙΛΕVC ΒΑCΙΛΕ - -. Mon. 142. Pl. IX. fig. 9.

From a coin in the cabinet of Dr. Swiney.

COPPER.

2. Round; large. Head of king, with helmet, to the left, with chlamys; right arm raised, holding a short lance. Mon. ␣ and 142. R. King on horseback, to the right; the right hand raised, holding apparently a hawk. CωΤΗΡ ΗΕΓΑ - -. Mon. in front of the horse. Pl. IX. figs. 8, 10.

From the Masson collection. Fig. 10 is much worn.

3. Round; middle size. Head of king, to the right; the hair in stiff curls, with fillet and rays; large ear-rings in the ears; the left hand holding a short lance. Mon. behind the head. R. King on horseback, to the right. CωΤΗΡ ΗΕΓΑC ΒΑCΙΛΕVC ΒΑCΙΛΕVωΝ. Pl. IX. figs. 11, 12.

4. Head of king, as before. R. Horseman, as before, but in a somewhat different costume. CωΤΙ (*sic*) ΒΑCΙΛΕVC ΒΑCΙΛΕωΝ. Mon. Pl. IX. figs. 13, 14.

5. Head, as before, without ear-rings; the lance has a tassel under the

head. R. Horseman, as before. ΗΡΕ ∇ΓΔ Β∇ - (*sic*) - - . Mon. Pl. IX. fig. 15.

6. Head, as before. R. Horseman, as before. - - - ΜΕΓΛϹ ΒΑϹΙΛΕVϹ. Pl. IX. fig. 16.

7. Head, as before. ϹѠΤΗΡ ΒΑϹΙΛΕVϹ ΒΑϹΙΛΕѠΝ. Pl. IX. fig. 17.

8. Head, as before. R. Horseman, as before. - - - ΛЄV ΒΑCΙΛЄVѠ. Pl. IX. fig. 18.

9. Head, as before. R. Horseman, as before. CѠΤΗΡ ΜЄΓΑC ΒΑCΙ-ΛЄVC ΒΑCΙΛΕVѠΝ. Pl. IX. fig. 19.

These are a few, out of an immense number in the collection, found in several topes, in the plain of Beghram, and in other places. They are also equally numerous of a still smaller size, as in Pl. X. figs. 1, 2, 3, 4, 6. Both large and small are of bold execution; but in many the legend is corrupt, as in fig. 4 of Pl. X., CIV ѠΝΙϹΙΓΙѠ; and the epithet ΜЄΓΑΣ is omitted, as in fig. 1 of the same Plate; in others, even of the small pieces, as in fig. 6, the legend is correct and complete. They are described and delineated in various places: As. Res. vol. xvii.; Burnes, vol. ii. Pl. IV. fig. 19; J. As. Soc. B. Jan. 1833, Pl. II. figs. 19, 20; Ibid. August, 1833, Pl. XIV. figs. 9, 10; April, 1834, Pl. X. figs. 26, 27, 28, 29; June, 1835, Pl. XXIII. fig. 26; J. des Sav. April, 1836; J. Asiatique, Feb. 1836; Mionnet, Supplement, viii. p. 505.

10. Round; middle size. King on horseback, to the right. - - - ΤΗΡ - - -. Mon. in front of the horse. R. Male figure, with cap and fillet, to the right, in a long robe; the left hand holds a staff, the right is stretched over a jar or fire-altar (?). Indian characters corrupt. [Indian characters] - - [Indian characters] - - -. Mon. or syllable [Indian character] *ti* behind the figure. Pl. IX. fig. 20.

11. Round; middle size. Horseman, as before. - - - - ΓΑC ΒΑCΙΛΕV. R. Figure, as before. Indian legend. Mon. [Indian character]. Pl. IX. fig. 22.

12. Round; small. Horseman, as before. R. Figure, &c., as before. Pl. IX. fig. 21.

These three coins are from the Masson collection, and are identifiable with the preceding by the Greek legend, which, although imperfect in each, is evidently intended to be ΒΑCΙΛЄCV ΒΑCΙΛЄѠΝ CѠΤΗΡ ΜЄΓΑC. Others have been described, J. As. Soc. B. June, 1835, Pl. XXIII. fig. 23;

J. Asiatique, Feb. 1836; Mionnet, Supplement, viii. p. 505. He calls the figure on the reverse "Roi diadèmé," and the supposed fire-altar a monogram, which he represents very differently from what appears on our coins.

SECTION III.—INDO-PARTHIAN DYNASTY.

VONONES.

The coins of this prince are rare, and appear to belong to the same series as the preceding, by the figure of the king on horseback, with his lance couched, observable on the hemidrachm. The types on his coins are borrowed from those of the Greek Bactro-Indian kings, as the Jupiter of Heliokles, the Hercules and Minerva of Demetrius, from which it may be a question if he should not be placed earlier even than Azilises. An argument also in favour of an earlier date may be drawn from the form of the Greek letters on his coins, which are of an earlier period than those of Palirisus. The imitations also of the Greek divinities are of a better style of execution, particularly on the square copper coin. On the other hand, the equestrian king is exactly in the same style as on the coins repeatedly noticed, so that they cannot be far apart. A striking proof of the coincidence is afforded by the mistaken appropriation of several of the coins of Azes to this prince by experienced numismatists.

A question of some interest is suggested by the name of Vonones, for it is also borne by two of the Parthian princes. The first of these, after having been some time at Rome as a hostage, became king of Parthia B. C. 6, and was killed A. D. 20. During the greater part of this period he was a fugitive in Asia Minor, having been driven from his throne and country by Artabanus, a Scythian prince of the Arsacidan race: although on one occasion he was victorious, yet in the following year he was again defeated and obliged to fly. It is scarcely likely, therefore, that any coins of his should be found at Kabul; and the improbability is further corroborated by a comparison of the coins that are found in Afghanistan with the genuine Parthian coins of Vonones, of which an example from a collection made by Sir H. Willock in Persia, and presented by him to the museum of the East India Company, is engraved. (Pl. XV. fig. 1.) Not only is the costume totally different, but the Greek characters are of a later and ruder period. With regard to the second Vonones, he reigned only a few months; and to him, therefore, conquests in India cannot be attributed.

The legends on the reverse of the coins of Vonones differ from the Greek. The epithets are 'great king,' and 'just'—dhamika; there is no equivalent for 'king of kings;' whilst the Greek has not 'Dikæus.' The name appears also as Palahara or Balahara. Professor Lassen suggests[1] the possibility that the latter may be intended for Volagases, the son and successor of the second Vonones, who reigned from A. D. 50 to A. D. 91, and whose name appears on the Parthian coins, ΒΟΛΑΓΑΣΟΥ. Balahasa, if the correcter reading, and, admitting that the initial P represents a B, differs only in substituting *h* for *g*; the coin thus expressing the names of both father and son. The name Balahasa, however, can be conjectured only on the hemidrachm, where the characters are rudely stamped, and more probably represent some other word. On all the square copper coins it is distinctly Balahara or Balahata, and therefore departs a little wider from Vologases. Mr. Prinsep, preferring the latter reading, conjectures the possibility that the coin was struck by some Indian dependant or tributary of the first Vonones.[2] The style of the coin renders it, however, almost impossible that it should have been the work of a period so late as the second half of the first century; and the authority of the Parthian king of Persia, Vonones, over any part of India is very problematical: at the same time the identity of name may be received in evidence of community of origin; and the Vonones of the coin may have been a Parthian adventurer who became possessed for a short time of a shred of the dissevered kingdom of Bactria.

COINS OF VONONES.

SILVER.

1. Hemidrachm. King on horseback, to the right, with lance in rest.

[1] Zur Geschichte, p. 63.

[2] J. As. Soc. B. July, 1838, p. 649.

ΒΑΣΙΛΕΩΣ ΒΑΣΙΛΕΩΝ ΜΕΓΑΛΟΥ ΟΝΩΝΟΥ. R. Jupiter, with sceptre and thunderbolt. Inscription imperfect, but name apparently 𐨤𐨯𐨱𐨪𐨯 Pasaharasa (?). Mon. 143. Pl. VIII. fig. 8.

From the collection of General Ventura. Described by Prinsep, J. As. Soc. B. June, 1835, Pl. XXI. fig. 5; also J. des Sav. March, 1836, Pl. II. fig. 10.

COPPER.

2. Square; middle size. Hercules standing, to the front; the club in his left hand, his right raised to his head. ΒΑΣΙΛΕΩΣ ΒΑΣΙΛΕΩΝ ΜΕΓΑΛΟΥ ΟΝΩΝΟΥ. R. Minerva, to the left; her shield on her left arm; her spear behind her; her right hand extended. 𐨨𐨱𐨪𐨗𐨯 𐨢𐨨𐨁𐨐𐨯 𐨤𐨫𐨱𐨪𐨯 Maharajasa Dhamikasa Palaharasa. Pl. VIII. fig. 9.

First described by Masson, J. As. Soc. B. April, 1834; but several other specimens have been received with his last collection. A similar coin was procured by Dr. Honigberger, J. des Sav. Oct. 1835; and one by General Ventura, J. As. Soc. B. June, 1835, Pl. XXI. fig. 10. M. R. Rochette also describes a coin which he considers to belong to Vonones; J. des Sav. March, 1836, p. 140, note; but which is a coin of Azes.

UNDOPHERRES.

Although the Vonones of the coins last described appears to stand in an isolated position, yet apparently he is not the only prince of Parthian origin of whose existence in connexion with India we have numismatic evidence. We have indeed historical evidence, as above alluded to,[1] of the presence of Parthian princes on the lower course of the Indus; and to some of these a portion of the coins now to be noticed may possibly belong: others may have held rule towards the Punjab, over some one of the five different and apparently independent cities of the Yu-chi; for there does not appear to be any wide difference between the two races. The Parthians were also Scythians. One of these princes may be the person

[1] Page 213.

whose name appears in barbarous Greek letters as Undopherres or Undophares, whose coins, although not very numerous, are found in the topes, and were therefore, as well as by their style, of a date not long if at all anterior to the æra of Christianity.

The head of the king and the Greek legend on these coins are evidences of a late and barbaric origin. The character of the head, with a long peaked beard, is peculiar, and is more akin to the Arsacidan coins than to any yet met with in Bactria or Kabul. The winged Victory on the reverse, although a common emblem on these coins, is also exhibited in a not dissimilar attitude on the later Arsacidan medals. No exact counterparts of them, however, have been described amongst the coins of the Parthian kings, and they are connected by the legend and by the style of the work, as well as by their being commonly found together in the topes, with the barbarous Su-Hermæus coins, showing it probable that they were current about the same time and in much the same tracts. On the other hand, they are allied by the name of the king, especially as it is read in the Arianian letters by Mr. Prinsep, with the following prince, whose coin has less of a Parthian than an Indo-Scythic character.

COINS OF UNDOPHERRES.

COPPER.

1. Round; middle size. Head of king, bearded, with crown and fillet, to the right. ΥΝΔΩΦΕΓΓοΥ ΥΑCΙΛΕΩΣ ΣΩΤΗΓΟC. R. Winged Victory, with palm-branch, wreath, and fillet, to the right. Inscription blundered, but the first word is 𐨨𐨱𐨪𐨗𐨯 Maharajasa. Pl. V. figs. 12, 13, 14.

2. Round; small. Head of king, to the right. - - ΕΛΓΥΩΩΛ - (*sic*). R. Winged Victory, with wreath and fillet, to the left. Inscription imperfect. Mon. 92. Pl. V. fig. 15.

The larger of these coins are found mixed with those of the ruder Hermæus type in some number, but in very inferior proportion: they are mostly much corroded, and indistinct; they are always of rude fabric; and no monograms are decypherable upon them. The smaller one is unique. In the head it agrees with the coins of Hermæus, and may belong to him, although identified with those of Undopherres by the Victory of the reverse. It is not easy to determine the arrangement or value of the Indian characters on these coins, as they are in some respects unusual, and always imperfect. The title Maharajasa may be made out on some. Mr. Prinsep thinks the reading should be 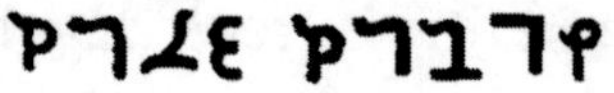 Farahatasa Nandatasa; J. As. Soc. B. April, 1834, June, 1835, and July, 1838; J. Asiatique, Feb. 1836; J. des Sav. April, 1836.

3. Head of king, to the left. - ЄωN MЄΓAC - - . R. Winged Victory, to the right. 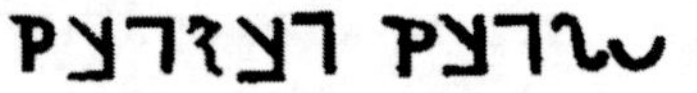 Maharajasa Rajadhirajasa.

This coin is described and delineated in the Phil. Trans. vol. L. Part I. p. 175, by Dr. Swinton, and is repeated by Dr. Grotefend in his work on the coins of the Bactrian kings. The Victory agrees with that on the coins of Undopherres, but the head has more the character of a Sassanian prince.

GONDOPHARES.

The presence of the king on horseback allies this coin with those of Azilises and Azes rather than with those of the prince last noticed; but the similarity of name indicates national connexion. In many instances, indeed, the name is the same, variously read Undopharou or Undapherrou; and it is not impossible that the coins may belong to the preceding prince. The Greek characters are, however, very barbarous, and their accurate representation of the name may be doubted; and it may also be observed, that the title differs, ‘great king of kings’ being substituted for ‘the king, the preserver.’ In the most distinct and best executed specimens the name is clearly Gondophares. The coins are distinguished from those of Azes and every other prince by the use of a peculiar monogram, No. 144^b. It is invariably in the same position, or in front of the horse; and in one instance is enlarged, so as to occupy the whole field of the reverse.[1] It is considered by Mr. Prinsep[2] to be a combination of the *b*, *m*, and *n* of the old Sanscrit alphabet; but the presence of a Nagari letter is inconsistent with that of Arianian letters, also commonly represented on the coins.

[1] Supplemental Plate, fig. 16.

[2] J. As. Soc. B. July, 1838, p. 653.

The name on the reverse, in Arianian characters, is not always decypherable; but where it is distinct, it is apparently Pharahatasa; offering some analogy to the name on the reverse of the coins of Vonones, and to that read by Mr. Prinsep on some of the coins of Undopherres. It seems not impossible that we have in this name the Phra-ates or Phrahates of the Greeks, an appellation given to four of the Arsacidan kings; but it does not appear very likely that either of those princes should be intended. The last of them, who was the fifteenth of the Arsacidan dynasty, discomfited in the early part of his reign the Roman legions under Mark Antony. Subsequently he was expelled from his throne for his cruelty; but he took refuge amongst the Scythians, and was replaced by them in his dominions. These were probably his neighbours the Scythians of Ariana, and his authority in that province would be incompatible with theirs. He enjoyed a long reign, being killed by his son Phrahatakes in A. D. 4; but he does not seem to have been engaged in any schemes of conquest towards the East, having constant occasions of dispute with the Romans on his western frontier. His son held the sovereignty but a few months, and to him therefore the coins cannot be referred. All that can be deduced from the appellation, therefore, is the possibility that the Gondophares or Pharahates of the coins may have been of Parthian descent, and a petty prince or satrap on the borders of India towards the close of the Arsacidan dynasty, or even later. Upon the coin in which the monogram is so conspicuous, the device on the obverse, the presentation of the wreath or fillet of royalty to the mounted figure, may possibly have some relation to the subject of that piece of sculpture at Nakshi Rustam[1] which represents two persons on horseback holding a similar circlet between them, in which case the coin will belong to an early period of the Sassanian dynasty of Persian kings.

In confirmation of a connexion between this dynasty and the first Sassanian king, it may be observed that the monogram, which may be regarded as one of the characteristic marks, is found upon a fire-altar on one of the Sassanian copper coins. See Pl. XVII. fig. 19.

[1] Porter's Travels in Persia, vol. i. p. 548, Pl. 23.

COINS OF UNDOPHARES OR GONDOPHARES.

PLATED.

1. Drachm. King on horseback, to the right; his right hand extended, holding a whip. ΟΑCΙΛΕΩΝ ΟΑCΙΛΕΩΝ (*sic*) ΓΟΝΔΟΦΑΓΟΥ. Mon. double, 144. R. Standing figure, to the front, with fillet and pallium; the right hand extended, the left leaning on a trident. - - [Kharoshthi] Maharajasa-jarasa (?) Mah - - - - - Pharahatasa. Mon. double, 145. Pl. V. fig. 16.

There are two of these in the Masson collection; on one of which, that which is engraved, the Greek legend and part of the Indian are very distinct. A similar copper coin, belonging to General Ventura, has been delineated by Mr. Prinsep, J. As. Soc. B. July, 1838, Pl. XXVIII. fig. 15.

COPPER.

2. Round; middle size. King on horseback, to the right, as before. ΒΑCΙΛΕΥΟ - - - - ΥΗΔΟ - - (*sic*). Mon. 144[b]. R. Female figure, Minerva (?), to the right; her spear and shield in her left hand; her right holding an indistinct object, a Victory (?). Inscription rude and doubtful, except the name, [Kharoshthi] Pharahatasa. Mon. double, 146. Pl. V. fig. 17.

Undescribed coin in the Masson collection. A plated coin of Azes, with a similar device on either face, occurs, but distinguished from this by the legends and monograms. A duplicate of this coin, belonging to General Ventura, is described by Prinsep, J. As. Soc. B. July, 1838, Pl. XXVIII. fig. 14.

3. Round; middle size. King on horseback, to the right. VΑCΙΛΕΩΙΙ ΙΛΕΩΝ ΜΕΓΑΛ - ΥΝΔΟΦΟΟΙΥ (*sic*). Mon. 144[b]. R. Male figure, to the right, in the Indian dhoti; the right hand extended, the left carries a sceptre. Inscription imperfect. Mon. double, 146[b] and 147. Pl. V. fig. 18.

Undescribed coin from the Masson collection.

4. Round; middle size. King on horseback, to the left; flying Victory placing a wreath and fillet on his head. ΟΑCΙΛΕΩC ΟΑCΙΛΕΩV ΜΕ-ΓΑΛΟΥ VΝΔΕΦΕΓΓΟΥ. Mon. 144[b]. R. Male figure in a dhoti, to the front; the right hand is raised to the head, the left holds a palm-branch (?).

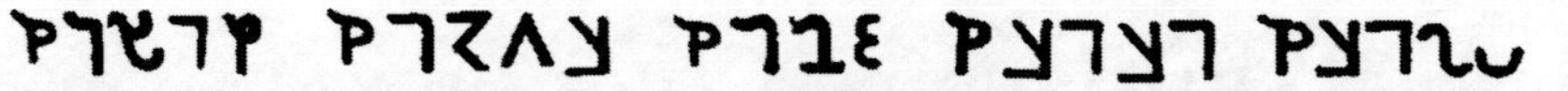 Maharajasa Rajarajasa Tadarasa Jayadharasa Pharahatasa. Mon. double, 148.

Described and delineated by Mr. Prinsep, from two coins; one in the collection of General Allard, the other in that of M. Court; J. As. Soc. B. July, 1838, p. 653, Pl. XXVIII. fig. 13.

5. Round; small. King on horseback, to the right. Inscription effaced. Mon. 149. R. Rudely executed female figure, to thé front, with fillets. No legend. Mon. various, 150. Pl. V. fig. 19.

6. Round; small. King on horseback, as before. ΟΛΙΛΙΙ Ι (*sic*). Mon. 144^b. R. Male figure, to the right; the right arm raised, the left holding a staff. Imperfect inscription. Mon. various, 151. Pl. V. fig. 20.

7. Square; middle size. Figure on horseback, to the left, and in front apparently a figure offering a wreath. R. A symbol or monogram, 144^b.  Maharaja-rajasa (?) Miramatasa. Mon. 152. Pl. VI. fig. 2.

Copied from a coin in the possession of Dr. Swiney. There are two in the Masson collection, but less distinct even than this.

8. Square; middle size. Figure on horseback, as before. ΜΕΓΑΛΟΥ ΓΟΝΔΑΦΑΓΟV. R. Symbol, or Mon. 144^b, magnified as in the preceding.  Maha - - - Dhamikasa Apatihatasa Jayadharasa Pharahatasa. Mon. double, 153. Supplemental Plate, fig. 16.

This specimen, which is amongst Mr. Masson's last collection, although it leaves something to be desired, is much more perfect than any preceding, and the inscription on both faces, as far as perfect, very distinct; the characters of the Arianian legend are rude, but no doubt can be entertained of their purport.

The attitude of the two figures suggests some resemblance to the sculpture on the rocks of Nakshi Rustam, where two mounted warriors jointly hold a ring or wreath, supposed by M. De Sacy to signify the victory of Ardeshir over the last Arsacidan king, but by Mr. Money, the association of the first two Sassanian princes, Ardeshir with his son Sapor.[1]

[1] Trans. R. As. Soc. vol. iii. p. 509.

ABAGASUS.

The general style of this coin, and the presence of the same monogram, allies the prince whose name it bears with the preceding, but no other conclusion can be hazarded respecting it. The Greek legend is mutilated and corrupt, and the Arianian letters are also apparently barbarized. The title Maharaja is legible, but the name seems to be Akajakubhasa. In the duplicate specimen of this coin it is something different.

COIN OF ABAGASUS.

COPPER.

Round; middle size. Figure, apparently female, with fillet, on horseback, to the left. Corrupt Greek legend. Mon. 144^{b}, and the Arianian letter [illegible]. R. Male figure, to the right, with fillet; the lower part of his body clothed; the right hand raised, the left holding a staff. [illegible] [illegible] Maharajasa Akajakubhasa. Mon. various, 154. Pl. VI. fig. 1.

From a coin in the possession of Dr. Swiney. The monogram on the obverse allies it to the coins of Undopherres; but a coin, from the collection of General Allard, similar to this in all respects except in the preservation of the lower part of the legend, has been lately described and delineated by Mr. Prinsep, in which the name ΑΒΑΓΑΣΟΥ, Abagasus or Abagases, distinctly appears. The Prakrit inscription is [illegible] - - - [illegible], which Prinsep thinks intended for [illegible] Abhakhafasasa; J. As. Soc. B. July, 1838, Pl. XXVIII. fig. 16.

KODES OR HYRKODES.

The chief inducement to the comprehension of this prince amongst the Indo-Parthians is the analogy which the portrait generally offers to those on the Arsacidan coins. It is very possible, however, that he is misplaced, and that he may belong to the Indo-Scythian family.

The name, whether Kodes or Hyrkodes, or Kodou or Hyrkodou,[1] is a suf-

[1] Die Munzen der Könige von Baktrien, p. 78.

ficient indication of a barbaric origin, although the characters on the coin are solely Greek: they are of a later and degenerate period. The coins are not very rare, though not numerous, and are procured at Kabul or still further north, and some have found their way to Europe through Russia. M. R. Rochette suggests, but merely as a conjecture, that they may have been struck by some of the barbarous tribes upon the borders of the Caspian, from whence they seem to have been brought.[1]

The devices on the reverse are a standing figure, with a halo round his head, or the head of a horse. Either device will ally the coins with those of the Indo-Scythians. On the reverse also occurs the legend - - **PΔHΘPº MAKAP** - -; in the former of which occurs an analogy to the terms Athro and Ardokro on the coins of Kanerkes. From these circumstances, and the locality in which the coins are found, Professor Lassen suggests that Kodes[2] may have been the founder of the Indo-Scythian dynasty of Kanerkes, and the first of the race who passed to the southward of the mountains. The data furnished by the coins themselves are insufficient to determine their origin.

COINS OF KODES OR HYRKODES.

SILVER.

1. Obolus. Head of king, bearded, to the right. **KωΔ.** R. Standing figure, to the front, in tunic; holding part of his robe in his left hand, a spear in his right. **OVA.** Pl. IX. fig. 1.

2. Hemidrachm. Head, as before. **KωΔ.** R. Warrior with spear. **PAHΘPºY MAK.** Pl. IX. fig. 2.

3. Hemidrachm. Head, as before. **KωΔºY.** R. Figure, as before. **PAHΘPºY MAKAP.** Pl. IX. fig. 3.

4. Hemidrachm. Head, as before, with fillet distinct. **KωΔ.** R. Standing figure. - - **HVI** - - **VKVº.** Pl. IX. fig. 5.

5. Hemidrachm. Head of king. R. Head of horse, to the right. Pl. IX. fig. 6.

6. Obolus. Head of king. **KωΔ.** R. Head of horse. **YHC.** Pl. IX. fig. 4.

[1] J. des Sav. July, 1834, p. 389.

[2] Zur Geschichte der Könige, pp. 104, 186.

7. Obolus. Head of king. R. Rude figure; intended, perhaps, for a horse's head. Pl. IX. fig. 7.

These coins are identifiable with Bactrian coins only by the situation in which they are found. They agree in the expression of the head better with the coins of Surashtra, to be hereafter noticed. The drawings are all taken from the J. As. Soc. B. vol. iv. Pl. XXV. figs. 11, 12, 13, and vol. v. Pl. XLVI., except the first, which is from a coin in the cabinet of Dr. Swiney. Similar coins, two with the standing figure on the reverse, and one with a horse's head, are described by the Baron de Chaudoir, in the Supplement to Sestini's account of his collection. On the obverse he reads the name ΥΡΚΩΔΟΥ; and on the reverse of the former, ΜΑΚΑΡΟ - - ΟΡΔΗΟΡΟΥ.

MISCELLANEOUS ARSACIDAN KINGS.

There can be no question of the origin of the coins noticed below; as although the head differs in some respects from the usual Arsacidan style, the seated figure on the reverse, with the bow in his hand, is a well-known device of the Arsacidan money. They offer one instance of identification, which is of some interest, as the coin with the two flying Victories presents a type which also occurs on a coin attributed to Phrahates IV., and which is dated in the year of the Seleucidan æra 311, or B. C. 2; Visconti, Iconographie Grecque, tom. iii. p. 93, Pl. XLIX. fig. 26. The others may be of about the same period, although probably they are the coins of different princes. The commercial and political intercourse which prevailed between Persia and Kabul may account for their presence in the latter country, without proving its subjection to the former under any of the Arsacidan princes.

MISCELLANEOUS ARSACIDAN COINS.

COPPER.

1. Small; thick. Head of king with crown, to the left. On either side of the head are two figures, which, though indistinct, may be intended for two Victories placing a wreath on the king's head. R. Seated figure with

bow extended, to the right; traces of characters possibly intended for Greek. Pl. XV. fig. 6.

2. Head of king, to the left, with bushy wig and fillet. R. Sitting figure; rude letters, apparently Arianian. Pl. XV. fig. 7.

Figures 8-11 of the same Plate represent diversities of this same coin. Nos. 9 and 10 have apparently a monogram resembling that on the coin of Gondophares, Pl. V. fig. 16.

These are from a considerable number of similar coins found by Mr. Masson at Beghram.

SECTION IV.—INDO-SCYTHIAN PRINCES OF KABUL.

KADPHISES.

We now come to a long and important series of coins, the issue of princes of well-defined names and of unquestioned Scythian descent; the duration of whose government must have comprised a considerable interval, and whose power, seated chiefly about Kabul and Jelalabad, must have occasionally spread along the Indus, and extended eastwards into the Punjab. That of these, Kadphises is the earliest, is evident from the style of his coins and the purport of the legends which they bear.

A very remarkable contrast to all that has preceded presents itself on the first consideration of the subject. Hitherto, with but two exceptions, in the unique gold coins of Diodotus and Euthydemus, the coins that have come under our observation have consisted of silver, of billion, or of copper. The coins of the Indo-Scythic princes are exclusively of copper and of gold. The solitary instance of a genuine silver coin of Kadphises confirms rather than invalidates the fact that gold and copper are the metals to which the discoveries in this branch of numismatic research have been hitherto confined. The gold coins are found in considerable number and variety; and the circumstance may be thought to indicate a material change in the political state of the country, the re-establishment of a season of tranquillity, and an advance in national wealth.

According to Arrian, the Indians with whom Alexander was engaged were without gold;[1] but, as Dr. Vincent remarks,[2] this cannot be reconciled with the ancient fable of the gold-making ants, and with the payment to Darius of the Indian tribute in gold, as affirmed by Herodotus. Arrian may perhaps have intended to say that they had no gold coins; but the material must have existed, as to some extent it still exists, in the upper course of the rivers that fall into the Indus. The quantity may, however, have been much less than that subsequently introduced into the country by extended foreign commerce, and the Greek princes, although they did coin gold, fabricated it in Bactria in a very inferior ratio to silver.

From the period of the reign of Kadphises the coinage of gold became evidently frequent, and continued to be so as late as the æra of the Mohammedan invasion; for, besides the gold coins of Kadphises, Kanerkes, and Ooerki, the coins of the Gupta kings are exclusively of gold, and the same metal prevails in the coins of the later Rajas of Kanoj. The total absence or great rarity of silver coins in all the series, and that of copper coins under the Hindu princes, is quite as remarkable as that of the limited gold currency of their predecessors. It can only be explained by the supposition, that during the whole of this term the currency of coins in the inferior metals was supplied from other sources. Under the Indo-Scythic kings the silver coinage was probably furnished by the abundant issues of the Greek princes. We know that at the end of the first century the drachms of Menander and Apollodotus were current at Baroach, and they must, therefore, have been equally current in the districts nearer to the original seats of the Greek Bactrian monarchy. Upon the decline of the Indo-Scythic dynasty the silver coinage of Kabul and Western India appears to have been derived from the money of the Sassanian kings, and to them succeeded, in the west of India at least, a native Hindu race, whose coins were chiefly of silver; and, as they are found in great quantities, they probably were sufficient for the wants of the circulation down to the twelfth century.

[1] Ἀχρύσους τε εἶναι Ἰνδοὺς ἐξήλεγξαν, ὅσους τε δὴ Ἀλέξανδρος ξὺν τῇ στρατιᾷ ἐπῆλθε: Book v. 4.

[2] Voyage of Nearchus, p. 82.

Again, it is clear that there must have been issued in the period of the Indo-Scythians an immense copper coinage, which continued to obviate the necessity of any other coinage of the same metal until the date of the Mohammedan invasion, when the small pyce, or copper coins of the Rajput princes, and next of the Patan kings of Delhi, became equally abundant. Of the place filled in the copper circulation of India by the Indo-Scythic coinage, no greater proof can be afforded than that of its being scarcely yet extinct. The copper coins of Kadphises and Kanerkes are found in considerable quantities in the hands of the money-changers of most of the large towns of Hindustan, and not unfrequently surpass, both in value and fabrication, the miserable copper currency of the actual rulers of the country.

The gold coins of Kadphises bear upon their obverse faces either a full-length portrait of the king sitting on a throne, or his bust in profile. In either case his costume is precisely that which prevails to the north of the Hindu Kush to the present day, and to a great extent also amongst the Afghans. He wears a conical cap turned up at the sides, a tunic close to the body, over which is a sort of straight coat: boots are invariably worn. The features are not those of the Mongol but of the Turk tribe. The name and title are clearly written in old Greek letters ΚΑΔΦΙCΗC ΒΑCΙΛΕΥC, 'Kadphises the king.' There are, however, some additional letters, as ΟΟΗΜΟ or ΟΟΚΜΟ, the purport of which is doubtful.

M. R. Rochette, and after him MM. Jacquet and Mionnet, considering the two last of the additional letters to be part of the name of the king, read it accordingly Mokadphises. As, however, Kadphises occurs without such a prefix on the barbarous coins described above, and as the doubtful word is not unfrequently written ΟΟΗΜ or ΟΟΚΜ without the final, Mr. Prinsep, Professor Lassen, Professor Müller, and Dr. Grotefend continue to omit the initial syllable, and consider ΟΟΗΜΟ as a distinct term, a title of the king, and to be read, as proposed by Müller,[1] Ovohemo or Ohovemo: the meaning of which title is, however, left undefined.

Upon the copper coins the titles of the king are extended to ΒΑCΙΛΕΥC

[1] Zur Geschichte der Könige, p. 78.

ΒΑϹΙΛΕѠΝ ϹѠΤΗΡ ΜΕΓΑϹ, but in both descriptions of coins the legend on the reverse is the same, and is evidently the equivalent of the longer series, with even additional titles. As already remarked, it includes letters which cannot be satisfactorily decyphered; and it presents unusual modifications of the characters previously known, showing that the alphabet had undergone alteration in the interval between Eukratides and Kadphises.

The obverses of the silver coin and of the copper coins offer the portraiture of the king at full length, in the same costume as those of the gold; the attitude and accompaniments are, however, remarkable. He appears to be offering incense upon a low altar, something of the form observable upon the copper coins of the early Arsacidan princes, without the supporters. (See Plate XVII. figs. 12, 13.) Behind the figure is a short club, and in front a trident, with an axe below the prongs on one side of the staff; a weapon of which an exact representation occurs in the monuments of Nepal.

Although the introduction of the fire-altar on the obverse intimates the recognition of the worship of fire, yet the presence of the trisula or trident is an indication of the concurrent adoption of the worship of Siva: and the trident, it may be remarked, is combined with an axe on one side of the staff, like the tridents at Barahat and Gopeswara, the latter of which is erected, according to the inscription it bears, at a tírtha, 'a holy spot,' sacred to Mahadeva or Siva.[1] These evidences of Saiva worship are corroborated by the types on the reverses. The most frequent, and that which is invariably presented by the copper coins, whilst it occurs also upon the silver coin and upon the large gold coins, is a figure of Siva, sometimes apparently naked, but at other times dressed in a short loose robe, such as is commonly worn by Hindus; being nothing more than a long piece of cloth thrown in variously disposed folds around the body, sometimes only over the lower part, but commonly covering the upper part also; sometimes covering the shoulders, sometimes leaving them bare; sometimes also it is carried over the back part of the head. The different modes of wearing it are represented on the coins, and are all decidedly Indian. The figure in many instances

[1] J. As. Soc. B. Aug. 1836, p. 485, Pl. XXX.

appears by the breasts and protuberant hips to be female; but it is not invariably so, and is sometimes, what it probably always should be, of an androgynous outline, the figure being that of Siva and his spouse in their composite character of Arrdha nárís'wara, Siva half-feminine. This is by no means an unusual form of the divinity, and is the type here represented. That this appropriation is correct, is confirmed by the chaplet which hangs over the left shoulder of the figure, and which has every appearance of being the Munda-málá, or necklace of skulls, worn both by Siva and by his bride in her terrific form. The trisula or trident, Siva's especial weapon, and the bull, Siva's particular váhana or vehicle (Nandi), are further confirmations of the Indian and Saivite character of the personage represented. The rays springing from his head are something unusual. The absence of sectarial marks from the forehead may only prove a date anterior to the use of such distinctions. The housings of the bull are such as may still be seen upon the Indian bull that is led about by mendicant Jangamas. Upon the reverse of the smaller gold coins the prevailing device is that of a man standing; he holds the trisula in his right hand, and in his left an object of doubtful specification, but it may be the short Indian club which in battle was hurled at an adversary. In one instance the figure is partly clad in a skin, the tail part of which appears to constitute a kind of cap. Figures of Siva are occasionally dressed with either the skin of an elephant or a tiger, and it may possibly be intended to represent the latter in this coin. Although, therefore, less decidedly characteristic of the Saiva faith, yet it does not militate against the conclusion irresistibly enforced by the common emblems on the other coins, that the Indo-Scythic princes either religiously adopted or politically encouraged the Hindu worship of Siva.

Equally characteristic of the coins of Kadphises, although not authorizing any deduction of their purport, are their monograms. They are two; one is analogous to that on the coins of the 'nameless king,' being a cross-bar, with prongs. There are four points, however, instead of three, and the handle is differently shaped. This is almost invariably on the obverse. The monogram on the reverse is also a species of trident, but it is of a different form from that on the obverse. In the case of the standing figure without the bull, both the monograms appear on the reverse. The meaning of these types cannot be satisfactorily conjectured, but they are of importance, as connecting the coins of Kadphises with those of the prince without a name, who we have suggested was probably Indian, and with those of succeeding dynasties down to a modern period in the history of the Hindus.

Besides the coins to which the preceding remarks more particularly apply, there are others of similar design, but of very inferior execution. The figure on the obverse is also in a somewhat different costume, the coat appearing as if quilted, or sometimes like mail. The left hand also supports a trident or spear. The figure on the reverse is in general more decidedly male; the dress, though a little varied, is still Indian; the head of the bull is always to the left, whilst, on the more perfect coins, it is as invariably to the right. Whether these differences denote a different period or a provincial origin it is hazardous to conjecture.

The other classes of copper coins which bear the name of Kadphises have been already the subject of remark. The name unequivocally attests their connexion with those now under consideration, but in what manner it is difficult to say. It seems possible that some of them, at least those which bear the portrait of Su-Hermæus, are of the earliest period, following closely upon the reign of Su-Hermæus, and imitated from his currency, and indicate a period of anarchy in which a prince of the name of Kadaphes or Kadphises was engaged in establishing a consolidated kingdom out of the conflicting elements of Greek, Scythic, and Indian rivalry. It is not unlikely that he was, as Grotefend conjectures, a different prince from the Kadphises of the coins now described, and that we might consider this prince as properly Kadphises II., who succeeded to the government after the transition period had passed, and a settled administration had been formed. There was then leisure and wealth for a reform of the currency, and gold and copper coins were fabricated, which, although of barbarous execution as compared with the best specimens of Grecian art, are not without considerable merit both in design and execution, and are infinitely superior to many of the coins which bear Grecian or Hellenised names.[1]

[1] The last dispatch from Mr. Masson has included a couple of small coins of base silver, on one of which something like the final syllables of Kadphises may be read. The bust, however, is like that of Eukratides, whilst upon the reverse appears an animal like those sculp-

The date of Kadphises, as inferrible from the relation of his coins to those of Su-Hermæus, and to those of the king known only by his title of Soter Megas, to both of which they are no doubt subsequent, cannot well be earlier than the commencement of the Christian æra: how much later it may have been it is difficult to conjecture; but as the coins of Kanerkes must be of a subsequent period, and as even they are found very commonly in the oldest topes along with the coins of Kadphises, it is certain that these latter must precede the third or fourth century, and it seems not unlikely that they were issued even earlier. Professor Lassen proposes the end of the first century as the term of the kingdom of Kadphises and the beginning of the Kanerkes period; and this appears not unlikely. That Kadphises reigned long and prosperously may be inferred from the material, the style, and the abundance of his coins.

The coins of Kadphises, with the device of the bull on the reverse, whether of the superior or inferior description, are exceedingly numerous. Many have been found in the topes, but vast quantities of them have been procured in the Punjab and along the Kabul river. Many were comprised in the collection of Colonel Tod, which was made chiefly at Mathura; and before his time a great number were collected at Allahabad, and presented to the Company by Mr. Tytler, a medical gentleman in their service. All these specimens, however, were much worn, and the inscriptions were so wholly obliterated that they offered no materials even for conjecture; and it was not until better specimens were found in the topes and the neighbourhood, that the name of the king was distinctly read.

COINS OF KADPHISES.

GOLD.

1. Large. Figure of king to the front, head turned to the left; dressed in a Tartar cap, with fillet, coat, tunic, and boots; sitting on a low bench, with pillow, and his feet supported by a footstool: he holds a flower in his

tured at Persepolis, and on either side of it is the word 'Nanaia.' If belonging to Kadphises, it would seem to intimate his having occupied, perhaps but for a time, a part of Persia. Supplemental Plate, fig. 18.

right hand; underneath is a club. **BACIΛEYC OOHMO KAΔΦICHC.** Mon. on the right, 155. R. Standing figure, front view, face to the left, with the hair combed to a point: the right hand, raised, rests on a trident; the left, bent, leans on the shoulder of an Indian bull, to the right, partly dressed with housings. [illegible]. Mon. on the right, 156. Pl. X. fig. 5.

This figure is copied from an engraving in the J. des Sav. July, 1834, Pl. fig. 7, taken from an impression of a coin in the possession of M. Dutrochet, brother-in-law of General Peyron, by whom it was brought from Delhi. It is described by M. R. Rochette, who read the name at first Mokaupsices, but subsequently Mokadphises.

2. Large. A coin precisely similar in all respects. Supplemental Plate, fig. 17.

This has been recently sent home by Mr. Masson. It seems doubtful if the figure be not clad in a thin robe. The Arianian inscription, as above inserted, is compiled from both these coins. (See p. 258.)

3. Middle size. Head of king, to the right, with Tartar cap and coat: the cap is surmounted by an ornament; the lower part of the bust has the appearance of characters, but they are probably only parts of the dress; the right hand holds a short club leaning on the shoulder. **BACIΛЄYC OOHMO KAΔΦICHC.** Mon. behind the head. R. Naked figure, to the front; the head in some instances wearing a cap, in others surmounted by a tapering flame: the right hand rests on a trident, half-way down which is apparently an axe; the left holds what seems to be a short club, and drapery or fillets hang from the fore-arm. Inscription incomplete, but same as above. Mon. double, 155, 156. Pl. X. figs. 7, 13.

Two coins out of four procured by Mr. Masson from the Tope of Guldára. A similar coin is figured, J. As. Soc. B. Nov. 1835, Pl. XXXVIII. fig. 3, procured by Colonel Smith at Benares; but the figure on the reverse wears what seems to be the dhoti or waist-cloth, and has a crescent on the top of the head.

4. Middle size. Head like the last, but turned to the left; the right hand projects, and holds the club upright. R. As before. Pl. X. figs. 8, 10, 11.

From three out of four coins obtained by Mr. Masson from Tope Guldára. A similar coin, found by Dr. Honigberger, is described by Masson,

J. As. Soc. B. April, 1834, Pl. XIII. fig. 24; also by M. R. Rochette, J. des Sav. Oct. 1835, Pl. II. fig. 22; and Mionnet, Supplement, viii. p. 496. The latter mistakes the cap, the front of which projects from the sides of it being turned up or cocked, as it is still worn in Tartary, for " le front ceint d'un diadème armé d'une corne sur le devant." He observes also, that the king " tient de la main gauche l'Ankouça," or Indian elephant-goad; but this does not appear upon Masson's coins. The reverse is the same on all.

5. Middle size. Figure of king, to the right, carried in a car drawn by two horses driven by a diminutive charioteer; cap and club, as before. **ΒΑCΙΛΕΥC ΟΟΗΜΟ ΚΑΔΦΙCΗC.** R. Standing figure, as before, but with cap well defined. Inscription, and double monogram, as before. Pl. X. fig. 9.

This coin, which is unique, was procured by Colonel Smith at Benares. It is copied from the J. As. Soc. B. Nov. 1835, Pl. XXXVIII. fig. 1.

6. Middle size. Bust of king, to the right, as before. **ΒΑCΙΛΕΥC ΟΟ - - - .** Mon. R. Figure of Siva, as in No. 1, but dressed, leaning on his bull, and holding his trident. Inscription imperfect. Mon. single.

This coin was likewise procured by Colonel Smith at Benares; J. As. Soc. B. Nov. 1835, Pl. XXXVIII. fig. 2. A duplicate was sent to Mr. Prinsep, from Afghanistan, by Karamat Ali; ibid. p. 631.

7. Small. Head of king, to the right, in a frame. **ΒΑCΙΛΕ - - Κ - - ΦΙCΗC** (?) R. Trident with axe, as on the large copper coins. 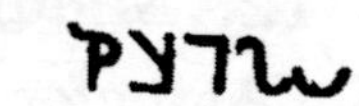  Maharajasa (Ra)jadhi(rajasa) Ma - ka - - - - sasa (?). Mon. double. Supplemental Plate, fig. 19.

Masson collection.

SILVER.

8. Small. Standing figure, to the left, with Arsacidan helmet and fillets; with tunic, coat, and trowsers; altar and trident in front, club behind; the right hand is in the usual position, the left holds a vessel (?). **ΒΑCΙΛΕVC ΒΑCΙΛΕΩΝ ΜΕΓΑC ΟΟΗΜΟ ΚΑΔΦΙCΗC.** Mon. R. Standing figure, with dhoti, leaning on the Indian bull, standing to the right. 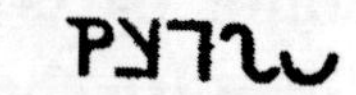 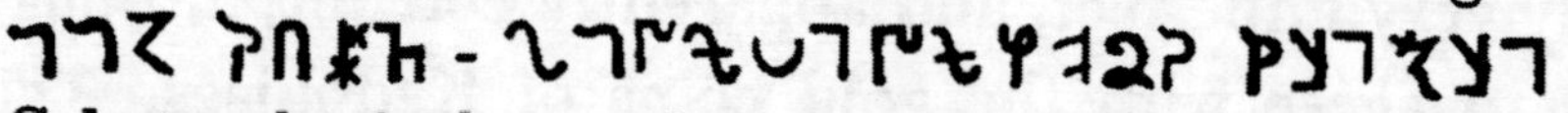 Maharajasa Rajadhirajasa Sabatraphatívahama ha varaha - Kapsisasa - dhanasa (?). Pl. XI. fig. 9. Procured by Mr. Masson, 1836. It has the singularity of being the only silver coin of the Indo-Scythian kings yet found. It is remarkably perfect.

COPPER.

9. Large. King standing, to the front; face, to the right, bearded, with conical cap and fillets; the right hand pointing downwards to an altar (?), the left resting on the hip; the figure dressed in coat, tunic, and boots; a trident to the left, a club to the right. **ΒΑϹΙΛЄΥϹ ΒΑΣΙΛЄѠΝ ϹѠΤΗΡ ΜЄΓΑϹ ΟΟΜΗΝ ΚΑΔΦΙϹΗϹ.** Mon. behind. R. Figure of Siva, to the front; head rayed, and surrounded by a sort of veil; body clothed in the usual Hindu dress, and a garland of flowers, or perhaps of skulls, hangs over the left shoulder; the right hand holds a trident, the left arm leans on the Indian bull behind, facing to the right. - - - - [illegible] [illegible] Maharajasa Rajadhirajasa - - - - ma - Kadphisasa dhanasa. Mon. Pl. X. figs. 15, 16, 17, 18, 20.

10. Small; Standing figure, &c., as before. R. Bull and figure. In some the latter appears to be a female. Pl. X. figs. 12, 14, 19, 21.

11. Middle size. Standing figure, with different costume from the preceding; left hand raised, and leaning on a spear. Inscription corrupt. R. Standing figure and bull, but the latter looking to the left. No inscription. Mon. double. Pl. XI. figs. 1, 2, 5, 6, 7, 8.

12. Middle size. Standing figure, as before, dressed in armour (?). R. As before, rude. Pl. XI. figs. 3, 4.

These coins are from a great number in the Masson collection, and have been found by him and the other labourers in the same field in many of the topes, as well as in the ground, or have been procured from the bazars. There are two chief descriptions of them; the coins which have the bull to the right, and those which have it to the left: the former are, in general, bold and handsome, whether large or small. The inscription is generally more or less worn, but the Greek legend is usually decypherable, at least in part. Some parts of the Indian inscription are also decypherable without much difficulty, but it is generally very imperfect, and apparently corrupt, although, upon the whole, appearing to agree with the gold coins of Kadphises. The term prefixed to the name in the Greek legend varies, appearing as **ΟΟΗ**, **ΟΟΗΚ**, **ΟΟΚΜ**, or **ΟΟΗΜΝ**; and the **Ο** preceding Kadphises in the gold coins very rarely occurs. One of the large coins was first delineated in the engraving to Colonel Tod's Memoir on the Greek, Parthian, and Hindu Medals; Trans. R. As. Soc. vol. i. Pl. XII. fig. 10. Several are described and engraved in the As. Res. vol. xvii. Pl. II. figs. 26-30, which are good examples of the state in which they are usually found. More perfect accounts and delineations are to be found; J. As. Soc. B. April, 1834, Pl. XII., XXVI., XXXIV.; J. Asiatique, Feb. 1836; Mionnet, Supplement, viii. &c.

13. Middle; thin. Head of king, to the right. ΚΟΓϹΟ ΚΟΖΟΥΛΟ ΚΑΔΦΙΖΟΥ. R. Standing Hercules. 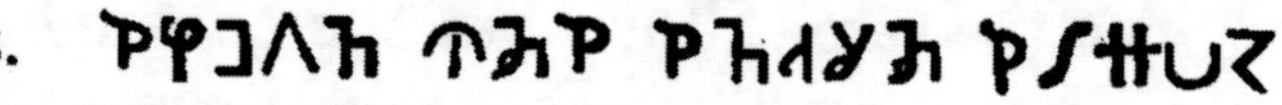 Maharajasa or (Dhamapidasa?) Kujulakasa Sakusa Kayadaphasa. Pl. XI. fig. 10.

14. Middle size. Head of king, to the right. ΟΣΟΝΗΛVΟ. R. Standing Hercules. Inscription as before. Pl. XI. fig. 12.

15. Middle size. Head of king. ΟΗVΟΧ ΦΗΟΜΟ. R. Standing Hercules. Inscription imperfect. Pl. XI. fig. 13.

These coins are found in considerable numbers in the topes and elsewhere, mixed with the coins of Su-Hermæus, as before observed, and agreeing with them in all respects except the Greek legend. On the reverse the Indian inscription is the same (see p. 309), as far as it can be decyphered upon either. These coins have been described and delineated by Prinsep, J. As. Soc. B. June, 1835, Pl. XXIV., and Sept. 1836, Pl. XXXV. They are also delineated by Masson, Jan. 1836, Pl. III.

16. Head of king, to the right. - ΑΟΟΥ ΚΟΖΟΛΑ ΚΑΔΑΦΕϹ - - - -. R. Figure seated, to the right; the right arm extended. Inscription indistinct, but apparently the same as in the last. Mon. 157. Pl. XI. fig. 14.

From a coin in the collection. Others, from coins found by different persons, are figured by Prinsep, J. As. Soc. B. June, 1835, Pl. XXIV. figs. 13, 14, 15; and Sept. 1836, Pl. XXXV. From these it appears that the entire Greek legend is ΖΑΘΟΥ ΚΟΖΟΛΥ ΚΑΔΑΦΕϹ ΚΟΓΑΝΟ.

KANERKI OR KANERKOU.

That this prince is later in the series than Kadphises is evident from various indications furnished by his coins. That the site of his power was the same is shown by the same evidence; as, whether it be in the topes, in the ground, or in the bazars, his coins are almost invariably mixed with those of his predecessors. In like manner also they consist of gold and copper, to which there is not even a solitary exception in silver.

The coins of Kanerki which approach most nearly to those of Kadphises are of copper. They bear upon the obverse a figure in the same attitude, and with the same altar; but the costume of the figure is something different. The coat is not open in front, but wraps the king round completely, and he has sometimes a cloak behind it. The head has either a kind of Phrygian cap or rays or horns rising from the hair. In some cases he has a bow behind his shoulders. The inscription is in Greek, of similar date as that of the coins of Kadphises, and, like that, also in the nominative case: **ΒΑϹΙΛΕΥϹ ΒΑϹΙΛΕΩΝ ΚΑΝΗΡΚΟΥ**. The copper coins with this form of the legend are comparatively rare; and the far larger proportion of the very numerous coins of this prince, of either metal, bear upon them, in Greek characters of a still more barbarous execution, the novel title of Rao Kanerki, **ΡΑΟ ΚΑΝΗΡΚΙ**; the name in which is probably a more exact representation of the denomination of the prince than Kanerkou. On the gold coins the legend is expanded to Rao-náná Rao Kanerki Koráno, **ΡΑΟ ΝΑΝΑ ΡΑΟ ΚΑΝΗΡΚΙ ΚΟΡΑΝΟ.** The title Rao, a vernacular corruption of Raja, is still borne by princes in Hindustan, and is, therefore, a genuine Indian word. The repetition of the term is probably the equivalent of 'king of kings,' and Náná must either be intended to import 'great,' or, which seems more likely, it should be thus divided, Raoná-ná-Rao, the first 'ná' being the plural termination, and the second being the sign of the genitive case, like 'dá' in Punjabi and Pushtoo, and 'ká' in Hindustani. In many of the coins, indeed, we have Nano, and the second syllable 'no' is the genitive sign in Guzarathi. The objection to this is, that in some examples we have Náná by itself on the reverse: it seems doubtful, however, if this is not an error for a different word, Nanaia, which will presently be noticed. With regard to the epithet, if it be an epithet, Korano, it has already been observed that Mr. Masson[1] considers it as denoting 'chief, or military leader,' at a time when the Indo-

[1] Page 78.

Scythians had substituted military chiefs for kings. No authority has been given for this meaning of the term, and it would be obviously incompatible with the use of the words Rao and Basileus, with which Korano is associated. No interpretation more satisfactory has been yet proposed. Besides the difference of the costume of the figure, and that of the legends, the obverse of the coins of Kanerki omits the hatchet-trident, club, and monogram, which occur upon the face of the copper coins of Kadphises.

It is, however, upon the reverses of these coins that the greatest departure from the analogous coins of Kadphises occurs. The difference is highly important, and indicates a total change in the political and religious principles of the princes or dynasties by whom these coins were issued.

The first remarkable distinction is the entire and final disappearance of the Arianian alphabet. In no one instance is the slightest vestige of the letters which have been so uniformly employed on the reverses of the coins from Menander to Kadphises to be discerned. In their place we have a brief legend in Greek characters, similar to those on the obverse, expressing words, of the general purport of which there can be no question, although the language from which they are derived has in all but two instances to be yet determined.

Upon the reverse of some of the small copper coins, which are of superior fabric to the rest, and in which Kanerki is styled ΒΑCΙΛΕVC, we find the legend Helios, ΗΛΙΟC. Upon some of the larger coins, where the name and title are ΡΑΟ ΚΑΝΗΡΚΙ, we have ΜΙΘΡΟ, ΜΙΟΡΟ, or ΜΙΙΡΟ. Professor Lassen remarks, after Müller, that ΜΙΙΡΟ appears to belong exclusively to the coins where the name is corrupted to ΟΟΗΡΚΙ; but this is not borne out by the fact (see Pl. XII. fig. 15, and Pl. XIII. fig. 16). The word has very reasonably been inferred by Prinsep and Müller to be intended for the Mithra, or solar divinity of the Persians. According to Lassen,[1] Mithra is a Zend or old Persian word, whence the modern Persian term Mihir is derived. The form Mi-iro may be, therefore, not a corruption, but a vernacular representation of the same. The termination of this and the following terms in *o* is that of the Zend masculine noun. It must be granted that

[1] Zur Geschichte, p. 98.

the terms Helios and Mithro indicate the relinquishment of all conformity to the Indian system of belief which prevailed under Kadphises, as shown by the types on his coins. The device accompanying this legend is that of a male figure, with the fillet of royalty on the head, which is also surrounded by a nimbus, with rays. The dress is something like that of the figure on the obverse, but the head is either bare, or covered with a kind of turban. It is, no doubt, intended for a personification of the Sun, who was usually represented in the costume of the Persian kings.[1]

Another legend which occurs on the reverses of these coins is a word equally recognisable, **MAO**, Mao, the Zend form of Más, which, both in that language and Sanscrit, means 'moon.' We have with this term a figure which on the copper coins does not materially differ from the representative of the Sun; but on the gold coins in which it occurs there rise from the shoulders of the figure what may be thought to be the horns of the moon. We have, therefore, in addition to the worship of the Sun, that of the Deus Lunus, with attributes like those with which he is represented on the coins of Asia Minor.

Thus far there is no great difficulty in interpreting the purport of the legends; but we come now to a variety of terms, meaning in all probability much the same things, but expressing them by denominations hitherto unknown. These and the preceding appellations have been investigated with much labour and research by Mr. Prinsep[2] and by the late celebrated scholar and antiquary K. O. Müller.[3] The conclusions of the latter are summarily stated and confirmed by Professor Lassen in his dissertation on the kings of Bactria.[4]

From these authorities, then, it appears that the Persians of the later period of the Arsacidan dynasty had departed from the spirit of the ancient elementary worship, and had grouped around the sovereign Sun a variety of deified beings unknown to the pure Magian religion; that the Indo-Scythians

[1] Hyde, Religio Veterum Persarum, p. 112.

[2] J. As. Soc. B. vol. iii. p. 449, and vol. iv. p. 629.

[3] In the Gelehrte Anzeigen of Gottingen, 1835 and 1838.

[4] Zur Geschichte, &c. This valuable memoir is translated and published in several Nos. of the J. As. Soc. B., beginning with No. xcix. p. 251.

adopted these divinities, and that we have now for the first time their names and representations on the coins of Kanerki and his successors. This theory is very probable, and the names accordingly should be discovered in ancient Persic, or in Zend if that be ancient Persic. This, however, is not invariably the case; and although the grammatical form of the words correspond, as above remarked, with that of the Zend noun, Professor Lassen is obliged to admit, of several of the words themselves, that Zend originals for them are not known.

A term of frequent occurrence upon both the gold and copper coins is **OKPO**, the meaning and origin of which are undetermined. Mr. Prinsep conceived it possible that it might be intended for the Sanscrit Arka, a name of the Sun. Professor Lassen suggests Ugra, 'the fierce,' a name of Siva; and he observes, as a confirmation of this origin, that the word is usually met with in conjunction with a figure of Siva holding a trident in his left and a noose in his right hand, and leaning on his bull Nandi. When combined with this device, however, it no longer belongs to the coins of Kanerki, but to a series of coins which we shall presently have occasion to notice. In the coins of Kanerki it is found upon a gold and a copper coin, associated with a figure having four arms, in one of which is not a noose, but the regal fillet; one arm holds a trident; another, a small Indian drum. On some small gold coins we have some indistinct object in place of the two upper arms, but this is no doubt either an error of the original die, or of General Ventura's draughtsman.

The costume and style of the figure, on the copper coins certainly, and possibly on the gold, are feminine, and in that case the person can scarcely be designated by a masculine noun. Although, therefore, the emblem is of a very Indian aspect, it is doubtful if Siva be intended. Ugra also, although it is an appellation of Siva, is not one of frequent use; and the objection urged by Müller against the derivation of Okro from Arka applies equally to its originating from Ugra, as it is to the Magian Persian, and not to the Indian Sanscrit, that we should naturally look for the appellations of Magian divinities.

A similar term to Okro occurs also on some of the coins of Kanerki, which has still less of an Indian aspect: this is **ΑΡΔΟΚΡΟ**, Ard-okro, in the first member of which, as Prinsep has conjectured, the Persian prefix Arda or Arta, as in Ardeshir, Artaxerxes, signifying 'great,' 'noble,' may very possibly be expressed. It is limited to a gold coin with the name of Kanerki, and accompanies the figure of a priest or priestess bearing a cornucopia. The name is more frequent as accompanying a seated female figure on coins which apparently belong to a different prince, and which will be again noticed. It is sufficient here to have specified its connexion with the uncompounded word Okro.

A word of not uncommon occurrence on the coins of Kánerki is Athro, ΑΘΡΟ, which Prinsep supposed to be derived from the Zend word Atars or Athro, a name of fire. It accompanies the figure of a man whose hair is rayed, in some small coins, as if with flames, but in others he resembles the figures with Helios and Mao: he holds the regal fillet in his right hand.

Upon one gold coin we have the legend ΟΡΔΑΓΝΟ, Ordagno, analogous in construction apparently to Ardokro; the figure of a warrior accompanies it. The word ΟΑΔΟ, Oado, is found, upon a number of copper coins, along with a figure running, invested in a transparent veil; and for the origin of this Lassen proposes the Zend Váto and Persian Bád, meaning 'wind.' Váta has the same sense in Sanscrit. The attitude of the figure is not out of keeping with the personification of this element.

Another term, and one of which the Persic origin can scarcely be disputed, Nanaia, ΝΑΝΑΙΑ, occurs upon very many copper coins, both large and small. In the same situation we have also ΝΑΝΑ and ΝΑΝΑ ΡΑΟ, but these are probably a corruption or inaccuracy. The title accompanies a female figure, in which we must have either the goddess Anaitis or Anahid of the Persians, or her priestess,—the Artemis, whose worship Artaxerxes Mnemon, according to Berosus, endeavoured to spread throughout Persia, and especially in Bactria, and whom Mr. Avdall has successfully identified as Anaia or Nanæa, the tutelary goddess of Armenia.[1] We find her also mentioned as Nanæa in the Apocrypha, as the goddess of Elymais, in whose temple Antiochus was slain.[2] It is very likely that her worship extended along the south coast of the Caspian, and thus reached some of the Indo-Scythic

[1] J. As. Soc. B. vol. v. p. 266.

[2] Maccabees, B. II. c. I. v. 13.

tribes, by whom it was imported rather late into India. Of the migration of Nanæa thither there is every probability that the memory survives in the Bibi Nani, or Lady Nani, who is reverenced by the Mohammedans, and worshipped as a form of Parvati by the Hindus in various parts of Afghànistan.[1] It does not appear that any vestiges of her temples have been yet found, but it is likely that they did exist where now the name of Bibi Nani is applied topographically to denote a particular locality, as, for instance, at the mouth of the Bolan Pass.[2]

These peculiarities of the coins of Kanerki sufficiently prove that upon his accession to the kingdom of the Paropamisus a modified form of the Magian religion was introduced into the countries bordering on the Indus, and that new divinities, with Persic denominations, were worshipped by the court: at the same time it can scarcely be doubted that the new religion exercised only a partial influence, and that even during the period of its especial patronage it was mixed up with the prevailing forms of Hinduism. At any rate it soon gave way to that faith, as we shall have occasion to notice; and Siva and his bull speedily resumed their place upon the Indo-Scythic coins. Even in the reign of Kanerki the new system did not monopolise the favour of the ruling authorities, and they struck some, although not many, coins in which the types of Buddhism appear to have been stamped upon the currency. Such is the case with the three copper coins particularized below, (Nos. 29, 30, 31,) on the reverse of which the figure standing to the front is manifestly that of Buddha or Sákya Sinha, in an attitude of preaching or prayer. The position, the tuft of hair on the top, and the large ears, characterize this figure too clearly to be mistaken. The comparative rarity of these coins, however, and the predominance of types unconnected with Buddhism, render it most probable that the Mithraic coins of Kanerki were current before the third century, by which time there is reason to

[1] As mentioned by Mr. Masson; J. As. Soc. B. vol. iv. p. 449. See also Prinsep's observations; ibid.

[2] "Our camp at Beeby Nanny was the first open spot we had seen in the pass on the bank of a beautiful stream, and where two valleys meet betwixt two different ranges of mountains:" Dr. Kennedy's Campaign in Afghanistan, vol. i. p. 216. "The spot was thirty miles from the entrance of the Bolan Pass:" Ibid. p. 215.

believe that the religion of Buddha was chiefly professed in the countries in which these coins are found.

It may be remarked, in conclusion, that the monogram, which in the coins of Kanerki is restricted to the reverse, is the same as one of those observable on the coins of Kadphises (No. 155): the second (No. 156) never recurs. From this and the other differences, and from the frequency with which the regal fillet is represented as being offered or bestowed by the personified elementary deity, we may infer that Kanerki founded a new dynasty, ruling over the same region as Kadphises,—the valley of the Kabul river, and perhaps the greater part of the Punjab. The identity of the monogram that is retained, and the purer style of the Greek inscriptions on some of the coins, tend to show that Kanerki must have come next in succession to Kadphises, and he may have reigned in the first half of the second century.

Although not connected with the history of Kanerki or his innovations, it seems not unlikely that the use of the term Nana on his coins may serve to elucidate some points in the history of Sanscrit literature. We find, for example, in the play called Mrich-chakati, in a Prakrit passage, and also in the Sanscrit text of the Mitakshara, the word Nánáka used to signify a coin.[1] No satisfactory etymology of this word can be offered, and it is in all likelihood not Sanscrit. It is possibly, therefore, derived from the Náná of the coins of Kanerki or his successors, from which Nánáka would be regularly formed. The commentator on the play describes a Nánáka as

[1] *Sakára.* एश्रा णाणक मूशिका 'this filcher of broad pieces;' Act I. Scene 1. The comment calls Nánáka शिवाङ्कटङ्कः 'a coin with the mark of Siva.' The text of the Mitakshara directs that the fabricators of false coins shall be punished, as also the assayer who gives a false valuation. तुलाशासनमानानां कूटकृन्नाणकस्य च 'the falsifier of weights, copper grants, measures, and also of the Nánáka.' And again, अकूटकं ब्रूते कूटं यश्चाप्यकूटकं । स नाणकपरीक्षी दाप्य उत्तमसाहसं ॥ 'the assayer of Nánakas who calls that which is genuine a forgery, or fails to detect a counterfeit, is to be punished in the highest degree;' Mit. Vyavahára, p. 80. The commentator evidently considers the Nánáka to be either a gold or silver coin, as he explains its being false or forged कूट to signify either its bearing an impression different from that legally struck, or its being adulterated with copper and the like. अव्यवहारिकमुद्रितत्वं ताम्रादि गर्भत्वं वा ।

a coin having upon it the figure of Siva; a description sufficiently warranted by the coins of this period. If this origin of the word be accurately conjectured, the age of Yajnawalkya's legal dicta and that of the Mrich-chakati must be subsequent to the æra of Kanerki; and whatever that may be, they will be of a less remote period than the age which popular belief assigns to them.

COINS OF KANERKI OR KANERKOU.

GOLD.

1. Middle size. Standing figure, to the left; a crescent or horns on his head; tunic, with cloak; bow behind his back, altar in front; his left hand holds a spear. ΒΑϹΙΛЄVϹ ΒΑϹΙΛЄωΝ ΚΑΝΗΡΚΟV. R. Figure, to the left, in a close dress and cloak; his left hand rests on a sword by his side, the right is held up; rayed nimbus, and fillets. ΗΛΙΟϹ. Mon. 155.

This coin, which corresponds in all respects except the wings (?) on the legs of the figure on the reverse with the copper coins, Pl. XI. fig. 16, was sent home lately by Sir A. Burnes.

2. Middle size. Figure, to the left, as before. - - - ΝΗΡΚΙ. R. Standing figure, to the left, with rayed nimbus. ΜΙΙΡΟ. Mon.

From Masson's last collection.

3. Middle size. Standing figure, to the left, bearded, with crown and fillets on the head; long coat, and boots; robe or cloak behind; bow across the back; the left hand holds a spear, the right is held over a low altar (?). ΝΑΝΑ ΡΑΟ ΚΑΝΗΡΚΙ ΚΟΡΑΝΟ. R. Standing figure, in tunic and robe; wings or a nimbus (?) behind the shoulders; the head rayed; a lance-like weapon held in his left hand; the right hand, extended, holds a short concave sword, the left grasps a short javelin. ΜΑΟ. Mon. Pl. XII. fig. 1.

From the Masson collection.

4. Standing figure, bearded, with cap and tunic, as before. ΝΑΝΟ ΡΑΟ ΚΑΝΗΡΚΙ ΚΟΡΑ - - . R. Figure, to the right, with halo round the head; fillet and crescent on the top, in a long robe; sword or club by the left side, and in the right hand a weapon or flower. ΝΑΝΑ ΡΑΟ. Mon. Pl. XII. fig. 2.

From the Masson collection; described also As. Res. vol. xvii. Pl. I. fig. 2, where the legend on the reverse is only NANA; that on the obverse is PAO NANO PAO KANHPKI KOPANO. See also J. As. Soc. B. Sept. 1834, p. 445, and Oct. 1836, Pl. XXXVI. fig. 4; Mionnet, Supplement, viii. p. 501.

A similar coin, with only NANA on the reverse, was sent home lately by Sir A. Burnes.

5. Middle size. Standing figure, with cap, but no crown; the left hand grasps an upright spear. PAO NANO PAO KANHPKI KOPANO. R. Standing figure, to the right, with cap, tunic, and boots; lance in his right hand, and sword by his side; a bird with expanded wings is perched on the top of his head (as a crest ?). ΟΡΔΑΓΝΟ. Mon. Pl. XII. fig. 3.

From the Masson collection; described and delineated also J. As. Soc. B. Oct. 1836, Pl. XXXVI. fig. 1.

6. Standing figure, as before. PAO NANO PAO KANHPKI KOPANO. R. Standing figure, to the left; halo round the head; four arms; the upper right holds a small Indian drum (?); the upper left, a trident, the shaft of which is behind the back; the lower right hand holds a short club (?), the left leans on the hip; the dress is Brahmanical; a fawn on its two hind-legs is by his left side. OKPO. Mon. Pl. XII. fig. 4.

Two of these are amongst Mr. Masson's last collections, which contain another exactly similar, except in being smaller. A similar coin is in the possession of Dr. Swiney, procured from Sayid Karamat Ali, and also figured, J. As. Soc. B. Nov. 1835, Pl. LI. fig. 1.

7. Middle size. Figure to the left, in cap, tunic, and boots, as before, with the bow in a case (?) behind his back. PAO NANO PAO KANHPKI KOPANO. R. Figure in long robe, to the right, with cap or turban, and halo round the head, holding a cornucopia. ΑΡΔΟΚΡΟ behind the figure. Mon. in front. Pl. XII. fig. 5.

Copied from Mr. Prinsep's engraving of a coin delineated by M. Court, J. As. Soc. B. Oct. 1836, Pl. XXXVI. fig. 9.

8. Standing figure, to the right, as before; he holds a hook or ankusa over the altar. PAO NANO PAO KANHPKI KOPANO. R. Figure, to the left, in tight dress and cloak, with fillet (?); flame from the shoulder; the right hand holds a fillet. ΑΘΡΟ. Mon.

From the Masson collection.

9. Small. Head of king, to the left, bearded; the left hand raised. ------ KI KOPANO. R. Standing figure, to the left, bearded, and partly clad; holding in the right hand a fillet, and in the left a noose? AΘPO. Mon. Pl. XII. fig. 6.

From a coin procured by Mr. Masson in 1836. One in the collection of Dr. Swiney, procured from Sayid Karamat Ali, is figured, J. As. Soc. B. Nov. 1835. Pl. LI. fig. 2.

10. Small. Standing figure, in cap and tunic; offering incense. --- PAO KANHPKI - KO --. R. Figure, as in the last, with fillet in the right hand. AΘPO. Mon. Pl. XII. fig. 7.

11. Small. Standing figure, as in the last; inscription mutilated. R. Standing figure, in robe, with four arms (?) OKPO. Mon. Pl. XII. fig. 8.

12. Bust of king, bearded, to the left. ---- KI KOPANO. R. Standing figure; the right arm, extended, holds a wreath; the left, a sceptre; object above the right arm like a double-headed snake (?); trowsers on the legs. OKPO. Mon. Pl. XII. fig. 9.

13. Bust of king, with peaked cap. PAO NANO PAO KA ---- KOPANOY. R. Standing figure, with four arms, as before. OKPO. Mon. Pl. XII. fig. 10.

These four coins were found by General Ventura at Manikyala, and are figured from Prinsep's delineations of them; J. As. Soc. B. Nov. 1834, Pl. XXXIV. figs. 15, 16, 17, 18.

14. Small. Head of prince, bare, to the left, with sceptre and lance. PAO. R. Standing figure, to the left; nimbus round the head. ONIP. Mon. Pl. XII. fig. 11.

Coin of General Ventura; J. As. Soc. B. Nov. 1835, Pl. XXXVIII. fig. 8.

15. Small. Standing figure and altar, as on the larger coins. R. Standing figure, with wreath, as in fig. 6.

Masson collection.

COPPER.

16. Middle size. Figure, to the left, in cap, coat, and boots, with fire-altar; the left hand grasps a spear. ---- EWN KANHPKOY. R. Figure, with turban and fillet, and tight dress covered by a transparent cloak; the right hand raised, the left rests on the handle of a short sword or dagger;

the head is inclosed by a nimbus with rays. **ΗΛΙΟC.** Mon. Pl. XI. fig. 15.

17. Middle size. Figure, to the left, bearded, with crescent on the head; a spear in his left hand; bow behind his back. **ΒΑCΙΛΕΥC ΒΑCΙΛΕΩΝ ΚΑΝΗΡΚΟΥ.** R. Standing figure, to the left, as in the last, with nimbus and fillet, but no turban; the style of the costume is somewhat different, and the legs have apparently small wings. **ΗΛΙΟC.** Mon. Pl. XI. fig. 16.

18. Middle size. King, to the left, as before. **ΒΑCΙΛΕΥC ΒΑCΙΛΕΩΝ ΚΑΝΗΡΚΟΥ.** R. Figure, to the right, of a priestess, in a long vest; the hair dressed after the Indian fashion; the right hand holds a sceptre (or a flower ?); nimbus round the head. **ΝΑΝΑΙΑ.** Mon. Pl. XI. fig. 17.

These are amongst a number of the same in the Masson collection, and are of better execution than any of the other copper coins of Kanerki.

19. Small. Standing figure, and altar. Inscription corrupt. R. Priest or priestess, to the right. **ΝΑΝΑ** (in barbarized letters). Mon. Pl. XI. figs. 18, 19, 20.

These are also numerous, but are of rude execution. The figure on the reverse allies them to No. 15, as well as to the gold coin, Pl. XII. No. 2.

20. Small. Figure, to the left; on his right the character ጎ *ti.* - **ΑΟΚΑ** -. R. Figure, with nimbus; spear, with flag, behind him. - **ΜΑ** -. Mon. Pl. XI. fig. 21.

A rude coin, from the Masson collection.

Of this and the preceding coins considerable numbers are found, varying in their degree of preservation, and occasionally in the legends; Rao Korano being sometimes substituted for Basileus, and the word on the reverse being read Nanaia, Nana, Anan, or Nanaid. They are found in the topes, as well as extensively elsewhere. One of them was the first of the Indo-Scythian series which presented a clearly legible inscription. It was procured by Sir A. Burnes near Manikyala. J. As. Soc. B. June, 1833, p. 314, Pl. XI. fig. 10; and Travels to Bokhara, vol. ii. App. Pl. IV. fig. 18. Similar coins are described, J. des Sav. Oct. 1835, Pl. II. fig. 24; and J. As. Soc. B. April, 1834, Pl. XII. fig. 1; Sept. 1834, Pl. XXV. fig. 7; and Nov. 1835, Pl. LI. fig. 4.

21. Large. Standing figure, with cap, lance, and cloak; bow behind the back; spear in his left hand. **PAO KANHPKI.** R. Priestess, with nimbus, to the right. **NANA.** Mon. Pl. XII. fig. 12.

22. Large. Figure, as before. **PAO KANHPKI.** R. Standing figure, with lance and cloak, fillet and nimbus, as in the smaller coin No. 14. **MAO.** Mon. Pl. XII. fig. 13.

23. Large. Figure, as before. **- NHPKI.** R. Figure, with rayed nimbus. **MIOP.** Mon. Pl. XII. fig. 14.

24. Large. Figure, as before. **- NHPKI.** R. Figure, as before. **MIIPO.** Pl. XII. fig. 15.

25. Large. Figure, as before. **PAO KA - - - .** R. Figure similar to that on the obverse; the right hand, extended, holds a fillet. **AΘPO.** Mon. Pl. XII. fig. 16.

26. Large. Figure, as before. **PAO KANHPKI.** R. Female figure, with four arms, each of which is decorated with bracelets; one holds a small drum, another a wreath or fillet, the third a spear, the fourth hangs down. **OKPO.** Mon. Pl. XII. fig. 17.

27. Middle size. Figure, as before. **PAO KANHPKI.** R. Figure, with four arms, as in the last. **OKPO.** Mon. Pl. XII. fig. 18.

28. Large. Figure, as before. R. A figure running, holding a transparent vest or cloak, otherwise naked or clothed in a light dress. **OAΔO.** Mon. Pl. XII. figs. 19, 20, 21, 22, 23.

These are specimens of coins, of which there are great numbers in the collection, and which are found extensively throughout India. Those with the two male figures and the legend **MIIPO**, or **MIOPO**, **MAO**, and **AΘPO**, are most numerous; next are those with the priestess and **NANAIA** on the reverse; next are those with the running figure and the term **OAΔO.** Those with the four-armed figure and the legend **OKPO** are comparatively rare. They are in general, however, much worn, and it is only upon select specimens that the devices are distinct and the inscriptions legible. There are slight variations in the style of the figures, and sometimes in the disposition of the inscriptions, but they are not of any importance, and are referrible to careless or unskilful fabrication, rather than to any purposed alteration. They have been described and delineated in various places, especially in the Trans. R. As. Soc. vol. i. Pl. XII.; As. Res. vol. xvii. Pl. II.; and J. As. Soc. B. April, 1834, Pl. XIII.; July, 1834, Pl. XXII.; September, 1834, Pl. XXV.; November, 1834, Pl. XXVIII.; and November, 1835, Pl. LI.

29. Large. Figure, to the left, as before. PAO - - PK - . R. Standing figure, to the front, in long robe; one hand raised, as if for benediction; part of the dress hanging over the left arm; nimbus round the head, which has a tuft of hair on the summit; the ears are large. AKAM - PAYO - - . Mon. Pl. XIII. fig. 1.

30. Middle size. Standing figure, to the left. PAO KA - - . R. Standing figure, to the front; both hands meeting on the breast. - - OKAMA - OAO. Mon. Pl. XIII. fig. 2.

31. Small. Standing figure, as before. PAO KA - - - I. R. As before. - AKA. Pl. XIII. fig. 3.

From the Masson collection, but they are rare. The legend on the obverse, although imperfect, identifies them with the coins of Kanerki. The figure on the reverse is like that of Sakya Sinha as usually represented, and resembles in its costume and character the principal figure on the gold cup found at Deh Bímarán. See Antiquities, Pl. IV.

KENORANO.

The only coins which bear the name of Kenorano, or, as it sometimes occurs, Kenrano, are of copper, and are distinguished by two devices. In one we have a figure seated or reclining on a couch, in the other a king riding on an elephant. The whole legend, which is never found entire, may be discovered from various coins to be PAO NANO OOHP KENOPANO. It may be a question whether the last three syllables should not rather be KOPANO, and the name be OOHPKE, being the same as that which appears to be OOHPKI on the gold coins to be next noticed. This would be consistent with the preceding examples of Kadphises and Kanerki. The distinction which the most obvious reading of the legend proscribes leaves to one prince an almost exclusive gold, and to the other an entirely exclusive copper, coinage; a peculiarity for which no precedent occurs. The legend, however, is more distinct upon the copper than it is upon the gold coins; and the style of their fabric, and the costume of the figures, seem to authorize their attribution to different princes.

The title of Nana Rao allies Kenorano to Kanerki; and the connexion is confirmed by the continuance of the same monogram, although in some instances it is slightly varied by the insertion of an additional cross-bar, as well as by the similarity of the figures and legends on the reverse. The latter are in general more rudely and indistinctly formed than on the coins of Kanerki, but we can distinguish **ΜΙΟΡΟ, ΜΙΙΙΡΟ, ΜΑΟ, ΟΚΡΟ, ΑΡΔΟΚΡΟ,** and other words, apparently blunders or corruptions for them. We have the standing figure, with cloak and rayed nimbus, the priestess and the four-armed figure, besides one or two others which are new and peculiar. They do not, however, add any positive data to those already furnished from which we may infer the continuance of the Mithraic worship introduced by Kanerki. The elephant possibly intimates the extension of this principality more into India proper. The number of the coins warrants a belief in a reasonable duration of this prince's reign.

COINS OF KENORANO.

COPPER.

1. Large. Figure, with cap and fillet, in a tight dress, reclining on a couch; the right leg raised, the left hanging down. **ΟΟΗΡ ΚЄΝΟΡΑΝΟ.** ℞. Figure, to the left, in armour (?); nimbus round the head, and fillet. **ΜΑ -.** Mon. Pl. XIII. fig. 4.

2. Large. Figure and couch, as before; the costume rather different, and the couch has an ornamented back. Inscription imperfect. ℞. Figure with four arms, as in No. 20 of Kanerki, but different costume, and a trident takes the place of what in No. 20 seems to be a spear. **ΟΚ - -.** Mon. Pl. XIII. fig. 5.

3. Large. Sitting figure, as in the last. **ΟΗΡ ΚЄ.** ℞. Figure, to the left, with sceptre in the left hand; the right extended; nimbus rayed. **ΜΙΟΡΟ.** Mon. Pl. XIII. fig. 6.

4. Large. Figure seated cross-legged, left arm raised; nimbus and fillet,

ЄNOPANO. R. Priestess, to the left; drapery very gracefully disposed. NANA. Mon. Pl. XIII. fig. 7.

5. Large. Figure sitting cross-legged on an ornamented scroll or lotus (?). ANO PAO OOHPKЄ. R. Figure, to the left, in tunic, short jacket, with cape and buskins; nimbus rayed. MIOPO. Pl. XIII. fig. 8.

6. Small. Figure on couch; very rude. R. Standing figure; rude. Characters imperfect. Mon. Pl. XIII. fig. 9.

7. Large. Seated figure, cross-legged; apparently female. PAO NONA OO R. Standing figure, as in No. 5. MAO. Mon. Pl. XIII. fig. 10.

8. Large. Figure sitting cross-legged. R. Female figure, rising apparently out of a pedestal; surmounted by a crescent. OKPO (?). Pl. XIII. fig. 11.

9. Middle size. Seated figure. Legend barbarous. R. Standing figure; rude. Pl. XIII. fig. 12.

10, 11. Small; thin. Sitting figure, cross-legged. R. Standing figure; rude. Characters illegible. Pl. XIII. figs. 13, 14.

These, with exception of No. 8, which is a unique in the possession of Dr. Swiney, are from the Masson collection. They are as numerous as the coins of Kanerki, and as extensively met with. They are in general much worn, and the small thin coins are particularly rude and imperfect.

12. Large. King, mounted on an elephant, to the right, with spear in his hand; nimbus and fillet; quiver (?) behind his back. PAO NANO PAO OOHP KЄNOPANO. R. Figure, to the left, in tunic and transparent cloak. MAO. Mon. Pl. XIII. fig. 15.

13. Large. King on elephant, with the ankusa or goad. R. Similar figure as on the last. MIIPO. Mon. Pl. XIII. fig. 16.

14. Large. King on elephant, with goad. OOHP KЄNOP -. R. Figure, as in the last. Inscription imperfect. Mon. Pl. XIII. fig. 17.

15. Middle size. King on elephant, with spear. R. Standing figure, with turban; the right hand, extended, holds a fillet. ωHVO. Pl. XIII. fig. 18.

16. Large. King on elephant. Inscription blundered. R. Female figure, to the front, with cornucopia. APΔOKPO. Mon. Pl. XIII. fig. 19.

From a coin belonging to Dr. Swiney. It is delineated also by Prinsep, J. As. Soc. B. vol. v. Pl. XLVI. fig. 13.

17. Large. King on elephant, with goad. Inscription blundered. R. Standing figure, to the front, leaning on a trident or spear; rude. Pl. XIII. fig. 20.

18. Large. King on elephant. **PAO NANO PAO OO - - .** R. Figure, in tight dress, with four arms. Mon. Pl. XIII. fig. 21.

19. Large. King on elephant. **KENOPANO.** R. Standing figure, to the front. **AΘPO.**

Delineated and described by Prinsep, J. As. Soc. B. Sept. 1834, p. 444, Pl. XXV. fig. 31.

20. Large. King on elephant. **OIΛHOH OIΛPOIΛHIΛ POΛIΩH.** R. Standing figure; the right arm holding a fillet. **ΛOH.** Mon.

A very perfect coin; one of the four procured in the Punjab by Colonel Stacey. Prinsep conjectures, with great probability, that the Greek legend on the obverse is a blundering imitation of **ΒΑΣΙΛΕΩΣ ΒΑΣΙΛΕΩΝ ΣΩΤΗΡΟΣ**; J. As. Soc. B. Nov. 1836, p. 722, Pl. XLVI. fig. 12.

These coins are also extremely numerous, and of very wide distribution. They are always of barbarous execution, but some are of ruder fabric than others. With exception of No. 16, those here represented are from the Masson collection. Many similar coins are described in the works already referred to: the Trans. R. As. Soc.; As. Res.; J. As. Soc. B., &c.; along with the coins of Kadphises and Kanerki, with which they are commonly found.

OOERKI.

The name of this prince appears rather to be Ookrki; but such a combination of letters is scarcely conceivable, and on some coins the first **K** has more the character of **H**. The letters are, however, rude, and offer a wider departure than even the preceding from the Greek model, from which may justly be inferred their later date.

The title of Rao Nana Rao, the same Mithraic legends on the reverse, and the same monogram, ally the coins of this prince with those of Kanerki. The costume of the king, however, undergoes a change; and whilst in some cases we have the same cap and garb which are worn by Kadphises, we have in others either a coat of mail or a coat thickly studded with jewels, and a richly ornamented helmet fastened under the chin. There is in this costume an approach to the first Sassanian kings; and we may, perhaps, regard Ooerki as nearly contemporary with them, as ruling at the end of the second or beginning of the third century.

The words Miiro, Mao, Athro, and the like, show that the religious system introduced by Kanerki still prevailed. We have one or two new terms also, as Pharo, Manaobago, and Kando-Komaro.

No satisfactory original has been suggested for Pharo, although, as observed by Prinsep, the elements of the word seem to be conveyed in the frequent Arsacidan appellation Phraates or Phraortes, or in the Undo-phares or -pherres of the coins. Lassen finds a Zend word, Frá, but does not pretend to explain its purport. In Manaobago, it has been conjectured that in the first part of it some affinity to Mao, 'the moon,' may be expressed, whilst in the latter we have the Sanscrit or Zend Bhaga or Bago, denoting splendour or beauty. These explanations, however, are far from satisfactory. The figure to which this title is attached is of a more decidedly Indian character than most of the rest. Komaro is a pure Indian word, meaning 'a youth' or 'prince,' in which sense it is also a name of the deity of war: the preceding words on the same coin are not very distinct; the first has been read Mao, but the initial letter is doubtful, and the word may be Rao. The first letter of the word following is also indistinct, and it is doubtful if it be a letter or only a mark. The word will be either Ikando or Kando, the nearest approach to which in any known Indian word will be Skanda, also a name of the Hindu Mars. Skanda Kumara, the prince Skanda, might be allowable, but then Rao would be out of place, and it is probable that we should have two names, as there are two figures upon the coin. There are two youthful divinities in Hindu mythology, the Aswini-kumaras, 'Sons of the Sun,' and therefore not unlikely to have been adopted into a Mithraic pantheon. They have no martial character, however, nor would any term like Kando be applicable to them. We must be content, therefore, for the present, with the conclusion that the device is Indian, without pretending to specify its application. The portrait on the obverse allies it with the coins of Ooerki.

COINS OF OOERKI.

GOLD.

1. Bust of king, with high cap and fillet, to the left, holding in his right hand two ears of corn (or two arrow-heads ?), and a flower in his left. PAO NANO PAO OOKPKI KOPANO. R. Standing figure of priest or priestess, to the right, as in the coin of Kanerki, No. 2. NANA. Mon. Pl. XIV. fig. 1.

From the Masson collection, from the Tope of Guldára; J. As. Soc. B. Oct. 1836, Pl. XXXVI. fig. 5.

2. Bust of king, to the left, with a mace (?) in his right hand, hook in his left. ---- PAO OOKPKI KOPANO. R. Standing figure, to the left, halo and rays round the head, with a close dress and robe; right hand extended, left holding the hilt of a sword (?). MIIPO. Mon. Pl. XIV. fig. 2.

From the Masson collection also; J. As. Soc. B. Oct. 1836, Pl. XXXVI. fig. 3.

A similar coin, but less perfect, and although of the same type, of a different mintage, is in the possession of Dr. Swiney.

3. Head of king, to the left, with ornamented helmet and halo; the right hand holds a short club, the left a lance or bill with tassels; the body appears to be dressed in armour. PAO NANO PAO OOHPKI KOPANO. R. Standing figure, with halo, close dress, and transparent robe; the right hand extended, the left leans on a lance. ΦΑΡΟ. Mon. Pl. XIV. fig. 3.

From the Masson collection.

4. Head of king, as in the last. PAO NANO PAO OOHPKI KOPANO. R. Figure in long robe, to the right, with cornucopia. ΑΡΔΟΚΡΟ. Mon. Pl. XIV. fig. 4.

From a coin belonging to General Ventura; J. As. Soc. B. Nov. 1835, Pl. XXXVIII. fig. 9; J. des Sav. July, 1834, Pl. fig. 10, and May, 1836; J. Asiatique, Feb. 1836. See also before, Pl. XII. fig. 5.

5. Head of king and legend, as before. R. Figure in long mantle, with cornucopia, to the left. ΑΡΔΟΚΡΟ. Mon. Pl. XIV. fig. 5.

From a coin in Dr. Swiney's collection.

6. Bust of king, as before, but with a hook or ankusa in his left hand.

Legend as before. R. Standing figure, with crescent-shaped wings behind his shoulders. **MAO.** Mon. Pl. XIV. fig. 6.

From a coin of General Ventura's collection; J. As. Soc. B. Nov. 1835, Pl. XXXVIII. fig. 10; J. Asiatique, Feb. 1836.

7. Bust of king, as before, with lance. Legend as before. R. Standing figure, the upper part of the body invested with flames (?), to the right. **AΘPO.** Mon. Pl. XIV. fig. 7.

8. Bust of king, with helmet; left hand holds a hook, the right a flower. Legend effaced. R. Standing figure, to the left, with halo and spear. **ωPOH.** Mon. Pl. XIV. fig. 8.

These two are engraved, J. As. Soc. B. Oct. 1836, Pl. XXXVI. figs. 6, 7, from drawings by M. Court of coins in his possession.

9. Bust of king, with short mace or sceptre and hook. Legend as before. R. Seated figure on a low chair, with footstool; helmet on the head; crescent wings behind the shoulders; four arms. **MANAOBA(ΓO).** Mon. Pl. XIV. fig. 9.

From a coin engraved in the As. Res. vol. xvii. Pl. I. fig. 1; J. As. Soc. B. July, 1834, Pl. XXI. fig. 2; and Oct. 1836, Pl. XXXVI. fig. 8.

10. Small. Bust of king, with mace and lance. R. Standing figure, with halo and spear. **MIPO.** Mon. Pl. XIV. fig. 10.

From a coin in the Masson collection.

11. Small. Bust of king, bearded; mace or sceptre in the right hand, hook in the left. **PAO NANO PAO OOKPKI KOPANO.** R. Two figures standing, a halo round each head, and each holding a spear. Monogram between them. Behind the figure, on the right, **- AO**; below, **IKANΔO**; and behind the figure, on the left, **KOMAPO**; above, between the figures, **B.** Pl. XIV. fig. 11.

A coin procured by Mr. Masson in 1836. A coin with similar devices, but having on the reverse the words **OKPO** and **NANA**, belonging to General Ventura, is figured in the J. As. Soc. B. Nov. 1835, Pl. XXXVIII. fig. 7; and described, J. Asiatique, Feb. 1836, No. LXI.; and by M. Mionnet, Supplement, viii. p. 502.

BARAORO, VARAORO, VARAHRAN, OR BEHRAM (?).

Although it seems probable that some such name may be read upon the obverse of these coins, yet the departure of the Greek letters from even the rude models of those on the coins of Kanerki renders the reading very uncertain; and the appellation here assigned to the prince whose portrait they bear is fully open to correction.

There can be little doubt that the letters are intended to be the same as those on the preceding coins, with which therefore they are allied. The types of the altar and the trident are the same as those on the coins of Kadphises; and we have here also a recurrence to the Hindu worship of Siva, in the displacement by that deity of the personifications of the elements on the coins of Kanerki. The continuance of the name Okro, if that be the word intended, may be accidental. In one of the monograms there is also a return to that of Kadphises.

The character of the altar now admits of no dispute, as the flame is evidently rising from it. The costume of the mailed monarch on the flat coins does not perhaps authorize our assigning to them a Sassanian origin, but there can be no question of the Sassanian character of the figures on the concavo-convex coins, as we find the same remarkable head-dresses on the acknowledged coins of the princes of that dynasty. The wings springing from the crown, observable on one of our coins, are found on the coins of Sapor II., and the kind of crown itself on those of Sapor III.; whilst the peaked cap on another coin is exactly like that worn by the young prince in the coins with three portraits of Varahran II.[1] These are evidently, therefore, coins of the first Sassanian princes of the third and fourth centuries. Whether the concavo-convex coins belong to the same dynasty as the flat coins here grouped with them may admit of doubt; and we may have different successions represented by them, beginning with Indo-Scythic or with Arsacidan princes, and terminating with Sassanian.

Although found in the valley of the Kabul river, these coins are most

[1] Médailles des Rois Perses de la Dynastie Sassanienne; by Adrien de Longperrier: Pl. IV. figs. 3, 4, 5, and Pl. VII. fig. 5.

plentifully met with in Badakhshan, where, according to information received by Dr. Lord, they are considered to belong to a race of Rajput princes once sovereigns of the province. Perhaps the rulers of the trans-Himalayan provinces may have been Hindu governors appointed by Sassanian superiors, or Rajas acknowledging their supremacy. This arrangement would explain the concurrence of Magian and Indian types.

COINS OF BARAORO.

GOLD.

1. Large. Standing figure, to the left, with nimbus and peaked helmet, and dress of mail; the left hand holds a trident, the right hangs over an altar, above which is a trident; a sword is at the side. **POO NO POO BO(P)OOPO KOB(P)OPO.** Mon. 156; also one between the feet, 157. R. Figure of Siva, in long robe, to the front, holding a trident in the left hand, and a fillet in his right; crescent on his head, surrounded by a nimbus: behind him his bull, to the left. **OKPO.** Mon. 158. Pl. XIV. figs. 12, 13.

There are several of these in the collection, differing only in the degrees of rudeness of execution. The legend on the obverse seems to be intended for Rao Nana Rao Baraono Korano. The letters, however, are much corrupted, and sometimes vary in form. Whether the vowel be A or O, the latter only is employed. The legend on the reverse has the appearance of Onro, but it is probably intended for Okro. The costume of the figure in front of the bull varies, and is sometimes a light vest, with pantaloons or a cloth wrapped round the hips.

2. Middle. Figure in armour, as before. No monogram. **PAO NANO PAO B(O)OANO KOPANO.** R. Figure of Siva, with hair like a wig; upper half of the body naked, the lower covered with the Indian dhoti, tucked up at the waist; bull. Mon. 159. **OKPO.** Pl. XIV. figs. 14, 18.

Several of these are in the Masson collection. Their execution, however barbarous, is very superior to that of the larger coins, and the letter alpha is distinguished from the omicron, being represented by an inverted **P** or **ꟼ**. There is also a character inserted after Bo- or Vo-, the value of which is unknown; it is something like the figure of the Sanscrit numeral two, २.

3. Small. Figure, to the left. Inscription worn. R. Siva, with the dhoti, in front of the bull. **OKPO.** Pl. XIV. fig. 15.

4. Large; convex. Figure, to the left, with beard and bushy hair, in armour; a crown with crest and wings, as on the Sassanian coins. Fire-altar with flames, and the king appears to be plunging a trident into it; his left hand also grasps a trident. Mon. 160. In place of the inscription a circle of **O**'s, occasionally varied with **P**. R. Siva, with dhoti, in front of the bull; the Sassanian wings extend from his head; a circle of rings; and, in place of **OKPO**, either a series of circles or Pehlevi characters (?). Pl. XIV. fig. 16.

5. Large; convex. Figure in armour, to the left, as before; with a cap bending in front, and terminating in the beak of a bird; altar with flame; trident, and Mon. 156. There is also apparently part of Mon. 158, and that between the feet, 157. R. Siva, with bushy hair, and flame (?) rising from his head; his right hand holds a fillet, his left the trident; bull behind. Inscription corrupt.

These are both from the Masson collection, which has a duplicate of No. 4, as well as another of a similar type, but of still more barbarous workmanship. Another has been sent by Dr. Lord from Badakhshan, differing, however, in the head-dress, which is a crown decorated with the horns of a ram. A duplicate of No. 5 has also been procured by the same gentleman at Kunduz.

Specimens of these coins, whether flat or convex, are not rare. They are all, however, although of different size and shape, with exception of the very smallest, of one weight, or about 124 grains troy. Several are in the possession of Dr. Swiney; others have been sent home recently by Sir A. Burnes and Dr. Lord. Some are described by Prinsep, J. As. Soc. B. Sept. 1834, Pl. XXVI. figs. 10, 11; Nov. 1835, Pl. XXXVIII. figs. 4, 5, 6. Of the three last, No. 4 has the Nagari syllable ঘ on the obverse, and **OKPO** distinctly legible on the reverse.

UNCERTAIN OR 'ARDOKRO' COINS OF THE INDO-SCYTHIC SERIES.

The occurrence of the term Ardokro on these coins allies them to the

Indo-Scythic series, and the discovery of the copper coins in such numbers in the vicinity of Kabul is further proof of the connexion. They were probably, however, some of the latest issued by these princes; for the same types, and particularly that of the sitting female, are found upon coins which are undeniably of Indian origin, bearing Hindu names and titles in Sanscrit letters, and being assigned to the Rajas of Kanoj. These have been therefore denominated by Mr. Prinsep not inappropriately 'link,' or transition coins,[1] as constituting a point of connexion between the coinage of foreign and of native princes. As some of the ruder forms have been met with in the topes, we cannot assign to the first of the Hindu imitations a later date than the fourth or fifth century; and consequently those which belong to the Indo-Scythic period will not be later than the third or fourth.

COINS OF ARDOKRO.

GOLD.

1. Middle size. Standing figure in cap and tunic, with wide sleeves, to the left; fire-altar and trident; halo round the head. - - - PKO KOPANO. R. Female figure, seated on a high-backed chair, her feet resting on a footstool; head encircled by a nimbus; her left arm supports a cornucopia; her right, extended, holds a fillet. Mon. 161. - PΔOKPO. Pl. XIV. figs. 19, 20.

Of these, fig. 19 is from the collection of Colonel Miles; the other belongs to myself, and was found at Hoogly in Bengal. They are inserted here as belonging to the same currency as the following copper coins, of which great numbers have been found at Beghram and in its neighbourhood. Two similar coins, but of ruder execution apparently, are delineated by Prinsep, from the Ventura collection, J. As. Soc. B. Nov. 1835, Pl. XXXVIII. figs. 11, 12. On the obverse of these is read PAO NANA PAO KOPANO.

COPPER.

2. Standing figure; imperfect. R. Female figure, on a high-backed chair, with fillet and cornucopia. APΔOXPO. Pl. XIV. figs. 21, 22.

[1] J. As. Soc. B. vol. v. p. 630.

3. Small. Part of a standing figure. R. Part of the female seated figure of the preceding.

Great numbers of these, and especially of the latter, have been sent home. Few have the figure and legend so entire as those of the larger two, which are delineated; but the disposition of the lower part of the garment, as in fig. 22, leaves no doubt of their identity. They are considered by Prinsep as imitations of what he terms his fourth series, J. As. Soc. B. Oct. 1836, p. 655, Pl. XXXIX. figs. 16-18; but they are probably original coins of a late period of the Indo-Scythian, and contemporary, at least, with the earliest of the Hindu or Gupta coins.

SECTION V.—COINS OF SASSANIAN KINGS.

Whatever may be the origin of the large concavo-convex and analogous coins, we have ample evidence of the influence, and possibly of the authority, of Sassanian princes in the presence of their coins in Afghanistan. We do not however meet with any of those which seem to be the very earliest,—those of the transition period between the change of alphabet, and of which a few found in Persia only are described below. They appear to be novelties in this branch of numismatic research, but there can be little room to doubt their appropriation. The costume of the persons on the obverse accords generally with that of the early Sassanian kings, and the fire-altar on the reverse is a further evidence of their having been issued by princes under whom the worship of the elements had revived in Persia. It is singular that these coins should have been obtained in Persia only; for they certainly present a mixture of the characters we have termed Arianian with those usually denominated Pehlevi. The inscription is evidently intended to be the same as the first two described below, and that published by Mr. Millingen; and whilst it seems to begin with the Pehlevi *a* and *ch*, it ends with letters with which we are familiar, as [illegible] Pala - - - paratisa, or something of the kind. That coins with such letters should have circulated in Persia proper indicates the use of an alphabet in that country, the existence of which we have never hitherto suspected. The Pehlevi alphabet is, no doubt, of comparatively modern growth.[1]

From Kabul and the neighbourhood, however, Mr. Masson has reaped an abundant harvest of Sassanian coins of various descriptions. We may class the silver coins, as they occur in the collection, under four different heads.

1. Coins of the Sassanian princes prior to the Mohammedan conquests. These are procured in various parts of Afghanistan, and comprise the coins usually attributed to Sapor II., Sapor III., Izdegerd I. or II., Hormizdas III., Firoz, and Kobad.

2. Coins found in the topes, and especially in the large tope at Hidda, (see p. 109). These are in much greater number and variety than the preceding. Many of them, although much oxydized, present with sufficient distinctness the types of the coins assigned to Sapor I., II., and III., to Bahram IV. and V., to Izdegerd I. and II., to Firoz, and Kobad. Amongst these, the coins of Sapor III. and Bahram V. are the most numerous. Along with these are found in considerable numbers the coins of a prince or princes in a costume and of features very different from those of the Sassanian kings in general (Pl. XVI. fig. 18). The bust is clothed either in a very tight dress, or is bare; the ornamented fillet rises from the shoulders, as is the case in the Sassanian coins from Izdegerd I. The head is either bare, or covered with a skull-cap, and in one or two instances with what may be intended for a sort of helmet surmounted by a bull's head, such as appears upon the coins of Hormuz III.[2] Other peculiarities accompany these coins, as noticed below; and it is important to remark, that they have been also found in considerable numbers at Beghram.

3. Coins which, concurrently with portraits of a Sassanian character, present names and titles in Nagari letters. They have double portraits in

[1] Kleuker, in his Remarks on the Zendavesta, as quoted by Milman, affirms that Pehlevi had fallen into disuse under the dynasty of the Sassanians, but the learned still wrote it. This is at variance with the received opinion of the use of both the language and letters upon the coins of all the Sassanian kings, and with the traditions of the translation of various works into Pehlevi in the reign of Nushirvan; Milman's Gibbon, vol. i. p. 335, note.

[2] Médailles des Rois Perses de la Dynastie Sassanienne; by M. Adrien de Longperrier: Pl. IX. fig. 1. There is some reason to question the appropriation, as we shall see hereafter.

the Sassanian style, one of which is identifiable with a similar portrait on the coins of Khosru Parvez. These are not numerous; specimens of one description of them were found in the Tope of Manikyala.

4. Coins which, although not of very certain attribution, are undoubtedly of the later Sassanian kings, and, from their being stamped with Arabic sentences on the margin, date subsequently to the Mohammedan conquest of Persia. These are procured in immense numbers at most of the principal cities of Afghanistan.

There are also in the collection, procured from various quarters, including Beghram, numerous copper coins, of apparently different æras of the Sassanian dynasty.

There is nothing extraordinary in the presence of the coins of the Sassanian princes, whether of an earlier or later date, in a country so contiguous as Afghanistan to the eastern provinces of Persia. There must always have been intimate commercial and political relations between the two, and it is not impossible that occasionally the authority of the Sassanian kings may have extended to Kabul. Oriental historians indeed do not hesitate to include Balkh, Khorasan, Kabul, and even India, amongst the dominions of the Persian monarchs; but it may be doubted if numismatic evidence confirms their assertions, although it agrees with the conclusions which a careful examination of historical probabilities suggests.

We do not find amongst the Sassanian coins of Kabul any of the coins of Ardeshir, the founder of the dynasty; yet both the Byzantine and Oriental historians assert that his empire extended to the Indus and Oxus; and upon their authority Gibbon somewhat unwarrantably observes, that he obtained easy victories over the wild Scythians and effeminate Indians.[1] It is not very likely that he was ever engaged in hostilities with either. The first years of his reign must have been fully occupied in establishing his sway and in reforming the national religion; and four years after his accession a war commenced between Persia and Rome, which was attended with many vicissitudes, in the course of which the flower of the Persian army was destroyed, and which was not terminated at the death of Ardeshir, A. D.

[1] Decline and Fall, vol. i. p. 349.

240. We may safely conclude from these circumstances that the absence of his coins in Kabul is not without meaning, and that the first Sassanian prince held no territory in the vicinity of India.

An interval of some duration elapsed before active hostilities were renewed between Sapor, the successor of Ardeshir, and the Byzantine emperor. It was not until A. D. 260, that Valerian was defeated and taken prisoner by the Persian king; and in this period it may be expected that we should find numismatic traces of the eastern conquests of Sapor. This does not appear to be the case; nor is the want of such evidence incompatible with history. The great object of the first years of the reign of Sapor was the establishment of his authority in Armenia,—an object he effected, after a long and arduous contest, only by the assassination of Khosru, king of Armenia.[1] He next wrested a tract between the Tigris and Euphrates from an Arabian ruler,[2] and then fell upon the Roman provinces. The wars that ensued probably left him little opportunity to prosecute schemes of conquest in a different direction. That he had not subjugated Bactria before this period is evident, as the Bactrians had promised to assist the Romans against Sapor at the time of Valerian's discomfiture.[3] Sapor I. died A. D. 271.

Hormuz, the son of the first Sapor, reigned one year. His son Bahram reigned three years and three months, during which Persia enjoyed perfect tranquillity.[4] We have none of their coins. The next king, Bahram II., excited a general rebellion in Persia by his cruelty; and after his escape from threatened deposal, his kingdom was invaded by Carus the Roman emperor, and saved from entire subjugation only by his death.[5] Then followed the recovery of Armenia from the Persian yoke by Tiridates. It is said of Bahram that he had subdued the Sejistans, one of the most

[1] Gibbon's Decline and Fall, vol. i. p. 457.

[2] Malcolm's Persia, vol. i. p. 96.

[3] "Lorsque Sapor, roi des Perses, eut fait prisonnier l'empereur Valérien, il écrivoit aux Bactriens pour leur en apprendre la nouvelle, mais sa lettre ne leur étant pas parvenue, ils promirent du secours aux Romains;" Mémoire sur l'étendue de l'empire des Parthes: par M. De Sainte Croix, Mém. de l'Académie, tom. l. p. 89.

[4] Malcolm, vol. i. 101.

[5] Gibbon, from Agathias, vol. ii. p. 91.

warlike nations of Upper Asia, and, according to the Rozat-us-safa, he was called Seganshah, King of Seistan, or Sejistan, because he had been governor of that province in the lifetime of his father. This title is also attributed to his son Bahram III.[1] If Seistan, however, was held by either of these princes, the supremacy of Persia was only temporary, as a prince of Sejistan appears as the ally or feudatory of a subsequent Sassanian sovereign, Sapor III. It is said, also, that at the time of the invasion of Carus, the greater part of the forces of Persia were detained on the frontiers of India. They must have been speedily recalled, even if they had ever been in such a position; and it seems improbable, therefore, that under these three princes any permanent accessions to the Sassanian monarchy were effected in the East.

The next princes were equally unlikely, from character and circumstances, to have been conquerors. Bahram III. reigned only four months:[2] his reign was followed by a contest between his sons Hormuz and Narsi. Of this the Oriental writers take no notice; but in the course of it, according to Western authorities, Hormuz called to his aid the Russians, the Sakas, and the Gelli.[3] In the Sakas we have by this time, as above observed, (p. 302,) the people of Sakastene or Sejistan; and whether they be meant, or any of the other Saka tribes who had spread over Khorasan, it is clear that the arms of Persia had not been carried with any success far from the provinces of Kerman and Fars. Narsi, having prevailed over his brother and his barbaric allies, directed his principal efforts to the recovery of Armenia: his policy provoked a war with Rome, the consequence of which was the humiliation and dismemberment of the Persian kingdom, by the cession of five provinces east of the Tigris to Diocletian and Galerius.[4] The power of the Sassanian princes must have been too much enfeebled by their losses to admit of their becoming formidable to their neighbours; and the reign of Hormuz II., the son of Narsi, was distinguished by no remarkable event.[5] These reigns

[1] De Sacy's translation from Mirkhond, in his Mémoires sur diverses Antiquités de la Perse, p. 299.

[2] Malcolm, vol. i. p. 103.

[3] Ipsos Persas ipsumque regem, ascitis Saccis et Russis et Gellis; Panegyr. Veter., cited by Gibbon, vol. ii. p. 139.

[4] Gibbon, vol. ii. p. 152.

[5] Malcolm, vol. i. p. 105. He married a daughter of the King of Kabul; Rozat-us-safa.

bring us to A.D. 310, up to which date we have no reason to expect any proofs of Persian domination in Ariana; and the negative evidence afforded by the absence of early Sassanian coins is in harmony with the inference authorized by history.

The second Sapor was acknowledged as king before he was born:[1] the consequence was a long minority, during which Persia was distracted by external and internal agitation. As soon as Sapor attained manhood, he retaliated first upon Thair, king of Arabia, and then upon the Romans. The war with the latter was long continued. Between A.D. 338 and 350, Nisibis was thrice besieged; and on the last occasion, the Persian monarch was called away to defend his eastern frontiers against an invasion of the Massagetæ; he therefore made a truce with Rome, and was occupied for nine years by a Scythian war.[2] According to the Greek writers, the site of the war was on the banks of the Oxus; but we have already seen that Getic tribes were established considerably to the south of the Oxus much earlier than the middle of the fourth century. It is possible that at this period the arms of Sapor II. may have been attended with some success in Ariana; but he appears to have converted his enemies into allies, or possibly have been contented with their nominal submission, rather than to have accomplished their actual subjugation. Upon the renewal of the war with Rome, Sapor was assisted at the capture of Amida by the Albanians, Chionians, Vartæ, and Segestans, under their own princes.[3] The first people need no further specification. In the Chionites we may have the Hiung-nu or the Huns: their king is named by the Byzantine writers Grumbates. The Vartæ are unknown: but the Segestans are the Sakas, or people of Sakastene, Sejistan, or Seistan: they are described as the bravest soldiers in the army of Sapor, and as covering their front with a line of Indian elephants. Thus, as Gibbon remarks, they appear as an independent nation, the ally of Persia, fourscore years after the boasted victory of Bahram. Consistently with these historical facts, we do not find the coins of the second Sapor in any number in Afghanistan, although there are a few.

[1] Malcolm, vol. i. p. 106.

[2] Gibbon, vol. iii. p. 142.

[3] Gibbon, vol. iii. p. 202, and note by Milman.

The invasion of Persia by Julian, and the events which followed both in Mesopotamia and Armenia, must have sufficiently engaged the attention of Sapor; but they were no sooner disposed of, than he was engaged in hostilities with Bactria.[1] He gained a victory over the Bactrians after having been in imminent danger of defeat and capture. As this occurred near the close of his glorious life and reign, he could not have reaped much advantage from his success: he died A.D. 380.

The succession of Ardeshir, the next king to Sapor, is differently described by the Oriental writers, according to most of whom he was the brother of his predecessor,—a fact incompatible with the story that Sapor was the posthumous and only son of Hormuz. We may infer that his title was defective, and that his short reign of four years, which ended in his deposal, was a period of civil commotion. Sapor III., the son of Sapor II., succeeded him. We have no particulars of his reign: he was entitled 'the warlike;' and as he preserved the peace with Rome, he must have indulged his martial propensities at the expense of his neighbours in the East. It is not improbable that he effected some conquests in that direction, and accomplished the annexation of Khorasan to Persia. His coins are found in the Hidda Tope in considerable proportion. He reigned from A.D. 384 to A.D. 389.

Varahran or Bahram IV., another son of Sapor II., who succeeded Sapor III., also furnishes a large proportion of the Sassanian coins of the Hidda Tope. History is silent as to his actions, beyond his foundation of the city of Kerman-shah, which is confirmed by the sculptured figures of himself and his father on the rocks at Tak-i-Bostan, in the neighbourhood of that city, with inscriptions in Pehlevi[2] bearing their names. He reigned ten years, and he may have extended the conquests to the east commenced by his predecessor.

Of the reign of Izdegerd, the successor of Bahram IV., no particulars

[1] Gibbon says Carmania; vol. iv. p. 300. But Ste. Martin, Histoire du Bas-Empire par Le Beau, with additions, &c., vol. iii. p. 387, has altered this to Bactria, and furnished some particulars of the war from Armenian writers. We can scarcely, however, admit with them that a branch of the Arsacidan dynasty was then reigning at Balkh, as the country had been previously occupied by the Sakas and the Getes.

[2] Translated by Silvestre de Sacy; Mémoires, &c., p. 211. See also Malcolm's Persia, vol. i. p. 113.

are recorded. According to the Oriental writers, he was a cruel and wicked tyrant; according to the Byzantine historians, a model of wisdom and virtue.[1] Neither character would become a conqueror. Bahram V., or Bahram Gor, is a prince whose fame is celebrated by the Oriental writers, although they record few circumstances of his reign of a historical character. He ascended the throne A. D. 420, and reigned twenty years. He received from his predecessor the legacy of a war with Theodosius, Emperor of Constantinople; but it was of short duration, and was followed by a treaty, of which the essential conditions were respected near fourscore years by the successors of Constantine and Artaxerxes.[2]

The establishment of peace between Persia and Rome could not have been attended with any permanent victories in the East; for Bahram was soon afterwards under the necessity of defending his kingdom against a more formidable enemy. It was in his reign that the people called White Huns, Euthalites, or Nephthalites,[3] made their appearance on the south of the Oxus, and advanced to Merv, or, according to some accounts, to Rei. Bahram fled into Armenia, but afterwards returned, and surprised the camp of the Huns, defeated them, slew their king, and chased them beyond the Oxus; on the banks of which he erected a column, to mark the boundary of his dominions. As De Guignes observes, these transactions, although from the succinct manner in which they are narrated

[1] Malcolm, vol. i. p. 114.

[2] Gibbon, vol. v. p. 408.

[3] Called also Atelites, Abtelites, Pidarites, and Haiatelites. Procopius writes the name Ἐφθαλῖται. According to De Guignes (Hist. des Huns, vol. ii. p. 326), their name was properly Te-le or Tie-le, to which, from their inhabiting the banks of the Oxus, the syllable Ab, 'water,' was prefixed. In the first part of the name Haia-telites we have an approach to the Hai-hajas of the Hindus; Vishnu Purana, p. 418, note 20. The Armenians call them Hephthal. They are commonly confounded under the denomination of Indo-Scythi with their predecessors the Sakas and Yu-chi; as is done by Gibbon when he observes, that the Indo-Scythæ reigned upon the confines of India from the time of Augustus to that of Justin the elder, A. D. 530. Up to the beginning of the fifth century at least, however, races different from the White Huns occupied Afghanistan and Sindh: at that time they were seated chiefly in Maweran-nahr and Khwarizm, and their capital, Gorgo, was probably identical with Korkenj; Ste. Martin, Additions to Le Beau, vol. iv. p. 254. According to the author of the Rozat-us-safa, the invaders of Persia were Turks; but this, as Malcolm observes, is a mistake; History of Persia, vol. i. p. 126.

by the Oriental writers they appear to have occurred in rapid succession, yet must have occupied a considerable time. It is not impossible that the tale of Bahram's visit to India *incognito*, and his marriage with the daughter of the Raja of Kanoj, may be founded either on a flight to that country when the Huns threatened to overrun Persia, or at least in negociations for an alliance with both the Yu-chi princes of Kabul, and the Rajputs of Central India, against a common enemy. The coins of Bahram Gor are found in some numbers in the Hidda Tope.

Izdegerd II., the son of Bahram V., succeeded him, and reigned eighteen years. He is entitled Sipah-dost, 'the soldier's friend,' and he is said to have displayed eminent military talents. As the peace with Rome was not seriously interrupted during his reign, the end of which brings us to A. D. 457, he must have acquired his cognomen and character in some other quarter, and this must have been Khorasan. History has not preserved any account of his wars against the Hephthalites; but as they continued to press upon his frontiers, it is most likely that he was engaged in frequent hostilities with them. That he engaged in schemes of conquest towards the Indus is incompatible with the progress of his Hun neighbours; and we have no proof of such attempts in his coins, of which a few only are met with in Afghanistan.

Hormuz III., the second and favourite son of Izdegerd, succeeded; but, after a short reign of one year, was deposed and put to death by his elder brother Firoz. It is therefore quite impossible that the coins noticed below (Pl. XVI. fig. 18, &c.) as being found in such considerable numbers at Hidda and at Beghram, should have been issued by him, as he could not have established any authority in Kabul. At the same time it is not unlikely that they were coins of or about this period.

The prince who asserted his birthright to the Persian crown, Firoz, reigned, according to the best authorities, thirty years, from A.D. 458 to A.D. 488.[1] He was of a warlike character, and thence termed Mardána,

[1] Malcolm, after the Oriental historians, says twenty-six or twenty-one years, and places his death in A. D. 484. According to some authorities he reigned but eleven. Gibbon places his death in A. D. 488; De Guignes, from Abu-l-faraj, A. D. 483; M. De Longperrier has A. D. 488. There are some difficulties in the chronology of this period; Hist. des Huns.

the manly or valiant.' He maintained amicable relations with Rome, but was engaged in perpetual hostilities with the Hephthalites. In his last campaign he was accompanied by Eusebius, the ambassador of the Emperor Zeno, who has described the manner in which Firoz was defeated and slain. It is said that the King of the Huns forbore to follow up his victory, but imposed a tribute on Persia. We can scarcely believe in such moderation, and it seems not unlikely that the Hephthalite king annexed the eastern districts of Khorasan and Kabul to his territories; and it is to this race that we must ascribe the coins in question. Their intercourse with the Persians, both in peace and war, had probably familiarized them with the religion and costume of the latter, and induced them to adopt similar types for their coins. The rude execution of these coins denotes a barbaric workmanship; but that they were not long subsequent to the end of the fifth century is rendered probable by their being found in the Hidda Tope with coins of the Greek emperors, dating from A.D. 407 to A.D. 474 (see p. 43). As these coins have not been found in Persia, they are not properly Persian coins; and as at the period conjectured it is not likely that any Persian prince held sway in Afghanistan, they must have been struck by either an Indian or a Scythic king. They are very unlike the coins of the Indo-Scythic princes; and if we refer them to Scythians, we must assign them to some new race, which at the end of the fifth century was that of the Hephthalites. If the portraits are those of the Hun princes, they were a better-looking race than the Huns of the western world; but the portraits may have been imitations of those on the Sassanian coins. If not the coins of this race, we must look for an Indian origin; and the traditions preserved by Firdusi are not incompatible with such a source, as the vice-royalty, or perhaps the sovereignty, of Khorasan and Kabul appears to have been held at the period of the death of Firoz, and for some time afterwards, by a chief whose name has a very Indian aspect. Firdusi calls him Suf-rai, the Marz-ban or governor of the frontier provinces of Kabulistan, Zabulistan, Bost, and Ghiznin.[1] Mirkhond terms him Sukhra, governor of Sejistan. Both these names are very like the common Indian appellations of Subh-rai

[1] Shah Nama, Calcutta edition, vol. iv. p. 1176.

or Subh-rao, or Sukh-rai, Sukh-rao; and the provinces of which this chief is styled the governor may have had during the reign of Firoz an Indian prince, who, in mark of fealty to Persia, adopted its devices on his coins. It is difficult, however, to believe that an Indian should have performed the part ascribed to him in the events which followed the death of Firoz, should have been guardian of Persia during the reign of Palash for five years, and should have held the same office under Kobad until assassinated by order of that prince. It seems more likely, therefore, that after the reign of Bahram Gor the Hephthalites occupied Kabul, and coined the rude imitation of Sassanian money which is still found there.

Kobad, the Kavades of the Byzantines, reigned for forty-three years. Although of this duration, his reign was full of trouble. After his removal of Suf-rai, his patronage of the religion of Mazdak provoked an insurrection, which compelled him to fly to the king of the Hephthalites for succour. He returned with an army of Huns, by the aid of which he recovered his throne, and in a war which ensued with Rome was enabled, by the valour of his barbarian allies, to carry fire and sword into Mesopotamia and Syria.[1] This war was concluded about A.D. 505. How Kobad was employed during the remaining twenty-six years of his reign does not appear. Part of his time and of his resources was expended on the construction of new cities in Persia, from which it may be inferred that the reign was prosperous; and it is very possible that the friendly relations he had established with the Hephthalites permitted them to extend themselves along the Indus without molestation.

Upon the death of Kobad in A.D. 531, he was succeeded by the celebrated Sassanian sovereign, Khosru Nushirvan the Just. That he was a monarch of great political power is undoubted: the Roman empire had repeated proofs of it.[2] According to the Oriental writers, he divided his kingdom into four great governments, of which the easternmost was composed of Khorasan, Seistan, and Kerman.[3] How far the limits of Khorasan extended is not stated, but they may have ultimately reached to the Oxus,

[1] Gibbon, vol. vii. p. 141.

[2] Ibid. pp. 318, 340.

[3] Malcolm, vol. i. p. 139.

as the power of the White Huns of Turkestan was annihilated in his reign, chiefly by the advancing progress of the oriental Turks.[1]

The historian of Persia affirms, that at one period of the reign of Nushirvan his mandates were obeyed from the Euphrates to the Indus; and, according to the Oriental historians, he subdued Kabulistan and a part of Hindustan.[2] Numismatic data do not confirm his having reigned at Kabul, as few or none of his coins are found there; and the historical accounts of his intercourse with India do not authorize the opinion that upon the upper course of the Indus it was one of aggression and conquest.[3]

In the beginning of the reign of Hormuz IV., A. D. 579, the Turks advanced in formidable force towards Persia, and occupied Badgis and Herat. They were defeated by the general of Hormuz, Bahram, and obliged to fall back; but these events were succeeded by civil commotions, in which Hormuz was killed. Bahram for a short period was king, but was deposed and put to death by Khosru Parvez, the son of Hormuz, with the assistance of the Romans. Whatever pretensions, therefore, Nushirvan may have had to kingly power on the confines of India, they were evidently not maintained by his successor.

Khosru Parvez, the last Persian prince of any celebrity, ascended the throne of Persia A. D. 591, and reigned thirty-seven years. He is described in the first years of his reign, as a brave and active, but subsequently as a luxurious and indolent prince, who nevertheless by his generals waged war against the Roman empire with extraordinary success; conquering Asia Minor, Syria, and Egypt; capturing Alexandria; and menacing for many years together Constantinople.[4] These successes were followed by proportionate reverses, and in the last six years of his reign Heraclius retaliated upon Persia the miseries which Khosru had inflicted upon the Roman empire. It is not likely that the Persian king would have been able to

[1] Malcolm, vol. i. p. 126. [2] Mirkhond, translated by De Sacy; Mémoires, p. 372.

[3] Even on the lower Indus, if native accounts are to be trusted, Nushirvan's victories were productive of no durable conquest. Sindh, although invaded by a Persian army in his reign, continued to be governed by its own Rajas. Pottinger's Beloochistan, p. 289.

[4] Gibbon, vol. vii. Malcolm, vol. i. p. 156.

recover that authority in Kabul which Hormuz had lost, although the coins seem to intimate that the princes now ruling there acknowledged some dependence upon Persia. It is to this period probably that we may refer the two descriptions of coins which bear upon one face, either in the area or the margin, inscriptions in Nagari letters, and upon the other face a head, which those numismatists who have made the Sassanian coins the object of their special attention recognise upon the coins of Khosru Parvez. If the appropriation is correct, the coins must be either of the time of Khosru or of his immediate successors; for, as some of these coins have been found in topes, they cannot have been current very long subsequent to the sixth century: and we may therefore presume that in the course of his reign, Indian princes, taking advantage of the reduction of the power of the Hephthalites by the Turks on the one hand, and the Sassanians on the other, had recovered possession of Kabul. They may have been indebted to the Persians for aid, and, in acknowledgment of such succour, adopted the Sassanian costume upon the coins, as far as the portraiture of the king extended, but dropping the emblems of the Magian religion. This is a reason, by the way, for not ascribing these coins to Turk princes, as they had first adopted the worship of fire, and afterwards deserted it for that of Buddha or Fo.[1] That Indian princes reigned at Kabul for some time after the Mohammedans had penetrated there, we know from their historians; and it is not inconsistent with this fact to suppose that they had re-acquired the sovereignty at the end of the sixth or commencement of the seventh century.

The short period that intervened between the death of Khosru Parvez and the conquest of Persia by the Mohammedans, was one of national distraction. In four years, from A.D. 628 to A.D. 632, seven princes ascended the throne, of whose coins our fourth class, no doubt, contains specimens. It becomes very difficult, however, at this period to decypher the Pehlevi legends, and much uncertainty prevails as to the appropriation of the individual coins. There can be no question also that in various instances the coins descend to a date posterior even to the last Sassanian king of Persia, Izdegerd III., as they bear upon the margin short sentences in Arabic

[1] De Guignes, vol. ii. p. 375.

characters, texts of the Mohammedan religion, as بسم الله Bism-Allah, 'in the name of God,' and لااله الا الله La Allah ala Allah, 'there is no God but God,' and لله الحمد Lillah-al-hamdo, 'praise be to God,' and others. The period of these coins has been shown by Dr. Fraehn [1] and M. de Sacy to have been that of the Khalif Omar, who, according to Makrizi, struck silver coins of the same type and form of those of the Khosrus of Persia, and upon some of them added his own name or texts from the Koran. Othman and Moawiạ did the same, and the latter struck also gold coins on which he was represented girt with a sword. There can be no reason to doubt that we have in these coins some of the pieces which Makrizi alludes to, and which were in all probability the work of the same artists who had been employed by the Sassanian kings, with the advantage of a better organised state of government, and means and time to bestow more care upon their work than under their latest native princes.[2] It seems much more probable that these are coins of the Mohammedan rule in Persia, than that they are the coins of the descendants of Izdegerd, who, whether they were settled for some time in Ghilan and Dilem, or in Sejistan, Zabulistan, and Kabul, were not likely to have had much money to coin, nor much time to coin it in, as the Arabs soon disturbed their dream of independence.[3] The great number and the perfect condition of these coins concur with their Arabic legends to render it most probable that they were the issues of the Khalifs.

It has been a question whether the legends within the area on either side of the head be not Arabic also; and Dr. Fraehn reads them الحجاج بن يوسف Al Hejaj bin Yusef, being the money of Hejaj, governor of Irak, who, Makrizi states, struck coins in his own name with the formula 'praise to God.' Marsden admits it possible that the sort of cypher observable behind the head may be intended for Hejaj, but cannot persuade himself that those

[1] Die Chosroen Münzen der früheren Arabischen Khalifen; von Dr. Fraehn zu St. Petersburgh. Des Monnaies des Khalifs avant l'an 75 de l'Hégire. De Sacy. Also Marsden, vol. ii. p. 445.

[2] J. Asiatique, vol. ii. p. 262. Mémoires sur l'Arménie, vol. ii. p. 18.

[3] Firoz, the son of Izdegerd, reigned, it is said, in Tokharestan, but he was expelled by the Mohammedans A. D. 661, or twenty-five years only after the battle of Kadesia; Ste. Martin, Mémoires, &c., tom. ii. p. 18, note 1.

of the second short line are intended for Beni Yusef. He remarks also, that the same characters occur on numerous specimens which contain no traces of the name of Hejaj.[1] They occur also, it may be added, on the reverses without the cypher; and there is also an inscription in front of the head upon the obverse, which presents considerable variety. At the same time, in many instances, the characters have an appearance very like Arabic, and it is possible that they were latterly intended for them, but were executed by Persian artists imperfectly acquainted with the Arabic characters.

The copper Sassanian coins sent from Afghanistan are evidently of two classes; in one the altar is simple, in the other it has supporters; and the figures of the large coin, which is unique, are remarkable for their entirely Indian costume. Both classes seem to be of local origin, from the characters which they represent, and which in the small coins have a great appearance of being intended for Rao Nana Rao, although they may possibly have a different value. This is especially the case in one instance, where upon the obverse a head is seen amongst the flames, and which should be, therefore, a Sassanian coin. These copper coins afford more reason than the silver to suspect at different periods the predominance of Sassanian rule in Afghanistan. The symbolical figures upon some of them are of value, as connecting them with other coins, as in Pl. XVII. fig. 19, where we have the emblem that occurs upon the coins of Gondophares (Pl. V. fig. 16). We may, at least, infer from it that the dates of the two coins were not very far apart.

SASSANIAN COINS.

SILVER.

1. Drachm. Head of king, with ornamented cap and fillet, to the left; long hair and beard; a crescent on the side of the cap; the bust dressed. R. A fire-altar on stand, a priest on the right. Mixed Arianian characters. Pl. XV. fig. 2.

2. Hemidrachm. Head of king, to the left, with ornamented crown and fillet; bushy hair and beard. R. Fire-altar and worshipper, on the right. Characters as in the last. Pl. XV. fig. 3.

[1] Numismata Orientalia, vol. ii. p. 446.

3. Diobolus. Head of king, to the left, with crown, bushy hair, and beard. R. King or priest, with star and crescent in front of him. Rude characters. Pl. XV. fig. 4.

4. Diobolus. Head of king, with crown, to the left. R. King, to the left, with star and crescent. Pl. XV. fig. 5.

These coins are in the collection presented by Sir H. Willock to the Museum at the India House. One, corresponding with the first, has been published by Mr. Millingen, from the collection of Mr. Thomas, Sylloge of Unedited Coins, 1837, p. 84. He considers it as a Parthian coin, but the fire-altar indicates its belonging to the Sassanian princes; the head-dress is also more Sassanian than Arsacidan. The legends which these coins present are evidence of an early period of Sassanian history, as they combine the characters of the Bactrian coins with a few apparently Pehlevi; belonging probably to the same period as the older inscriptions at Nakshi Rustam.

5. Large. Head of king, with crenellated crown and globe, fillet, and bushy hair, to the right. Pehlevi legend defective, but apparently 'Shahpuri.' R. A fire-altar; in the midst of the flames a head turned to the right; king and one of the Magi guarding the altar with drawn swords. Pl. XVI. fig. 1.

6. Middle size. Head of king, to the right, with crenellated crown and globe. Pehlevi legend, 'Shahpuri.' R. Fire-altar, with head amidst the flames; figures by the side. Pl. XVI. fig. 2.

Similar coins are given by Visconti, Pl. LI. fig. 8, and Steuart, Pl. IV. figs. 3, 4, as the coins of Sapor II. See also Mionnet, v. p. 696.

7. Large. Head of king, to the right, with flat crown and globe; fillets turned up behind. Legend indistinct. R. Fire-altar, with head amidst the flames, to the right; figures on either side, with swords. Pl. XVI. fig. 3.

See also Steuart, Pl. IV. fig. 7; De Longperrier, Pl. VII. fig. 5; according to whom this is a coin of Sapor III.

8. Small. Head of king, to the right; crenellated crown, crescent, and globe; and a crescent in front of the crown. R. Fire-altar, and guards with spears; two crescents on either side of the flame. Pl. XVI. fig. 4.

The coin has been cut at the edges, so that the inscription has been removed. A similar coin is assigned to Artaxerxes III. by De Longperrier,

Pl. VII. fig. 2; but Steuart ascribes it to Izdegerd I., Pl. V. fig. 1. The legends on the engravings of his coins justify his reading.

9. Large. Head of king, to the right; crenellated crown, crescent, and globe rising above the beading of the margin. Legend imperfect. R. Fire-altar and guards, with spears. Pehlevi letters on the pedestal of the altar. Pl. XVI. fig. 5.

This is a coin of either Izdegerd I. or II.: Longperrier, Pl. VIII. fig. 4; Steuart, Pl. V. fig. 4.

10. Head of king, to the right, with remarkable features; diadem surmounted by the head of a buffalo; collar and cross-band of pearls on the bust, and wings or fillet rising from behind the neck. Characters, (Auh)rimazd. R. Fire-altar and Magi; behind the one on the left, the letter ٦; above the heads of both, crescent and wheels. Pl. XVII. fig. 5.

11. Head of king, to the right, resembling the preceding; the summit of the diadem partly effaced. Characters (A)uhrimazd (?). R. Fire-altar and attendants; above the heads, dotted rings or wheels. Pl. XVII. fig. 7.

These, in costume and types, are the same as the coin ascribed to Hormuz or Hormizdas III.; De Longperrier, Pl. IX. fig. 1. There are several in the Masson collection, procured with others at Kabul. They are generally worn.

12. Large. Head of king, to the right; crenellated crown and globe; crescent in front; a crescent or the letter ᴗ in front of the neck. R. Fire-altar and figures; a star and crescent on either side of the flame. Pl. XVI. fig. 6.

The types of this coin identify it with the coins of either Firoz or Kobad or Kavades; De Longperrier, Pl. X. fig. 1; Steuart, Pl. V. fig. 12.

These coins are from a number obtained by Mr. Masson at Kabul and Beghram.

TOPE COINS.

13. Large. Head of king, to the right. Pehlevi legend. R. Fire-altar; two royal persons with spears, turning their backs to the altar. Pl. XVI. fig. 7.

Although much worn, this coin is evidently the same as the coins of Sapor I.; figured, De Longperrier, Pl. III. fig. 2; Steuart, Pl. II. fig. 8. This, and the following, to No. 25 inclusive, are of great interest, being taken from the two hundred Sassanian coins found in the large Tope at Hidda. See p. 108.

14. Large. Head of king, to the right, with peculiar head-dress; an altar in front. Characters, like Greek or Indian: behind the head, part of a symbol, No. 163, apparently the same as on the reverse of a copper coin, (Pl. XVII. fig. 20.) R. A fire-altar, with head amongst the flames (?). Pl. XVI. fig. 8.

This is also from Hidda. I have not met with any like it in the authorities consulted.

15, 16. Head of king, to the right, with crenellated crown and globe; crescent behind the head. Mon. 163 in front. Legend in peculiar characters, differing mostly from Pehlevi. R. Fire-altar and attendants; head amongst the flames. Pl. XVI. figs. 9, 10.

The presence of the head on the reverse renders it likely that these belong to Sapor II. and III.; but none exactly like them are delineated elsewhere. The monogram or altar on the obverse is the same as that referred to in the preceding number. From Hidda Tope.

17. Large. Head of king, to the right, with a crown terminating behind in wings. Pehlevi legend, Mazdiesn - - - - - - rahran. R. Fire-altar and attendants; head amongst the flames. Pl. XVI. fig. 11.

The peculiar winged crown and the head amongst the flames identify this with the coins of Varahran IV.; De Longperrier, Pl. VIII. fig. 1; Steuart, Pl. IV. fig. 9. It is from Hidda.

18, 19. Head of king, to the right, with cap like the preceding. Pehlevi legend. R. Fire-altar and attendants. Pl. XVI. figs. 12, 13.

Though agreeing in the head-dress of the king, the reverse differs in omitting the head on the altar. Similar coins are ascribed by Steuart to Varahran V. or Behram Gor. Pl. V. fig. 2. From Hidda.

20, 21. Large. Head of king, to the right, with crenellated crown and ornamented crescent; fillets turning up. Legend on the second distinct: Mazdiesn beh - - - Izdegerd mal - (kan). R. Fire-altar and attendants. Pl. XVI. figs. 14, 15.

Coins of Izdegerd II.; Steuart, Pl. V. figs. 4, 5.

22. Head of king, to the right, with crown, crescent, and globe; crescent

in front. R. Fire-altar and priests, with crescent and star on each side of the flame. Pl. XVI. figs. 16, 17.

There are some on which the legend agrees better with that on the coins of Kobad or Kavades; De Longperrier, Pl. IX. figs. 2, 3, and Pl. X. figs. 1, 2; also Steuart, Pl. V. figs. 8-13.

23. Large. Head of king (?), to the right, with either a small cap or the hair in a tuft; a necklace and ear-rings, and the fillet rising apparently from the collar; the breast bare; a wreath (?) under the bust. Mon. behind the head, 163, (?). R. Slightly hollowed, and device effaced. Pl. XVI. fig. 18.

24. Large. Head of king (?), to the right; costume as before, but tufts of feathers (?) springing from the shoulders; a few characters on the margin. R. Fire-altar and attendants, and head amongst the flames, but very indistinct. Pl. XVI. fig. 19.

25. Head of king, to the left; costume as in No. 19, but a trident in front. Characters, intended for Pehlevi perhaps, on either side of the head. R. Fire-altar and attendants. Pl. XVI. fig. 20.

A number of these coins were found in the great Tope of Hidda, and great numbers of them are met with at Beghram. They are of base metal and rude fabric. They are slightly concave on the reverse, the impression of which is always very indistinct. The appearance of the bust is almost feminine, but the features are male. They are those of an Indian rather than of a Persian. There is, however, a decided similarity of style between these busts and that of Hormizdas III.; and in some of them the buffalo's head and the diadem are indistinctly visible. Supplemental Plate, fig. 21.

Mr. Masson, indeed, states that these busts have several bulls' or buffalos' heads round them, but in general one only surmounts the cap; the former are not visible in those sent home, nor in Mr. Masson's own delineation of them; J. As. Soc. B. January, 1836, Pl. III. figs. 2-6, Sassanian coins, 1-6; ibid., April, 1837; Memoir on Indo-Sassanian coins, by Prinsep, p. 288, Pl. XIV. figs. 3, 4, 5.

INDO-SASSANIAN COINS.

26. Large. Head of king, to the right; ornamented crown, with upright

crest and wings. Inscription in front of the head, in Nagari letters of an unusual form, श्री बहमन Sri Bahmana; and, behind, वसुदेव. The latter word is unequivocal, but the two last letters of Bahmana are doubtful. Margin covered with characters undecyphered. R. Fire-altar and Magi; crescent and star above their heads; characters on either side; and the margin covered with others similar to those of the last. Pl. XVII. fig. 8.

One of two coins in the Masson collection; engraved by Prinsep, J. As. Soc. B. April, 1837, Pl. XIV. fig. 6. A similar coin, from Kabul, was previously described and figured by Prinsep, J. As. Soc. B. Sept. 1834, p. 441, Pl. XXV. fig. 6.

27. Large. Full face of king, with crown and upright crest. An inscription on each side of the head, also round the margin. R. A head, with full face, cap enclosed with flame. Inscription on the right in Pehlevi, on the left in Nagari, श्री वसुदेव Sri Vasudeva. Characters on the margin; Pehlevi (?). Pl. XVII. fig. 9.

One of four coins in the collection; three of them have been punched in the same spot on the left of the head of the obverse, and apparently with characters, but they are illegible. The portraits are precisely those on the coins of Khosru Parvez; De Longperrier, Pl. XI. fig. 3. And the name Khosru may be conjectured in the legend of the obverse in front of the face. His coin is without Nagari, and without marginal characters.

28. Head of king, to the right; flame rising from his head. In front, in Nagari letters, Sri-mahe-(ndra ?). R. Fire-altar and attendants, but worn. Pl. XVII. fig. 11.

29. Head of king, as before, with a banner, in front; and Nagari inscription, Sri-mahe-(ndra ?). Pehlevi letters behind the head (?). R. Obliterated. Supplemental Plate, fig. 20.

30. Head of king, to the front, with very peculiar crown: before him, characters uncertain. Round the margin a Nagari inscription. R. Same head as No. 27. Pehlevi inscription on either side. Supplemental Plate, fig. 22.

From one of two coins in the Masson collection. Two of the same description were obtained by General Ventura from the great Tope at Manikyala; J. As. Soc. B. July, 1834, Pl. XXI. figs. 10, 11; ibid., Sept. 1834, p. 438; and three others were sent to Calcutta by Sir A. Burnes for Mr. Prinsep's examination, who has given a detailed account and accurate delineation of them in the Journal of May, 1838. Those coins, and several more of the same kind, have since been sent home, but nothing can be added to Mr. Prinsep's description, although it may be doubted if his reading of the inscription be entirely correct. The characters of both kinds appear to be distinct, but it is difficult to offer any interpretation of them throughout. The Nagari legend runs apparently Sri Hinivira Rajadhiraja (?) Parameswara (?) Sri cha Hinivira deva janita. Prinsep has Sri Hitivira Airana cha parameswaru Sri vahitigan deva janita. The middle portion is very doubtful. In the Pehlevi the inscription on the right may be read, as the characters are usually explained, Mazdiesn beh; and they are followed by a group of letters which M. De Longperrier conjectures to represent Sarbaraz; Médailles Sassaniennes, p. 81. On the left they seem to express Artachhatr, or Artaxerxes, but whether these readings are correct must be left to further examination. A considerable number of small Indo-Sassanian coins, peculiar apparently to India, and bearing imperfect legends in Nagari letters, are also described by Mr. Prinsep in the Bengal Journal, April, 1837, Pl. XIV. XV. They are very rude, and afford no clue to the Persian princes whose effigies they may be supposed to bear.

LATER SASSANIAN COINS.

31. Large. Head, to the right, with flat coronet, surmounted by an upright crest with wings; dress richly ornamented; characters effaced. On the outer margin, on three sides, a crescent and star. R. Fire-altar, of a peculiar form; a star and crescent on each side of the flame; Magi attending; stars and crescents on the outer rim. Characters doubtful. Pl. XVII. fig. 1.

The feminine appearance of the face, the absence of beard, and the large eye, as well as the style of the coin, which is that of a declining age, render it possible that this may be a coin of one of the two princesses, Purandokht or her sister Azermi-dokht, who reigned for a short time in Persia not long before the Mohammedan conquest, or in A. D. 630, 631.

32. Large. Head of king, to the right, with crown and upright crest, with wings terminating in a crescent and star; star in front of the helmet. Characters both before and behind the head, in two rows; a double border

of pearls, forming an inner margin; on the outer rim, three stars and crescents, and characters like Kufic بسم الله and الحمد (?) in another. R. Fire-altar, and Magi with horns (?), leaning on sticks or staves, to the front; moon and crescent on each side of the flame. Characters doubtful. Inner margin, three rows of pearls; four crescents, with stars, on the outer. Pl. XVII. fig. 2.

33. Large. Head of king, to the right, as in the last. Characters, behind the head, the same; those in front something different. Margin plainly بسم الله R. Fire-altar and Magi, as in the last. Characters on both sides. Pl. XVII. fig. 3.

34. Large. Head of king, to the right, with upright crest; similar in costume and countenance to the two preceding. Inscription, behind the head, same as the two last, that in front different; outer margin بسم الله and another in similar characters لله الحمد (?) R. Fire-altar and Magi, as in the two last. Characters different from the preceding; margin nearly covered with undecypherable letters.

These are from a great number of coins procured at Kabul and in the neighbourhood. They are well-known coins, and have been often described and discussed, as noticed above. Marsden, Numismata, No. DXL.; De Longperrier, Pl. XII. figs. 2, 3, 4; Steuart, Pl. II. figs. 11-14. One was found by General Ventura in the great Tope of Manikyala; J. As. Soc. B. July, 1834, Pl. XXI. fig. 8. Porter has one, Pl. 58. fig. 8, which he attributes to Shahpur II., reading Shahpur Mazdiesn on the obverse; Travels, vol. ii. p. 130. As M. De Longperrier observes, the letter of the word which Porter reads *p*, elsewhere represents *t*. The style of these coins evidences a much more modern date than that of either of the Sapors.

COPPER.

35. Large; thin. Head of king or queen (?), to the right. Characters unknown. R. Fire-altar, with attendants in Indian dress, and by the stand of the altar Indian letters, apparently Sri-mad deva bhadra sri. श्री मद् दे (व) भद्रश्री or श्रु. Pl. XVII. fig. 6.

From Beghram. Some of the Nagari letters are doubtful, and the last word may possibly be Khosru.

36. Large; thin. Head of king, to the right. Pehlevi letters (?). R. Two fire-altars, with Magi; starred circles above their heads, as in the silver coin of the same Plate, fig. 7. Pl. XVII. fig. 10.

37. Small; thick. Head of king, to the right. R. Fire-altar. Characters. Pl. XVII. fig. 12.

38. Small; thick. Head of king, with crenellated crown. Characters, Rao Ma-rao (?). R. Fire-altar. Pl. XVII. figs. 13, 14.

39. Small; thick. Head of king, with crown of different shape. Nano Rao (?) R. Fire-altar, with head amongst the flames. Pl. XVII. fig. 15.

40. Small; thick. Head of king, crown different, and different characters. R. Fire-altar. Pl. XVII. fig. 16.

41. Small; thin. Head of king, to the right, with rayed cap. R. Fire-altar and supporters. Pl. XVII. figs. 17, 18.

42. Small; thick. Head of king, to the right. R. Fire-altar, with monogram, as on the coins of Gondophares. Pl. XVII. fig. 19.

43. Small; thick. Head of king, with crown, to the right. R. Altar (?) of a peculiar shape. Pl. XVII. fig. 20.

44. Small; thick. Head of king. R. Trident between two letters (?). Pl. XVII. fig. 21.

These have been selected, as the most distinct, from a great number found at Beghram.

SECTION VI.—HINDU COINS.

Doubts have been entertained of the existence of a native Indian currency prior to the introduction of the art of coining by the Greeks of Bactria,[1] and certainly there are strong grounds for admitting the probability that the fabrication of money in India originated with them. There are some considerations, however, which militate against it. That the want of a specific denomination of money is not incompatible with a metallic medium of exchange, we know from the practice of the Chinese and the Indo-Chinese nations to the present day, amongst whom certain weights of gold and silver, sometimes bearing a stamped attestation of their standard value, take the place of coined money. This may have been the case

[1] Prinsep; J. As. Soc. B. vol. i. p. 394.

also with the Hindus; and as the different tables, which are given in their law-books, of the several values of gold and silver refer to weight, not to number,[1] it is likely that the currency of the country consisted chiefly, if not exclusively, of lumps of gold and silver not bearing any impression, until the Hindus had learned the usefulness of money from their Bactrian neighbours, and from their foreign commerce, especially with Rome. At the same time it seems likely that they had a sort of stamped coin even before the Greek invasion.

In all parts of India numerous small pieces of silver have been found in the ground, some oblong, some square, some round, and which were, no doubt, once employed as measures of value.[2] They commonly, but not always, bear upon them rude symbols of the sun or moon, a star or nondescript mark, to which it is not easy to assign a definitive import, but the application of which gives to them the character of a coinage. The style of these pieces and the rudeness of their execution are in favour of their ancient date, as it is scarcely probable that after the art of fabricating money had been introduced, the making of such coins would have been continued. They must have preceded also, it may be supposed, the law which inflicts punishment on the falsifier, not only of the standard, but of the fabric and stamp of the coin, as has been noticed above (p. 364, note). Again, it is well known that the chief punishments in the penal code of the Hindus are fines, and it is difficult to reconcile such a penalty with a mere weight of metal. The one hundred, five hundred, and one thousand Panas, which are the several series of mulcts in Manu, might possibly have intended so many pieces, or their equivalent in weight in some other metal; the Pana being either a copper weight or coin of about two hundred grains, which may be considered as that of the native Pice or copper coins. That it was a coin is so understood apparently by the commentator on the text of Yajnawalkya, in which he explains the word Karsha or Pana to denote a fabricated form of copper (támrasya vikára), and a text of Vachaspati is quoted in law-books, which defines a Karsha or Pana to be a stamped coin. That it had come to signify a piece of money there is no doubt, although

[1] They are collected by Colebrooke, As. Res. vol. v.

[2] As. Res. vol. xvii. p. 596, Pl. V.

at what period is open to conjecture. It is not unlikely that Hindu artists were employed by some of the Greek princes. The expression of the old native characters on the coins of Agathokles and Pantaleon is very national, and the accompanying devices are not beyond Indian skill.

1. SAURASHTRAN COINS.

That the Hindus, however, learnt to imitate the fabrication of coined money, is proved by the various kinds now to be noticed, and of which some of the earliest are possibly the coins that are called Saurashtran, from their having been found chiefly within the limits of Surashtra or in Guzerat and Cutch. None of them have been found in Afghanistan, and any detailed notice of them would be here out of place. A few, from a small collection presented to the Royal Asiatic Society by Lieutenant Postans, are delineated in Pl. XV. figs. 12-20. Others, in greater number, have been published in the Royal Asiatic Society's Journal, from Plates engraved for Mr. Steuart; and still more have been drawn and described by Mr. Prinsep, to whom belongs the merit of decyphering the characters on their reverse. These are a modification of the Sanscrit or Nagari alphabet, not of the highest scale of antiquity, and contain the names of a dynasty of princes bearing the family name of Sah, and the title of Raja Kshatrapa, or Raja Maha Kshatrapa.[1] The name Sah, as it occurs in the modern dialects, is apparently a corruption of Sádhu, 'good,' 'excellent.' Kshatrapa admits etymologically of its being explained chief or protector of the Kshatriya, or martial race, and may possibly be the origin of the Persian title Satrap, as Prinsep supposes, although there is some incompatibility in the assignment of the titles Raja and Satrap to the same individual. The names are less questionable than the titles, and Prinsep has made out those of twelve princes, from the coins, and from an inscription found at Junagarh in Guzerat:

1. Rudra Sah I.
2. Aga Dama, his son.
3. Dama Sah.

[1] Prinsep; J. As. Soc. B. Dec. 1835, p. 684; May, 1837, p. 337; and April, 1838, p. 345.

4. Vijaya Sah, his son.
5. Vira Dama, son of Dama.
6. Rudra Sah II., son of Vira.
7. Viswa Sah, son of Vira.
8. Rudra Sah III., son of Rudra II.
9. Atri Dama.
10. Viswa Sah, his son.
11. Swami Rudra Dama.
12. Swami Rudra Sah.

The coins which are described below appear to belong to Viswa Sah, Rudra Sah II., and Rudra Sah, son of Rudra Dama. For the periods at which these princes flourished we have not data on which dependence can be placed. Mr. Prinsep had suggested a principle of decyphering dates upon these coins, which, however, requires to be further investigated.[1] If he is correct, they may have reigned from the beginning of the second to the middle of the fourth century of our æra. In Prinsep's first paper he considers the Sah Rajas to have reigned till the close of the sixth century; but this is founded on the supposition that Sah is the same as Sasí Raja, who, according to Colonel Pottinger, was contemporary with Nushirvan:[2] this identification of name cannot be admitted.

There is some resemblance between the costume of the head and that upon some of the Arsacidan coins, but it is not so striking as Prinsep represents it; the general style is also that of the coins of Kodes (see p. 344), but the difference of the sites in which his coins and the Saurashtran are found, renders it difficult to understand any connexion between them. Nor is it an easy matter to divine from such historical notices as are available any ancient æra in which to locate them. If they were of the period of Parthian rule, upon the lower Indus, they would belong to the first century of the Christian æra; but as the Indo-Scythi were in the same locality, either then or shortly afterwards, it might be expected that their coins would succeed to these Saurashtran coins. This is not the case: the series continues uninterrupted until it merges into coins belonging to a different dynasty, and to a different state of things. The family name of Gupta takes the place of

[1] On Ancient Sanscrit Numerals, J. As. Soc. B. April, 1838, p. 348.

[2] Travels in Beloochistan, p. 386.

Sah, and the title Nandi, a type of Saivaism, is substituted for the Buddhist Chaitya which accompanies the coins of the Sah dynasty. Of the Gupta princes, as we shall have occasion presently to notice, we have authentic traces in the seventh century; the coins of the Sah princes must therefore have been prior to that age.

There is, however, still a difficulty in the way of this appropriation. Inscriptions have been found confirming the traditional accounts of the importance of a city in Guzerat termed Vallabhi or Ballabhi; traces of which still exist at Balbih, to the north-west of Bhaonagar, and considered by Colonel Tod to be the same as the Byzantium of Ptolemy.[1] According to him, the Gehlote Rajputs either founded or became possessed of this city some time after the middle of the second century. The only names of its princes which he particularizes are, Kanaksen, who came into the province from Upper India about A. D. 144; Vijaya, who, four generations afterwards, built several cities; and Siladitya, in whose reign, A. D. 524, Vallabhi was besieged and taken by barbarians;[2] Indo-Scythians, according to Tod: but supposing the event and the date to be accurately recorded, more probably the Hephthalites, or White Huns. In two inscriptions found in the earth at Guzerat, one at Danduka, the other at Bhaonagar, described and translated by Mr. Wathen,[3] we have a series of Vallabhi princes named for eighteen generations. They are,—

1. Senapati (the general) Bhattaraka.
2. Senapati Dhara sena.
3. Maharaja Drona sinha.
4. M. Dhruva sena I.
5. Dharapattah.
6. M. Griha sena.
7. M. Sridhara sena I.
8. Siladitya I.
9. M. Charagriha.
10. M. Sridhara sena II.
11. M. Dhruva sena II.

[1] Annals, &c., of Rajasthan, vol. i. p. 83.
[2] Ibid. p. 216.
[3] J. As. Soc. B. Sept. 1835, p. 487.

12. Sridhara sena III.
13. Siladitya II.
(Two other names obliterated.)
16. M. Charagriha.
17. Siladitya III.
18. Siladitya Musalli IV.

The seventeenth Mr. Wathen considers to be the prince in whose reign Vallabhi was destroyed; and admitting the date of this to have been A. D. 524, then a calculation of seventeen reigns, at an average of twenty years, would bring the first of the race near the period assigned by tradition to the origin of the power of the Vallabhi princes, or the end of the second century. If, however, they were paramount in Guzerat from the second to the sixth century, where flourished the Kshatrapas whose coins are supposed to be of this same period? The same objection will not so strongly apply, however, if the dates of the inscriptions are altered according to the computation rendered necessary by the Chinese evidence adduced by M. Jacquet.[1] He quotes the relation of a religious Buddhist, a native of China, who visited India in the year 632 and following years of our æra, and describes Fa-la-pi or Balabhi as a flourishing city at the time of his journey, a century after it had been destroyed by barbarian invaders according to Colonel Tod's authorities. The king then ruling he names Thu-lu-fo-po-cha, which M. Jacquet considers to be Dhruva-bhatta, the same as the second Dhruva sena of the inscriptions, the eleventh of the series. If this is to be relied upon, the commencement of the Vallabhi princes of the inscription will be brought down ten reigns, or two hundred years prior to the travels of the Chinese in the years succeeding A. D. 632, or to about A. D. 435.[2] This would afford an opening for an anterior race

[1] J. As. Soc. B. Nov. 1836, p. 687.

[2] An inscription found at Kaira by Dr. Burnes confirms the descent of the princes specified in those discovered by Mr. Wathen, furnishes corrections of some of the names, and adds some genealogical particulars. It records a grant made by Dhruva sena III., a son of the first Siladitya, the eighth of Mr. Wathen's list; the princes succeeding in his list belonging to the junior branch which, down to Sridhara III., had usurped the right of the elder: the grant is dated in ancient figures, which are read Samvat, 365. It seems probable that we are to understand the

of Parthian or Scythian origin prior to the Bhattaraka family, as well as for the Gehlote Rajputs by whom Vallabhi was founded, and who preceded the descendants of Bhattaraka Senapati.[1] It leaves us uncertain, however, what we are to do with Kumara Gupta and Skanda Gupta, who must have been contemporary with the Gehlote family. It might be thought possible, indeed, that they did not reign in Guzerat; but the identity of the style of their coins shows that wherever the Sahs had reigned they must have succeeded. Now, as the Gupta kings reigned in Upper Hindustan, very probably at Kanoj, the presence of their coins in Surat with a character of local fitness is something unaccountable. If they ruled in Guzerat or Cutch they must have ruled as paramount sovereigns or conquerors. They could not have been lords paramount of Vallabhi, for that was independent in the period of the Guptas; and whilst the princes of that city reigned over the adjoining provinces, how could princes from the north have also exercised supremacy? There is, however, a curious passage in the extract from the Chinese traveller quoted by M. Jacquet, which may furnish a clue to the difficulty. He expressly states that Dhruvabhatta, king of Fa-lu-pi, was the son-in-law of the king of Kie-nu, Kieu-che, Kanyakubja, or Kanoj. There were relations then of amity and alliance between the kings of Vallabhi and Kanoj in the seventh century; and the

Vallabhi æra in this place, which commenced A. D. 319, and the date of the inscription would then be A. D. 684, a date not irreconcileable with that of the king named by the Chinese, Dhruvabhatta, or Dhruva sena II. In this case, however, we must bring the commencement of this dynasty still lower, for Dhruva sena III., although thirteenth in the succession, is but the ninth in the genealogy, and eight descents prior to 684 could not be much anterior to A. D. 524. That this family, however, was preceded by a different Hindu race at Vallabhi is also proved by inscriptions; J. As. Soc. B. Nov. 1838.

[1] An inscription also found at Kaira by Dr. Burnes is evidence of a different family reigning in Guzerat, in a grant made to Brahmans by Prasanga Rága, son of Vijaya-bhatta, son of Samanta Datta. It is dated in the Samval year 380, which is most probably, in this place, the æra of Vikramaditya, or A. D. 323, a few years after the foundation of Vallabhi pura; J. As. Soc. B. Oct. 1838. We should then have Parthians and Indo-Scythi in Surashtra to the middle or end of the second century; the Buddhist Sah Rajas succeeded and ruled till the beginning of the fourth century. They were displaced by the Rajputs, who may have been dislodged by the White Huns at the end of the fifth, and who, as their power was broken up about that time, gave way to another Rajput race in the beginning of the sixth century.

former may in compliment, if not in necessity, have acknowledged the supremacy of his father-in-law, and struck coins in his name, modelled upon the currency of the province, which was still that of the Sah Rajas. There is another bond of union between them. Notwithstanding the traveller's assertions of the prosperous state of Buddhism in Vallabhi, all the inscriptions show unanswerably that the royal family was devoted to the worship of Mahadeva. The Saurashtran coins of the Gupta kings bear the great type of the Saiva faith, the bull of Siva. It seems possible, then, that the Buddhist Saurashtran coins of the Sah Rajas were the work of a dynasty ruling in Guzerat anterior to the fourth century, and that the Saurashtran Gupta coins were struck by some of the second race of Rajputs, in honour or in deference to their connexions, the Rajas of Kanoj.

There are some rude silver coins usually grouped with the Saurashtran, but which appear to be found more numerously in Malwa. They are commonly known, it appears, by the name of Gadhia pysa, or 'ass-money,' or rather, as Mr. Prinsep observes,[1] the money of Gadhia, a name of Vikramaditya, whose father, Jayanta, one of the Gandharbas or 'heavenly choristers,' is reported to have been cursed by Indra, and transformed into an ass. There are some curious legends, current in the west of India, as Mr. Prinsep has noticed, and which were collected by Colonel Wilford,[2] of this metamorphosis of the ancestor of a Raja of Ujayin, but not of the father of Vikramaditya, the enemy of the Sakas. The legend has probably grown out of the name of a peculiar dynasty, that of the Garddhabins, who, according to the Vishnu Purana,[3] ruled in India contemporaneously with the Yavanas, the Sakas, and Tusharas; that is, in the early ages of the Christian æra. The word Garddabha means 'an ass,' and hence the story in place of that which may have once existed, accounting for the family name.

These Gadhia coins then are the coins of the Garddabha dynasty; they are not so ancient as I have elsewhere conjectured them to be,[4] and this is

[1] J. As. Soc. B. Dec. 1835, p. 687.

[2] As. Res. vol. ix. p. 155.

[3] J. R. As. Soc. vol. iii. p. 384.

[4] Mr. Prinsep, J. As. Soc. B. May, 1837, supposed that I had applied the term to the Saurashtran coins; which, however, was not the case. I had confined it, as he had done before, to the silver coins delineated in the J. As. Soc. B. Dec. 1835, Pl. XLIX. figs. 13, 14, 15, and which

established by the presence of the Sassanian fire-altar of a late date on their reverse, as well as the syllable Sri, and traces of other Sanscrit letters of a date subsequent to the seventh century. It seems possible, however, that these are not properly the Gadhia pysa, but that the name applies to some copper coins, found also in Guzerat, bearing the effigy of an ass. Upon these, Nagari letters of an early period are very legible, but the words, although apparently Sanscrit, do not offer familiar or recognisable combinations.

SAURASHTRAN COINS.

SILVER.

1. Head of prince, to the right, with a low cap and long hair. R. A Chaitya or type of a Buddhist temple, two crescents on the left (?) above it, and a star or sun of dots on the right. Inscription partly defective. (Raja) Kshatrapasa Viswa Sahasa Raja Maha Kshatrapasa Rudra Saha putasa. Pl. XV. fig. 12.

Coins of Viswa Saha are described and figured by Prinsep, J. As. Soc. B. May, 1837, p. 381, Pl. XXIV. fig. 5; April, 1838, Pl. XII. fig. 6.

2. Head, as before, with neck, and the upper part of a garment or collar. Characters indistinct. R. Chaitya, with sun and moon (?), and a wavy line underneath. Legend imperfect. Rudra (?) Sahasa Rajna Maha Kshatrapasa. Pl. XV. fig. 13.

See coins of Rudra Sah; J. R. As. Soc. April, 1838, p. 351, Pl. XII. fig. 1.

3. Head, as in No. 1. Greek letters in front. VC NAC -. R. Chaitya, crescents, and star of rays. Characters indistinct, and apparently corrupt. Pl. XV. fig. 14.

A coin with a similar star is figured by Prinsep, J. As. Soc. B. April,

are marked S. He adds, in his note in the Journal of May, 1837, that the Gadhia paisa are generally of copper. A large collection of all the varieties of Saurashtran coins dug up at Kaira has been recently brought to England by Dr. Burnes, and from him I learn that the natives apply the term Gadhia-money to all these small coins indiscriminately. The greater number are very probably issues of the Garddabha princes, who may have been Buddhists.

1838, Pl. XII. fig. 12. He assigns it to a Rudra Sah, son of Rudra Dama; it was brought from Ujayin; ibid. p. 355.

These three coins are from the collection of Colonel Miles, and were obtained by him in Guzerat.

4. Head of king, to the right. Characters, imperfect, behind the head. R. Chaitya, without crescents and star. Characters indistinct. Pl. XV. fig. 15.

5. Head of king, to the right, imperfect. R. Ox recumbent. Legend indistinct, but containing apparently the name of Kumara Gupta. The coin has been struck with two uneven blows, and the lines are intermixed. Pl. XV. fig. 16.

6. Head of king, to the right. R. Ox recumbent. Legend, Sri (Vikrama) jitya paramaha (?) Raja. Pl. XV. fig. 19.

The presence of the bull in place of the Chaitya is a novelty in this class of coins. A bull standing on the obverse of one of these coins, brought from Ujayin by Lieutenant Conolly, is figured by Prinsep, J. As. Soc. B. p. 356, Pl. XII. fig. 14.

7, 8. Head of king, to the right, with a crescent in front of the cap, and by the side of the other; ONO behind the head of the second. R. Emblem or figure in the centre. Parama bhattaraka (?) Rajadhi raja Sri Kumara Gupta Mahendrasya. Pl. XV. figs. 17, 18.

Coins similar to these are delineated by Prinsep, J. As. Soc. B. April, 1838, Pl. XII. figs. 16, 17. On one of his is the word ONONO. The same occurs on several similar undescribed coins in his cabinet, in some of which NONO is seen in front of the head; he suggests its being intended either for Nana Rao or for Vonones, p. 356.

9. Head of king. R. An ornament like a disintegrated Chaitya. Sri Skanda Gupta krama-(ditya parama bhattaraka). Pl. XV. fig. 20.

The name in the last coin is unusually legible; the rest of the legend is for the greater part indistinct. Prinsep gave several specimens from different parts of Cutch, Kattywar, and Guzerat; he reads the inscription, Parama bhagadata(ma)ha Raja Sri Skanda Gupta (Vi)kramaditya; J. As. Soc. B. April, 1838, p. 356, Pl. XII. figs. 18-21, and Pl. XIX.

The last six coins are from the cabinet of the Royal Asiatic Society, to which they were presented by Lieut. Postans: they were from a number dug up near Somnath.

10, 11. Head, uncouthly delineated, chiefly in dots, but distinguishable, to the right; various marks and dots, some intended, perhaps, for characters, especially for *Sri*, behind the head. R. An altar; the face of the coin covered with dots and lines of no determinable figure. Pl. XV. figs. 21, 22.

These are from the Company's cabinet. They are found numerously both in silver and copper in Guzerat and at Ujayin, where they are known as Gadhia pysa or ass-money, according to Prinsep, J. As. Soc. B. Dec. 1835, p. 687, Pl. XLIX. figs. 13-16.

COPPER.

12, 13. An animal, a horse or ass (?), to the left; a snake (?) above it. R. A man standing, a double trident on his left, a staff on his right. Legend in old Nagari. Vitapasa pagi maharajasa (?). Pl. XV. figs. 24, 25.

These, which are very rude coins, seem to deserve the name of Gadhia pysa, or ass copper money, rather than the preceding silver, and they appear to be the same as the coin of which one side only is given by Mrs. Postans in her account of Cutch, p. 22, and which she terms Gundhurvu pice. A similar coin was delineated by Prinsep, J. As. Soc. B. Dec. 1838, Pl. XXXII. His brother, by whom the Plate was published, for he had then left India never to return, reads the legend, Sarva tapasa patamapasa, p. 1051.

2. BUDDHIST COINS.

A few thick and rudely executed copper coins have been found at Beghram, which, from the devices they present, are undoubtedly the coins of Buddhist princes, but of what period it is impossible to say. Mr. Prinsep has occasionally been inclined to class them with the coins of Agathokles and Pantaleon, from a supposed analogy of form and style. They are both rude lumps of copper, it is true, but they have nothing else in common, and the style of the Greek coins, however barbarous, is very superior to that of these Buddhist coins. They have no legends, and are not numerous. We have seen that coins with Buddhist emblems were issued by Kanerki, and these may be of the same period. There are some other copper coins with the peculiarity of being blank on one face; and others, again, of a different character; but none of these coins present any inscription by which their origin or date may be conjectured. The characteristic device upon all is the same,—a Chaitya, a Buddhist temple surmounted by a crescent, with or without monograms, and symbols probably significant in the Buddha religion, but respecting the import of which we have no authentic information.

As a further illustration of the Buddhist coins, one of the most remarkable of the class is described below, and has been engraved, although no such coins have been yet sent from the west of the Indus. We have upon this a collection of various devices, which are, no doubt, eminently Buddhist, although why they are so we are not apprised. The principal object is a female figure, in front of a stag, the meaning of which does not derive much light from the passage quoted by Mr. Csoma from the Dul-va, that "a man of the religious order may have on his seal or stamp a circle with two deer on the opposite sides, and below, the name of the founder of the Vihára or monastery."[1] On the reverse of this coin we have a Chaitya of three tiers, surmounted by an umbrella; a tree with three ranges of branches rising from a square pedestal divided into compartments: upon the left of the Chaitya is a symbol of good fortune, usually termed Swastika, and below it an emblem of less familiar occurrence; above the Chaitya is an emblem which, it is worthy of observation, corresponds with the monogram on the coins of Kadphises. There are inscriptions on both faces of this coin, the one in Sanscrit letters of an ancient date, but perfectly legible, Maharajasa Ranakanadasa Amoghabhatasa; the other is incomplete and corrupt: whether it may be read, as proposed below, Ranakanadasa, is very doubtful. This combination of elements, however, renders it likely that the Buddhist prince, by whom the coin was issued, may have reigned in India, possibly on the borders of the Punjab, about the time of Kadphises or Kanerki. The data furnished by these coins can only become of value when we shall be able to compare them with those derived from other sources.

[1] J. As. Soc. B. Nov. 1835, p. 625.

BUDDHIST COINS.

SILVER.

1. Round. Stag, to the right, with female figure in front; above the back of the animal a symbol, Mon. No. 164^{a}, and between its horns another (?), No. 164^{b}. Legend, Maharajasa Ranakanadasa (?) Amoghabhatasa. R. A Chaitya surmounted by an umbrella, and Mon. No. 156; on its right a square Mon. No. 165, surmounted by a triple tree; on its left two symbols, No. 166, and the sign familiar to the Hindus by the name of Swastika. See No. 158. Legend  Ranakanadasa (?). Pl. XV. fig. 23.

Several of these coins, varying in size, and sometimes in design, but retaining the stag, being also of copper, have been found in different places. The first was sent from Behut by Captain Cautly, J. As. Soc. B. May, 1834, p. 227, Pl. IX. fig. 1; the next from the Punjab by General Ventura, Nov. 1835, Pl. XXXIV. fig. 16; also one of copper, ibid. Pl. XXXV. fig. 48. Two of copper, with a figure of a man with trident on the reverse, were obtained by Dr. Swiney at Saharunpur, ibid. Sept. 1834, p. 435, Pl. XXV. figs. 4, 5: for others see the same work, Dec. 1838, Pl. XXXII. On some of the latter the Nagari letters are read Amapasaté and Maharajasa, and on the reverse Maharajasa in Arianian letters, .

The coin here engraved was procured by Mr. Thomas at Kunkul, near Haridwar, and presents a more complete inscription than any other yet discovered; it agrees for the most part with the similar silver coins described by Prinsep. Some difference prevails in a few of the letters, and the reading of the inscription is open to correction, but the value of the principal characters admits of no doubt.

2, 3. Square; thick. An elephant, to the right, with Chaitya topped by a crescent over his back. R. Lion, to the right or left; Chaitya, with crescent, in front; over his back the character or symbol . Pl. XV. figs. 26, 27.

4, 5. Square; thick. Chaitya, with crescent, as before, and a second (?) formed of dots; a waving line (or snake) underneath, and sometimes other symbols beneath it; No. 4 has the same symbol as the last, . R. Blank, never having been stamped. Pl. XV. figs. 28, 29.

6, 7. Round; thin. Chaitya and crescent; worshipper, on one side, either left or right. Characters uncertain. R. Blank, never stamped. Pl. XV. figs. 30, 31.

These are from a number of coins found at Beghram. Those which have the lion on the reverse are thought by Prinsep to bear an analogy to the copper coins of Agathokles, but the figure of the animal differs; it agrees better with that on the coins of Azes (see Pl. VII. figs. 8, 9). They have been described and delineated on various occasions by Masson and Prinsep; J. As. Soc. B. April, 1834, Pl. IX. fig. 19; ibid. Nov. 1835, Pl. XXXV. figs. 50, 51.

8. Small; round. Elephant (?), to the left. R. Chaitya, with crescent. Pl. XV. fig. 33.

From Beghram.

9. Small; square. Elephant, to the left; various symbols, Nos. 166, 167, and the character or symbol ᚷ. R. Chaitya; trident rising from a square symbol; other symbols or characters (?) below the Chaitya. Pl. XV. fig. 32.

From a few in the Masson collection. These are found frequently in Hindustan; As. Res. vol. xvii. Pl. III. figs. 68, 69; J. As. Soc. B. May, 1834, Pl. IX. fig. 22; Nov. 1835, Pl. XXXIV. fig. 15; Pl. XXXV. fig. 38, &c.

3. GUPTA COINS.

An extensive and interesting series of coins, almost exclusively of gold, has been found in various parts of Hindustan, which bear in Sanscrit letters the names of Indian princes, with the family designation of Gupta. Some coins, which are either very rudely executed specimens or barbarous imitations of them, have been procured in a few of the topes in the Punjab and in Afghanistan; but the greater number are from other parts of India, and might therefore have been passed by on the present occasion without further notice. Having, however, been favoured with the opportunity of obtaining delineations from the very rich collection of Dr. Swiney, in this department, I have availed myself of it to bring them before the observation of Indian numismatists. A few are also contained in the Company's cabinet, although not part of the Masson collection.

From the circumstance of the rude coins of this class having been discovered in the topes of Afghanistan, we have in some degree an indication of their date, at least of its latest limitation, as it is not likely that the more perfect coins were subsequent to those of inferior fabrication. This limit we may take to be the end of the seventh century. It is not so easy to define the place of their issue. From many having been met with at Kanoj, it has been thought likely that they belonged to Rajas of that principality;[1] but they have been obtained in many other situations, and all that can be affirmed of them with any degree of certainty is, that they are coins of the west and north-western provinces of Hindustan.

The prevailing device on the obverse is a standing male figure, in a costume which is unlike any thing Indian that is known, or an ornamented coat with skirts and trowsers; the head is bare, and not shaven, but surrounded by a nimbus. In some instances the garb resembles plate armour. The figure usually holds a bow, and is sometimes represented as using it, shooting an animal, a lion. A banner with a bird, probably the Garuda, the winged vehicle of Vishnu, stands by his side; and he is sometimes attended by a follower holding an umbrella, a sign of royalty, over his head, or sometimes accompanied by a female. This association suggests the idea that the figures represent Rama and Sitá, and the other parts of the type would be not incompatible with these. We know that in the south of India there are old coins bearing the effigies of this incarnation of Vishnu, thence called Ráma-tankas;[2] and although they are of a totally different description from those of Hindustan, they show that there would have been nothing exceptionable in the representation of such types upon Hindu coins.

The reverse has in almost every instance a seated female figure holding the wreath of royalty, and connected by this emblem with the Victory reverses of so many of the Greek Bactrian coins, as well as with the Lakshmi or Sri, 'the goddess of fortune,' especially of regal fortune, of the Hindus; and the accuracy of this identification is confirmed by her bearing the horn

[1] Prinsep; J. As. Soc. B. Nov. 1835, p. 640.

[2] Marsden, vol. ii. p. 731, Pl. XLVIII. As. Res. vol. xvii. Pl. IV. figs. 74-78.

of plenty in her left arm. In many specimens she is seated on a high-backed chair, with a footstool at her feet; but in others she sits cross-legged upon a cushion or a lotus. Sometimes she sits upon a morah or Indian stool, sometimes upon a lion; in which case she may typify Durgá, who is ordinarily so represented.

The introduction of the cornucopia, although not incompatible with the character of Lakshmi, indicates the imitation of a foreign design. The type is not known to the Hindus, and in this particular, in the device of the high-backed chair, and in the general style and attitude of the seated female, there can be no question that we have the prototype in those coins which bear the legend Ardokro, and which belong to the Mithraic coins of Kanerki or his successors. There is also another remarkable proof of the connexion, in the use of the same monogram that is found upon the coins of Soter Megas, Kadphises, and Kanerki. Agreeably to the purport which there seems reason to assign to these monograms, the recurrence of this emblem on all these coins should denote the place of their coinage; but, as above observed, we have no reason to place these princes on the west, any more than we have to bring the Indo-Scythians far to the east of the Indus. It is therefore, perhaps, merely a proof of imitation, and has been introduced without any definite object. It is of use, however, in addition to the other resemblances, as evidence that the coins of the Gupta princes succeeded immediately to those of the Mithraic princes, and that the former, therefore, reigned from the second or third to the seventh century of our æra. We have other indications of a similar date.

In the first place, the Vishnu Purana[1] prophesies that at a late period of the Kali age a race of princes called Guptas will reign in Magadha or Behar, from Champavatí (Bhagalpur) to Prayaga (Allahabad). From the manner in which they are mentioned, the close of the dynasty was probably not very long anterior to the compilation of the Purana, which may have been the work of the tenth or eleventh century. Some time before this, the princes ruling on the Ganges were Chouhan Rajputs;[2] but Gupta usually implies that the dynasty so termed was of Vaisya descent,[3] and at any

[1] Page 479, and note 70.

[2] From the Prithwi Raja Rayasa; Calcutta Quarterly Magazine, Sept. 1827.

[3] Vishnu Purana, p. 298.

rate it is not a Chouhan designation, and consequently they had ceased to reign. These considerations harmonise with the inference afforded by the coins, and restrict the most modern period of the Gupta kings of Magadha to the seventh or eighth century.

We have other testimony of the existence of princes of the family name of Gupta in the second inscription on the pillar at Allahabad, decyphered by Captain Troyer,[1] and again revised and translated by Dr. Mill, recording the erection of the column by the great king of kings, Samudra Gupta, son of Chandra Gupta, son of Ghatotkacha, son of Gupta or Sri Gupta. And, again, we have a further series of the same dynasty from an inscription on a column at Bhitari, near Ghazipur,[2] also translated by the same distinguished Sanscrit scholar. This, after enumerating the same descent as the Allahabad column, adds the names of Chandra Gupta II., the son of Samudra Gupta, to whom succeed Kumara Gupta and Skanda Gupta, and a young prince, a minor, whose name is supplied from conjecture as Mahendra Gupta, a worshipper of Siva; thus giving an authentic series of eight connected descents. In the first of these inscriptions, these Gupta princes claim to belong to the Solar dynasty or to be Rajputs; and this would be more consistent with the martial character assigned in the inscription to Samudra Gupta, as well as to the personations on the coins. It is not impossible that a man of the military caste might take such an appellation, or term himself 'the protected' (Gupta) of a deity; although, as above observed, it is contrary to holy texts. But this is of no importance. We have in the Allahabad inscription positive proof of the authority of a royal family of the name of Gupta at Prayaga, recorded in a form of the Sanscrit alphabet, which we now know to be anterior to the seventh century. The inscription, the Puranas, and the coins, are therefore remarkably consistent as to the existence and probable date of this dynasty.

With regard to the individual princes, we derive from the coins many additions to the names on the Allahabad column, whilst we have not the second name there specified, Ghatotkacha. Nor have we met with the name of Gupta alone, or Sri Gupta. Prinsep has given no fewer than

[1] J. As. Soc. B. March and June, 1834.

[2] Ibid. Jan. 1837, p. 1.

thirteen names from the coins;[1] but exceptions may be reasonably taken to some of his readings, and it may be doubted if others belong to this dynasty.

The characters which occur upon the coins are of the same style as those on the Allahabad and Bhitari columns, and express several similar names. We have upon them the appellations of Samudra Gupta, Chandra Gupta, Kumara Gupta, Skanda Gupta, and Mahendra Gupta. The name alone without the family designation is usually arranged perpendicularly under one arm of the standing figure on the obverse; but it is commonly repeated on the margin with some additions, either of name or title, as Sri Chandra Gupta, Sri Gupta Mahendra Jaya, and in one instance we have Maharaj dhi raj Sri. On the reverses are also titles; of which it may be observed that Sri Vikrama, 'the illustrious hero,' occurs wherever the name of Chandra Gupta is read on the obverse, and Apratiratha, 'the unsurpassed warrior,' when Samudra Gupta is the name. Other combinations occur, of which the correct reading is doubtful, and of which, when decypherable, the meaning cannot be satisfactorily rendered. On one of these coins Mr. Prinsep conjectures that part of the name of Ghatot-kacha may be read.

There are also some names, apparently of the same dynasty, which may either belong to other individuals than those particularized in the inscriptions, or may be modifications of their names and qualities not there alluded to. The name Samara occurs distinctly on several coins, and with a rather complicated legend, which Prinsep has rendered "more invincible in battle than a hundred wild elephants," but upon rather questionable grounds. This inscription occurs in part also upon a coin of Samudra Gupta, and it may be possible that Samara is an error for Samudra. On the reverses of the coins with the name Samara occurs Parakrama, 'the powerful.' Again, upon some of the coins of Kumara we have upon the reverse Jayati Mahendra, and upon another, Sri Skanda, as if those princes had been contemporary. Upon the reverses of coins upon the obverse of which no name is decypherable, we have the name or title Sinha Vikrama; whilst upon others which bear the name of Mahendra Gupta

[1] J. As. Soc. B. Nov. 1835, p. 643.

we find upon the reverses Ajita Vikrama, Ajita Mahendra, and Parakrama deva. It is possible that these variations may be reduced to method by the examination of additional specimens of these coins, but at present they are somewhat perplexing.

In one instance we have a very remarkable name, that of Vikramaditya. As it occurs on the reverse, however, it may be like the Vikrama, concurrent with Chandra Gupta, a title only of one of the Gupta princes. It would be highly interesting if this coin could be considered as the coin of the great patron of Hindu literature and the defender of his country from barbaric devastation, Vikramaditya, king of Ujayin, B. C. 56.

Another very remarkable coin connected with this class by its general style, although differing in its types, is the coin with a female figure, and chowri, on one face, and a standing uncaparisoned horse on the other. That the steed represents one dedicated to the Aswamedha, or solemn sacrifice of a horse, performed only by paramount sovereigns, cannot be doubted, from the inscription Aswamedha-parakrama, 'he who has the powers of the Aswamedha rites.' Who this prince was, is no further intimated, but he may have been one of the Gupta dynasty, and certainly he reigned in the same part of India and in a similar period.

The great number of coins of the Gupta type, in all degrees of deteriorated execution, which are found in different parts of Hindustan, show that the family must have enjoyed extensive power for some considerable period. Some of these rude coins may be modern imitations, but they have been found in situations and under circumstances where it was impossible that they could have been of recent fabrication, and the greater portion of them must be admitted to be genuine. They confirm the deductions derived from the more perfect coins, and leave no doubt of a connexion between the Hindu coinage of the Gupta princes and that of the Indo-Scythians on the west of the Indus, to whom they must have succeeded.

GUPTA COINS.

GOLD.

1. Standing female figure, to the left (Victory?), holding a regal fillet in

her right hand, bangles (Hindu ornaments) on the wrists and ankles; staff or back of chair (?) on her left, on the right of which occur characters, indistinct. R. Figure of Raja, to the left; attendant behind, holding a chattah or umbrella over his head. Legend indistinct. Pl. XVIII. fig. 1.

In the Company's cabinet. A similar coin, in some respects better preserved, is engraved, J. As. Soc. B. Nov. 1836, Pl. XXXVIII. fig. 7. It belonged to Mr. Tregear. Prinsep read the legend on the reverse Vikramaditya, and his reading is confirmed by Mr. Tregear; ibid. p. 650. The characters on our coin are indistinct, and are still more so in the engraving; but in the former they may be distinguished, when their value is known as representing Vikramaditya.

2. Female figure, with halo round the head, to the left, supporting a chowri, or tail of the Tibetan ox, with handle; a spear in front: Aswamedha-parakrama. R. Horse, without saddle or bridle, to the left; altar in front, whence rises a waving flame (?). Characters above, imperfect: under the horse, 'Deva' (?) Pl. XVIII. fig. 2.

From a coin procured by Mr. Thomas at Saharanpur. Two similar coins are described by Prinsep, J. As. Soc. B. Nov. 1835, p. 638. Pl. XXXIX. figs. 31, 32.

3. Two figures, one on the left a female, that on the right a warrior, in a kind of coat and trowsers, holding a trident. Sitá and Rama (?). Characters on the left, indistinct. Under the arm of the male, Chandra (Gupta). R. Female (Durgá ?) sitting on a lion, a fillet in her right hand, a cornucopia in her left; upon her right, Mon. No. 160, and on her left, Pachchawaya. Pl. XVIII. fig. 3.

From a coin in Dr. Swiney's collection. One is engraved by Prinsep, J. As. Soc. B. Oct. 1836, Pl. XXXV. fig. 15. He mentions having received another, on which a parallel line under the arm of the male figure adds Gupta to Chandra,—Chandra-Gupta. Marsden has another of this coin, No. M.LVIII.

4. Male figure, to the left, in a sort of ornamented coat; a halo round the head; an arrow in his right hand, a bow in the left; in front of him a standard surmounted by a bird or by Garuda (?). Characters on the margin, imperfect. Under his arm, Chandra, as in the last. R. Female

seated cross-legged on a lotus; halo round the head; fillet in her right hand, her left raised. Mon. No. 159. On her left, Sri Vikrama. Pl. XVIII. fig. 4.

From the Company's cabinet. Many coins, with similar figures on either side, are given in the Journal, from the collections of Mr. Tregear, Lieutenant Cunningham, and others; but, although the general devices agree, the legends show them to belong to different princes. Instead of the lotus also, and the Indian mode of being seated, the female is often represented as sitting on a high-backed chair, with her feet on a footstool. There is not one that exactly corresponds with our coin, although several differ very little. The nearest to it is delineated, J. As. Soc. B. Oct. 1836, Pl. XXXVIII. fig. 9. This has the inscription on the margin of the obverse legible, as Sri Chandra Gupta.

5. Archer, in the attitude of shooting with a bow, to the right. R. Female seated on a lion (?); her right hand over an altar (?), her left holding the cornucopia. Mon. rude, 160. Sinha Vikrama. Pl. XVIII. fig. 5.

From a coin in Dr. Swiney's collection. The execution, though spirited, is rude, especially on the reverse. Coins, with similar subjects, but differing in the representation, are figured by Prinsep, J. As. Soc. B. Oct. 1836, Pl. XXXVIII. figs. 1, 2, 8. In them the legend is distinctly Sinha Vikrama. In others, which he has described and figured in the Journal, May, 1834, Pl. XVIII. fig. 24, and Nov. 1835, Pl. XXXIX. figs. 25, 27, 28, the position of the archer is reversed. Their legends differ; on one the obverse has plainly Maharaj dhi raj Sri. The reverse is read by Prinsep Sri Sachha Vikrama; but, as he observes, the second word is doubtful. Comparing the letters with those of coins Nos. 1, 2, of Oct. 1836, there can be little doubt that the correct reading of this coin, as well as of Prinsep's No. 27 in the same Plate, and of our coin, should be Sinha Vikrama also. No. 27 of Prinsep's Plate has an inscription on the obverse, which he reads Vikrama nari nama Gupta. The second word he conjectures to be an error for Narayana: it is, no doubt, incorrect. No. 8 of Prinsep's October Plate has different legends, or, on the obverse, Sri - - - pta Mahendra Jaya; on the reverse, Sri Mahendra Sinha. There is another coin, with the archer and animal to the left, in the cabinet of Dr. Swiney; and on the reverse a female feeding a peacock. The inscription of the obverse is indistinct, but it may be Vikrama Sinha; that of the reverse is Kumara Gupta.

6. Standing figure, to the left; halo and fillet; the Garuda banner in front; the right hand is dropping incense upon an altar, the left rests upon a staff or sceptre. Characters under the arm, Samu - -, and in the margin; the latter are Samara - - - - -. R. Female sitting on a couch with legs, her feet upon a stool, holding the fillet and cornucopia. Mon. 159. Parakrama. Pl. XVIII. fig. 6.

Prinsep has several of these; J. As. Soc. B. Nov. 1835, Pl. XXXVIII. figs. 16, 17; Oct. 1836, Pl. XXXVI. fig. 14. From a collection of several he made out the entire inscription on the obverse to be Samara-sata-mata ga-(ja) vijaya-tara, 'one who is more invincible in battle than a hundred wild elephants;' but this seems very doubtful. There can be little question as to his other verifications. The letters under the arm express Samara Gupta; J. As. Soc. B. Oct. 1836, p. 646.

7, 8. Figure, to the right; costume somewhat different from the preceding; halo round the head; the left hand holds a bow, the right an inverted arrow; standard in front. Under the arm, Samudra. Characters in the margin imperfect, - - - vijaya - - - (?). R. Female figure, on a bed with back; her right hand holds a fillet. Apratiratha. Mon. No. 160. Pl. XVIII. figs. 7, 8.

No. 7 is from Dr. Swiney's collection; No. 8, from the Company's cabinet. Similar coins occur in the Journal, Nov. 1835, Pl. XXXIX. fig. 19. Prinsep read the legend at first Apatirurha, which has no meaning, but he corrected it afterwards to Apratiratha.[1] This, 'the unsurpassed warrior,' is a genuine Sanscrit title.

9. Figure, to the right, as in No. 6; the altar distinct. Under the arm, Samudra (?). In the margin, Samara sata vataga (?). R. Sitting female, as before, with cornucopia. Parakrama. Pl. XVIII. fig. 9.

10. Warrior, in Roman armour (?), with right hand resting on trident with hatchet; a short sword or dagger at his waist; in front his standard-bearer (?), with standard surmounted by a crescent; between the figure, Samudra (?). R. Female, seated on couch, with fillet and cornucopia; flames (?) at her feet. Mon. Kratu-paraga (?). Pl. XVIII. fig. 10.

From the collection of Dr. Swiney. Prinsep has engraved two coins with

[1] J. As. Soc. B. vol. v. errata.

a similar device, but the figures are reversed, J. As. Soc. B. Nov. 1835, Pl. XXXIX. fig. 23, and Oct. 1836, Pl. XXXV. fig. 11. In his drawings, instead of seeming flame, the footstool is composed of leaves of the lotus. Prinsep's corrected reading of the whole decypherable inscription is Kubhava-paraguja; but his attempts to give a meaning to these syllables are very unsuccessful; Journal, Oct. 1836, p. 645. The inscription under the arm is in one instance Samudra; in two others he thinks it Asa, as if it were intended for Azes; but the former is the preferable reading.

11. Warrior, with bow, to the left; attitude different from the preceding. No letters under the arm; but, behind the bow, Kumara (?): others, in the margin, indistinct. R. Sitting female figure; string of pearls in her right hand (?), flowers (?) in her left. Pa - - - . Pl. XVIII. fig. 11.

A very rude coin.

12. Figure, with bow; his right hand extended beyond the staff of the standard. Under the arm, Sri-ku (?); margin, Jayati Mahendra Gupta. R. Female, seated cross-legged on a lotus; a fillet in her right hand, her left resting on her knee. Sri Mahendra (?). Pl. XVIII. fig. 12.

Two of these are engraved by Prinsep, J. As. Soc. B. Oct. 1836, Pl. XXXV. figs. 19, 20. The latter has precisely the same legends as our coin; the former differs, having Parama Raja (?) on the reverse, with Sri between the legs of the figure, and Gu near the hand. Mahendra, on the reverse, is distinct. For a coin of Mahendra Sinha see remarks on No. 5.

13. Male figure, to the left, playing with a peacock. Inscription imperfect. R. Figure (female ?), holding a trident in the left hand, riding on a peacock, in front of an altar. Sri Skanda - - - (?) Pl. XVIII. fig. 13.

From a coin belonging to Dr. Swiney, hitherto undescribed.

14. Standing figure, to the left, dropping incense on a fire-altar, spear behind. Under the arm, Kcha. On the left, Kumara Guptasya Jaya. R. Female, with ring and cornucopia, standing, to the left; halo round the head. Mon. 160. Sri vairajich-chatra. Pl. XVIII. fig. 14.

From Prinsep's drawing of a coin found by Mr. Tregear; J. As. Soc. B. Oct. 1836, Pl. XXXVI. fig. 12: he reads the inscription, Sarva rajochhatra Kama-naruttama-ja Gha - - -, and under the arm, Kacha; conjecturing it to be a coin of Ghatotkacha Gupta, one of the earliest of the dynasty.

15. Raja, on horseback, to the right, with bare head. Inscription indistinct, - - - hendra Gupta (?). R. Female, sitting on an Indian stool; halo round her head; fillet in her right hand, fan (?) in her left. Ajita Mahendra. Pl. XVIII. fig. 16.

16. Raja, on horseback, to the right, apparently naked, with a rayed turban on his head. - - - ndra Gupta. R. Female, on seat; fillet in right hand, a sceptre or staff, with Garuda on the head, in her left. Mon. 160. Ajita Vikra(ma). Pl. XVIII. fig. 17.

17, 18. Raja, on horseback, running a spear through the jaws of a lion. R. Female, seated on lotus; fillet in her right hand, sceptre in her left. Mon. 160. Sri Prakrama deva (?). Pl. XVIII. figs. 18, 19.

These coins, which are rude, are not very uncommon: two are given in the As. Res. vol. xvii. Pl. I. figs. 17, 18; Prinsep has two, J. As. Soc. B. Nov. 1835, Pl. XXXIX. figs. 29, 30; and four, Oct. 1836, Pl. XXXVIII. figs. 3, 4, 5, 6. All these have the female and peacock reverse. From these different specimens Prinsep finds the legend on the reverse, Ajita Mahendra, or, in one case, Ajita Vikrama. The inscription on the obverse is always more or less imperfect; and such characters as are decyphered offer no satisfactory reading. In one, No. 6 of his Plate of October, the inscription on the obverse is Paramesa - - - - ndra Gupta. He has not published any with the lotus-throned female on the reverse.

19. Female figure, with bow and standard; a border round the margin. R. Winged Victory, to the right. In the margin, characters, undecyphered. Pl. XVIII. fig. 20.

From a coin belonging to Dr. Swiney; of doubtful authenticity.

20-23. Figure, sometimes female, with bow and arrow; standard in front. Characters under the arm. R. Seated female figure on lotus, with fillet, and characters in the margin. Pl. XVIII. figs. 21-24.

These are from a number of similar coins in the Company's collection, of rude execution and debased metal. They are part of two hundred found in a jar in Bengal in the time of Warren Hastings, and sent by him to be distributed to public institutions at home. There are some in the British Museum, some in the Ashmolean Museum at Oxford, and some in the Public Library at Cambridge. (See Marsden, vol. ii. p. 726.) They have different legends, but not often decypherable. Under the arm of the standing figure are the syllables Ku, Vi, Chanda, for Kumara, Vikrama, Chandra Gupta (?). On the reverses may be conjectured Sri Vikrama, or Prakrama, or Ajita Mahendra Gupta; and they are, no doubt, imitations of the coinage of the Gupta princes, or an inferior class of coins issued by them in times of difficulty or for provincial currency.

24-27. Standing figure of king; the right hand extended over an altar, the left resting on a spear or trident. Characters under the arm. R. Female, sitting on a seat, fillet in her right hand, and cornucopia in the left. Mon. 159, 160. No legible inscription. Pl. XVIII. figs. 25-28.

Rude coins, frequently found in various parts of India. The attitudes of the figures, and their accompaniments, and the characters under the arm of the male figure, intended apparently for Ku, Chan, Vi, &c., connect these coins with those of the Gupta princes, and especially with those which, by the chair on which the female sits, and in the introduction of the fire-altar, are evidently allied to the coins of the Ardokro type. Many specimens of these coins are given by Prinsep, Nov. 1835, Pl. XXXVIII. figs. 13-15, and Oct. 1836, Pl. XXXVIII. figs. 15-20. At the time he last wrote he observed correctly, that none of them had been found at Beghram. They have, however, since been found in Afghanistan, as those now delineated are from Mr. Masson's collection. Two of them, Nos. 25, 26, are from the Great Tope of Hidda; consequently, even these rude imitations of the Gupta coins are earlier than the sixth or seventh century at the latest. (See p. 109.) Other diversities of these coins, of a still ruder description, are given, Supplemental Plate, figs. 23, 24. Silver and copper coins of the same kind are figured by Prinsep, J. As. Soc. B. Oct. 1836, Pl. XXXIX. figs. 1-10. The word Sri is legible on many, so is Yaga, or, as Prinsep proposes, Yasa; but on some it appears to be Yoga, perhaps part of Yogeswarí, a name of Durgá, who is intended by the sitting female. On others are the words Sri Pratapa; in one, Sri Vijaya Mahendra very legibly occurs.

COPPER.

28. Head of female (?), to the left. Characters underneath, indistinct.

R. A bird, standing on a base; below, (Sr)i Chandra Gu(pta). Pl. XVIII. fig. 15.

From Dr. Swiney's collection. The same coin is figured by Prinsep, J. As. Soc. B. Oct. 1836, Pl. XXXVIII. fig. 14, as well as others, figs. 11-15; from which may be made out, with certainty as to the name at least, Sri Vikrama deva (Ma)haraja Sri Chandra Gupta.

4. RAJPUT COINS.

Another series of Hindu coins is found in considerable numbers in the west and north-west of Hindustan, extending to the Punjab and Afghanistan, and occasionally in the eastern provinces of Persia; although not upon the lower course of the Indus, in Sindh or in Guzerat. These it has been agreed to designate Rajput coins, and the name is sufficiently appropriate to them, in what appears to be their most early and authentic form. They bear upon one face a mounted horseman, piercing some undefined object with his lance; and upon the other the bull of Siva, Nandi, recumbent and caparisoned, as he is seen in temples dedicated to his master. They are of distinct though rude execution, and bear upon them, in Sanscrit letters, names and titles which are undoubtedly those of Hindu princes. It is remarkable, however, that the name which is of most frequent recurrence, particularly upon the best-executed silver coins, is not an ordinary Indian appellation. The whole is Sri Samagu deva, of which, although the first and last are genuine Hindu titles, the intermediate denomination is very equivocal. It has been proposed to read it Samanta, which would get rid of the difficulty; but it is doubtful if this can be allowed. The last syllable is of an unusual form, it is true, but it can scarcely be *nta*; it is more obviously *gu* in most specimens, although sometimes it looks like *gri*, or *tri*, or *ntri*. None of these would furnish a more satisfactory reading. The unfamiliar form of the name does not, however, preclude the probability of its Indian origin, for we still find amongst the Rajputs names not readily traceable to the Sanscrit language, and this may be therefore an Indian although not a Sanscrit word.

The name and titles of Samagu deva occur over the couchant bull, and in the same place we have upon other silver coins the equally Indian inscription of Sri Syalapati deva; whilst upon the reverse of the former we have also the Hindu designation Bhíma.

The greater number of this class of coins consists, however, of very base silver or of copper. A few of the latter vary in type from the rest, having an elephant on one face and a lion on the other, with the name of Samagu deva, or, in one instance, of Sri Vanka deva. In general, however, the copper retain the devices of the silver coins, the horseman and the bull. Over the latter we have the same names of Samagu and Syalapati deva, preceded sometimes by the word Asavari, with other Hindu names on the reverse, as Sri Raja, Sri Madana Pala, and, which is of more interest, as readily identifiable, that of Sri Prithwi Pala deva, in whom we cannot hesitate to recognise the gallant Prithwi Raja, the patron and friend of the bard Chand, and who, after a long and gallant resistance to the Mohammedan arms, lost his freedom and his life in battle with Mohammed Sam in A. D. 1192. It is undeniable, therefore, that these coins are the coins of the last Hindu princes of Hindustan. The copper coins of Prithwi Pala are evidently of a later æra than the best of the silver coins; and the latter may perhaps be dated a century or so earlier, having been struck by the Pala princes of the Punjab, who were first attacked, but not wholly subdued, by Mahmud of Ghizni and his successors at the end of the tenth and beginning of the eleventh century, terminating with Prithwi Pala at the end of the twelfth.

RAJPUT COINS.

SILVER.

1-5. Indian bull, caparisoned, couchant. Sri Samagu deva. R. Raja, on horseback, to the right, with lance. Bhíma. Pl. XIX. figs. 1-5.

6-10. Indian bull. Sri Syalapati deva. R. Horseman, as before. Pl. XIX. figs. 6-10.

These are from a considerable number procured at Kabul and in the neighbourhood. Similar coins are found in great numbers in Western India. A number are described by Prinsep, J. As. Soc. B. Dec. 1835, Pl. XXXVI.

COPPER.

11. Elephant, to the left. - - Samagu deva. R. Lion, to the right. Pl. XIX. fig. 11.

12. Elephant, to the left. Sri Vanka deva. R. Lion, to the right. Pl. XIX. fig. 12.

13. Bull, couchant. Sri Syalapati deva (?). R. Horseman. Pl. XIX. fig. 13.

14. Small. Nagari letters, imperfect. Sri Hari (?). R. Horseman. Pl. XIX. fig. 14.

15-17. Bull, couchant. Samagu deva. R. Horseman. Sri Raja. Pl. XIX. figs. 15-17.

18. Bull, couchant. Asavari Sri Samagu deva. R. Horseman. Sri Prithwi Raja deva. Pl. XIX. fig. 18.

19. Bull, couchant. Sri Samagu deva. R. Horseman. Madana Pala deva. Pl. XIX. fig. 19.

20. Bull. Asavari Sri - - - - . R. Horseman. Sri - - - - . Pl. XIX. fig. 20.

21. Bull. - - - ta deva. R. Horseman. (A)la(ud)din (?). Very rude. Pl. XIX. fig. 21.

22. Bull. Sri Samagu ma - - . R. Horseman. Coin rude. Pl. XIX. fig. 22.

23. Bull. Madhava (Sri) Sama. R. Sri Madana (Pala ?). Pl. XIX. fig. 23.

5. INDO-MOHAMMEDAN COINS.

That the types in use upon the coins of the Rajput princes were popular with the people of Upper Hindustan, may be inferred from their continuance by their Mohammedan conquerors, the princes of the house of Ghor, and the first kings of Delhi. The bull of Siva, and the mounted cavalier, do not disappear with the Deva or Pala families, but proceed for some time, accompanied either wholly or in part by Mohammedan names and titles, expressed at first in Nagari but ultimately in Arabic letters, until at last the latter take entire possession, and the traces of Hinduism entirely disappear. Thus we have in Nagari, over the bull, Sri Mohammed Sam, that is, Mohammed Ghori, the conqueror of India, or Sri Sams-ud-din, referring, no doubt, to Shams-ud-din Altamsh, who ascended the throne of Delhi in A. D. 1210. These appear to be the only names written in Nagari, except in one instance noticed by Mr. Prinsep, where Mawwaj occurs on one side with the title Al Sultan, whilst on the other we have in Arabic letters, Al Sultan Al Azim Maiz-ud-dunia wa ud-din. Here, however, we have no Hindu device, although the coin is, no doubt, that of Mohammed Sam, called Maiz-ud-din, whilst acting as the general of his brother Ghias-ud-din.[1]

The next step is the adoption of Arabic letters along with one or other of the Indian types, of which an example apparently of a still earlier age seems to have been set by one of the princes of the house of Ghizni; as upon the reverse of coins of Samagu deva with the Indian bull, we have in Kufic the names and titles of Ibrahim, the son of Masaud, who reigned from 1059 to 1088. Of other names with Indian types, but in Arabic characters, we have Maiz-ud-din, that is, Mohammed Ghori; or Mohammed bin Sam; Shams-ud-din Altamsh; Sultan Al Azim al Fateh Bulbun. Concurrently with these coins we have others similar in size and style, but wholly Mohammedan, omitting the Hindu types, and having in Arabic letters on both sides the names of the same princes, Ghias-ud-din, and his brother Maiz-ud-din, and Shams-ud-din Altamsh, with the addition of Ala-ud-din, Nasir-ud-din, and Khosru Malek, who is probably the last of the Ghiznevide princes, and reigned more in India than in his paternal dominions. The period of these mixed coins, from Ibrahim to Bulbun, extends from A. D. 1059 to A. D. 1286,[2] during which period it was no doubt often the interest and the policy of the first Mohammedan conquerors to conciliate their Hindu subjects. It is worthy of remark, that as long as the figure of the horseman is preserved, there are Nagari letters accompanying, expressing Sri Hamíra.

[1] Prinsep ascribes it to Ghias-ud-din Toghlak Shah, A. D. 1321, mistaking him for the Ghori prince, who is undoubtedly intended on the coins, as he is so constantly associated with Maiz-ud-din, his brother.

[2] Briggs' Ferishta, vol. i. p. 168. It may also be observed, that with the change of dynasty to that of Khilji, the conduct of the Mohammedan princes towards the Hindus became more intolerant and cruel.

This, Prinsep says, can be no other than the celebrated prince Hamíra of Mewar, who succeeded to the throne in A. D. 1300.[1] But this cannot be correct, for Hamíra is contemporary on the coins with Shams-ud-din, a century before, and he cannot be the same person with the Raja of Mewar. He was more probably the Hamíra who was governor of Hansí in the time of Prithwi Rai, and was killed by the Raja's uncle Kilhana, as recorded by an inscription found in that fort.[2] He may have provoked the enmity of his countrymen by his connexion with Mohammed Ghori, under whom he may have held the fortress, and thence the appearance of their names conjointly upon the coins. The continuance of his name after the conquest of Delhi was probably mere imitation; it formed part of a die which was not changed until the devices of Hindu idolatry were altogether discarded.

INDO-MOHAMMEDAN COINS.

COPPER.

1-4. Bull, couchant. Sri Mohammed Sam. R. Horseman. Sri Hamíra. Pl. XIX. figs. 24-27.

5. Bull. Sri Sams-ud-din. R. Horseman. Sri Mohammed (?). Pl. XIX. figs. 28, 30.

6. Bull. Sri Sams-ud-din. R. Horseman. Sri Hamíra. Pl. XIX. fig. 31.

7, 8. Bull. Sri Sams-ud-din. R. Horseman. Letters imperfect. Pl. XIX. figs. 32, 33.

9. Bull. Asavari Sri. R. Horseman. Sri Raja. Pl. XIX. fig. 34.

10, 11. Bull. Sri Mohammed. R. Horseman. Sri Hamíra. Pl. XIX. figs. 35, 36.

12. Bull. Sri Sams-ud-din Mohammed. R. Horseman. Sri Hamíra deva. Pl. XIX. fig. 37.

13. Rude figure of a horse. ناصر الدنیا و الدین Nasir-ud-dunia wa ud-din. R. Letters intended for Sanscrit, but not offering any intelligible legend. They are probably designed to express the title on the obverse. Pl. XIX. fig. 38.

[1] J. As. Soc. B. Oct. 1835, p. 682.

[2] As. Res. vol. xv. p. 444.

14. Bull. Sri Samagu. R. السلطان الاعظم ابو ال مظفر ابرهيم Al Sultan al Azim Abu-l-muzaffar Ibrahim. Pl. XIX. fig. 39.

15, 16. Bull and horseman, but very rude; and characters, indistinct. Pl. XX. figs. 1, 2.

17. Bull. Sri Mohammed Sams-ud-din. R. Horseman. Sri Hamíra. Pl. XX. fig. 3.

18. Bull. - - - - Sam. R. Al Sultan al Azim al Sultan. Pl. XX. fig. 4.

19. Bull. Sri Samagu deva Shah al Sultan al Azim Abu-l-muzaffar Ibrahim. Pl. XX. fig. 5.

20. Bull (very rude). R. Sultan al Azim Maiz-ud-dunia (wa ud-din?). Pl. XX. fig. 6.

21. Horseman (rude), to the left. R. Sultan al Azim (Mohammed) bin Sam. Pl. XX. fig. 7.

22. Horseman, to the right. R. Sultan al Azim Mohammed al Sultan. Pl. XX. fig. 8.

23. Horseman. R. Sultan al Azim al Fateh Bulbun (?) Sultan. Pl. XX. fig. 9.

24. Horseman. R. Al Sultan al Azim Maiz-ud-dunia wa ud-din. Pl. XX. fig. 10.

25. Horseman, indistinct, or characters (?). R. Al Sultan. Pl. XX. fig. 11.

26. Horseman (very rude). R. Sultan al Azim Abu-l-muzaffar Ibrahim (?). Pl. XX. fig. 12.

27. Horseman (rude). Sri. R. Al Sultan al Azim Altamsh. Pl. XX. fig. 13.

28. Al Sultan (?) Maiz-ud-dunia. R. wa ud-din (in a frame). Pl. XX. fig. 14.

29. Rude lines for the horseman. R. Abu-l-fateh Mohammed al Sultan. Pl. XX. fig. 15.

30. Al Sultan al Moazim Al-seraj-ud-daulet (?). R. Khosru Malek. Pl. XX. fig. 16.

31. Mohammed - - - ud-daulet - . R. Nasir-ud-dunia wa ud-din. Pl. XX. fig. 17.

32. Al Sultan al Azim Maiz-ud-dunia wa ud-din. R. Sultan al Azim Ghias-ud-dunia wa ud-din. Pl. XX. fig. 18.

33. Horseman. R. - - - - Fateh al Sultan. Pl. XX. fig. 19.

34. Bull. Sri Sam (?). R. Adel Al Sultan al Azim Muzaffar Ibrahim (?). Pl. XX. fig. 21.

35. Horseman (rude). R. Maiz-ud-dunia wa ud-din Al Sultan Altamsh. Pl. XX. fig. 20.

These, as well as the preceding Rajput copper coins, are chiefly from a large number in the Masson collection, of which many were found at Beghram. Some are from an extensive collection made by Mr. Thomas, chiefly at Saharanpur and Karnaul. They are numerously found in Western and North-western Hindustan; Tod, Rajasthan, vol. i. p. 698; Prinsep, J. As. Soc. B. Dec. 1835, Pl. XXXVI., XXXVII., and XLIX.

6. LATER KANOJ. HINDU AND INDO-MOHAMMEDAN COINS.

However uncouth and distorted the sitting female may be which is seen upon one face of these coins, its general character and attributes show it to be the genuine descendant of the seated figure on the reverse of the coins of the Gupta princes. The Deva Nagari inscription on the other face identifies these coins with a dynasty of princes who we know, from the authentic testimony of inscriptions, confirmed by history, reigned at Kanoj and over the adjacent provinces, as far as to Benares, and perhaps to Allahabad, from the middle of the eleventh to the end of the twelfth century.[1]

That they did not immediately succeed to the Gupta princes, but that some considerable period intervened, is probable from the rude execution of their coins, and the modernised form of the Sanscrit letters. By what race of princes the interval was filled up, we have not yet means of ascertaining, although one or two names are derivable from collateral sources,[2] which are not found either amongst the Gupta kings or those of a later æra.

[1] As. Res. vol. xv. p. 461.

[2] As, Yasovarma, Sáhasanka, and Kora; ibid. p. 463.

The names of the last dynasty of Kanoj found upon the inscriptions above referred to are:

1. Yasovigraha.
2. Mahí Pala.
3. Madana Pala.
4. Govinda Chandra.
5. Vijaya Chandra.
6. Jaya Chandra.

The last shared the fate of his contemporary and rival Prithwi Rai, and was slain in battle with the Mohammedans in the same year, A. D. 1192. Upon the coins here delineated we have but one of these names, that of Govinda Chandra. Coins of Vijaya Chandra, and of Jaya Chandra, have been found elsewhere.[1] On the other hand, we have in these coins names which do not belong to the Kanoj dynasty, and which may designate princes more to the west, as Jadjeya deva, and Kumara Pala. We have also the same amalgamation of Mohammedan names with the Hindu device; and the coins of this class with the name of Mir Mohammed Sam, or Mohammed the son of Sam, convey the same intimation of his policy as was expressed by the copper coins last described. These late Kanoj coins are exclusively of gold.

LATER KANOJ. HINDU AND INDO-MOHAMMEDAN COINS.

GOLD.

1. Rude figure of seated female. Durgá or Bhavaní (?). R. Sri mad Govinda Chandra deva. Date, 11- - . Pl. XX. fig. 22.

2. Figure of seated female, rather less rude than the preceding. Ornamented margin. R. Sri mad Jadjeya deva. Pl. XX. fig. 23.

3. Female figure, as before. R. Sri mad Kumara Pala deva. Pl. XX. fig. 24.

4. Figure, as before. R. Sri Mohammed bin (?) Sam. Supplemental Plate, fig. 25.

5. Figure, as before. R. Sri mad Mir Mohammed Sam. Pl. XX. fig. 25.

[1] As. Res, vol. xvii. p. 585.

6. Figure, as before. R. Sri mad Mir Mohammed Sam. Pl. XX. fig. 26.

7. Figure, as before. R. Mohammed Chhám. Pl. XX. fig. 27.

These are from several procured at Kabul by Mr. Masson.

The Hindu coins of this series, usually denominated Kanoj, from their being commonly procured at that city, were first delineated in the As. Res. vol. xvii. Pl. III. figs. 48-50. Others are noticed by Mr. Prinsep as in different collections, and particularly in that of Colonel Stacey, which has similar coins of silver and copper, as well as gold; J. As. Soc. B. Dec. 1835, p. 668, Pl. L. The smaller Mohammedan coins appear to have been found only in Afghanistan. One of the larger (No. 4 of the above list) is described and delineated by Prinsep as above (Pl. L. fig. 3); but, impressed with the belief that it was Hindu, he was perplexed by the inscription, and read it Sri mad Rama haveche nam. He observes, however, that other specimens are required to determine the name. There can be no doubt of it from that which is here engraved, and which is one out of five last received from Mr. Masson.

MOHAMMEDAN COINS OF GHIZNI AND GHOR.

We might reasonably expect to find Mohammedan coins of all periods in Afghanistan having upon them indications of their character and origin, unaffected by contact or collision with the Hindus. A considerable number has accordingly been sent from Kabul by Mr. Masson. Some of these, of later date, the coins of the kings of Delhi, are more modern than the limit to which it is proposed to bring these numismatic witnesses of historical events, and are too well known to need description. Amongst the rest are a few of an earlier period, that of the Abbasside Khalifs; but the greater number are coins of the princes of Ghizni and Ghor, or Mahmud, Masaud, Modud, Behram, and the two first Ghorian princes, Ghias-ud-din and Maiz-ud-din conjointly; and the latter also separately, as Mohammed the son of Sam. A very considerable number of gold coins has been also procured, the legend upon which, and the date and place of coinage, Ghizni, prove them to belong to Mohammed VI., prince of Khwarizm, after his capture of Ghizni in the year of the Hijra 614, or A. D. 1217.[1] According to Professor Fræhn,[2] the gold coins of this prince have been hitherto exceedingly rare. The Company's cabinet contains nearly a hundred, besides several silver.

MOHAMMEDAN COINS OF GHIZNI AND GHOR.

GOLD.

1. Centre. لا اله الا الله محمد رسول الله الناصر الدين الله امير المومنين 'There is no God but God. Mohammed, the messenger of God. Nasir-ud-din Allah, the Commander of the Faithful.' Margin imperfect, but it is the second symbol of Marsden. محمد رسول الله ارسله بالهدي و دين الحق ليظهره علي الدين كله 'Mohammed, the messenger of God, whom he sent with guidance and true faith, that he might exalt (the true) religion above all.' Koran, Surahs 9 and 61. R. Centre. السلطان الاعظم علا الدنيا و الدين ابو الفتح محمد بن السلطان 'The mighty sovereign, over the world and religion; the father of victory; Mohammed the son of the Sultan.' Margin. ضرب هذا الدينار ببلده غزنه في شهور سنه سته عشره و ستمايه 'This dinár is struck in the city Ghiznah, in the year 616.' Pl. XX. fig. 28.

One of a considerable number of similar coins purchased at Kabul by Mr. Masson.

SILVER.

2. Centre. La Allah, &c., and ناصر الدين (بالله) سلطان الاعظم غياث الدنيا و الدين ابو الفتح محمد 'There is no God, &c., (the Khalif) Nasir-ud-din billah; The defender of the world and religion, the victorious Mohammed.' Margin. The same passage as in the last. R. Centre. 'Mohammed, the messenger of God,' and السلطان المعظم معز الدنيا و الدين ابو المظفر محمد 'The great Sultan, Maiz (the venerator) of the world and religion, the victorious Mohammed.' Margin. ضرب هذا الدر هم ببلده غزنه في شهور سنه - - -

[1] Price's Mohammedan History, vol. ii. p. 401.

[2] Numi Muhammedani, Ch. M. Fræhnii, Petersburg, 1826, vol. i. p. 146.

'This dirhem struck at Ghiznah in the - - - of the year - - - .' Pl. XX. fig. 29.

3. لااله الا الله وحده لا شريك له الطايع لله 'There is no God but God, the only one, without any partner. The obedient to God.' Margin, characters, imperfect. R. لله محمد رسول الله ابوالقاسم محمود سبكتكين 'To God, Mohammed, the messenger of God. Abu-l-kasim Mahmud Sabektegin.' Marginal legend imperfect. Pl. XX. fig. 30.

4. Formula, as in the last; with a doubtful word, سرى in place of the two last. R. لله محمد رسول الله القادر بالله يمين الدوله محمود 'Mohammed, the messenger of God; Al Kader billah (the Khalif), the support of the state, Mahmud.' Pl. XX. fig. 31.

5. Formula, as before. R. القادر بالله مسعود 'Mohammed, &c., (the Khalif) Al Kader billah, Masaud.' Pl. XX. fig. 32.

6. Formula, as before, with the addition of the name of the Khalif Al Kaim b'amr Allah. R. لله محمد رسول الله شهاب الدوله - - - - - - مودود 'Mohammed, &c., the light of fortune (a word doubtful), Modud.' Pl. XX. fig. 33.

7. Formula, as before. R. السلطان بهرام شاه خلد ملكه سنه 'Sultan (?) Bahram Shah; may his kingdom endure - - - year (?).' Pl. XX. fig. 34.

8. Inscription on both sides. Circular. Formula as usual. ابولفتح غياث الدنيا و الدين محمد بن سام 'The father of victory, the defender of the world and of religion, Mohammed, son of Sam.' R. (السلطان) الاعظم معز - - - - - - ابو المظفر الدنيا و الدين - محمد بن سام 'The great (Sultan?) Maiz (?). The victorious (protector) of the world and religion, Mohammed bin Sam.' In the margin, سته و سبع - - - - Pl. XX. fig. 35.

9. Centre. Formula as usual. Margin. 'In the name of God; this dirhem is struck in the city of peace (Baghdad) in the year 188.' R. Centre. 'Mohammed, the messenger of God,' &c. Pl. XX. fig. 36.

This coin corresponds in all respects with one described and delineated by Marsden, and is referred by him to the Khalif Harun al Rashid, vol. i. p. 41. No. XLI.

These coins are selected from a number procured in Afghanistan by Mr.

Masson. They comprehend others of the same princes, or of their successors in Hindustan. There are a few also of the princes of Turkestan.

The coins which have been described in the preceding pages afford a remarkable proof of the advantage of numismatic studies. Extending through a period of more than fifteen centuries, from the middle of the third century before the Christian æra until the commencement of the thirteenth century after that epoch, they furnish a distinct outline of the great political and religious vicissitudes of an important division of India, respecting which written records are imperfect or deficient. To the scanty notices left us by classical writers of the Greek kings of Bactria they have added the names of many different princes, and enabled us to bring down the total subversion of Grecian authority on the confines of India to a period considerably later than that assigned, upon the evidence of Chinese writers, to the downfall of the Bactrian kingdom. They show that the latest of the princes of Greek origin must have ruled until within a brief interval of the æra of Christianity; and although it is manifest, from the degenerate style of the coins, that the arts and the religion of Greece had yielded to the effects of time and expatriation, yet it is impossible to imagine that the presence of Greek principalities upon the confines of India for more than two centuries should have failed to exercise some influence upon the arts and the knowledge of the Hindus. The amount may not have been considerable, but it was not likely to be totally wanting; and, indeed, it is recognised by the Hindus themselves in the frequent allusions to the Yavanas which occur in their mythological and heroic poems.

That barbarians succeeded to the Greeks in Bactria a little more than a century B.C., was made known to European literature by the Chinese scholars of Paris in the beginning of the last century. The details were meagre; and although they have been amplified by more recent researches, they derive still more abundant illustration from the coins to which the designation of Indo-Scythic has been applied. In them we may trace several and successive dynasties of barbaric rulers, Sakas, Getæ, Parthians, Huns, and Turks, who from the beginning of the Christian æra, or a brief period before it, to the fifth or sixth century after it, occupied with fluctuating fortunes the country on the west of the Indus, from the Hindu Kush to the Indian Ocean. At the date of their first establishment some of them apparently retained the divinities of the Greeks; others adopted an eclectic form of faith, and endeavoured to combine the worship of fire with the polytheism of the Hindus; whilst at a subsequent period different dynasties attempted to introduce, seemingly with little success, the deities of a form of the Mithraic faith, with many of the objects of which we are now for the first time made acquainted. With this Mithraic worship was combined a partial encouragement of the doctrines of Buddha; but both disappeared when the ascendancy of Indian princes was re-established, and Hindu sovereigns, after a long interval, once more reigned in the country of the Paropamisus. Their domination, which appears to have been partially recovered about the third century, was not undisturbed; and that other Scythian tribes from the north, and Sassanian princes from the west, encroached from time to time upon the limits of Hindu sovereignty, is proved by the presence of coins probably or with certainty attributable to such sources. That Hindu rule was not totally extinguished, however, is confirmed by the same testimony; and the different coins of a purely Indian character which are found in the Punjab, upon the Indus, and in Afghanistan, confirm the accounts given by Mohammedan historians, of the presence of Hindu Rajas in the eighth century in Sindh, at Kabul, and in its vicinity. That the coins are trustworthy records is still more fully demonstrated when we come to later periods, and find those of Hindu Rajas gradually merging into those of Mohammedan Sultans, agreeably to the assertions of authentic history. They supply, however, even here some very important facts; for they prove that the extension of Mohammedan conquest in India was gradual and slow, and that it was the policy of the first conquerors, the princes of Ghor, to conciliate the prejudices of their Indian subjects, when, in contradiction to the precepts of Islam, and still more to its spirit, they preserved the symbols of the Hindu religion upon their coins. Even the Mohammedan kings of Delhi were slow to abandon this practice, and it was not until the accession of the dynasty of Khilji that it was totally relinquished. From this time forward the principal currency of India became entirely Mohammedan, until in our own days the coinage of the East India Company with European blazonry and with English inscriptions has supplanted the texts of the Koran, the alphabet of Arabia, and the pompous titles of the Mogul; the numismatic records of Indian history thus faithfully following the destinies of the country for more than two thousand years. That the latest alteration is prophetic of a longer period of national prosperity than India ever enjoyed under any of those types of sovereignty which formerly circulated there, is no more than the world has a right to demand from the superior civilization and the purer faith of those who have succeeded to Greek, Scythian, Parthian, Persian, and Turk, in wielding the sceptre of foreign sway over the native millions of Hindustan.

INDEX.

THE END.

PRINTED BY W. HUGHES,
KING'S HEAD COURT, GOUGH SQUARE.

Plate I

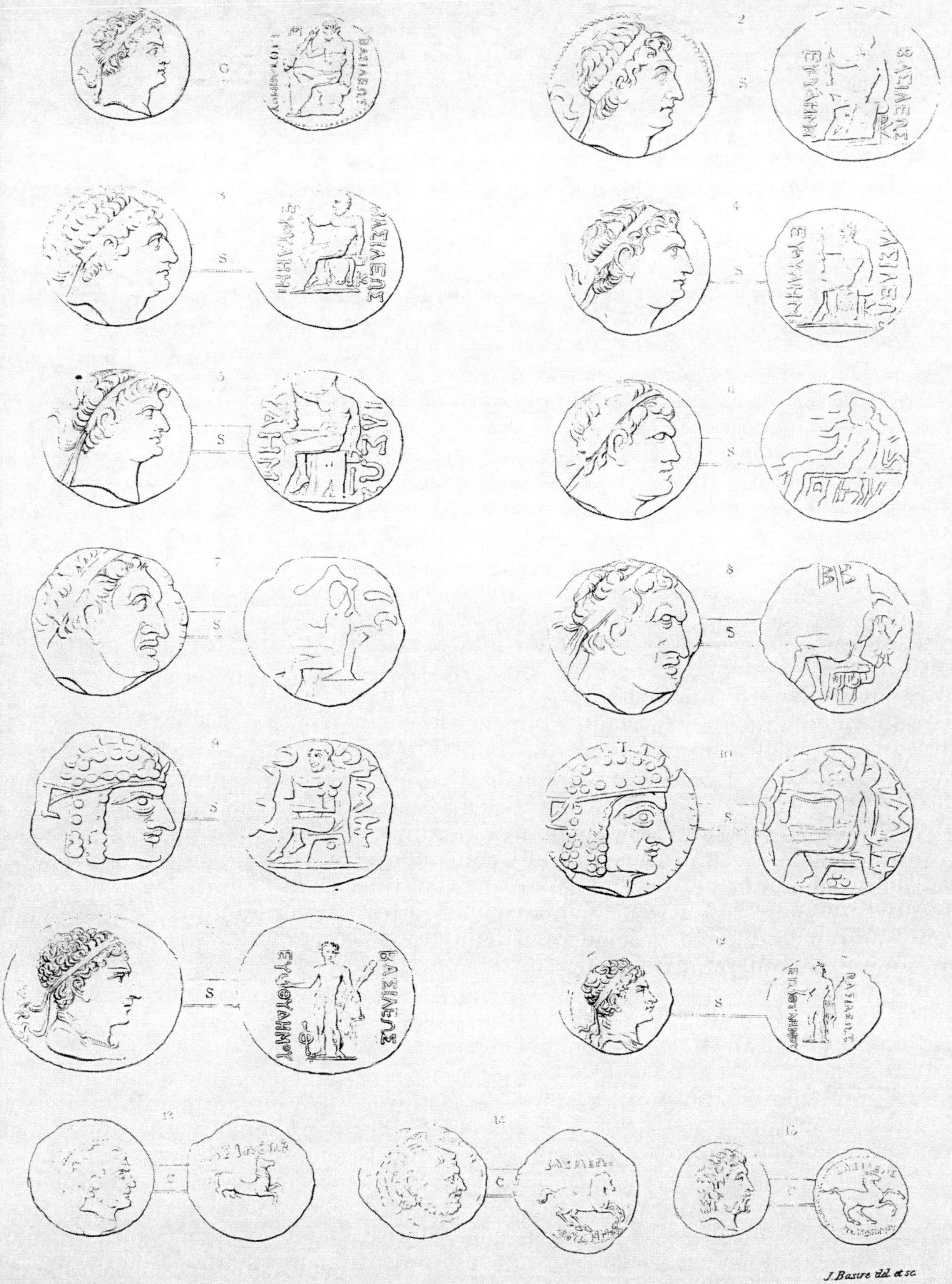

J. Basire del. et sc.

Plate·II

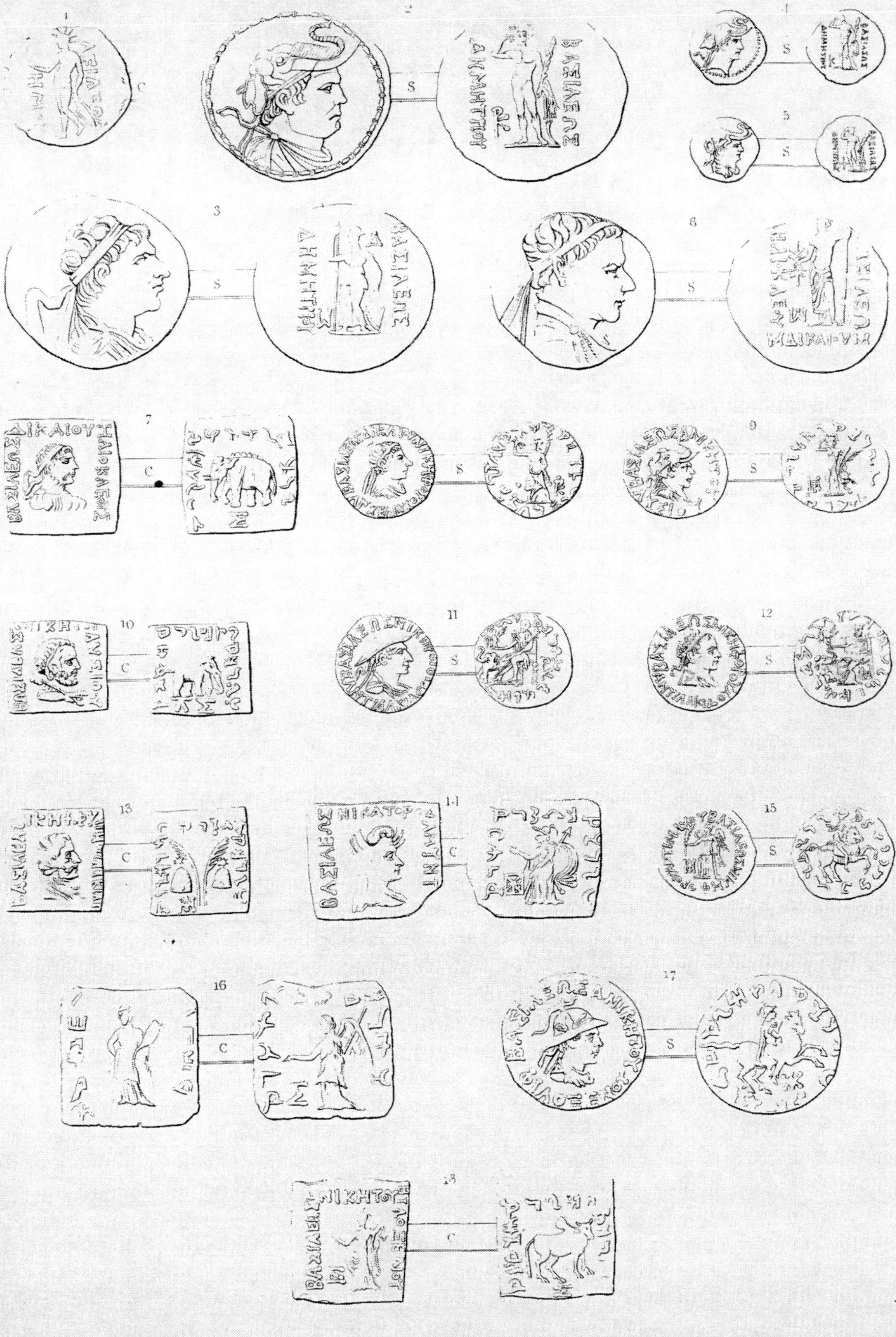

J Basire del. et sc.

Plate III

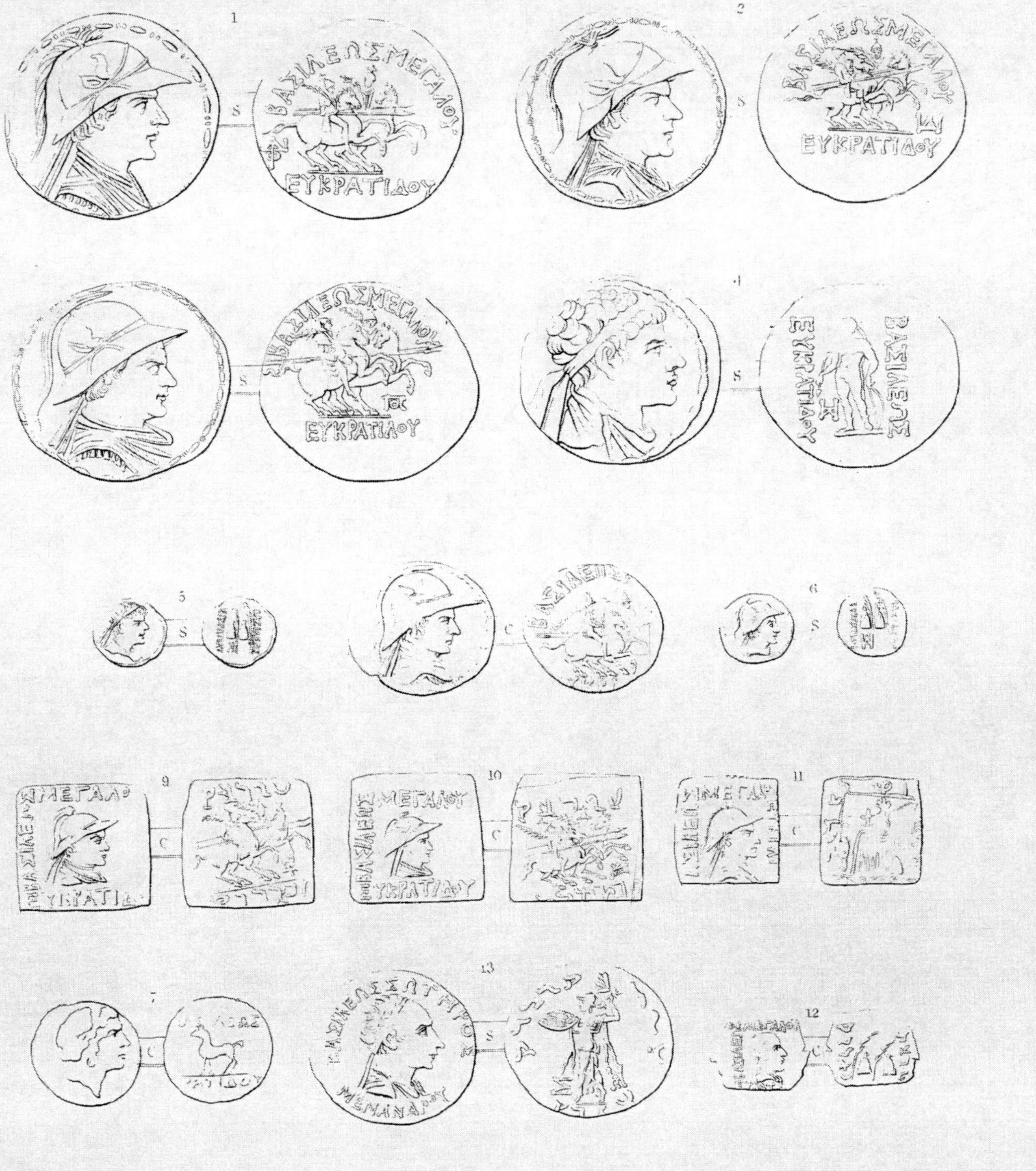

J Basire del et sc

Plate IV

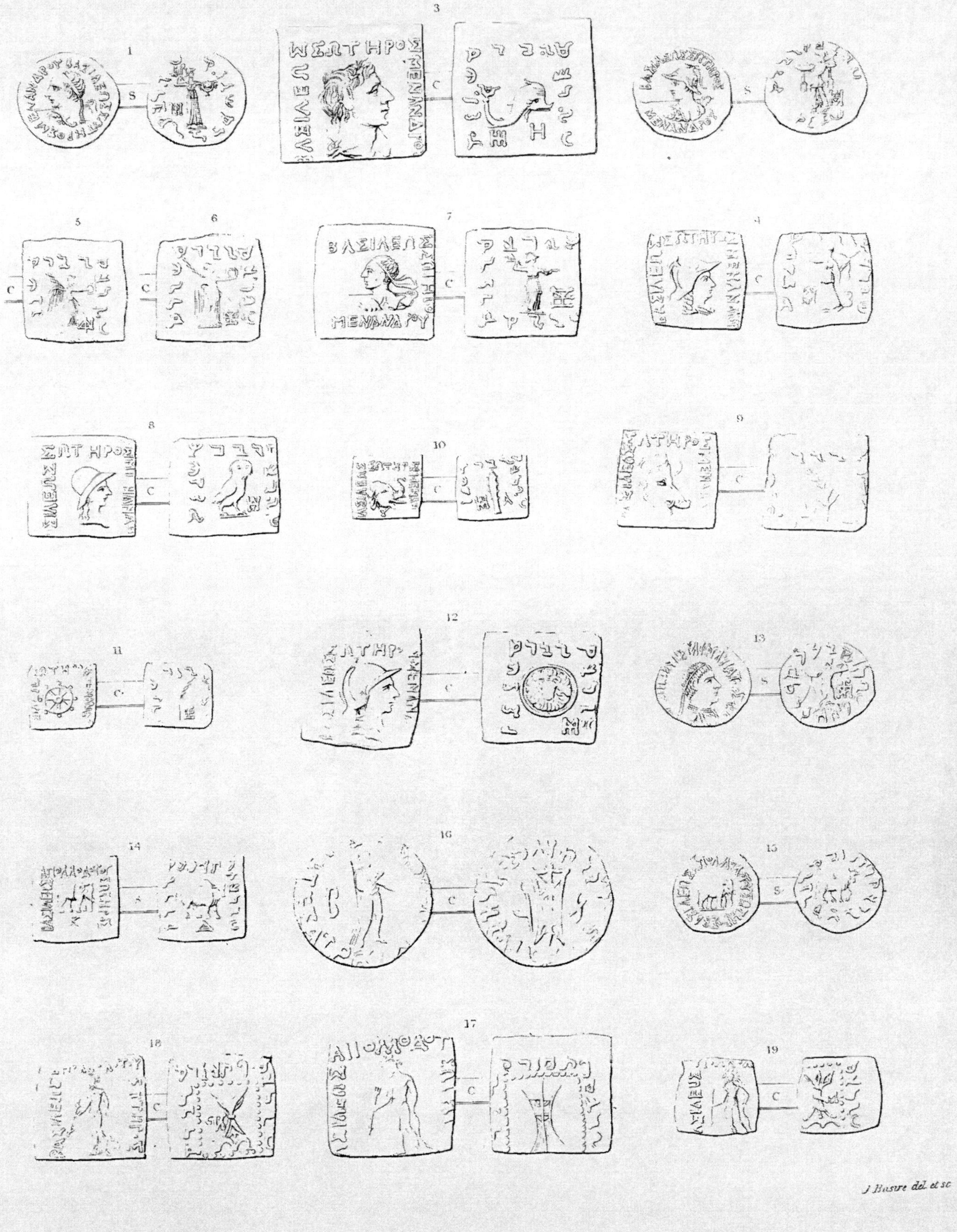

J Basire del. et sc

Plate V

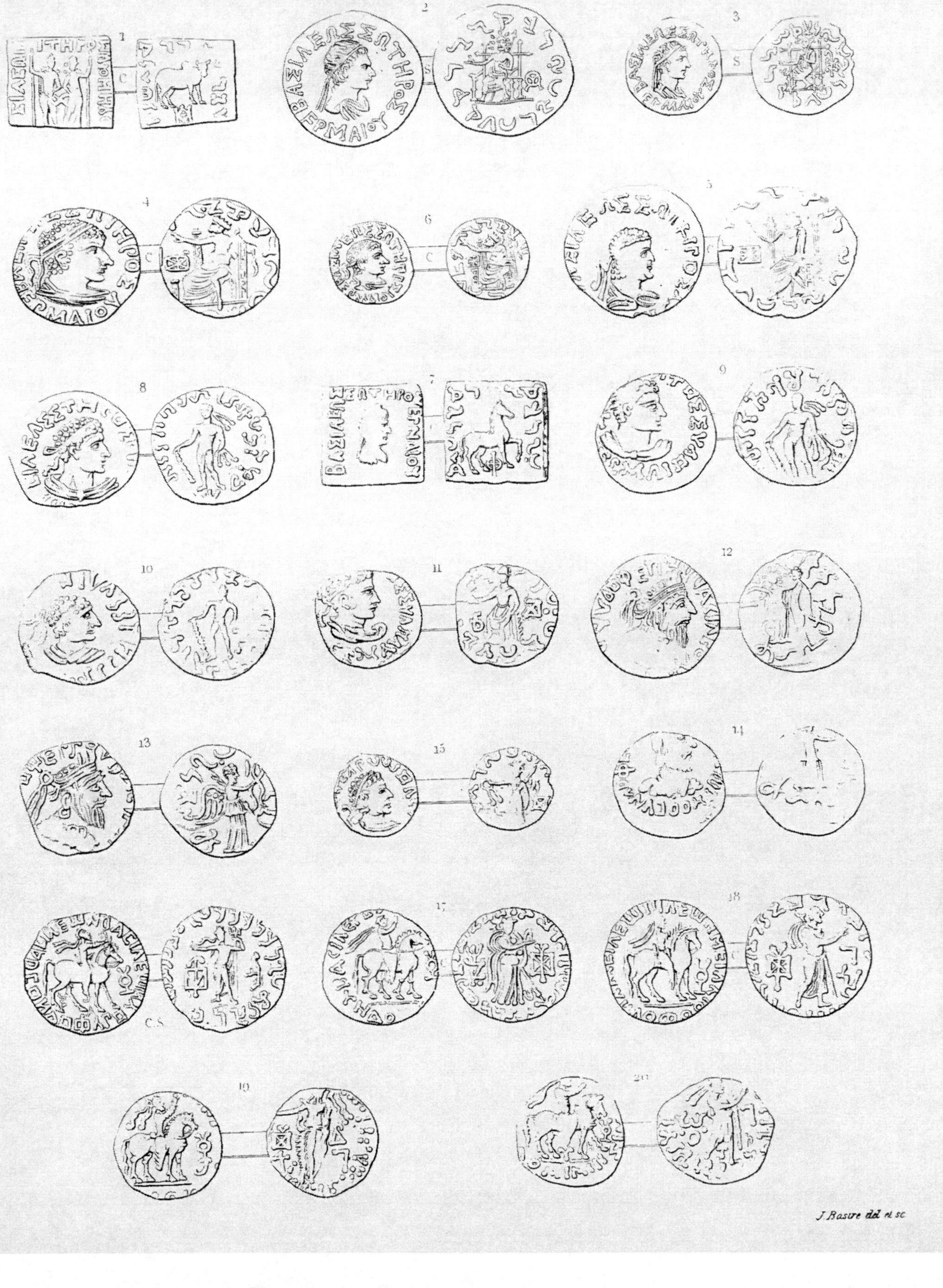

J Basire del et sc

Plate VI

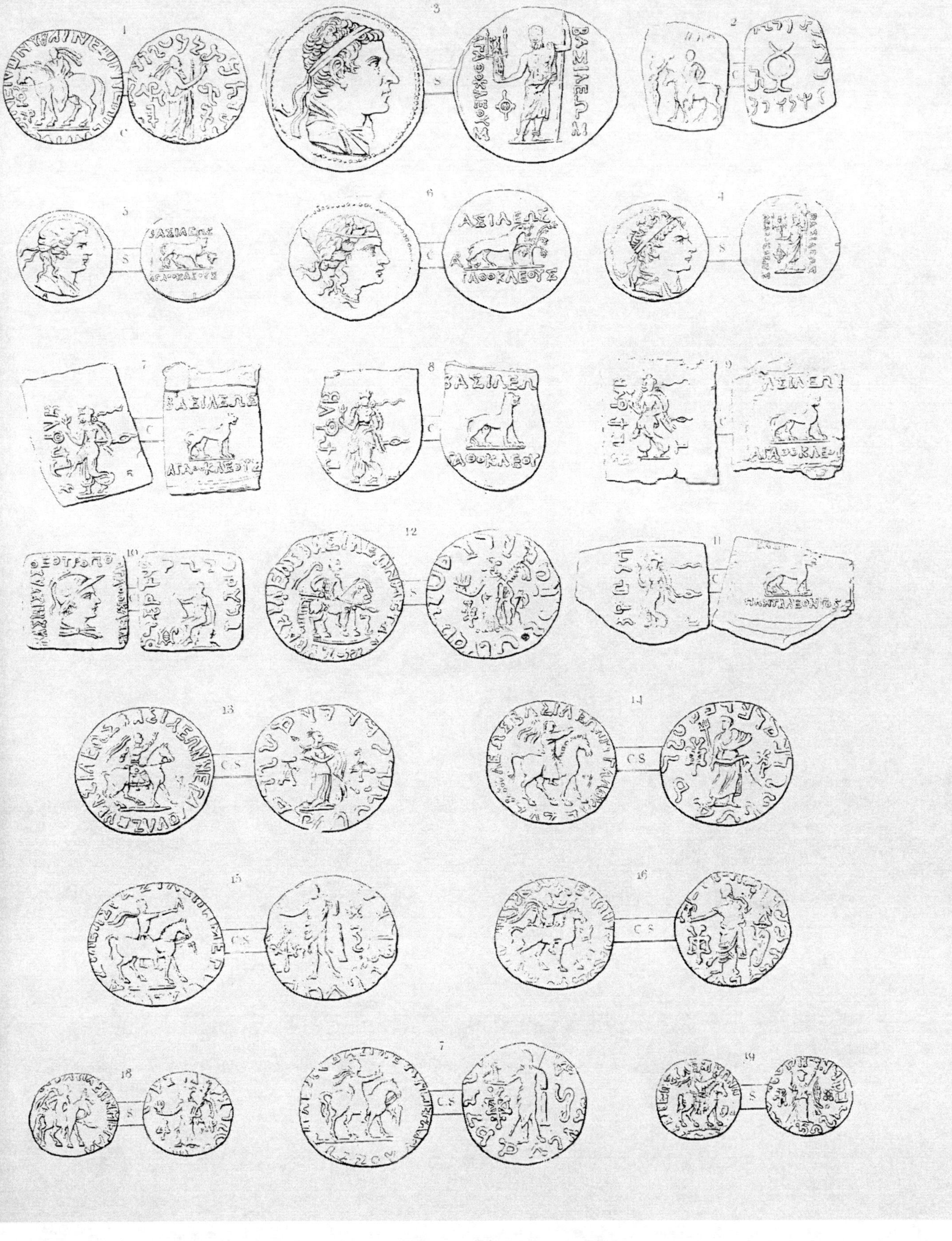

Plate VII

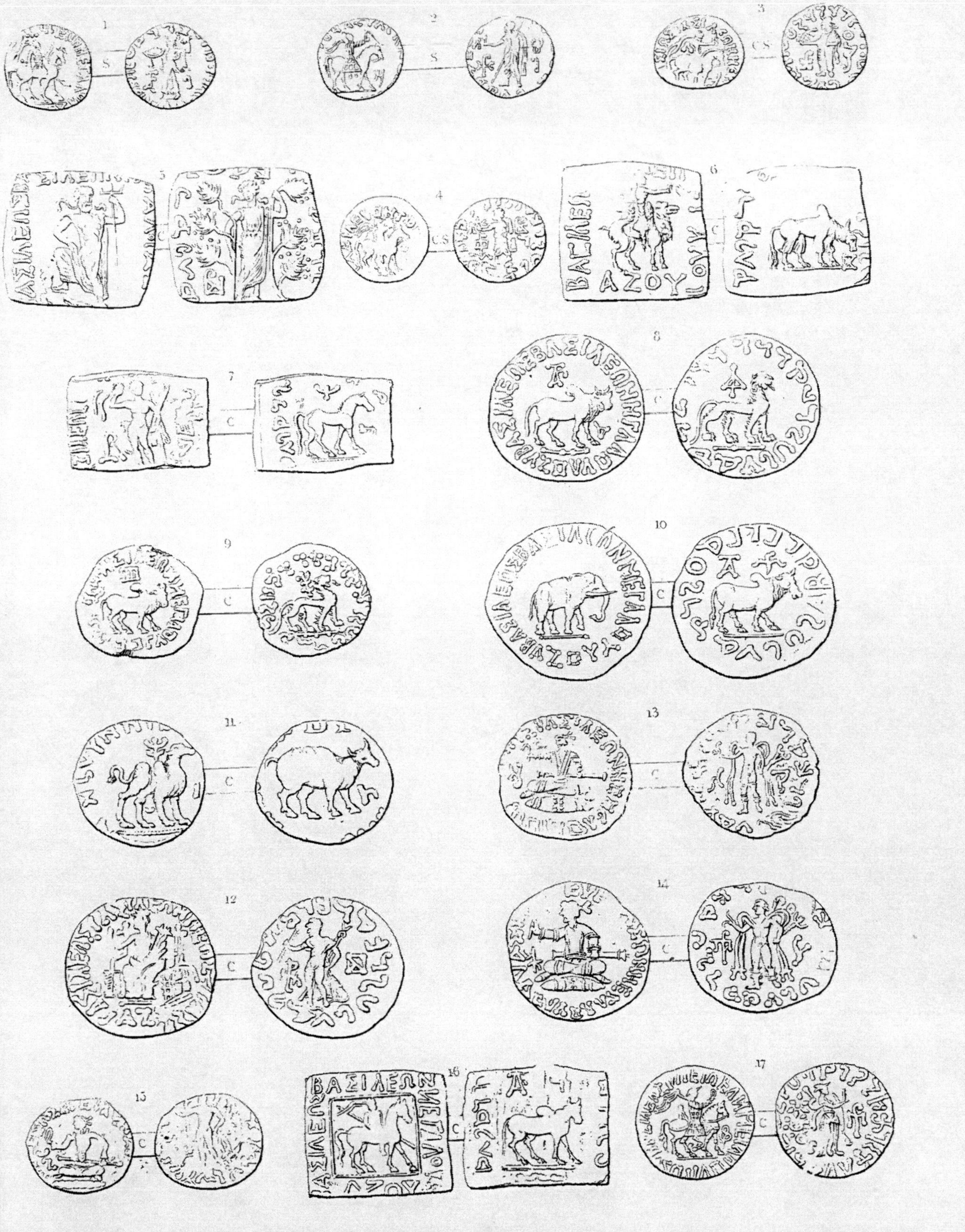

Plate VIII

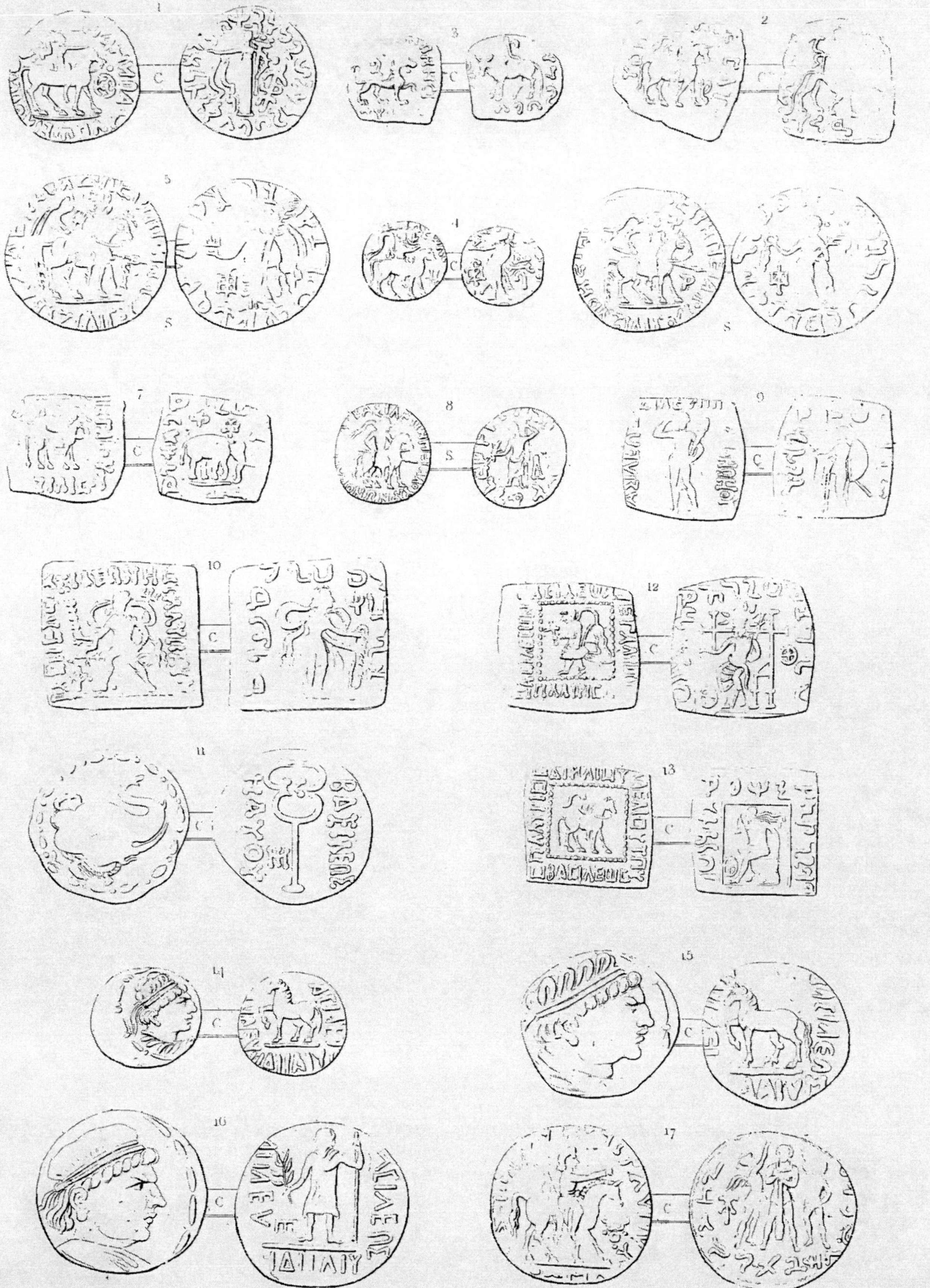

J. Basire del. et sc.

Plate IX

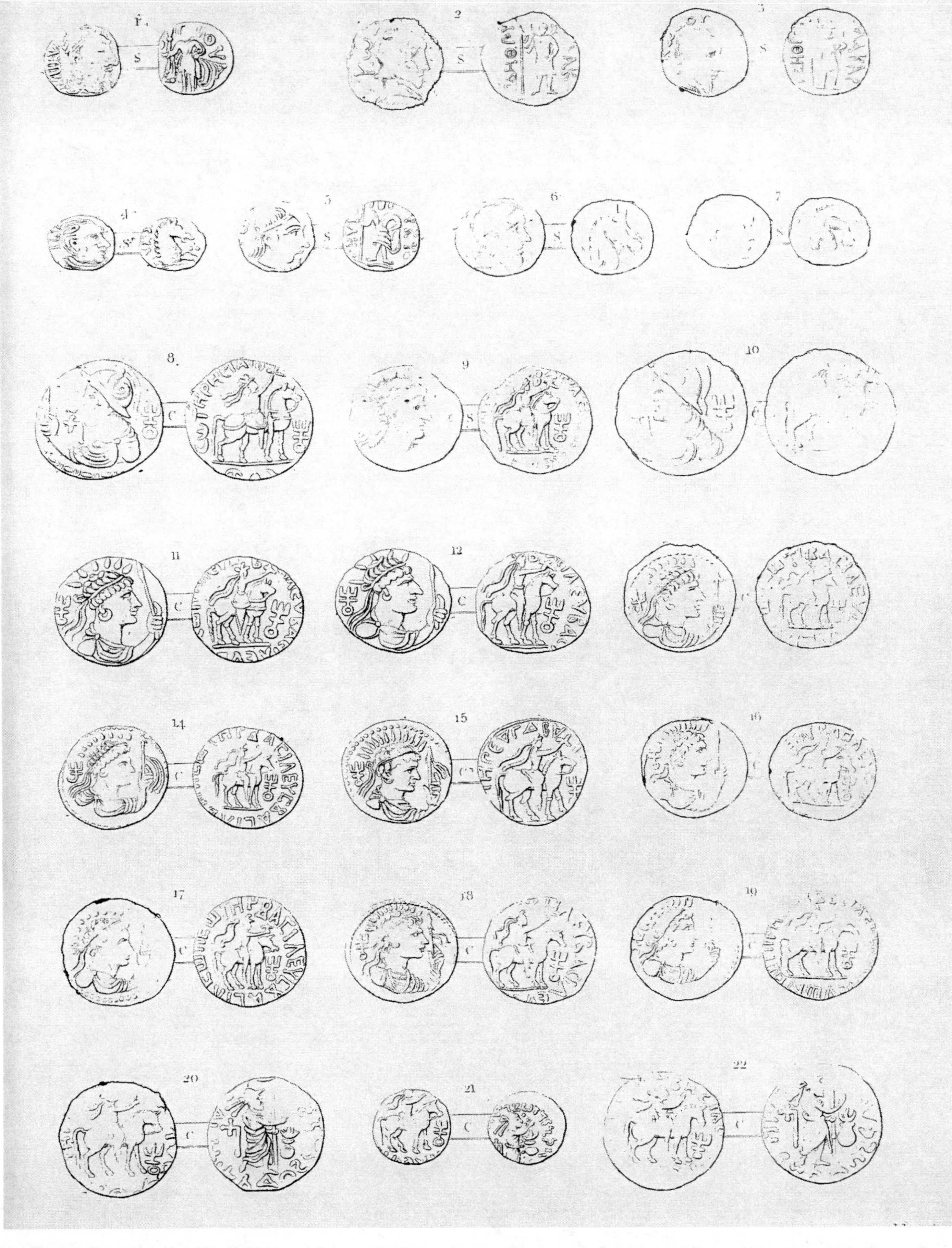

Plate X

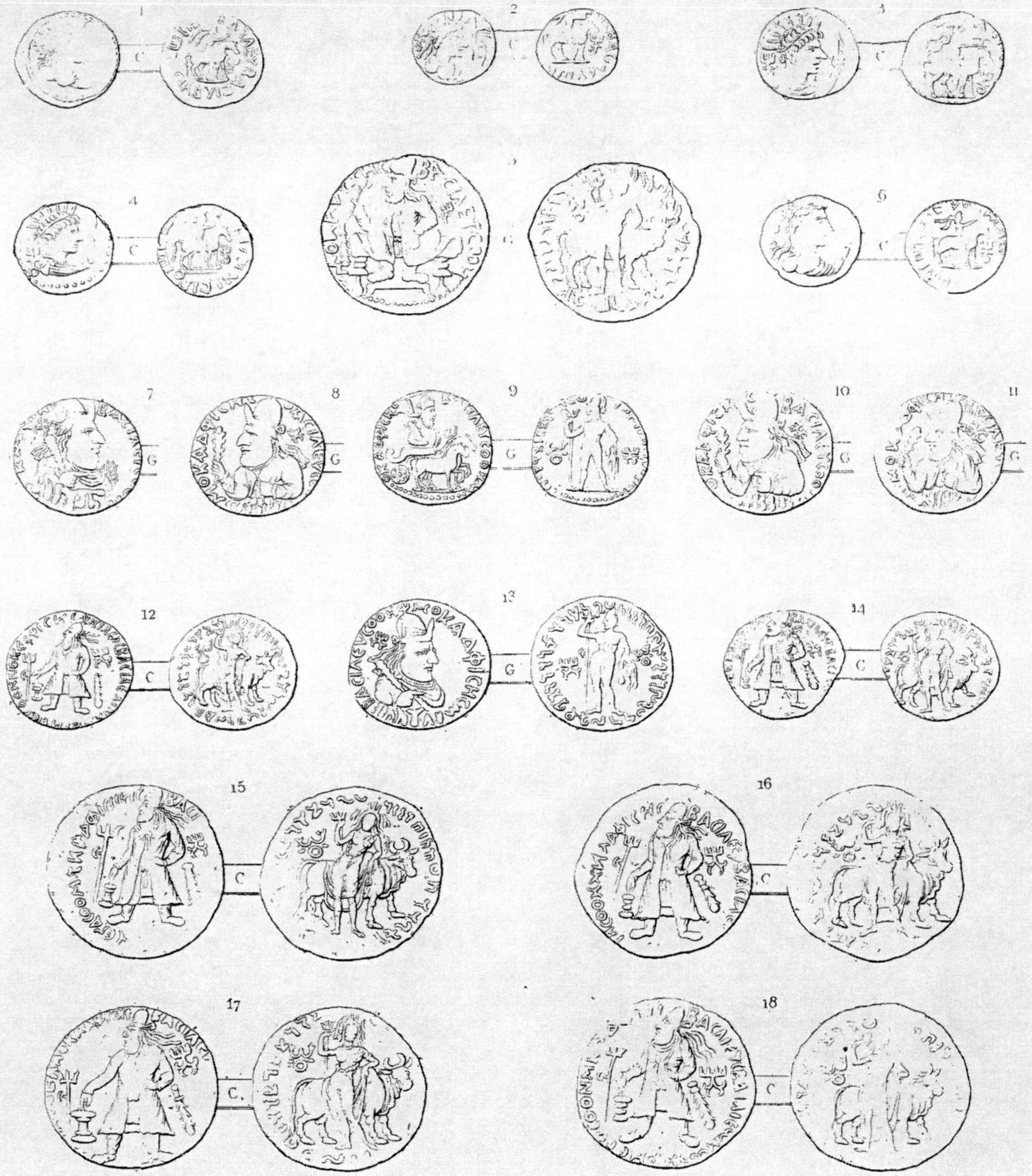

J^s Basire del. et sc

Plate XI

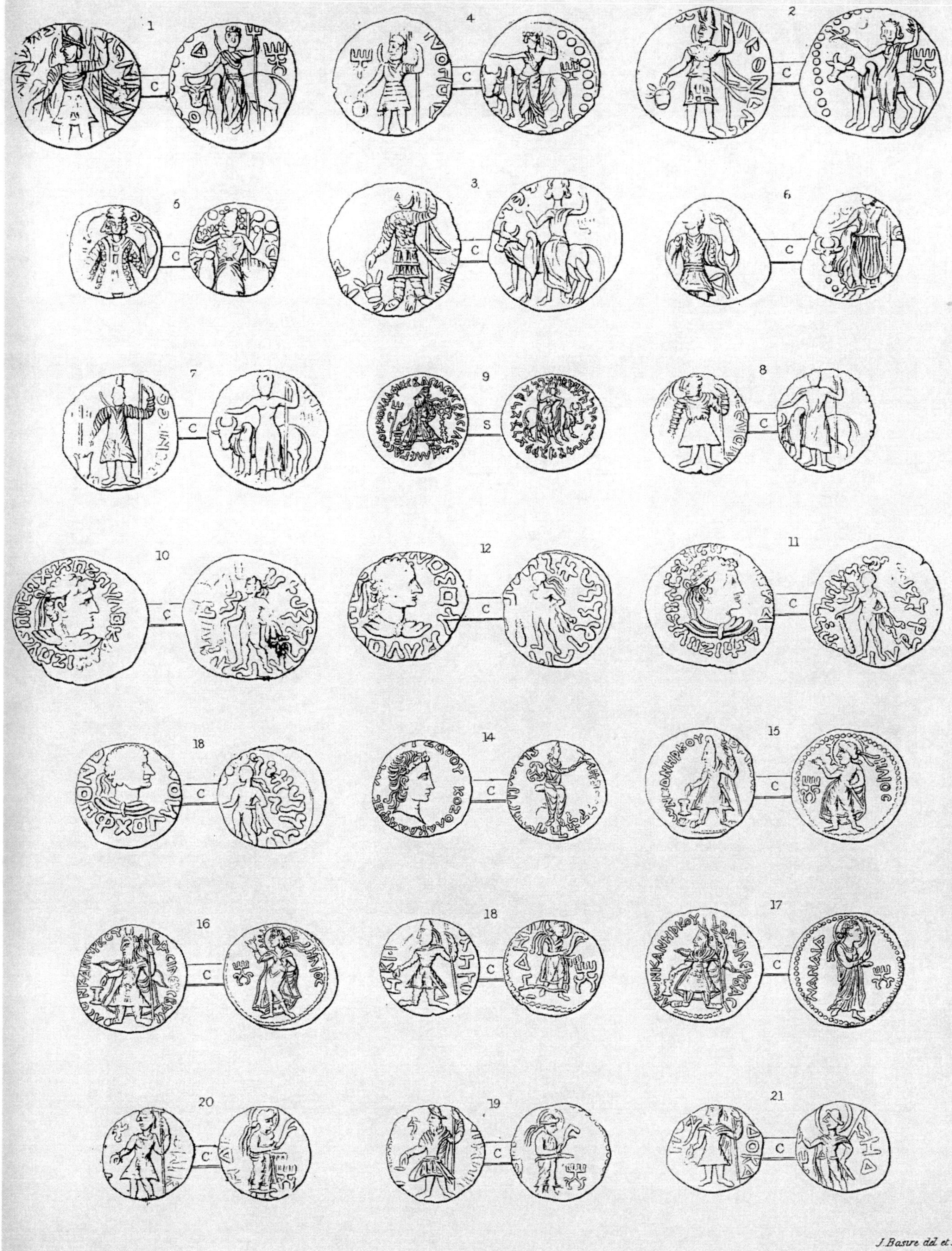

J. Basire del. et sc.

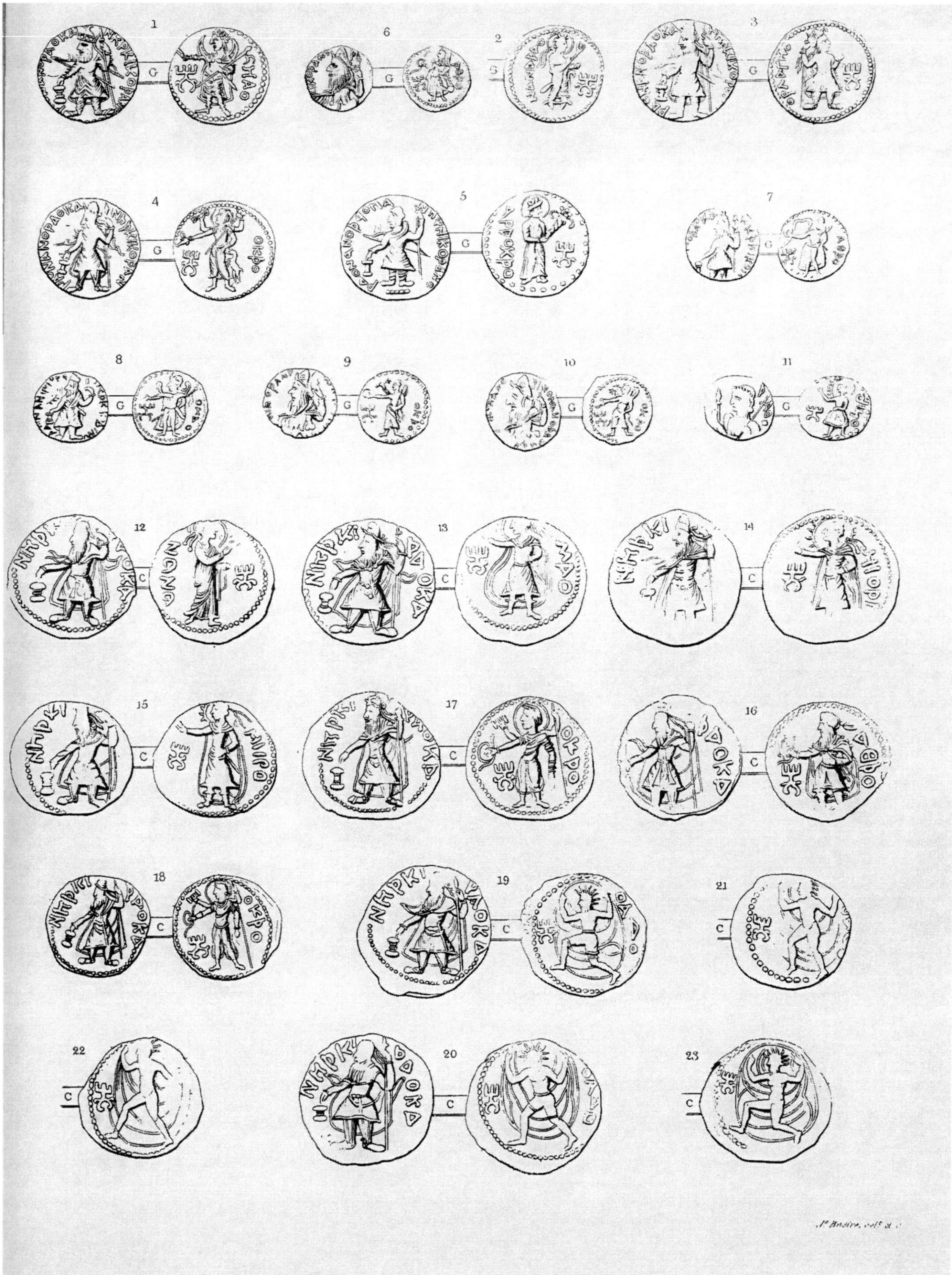

Plate XIII.

J Basire del. et sc

Plate XIV

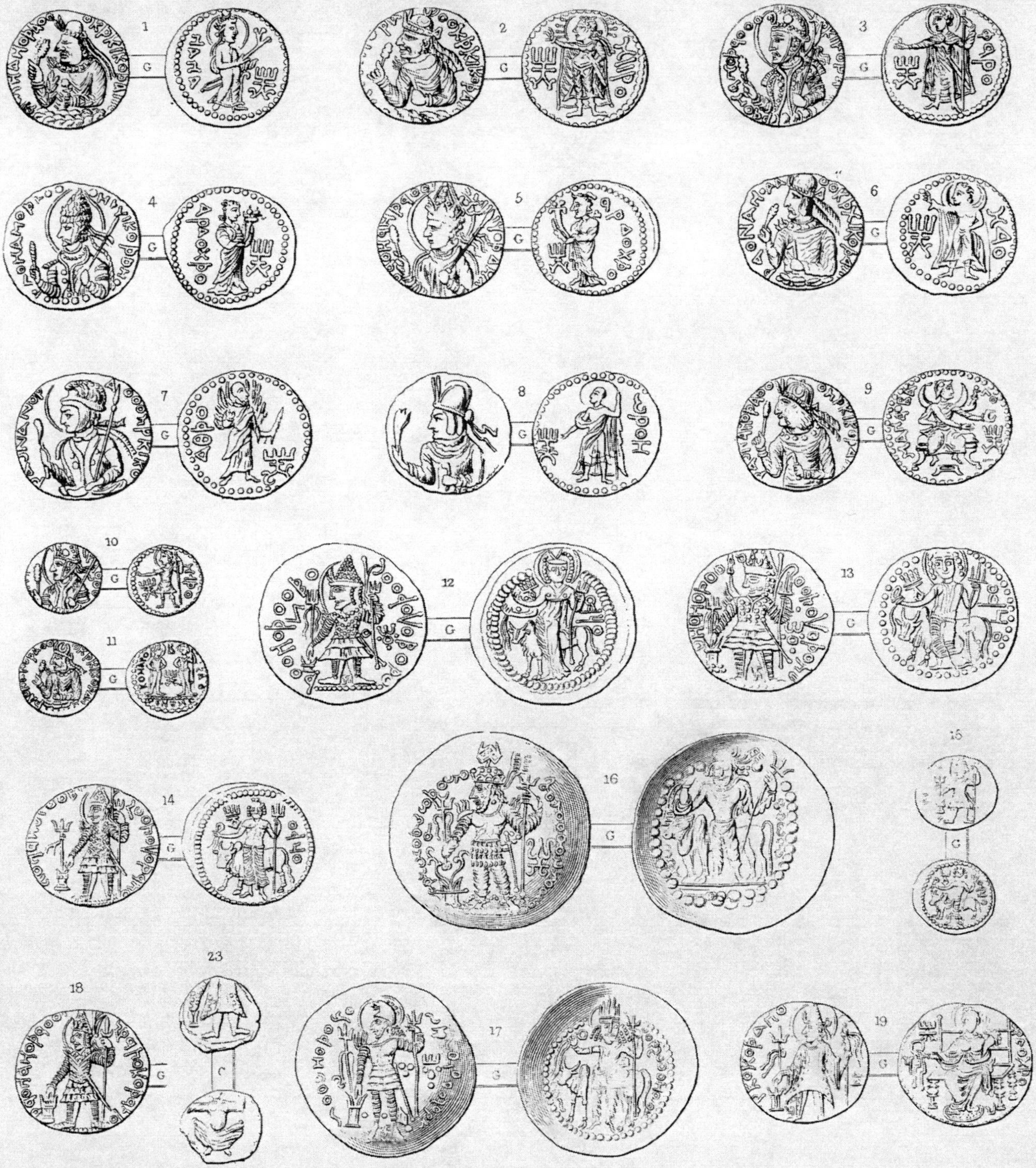

J. Basire del. et sc.

Plate XV

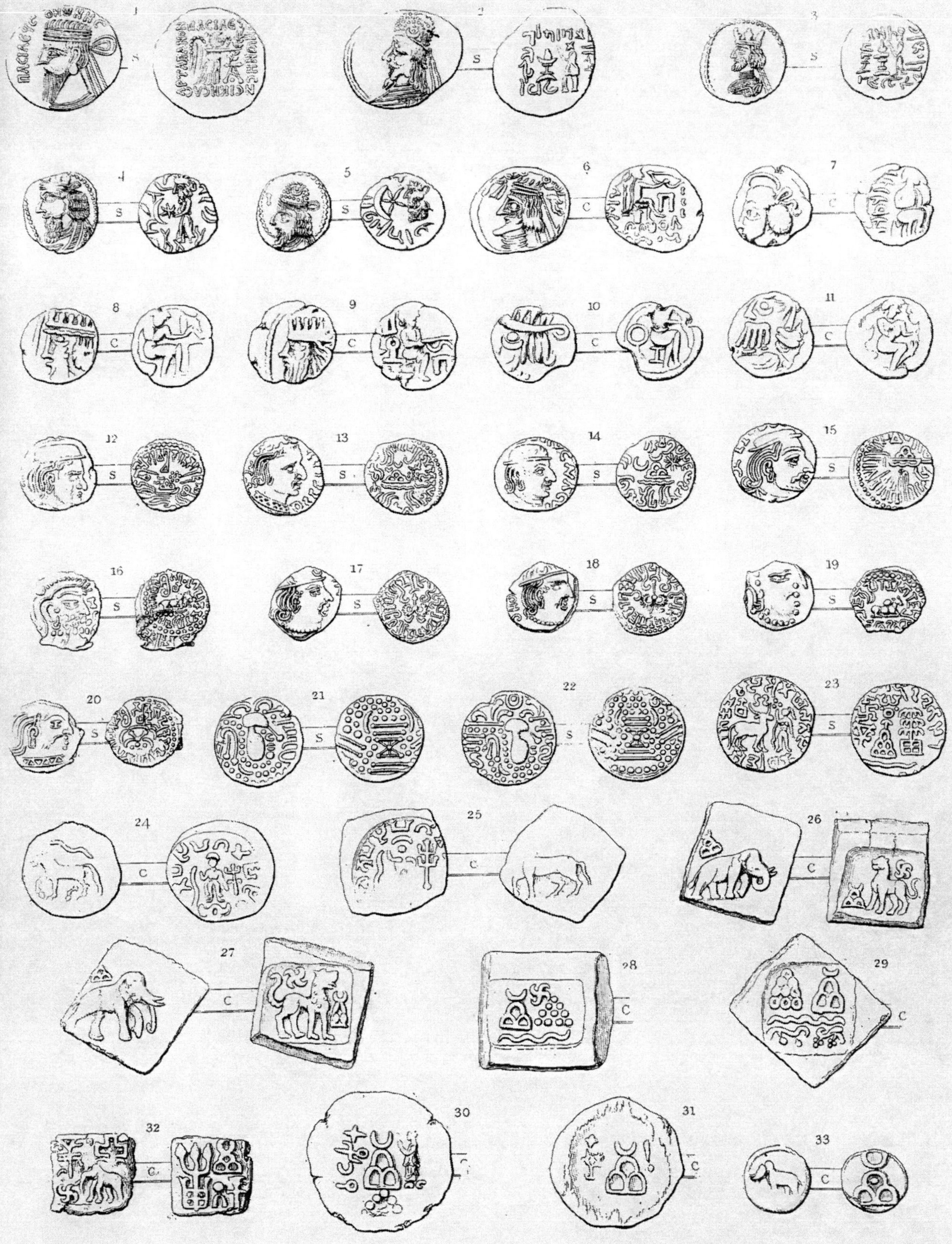

Plate XVI

J. Basire del. et sc.

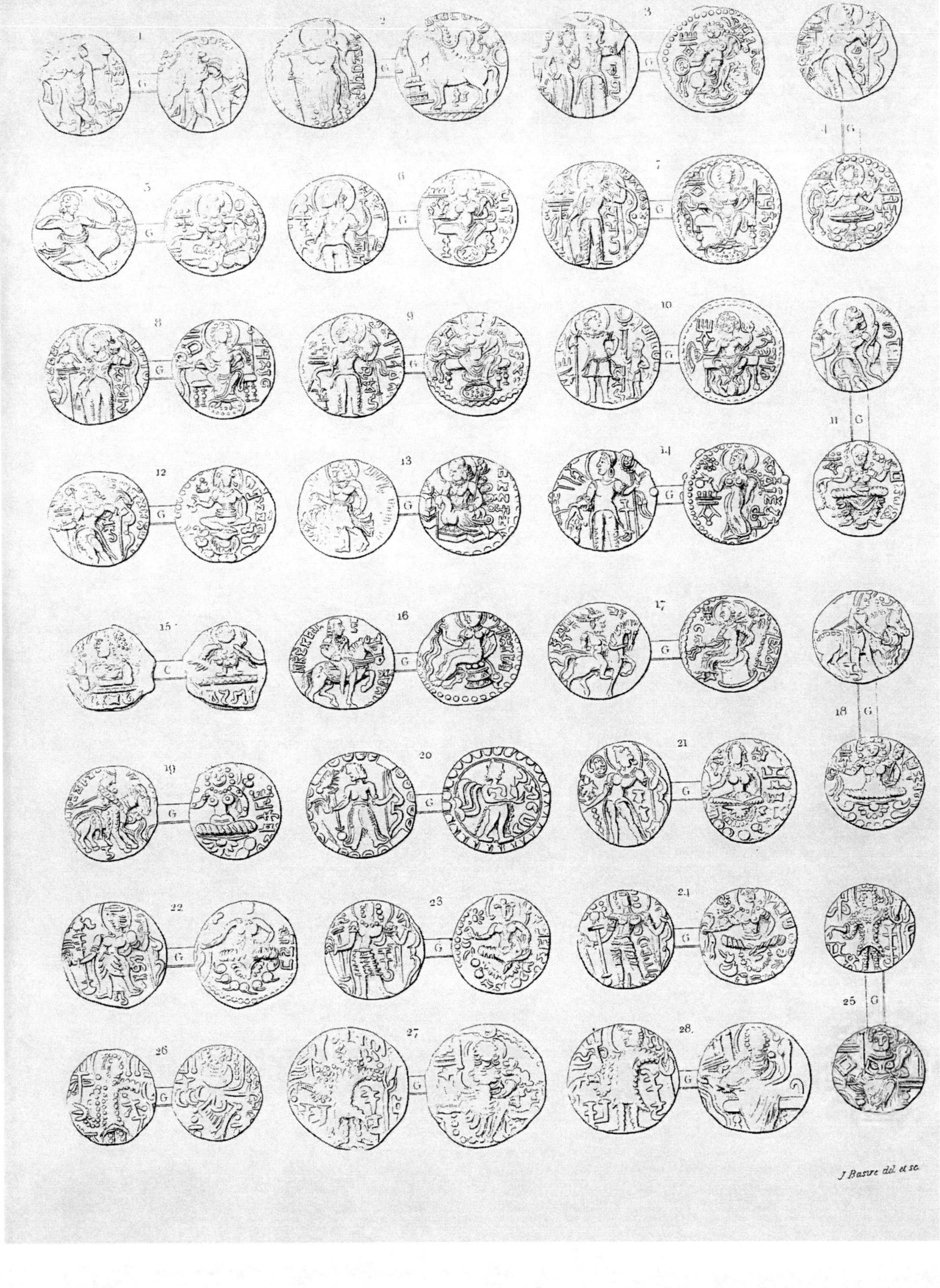
J Basire del. et sc.

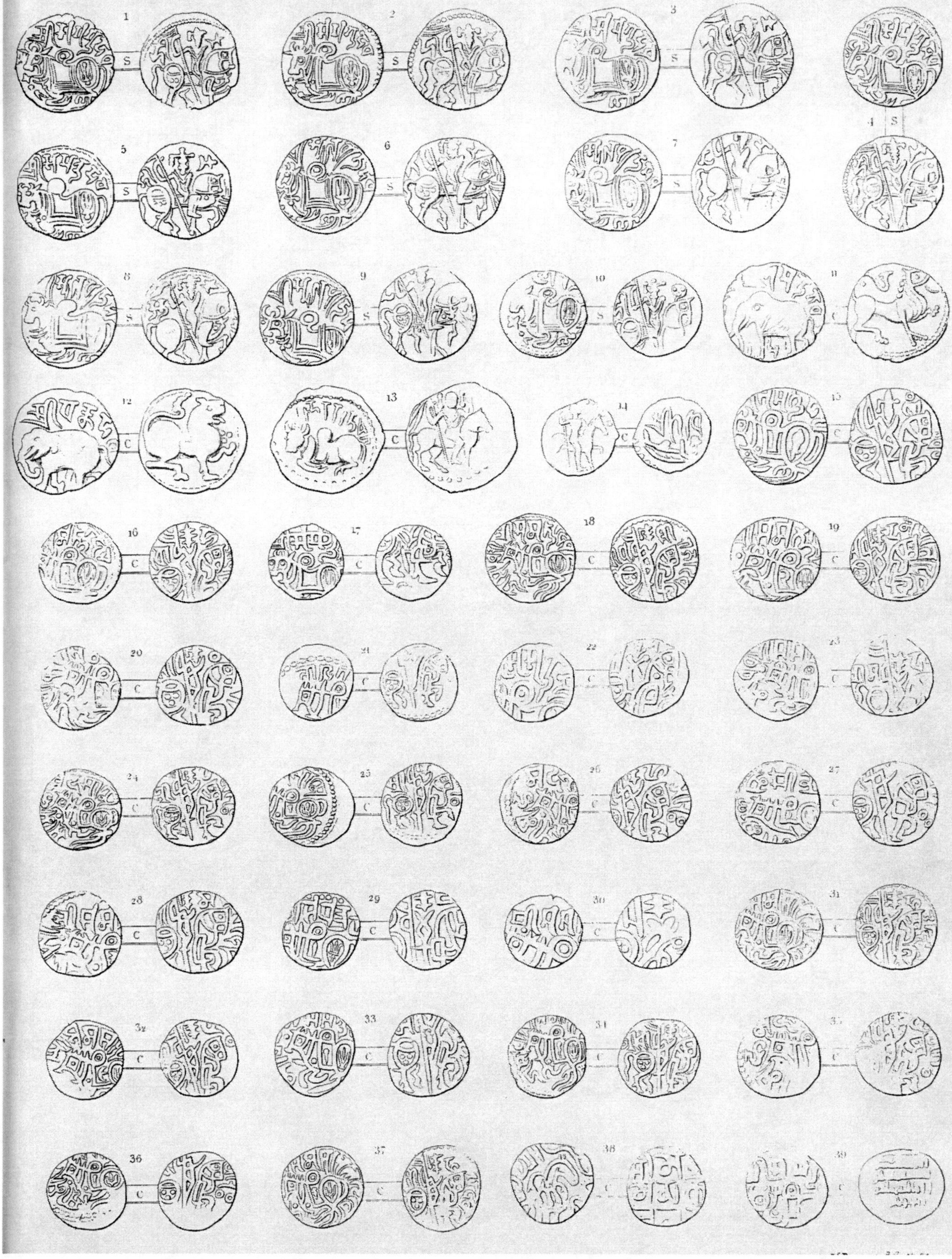

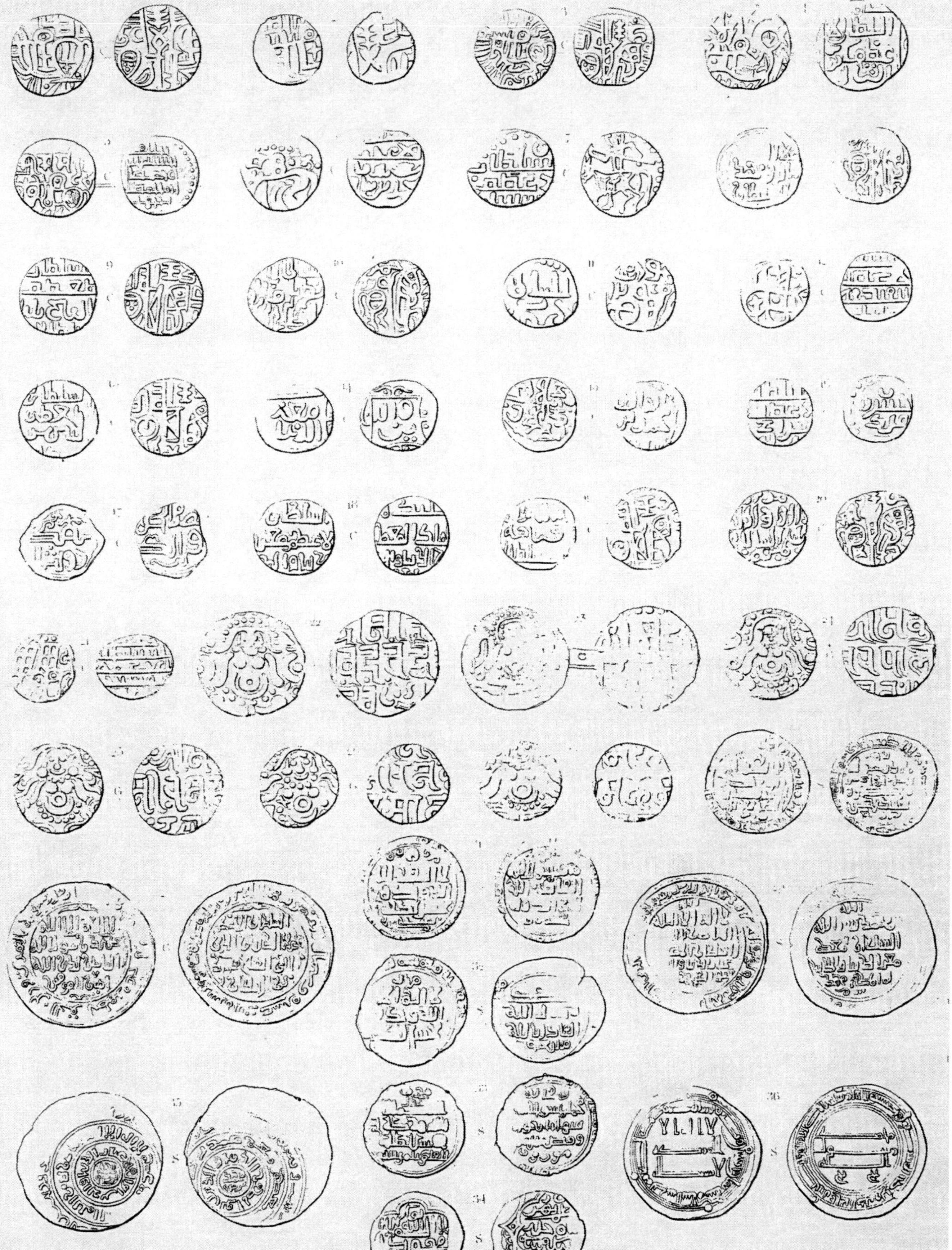

J Basire del. et sc.

Plate XXI

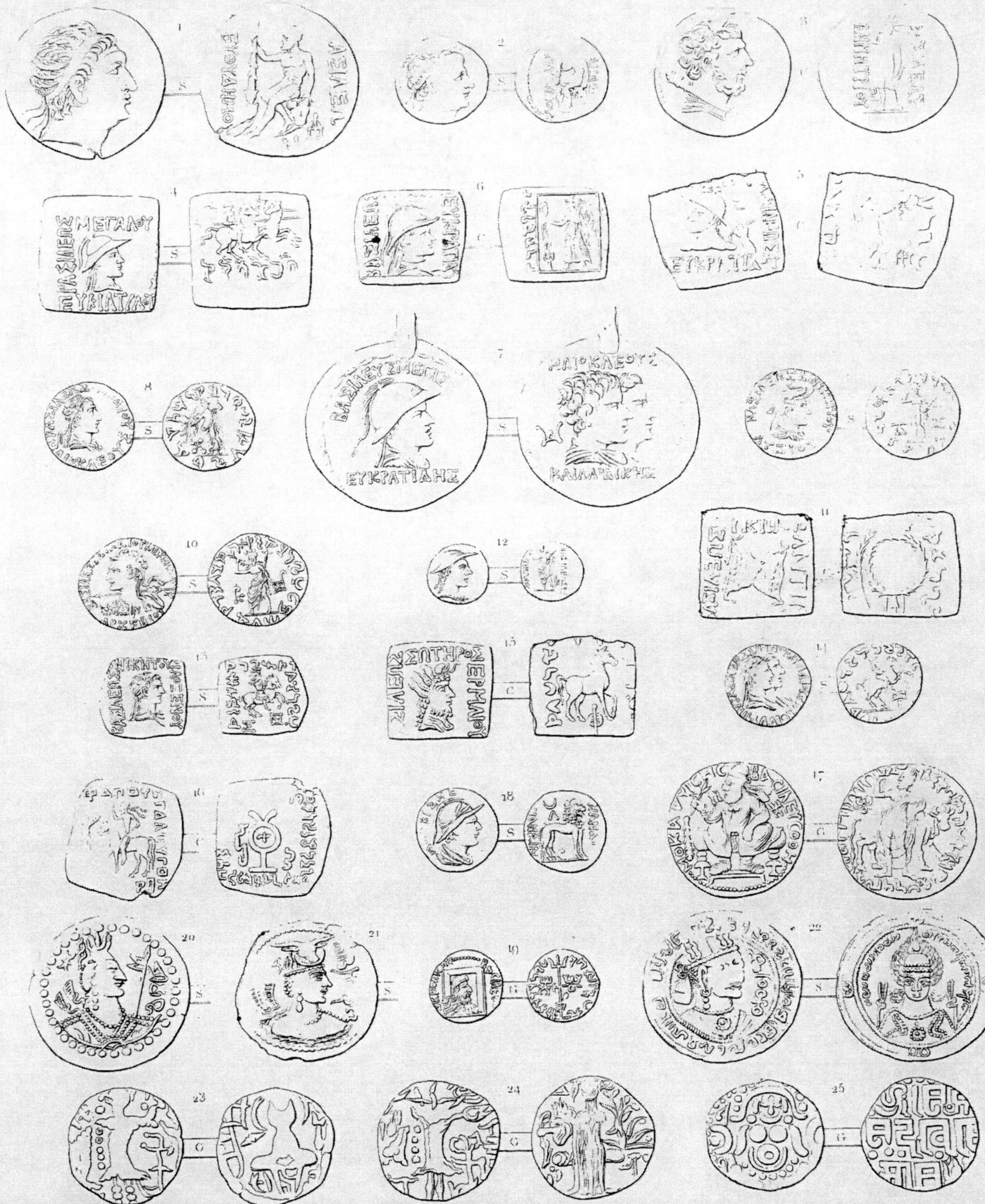

Plate XXII

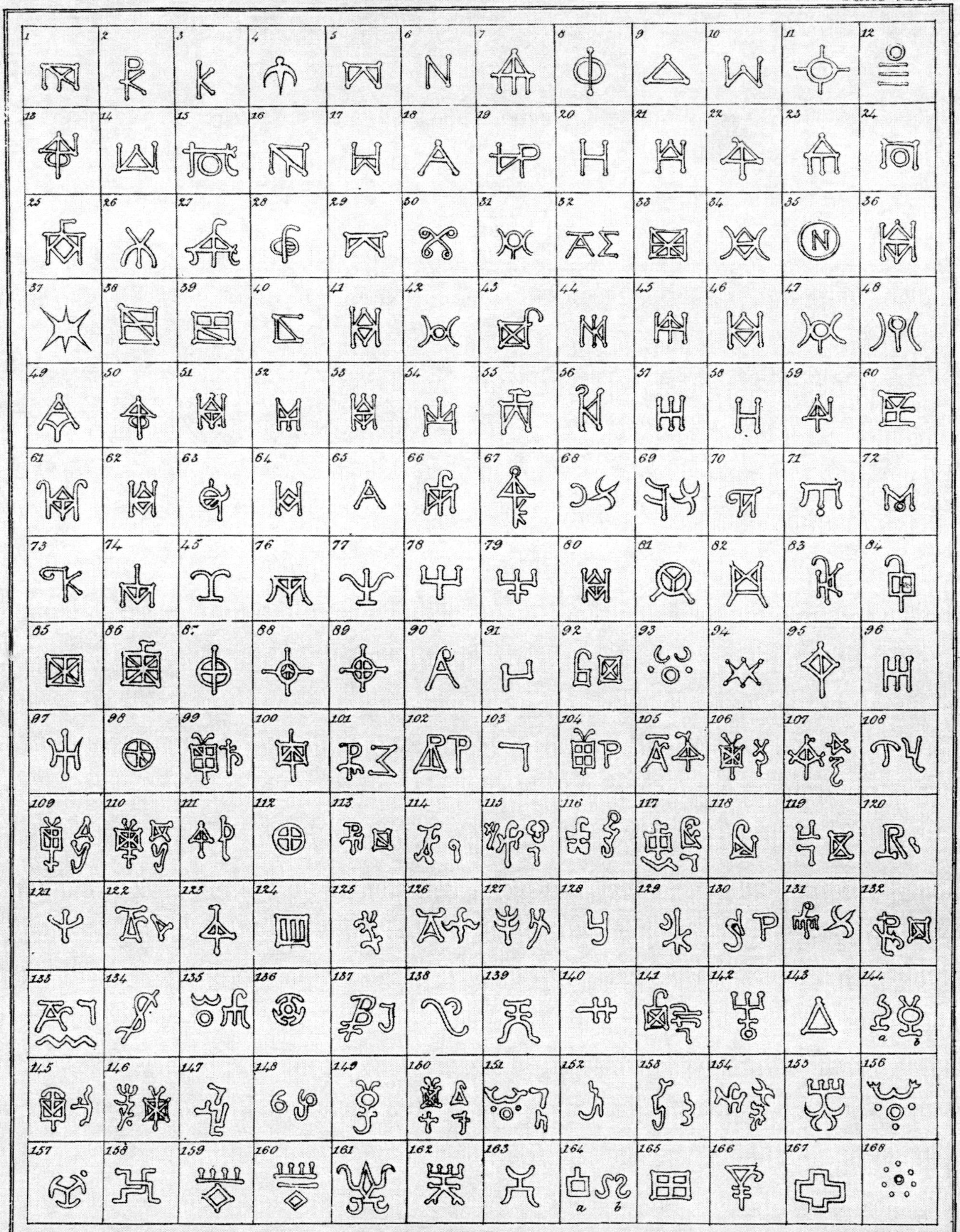

J. Basire, lithog.